ISBN 978-1-4400-7013-6
PIBN 10024627

FB &c Ltd, Dalton House, 60 Windsor Avenue, London, SW19 2RR.
Company number 08720141. Registered in England and Wales.

For support please visit www.forgottenbooks.com

A MANUAL OF MODERN SCHOLASTIC PHILOSOPHY

By
CARDINAL MERCIER
And
PROFESSORS OF THE HIGHER INSTITUTE OF PHILOSOPHY, LOUVAIN

Authorized Translation, and Third English Edition, by
T. L. PARKER, M.A., and S. A. PARKER, O.S.B., M.A

With a Preface by
P. COFFEY. Ph.D.(Louvain)
Professor of Philosophy at Maynooth College, Ireland

VOL. I

COSMOLOGY, PSYCHOLOGY, EPISTEMOLOGY (CRITERIOLOGY), GENERAL METAPHYSICS (ONTOLOGY)

WITH FRONTISPIECE AND FIVE PLATES

THIRD ENGLISH EDITION

LONDON
KEGAN PAUL, TRENCH, TRUBNER & CO., LTD.
ST. LOUIS: B. HERDER BOOK COMPANY
1923

Nihil obstat:
J. Cuthbertus Almond, O.S.B.

Imprimi potest:
E. Cuthbertus Butler,
Abbas Præses Congr. Angl. O.S.B.
die 6 Junii, 1916.

Nihil obstat:
Fr. Innocentius Apap. S.Th.M., O.P.
Censor deputatus.

Imprimatur:
Edm: Can: Surmont
Vic. Gen.
Westmonasterii, die 21 Augusti, 1916.

This translation has been made from the fourth French edition, with the aid of the second Italian.

Printed in Great Britain by Butler & Tanner Ltd., *Frome and London*

AUTHOR'S PREFATORY LETTER

ARCHEVÊCHÉ
DE MALINES.

MALINES, 10 *Juin*, 1916.

CHERS MESSIEURS,—

Très aimablement vous avez pris la peine de traduire en langue anglaise, le cours de philosophie néo-scholastique édité sous ma direction et mon patronage, à l'Université de Louvain.

De tout cœur, je vous remercie de votre collaboration à une œuvre, qui a fait l'objectif de ma carrière professorale, et dont l'importance a grandi encore, à mes yeux, à la lumière des événements que nous vivons à l'heure présente.

Les pays anglo-saxons ont subi l'influence de l'empirisme, et nombreux étaient les esprits qui couvraient du nom d'agnosticisme leur dédain inconscient pour les réalités d'ordre métaphysique. D'autres, tributaires de Kant, cherchaient dans un idéalisme nébuleux, teinté de subjectivisme et de monisme, un terme aux aspirations qui les soulevaient au dessus de la région de la pure expérience sensible.

Or, les événements sinistres de ces deux dernières années ont secoué les âmes.

Le besoin d'idéal, d'une part, est devenu plus impérieux. Quiconque a senti que le Droit, l'Honneur, la Vérité habitent une autre sphère que la force brutale, appelle, de toute la puissance de son être, un Absolu. Ces millions de héros, qui, sur les champs de bataille font ou sont prêts à faire le sacrifice de leur vie ; les peuples, témoins émerveillés de leur héroïsme, ont entrevu autre chose que le rêve d'une poésie charmeuse ; leur volonté, si pas encore leur raison, a dépassé l'empirisme agnostique et affirme la nécessité et la réalité d'un monde transcendant, dont le philosophe sera contraint de rechercher la nature.

D'autre part, le Kantisme et ses corollaires se disloquent. Dès avant la guerre, une poussée vigoureuse vers le réalisme s'accusait en Angleterre, aux Etats-Unis, en France, même en Allemagne. Cette réaction se fortifiera.

Le moment est propice de présenter aux esprits inquiets une solution adéquate aux appels de la totalité de la conscience.

Cette solution fera la part à l'expérience ; elle la fera aux aspirations métaphysiques. Elle tiendra compte des conditions du sujet et des lois de la réalité objective. Elle verra dans l'homme un "cerveau pensant," mais elle le regardera aussi agissant, doué de moralité ; rattaché, par ses racines, à une organisation sociale qui conditionne le développement normal de sa vie.

Aucune philosophie n'a l'ampleur de la "Modern Scholastic Philosophy," pour répondre à cette multiplicité d'exigences.

Votre noble tâche, Chers Messieurs, est de montrer à vos contemporains—que le mot "scholastique" effarouche, peut-être, encore—qu'il en est bien ainsi.

Les professeurs de l'Institut Supérieur de philosophie de Louvain ont eu à cœur de soumettre les doctrines traditionnelles des grands Docteurs du Moyen-Age au double contrôle de la science moderne et de l'histoire des idées philosophiques ; vous-mêmes, en un langage à la fois élégant et sobre, vous avez adapté le traité élaboré par vos anciens maîtres aux habitudes d'esprit de vos compatriotes.

Il y a donc tout lieu de penser que le succès est assuré à votre travail.

Je m'en réjouis par avance et vous renouvelle, Chers Messieurs, l'expression de mes sentiments dévoués et reconnaissants.

THE work here offered to the English-speaking public will have a twofold interest.

The one arises from the tragic fate that befell the University of Louvain when the tide of the present ruthless war swept over the plains of Flanders. . . . The halls where courses of Philosophy were delivered are now the wards of a Red Cross Hospital. . . . The professors of the Institute of Philosophy are scattered, and some are in exile. . . . The illustrious founder of the Institute, and author of most of these pages, is the Prelate who now consoles his stricken people, while his name is held in benediction in every corner of Christendom. . . . Had the world but hearkened to the truths proclaimed by such as he and embodied in lives like his, had it but held fast to the *Christian Philosophy of Life*, well—the twentieth century might have dawned without such a baptism of blood. . . .

The other interest attaches to the subject-matter of the work on its own intrinsic merits. It is an English version of the Louvain *Traité élémentaire de philosophie*. The original is in part an abridgment of the larger *Cours de philosophie* [1] published by the various professors of the Philosophical Institute. It was intended partly as an introduction to the larger course, and mainly for the use of clerical students in Catholic seminaries. But not exclusively in either respect: for on the one hand, though undoubtedly elementary, it contains a clear, simple and methodical exposition of the principles and problems of *every* department of philosophy; and on the other

[1] Six volumes of this larger series have been published: *Logique* (Mercier, 5th ed., 1910); *Métaphysique générale ou ontologie* (Mercier, 5th ed., 1910); *Psychologie* (Mercier, 9th ed., 1912); *Critériologie générale ou traité générale de la certitude* (Mercier, 6th ed., 1912); *Histoire de la philosophie médiévale* (De Wulf, 4th ed., 1912; 3rd ed., English tr. London, Longmans, 1909); *Cosmologie ou étude philosophique du monde inorganique* (Nys, 3rd ed.). Before the war the other volumes were in preparation. Perhaps the *Traité élémentaire* may be considered to give an outline of these future volumes in its sections on *Critériologie spéciale*, *Théodicée* and *Morale*, and in so far may now be regarded as a doubly valuable supplement of the Louvain *Cours* of philosophy. Volumes of the *Cours* are to be read in seven of the European languages, and this Manual in four of them.

hand its appeal is not to any particular class, but is broadly human and universal.

Surely the shock of a world-catastrophe will be followed by graver and deeper heart-searchings about the guiding principles which have been 'civilizing' peoples by ripening their human forces for mutual slaughter and annihilation. The cult of material might and its supplanting of moral right, the gospel of individual self-sufficiency and emancipation from religious restraints, the deification of the State and extinguishing of the lights of heaven—have *these* tendencies and achievements heralded human progress, or have they brought on humanity a terrible nemesis? Perhaps the cry of a chastened Europe will be—Back to *Christ!* Back to *the Christian Philosophy of Life!* Let us hope so. . . .

The truth is found in unpretentious places. Of late years, and in no small measure owing to the repute of the Louvain teaching, the *philosophia perennis*, the *old and new* philosophy of the Christian Schools, had been attracting the notice and claiming the attention—both hostile and sympathetic—of many leading thinkers in both hemispheres. It is sure to command wider and more friendly attention in the near future—now that the scales are falling from the eyes of some of those who were blinded by the erring lights of 'modern thought,' and are at least loosened on the eyes of many others. . . . The great basic truths, both speculative and practical, of this perennial philosophy will be found between the covers of the present little volume.

We therefore think that its translation deserves well of the English-speaking public generally, of the students of our Catholic schools and colleges in particular, and also of Catholic ecclesiastical students preparing for the study of theology.

Even if it were meant for these latter exclusively, we do not believe an apology would be needed for presenting them with such a manual in the vernacular. The Scholastic philosophy can be studied and taught successfully in the vernacular. But the student of it, and for special reasons the ecclesiastical student, should at the same time have access to the works, or suitable passages from the works, of the mediaeval masters in the Latin originals: under the guidance of his professors he can be made familiar with its admirable Latin terminology.

Indeed it is by this sort of bilingual formation he will most effectively master its rich wealth of wisdom.

In his preface to the first edition Cardinal Mercier makes a valuable contribution to the much-discussed question as to whether the student of Scholastic philosophy, preparing for the study of theology, should be taught in Latin or in the vernacular. He speaks from a ripe experience of more than twenty years spent in teaching such students. During those years he tried both methods, that of teaching exclusively in Latin, and that of teaching mainly in the vernacular but revising and summarizing the lessons in Latin, with simultaneous recourse to the Latin sources, and occasional oral repetitions and discussions with the pupils in Latin. The results were incontestably in favour of the latter method; and with these undeniable facts he meets all theorizings to the contrary.

The world has heard much *about* Louvain. In these pages is a message *from* Louvain, a little of the truth that is indestructible. For the time a great seat of learning lies desolate. For the time: its voice will be heard again: *rescissa vegetius resurget.*

P. COFFEY.

MAYNOOTH, *Feast of the Exaltation of the Holy Cross*, 1915.

TRANSLATORS' NOTE TO THE THIRD ENGLISH EDITION

It has been no small satisfaction to the translators to see that in addition to the many French, Italian and Spanish editions a third English edition has been called for in so short a time. They wish to state that this new edition contains besides minor changes a special appendix to Cosmology upon modern conceptions of the atom written by Prof. Nys, the translation of which he has read and approved of; it will be found at the end of Volume I. The translators also wish to take this opportunity of placing on record their gratitude to Prof. A. O'Rahilly, of Cork University, for the able Appendix upon the same subject which at their request he wrote for the first English edition at a time during the war when communications between Louvain and England were extremely difficult. They wish to express their indebtedness too to Fr. C. W. O'Hara, S.J., of St. Mary's Hall, Stonyhurst, for valuable suggestions in the work of translation.

THE TRANSLATORS.

ST. BEDE'S COLLEGE, MANCHESTER, 1923.

CONTENTS OF THE MANUAL

VOL. I.

VOL. II.

ILLUSTRATIONS.

Analytical Contents of Volume I

PAGE

PART III

Dynamic Atomism

PART IV

Dynamism and Energism

ART. I. STATEMENT OF DYNAMISM

ART. II. CRITICISM OF DYNAMISM

ART. III. STATEMENT OF THE THEORY OF ENERGISM

ART. IV. CRITICISM OF THE THEORY OF ENERGISM

APPENDIX

Time and Space

ART. I. TIME

PSYCHOLOGY

PART I

Organic or Vegetative Life

PART II

Sensuous or Animal Life

PART III

Rational Life

CRITERIOLOGY

PART I

General Criteriology

CHAP. I. PROBLEMS TO BE SOLVED

CHAP. II. SOLUTION OF THE PRELIMINARY PROBLEM: CONCERNING THE INITIAL STATE OF THE MIND

CHAP. III. OBJECTIVITY OF PROPOSITIONS OF THE IDEAL ORDER

METAPHYSICS

PART 1

Being

PART II

The Transcendental Properties of Being

PART III

Substance and its Determinations or The Principal Divisions of Being

CHAP. I. SUBSTANCE AND ITS ACCIDENTS

CHAP. II. ACTUAL BEING AND POTENTIAL BEING

CHAP. III. CREATED BEINGS AND THE UNCREATED BEING

INTRODUCTION TO PHILOSOPHY *

1. General View of Philosophy at the Present Day.—Has philosophy the right to be named among human sciences? What is its legitimate place among them?

According to one opinion which is seldom expressly formulated but which we may say is none the less 'in the air', the special sciences have nowadays monopolized everything that can be the object of such knowledge as is certain and can be subjected to verification. In proportion as our instruments of observation have become more perfect, the number of special sciences has increased; and as each special science maps out for itself a definite field of research, it would seem that there is no room for any science other than the positive sciences. If then philosophy has a claim to exist, it can only be as a science outside positive science, busying itself with shadowy speculations and contenting itself with fictions for its conclusions or, at least, with conjectures that cannot be verified.

Such an opinion arises from a failure to understand the rôle philosophy thinks it right to assume and, in consequence,

* Books for study or consultation :—

S. Thomae Aquinatis *Opera*; a translation of the *Summa Theologica* by the Dominican Fathers has now been published (Washbourne, London) and the *Contra Gentes* has been translated, in a somewhat abbreviated form, by Fr. Rickaby, S.J. (Burns & Oates, London, 1905).

Aristotle's Works; some isolated volumes have been translated. Of the 'Oxford Translation', edited by Smith & Ross, nine volumes have already appeared and others are in course of translation (Clarendon Press, Oxford).

Cardinal Mercier, *Logique*, one of the larger volumes of the *Cours* of the Institut Supérieur de Philosophie, Louvain (5th ed., 1910); the Introduction contains a fuller treatment of the ideas in this introductory section of the Manual.

M. De Wulf, *Scholasticism, Old and New* (trans. P. Coffey, Longmans, London, 1907).

Catholic Encyclopedia; see Volume xv. Index, heading 'Philosophy'; many of the articles have been written by Louvain professors.

Many other references to books will be found in their proper place in this Manual. The translators hold themselves responsible for all references to English Books.

the scope of its claims. Philosophy does not profess to be a particularized science, with a place *alongside* other such sciences and a restricted domain of its own for investigation; it comes *after* the particular sciences and ranks *above* them, dealing in an ultimate fashion with their respective objects, inquiring into their connexions and the relations of these connexions, until finally it arrives at notions so simple that they defy analysis and so general that there is no limit to their application. So understood, philosophy will exist as long as there are men endowed with the ability and energy to push the inquiry of reason to its furthest limit. So understood, it is a living fact, and it has a history of more than two thousand years.

Indeed it is strange that those who speak with contempt of philosophy, who glory in the name of *positivist* to emphasize they only profess knowledge of positive facts,[1] or of *agnostic* to signify their unwillingness to concern themselves with whatever may lie beyond immediate facts, have their own general theories about things. *Evolutionism*, for example, asserts that the universe is for ever in process of becoming something other than it is; *mechanism*, that the happenings in the world are all of them mechanical and hence their laws are in all cases to be identified with the laws of mechanics; *phenomenalism*, that the mind knows only fleeting, relative phenomena. It would seem, indeed, that these names are but titles of so many general theories of philosophic speculation.

The discoveries the sciences of observation make and the practical solutions they afford do not bring the mind a full and abiding satisfaction. It is driven to seek the connexion which links together the scattered results of these special sciences, it seeks to unify them and so learn how they fit in with the conditions of human life. Of this necessity a sincere as well as independent thinker has recently written:—

> 'The farther science has pushed back the limits of the discernible universe, the more insistent do we feel

[1] So, for example, Auguste Comte, who has done most to discredit metaphysics in favour of the 'positive' sciences, has been obliged to recognize that beyond the sciences strictly so called there is scope for the study of the 'generalities' of the different sciences, conceived as submitted to a single method and as forming so many parts of a general plan of investigation. See Introduction and First Discourse of his *Cours de philosophie positive*.

the demand within us for a satisfactory explanation of the whole. The old, eternal problems rise up before us and clamour loudly and ever more loudly for some newer and better solution. The solution offered by a bygone age was soothing at least, if it was not final. In the present age, however, the problems reappear with an acuteness that is almost painful: the deep secret of our own human nature, the questions of our origin and destiny, the intermeddling of blind necessity and chance and pain in the strange, tangled drama of our existence, the foibles and oddities of the human soul, and all the mystifying problems of social relations: are not these all so many enigmas which torment and trouble us whithersoever we turn? And all seem to circle around the one essential question: Has human nature a real meaning and value, or is it so utterly amiss that truth and peace will never be its portion'?[1]

It is true that in the present age the task of the philosopher is more arduous than ever before. Materials continue so to accumulate, discovery follows discovery so rapidly, that it has become impossible for a single mind to obtain a complete grasp of everything. This absence of a *complete philosophy adequate to all the present results of science* is accountable for the attitude of those who contemn or ignore philosophic speculation. Yet it is a mistake to imagine that what is impossible to the isolated individual is beyond the concerted effort of many; and that what cannot be done to-day may not perhaps be done to-morrow. It was the urgency of this feeling, we may remark in passing, of the incompetency of the individual to deal with the task now confronting philosophy which inspired the foundation of the School of St. Thomas Aquinas at the University of Louvain. 'Since individual effort feels itself wellnigh powerless in the presence of the field of observation which daily continues to widen, it is necessary', we suggested in 1891, 'for association to make good the insufficiency of the isolated worker and for men of analysis and men of synthesis to come together and form, by their daily

[1] RUDOLF EUCKEN, *Gesammelte Aufsätze zur Philosophie und Lebensanschauung*, p. 157. Leipzig, 1903.

intercourse and united action, an atmosphere suited to the harmonious development alike of science and of philosophy '.[3]

What are these simplest notions by means of which a higher science lays claim to explain the particular sciences? *How* comes it that philosophy holds the hegemony of thought? The answer to this question calls for a few preliminary words on the twofold rôle—abstractive and unitive—of intellectual knowledge, or, in other words, on the simplicity and universality of ideas.

2. The Distinctive Feature of Thought is the Simplicity and Universality of Ideas. General Notion of Philosophy.—We are unable, as soon as we are presented with some object of nature, for example a piece of sulphate of copper, to grasp all at once the sum-total of reality therein contained. When the mind has been awakened by the excitation of the senses set up by something external to itself, it falls to considering the thing's various aspects one by one. The separate consideration of the manifold aspects, ' separatim considerare ', is what is called in philosophical language *abstraction*. *To abstract* is that distinctive function of intelligence, by which man differs from beast, which is common to all men and is present in every kind of intellectual act, whilst it is wholly wanting in animal perception.

When the mind is confronted with crystals of copper-sulphate, it *abstracts* from them their various peculiarities in turn—their hardness, their bluish colour, their geometrical form, their dimensions and so forth. Each of these properties that the mind lays hold of in this one thing that constitutes this crystal, is a partial intelligible object—aliquid *objectum* intellectui—an element, a feature or ' note ', a ' characteristic ' of the whole object; and the union of all these notes into one whole intelligible object gives the mind the most complete and faithful representation possible of the thing under inspection. Thus we see that after examining separately, the mind

[3] *Higher Studies in Philosophy*, a paper read at the Congress at Malines in 1891. For an account of the recent work of Louvain professors see *Appendix* by Dr. Coffey in *Scholasticism Old and New*, an article *Science and Philosophy at Louvain* by Dr. Vance in the *Dublin Review*, July 1913.

puts together the several notes it has grasped; it first *abstracts*, then *unites*; or, if we may be allowed the words, intellectual knowledge is first *abstractive*, then *unitive*.

The sum of the notes that put together make up an object of mind is called the *comprehension* of the idea. The range of application an idea has, the greater or less number of subjects it applies to, is called its *extension*.[4] Now between the comprehension and extension of an idea there exists a relation of inverse proportion—the greater the comprehension the less is the extension; or, in other words, the simpler an idea, the more general its application; those of our ideas which have the minimum of comprehension have the maximum of universality, those which contain the fewest notes are the most general. For example, the idea that comprehends the following notes—'extended thing, of prism-shape, bluish colour, resting at this moment on the end of my finger'—applies to this copper-crystal and to nothing else. The idea of 'extended thing, of prism-shape and bluish colour' applies to all crystals of copper sulphate wheresoever and whensoever they may be. The idea of 'extended thing of prism-shape' applies to several other crystals besides those of copper sulphate. Further, the still simpler idea of 'extended thing' applies to all material bodies of the universe, crystalline and amorphous. And lastly the simplest idea of all, the idea of 'thing', is of unlimited extension. Hence the simplicity of an idea and its universality go hand in hand.

Now since simplicity and universality go together, it is easy to understand how it is that, in order *to explain* anything, we have to pull it to pieces, to split it up, into its simplest elements, with a view to putting it together (cum-prehendere) and so understanding, *comprehending*, the complex thing by means of the simple. In brief, it is by the most general ideas

[4] These two fundamental words appear again in Logic, but we may remark now once and for all that *connotation* (a joining-of-notes) is the more current English word for *comprehension* (a grasping or putting-together; cp. synthesis, *συντίθημι*, which ensues after analysis, *ἀνα-λύω*, an un-loosening, taking-to-pieces) and it has for correlative *denotation*. Another further variant for comprehension is *intension*, a word formed obviously to be the correlative of *extension*, matching it even in spelling.

We may take the opportunity to add that *abstraction* nowadays often means the very reverse process Scholastics understood it to mean; for *abs-trahere* (to take from, apart) is nowadays construed into leaving part behind, *ignoring* some elements rather than *attending* to them separately.—Trs.

of the simplest objects that we come to understand the more particular ideas of more complex objects.

However, the process of splitting up cannot go on for ever; a time comes when ideas resist further analysis; they no longer continue to be explained by previous ideas, but on the contrary are such that they explain everything else. These most elementary objects of thought by means of which others are understood are called the *principles* of things. They are called, too, the *reasons* of things, inasmuch as they give an explanatory reason of the complicated objects the human mind is faced with whenever it interrogates nature or attempts to sound its own consciousness. Principles or fundamental reasons are the ultimate solutions to the problems the human mind inevitably proposes every time it sets itself to reflect upon the world or upon itself. They supply the answers to the last *why and wherefore* that reason asks.

Philosophy then, which by definition is the most general science, has for its object the simplest principles whereby other objects of thought are explained. By means of these principles, Aristotle says, we get to know what other things are, but other things do not tell us what they are.[5]

After this very general view of philosophy it behoves us to enter upon some detailed explanations in a more didactic form. First of all let us inquire in what precisely philosophical knowledge differs from other kinds of intellectual knowledge.

3. Stages in Human Knowledge.—1. The first intellectual knowledge a child has is *spontaneous*; it is knowledge begotten entirely through the things of nature stimulating the sense-organs. As one thing gives place to another and they vary according to the chance of circumstances, the ideas they engender succeed one another correspondingly, thus being rather juxtaposed than connected according to any determined order. Science or knowledge proper begins only when all the fragmentary pieces of information relating to one object are connected and systematized, and thus the merely spontaneous activity of the mind is incapable of forming a science.

2. The formation of a science is attained by concentrating *reflective thought* upon some given object. The will has the

[5] Διὰ γὰρ ταῦτα καὶ ἐκ τούτων τἆλλα γνωρίζεται, ἀλλ' οὐ ταῦτα διὰ τῶν ὑποκειμένων. *Metaph.*, I.

power of controlling the exercise of the other faculties, and it can apply and hold the attention of the mind to the study of some one object, making it examine this under all its aspects until it has analysed as far as possible, and discovered its content through successive abstractions, in order afterwards to reunite its several notes in one total object. In this way a particular science comes into being.

The *particular sciences*, or as Aristotle calls them the 'partial sciences: αἱ ἐν μέρει ἐπιστήμαι', each regard an object which is common to a larger or smaller group of real things and which, in consequence, is relatively simple; thus for example, crystallography studies crystalline form and the influence it has on physical properties; physiology, the functions common to living organisms. But no particular science can exceed the limits which bound its special object; it is concentrated wholly on this without attempting to connect itself with the neighbouring sciences: it has its own processes of investigation and applies them, but it does not submit them to the higher principles that justify them.

3. It is evident that knowledge of this sort is imperfect: even should it have assimilated all the particular sciences one after another, the mind would still not be satisfied. It would possess an encyclopedic knowledge of things, and yet the law of its nature to *unify* the sundry results of its first inquiries would urge it to ask if the several objects of the particular sciences, or perhaps all of them, have not one or more common features and, in consequence, simpler ones. Such is the tendency of the mind towards *science* in the highest acceptation of the word, towards *philosophy*: a tendency to find for the many objects of the particular sciences one which is common and simpler than any of them.[6]

In this inquiry Aristotle has succeeded better than any one and he has found a threefold object common to all the things of nature: namely, 'movement' or change, quantity, and substance. The insight into things by means of this triple object deserves above all to be called the *most general science*,

[6] The word *philosophy* (φιλεῖν, σοφία) means the search after Wisdom. According to a tradition related by Diogenes Laertius (I, 12; VIII, 8), Pythagoras was the first to substitute the word 'philosophy' for 'wisdom'. Plato frequently employs the words φιλόσοφοι, φιλοσοφία, but with a sense not yet accurately determined. Nevertheless he gives in particular the name *philosophy* to the universal science (*Repub.*, V.).

philosophy. So now we may proceed to give a formal definition of philosophy.

4. Definition of Philosophy.—Philosophy is the comprehensive, or synthetic, explanation of things, and may be defined as *the science or understanding of all things through their simplest and most general reasons.* As the knowledge of the simplest and most general reasons requires the greatest degree of mental penetration, the definition may be resolved into: *The science of all things through their ultimate or deepest reasons.* Both these definitions are only the translation of Aristotle's: τὴν ὀνομαζομένην σοφίαν περὶ τὰ πρῶτα αἴτια καὶ τὰς ἀρχὰς ὑπολαμβάνουσι πάντες. St. Thomas' definition is: 'Sapientia est scientia quae considerat primas et universales causas. —Sapientia causas primas omnium causarum considerat'.[8] Let us explain each of the terms of this definition.

1. Philosophy is a *science.* It is therefore opposed to: (*a*) *spontaneous* intellectual knowledge, which gets scarcely beyond the surface of things and does not centre in a systematic way around any one object. The knowledge of the 'man in the street' is for the most part this spontaneous knowledge; it limits itself to the mere registration of facts without looking for any explanation of them. (*b*) It is opposed to *belief* and *historical* knowledge. 'To know' (*scire,* science) is not to accept on the authority of another but to have a personal understanding. (*c*) Lastly it is opposed to *uncertain, conjectural* knowledge: for science implies *certitude.* Now, as St. Thomas well remarks, we have a definite, tranquil certitude of a thing principally when we have been able to give the reason why it is what it is.[9] Every science, even a particular

[7] Aristotle at the beginning of his Metaphysics shows how science deals only with universals; the individual is the object of experience and not the object of scientific knowledge. In every fact two elements must be distinguished, one transient and accidental, the other permanent and general; the man of experience knows that a thing is so but does not know why, the wise man knows the 'why' and the cause.

'A thunderbolt that traverses a definite area at a definite time and kills this man or strikes this tree is an individual fact which happens only once and can never admit of an identical repetition however long the world may last. Yet it is an object of science inasmuch as, besides its accidental elements it comprises others which are general in character and common to all thunderbolts, to all electric flashes'. HAUSER, *L'enseignement des sciences sociales,* p. 64.

[8] ST. THOMAS. *In Met.,* I. lect. 2.

[9] 'N men scientiae importat quamdam certitudinem judicii . . . Certum

one, comprises the explanatory reasons of a certain number of things which have a common formal object.[10] Hence that knowledge alone strictly merits the name of science which supplies the explanations of the things submitted to its examination. A science means, then, a synthetic view of its object.

2. Philosophy is the science of the *totality of things.* The particular sciences are directed to groups of objects more or less restricted: philosophy, the general science, regards the sum-total of reality.

3. Philosophy is the science of things *through their simplest and most general reasons,* or again, *through their most far-reaching causes.* Since philosophy embraces all things, its formal object must be common to everything; and therefore it must be very simple, the simplest possible [11]; drawn by abstraction from the very depths of reality. Now, the human mind is capable of a threefold process of abstraction corresponding to which are the three objects of the general science in its three stages,—'movement' or change, the object of Physics; 'quantity', of Mathematics; and 'being', of Metaphysics. This classification we shall have to come back to later.

Corollary.—It follows from what has been said that between science in the higher sense of the word and philosophy there is no difference but of degree; philosophy is only science at its *highest degree of perfection, that knowledge which penetrates to the bottom* [12].

autem judicium de aliqua re maxime datur ex sua causa'. *Sum. Theol.* I–II, q. 9, art. 2, c.

[10] Each science derives its unity and its distinctive character from the formal object it contemplates. 'Knowledge forms true science when it is concerning a single class of objects considered formally . . . Material diversity of the knowable objects does not differentiate science, but their formal diversity—Illa scientia est una, quae unius generis subjecti formaliter sumpti . . . Materialis diversitas scibilium non diversificat scientiam, sed formalis." St. Thomas, *Totius Logicae Summa*, Tract. VIII, c. 14.

The *material* object of a science is that which it contemplates considered apart from its qualities, apart from any aspect it presents; the *formal* object is the definite point of view from which the science contemplates it.

[11] 'In omnibus scientiis . . . oportet quod illa quae est altior . . . consideret rationes magis universales, eo quod principia sunt parva quantitate ex maxima virtute, et simplicia ad plurima se extendunt'. St. Thomas, *I. Sent.*, Dist. III, q. 3, art. 2, sol.

[12] Yet such science, however perfect, is not the highest ideal of the Christian, for *Christian wisdom* consists in judging all things according to their relations with God: 'Ille qui cognoscit causam altissimam simpliciter, quae est Deus, dicitur sapiens simpliciter, in quantum per regulas divinas omnia potest

5. The Principles, Causes or Reasons of Things.—What do we mean by principles, causes, and reasons which it is the aim of philosophy to discover and by means of which it is to explain all reality? Both the sciences and philosophy make answer to the 'How?' and 'Why?' the human mind is ever proposing to itself; but whereas the former give only a comparatively superficial answer, only the proximate and immediate solution, the endeavour of philosophy is to probe deeper, to get at the bottom of everything, to give the last answer, and this it draws from the principles, causes and reasons of things.

Principle (principium, principe, ἀρχή) etymologically means nothing more or less than 'beginning', something previous to something else; thus the starting point of a movement may be called its principle [13]. In philosophical language it means something antecedent which exercises a real, positive influence upon its consequent. Of the two kinds of principles in this stricter sense, ontological principles, or those from which things draw their origin, are exactly the same as causes, for a *cause* is whatever a thing is positively dependent upon either for its reality or for its coming into existence. When they are considered in relation to an intellect understanding or trying to understand things, principles or causes are spoken of as *reasons*: they are then the answers to a mind's question '*Why* reality is so'. Yet, although every cause viewed in reference to a mind investigating it is known as a reason, not every reason is a cause; for whereas there is a real distinction between a cause and that which depends upon it, in the case of a reason and that of which it is the reason there may be only a logical distinction. Thus geometry and the exact sciences aim at giving the 'reasons' of properties enunciated

judicare et ordinare'. *Sum. Theol.* II–II, q. 45, art. 1, c. Wisdom thus understood is a supernatural gift: 'Non acquiritur studio humano, sed est desursum descendens'. *Ibid.*, ad 2.

The effort of natural reason will of course enable us to know God, but to know Him through creatures rather than to know creatures through Him. Wherefore says St. Thomas: 'Cum homo per res creatas Deum cognoscit, magis videtur hoc pertinere ad scientiam, ad quam pertinet formaliter, quam ad sapientiam, ad quam pertinet materialiter; et e converso cum secundum res divinas judicamus de rebus creatis, magis hoc ad sapientiam quam ad scientiam pertinet'. *Sum. Theol.*, II–II, q. 9, a. 2, ad 3.

[13] For a full development of the ideas here outlined see *Métaphysique générale*, 5th large edition 1910, p. 527 ff., and this volume p. 553.

by figures, numbers and ratios; we see in the light of the definitions of triangle and right angle the reason why a triangle has its three angles equal to two right angles, but we do not demonstrate its cause since triangle is not the 'cause' of the property we predicate of it [14]. So likewise the philosopher who explains the immortality of the soul by its simplicity does not proceed from an effect to its cause but from a quality of the soul to its explanatory 'reason'; yet he does arrive at a real 'cause' when he puts down the origin of the universe to the creative action of God. This subject of causes is worthy of more attention [15].

A cause we have just defined as a principle in virtue of which a being is what it is or becomes this thing or that thing; it has a direct influence upon the existence and properties of a being. Now we can distinguish four different kinds of causes, corresponding to four different kinds of questions [16]. To exemplify them let us consider a marble statue of Apollo sculptured by Polyclitus:

1. *Formal Cause. Specific Form.*—We may ask, What is this thing? and when you say, It is a statue, then, *Why* is it a statue? What precisely is it *that makes it a statue*? A shapeless block has been made to assume a special *form*, and in virtue of this form it has become a statue. It is this which makes the stone a statue. It is this, the *form* or *formal cause*, which makes a thing what it is, determines it to be what it is and thereby to be distinct from everything else.

But there is more than one kind of form or formal cause.

[14] 'Et dico quod definitio dicens quid et propter quid . . . id est ex definitione subjecti et passionis, est medium in potissima demonstratione propter quam praedicatur passio propria de subjecto universali et adaequato; v. g., omnis figura plana tribus lineis contenta, habens angulum extrinsecum aequalem duobus intrinsecis sibi oppositis, habet tres angulos aequales duobus rectis.' St. Thomas, *Opusc. de Demonstratione*.

[15] On this subject Bossuet's *Traité des causes* in his *Traités de Logique et de Morale*, edited by M. l'abbé M.*** (Paris, Lecoffre) p. 207, will prove helpful, if read throughout.

[16] 'Evidently we have to acquire knowledge of the original causes (for we say we know each thing only when we think we recognize its first cause), and causes are spoken of in four senses. In one of these we mean the substance, i.e. the essence (for the 'why' is reducible finally to the formula, and the ultimate 'why' is a cause and principle); in another the matter or substratum, in a third the source of the change, and in a fourth the cause opposed to this, the purpose and the good (for this is the end of all generation and change).' Aristotle, *Met.*, I, ch. 3 (Tr. Ross).

The statue of Apollo has its own particular form distinguishing it, say, from the statue of Minerva; which form, since it is a sculptured one, presupposes for its realization something out of which it has been cut. We call it therefore an *accidental form*, since it needs a subject or substance to adhere or belong to before it can exist. The marble is this substance. Before it was worked upon by the sculptor, though from an artistic point of view it was formless, it had nevertheless its specific form. Compared with wood or iron or gold, it had its own nature, which even the chisel of Polyclitus did not destroy; it possessed and still possesses *that by which the substance of marble is specifically marble* and has the natural properties belonging to marble. This specific form of the substance marble is called a *substantial form*—its own form in the chief and deeper meaning of the word.

The formal cause or form, whether substantial or accidental, is the *determining* principle, that by which a being, substance or accident, is what it is, *id quo* ens est id quod est (τὸ διὰ ὅτί qua re). The other element, the subject capable of being determined by the form is called *matter* or *material cause.*

2. *Material Cause. First or Primary Matter.*—The shape or form of the statue does not exist by itself; it has been given to a previously existing block of marble and rests in it, or on it, as in a subject. *That out of which* the statue is made (*id ex quo*), as opposed to the shape (forma) which is made up out of it, is called *matter*, or *material cause* to distinguish it from the formal cause. It is also termed *subjective cause*, inasmuch as it is the subject which receives the form (*id in quo*) 'Materia est id *ex quo* aliquid fit et *in quo* forma existit' (ἡ ὕλη καὶ τὸ ὑποκείμενον).

The *accidental* form of the statue of Apollo is brought out of the block of marble that the artist has at his disposal; it inheres in it; and therefore between the accidental form of the statue and the sensible matter which supports it there exists a relation of dependence: the sculptured form in one sense owes its existence to this marble, and the sensible matter is in a true sense a *cause* of the statue.

Substantial forms, independently of any accidental forms that may accrue in addition, are the cause of material substances—whether elements or compounds—being specifically different and having distinctive natural properties. The *first* subject of these forms—that which remains when as the result of chemical reactions new forms are generated and old ones perish, succeeding one another without interruption of any sort; that which the senses perceive not, but whose existence reason infers—is the *first material cause*, or as we call it for short, *first* or *primary matter*, the first substratum of the manifold substantial forms of the corporeal world.

We have then discovered two classes of causes: *formal* and *material*. And two groups of such correlative causes: *accidental* form and *sensible* body, and *substantial* form and *first* matter. Of these the latter couple, which are of chief interest to the philosopher, are so intimately dependent upon each other that they cannot exist apart but only as united to constitute a material *substance* (ἡ οὐσία), whereby indeed they answer to the question, *What* is this or the other material thing? What is the specific *nature* of this body? (τί ἐστιν, τὸ τί ἦν εἶναι).

A further inquiry is whether every substance is a material one and therefore a composite of first matter and substantial form. Whether, in other words, there are forms that can or do exist without matter? and if so, what is their precise nature? Questions which belong to metaphysics.

3. *Efficient Cause.*—Where did the statue come from? (ὅθεν). Who made it? Polyclitus, the artist. The artist is the efficient cause, *id a quo* ens fit id quod est (ἀρχὴ τῆς κινήσεως).

But where did the artist himself come from? Who made him, and the marble that he sculptures? There is the further question requiring answer, of the *first* origin, the *supreme* efficient cause of everything that exists.

4. *Final Cause.*—Why (*ad quid*) did Polyclitus make the statue? Had he an object in view? Yes, his fee of a talent of gold and to gain a reputation for himself. The purpose he had was the *final cause* of his work, *id propter quod* or *id cujus gratia* aliquid fit (τὸ οὗ ἕνεκα).

Then further, Why did Polyclitus and why do men in general seek money and reputation? If it is because they reckon gold and reputation as steps to happiness, what is the meaning of this natural tendency towards happiness? What is happiness, regarded as a goal or *end*? What is the ultimate, *supreme end* of man and of all things?

Here we may end our brief analysis of causes. In order to find the way of getting at the unknown, we have considered what there is to know in a particular case, about the statue of Apollo sculptured by Polyclitus. And we have found that for the sake of a talent of gold (*final* cause) the artist Polyclitus (*efficient* cause) gave to a block of marble (sensible *material* cause) the shape of Apollo (accidental *formal* cause) [17]. Then generalizing and widening the subject, we have seen that if the inquiry is to be most general, i.e. all embracing, and to reach to the bottom of everything, we come up against the formal and material causes of corporeal *substances*, and, what is more general still, the *nature* of things, together with the *first efficient* cause and the *supreme final* cause of reality.

To study these causes is the business of philosophy. Since they have in common between them that the reality of which they are the causes truly depends upon them for being what it is, and so 'cause' comes to stand for whatever has a real influence on the nature and existence of a reality, we are brought back again to the statement that the *Why* of a thing expresses several different concepts and that the word 'cause' has several different meanings.

Thus are we now enabled to get at the meaning of the definition of philosophy with which we set out, that it aims at the true understanding of things through their ultimate causes and reasons, that it is the *understanding of the causes and reasons* of things, or in other words, of what reality is at bottom. If in all the beings of the universe, taken singly and together, the human mind could thoroughly grasp these different principles and by them understand all effects and consequences, then the definition of philosophy would be adequately verified in fact. But such is an ideal which in the present conditions of human life we can only approach and never attain.

6. Another Definition of Philosophy.—Since order (*Gen. Metaph.* **168**) is nothing more or less than relations of causality whereby the things of the universe have a bearing upon one

[17] To these causes we might add the *exemplary* cause, or the ideal type conceived by an artist which directs him in the execution of his work. But as sufficient has been said to make it clear what is the object of philosophy, we defer a fuller treatment of these notions for *General Metaphysics* (**131** ff.).

another, the definition of philosophy may be re-formed into *a complete grasp of the order of the universe.*

In the universe contemplated by philosophy is man himself, and therefore man's relations with the physical world, as also with Him Who is the First Cause and Supreme End of the universe, come within the sphere of philosophy. Man is a free agent, capable of choosing between various ends compatible with the circumstances of his life, and in so far he is responsible for those relations; and, on the other hand, he has an end appointed him by nature which is obligatory upon him as his moral end. A philosophical knowledge of the universe, then, must entail a philosophical knowledge or thorough explanation of the reasons of man's duties flowing from his relation to things and to Him Who is their First Cause and Last End. Furthermore, man has the power of reflecting on his own knowledge; as is seen from the fact that the understanding of what knowledge is is distinct from knowledge, that the study of the logical structure of science is distinct from the knowledge he acquires of real things. Hence do we arrive at the more comprehensive definition, that philosophy is the full understanding of the order in the universe, of man's moral duties resulting from it, and of his knowledge of reality.

7. General Division: Speculative and Practical Philosophy.—A general division of philosophy may be made according to the two kinds of order which are present to the philosopher's attention, namely, the order already existent in nature—things—and the order we bring into existence—our acts. The former kind, the order of nature, exists independently of us, and all we have to do is to look carefully at it, to investigate it (*speculari*, θεωρέω), not to create it. The latter kind, the *practical* order, we have ourselves to form, first in our acts of *thought* or of *will*, then in our external use of things to which our internal acts give rise, in the *arts*. Corresponding are *speculative* or *theoretical* philosophy which is a group of ultimate investigations making up the philosophy of nature, and *practical* philosophy, which comprises the following branches [18].

[18] St. Thomas explains and justifies the division of philosophy into speculative and practical philosophy as follows: 'Sapientis est ordinare, dice commentando Aristotele. Cujus ratio est, quia sapientia est potissima per-

8. Subdivision of Practical Philosophy.—This falls naturally into three parts: *logic*, which treats of the acts of the mind; *moral philosophy* or ethics, which deals with the acts of the will; *aesthetics* or the *philosophy of the arts*. The full significance of this division will appear presently.

9. Subdivision of Speculative Philosophy according to the Scholastics and to Modern Philosophers.—Following upon the study of the particular sciences, further reflection finds that the things and groups of things severally observed in those sciences have something knowable in common, which is that whereby we are enabled to bind together or synthesize the various findings obtained by the previous work of analysis. This *common intelligible object* is the object of philosophy.

The object common to things is threefold—movement, quantity and substance—and furnishes ground for a triple division of speculative philosophy. This division corresponds to three stages or degrees of mental abstraction that the mind makes in its endeavour to obtain a complete, synthetic grasp of the order of the universe.

(*a*) What *takes place* in nature—understanding thereby the ensemble of things presented to our observation—we may describe in general language as *change, movement*. To use the ancient words, the body in which the change takes place is a *moving* thing (ens mobile); the efficient cause of the change the *motor*-agent; the change itself *movement* (motus, ἡ κίνησις). It is the profound explanation of movement so understood which provides the subject-matter of the first part of the philosophy of nature, namely of *physics*.

fectio rationis, cujus proprium est cognoscere ordinem. . . . Ordo autem quadrupliciter ad rationem comparatur. Est enim quidam ordo quem ratio non facit, sed solum considerat, sicut est ordo rerum naturalium. Alius autem est ordo, quem ratio considerando facit in proprio actu, puta cum ordinat conceptus suos ad invicem, et signa conceptuum, quae sunt voces significativae. Tertius autem est ordo quem ratio considerando facit in exterioribus rebus, quarum ipsa est causa, sicut in arca et domo. Et quia consideratio rationis per habitum perficitur, secundum hos diversos ordines quos proprie ratio considerat, sunt diversae scientiae. Nam ad *philosophiam naturalem* pertinet considerare ordinem rerum quem ratio humana considerat sed non facit; ita quod sub naturali philosophia comprehendamus *et metaphysicam*. Ordo autem quem ratio considerando facit in proprio actu, pertinet ad *rationalem philosophiam*, cujus est considerare ordinem partium orationis ad invicem et ordinem principiorum ad invicem et ad conclusiones. Ordo autem actionum voluntariarum pertinet ad considerationem *moralis philosophiae*. Ordo autem quem ratio considerando facit in rebus exte ribus constitutis per rationem humanam, pertinet ad artes *mechanicas*'. *In X Ethic. ad Nic.*, I, lect. 1.

(*b*) What *is* in a thing, if we consider it apart from its movement, what is the permanent reality in nature (τὸ ἀκίνητον), comes before the mind first as something quantified—to use an Aristotelian phrase, ἀκίνητον ἀλλ' οὐ χωριστόν, as 'an object without movement but not separated from matter'. This object the mind can strip of all its sensible properties on which its mechanical, physical changes and chemical transformations depend, and then there remains in the mind merely a something formed of parts in respect of other parts according to the three spatial dimensions of length, breadth and thickness: which furnishes the object of a general science, the science of *mathematics*.

(*c*) We can still further abstract from an object of thought even this mathematical attribute and we are then left with mere *being*, thing, subject, principle of action, which has nothing in common with quantity and quantitative attributes, τὸ ἀκίνητον καὶ χωριστόν, and provides us with matter for an even more general science than mathematics: *metaphysics* or *first philosophy*.

In consequence of the very great development of the experimental sciences in modern times, natural philosophy is now concerned only with the very broadest problems of physics and these are studied in two separate branches of philosophy, *cosmology* or the physics of the inorganic world, and *psychology* or the physics of the organic world.

Natural theology, the crown of the ancient physics inasmuch as it treats of the First Efficient Cause and the Supreme Final Cause of nature, forms in the modern division a third branch of study, frequently known also as *theodicy*.

Further, although the problems concerning the origin and validity of our intellectual cognitions belong really to psychology, their exceptional importance since the time of Kant has led philosophers to treat them apart and to regard them as a separate branch of study under the name of *ideology* or *theory of ideas*, and *epistemology* or *criteriology*.

We may note that the ancient general metaphysics [19] is

[19] According to the old definition Metaphysics studies Being considered apart from matter. As Physics can demonstrate in the case of man the existence of a soul capable of existing in separation from the body, as well as the necessity of asserting the existence of a supreme immaterial Cause, to

to-day frequently called *ontology*. Mathematical studies no longer are included as a branch of philosophy, but the fundamental ideas of unity and number are investigated in ontology, and those of quantity, extension and space in cosmology.

To sum up: speculative philosophy (1) according to the ancient and mediaeval classification covered all the sciences grouped under the three great headings of physics, mathematics and metaphysics [20]; (2) according to the modern classification it comprises: ontology or general metaphysics; cosmology, or transcendental cosmology as distinguished from experimental physics; psychology, or rational psychology as distinguished from the sciences of anatomy and physiology; theodicy or natural theology. Criteriology or critical philosophy has also in these days a separate treatment even with those who keep to the ancient classification.

In what order ought we to arrange the different branches of philosophy?

account for the material universe, there are two branches of Metaphysics: one, *General Metaphysics*, to treat of the material world considered apart from matter; the other *Special Metaphysics*, to treat of Being actually immaterial or spiritual. Yet metaphysics makes *one* science inasmuch as its object is *formally one*, as will be explained in *General Metaphysics*, **3**. The division invented by Wolff, according to which not only Natural Theology, but also Psychology and Cosmology are included in Special Metaphysics, is an unfortunate one: see *ibid.* **4**.

[20] 'Theoricus sive speculativus intellectus, in hoc proprie ab operativo sive practico distinguitur, quod speculativus habet pro fine veritatem quam considerat, practicus autem veritatem consideratam ordinat in operationem tamquam in finem; et ideo differunt ab invicem fine; finis speculativae est veritas, finis operativae sive practicae actio. . . . Quaedam igitur sunt *speculabilium* quae dependent a materia secundum esse, quia non nisi in materia esse possunt; et haec distinguuntur quia dependent quaedam a materia secundum esse et intellectum, sicut illa in quorum definitione ponitur materia sensibilis: unde sine materia sensibili intelligi non possunt; ut in definitione hominis oportet accipere carnem et ossa: et de his est *physica* sive scientia naturalis. Quaedam vero sunt quae, quamvis dependeant a materia sensibili secundum esse, non tamen secundum intellectum, quia in eorum definitionibus non ponitur materia sensibilis, ut linea et numerus: et de his est *mathematica*. Quaedam vero sunt speculabilia quae non dependent a materia secundum esse, quia sine materia esse possunt: sive nunquam sint in materia, sicut Deus et angelus, sive in quibusdam sint in materia et in quibusdam non, ut substantia, qualitas, potentia et actus, unum et multa etc.: de quibus omnibus est theologia, id est divina scientia, quia praecipuum cognitorum in ea est Deus. Alio nomine dicitur *metaphysica*, id est transphysica, quia post physicam dicenda occurrit nobis, quibus ex sensibilibus competit in insensibilia devenire. Dicitur etiam *philosophia prima*, in quantum scientiae aliae ab ea principia sua accipientes eam sequuntur.' St. THOMAS, In lib. Boet. *de Trinitate*, q. 5, a. 1.

10. Hierarchy of Philosophical Studies.—Observation, alike of the external world and of consciousness, is the philosopher's only source of information, and therefore the mind must commence with observation of reality. Hence the sciences of observation, which verify and enrich cursory popular observation, must come first of all, supplying, as they do, the material for philosophy. Their philosophical complement is *general physics*. Physics is to-day represented by cosmology, psychology and natural theology [21], and to psychology belong epistemological questions as well as the fundamental principles of ethics or the science of conduct. *Mathematics* comes after physics. *General metaphysics* or *ontology* then gathers together in a synthetic conception the results obtained by physics and mathematics. Finally, as scientific knowledge—alike of physics, mathematics and metaphysics—is formed by grouping together relations and so constitutes order in the mind, *logic* comes in as the science of reasoning or science of this mental order. With logic speculative philosophy, which embraces all that is essential in philosophy, is complete.

The ideas of logic put forward in the Introduction as prenotions do not strictly speaking belong to logic *qua* a science. And the theses on ethics and natural law that we discuss after the treatise on logic are in reality only applications of moral science to conduct in individual and social life, and therefore really belong to psychology, seeing that the general principles of moral science are borrowed from it. The moral act, which is the object of ethics, is that performed by man in view of his proper end, and it is in psychology that the end of a rational being is determined, his free act investigated and the habits —virtues or vices—brought about by the use or abuse of soul-freedom discussed. The theoretical principles of moral philosophy are, then, part of psychology, and the application of these principles, as given in this Manual after logic, must be regarded as a complement rather than a department of philosophy. So, too, the arts are applications of the science of aesthetics, and aesthetics or the study of the beautiful and man's sense of the beautiful belongs, in its principles, partly to general metaphysics and partly to psychology. As for the history of philosophy, which is given as an appendix to the Manual,

[21] For the double place Natural Theology may take see that treatise, 2.

it is a parallel study, closely interwoven with the study of philosophy itself [22].

11. Philosophy and the Particular Sciences.—Man's distinctive perfection whereby he is superior to the animal consists in his power of mental abstraction. The study of philosophy in its various branches is this work of abstraction carried to its furthest limits. Thus philosophy, in its various forms, has an inherent perfection of a higher order than that of other branches of study. Mathematics stands on a higher plane than the several physical sciences; so metaphysics, in its turn, carries off the palm of nobility and ranks above the former as well as the latter.

For the sake of those who may be tempted to regard philosophy with distrust rather than esteem, we may briefly recall the arguments on which Aristotle bases the superiority of metaphysics over other branches of human study.

[22] The Translators wish to acknowledge that they are responsible for the insertion of the popular sub-headings in the Table of Contents. Their endeavour has been to make clear at a glance the logicality of the order of the treatises. Philosophy is by definition an attempt at the most ultimate explanation of whatever there is to know. When the particular sciences have offered their partial explanations of reality, philosophy commences, and begins, like all science, from the data of experience: of the total reality directly disclosed to our experience part is seen to have the feature of being inorganic, part the additional feature of being living, whilst some living being has a yet further (accidental) reality in the truth of mental acts. After three separate investigations (*Cosmology, Psychology, Epistemology*) of these three very different kinds of material 'being' of which we have direct experience, it remains only to press the inquiry further and explain them in terms of what is common to all being (*General Metaphysics*), and finally to press it still further and find the ultimate understanding of all being in the First Being, Being Itself (*Natural Theology*). Here the explanation of reality might seem complete and speculative philosophy to have attained its goal, did it not happen that two properties of some living being, viz., man's power of knowledge and his power of free-action, remain not fully explained. Now since the object of the science of knowledge is knowledge, *Logic* as a speculative science should come after the knowledge of real being has been acquired, after the sciences, after philosophy, the acme of science, (as an art it draws its rules directive of thought from it as a science, and as far as it has been deemed useful these have been anticipated in the second half of this Introduction to Philosophy.) The treatise on *Ethics* is only a development of the philosophy of man's other peculiarity, his free-act; it is consequently natural to study it after the reality of the last end has been established and when, as a special development, it will not interfere with the flow of the main train of philosophic thought. The *History* is an appendix, meant for reading at all times, which by presenting other Theories broadens the mind and more often than not shows up the Scholastic Theory as a mean between two extremes. —Trs.

He says: Breadth of knowledge has a better claim to be considered scientific knowledge than knowledge of detail; one who has knowledge of a whole must have some knowledge of each and all of the parts of it. Secondly, a comprehensive knowledge is the better reasoned knowledge; and the reason of things is expressly the knowledge of them. Then, speaking directly of first principles, he says: General knowledge has more scientific precision: it studies the causes and so busies itself with what may, in the result, prove the more complete knowledge, since we cannot really know anything until we have learnt its cause. Finally, the science which goes furthest into the beginnings of things and best helps us to comprehend them is the one which knows to what end each thing must have been made. With each thing this final end is its good; and the universal final end is the one greatest possible good to be found in nature [23].

12. Philosophy and Revealed Truth.—In the eyes of theologians philosophy is regarded as a 'natural' science, in this sense that it deals with an order of knowledge to which man can attain by the light of unaided reason and is opposed to that order of knowledge which, because it surpasses the power and needs of created nature, is called 'supernatural'. The latter order of knowledge deals with the truths proposed to our faith by divine revelation and the profound study of this concerns not the philosopher but the Christian theologian [24]. Yet that there is a certain connexion between human sciences and revealed truths we may see from the fact that both these natural and supernatural spheres of knowledge meet in the mind of the Christian scientist or philosopher.

It is important to determine the relations between them.

1. Philosophy is a study formally independent of all authority. Indeed, for the constitution of a science two things are essential: that it have certain principles and the means of drawing such conclusions from these principles as are contained by them in germ. Just like all science, philosophy has its own principles and its own distinctive methods. Both alike deduce their principles from the analysis of a given subject-matter, which so analysed discloses the existence of various

[23] *Metaph.* I, c. II.—Cp. BARTHÉLEMY SAINT-HILAIRE, Préface à la *Métaphysique*, pp. CXCI–CXCII.

[24] Cp. ST. THOMAS, *Sum. Theol.* I, q. 1, art. 2, 5, 8.

relations; the simplest and most general of these furnish the formative principles of our knowledge. The mind recognizes these relations with certitude because they furnish their own evidence. When the combination of these simple relations leads the mind to more complex conclusions, it is precisely the evidence of the connexion between the latter set and the former that is the sole motive which induces the reason to assent to the results obtained by the demonstration. Hence the essential elements of science—principles, conclusions and the certainty of the evidence between them—are independent of all Church authority.

This general argument is confirmed by the fact that science and philosophy existed before the foundation of the Church, and the Author of Christianity came not to destroy the natural endowment of man but to enrich it with better gifts. Moreover, when in the first half of the last century De Bonald and La Mennais sought to oblige the human reason to receive its first principles and its primary motives of certitude from revealed teaching, Gregory XVI, far from accepting this dutiful subjection offered to the Church, publicly reproved and condemned the mistaken loyalty of its authors.

2. Are we then to conclude that the Christian scientist and philosopher may show a complete disregard of the teachings of revelation? Certainly not, for the Church has received from God the deposit of revealed truths and it is her mission to hold it intact. Thus when in the name of science or philosophy the imprudent or the rash advance theories which contradict the teachings of revelation, the Church cautions those who trust to her for guidance, and denounces the error the acceptance of which would run counter to belief in divine revelation. Her guardianship is thus negative and she herself does not *positively* teach either science or philosophy. She leaves entire liberty to those who study them, and history and individual experience testify to her zeal in encouraging them. She uses no voice of authority in such matters; men are left to their own reflection and research; her only authoritative mission is to teach the dogmas of revelation. But such being her mission she cannot allow, still less approve, anything that may be detrimental to the divine teaching. As long as scientists and philosophers do not put themselves in opposition to what she knows to be revealed by God, and

in consequence most certainly true, she respects the freedom of human learning; but when any one puts forward as science what is only mistaken conjecture, she calls for a revision of such hasty conclusions, and thus shows herself the helpmate of the human reason by her assistance in disclosing to it its errors.

In short, philosophy and the sciences are autonomous in this sense that in their case the supreme motive of certitude is the intrinsic evidence of the object they study, whereas in matters of faith the ultimate motive of belief is the authority of God, the author of supernatural revelation. Revelation is not a motive of assent, a direct source of knowledge for the scientist and the philosopher, but rather a safeguard and *negative* standard. The Christian philosopher from the moment that he undertakes his investigations has full liberty of interrogating nature or his own consciousness and of following the direction of his reason. But if it should happen that he finds his conclusions at variance with revealed truth as proposed to his belief by legitimate authority [25], he is bound alike in the interest of faith and of scientific truth to trace back his inquiries until his difficulties find a solution in accord with

[25] The authority to which the interpretation of the sacred deposit of revelation has been entrusted is primarily the *ecclesia docens*, that is to say, the episcopate in communion with the Sovereign Pontiff or the Sovereign Pontiff alone in the infallible exercise of his supreme office. The *ecclesia docens* has an *ordinary* magisterium which is permanent and an *extraordinary* magisterium which is intermittent; the teaching of the latter is contained in the definitions of the œcumenical councils and the *ex cathedra* decisions of the Popes.

Under the guardianship of the *ecclesia docens*, the beliefs of the *ecclesia discens* constitute a Christian rule of faith; for the unanimous beliefs of the faithful—the expression of the *sensus catholicus*—in matters which are within their competence, can but be an echo of the authoritative teachings of the Church. In matters which are beyond the general competence of the faithful, the only authorized judges are the Fathers, the Doctors and the Theologians. To these, then, subject to the higher decisions of the *ecclesia docens*, the human mind must have recourse in all that concerns the faith or truths in close connexion with the faith; their unanimous agreement in these matters furnishes the scientist and the philosopher with a negative, at least a provisional, rule of assent; it is indeed an authorized *intermediary* between them and the supreme magisterium of the Church.

Yet in secular matters which have only indirect bearing on revealed truths it is wise to call again to mind the assurance expressed in St. Thomas' words 'locus ab auctoritate quae fundatur super ratione humana est infirmissimus'—the argument from authority is the weakest of all arguments (*Sum. Theol.* I, q. 1, a. 3, ad 2).

the teachings with which at first sight they seemed to conflict. Divine truth cannot be erroneous; whatever is a certain contradiction of a dogma certainly revealed cannot but be error and to repudiate error is surely an act of reason.

3. But, it may be asked, if the case should arise of an evident contradiction between faith and reason, must we abdicate the rights of reason? We who are believers do not admit the possibility of such a contradiction. To answer the unbeliever, we must make an appeal to experience. Can he bring a proof, even a single proof, of a manifest contradiction between an evident truth of reason and a dogma of the Church? We confidently assert that there never has been found a manifest conflict between a dogma and a certain conclusion of science. Where discrepancies have arisen and doubts have been introduced they have always been the outcome of hasty observation, premature induction or ill-considered hypothesis, or, on the other side, of inaccurate definition of belief or the personal opinion of isolated theologians. When it is not immediately apparent wherein lies the explanation of a seeming disagreement between what is put forward as of faith and what is put forward as a scientific conclusion, the prudent and wise Catholic scientist will for the time suspend his judgment and await with confidence for the real truth to be brought to light [26].

[26] We may quote the testimony of two who are great scholars and whose loyalty to the Church is above suspicion. First, H. de Smedt, S.J., who has devoted his life to the study of ecclesiastical history. He writes thus, in his *Principes de la critique historique*: 'To be called upon to make a sacrifice on these matters presupposes the possibility of a genuine opposition between historical truth and revealed truth. But since such an opposition is quite beyond all question, the critic has no ground for anxiety. It may happen, we agree, that some fact asserted by historical documents of unquestionable authority seems at first sight to be in contradiction with the teachings of faith. But more attentive examination of the fact in question and the doctrine opposed to it soon reveals that there is no difficulty in reconciling them and that the supposed contradiction is in reality only the result of inaccurate knowledge of either or both. And further, even if it should happen that all attempts at reconciliation prove at first to be fruitless, and the most searching examination furnishes no means of agreement—an event which has never yet come within our experience—this need never disquiet the Catholic savant. He will wait again for light without being troubled by the shouts of triumph of the enemies of religion who are always so alert to claim a victory despite the many hard lessons such hasty folly has brought against them. This patience will be in every respect and particularly for the sincerity of his faith and the peace of his soul far preferable to the violent effort he would have to make to twist the evidence of a fact which for the moment stands

The Vatican Council sums up Catholic teaching concerning the relations of rational conclusions and revealed dogmas in these words: 'Although faith is above reason there can never be a true discord between faith and reason; for the God Who reveals mysteries and bestows the gift of faith is He Who has also illuminated the human mind with the light of reason; but we cannot find contradiction in God and neither can truth be opposed to truth. If the vain appearance of such contradiction should arise, this is either because the dogmas of the faith have not been understood and expounded according to the mind of the Church or because arbitrary opinion has been mistaken for judgment founded on reason' [27].

opposed to convictions reached from a source higher than science' (pp. 20, 21).

Our second witness is M. Paul Mansion, a scientist and mathematician of the first rank, who when attacked by an anti-Catholic newspaper gave this decisive answer: 'The greatest savants of the nineteenth century, with but few exceptions, have been Christians: Cauchy and Weierstrass, the two leading mathematicians, were Catholics. Amongst physicists, Ampère, Faraday, Clausius, Mayer, Joule, Maxwell were believers. So too in the natural sciences, not to mention others, there were Cuvier and Geoffroy Saint-Hilaire; and Leverrier and Secchi, the two princes of mathematical or physical astronomy were Catholics, as also were Lavoisier, Chevreul, Dumas and Pasteur. Darwin hesitated all his life but very many evolutionists are believers, amongst others Gaudry and the Belgian d'Omalius, and I need hardly mention André Dumont and many other geologists. Among the 'old' mineralogists Stenon, Agricola, Werner, Hauy. . . . The founders of modern science in the past—Kepler, Descartes, Newton, Leibniz—were all ardent believers.

'With these illustrious names before me, I look in vain for an antagonism between scientific truths and religion. If this antagonism were real there could not possibly have been Catholic scientists, and yet Catholic scientists there have always been. . . . It is not scientific to speak insistently of the antagonism between Science and Catholicism in a vague and general way without ever coming down to detail. If the anti-Catholic press is so sure of this antagonism, why is it not more explicit in stating wherein the claimed opposition between science and faith lies. Let its writers set down in two parallel columns the scientific truths reached by physics, chemistry, astronomy, mineralogy, geology, botany, zoology, anthropology, biology, etc., and—if any such they can discover—the contrary decisions of the Councils and Popes, as they are to be found, for example, in Denzinger's *Enchiridion*.

'We are bold enough however to predict that the second column would never be filled in if it were to contain only the authorized interpretations of Scripture and Catholic Tradition and if indefensible assertions were not inscribed under the pretext of science in the first column'.—Cp. Donat, *The Freedom of Science* (Wagner, New York, 1915); B. Windle, *A Century of Scientific Thought* (Burns and Oates, London, 1916).

[27] 'Verum etsi fides sit supra rationem, nulla tamen unquam inter fidem et rationem vera dissensio esse potest: cum idem Deus, qui mysteria revelat et fidem infundit, animo humano rationis lumen indiderit; Deus autem negare seipsum non possit, nec verum vero unquam contradicere. Inanis autem hujus contradictionis species inde potissimum oritur, quod vel fidei dogmata

13. Prominent Names in the History of Philosophy.—Beginning with the seventh century B.C. we see the rise and development, one after another, of several Schools of Greek philosophy—the *Ionian School* (Thales, Anaximander, Heraclitus, Anaxagoras); the *Atomist School* (Leucippus and Democritus) in Asia Minor or the greatest part of the modern Turkey in Asia; the *Italian School* founded by Pythagoras in Sicily; the *Eleatic School* (Xenophanes, Parmenides and Zeno of Elea) and that of Empedocles, in the isles of the Aegean (the modern Archipelago) and the Magna Graecia (Sicily and Southern Italy).

Towards the middle of the fifth century B.C. several brilliant rhetoricians, notably Gorgias and Protagoras, gathered at Athens and formed a school under the name of *Sophists*. *Socrates* (470–399) who was their great opponent created what in some sense may be called a moral philosophy and a psychology and inaugurated the celebrated 'Socratic method' of instruction [28]. But it was in Plato and Aristotle that the philosophy of the ancients reached the zenith of its power. *Plato* (427–347) established at Athens a systematic course of teaching which became known as the *Academy*. Later Arcesilaus (*b.* 315) and Carneades (*b.* 213), introduced a considerable departure from his doctrines and the Platonic tradition developed under the name of the *New Academy*. *Aristotle* (384–322) who had been a disciple of Plato founded the Lyceum or *Peripatetic School* in opposition to the Academy [29]. A little later there arose a body of sceptics under the leadership of *Pyrrho*, the *School of Epicurus*, and its rival the *Stoic School* (Zeno of Citium). All these flourished in the fourth and third centuries B.C.

The conquest of the East by Alexander changed the centre of the philosophic world. Alexandria in particular became the home of philosophy and during the first years of the

ad mentem Ecclesiae intellecta et exposita non fuerint, vel opinionum commenta pro rationis effatis habeantur.' *Const. Dei. Filius*, cap. IV. De fide et ratione. DENZINGER, *Enchiridion Symbolorum* (Ed. 1911), n. 1797.

[28] The Socratic method consists in a series of questions adroitly framed so that the answers elicited from the pupils gradually lead them on to a discovery of the truth for themselves.—See ZELLER, *Socrates and the Socratic Schools*.

[29] Aristotle taught in a gymnasium called the *Lyceum*, discoursing with his favourite pupils whilst strolling up and down (περιπατέω) the shaded walks: whence his school were called the Peripatetics.

Christian era there flourished there several schools : the *Jewish School* (Philo), the *Gnostics*, the School of *Christian Apologists* (Clement of Alexandria, Origen), the *neo-Platonic School* organized by Plotinus (205–270) and his disciple Porphyry (233–304) the author of the much-discussed *Isagoge*.

The early Christian writers, always subsequently known as the Fathers, aimed mainly at achieving a scientific exposition of the revealed truths of religion, but from the nature of the case they could not fulfil their task of defence against the paganism with which they were everywhere surrounded without touching on most of the questions that belong to the domain of philosophy. Therefore in this chapter of the history of philosophy, covering the first centuries, especially the fourth, of the Christian era, the *Philosophy of the Fathers* and other ecclesiastic writers occupies an important place. The chief writers were St. Justin, Athenagoras, St. Irenaeus, Tertullian, St. Methodius, St. Clement of Alexandria, Origen, St. Cyril of Jerusalem, St. Basil, St. Epiphanius, St. Gregory Nazianzen, St. Gregory of Nyssa, St. John Chrysostom, St. Augustine ; and we should mention, too, Denis the pseudo-Areopagite (towards end of fifth century) who had a great influence on the mystical and philosophical developments of the Middle Ages.

The Greek philosophy was never entirely abandoned. Banished from Athens in the fourth century and from Alexandria, it flourished at Byzantium throughout the Middle Ages until the thirteenth century, developing on parallel lines though never coming in contact with the march of ideas in the civilized countries of the West. But from the end of the thirteenth century there came about an interchange of ideas between East and West, and the Byzantines introduced the Scholastics to a number of works hitherto unknown, though it was chiefly from the Arabian philosophers that the latter became acquainted with the scientific and philosophical writings of ancient Greece.

Scholasticism became a school of philosophy not because it was the growth of any particular epoch or place, or from any external circumstances, but because it stood for a single body of fundamental doctrines peculiar to itself [30]. Already

[30] See M. De Wulf, p. 101 ff. *History of Medieval Philosophy* (trs. Coffey, Longmans, London, 1909).

in the eleventh century *St. Anselm of Canterbury* (1033–1107) had endeavoured to unify the fragmentary teachings of the earlier Scholastics into one system. In the twelfth century *Peter Lombard* (*d.* 1160) wrote his famous *Summa sententiarum*, which was a kind of encyclopedia of matters theological and philosophical and destined to become the groundwork of innumerable commentaries made by the great thinkers of mediaeval philosophy.

The thirteenth century marked the golden age of Scholasticism. Three facts we may emphasize as contributing to this result: the introduction of the Scholastics to the *Physics*, *Metaphysics*, and the *De Anima* of Aristotle, through the medium of translations from the Greek and Arabic (about 1200); the rise of the great universities, particularly that of Paris; the foundation of the Dominican and Franciscan Orders. *Alexander of Hales* (*d.* 1245), *Albert the Great* (1193–1280), *St. Thomas Aquinas* (1227–1274) surnamed the Angelic Doctor or the Angel of the Schools, *St. Bonaventure* (1221–1274) surnamed the Seraphic Doctor, *Henry of Ghent* (*d.* 1293) and *Duns Scotus* (1266?–1308) were chiefly instrumental in making the thirteenth century the most glorious period in the history of Christian philosophy [31].

The sixteenth century marks the period of the decadence. Yet this was not general. Two minds of high calibre, *Francis a Sylvestris* or Ferrariensis (1474–1528) and Thomas del Vio, better known as *Cardinal Cajetan* (1469–1534), have left what still remain the classic commentaries on the *Summa contra Gentiles* and the *Summa Theologica* of St. Thomas. About 1563, after the Council of Trent, there was a revival in theological and philosophical studies. A neo-Thomism made its appearance under the initiative of the University of Salamanca, and the universities of Alcalá, Seville, Valladolid, of Coimbra and Evora in Portugal were not slow in following. *Dominicus de Soto* (1494–1560) and *Bañez* (1528–1604) among the Dominicans; *John of St. Thomas* (1589–1644) whose *Cursus philosophicus* is still greatly valued; and *Suarez*, the Jesuit (1548–1617), known as Doctor Eximius, are names worthy of particular mention.

[31] We must not omit the name of Dante Alighieri (1265–1321) whose *Divina Commedia* has been very aptly described as 'Aquinas in verse'. See Ozanam, *Dante et la philosophie catholique au XIIIe siècle*. WickstEED, *Dante and Aquinas* (1913).

With the period of the decline of Scholasticism coincides the gradual growth in literature and philosophy of ideas born of the Renaissance. The rehabilitation of the literature and philosophy of the ancient world, the Protestant Reformation, the enthusiasm for the various experimental sciences, brought about the introduction of what is known as Modern Philosophy. The notable men of influence were *Giordano Bruno* (1541–1602) and *Campanella* (1588–1639) in Italy; *Francis Bacon* (1561–1626) and *Hobbes* (1588–1679) in England; *Descartes* and his numerous disciples in France. René Descartes (1596–1650) was in reality the chief initiator of the new movement, and his influence was very widespread, not only in France, over such men as Pascal, Bossuet, Fénelon and Malebranche, but in Holland where *Spinoza* (1632–1677) permeated the Cartesian doctrines with a species of Oriental pantheism, and also in Germany where *Leibniz* (1646–1716) surrendered himself very largely to his tone of thought, though in reality he must be classed as an eclectic philosopher.

The eighteenth century contains many great names, especially those of *Locke* (1632–1704), Newton (1642–1727), *Berkeley* (1685–1753), *Hume* (1711–1776), Adam Smith (1723–1790) and Bentham (1748–1832) in England; those of *Condillac*, Montesquieu, Voltaire, Rousseau, Turgot and Condorcet in France; those of Wolff, and above all, *Kant* in Germany.

At the commencement of the nineteenth century the chief centres of philosophic influence were Glasgow where *Reid* (1710–1796) had founded the Scottish School and Königsberg where Kant (1724–1804) had inaugurated a new movement. This double current was fused, in France, into an eclectic spiritualistic philosophy by such men as Royer-Collard, Jouffroy and Victor Cousin, and finally by Caro and Paul Janet.

In the course of the nineteenth century, alongside the Christian schools arose positivism under *Comte*, Littré and *Taine* in France; in Germany the pantheist school of Kant's successors, notably *Fichte, Schelling, Hegel*, and later, with some qualification, *Schopenhauer* and *Hartmann*; in England associationism and evolutionism under the patronage of *John Stuart Mill, Herbert Spencer* and others [12]. Alike in Germany,

[12] See the author's *Origins of Contemporary Psychology* (translated by Mitchell, London, 1917); or MERZ, *History of European Thought in the Nineteenth Century*, 3 vols. (Edinburgh, 1904, etc.).

France and Italy there spread a neo-Kantianism. The German group comprises Liebmann, Cohen, Natorp, Vaihinger and others; and the same influence is manifest in the work of Wundt who was the chief promoter of a psycho-physiology, and in the German and American psychologists of his school. Kant was introduced chiefly by Charles Renouvier and Lachelier into France, where the most prominent names are Boutroux, Fouillée, Liard, and Bergson.

Among believers in Christianity were many attempts to restore a sound philosophy but some of these were marked more by the excellence of their motive than by a full appreciation of their results. Thus the schools—Traditionalism, Ontologism, Rosminianism—founded by de Bonald (1754–1840), La Mennais (1782–1854), Bautain (1796–1867), Gioberti (1801–1852) and Rosmini (1797–1855) were destined to have but a short existence.

At Naples, Rome, and in Spain, however, much modest and untiring work has slowly brought back again the Aristotelian and Scholastic tradition. Its influence has steadily grown, and under the impetus given by the publication in 1879 of the Encyclical *Æterni Patris* of Leo XIII has led to a movement of considerable power back to the great system of the philosophy of the Scholastics and above all of St. Thomas Aquinas.

14. Leading Features of Thomistic Philosophy.—One system of philosophy alone, amidst the incessant endeavours of the many systems through three centuries to investigate the inmost mysteries of reality, has been able to stand without modification in its fundamental tenets, and this is the philosophy of St. Thomas. To-day its stability and breadth is such that it serves as an excellent basis and principle of unification for all the results of philosophical speculation reached by the various sciences of modern times. We are convinced, and in this we feel confident we are not mistaken, that all who have the courage to pursue his philosophy to the bottom and follow its logical conclusions will agree with us that concerning the analysis of the activity and processes of the mind, concerning the inner nature of body, living being and man, concerning the foundations of speculative science and ethical philosophy, no other man has ever thought and written with the power of St. Thomas Aquinas [33].

[33] Whilst it is true that our course of philosophy is intimately associated

For the purpose of examining what are the particular characteristics of his philosophy, we may distinguish between the substance of his teaching, and the form and method of his exposition.

With regard to the substance we may point out three particular features—its attitude of fidelity to the revealed truths of religion, its happy combination of the work of personal investigation with a respect for traditional teachings, and its maintenance of a right balance between methods of observation and speculations of the reason, or its union of analysis with synthesis, of induction with deduction. Three characteristics indeed which are worthy of close attention.

with the name of St. Thomas, we wish it to be understood that we do not regard the Thomistic philosophy either as an ideal which one must not attempt to surpass or as a boundary which sets limits to personal activity of thought; but our position is that we regard it as a mark no less of prudence than of modesty to make use of his teaching as a starting-point from which we may go further afield in original speculations and as a constant standard of reference. This we feel called upon to say in reply to those, whether opponents or friends, who may feel tempted to ask if it is our intention to lead back the modern mind to the outlook of the Middle Ages or to identify Philosophy with any particular system of philosophy.

There is no question of retracing our steps back to bygone centuries; Leo XIII, who has been greatly instrumental in bringing back the Scholastic philosophy to a place of honour, lays emphasis on the welcome that should be given by all to the discoveries and speculations of any modern philosopher in so far as they are sound and helpful to the cause of truth: 'Edicimus libenti gratoque animo recipiendum esse quidquid dictum, quidquid utiliter fuerit a quopiam inventum atque excogitatum'. And St. Thomas himself would have condemned any servility in adherence to his own thought, since at the beginning of his *Summa* he bids us beware of exaggerating the value of arguments resting merely on human authority, which he describes as the weakest of all arguments: 'locus ab auctoritate quae fundatur super ratione humana est infirmissimus'.

But respect for tradition is no indication of servility of mind but rather one of elementary prudence; respect for a doctrine whose merits have been personally ascertained and verified is no mark of a blind devotee, but of a dutiful disciple of the truth. Neo-Scholasticism, taught by the history of the philosophic strife of the sixteenth and seventeenth centuries, is little likely for the future to renew the failings of its predecessors; it will keep in close contact with the march of contemporary thought and the discoveries and speculations of the various particular sciences which are the handmaidens of Philosophy. We have done our best to insist on the necessity of this in chapter VIII of *The Origins of Contemporary Psychology* and in an article *Le bilan philosophique du XIX*ᵉ *siècle* (*Revue Néo-Scholastique*, 1900); and also, in the matter of teaching, in *Rapport sur les études supérieurs de philosophie*, 3rd Edit. (Louvain, 1901).

For an outline of Scholastic Philosophy and its development by the neo-Scholastics of Louvain, see *Scholasticism Old and New* already referred to.

1. It is worthy of notice that St. Thomas, after a careful introspection into the facts revealed by personal consciousness and after learning the lesson written across the pages of history, lays stress at the beginning of his *Summa Theologica* on the moral necessity for a religious teaching for man, a teaching to which the human reason must conform.

> 'It was necessary for the salvation of man that certain truths which exceed human reason should be made known to him by divine Revelation. Even as regards those truths about God which human reason could have discovered, it was necessary that man should be taught by a divine revelation; because the truth about God such as reason could discover would only be known by a few, and that after a long time, and with the admixture of many errors. Whereas man's whole salvation, which is in God, depends upon the knowledge of this truth. Therefore, in order that the salvation of men might be brought about more fitly and more surely, it was necessary that they should be taught divine truths by divine Revelation '[34].

2. Whilst he asserted the right, and confirmed it by his

[34] *Summa Theol.* I, q. 1, a. 1 (Dominican translation). *Contra Gentiles*, I, 4. Monsabré has devoted one of his excellent conferences (*Introduction au dogma catholique*, Confer. 6) to commenting upon this passage and explaining the meaning of this *moral* necessity. He observes that in dealing with intellectual problems we must notice that there are two points of view. If we consider natural truths in themselves, we may say that it is possible for the human mind, by a sustained application, to form a conception of them, following as they do one from another; if we consider the human intelligence in the application it brings to bear upon these truths, we find that as a matter of fact it does not reach a conception of them. From this second point of view, when we look at the weakness, in one form or another, of the majority of men we may say that it is impossible for them to arrive at a knowledge of natural truths in their entirety. Hence it is befitting that God in His mercy should have provided for the needs of the human race by granting that men should hold by the light of faith what reason could know by its natural power, and that thus all should be able easily to share in a knowledge of things divine, and this without any obscurity arising from doubt and without fear of error. And he goes on to give various reasons why, as all know to be a matter of common experience, the majority of mankind cannot without this supernatural aid become possessed fully and easily of all natural truths: for instance, some are incapable, through natural feebleness of mind, others are hindered by social duties and family ties, whereas leisure and solitude are indispensable for real scientific knowledge; others again are held back by a defect of will arising from indolence of character or the restlessness caused by the passions. In short, Revelation is a moral necessity.

constant practice, of checking by his own personal work that of his predecessors, he never overlooked the value of their labours [35]. He was well versed in the writings of the Greek philosophers [36], the Fathers, Cicero and Seneca, and the Arabians; far from wishing to be entirely original, he impregnated all his own work with the wealth of ideas he inherited from the past. He had no share in that naïve vanity displayed by Descartes in his third rule for the guidance of the mind: 'In our study we must look not to what others have thought about it but to what we ourselves are able to see clearly and evidently or to deduce with certainty; this is the only means of arriving at the truth'. His commentaries on the works of Aristotle and Peter Lombard are sufficient testimony to the respect he had for the thought of others, little matter whether it came from a Christian or from a pagan source.

3. As a third characteristic, we may point out that this philosophy is remarkable for the harmonious alliance it displays between inductive reasoning which carefully observes facts and deductive speculation, or what is now frequently spoken of as analysis and synthesis. It avoids on the one hand the false empiricism of the positivist and on the other the false idealism of the pantheist, which are the two tendencies which have directed all non-Scholastic systems of philosophy.

Here we must content ourselves with pointing out the fact without offering a proof, but it will be seen to be borne out by each of the leading theses treated in this Manual and, at greater length, in the large volumes of the *Cours de philosophie* published by the *Institut.*

Whilst such, then, are the characteristics which appeal to the student of St. Thomas' philosophy if attention is paid to the substance of his teaching, no less admirable qualities are presented by the *form* and *method* of its exposition. Its style is clear, crisp and concise; it is simple and straightforward in its manner of unfolding ideas and without any of

[35] See TALAMO, *L'Aristotélisme de la scholastique*, chap. X (Paris, 1876).

[36] It is interesting to note in this connexion, as a proof of the critical spirit of St. Thomas, that conscious of the many errors shown in the different versions of Aristotle's works then in vogue, he went to the trouble of collating the various translations and to this end obtained permission of his superiors for a Dominican—a Belgian, William de Moerbeke—to journey to Greece to discover a more faithful text. See Introduction to the Leonine edition of St. Thomas (1882 etc.). Dissert. XXIII, Cap. 2.

the florid language or embellishments of the poet or the orator, such for instance as we find in Plato where allegories and myths so often break up the regular sequence of thought. Those who accuse the Scholastic style of want of elegance and of severity in its terminology forget that the Latin tongue had produced no philosophers—unless we may mention the poet Lucretius and the orator Cicero and certain ethical writers—and that the Middle Ages had the difficult task of creating a language suitable for the expression of philosophical truths. In his argumentation St. Thomas usually employs the clear-cut form of the syllogism. Lastly, his method of exposing a truth is peculiarly his own, inasmuch as in most of his works he first of all begins by setting forth sundry arguments from authority and certain objections that militate against his thesis in point, thus bringing out the exact state of the question and focusing the attention on the problem to be solved; then he handles the question directly, subjecting it to the severe logic of the syllogism until gradually all the obscurities and difficulties he himself at first introduced are cleared up. Thus when his proof is completed he leaves the mind so clear that usually all the difficulties previously proposed are easily seen through and vanish of their own accord.

These characteristics both in doctrine and in method which go to make the attractiveness of St. Thomas' work will appeal to all his readers, whose judgment, we feel sure, will endorse to the full what we have been saying [37].

[37] Since we shall have very frequently to quote St. Thomas in the course of this Manual we give a list of his chief philosophical works, following the Parma Edition (1852–1869).

The *Summa Theologica* (which with the *Summa contra Gentes* form his chief works) is divided into three parts which treat respectively of God, of the tendency of the creature towards God, and of Christ the mediator between the creature and God. The second part is subdivided, prima pars and secunda pars. Each part is again subdivided into questions, and each question into articles, which contain first the objections, then the body of the article—the exposition and proof of his thesis—and finally answers to the objections. We shall in giving references abbreviate thus: I (pars prima), I–II (prima pars secundae partis), II–II (secunda pars secundae partis), III (tertia pars), supp. (supplementum tertiae partis), q. (quaestio), a. (articulus), c. (corpus: the body of the article), ad 1 or ad 2 (answer to first, or second, objection)—Thus II–II, q. XIII, a. 4, ad 3.

The *Summa de veritate catholicae fidei contra Gentiles*, frequently known as the *Summa Philosophica*, contains four books, the first three treating of God *secundum rationem*, the fourth *secundum fidem*. (Thus *Cont. Gent* lib. II, cap. 34). Next come his commentaries on the Books of Sentences of Peter

15. Some Important Preliminary Ideas.—Whatever be the order adopted in the teaching of the different branches of philosophy there will always be certain notions which belong partly to one, partly to another of the various sections of study. Usually logic is taught first, and general metaphysics immediately follows. But even in logic the most elementary notions presuppose various notions that belong to psychology, epistemology and general metaphysics; for example, mental abstraction, the relations of idea and word, scientific certitude, the opposition between *ens reale* and *ens rationis*, the idea of truth, etc. Again, general metaphysics relies on cosmology for its meaning as a study. We have endeavoured to avoid these inconveniences by placing cosmology and psychology first in the order of instruction designed in this Manual and by emphasizing the fact that these hold

Lombard. Each book contains various studies grouped under the wide heading of *Distinctio*, each of which is subdivided into *Quaestiones* etc. as in the *Summa*. (Thus 3 *Dist.* 6, Q. 2, a. 1, ad 2).

Volumes VIII and IX contain a collection of writings, philosophical and theological, called *Quaestiones Disputatae*, in particular those bearing subtitles *De potentia, De malo, De spiritualibus creaturis, De anima, De veritate* and similar treatises, including also some on Canon Law and liturgy called *Quaestiones quodlibetales* or more briefly *Quodlibeta*. (Thus *Qq. disp. De pot.*, q. 7, a. 2, ad 1.—*Quodlib.* 12, a. 10, ad 1.)

Volumes X–XV are devoted to the exegesis of S. Scripture and to spiritual writings.

Volume XVI publishes some theological and philosophical minor works or *Opusculae*, some of which are of doubtful authenticity. The most interesting from our present point of view are:—*Compendium theologiae; de natura verbi intellectus; de regimine principum* (the last two books of which are not authentic); *de aeternitate mundi contra murmurantes; de principio individuationis; de ente et essentia; de principiis naturae; de natura materiae; de mixtione elementorum; de differentia verbi divini et humani; de unitate intellectus contra Averroistas; de potentiis animae* (?); *de totius logicae Aristotelis summa* (?); *de universalibus* (?); *in libram Boetii de Trinitate.*

Volume XVIII opens the series of Commentaries on Aristotle, notably—*Commentaria in libros Perihermeneias; de generatione et corruptione; de anima; de sensu et sensato; in XII libros Metaphysicorum, in X libros Ethicorum, in VIII libros Politicorum* (parts of doubtful authenticity). These commentaries are divided into lessons. (Thus: In IV Ethic., lect. 3).

Considered chronologically St. Thomas' writings stand in the following order:—About 1250 *De ente et essentia*, at Cologne; from 1252 the *Commentaries on the Sentences* and probably some of those *on Aristotle* at Paris; commencement of *Contra Gentiles* which was completed in Italy; about 1272 commencement of *Summa*, at Bologna; we must place about 1270 his *De unitate intellectus* and probably between 1268 and 1271 most of the *Quaestiones*. The *Supplementum tertiae partis* is an extract from the Commentary on the Sentences inserted by another author into later editions of the *Summa* the chief place in constructing a system of philosophic study. But at the same time we recognize that this does not avoid certain difficulties which must be met with in any arrangement. In our view the best course is to present, as we have already done in this Introduction, certain preliminary ideas, and in the ensuing pages to add to and complete these necessary propaedeutical notions.

It is impossible to help the student to a study of philosophy, whatever form it may take, unless we first insist on what he may and must expect from such a study, namely, to learn about reality from the most general of all points of view, to gain a comprehensive or synthetic view of all things by their most fundamental causes or principles. To aid him in appreciating this point of view we have traced with him the different stages of human knowledge, first leading him to recognize that all operations of the mind have an abstractive character in common; next delineating the three distinct stages of these abstractive processes; then defining terms, namely principles, reasons, causes; and lastly showing what principles, reasons, causes are the concern of the philosopher. It remains to notice briefly those ideas from logic and metaphysics which have a frequent and important bearing on the study of cosmology and psychology.

16. Important Ideas from Logic.—It seems indeed almost superfluous to make even a brief mention of the logical ideas we propose to give, for they are merely applications of common sense.

Logic furnishes certain rules for the right guidance of the operations of the mind. Logicians are accustomed to distinguish three kinds of operations: (1) *Simple apprehension* consists in representing an object without affirming or denying anything about it. Thus by a simple apprehension of the mind I conceive the idea 'being', 'tree', 'man'. (2) *Judgment*—and a *proposition* is merely its oral or written expression—is the act by which under the form of affirmation or negation one object already known, viz., the *predicate* of the judgment, is brought into mental relation with another object known, viz., the *subject* of the judgment: e.g. 'This tree is high', 'the whole is greater than one of its parts'. (3) *Reasoning* or ratiocination, of which the *syllogism* is the expression, is the act by which the mind compares with a third idea (called the *middle term*) two notions (the *extreme terms*) between which it does not immediately perceive the agreement or disagreement, identity or non-identity. This comparison of each of the extremes with the middle term is made in the *premisses* of the reasoning (propositiones quae praemittuntur), and the result of the twofold comparison finds expression in the *conclusion* of the syllogism. The two premisses together are known as the *antecedent*, and the conclusion as the *consequent*; the logical bond or nexus between antecedent and consequent is the *consequence*.

When each of the extreme terms agrees with the middle term, the conclusion is affirmative; when one agrees and the other does not, the conclusion is negative.

A judgment, as opposed to the conclusion of an argument, is said to be *immediate*; and the conclusion of a reasoning process *mediate*.

A conclusion strictly deduced from two certain premisses is itself certain; a conclusion deduced from two uncertain premisses or from one certain and another uncertain premiss is itself uncertain, i.e. doubtful or only more or less probable.

A reasoning-process which leads to a certain conclusion is a proof or *demonstration*.

Demonstration in the strict sense, however, requires something more than mere certain reasoning: it requires that the premisses be based not on extrinsic considerations—which would be an extrinsic proof,—nor upon the absurdity that would result from the conclusion being false, upon a reductio ad absurdum; but it requires that they be drawn from the analysis of the subject. This intrinsic, causal, a priori, (διότι), demonstration is the only one which in the Aristotelian terminology is strictly speaking *scientific*. To attain to this is the constant aim of the true scientist and philosopher; by this alone is *Science* built up, if we use the word in its highest sense.

Deduction is the demonstration of a conclusion from an examination of the premisses. *Scientific induction* is a different process; it is that by which the scientist finds out the laws of nature. The law of a natural body is the manner in which it exercises its actions: e.g. it is the law of chlorine and hydrogen, under certain conditions of temperature and pressure, to combine in the proportion of 35·5 and 1 to form by their union 36·5 of hydrochloric acid (HCl.). A law is the natural outcome of the *properties* a body has, i.e. certain qualities necessarily inherent in the body. The rational, exact sciences are deductive in method; the sciences of observation, the experimental or empirical sciences, are inductive, albeit their logical validity, as will be proved in Logic, rests on a deduction.

Demonstration or demonstrative proof is not the only process necessary for the constitution of science: *definition* and *division* must also be added. For, demonstration presupposes premisses; and it cannot be—if we are ever to arrive at a certain conclusion—that all the premisses of a science should have to be demonstrated; there must be some which carry the evidence of their truth with them without needing proof and which serve as the formative principles of the science in question. The formulation of these principles for each science constitutes the initial *definitions* of that science.

Division is a complementary process of definition. Definition gives us to understand what something is,—what 'quantity', e.g., is, the object of mathematics;—division establishes a relation of identity between the definition and the object defined and thereby makes the definition to belong to this object and it alone: whence the rule essential to good definition, 'conveniat *omni* et *soli* definito'.

To take as a starting-point for argument (principium) a proposition which because it is not evident still requires to be proved, is to fall into the fallacy known as 'begging the question' (petitio principii).

These notions we have given belonging to logic teach us the structure essential to a perfect science and bring before us, therefore, the ideal of the scientist and philosopher and the criterion by which we judge the value of their work.

17. Important Ideas from Ontology.—When the mind considers a natural body under all its aspects, it forms for itself an object of thought (objectum intelligibile), and the following are its '**notes**':—

Considered in so far as it is something, every body is a substance, determined by certain accidents, some of which are necessary and others contingent, and in itself composed of metaphysical parts, namely potential subject and specific form.

Considered in so far as it is capable of action, every body is a nature endowed with operative powers—forces or faculties

—by virtue of which it acts or is acted upon in such a way as to realize an end which is proper to itself, called its intrinsic or natural end.

The subject, whether we call it substance or nature according as we view it from the static or dynamic point of view, is made actual by existence.

But we must notice at the outset that though these characters or 'notes' by which we represent to ourselves a natural body are manifold, this by no means implies that the thing itself is not one single thing; it is our concepts that are many, for the reason that we are incapable of forming a single conception of a thing which adequately expresses to us its reality; the reality itself is not manifold, it is individualized, that is to say, it is undivided in itself, one, distinct from every other thing. That we have to employ many concepts for the representation of a thing that is single is due to the law of the mind's activity which *abstracts*, and this process of abstraction means to take apart (abs-trahere) in our consideration different characters of a thing which are ontologically or in the order of reality not separate from one another.

The first stage is when the mind represents to itself a natural object, e.g. this table, this tree, as a something placed before it and capable of being referred to by the demonstrative pronouns 'this', 'that'. The philosopher calls the object, at this stage of knowledge, an *essence*, what-a-thing-is. The question, 'What is this? What is that?' is answered by the essence of the thing. Thus what-ness, essence, quiddity (quid est?), τὸ τί ἐστι, are synonymous terms; each signifies that by reason of which a thing is what it is.

Essence is also called *substance*, a word used when we wish to emphasize its distinction from *accident* (accedens, ἐπισυμβεβηκός). Both substance and accidents are realities; accidents are secondary realities which supervene upon a substance and determine it, whereas substance is a presupposed reality, determinable by the accidents: e.g., extension is an accident, the quantified body is a substance. An accident is inherent in a substance and—if there be no derogation from the natural law—is incapable of existence except as existing in a substance; substance on the contrary has no need of something else in which to exist. Whence these two definitions: 'Substantia est ens in se; accidens est ens in alio'. Or to speak more accurately in view of the possibility of a miraculous exception to the natural law: 'Substantia est ens in se; accidens est ens cui debetur esse in alio'.

An accident is never an intrinsic part of its substance, seeing that it presupposes it and adds something to it; yet among accidents some are necessarily united to their substance —called *properties* (proprium, ἴδιον). The word property is used as opposed to *contingent* accident; accordingly when in logic we distinguish between what is necessary and what is accidental, it must be noted that 'accidental' is used as a synonym with 'contingent': that is said to be necessary which is not able *not to be*, that is said to be contingent which is but is able *not to be*—contingit ut sit vel non sit.

Substance is made known to us by its accidents, especially by its properties, 'as the properties, so the substance'. Thus we are led to distinguish various kinds or species of substances, *specific types*. We shall see in cosmology in the case of mineral substances, and in psychology in the case of organized substances, that each substance is composed of two constitutive parts, primary or first matter and a specific substantial form. The latter presupposes the former as that by which a compound is specifically determined presupposes a determinable subject. The relation between what is determinable and that by which the determination is effected, is, in the language of metaphysics, the relation of potency or *potentiality* and *actuality* (potentia, actus) or again, of *matter* and *form* (materia, forma); in fact potency and actuality, matter and form, determinable and determinant are interchangeable couples.

The object we have been speaking of as submitted to the analysis of the mind's abstraction we have hitherto considered as a thing. A thing, if we look at its whole meaning, is itself an essence in the state of being potential to existence and its existence is its actuality; in other words, *existence* makes an essence actual. Thus 'esse est ultimus actus', to use the Scholastic terminology.

We have now to attend to another point of view. We observe that things act upon other things or undergo action from them. Whilst in God action and substance are identical, no creature is an agent directly by virtue of its substance; its substance has operative powers which serve as means of action. These operative powers, called *forces*—mechanical, physical, chemical—in the corporeal world, and *faculties* in the case of man, are then *immediate principles of action*, whereas the substance is the first, mediate principle of action. Considered from this point of view substance bears another name; it is called a *nature*.

We have just said that it is from their properties that we are able to learn of the varieties of specific substances. Specific natures too are in the same way diversified according to the powers of actions proper to them. By means of these powers they accomplish the purpose they have, their rôle or peculiar end.

Speaking generally, then, we may say that a *nature* is a substance considered in so far as it is the first intrinsic principle of the activities it is capable of and of the determinations which it may undergo by means of the powers which properly belong to it.

There is thus a correspondence between a *nature*, which is the source of activities, and its *end*, which is the purpose and finish of these activities; whence, too, various expressions such as the *natural end* of a being, the *natural tendency* of a being towards its end, *natural law* according to which it acts in the direction dictated by its end, *natural action*, i.e. in conformity with the exigencies of its end and thus in conformity with the natural law of its being.

The natural end of a being is inherent in it, *intrinsic* to its nature. As each nature tends towards its own intrinsic end, the activities of all natures harmonize together and arrange themselves in mutual relations, and thus bring about *extrinsic* ends and work out the intentions of Him Who both wills and accomplishes the general order of nature.

Philosophy is the study of this order of the universe and of the means which bring it into effect.

We pass on now from what is introductory to the definite study of the different branches of philosophy. Physics, in the Scholastic use of the word, is the first part of philosophy It embraces, according to the universal division in vogue, two parts, *Cosmology* and *Psychology*.

COSMOLOGY

INTRODUCTION *

1. Definition of Cosmology.—Cosmology is the *philosophic study of the inorganic world*. This concise definition embodies, on the one hand, the *material* object or subject-matter which cosmology proposes to study—the inorganic world; on the other, the *formal* object or the special aspect under which it regards it—the philosophic point of view.

2. Material Object of Cosmology.—Our definition of cosmology limits the field of cosmology to the inorganic world and leaves to psychology the philosophic study of plants, animals and men. As the name implies (ψυχή and λόγος), psychology concerns itself with the soul, that is, with the first principle of life in organic beings. Yet this first principle of inherent activity is not confined to the human being but exists also in all beings endowed with sensitive or vegetative life. If therefore we would avoid an arbitrary classification we must exclude from the scope of cosmology life under any of its forms.

3. Formal Object of Cosmology.—The inorganic world forms the object of five different sciences: physics, crystallography, mineralogy, chemistry and geology. After we have assigned to each its own proper field of investigation, it becomes evident that there remains, outside their respective boundaries, another field proper to cosmological speculation.

Thus, physics has for its object the properties common to matter: weight, sound, light, heat, electricity, magnetism, together with local movement that accompanies the exercise of these forces; it deals with inorganic matter under a special aspect, and that only a *superficial* one. Crystallography considers a particular *state* of mineral substances, the crystalline state and the geometric forms which are its sensible manifestation. Mineralogy is the *descriptive* study of the minerals of which the crust of the earth is composed; it classifies them according to their physical and chemical analogies, or even according to their geological position. Chemistry investigates

* For a fuller treatment see Nys, *Cosmologie*, 3rd Edit., 3 volumes (Louvain); Schaaf, *Institutiones Cosmologiae* (Rome, 1907, printed privately).

those transformations of corporeal substances which affect and deeply modify their inner nature, and describes to us what are the *factors* which combine to effect these intimate modifications, the thermic, electric and luminous phenomena which *accompany* their combination, and the properties and the chemical constitution of the *new body* that results from the reaction. Geology takes a more general point of view: far from limiting itself to the consideration of the *simple ingredients* of the earth's crust, it takes cognizance of the various aggregations of mineral particles that have been brought together according to the fixed laws of nature; and in the light of the actual phenomena that are unceasingly modifying the earth's crust, it investigates their origin and the manner of their formation; in a word, it endeavours to reconstruct the past history of our globe.

But however adequate may be the methods of investigation employed by these five sciences, they cannot throw any light on, and still less solve, many problems of the very first importance. Geology in retracing the history of the earth takes the mind back to the most distant ages. But as this history presupposes at the outset the existence of matter, we may push our inquiry further and ask from whence it came. This question deals with its very first *origin*, its *first efficient cause*.

The same problem presents itself again when we consider simple bodies and their compounds, the subject-matter of chemistry; we have to face the problem of the *ultimate constitutive causes of the inorganic world*. What is the essential nature of the chemical elements which result from the analysis of the natural scientist? Is matter altogether homogeneous? Has it, as the purely mechanical theory maintains, no other energies than that of local motion? Or must we regard it, with the dynamist, as an aggregation of simple unextended forces? Or, lastly, ought we to agree with the Schoolmen and explain it by a double principle: one common to all matter, a permanent substratum enduring through all its transformations however intimate; another, special to each of them and the formative principle to which they owe their specific nature? Finally, as physics, mineralogy, crystallography and each of the other natural sciences are confined by their very object to the specific investigation of some particular province of the material world, none of them make an attempt to deal with the entire cosmic order as such, to discover the principles that determine it or the end for which it exists. Nevertheless, the human intellect cannot refrain from asking what are the *destinies* of our world, what is its *final cause*.

Cosmology has then to solve three questions which are outside the scope of the special sciences: (*a*) *What is the first efficient cause of the inorganic world?* (*b*) *What are its ultimate constitutive causes?* (*c*) *What is its final cause?* These three questions express the *formal* object of cosmology and justify the use of the term 'philosophic' in our general definition: for it is the province of philosophy to explain things by their ultimate causes.

4. Division of Cosmology.—Cosmology comprises three parts, the respective objects of which are: (*a*) The origin of the inorganic world or its first efficient cause; (*b*) its intrinsic constitution or its ultimate constitutive causes; (*c*) its destinies or its final cause. As the second of these problems belongs exclusively to cosmology and cannot be treated elsewhere, we propose to devote our attention to it alone in this treatise.

5. Method Followed in this Treatise upon the Constituent Causes of the Inorganic World.—The mind has no immediate or intuitive knowledge of the essence of material bodies. This knowledge is attainable only by the study of the phenomena which are its visible expression. Hence the more careful and thorough the investigation of all these visible phenomena, the more complete will be our knowledge of the substantial reality underlying them. It follows, then, that cosmology is essentially an inductive science, necessarily dependent upon matter supplied by the natural sciences. It presupposes as its starting point an impartial examination of all those scientific facts and phenomena which reveal more or less clearly the nature of material substance.

6. Theories of the Constitution of Matter.—The study of the intrinsic constitution of matter has given rise to four great cosmological systems:—

(1) *Pure Atomism*, now more commonly known as Mechanism.

(2) *Hylomorphism* or the Scholastic Theory of Matter and Form.

(3) *Dynamic Atomism.*

(4) *Dynamism.*

PART I

Pure Atomism or Mechanism

CHAPTER I

OUTLINE AND HISTORICAL DEVELOPMENT OF THE MECHANICAL THEORY OF THE UNIVERSE

7. Mechanism among the Ancients.—Mechanism as a philosophical system possesses a very high antiquity. *Thales* (B.C. 624), *Anaximander* (B.C. 611), *Anaximenes* (B.C. 588) and *Heraclitus* (B.C. 535) derived the universe from one primitive homogeneous substance, and thus they laid down the first principle of that evolution on which the modern theories of mechanism are based. Water, a subtile matter spread through infinite space, air and earth, were the bodies successively considered by these philosophers as the primary substratum of our world.

A little later, in the speculations of *Empedocles* (B.C. 495–435) these four bodies (water, fire, air, earth) played a more honourable rôle as being together the elements constitutive of the universe. Thus arose the celebrated theory of the four elements which science preserved as a sacred deposit until the time of the epoch-making discoveries of *Lavoisier* (1790). Empedocles asserted the essential intransmutability of the elements; and he attributed to them two forces—one of attraction, the other of repulsion, which he poetically called 'love' and 'hatred'. In this system the fundamental idea of modern mechanism, namely the reduction of every compound to a simple juxtaposition of immutable elements, is already outlined.

According to *Anaxagoras* (B.C. 500), each body contains particles of all the other elements, in such a way as to constitute a world in miniature, 'omnia in omnibus'. Although he has recourse to motion for the explanation of the union and dissolution of the particles of matter, nevertheless the efficient causality of all natural activities he attributes to some higher principle, to a being endowed with intelligence.

Democritus (B.C. 460) in his turn developed still further the mechanical theory. The identity or homogeneity of cosmic matter, the atomic constitution of bodies, the reduction of all material forces to local motion, were laid down by him as indisputable first principles of physics. His system is the complete negation alike of any first efficient cause, as of any final cause. Movement is as purposeless as it is without beginning and end. Everything is explained by the eternal motion of matter and the laws of an absolute determinism.[1]

Epicurus (B.C. 342–270), an ardent follower of Democritus, whilst adopting the fundamental principles of his predecessor's cosmology, introduced a slight modification with regard to the cause of motion. In the Epicurean theory the atom is self-moving. Although subject to the action of gravity which gives it the tendency to fall in a straight line, it has the power of changing the direction of its movement without any internal or external cause determining this deviation. By this extraordinary hypothesis Epicurus sought to reconcile the cause of motion with the possibility of the collision and of the combination of the material particles.

8. Mechanism after the Fifteenth Century.—After Epicurus atomism disappeared almost completely from philosophic thought for many centuries. It was only at the Renaissance that it reappeared in the speculation of Francis Bacon, Magnen and Gassendi. These revivals of mechanism, though at first isolated, were not slow to obtain a sympathetic reception in philosophic and scientific circles, for this was the epoch of Descartes, the real founder of modern mechanism. With his essentially mathematical mind, Descartes (1596–1650) endeavoured to build up his system of cosmology on the methods of geometry.[2] As geometry sets out from the simplest propositions and arrives by a chain of deductive reasoning at the most complex truths, so the French philosopher sought, among the attributes of bodies, for the property which is at once the most

[1] Consult BURNET, *Early Greek Philosophy* (London, 1892); ZELLER, *History of Greek Philosophy*, trans. ALLEYNE (London, 1881).

[2] See MAHAFFY, *Descartes* (Edinb. and Philadelphia, 1894).

fundamental, the most evident, the most universal. This property he thought he discovered to be extension. We may, he says, by an act of thought strip off all the qualities from a body without making it cease to be a real body so long as we retain its extension in length, breadth and thickness[3]. Extension was for him the fundamental, sole constituent of material being, its essence.

This principle established, Descartes denied to matter all properties which cannot be logically deduced from the analysis of extension:

1. First, he denied all intrinsic activity to bodies because the nature of extension contained no ground for such activity. He therefore rejected substantial forms, final causes and active qualities.

2. In the second place, since extension is everywhere and always homogeneous, he concluded that matter, the essence of which is extension, must therefore also be homogeneous.

3. From the above principle he further inferred the absolute impossibility of a vacuum. For, a vacuum is a kind of extension; but extension constitutes matter; therefore to admit a vacuum in the world is tantamount to identifying this vacuity with the presence of matter—which would be a contradiction.

4. Finally since extension is divisible *ad infinitum*, the existence of atoms or small particles of matter incapable of further division is inconceivable.

5. All phenomena are modes of motion communicated by God to the masses of matter at the very moment of creation: for since motion cannot be accounted for by passive extension, it must proceed from an extrinsic cause.

Cartesian mechanism lacked a scientific basis. It had been built up a priori, that is to say, on the mathematical concept of extension. With the nineteenth century mechanism entered on a new phase, and was adopted by a great many scientists as a convenient basis for the philosophic unification of the results obtained by science[4].

[3] DESCARTES, *Principiorum philosophiae*, P. II, n. 3, 4, 5. Abridged translation (Edinburgh and London, 1870).

[4] DUHEM, *La théorie physique, son objet et sa structure* (Paris). For a critique of the mechanical-materialistic theory from the standpoint of idealism see JAMES WARD, *Naturalism and Agnosticism*. For the mechanical theory in its broader and more inclusive interpretation, see A. BALFOUR, *Foundations of Belief* (London, 1895); B. RUSSELL, *Free-man's worship* in *Philosophical Essays* (London and New York, 1910).

One of the facts which have contributed most to the success and popularity of mechanism was the application by Dalton of the atomic hypothesis to chemistry.

9. Mechanism in Modern Times.—Before entering upon the study of this latest phase of the system, we must carefully distinguish two kinds of atomism: one purely scientific, called *chemical atomism*; the other metaphysical, called *philosophical atomism* or simply *mechanism*.

10. Chemical Atomism.—In chemistry we distinguish two kinds of bodies—simple bodies, and compound bodies which result from the combination of the former according to invariable laws of weight and volume.

Simple Bodies.—According to modern chemistry, elementary substances are composed of atoms, that is, of extremely minute particles of matter that are incapable of real division by any known chemical agent and yet possess the properties of the sensible body of which they are the smallest possible representatives.

These atoms are seldom found to exist in isolation. They have a tendency to form intensely compact little groups of two, of four, or sometimes even of a greater number of atoms. These groups, which ordinary physical agencies can only dissolve with great difficulty, are called the 'chemical molecules' of a body. These chemical molecules themselves unite to form more complex wholes, called 'physical molecules'. It is by the union of these latter that the body which is perceptible by the senses is finally built up.

Compound Bodies.—As the word implies, every compound results from the combination of several simple bodies, and therefore the chemical molecules composing it must contain several atoms *specifically different* from one another. The name 'chemical molecule of the compound' is given to the smallest quantity of this body that is capable of enjoying isolated existence. For example: NaCl.

As in the case of simple bodies, these molecules unite to form more complex physical molecules the resultant of which is a body as we see it.

Such, in outline, is the hypothesis of the atomic constitution of matter.

In accordance with this hypothesis chemistry describes in

detail the physical and chemical properties of the combining elements, the resultant compound, the phenomena which accompany the chemical combination and the laws which govern the natural transformations of bodies. The chemist describes each compound by a *molecular formula* that indicates what are the simple elements that have united to form the compound, and the number of atoms of each element contained in a chemical molecule; e.g. CO_2. Moreover by a *structural formula* he indicates the play of the atomic activities which results in the formation of the new compound.

The atomic theory, as thus conceived, belongs exclusively to the province of the natural sciences. Unconcerned with any opinions either about the nature of simple bodies and their properties, or about the substantial essence of the molecule of the compound, it leaves an open field to philosophic speculations which transcend empirical data.

11. Philosophic Atomism or Modern Mechanism.—This system is the philosophic interpretation of chemical atomism. Its leading tenets may be expressed in the following propositions:

1. The atoms of simple bodies are homogeneous, i.e. of the same nature. They are distinguished only by a quantitative difference of mass and motion.

2. All corporeal properties are reducible to modes of local motion.

3. The substantial being of the atom is itself inert, possessing no inherent principle of activity. Communicated local motion constitutes the whole of its energy, which is therefore merely borrowed.

4. Intrinsic finality or the substantial adaptation of beings to predetermined ends is for modern cosmology a useless fiction. The working of natural forces and the harmonious succession of material phenomena is adequately explained by mechanical laws.

5. The molecule of the compound is a microcosm formed of various atomic masses each of which has its own indestructible existence.

In a word, two factors alone are needed to explain the world: *homogeneous mass* and communicated *local motion*, capable of being transmitted and transformed in numberless different modes. Such is the theory adopted by the majority of modern scientists.[3]

[3] For instance: SECCHI, *Unité des forces physiques* (Paris, 1869); CLAUSIUS, *Théorie mécanique de la chaleur* (French translation, Paris); TYNDALL, *Heat as a Mode of Movement* (Lond., 1868); TAIT, *Sketch of Thermodynamics* (Edinb., 1877); BALFOUR STEWART, *Conservation of Energy* (Lond., 1890); HELMHOLTZ, *Mémoire sur la conservation de la force* (Paris, 1879). For modern theories see also L. POINCARÉ, *The New Physics*, III (Lond., 1907); H. POINCARÉ, *Science and Hypothesis* (Lond. and New York, 1905).

Of late years pure mechanism has been steadily losing ground in favour either of *neo-mechanism* or of *energism*. The neo-mechanists are less dogmatic than their predecessors; in place of laying down categorically that all properties of matter are only local motion, they are content with saying that the reduction of all properties to motion ought to be the aim of all scientific explanation, and that this end will perhaps be attained by the science of the future. They admit, however, that up to the present day such an explanation is faced with great difficulties, if indeed it does not lead to real contradictions. In the second place neo-mechanists refuse to pass any judgment as to the real nature of things, on the ground that it is not the province of science to solve metaphysical problems. Such are the two differences that distinguish pure mechanism from neo-mechanism. As a matter of fact, these differences are of secondary importance. For in both systems, the only accidental reality which is taken into account is local motion; it is the sole agent admitted, whether definitely or tentatively, to explain the entire order of material phenomena. With regard to the substance of bodies, although neo-mechanists are unwilling either to define or even to admit it, it remains true that logically this substance must be homogeneous; since if all properties are reducible to motion and are therefore homogeneous, it is arbitrary to introduce qualitative distinctions between the substances which support these different properties. The chief advocate of neo-mechanism to-day is M. A. Rey. See *La Théorie de la physique chez les physiciens contemporains* (Paris, 1907); *La Philosophie moderne* and *L'énergétique et le mécanisme* (Paris, 1908).

The *theory of energetics* or, as it has been called, *energism* is a reaction from mechanism, a new form of dynamism. An outline and criticism will be found p. 137 ff.

The Translators wish to add that the above note and the later section on the new dynamism are additions of the Author to the fourth French edition of 1913. He also recognized that now a further word regarding the Harmony of the Scholastic Theory with Facts requires to be said in view of the latest ascertained scientific facts, and in order to show that the Theory of Matter and Form has been in no way radically impaired. M. Nys wrote in the *Revue Néo-Scolastique de Philosophie* Mai, 1914, the first portion of an article, intending no doubt to embody his views in the next edition of this Manual. This first portion recounts the advances of natural science, and was to be followed up by their bearings upon philosophy. Unfortunately this important instalment was to have appeared in the fatal August which saw the sack of Louvain. Since that August the Translators have up to the present had no communication with M. Nys. If the rest of the article in question comes into their hands, they will append it at the end of volume II; if not, a few remarks may be added instead, for which of course the Author will be free to disclaim responsibility.

CHAPTER II

EXAMINATION OF THE MECHANICAL THEORY

A THEORY can rank as scientific only in so far as it offers a solution of the problems it professes to explain. Now the mechanical theory is unable to meet these problems.

ART. I. FACTS OF CHEMISTRY

I. ATOMIC WEIGHTS

12. Diversity and Constancy of Atomic Weights.—Each of the 85 simple bodies at present known has its own specific atomic weight. These atomic masses are ranged in ascending scale beginning with hydrogen whose atomic weight is represented by unity, up to uranium whose atomic weight is 238·5. Now it is a remarkable thing that these elementary bodies which differ so much from one another in their relative masses, all show an equal resistance to further division. They preserve their integrity throughout all chemical reactions.

13. Examination of the Mechanical Explanation.—In the mechanical theory the constant persistence of atomic weights is explained simply by two realities, *mass* and *motion*; for the whole universe is reducible to these two factors. But neither of these two can explain the fact. If *mass* is homogeneous, why does the divisibility of matter stop short at atomic masses that are unequal in quantity? To say that the secret of the constant diversity of these weights lies in the homogeneity of matter is surely to attribute a diversity of effect to an absolute identity of cause. On the other hand, equally incapable is *local movement* of accounting for the constant inequality of atomic weights. It is by a series of chemical reactions that all atoms undergo those manifold changes which transform their intrinsic energy, or reduce it to a minimum; but the forms of motion, to which mechanists attribute the permanence of the atomic nature, are essentially variable and reducible, and therefore we have no explanation how the elementary masses, once deprived of their protecting agents, always triumph over all physical and chemical causes that tend to disintegrate them [6].

II. Chemical Affinity

14. Meaning of Affinity, and Criticism of the Mechanical Conception of it.—Affinity is an elective tendency in virtue of which some bodies tend towards other bodies to make definite combinations. Each simple body has its own specific tendency, its own circle of sympathetic elements.

According to the mechanical hypothesis, two bodies have a mutual affinity if their motions are able to harmonize, to coalesce, to result in a state of stable equilibrium. The tendency of the elements is entirely extrinsic; it depends solely upon the impulse communicated to the atoms and on the direction that results from it.

Now it is an undeniable fact that the impulse and direction of motion can vary indefinitely in the molecules of bodies subjected to the influence of heat, of electricity, or of other physical forces. The affinity should therefore undergo the same variations and in this case we rightly ask how it is that any one body will not combine with any other. Experience attests that nothing can overcome the perfect indifference of some bodies for one another, as also the specific and invariable character of the affinity existing between others.

III. Valence or Atomicity

15. Meaning of Valence and Criticism of the Mechanical Explanation.—Valence is the name given to the property, possessed by each of the atoms of a given element, of uniting itself to 1, 2, 3, . . . *n* atoms of hydrogen or chlorine.

Although valence is not absolutely constant, it would be false to conclude that it is subject to the caprices of chance. It depends on the nature of the elements, yet it is subject, within well-defined limits, to the influence of certain extrinsic causes. This we express by saying that it is *relatively constant*.

Now does the mechanical hypothesis supply any cause capable

[6] Secchi has himself acknowledged 'that hitherto no one has been able to furnish a reason for the constant diversity of atomic weights.' See *Unité des forces physiques*, p. 133.

of guaranteeing this relative constancy? Evidently not. Local motion, we are told, is the only agent put forward to determine the number and the manner of the arrangement of the atomic masses that are contained in the molecule of the compound. But, on this hypothesis, the variations of the internal movements would always correspond to all the variations of external causes, and thus valence would lose its constancy.

IV. Chemical Combination

Between a chemical combination or compound and a simple mixture there is an essential difference of a threefold nature:—

1. Every compound is characterized both by the entire disappearance of the greater number of the physical and chemical properties of the component elements, and by the appearance of *new stable properties.*

2. A second sign showing that a combination has taken place is given by the considerable quantity of *heat* which is discharged in the process of the chemical reaction.

3. Combinations are regulated by *laws of weight* which are not observable either in physical actions or in simple mixtures.

16. First Sign: The Appearance of New Properties.— The supporters of mechanism do not all share the same opinion concerning the nature of these changes.

First opinion. According to some, the atoms preserve their properties within the compound. The combination, it is said, is a stable equilibrium, a co-ordination of the movements of the atoms. It takes place without destroying in any way the natural properties of the elements. But, as these movements of the elements when combined can no longer manifest themselves in the same way as in the state of isolation before combination, they produce on our sense-organs an impression of a new form, which leads us to conclude that a great change has taken place within.

But this opinion cannot be reconciled with the principle of the conservation of energy. Many combinations are accompanied with an enormous discharge of heat, electricity, light and chemical energy. The immediate surroundings are affected by it, becoming heated, illuminated and charged with electricity. Now every increase of energy gained by a body of any kind always implies, according to the above-mentioned principle, a corresponding loss suffered by some other bodies. The enormous quantity of forces set free by the reactions is accordingly the measure of the real loss sustained by the new compound; in other words, it measures the importance of the changes that have taken place in the elemental properties.

Second opinion. By paying greater attention to the facts of experience, many mechanists recognize that chemical combinations involve some profound modifications in the characters of the atomic masses. This concession is important. But as every mistake carries with it serious consequences, the result of this acknowledgment is that the mechanical theory, as we shall see later, cannot reconcile with its own principles either the regular decomposition of bodies or the return of the elements back to their natural state.

17. Second Sign: Thermal Phenomena.—According to mechanists, the generating cause of the heat discharged by chemical combinations is twofold; it is due partly to the intensity of the molecular collisions, partly to the breaking-up of the equilibrium existing between the atoms.[7]

This explanation of the mechanical theory appears certainly insufficient when we take into consideration the two distinctive characteristics of thermal phenomena, namely, *intensity* and *invariability*.

Thermo-chemistry teaches us that 16 grammes of oxygen combining with 2 grammes of hydrogen sets free 59 calories, or units of heat, that is, a force capable of lifting (59×425) 24·745 kilogrammes one metre high in a second. But is it not incredible that 18 grammes of matter, whose atoms moreover are in close proximity to each other, could by a simple modification of their spacial relations suddenly generate such an enormous display of energy[8]?

Yet be this as it may, the invariability of this phenomenon in a given combination is in manifest opposition to the mechanical theory. As soon as we were to identify all chemical energies with local motion pure and simple, the constancy of the phenomenon and its absolute independence in the presence of alien energies which provoke it, would disappear entirely. An effect that is always constant demands a cause that is stable, permanent

[7] Cp. SECCHI, chap. 14, and BERTHELOT, *Essai de mécanique chimique*, p. xxvii (Paris, 1874).

[8] See STALLO, *Concepts and Theories of Modern Physics* (Lond.. 1882).

and invariable. And, it is needless to say, local motion in no way possesses these qualities.

18. Third Sign: Laws of Weight.—Most chemists regard the physical indivisibility of atoms as the real foundation of the laws of weight. Such was notably the opinion of Dalton, who revived Greek atomism. However well-founded this may be, it is astonishing that mechanists look to the indivisibility of atoms as a self-evident postulate, when, of all chemical facts, perhaps none is more manifestly opposed to their principles (**13**).

V. The Recurrence of Chemical Species

19. Statement of the Fact.—An element under the stress of chemical agencies can pass through a countless number of compounds in each of which it assumes new properties. Molecular structures are scarcely formed before nature, with higher designs, either releases their elements again, or uses them for the formation of more complex compounds. Nevertheless, in spite of these great transformations in which the distinctive characteristics of the bodies appear to be the sport of material forces, there are invariably presented to us the same species, simple or compound, endowed with the same chemical and physical properties.

20. Reasons for This Fact.—Among the immediate and manifest conditions to which this fact is subject, there are at least three which chemists unanimously agree in asserting to be absolutely necessary:—

1. The *constancy of elective affinities.*—Most strange and disordered aggregations would be brought into existence at every moment if the affinities of bodies were open to the whims of chance or the contingent circumstances of reactions.

2. The *fixity of the laws of weight,* since every change in the relations of weight on the part of bodies subject to reaction has an infallible influence upon the specific characteristics of the compound.

3. Since the elements are deprived in the compound of their distinctive characteristics in order to assume in common a number of new properties, it is necessary that there be in the compound itself *a cause* that can control the exterior action and can differentiate its effect; otherwise, the simultaneous

re-appearance of the elements with their natural properties would remain inexplicable.

21. Insufficiency of the Mechanical Explanation.—Neither the laws of weight nor affinity, we have shown above, are sufficiently explained by the principles of mechanism. The only condition which still calls for special examination is the third. Here we are faced with two hypotheses: either we may say that the atoms remain unchanged in the heart of the compound—and this is the opinion adopted by a great number of mechanists—or that they there receive certain new properties.

Mechanism, should it choose the first, can explain the re-appearance of the elements and their properties under the influence of a similar extrinsic cause; but it would contradict the principle of the conservation of energy (**16**) and refuse all credence to the universal testimony of the senses which assure us of the existence of momentous changes in the elements gathered in the compound.

Should it prefer the second, it assumes a hypothesis quite incapable of explaining the fact in question. For, on the one hand, the atoms when combined are deprived of their natural properties; on the other, because of their essential identity, they cannot have any special aptitude to receive these or those determinate properties,—any specific aptitude being incompatible with the homogeneity of the atomic masses. There is then no reason why the extrinsic agent, which releases from a compound one or more of its component atoms, should invariably restore to each its original motion.

ART. II. PHYSICAL FACTS

I. Crystalline Form

22. Statement of the Fact.—Many bodies when they pass, slowly and guarded from all disturbing influences, from a liquid or gaseous state to a solid state assume geometric forms. They are then said to be crystallized. In point of fact the regularity which the plane surfaces of a crystal present is only a sensible manifestation of an internal and invisible regularity which governs the orientation and distribution of the crystalline matter.

What is of most interest among crystallographic phenomena is the law enunciated by Abbé Hauy: 'Bodies of the same chemical composition have the same crystalline form, bodies of different composition have a different crystalline form'.[9]

23. Criticism of the Mechanical Explanation.—For the explanation of the properties of crystals, crystallographers suppose the molecule of the crystallized body to be itself endowed with the specific form of the sensible crystal. This molecule, which is often called the *crystalline embryo*, is a very complex structure, made up of a great many chemical molecules. Scientists have not yet been able to determine the number of elements which constitute the crystalline molecule, but it is well ascertained that these elements are arranged in fixed directions and in an order characteristic of each body. Hence it is necessary that a governing principle should direct the arrangement of the molecules within the crystalline polyhedron by fixing their number and eventually determining their mode of union.

Now the motion of homogeneous particles, deprived by mechanists of any inherent tendency towards a determined end and of any element of finality, is manifestly incapable of producing this harmonious convergence of the manifold constituent parts of the crystalline molecule and cannot give it, with mathematical precision, its specific form. The order which we find realized in these extremely minute particles of matter is one that is stable, complex and distinctive of the species. The reasons put forward by mechanism leave both the specific nature of the phenomenon and its constancy alike unexplained.

[9] There are two apparent exceptions to this rule: isomorphism and polymorphism. By *isomorphism* is meant that property which certain bodies possess of being able to crystallize together and of assuming a common form. By *polymorphism* that property in virtue of which a body can crystallize under different primitive forms. A careful study of these facts has made it possible for crystallographers to put them under the general law.

However, some recent experiments have proved that the crystalline form sometimes undergoes numerous variations under the influence of temperature. Some bodies can assume seven different crystalline forms. The law of Abbé Hauy has, then, less importance than was at first attached to it; but it remains true that in the same physical conditions of pressure and of temperature different bodies, crystallizing in isolation, usually take different crystalline forms.

II. Physical Facts properly so called

24. Statement of these Facts, and Criticism of the Mechanical Explanation.—From the study of physical phenomena there follows a general conclusion which it is important to describe, namely that all bodies of nature are distinguished by a collection of properties that give them a definite place in the scale of beings. Natural state, density, crystalline form, properties relating to sound, heat, light, density, magnetism and electricity are all so many criteria of differentiation at the disposal of the physicist.

Secondly, a fact which is no less remarkable is that of the invariable recurrence of these physical species throughout the incessant transformations of matter. The same bodies ever re-appear with the same group of properties, a group so well determined that it is enough for a physicist well-versed in the study of matter to know only a single one of these properties in order to give a complete description of the species to which it belongs.

Thirdly, although these properties are independent of each other and are therefore each capable of receiving separate modifications, they are always to be found united in an indissoluble group in which each of them, either by its degree of intensity or by its conditions of activity or by other distinctive characteristics, appears as a visible manifestation to us of the corporeal nature of which it is the property.

Does mechanism, we ask, explain this threefold fact? We think not. This connexion which invariably associates a given group of properties with a determined substance finds no explanation in the hypothesis of homogeneous matter. Either matter should always and everywhere manifest the same exigences, or it should show itself indifferent to receiving one group of accidental qualities rather than another. In the latter case, there is nothing to prevent the same substance, e.g. hydrogen, from assuming successively the properties of nitrogen, carbon or of any other body whatever. In the former case, it is equally difficult to see why a given body should always possess a given group of properties in preference to any other, since the homogeneity of matter is incompatible with specific exigencies.

ART. III. MECHANICAL FACTS

I. THE KINETIC THEORY OF GASES

25. Statement of the Theory.—The particular object of this hypothesis is to explain the characteristic properties of the gaseous state, especially of the pressure that every gas exercises upon the sides of the vessel which contains it.

It rests on the following postulates :—

1. A gas is composed of solid particles, having a constant *mass* and *volume*.

2. These particles have *perfect elasticity*.

3. They are in *continual motion* and have no influence, except at very slight distances, upon one another, so that their movements remain *free* and therefore *in a straight line.*[10] According to this theory, the pressure exerted by a gas upon the sides of the vessel in which it is contained is due to the countless collisions of the moving particles with these sides.

26. Criticism.—None of the three propositions upon which the theory rests is capable of being proved by experience. This is the first ground for adverse criticism.

In the second place, the theory regards the perfect elasticity of the particles as an indispensable condition for securing the perpetuity of the movement and of the pressure : without this perfect elasticity the particles would sustain at each new contact a loss of motion and the gaseous body would eventually be in a state of rest. But this supposition introduces a real contradiction into the mechanical system, for the same atom which in physics is declared to be absolutely elastic, in chemistry is considered as devoid of all elasticity. Is it possible that the same individual atom can simultaneously possess two attributes mutually exclusive, or can change its nature suddenly according as the cause demands ?

Furthermore, by admitting the elasticity of the particles, the mechanist is obliged to re-introduce into the world of matter that element 'force' which he has banished from it. For suppose that two elastic atoms of the same mass are moving with equal velocity in opposite directions, and eventually meet along their line of motion and the line joining their centres of gravity. Having come into contact they press upon each other until at length their respective motions cease. As these

[10] Cp. CLAUSIUS, *op. cit.* II, 186 ff.

atoms must rebound, it is necessary that the movement which starts again after their contact be preceded by a moment, however brief, of complete rest. But if complete immobility precedes the reverse movements of these bodies, it is impossible that these movements arise from another movement. And therefore, unless we are to admit an effect without a cause, it is necessary to have recourse to a dynamic power essentially distinct from motion and intrinsic to the atoms, in a word, to the *force of elasticity*.

II. Gravitation

27. Mechanical Conception of Gravitation.—Modern science endeavours to reduce all the forces of nature to modes of universal attraction—the law of which was thus stated by Newton: 'The attraction between bodies is proportionate to their masses, and varies inversely as the square of the distance between them'. To account for this property by the sole factors of mass and motion would be, therefore, to justify mechanism in the triple sphere of physics, chemistry and astronomy. The most celebrated theory invented for this purpose is the *collision-theory* of Le Sage of Geneva (invented 1818). Briefly it is: Space is constantly traversed by flowing multitudes of extremely minute bodies, moving with more than lightning speed and coming from unknown regions of the universe. On account of their smallness most of them easily penetrate through ordinary sensible bodies in such a way that all parts of these bodies are equally struck by the corpuscles. If there were in space but one elementary body or one atom, this would be struck equally from all sides. But any two bodies naturally act as screens, with the result that each receives fewer shocks on the side which faces the other body, and they are thus attracted towards each other[11].

This theory, we notice, eliminates the element of force to the advantage of motion pure and simple.

28. Criticism.—We must choose one of two hypotheses, as Clerk-Maxwell observes: Either the particles are elastic, and in this case the action of gravity is reduced to nothing. For, owing to their elasticity, the particles rebound from the body with the same velocity as they had in approaching it and

[11] See Tait and Stewart, *The Unseen Universe*, § 141 (London, 1875, and New York, 1901).

preserve their energy unimpaired. But, in whatever direction they rebound from the body, they will be in the same number and have the same speed as the particles which are tending towards the body. Or, on the other hand, if the onrushing atoms are inelastic, the energy of the collisions will be converted into heat, and under the influence of this liberated heat the bodies will in a short time become white hot[12].

ART. IV. THE PHILOSOPHIC ASPECT OF MECHANISM

Mechanism attributes to motion three fundamental properties :—

1. Motion is the *principle of all material activity*; it is to be held to account for the birth of all new phenomena that occur in the world.

2. It has the aptitude of *transforming* itself into numerous modes, such as heat, magnetism, electricity, light and weight.

3. It passes unchanged from one body to another, in a word, it is *transmissible*.

Before undertaking to examine these propositions, we should be sure that we have a clear notion of what 'motion,' or 'movement', means.

29. Metaphysical Analysis of Local Motion.—'Movement' says Aristotle 'is the actuality of a being which is formally potential', i.e., which is capable of having some further reality [13].

Movement is an actualization, a determination which it is necessary carefully to distinguish from a simple power to act or to receive perfection in being. A stone when lying still is *susceptible* of movement, but it is not in movement. Movement commences when that susceptibility, or potentiality, begins to be actualized. It is therefore the actuality of a being still potential to possess further reality, to be something else.

Yet, this actuality which gives bodies a new position and constitutes all the mobile reality of movement cannot be anything terminated or complete in all respects. If you con-

[12] For further criticisms see PICTET, *Étude critique du matérialisme et du spiritualisme*, p. 239 (Paris, 1896).

[13] ARISTOTLE, *Physic.*, III, c. I. In the Oxford translations of Aristotle edited SMITH & ROSS) the *Physics* is in preparation. For a fuller metaphysical analysis of this definition see *General Metaphysics*, 115.

sider the stone you have thrown into space, at the precise moment when it receives its new place, you can say that it has been moved, but it is no longer in movement. If, then, you wish to conceive it in the state of movement, you must consider it as on its way towards a new position which is no longer its starting-point nor yet its final resting place.

In other words, although determined by a new position, the moving object would appear in movement only on the condition of its being in proximate passive potentiality with regard to a further actualization.

The actuality constitutive of movement is thus seen to be an incomplete reality bearing a twofold relation—on the one hand to a receiving or movable subject which it determines by placing in a new position in space, and on the other to an ulterior perfection or new position which the moving body continuously receives.

I. First Principle of Mechanism: Local Movement is a Force and a Cause capable of Producing a Mechanical Effect

30. Criticism.—According to the definition given above, movement comprises three elements indissolubly united. (1) First there is a movable thing in passive potentiality; (2) an actuality or determination which realizes the passive potentiality of the subject by giving it a new localization; (3) the tendency on the part of the subject to receive *hic et nunc* other spatial determinations.

Now in these elements, whether considered individually or together, there does not appear the least indication of any power of action.

1. In virtue of its aptitude to pass from the state of rest to that of movement, the subject of movement manifestly cannot communicate anything or produce anything; it is capable only of receiving something under the influence of an external cause. *Passivity*, which excludes all dynamic power, is the essential characteristic of this first element which constitutes movement.

2. Whatever reality exists in movement consists in the continuous determination by which the body is fixed at each

moment in different positions in space. Now this actualization has only this one effect, of giving to the body which receives it positions so fleeting that one disappears as another becomes real.

3. The tendency possessed by the moving body constantly to receive further actualizations is clearly a passive tendency and accordingly one incapable of producing an effect of any kind.

Local movement, therefore, considered in its separate elements and in its whole reality, is powerless to exercise any causal influence whatever.

31. An Objection.—Is not every body in movement endowed with a dynamic power proportionate to the intensity of the movement by which it is animated? Must we not then conclude that movement is the source of this energy?

A body in movement can certainly produce mechanical effects. Yet, the real cause of these effects is not the local motion, but a force properly so-called, a motor-quality inherent in the mover.

In the first place, the study of movement proves that this accident is incapable of exercising an efficient causality.

Secondly, experience confirms this deduction. A billiard ball which is at rest on the table, you may put into motion by a sharp stroke with the cue. As long as your cue is in contact with the ball you can attribute the movement to the exercise of a force that is within you. But once the contact has ceased and your action is finished, the cause of the movement which continues and even would never cease, were it not constantly lessened by the resistance from exterior things, must lie elsewhere. In fact either the new positions of the ball are not real, and in this case it is foolish to attribute a dynamic power to this movement; or these new positions are real, and in this case they demand a permanent stable cause which is present during its effects and consequently resides in the moving subject itself. For it is no longer you who are producing the fleeting and constantly renewed series of the movement, for you have ceased altogether to influence the ball. Whence then comes this energy? It was communicated to the ball at the moment of the shock; it is the immediate effect of your action, and the movement is only the result and partial measure of it. Like all other qualities, this force is by its nature stable and permanent, and cannot be destroyed except by a contrary force.

32. A Second Objection.—Does not movement, when it has once been started, carry along in itself the principle of its continuity, in the sense that every spatial position is itself the cause of the position which immediately follows it?

This hypothesis is overthrown by the mechanists themselves. For, to say that each position occupied by a body gives it the power of procuring the next is to affirm that matter at rest can by its own initiative communicate movement to itself, and thus to deny the law of inertia. The successive positions through which the body in motion passes in its action are not of a different nature from the last position where it comes to rest. There is no real difference between them. If the first ones form part of the movement, it is solely because each supplies a stage in the progress.

II. Second Principle of Mechanism: Movement is Transmissible from one Body to Another

33. Criticism.—Like all other accidental realities, movement is made concrete and individual by the subject in which it inheres; it is dependent on it intrinsically and must remain attached to it, otherwise it would disappear from the world of reality.

The hypothesis that movement is transmissible is moreover condemned by experience. If two bodies meet, the one being in a state of motion, the other at rest, the result is that the moving body comes to rest and the stationary one is set in motion. Now where does this new motion come from? Has it been transmitted from the body in motion? Evidently not. At the moment of contact, the moving body could not transmit the positions through which it had passed, since they no longer existed; nor again its present position, or else it would no longer have a place in space; nor again the future positions it could have received, since they yet exist only in the domain of pure possibilities. No particle of the movement of the moving body has then been transmitted to the body put in motion. And as the new movement demands a cause, recourse must be had to the motor forces brought into play by the contact.

III. Third Principle of Mechanism: Local Movement transforms itself into Heat, Electricity, Light, Magnetism, etc.

All the forces of nature are said to be modes of movement that are capable of being transformed into one another.

34. **Criticism.**—For one thing to be transformed into another, it is necessary (*a*) that it be deprived of some modes of being that characterize its present state, and (*b*) that part of the original thing remain in the final stage of the transformation. In default of the first condition, if the thing remains identically as it was, it will undergo no transformation; in default of the second, there would be an annihilation and a subsequent creation.

Now, in any case, a new movement does not contain a part of the movement which preceded it. For, the transitory actualizations which constitute the whole reality of movement are susceptible of two changes—change of velocity and change of direction. Let us consider each of these:

1. *Change of velocity*: On receiving an impulse, a body already moving with a velocity of two metres a second acquires a speed twice as great. Now the only connexion there is between these two movements is that one succeeds the other. To the series of positions occupied by the body in motion and now no more, at the moment of impulsion there succeeds a new series of transitory localizations. It is impossible to see in this second phase of the phenomenon the least trace of the former phase.

2. *Change of direction*: If a body in motion receives a lateral shock, it changes its direction. Now in this new direction, be the motion rotatory, vibratory or undulatory, one cannot discover any trace of the movement which preceded it, since at the moment of the shock all the previous spatial determinations had completely disappeared one after the other.

Hence movement is never the subject of any transformation.

It is true that the succession of the phenomena which we have just analyzed awakens the idea of a change, or rather, of a certain transformation. But where mechanism errs is to place it in movement rather than in its real cause. In the cases cited the motor force of the bodies, and that alone, has undergone the modifications or alterations which have produced the changes of velocity and of direction.

IV. Conclusion

35. General Reasons for the Repudiation of Mechanism.— 1. Mechanism has exaggerated the part played by movement and has falsified the notion by making it the principle of all the changes that take place in the universe. Hence arise contradictions when it is considered metaphysically, as well as its incapability to account for that vast array of facts where it is evident movement cannot take its origin from movement [14].

2. The second cause is its rejection of the teleological point of view in the explanation of scientific facts. The invariable recurrence of the same chemical and physical phenomena, the indissoluble union of fixed properties with fixed substances, in a word the cosmic order, demand a permanent and stable cause, an immanent directive power or principle of finality proper to each body and really specific. But such a principle mechanism rejects by substituting for it its dogma of the homogeneity of matter.

3. A third cause is its reduction of all the forces of nature to different modes of local movement. Although all corporeal activities are accompanied by movement and on this account make the formation of mathematical physics possible, it is undeniable that they also present a *qualitative* and differential aspect which cannot be discovered in the modes of local movement, and this aspect mechanism fails to consider, thereby dooming itself to give but an incomplete explanation of the physical properties of matter [15]. Furthermore the doctrine of the transmissibility and the convertibility of movement into light, heat, electricity and magnetism is the necessary consequence of the theory which reduces all to motion.

[14] See above concerning chemical affinity, the kinetic theory of gas, weight, metaphysical analysis of movement, etc.

[15] Cp. Duhem, *Sur quelques extensions récentes de la statique et de la dynamique* (in *Revue des Questions scientifiques*, Vol. I, April 1901).

PART II

The Scholastic Theory

CHAPTER I

HISTORICAL SKETCH [16]

36. Historical Development of this Theory from Aristotle to the Present Day.—The founder of this system was Aristotle (B.C. 384–322), who in the year 334 founded the Peripatetic School at Athens. His disciples remained for the most part faithful to his thought until the first century before Christ. But from that time till the sixth century, the epoch of the dissolution of the Greek Philosophy, Peripateticism underwent great modifications under the influence of Pythagorean and Platonic infiltrations.

During the first period of the Middle Ages, which extend from the ninth to the twelfth century, Western Philosophy did not remain indifferent to the hylomorphic system of the Stagirite. Yet this doctrine had but a second place and was always misunderstood. During this period the two most celebrated commentators were Avicenna (980–1036) and Averroës (1126–1198).

The thirteenth century was the golden age of Scholasticism. Through the medium of the Arabians and of the Greeks of Byzantium, the West became acquainted with the original works of Aristotle. Physics and metaphysics, in which the cosmological theory is contained, being popularized by means

[16] Cp. DE WULF, *History of Medieval Philosophy*, trans. COFFEY (Longmans, 1909), p. 35 ff. This theory has received different names: the Aristotelian Theory, after the name of its founder; the Peripatetic Theory or Peripateticism, because the School of this name, founded by Aristotle, was in ancient times its official depository; the Scholastic Theory, on account of the prominent place it occupied in the teaching of the Schools during the Middle Ages; the Thomistic Theory, in memory of its principal representative, St. Thomas Aquinas; and finally Hylomorphism or the Theory of Matter and Form, since this conception of material essence is one of its fundamental doctrines

of numerous Latin translations became the subject of keen controversies. A galaxy of distinguished philosophers gave their attention to this newly found mine: Alexander of Hales, Albert the Great, St. Bonaventure, Henry of Ghent and St. Thomas Aquinas.

The period of decadence began with the second half of the fourteenth century and the first half of the fifteenth. The most distinguished Thomist of the fifteenth century was Capreolus, called by his contemporaries 'Princeps Thomistarum'.

From the fifteenth to the seventeenth century, the traditional philosophy had to battle against the tide of new ideas, the Renaissance and the Reformation, to which it offered but a feeble resistance. The indifference of the Thomists with regard to the rapid progress made by the natural sciences and the contempt of the men of science for speculative study continued to discredit the old Scholasticism. However, this period was not without individual theologians and philosophers of note, such as Cajetan, Sylvester of Ferrara, Soto, Bañez, John of St. Thomas, Fonseca, Vasquez and Suarez.

At the beginning of the seventeenth century, the works of Copernicus, Galileo and Kepler gave a great impetus to astronomy and physics. But these important discoveries which marked the awakening of scientific thought dealt a great blow to the Aristotelian physics. It then happened that, owing to the disfavour which resulted from confusing the philosophic system of Aristotle and the scientific conclusions to which this system is in no way necessarily bound, both scientists and philosophers abandoned altogether the Peripatetic-Scholastic philosophy. Only during the second half of the last century was a restoration inaugurated by Liberatore and Sanseverino in Italy, and Kleutgen in Germany. These attempts, generous but too isolated, exercised only a limited influence until Pope Leo XIII, witnessing the babel of confusion in philosophic thought and dismayed at the progress of so many false systems, urged the Christian world in his encyclical *Æterni Patris* to return to the Scholastic teaching so admirably systematized by St. Thomas Aquinas.

CHAPTER II

EXPOSITION OF THE SCHOLASTIC THEORY

37. Leading Ideas of this Theory.—This system can be reduced to three fundamental propositions:

1. Simple bodies and chemical compounds are beings endowed with *substantial unity, specifically distinct* from one another, and naturally *extended* [17].

2. These beings possess *active and passive powers* which belong to them in virtue of their substantial essence and are indissolubly bound up with it [18].

3. They have an *inherent tendency* to realize by the exercise of their native energies certain special ends [19].

From these principles there follows an important corollary: the possibility, or rather the necessity of substantial transformation and, in consequence, the existence in every natural body of two constitutive principles, *matter* and *form.*

38. Analysis of Substantial Transformation.—If the chemical compound is substantially one, if it constitutes, as such, a new species, the elements which form it must have been dispossessed of their own specific essential notes in order that they may receive in exchange a specific common determination, namely that of the compound.

On the other hand, it is clear that in this change an essential indeterminate part of each elemental being must persist unchanged in the final resultant of the transformation. For if not, the transformed substances would be annihilated and replaced by a new substance, drawn in its entirety from nothing. The name *substantial form* is given to that specific determination from which the nature and the actuality of the body result; it is the principle which comes into being and disappears at each intimate transformation of matter. The

[17] ST. THOMAS, Opusc. *De natura materiae*, c. VIII. *De principiis naturae. De pluritate formarum. De mixtione elementorum.*

[18] *Id.*, Opusc. *De ente et essentia*, c. VII, *Sum. Theol.* I, q. 77, a. 6, ad 3.

[19] *Id. Cont. Gent.*, IV, c. 19.

indeterminate part of the being which serves as a substratum for the reception of the essential forms is called *primary matter.*

ART. I. PRIMARY MATTER

39. Meaning and Reality of Primary Matter.—What in ordinary speech we call 'raw material' we might also call 'first, or primary, matter'; it stands for some indeterminate material which in respect of forms it may assume is imperfect and not fully determined. Cotton, flax, wool, are instances of 'first matter' in regard to the fabrics into which they are made. In philosophy the phrase, while retaining certain analogies with its original meaning, has a deeper signification: here 'primary matter' stands for something that is *absolutely indeterminate,* something that is not only without certain accidental determinations but lacking also substantial determination. Primary matter, in this philosophical conception, is a real part of a material being, but it is not a being in itself, it carries no stamp such as differentiates all corporeal beings from one another. And lacking all substantial determination, it of course still more lacks the chemical and physical properties with which the different kinds of inorganic bodies are endowed. It is itself neither gold, nor silver, nor copper, although it can be brought to the perfection of these metals by the reception of the determining principles peculiar to each of them. Primary matter is a substantial principle which in conjunction with the form it assumes constitutes a physical body: it would then be quite wrong to relegate it to the category of mere logical entities. Nevertheless, because of its complete indetermination, we conceive it as not capable of being realized except in union with a form, that is, except in some corporeal being.

40. Passivity of Primary Matter.—By its essence it is destined to receive a determining principle or form; by its essence also it is a passive potentiality [20]. Accordingly its universal passivity extends to all essential perfections as well as to all accidental properties.

41. Dependence of Matter on Form.—Primary matter would return to nothing were it deprived of all essential form, for what is entirely indeterminate can have no proper existence. It depends therefore on essential form *intrinsically* and *abso-*

[20] ST. THOMAS, *In I physic.* lect. 14.

lutely. In other words, what exists is not exactly the material substrate in an isolated state, but matter determined and made specific, *the body*.

42. Evolution of Primary Matter.—Conceived in the abstract, first matter may be regarded as a subject capable of receiving any and every essential form of nature. But as it is in reality, as individualized in this or that body of the universe, its natural receptivity is limited, inasmuch as the manner and extent of its evolution in point of fact depends upon the material beings which contain it and upon the laws governing chemical combinations. The matter of a simple body, for example, can never become the matter of another simple body, since the elements are not transformable into one another [21]. With this one reservation, then, we may say that primary matter admits of a passive evolution to an unlimited extent. It may abandon its elementary forms to receive in their stead, under the violent influence of chemical reactions, the form of a compound body. Then from relatively simple compounds, it may pass to others more and more complex until finally, after many transformations, it takes its place in the living substance, either of a vegetable, or of an animal, or even of man where it concurs, in its own sphere, in the highest functions of sensitive and intellectual life.

43. Unity of Primary Matter.—Primary matter is, from the logical point of view, *one*. By a mental abstraction, we strip it of the various essential forms which determine it and of the special powers it possesses in virtue of these forms, and it then stands before the mind as something truly one. Ontologically, however, or in point of fact, there are just as many

[21] We venture as meticulous critics to suggest that the results of scientific research, notably with regard to radio-activity, which has detected detached corpuscles from elements and given currency to the electric theory of matter, may allow one even to modify this one reservation. We do not wish to imply, however, what indeed some who seem to profess Scholasticism suggest, that these minute corpuscles, howsoever named, or the homogeneous ether by which they are ensphered, are primary matter: for were they such, then a reality would be a substance, a determinate kind of being, and yet by the definition of primary matter wholly indeterminate (Cp. *Scholasticism and Modern Thought* by Dr. Coffey, Irish Theological Quarterly, 1909). We merely say that to-day it would not seem contrary to fact to assert that the matter, or at least part of the matter, of some elements may become that of others. If some elements can be wholly transmuted, there is less difficulty in modifying the reservation.—Trs.

examples of it as there are distinct bodies; for each material being has its own allotted quantity of matter.

44. Our Knowledge of Primary Matter.—Neither our senses nor our imagination is able to afford us an adequate representation of this indeterminate element; for whatever falls under the perception of our senses is concrete and individualized—namely, the phenomena of material substances, or, to speak more precisely, the compound of substance and accident which we knew as a 'body'. Only by our reason can we indirectly form an idea of primary matter; an idea, partly positive and partly negative, which represents it as the *potential subject* of the specific types of being which are realized in the material world [22].

ART. II. SUBSTANTIAL FORM

45. Meaning and Function of Substantial Form.—Beneath the manifold accidental determinations by means of which we distinguish one body from another lies something much more radical which is the cause of one body being of an essentially different kind from another body. This deeper determination which is at the very bottom of a being and makes it to be of the kind it is, is all that is meant by *substantial form.*

Substantial form, or as it is also called essential form, is, logically conceived, anterior to all accidental realities, for these are nothing but its visible manifestation. Yet although it is thus anterior to and the primordial source of all the perfections a body possesses, it is itself dependent upon primary matter inasmuch as it can neither come into existence nor continue in it apart from this, its connatural subject.

1. Part of the function of substantial form is to determine primary matter, to confer on material essence that intrinsic complement which it needs before it can exist: for only a complete essence of a determinate species is capable of existence [23]. On this account, therefore, the form is said to be the *principle of being.*

2. Substantial form is also called the *principle of action.*—According to St. Thomas, activity is the operation of the physical compound, of the 'body' made up of matter and form; the body alone can act, since action is an unfolding or

[22] St. Thomas, *De natura materiae*, c. 2. *In I physic.*, lect. 14.
[23] St. Thomas, *Cont. Gent.*, II, c. 54, n. 3.

display of being and only the compound-body enjoys proper existence. But whilst this is true, we must remember that substantial form is the first cause of all the determinations a compound possesses, and therefore, on the ground that every being acts according to the measure of its perfections and as it is actual, substantial form must be the foundation of a body's activities [24].

3. Finally, it has the further name of *principle of finality*. When the form gives to the body its specific nature, it impresses upon it an inclination towards the ends ordained for it, and this inherent tendency controls all the properties that result from the essence of the body [25].

46. Does a Substantial Form admit of Increase or Decrease ?—The whole content of the form is of the substantial order. Hence it follows that it cannot undergo any *qualitative* change without involving corresponding change in the being it constitutes, in the substance as such : every modification introduced into the intrinsic perfection of the principle which determines a being necessarily brings about a change of species [26]. As a matter of fact, it is impossible for us to conceive that a molecule of water can be more or less of the nature of water. Although we may observe accidental differences of state, of limpidity or of freshness, between the specimens of water we examine, the specimens as such, or the molecules, always possess the total perfection of the nature of water. Viewed in this way, the substantial form does not admit of any degrees of increase or decrease.

Nevertheless, as we shall see later, the form can lend itself to real division in the purely *quantitative* order. In this case, it diminishes in extent without losing anything of its qualitative perfection.

47. Classification of Forms.—The name *material* or *purely corporeal forms* is given to those specific principles which are intrinsically dependent on matter : such are the forms of chemical bodies, vegetables and animals.

The name *immaterial* or *subsistent forms* is given to those

[24] St. Thomas, *Sum. Theol.*, I, q. 97, a. 1, ad 3.

[25] *Id.*, *In II physic.* lect. 14.— *Quaest. disp.*, q. 12, a. 1.

[26] *Id.*, *Sum. Theol.*, I, q. 118, a. 2 ; q. 76, a. 1. — *Quaest. disp. de virt. in communi*, q. 1, a. 11. 'Et propter hoc forma substantialis non recipit intensionem vel remissionem quia dat esse substantiale, quod est uno modo : ubi enim est aliud esse substantiale, est alia res.'

which, while naturally destined to inform matter, are nevertheless capable of existing and acting without it; among such is the human soul.

According to Aristotelian physics there are also *permanent* and *transitory* forms. The former determine individual substances that are endowed with stable and permanent existence. The latter mark the different stages through which a substance passes before acquiring its final perfect state. According to St. Thomas, the human foetus is successively informed by three essential forms—a vegetative soul, a sensitive soul, and finally a rational soul. The first two have a function essentially transitory, that of predisposing the matter for the reception of the rational soul.

48. Can there be several Essential Forms in the Same Being?—A single essential form determines a being in its specific nature and subsistence.

1. There can be nothing intermediary between substantial forms and accidental forms. If it is of the function of substantial form to constitute in conjunction with matter a complete substance, any additional form is necessarily foreign to the essence and consequently is accidental to it [27].

2. Substantial form communicates to a body its essential unity. If, then, several forms could simultaneously belong to the same material subject, this latter would belong to several distinct bodies—which entails a manifest contradiction [28].

3. A form can come into existence only in matter which is predisposed to receive it. In order to receive simultaneously several forms, the same material substrate would have to present several different and opposite dispositions, and this for obvious reasons cannot be allowed [29].

4. Finally, since a specific determining principle is the cause not only of a body's essential perfection but also of all the determinations proper to its inferior principles, the hypothesis of a plurality of forms, even subordinated to one another, is useless.

49. Divisibility of Essential Forms.—According to St. Thomas and the majority of the Scholastics later than the thirteenth century, all corporeal forms are divisible except

[27] St. Thomas, *De potentia*, q. 3, a. 9, ad 9.
[28] St. Thomas, *Sum. Theol.*, I, q. 76, a. 3.
[29] *Id.*, *Opusc. De pluralitate formarum*, p. I.

the principle of life in the higher animals [30]. In the light, however, of the present data furnished by science, this opinion requires certain modifications.

The Inorganic World.—It is now admitted that the atom of simple bodies and the molecule of compound bodies constitute true individualities, beings endowed with their own existence. Now although the form of these bodies is theoretically divisible, as a matter of fact the parts which would result from a division, would not be—contrary to the opinion of St. Thomas—of the same species as the integral being from which they took their existence: for every separation of the chemical constituents of a mineral substance brings with it a change of species. So great is the imperfection of essential forms in the inorganic world that they are not only immersed, to use St. Thomas' word, in matter, but are dependent for their generation and existence upon a *determined quantity* of matter. The atomic weights, 16 of oxygen, 32 of sulphur, 35·5 of chlorine, are so many definite masses of matter necessary for the very existence of these bodies. Here the subjection of the form to its substrate is as profound as possible; the physical impossibility of breaking it up without destroying it provides us with an evident proof. The case becomes otherwise, how-

[30] *Id.*, *De anima*, q. I, a. 10. — *De natura materiae*, c. IX. 'Unitas continuitatis in re reperta maxime potentialis invenitur, quia omne continuum est unum actu et multiplex in potentia . . . unde in divisione lineae non inducitur aliquid novi in ipsis divisis, sed eadem essentia lineae quae prius erat actu una, et multiplex in potentia, per divisionem facta est multa in actu. . . . Consimile penitus reperitur in lapide, et in igne, et in omnibus corruptibilibus et generabilibus inanimatis: forma enim totius in eis, per quam habent quandam unitatem suae naturae super unitatem quantitatis, secundum totam rationem formae est in qualibet parte talium rerum. Unde facta divisione manet essentia ejusdem formae in partibus ab invicem divisis: quaelibet enim pars ignis est ignis, et quaelibet pars lapidis est lapis. . . . Super haec autem sunt animata imperfecta, ut plantae, et quaedam animalia imperfecta, ut sunt animalia annulosa; et in ipsis idem invenitur: quia cum evellitur ramus ab arbore, non advenit nova essentia vegetabilis, sed eadem essentia vegetabilis quae una erat in arbore tota, etiam actu uno, simul erat multiplex in potentia, et per divisionem novum esse perdit, et actus alius et alius secutu est. . . Similiter est in animalibus annulosis una anima in actu et unum esse, sed multiplex in potentia accidentali . . . et hoc totum contingit propter imperfectionem talium formarum: quia cum sint sub uno actu, simul sunt sub potentia multiplici respectu esse diversorum quae acquiruntur eis sine aliqua corruptione in suis essentiis sed sola divisione. In animalibus vero perfectis, praecipue in homine, forma quae est una in actu, non est multiplex in potentia, ut per divisionem constituatur eadem essentia formae sub diversis esse.'

ever, according as one ascends in the scale of beings, when the subordination of forms to the *quantity* of matter progressively diminishes.

The Vegetable Kingdom.—It is easy to multiply a plant, either by cuttings, graftings, layers, or inoculations. The individuals thus obtained faithfully preserve the characteristics of the parent-stock; they continue its course of life, undergoing the same development without any appreciable change marking the passage from the common life to the individual life. The specific principle uniformly spread throughout the parent-stock can, then, be divided into parts each of which preserves, yet with complete independence, the being which it recently had in common with the other parts produced along with it. Hence it is said that the form of a plant is *actually one* and *potentially manifold*. Here the cosmological theory of the Middle Ages is seen to be in perfect harmony with the data of botanical science.

The Animal Kingdom.—The division of the lower animals such as hydras and earth-worms, leads to the same conclusion. Here again the new beings constituted by detached portions are clearly of exactly the same nature as the trunks from which they are detached. Moreover, there seems no reason why such divisibility must be said to be confined only to the lower grades of the animal kingdom. For if we inquire what is the basic reason of the divisibility of corporeal forms, we find it is simply their intrinsic dependence upon matter: the formative principles, since they are necessarily united to this substrate, necessarily partake of the natural imperfections of the body, they constitute with the matter the immediate subject of extension, and with it make up one quantified whole of which divisibility is an essential property. It may often be the case with the higher animals that, owing to the division of labour and to the multiplicity of the organs required for the normal functioning of sensitive life, detached portions are unfitted to survive and die before they can reproduce the complete type of the species. But there seems no sufficient reason for refusing to their vital principle a really quantitative character.

50. Gradation of Substantial Forms.—From the simplest body up to man, between the world of matter and that of spirit, there stretches a continuous series of essential perfections. According to the Thomistic theory, a single form fixes each of these beings in its nature and subsistence, since every higher form contains virtually, despite its unity, all the perfections of the other forms which it supplants [31]. In the chemical compound, the substantial form is the natural substitute of the elemental forms which have disappeared. In the vegetable it is the source of the chemical, physical and mechanical activities of the mineral substances which are incorporated in it; it makes them all converge to one end, which is the nutrition and development of the being. In the animal it is the one and ultimate principle of the energies of the brute matter and of vegetative and sensitive life. And in man it is his rational soul, the single principle, as will be seen in Psychology, which makes him at once a living, sentient and intellectual being.

ART. III. THE SUBSTANTIAL COMPOUND

51. The Union of Matter and Form.—Since they are intrinsically dependent on each other, the two essential principles of being exist only in virtue of their union. The primary exigence of matter is to receive a profound, specific impress, an essential form, in order that it may become some specific kind of body. The form, on its part, is essentially nothing but the determination of its potential subject, matter, which from being merely potential it makes definite and actual. *Together they make up one complete essence,* one basic principle of action, a single material being.

But in spite of this mutual and essential interdependence the matter and the form that are united in the compound are nevertheless *two distinct realities.* For it is impossible to conceive that two realities having characteristics diametrically opposed should be converted into a third reality without either of them undergoing some change in its nature. Now neither matter nor form changes by having to constitute the compound essence: did it do so it would cease to verify the idea of material or of formal cause and would be an efficient cause rather than a constituent one.

Lastly, inasmuch as neither matter nor form is the reason whereby the essence they constitute is existent, this further

[31] St. Thomas, *Quaest. Disp. de anima*, q. 1, a. 1; and cp. a. 7.

determination, this ultimate actuality, *existence*, must needs be something additional to, and distinct from the subject that receives it [32]. Hence the concrete essence, compounded of matter and substantial form, is potential with respect to its further completion, namely, to existence; this is its last determination or actuality which clinches the compound and makes it a *being* in the strictest sense[33].

ART IV. PROPERTIES

I. Properties in relation to Substance

52. Natural Connexion between Properties and Substance.—There are two kinds of accidents: *contingent accidents* and *necessary accidents* or *properties*.

When we glance at the material world, some accidents immediately strike us as not attaching necessarily and invariably to the bodies in which we see them; they may come and go without the bodies changing essentially—such as local movement, mechanical impulse, colour, etc. These are called *contingent accidents*.

On the other hand, other accidents are *properties*—quantity, extension, and active and passive powers, notably calorific, electric and magnetic forces, and chemical affinity—which not only are never entirely absent but may even not undergo more than certain modifications, fixed by the nature of each body, without involving a change of species. It is these necessary accidents of a body which together characterize it and, as experience shows, serve as the basis of scientific classification.

Now how is it that each different kind of inorganic being invariably possesses a definite group of properties?

53. Reason of the Natural Connexion between Properties and Substance.—St. Thomas seems to have given the reason in a sentence that is brief but sufficiently expressive: 'The subject is both the *final* cause, and *in a way the active cause*, of its proper accident. It is also as it were the *material* cause,

[32] St. Thomas, *Quaest. Disp. de Spir. creat.*, q. 1, a. 1; and *De anima*, q. 1, a. 6. — *Sum. Theol.*, I, q. 54, a. 3; q. 3, a. 4; q. 4, a. 1.

[33] Wider meanings of the word 'being' are expounded in *General Metaphysics*, 35. Individual things that are concrete, substantial objects of experience are 'beings' *par excellence*, they merit the name in the first or strictest sense, which is sometimes defined as 'that which exists'

inasmuch as it is receptive of the accident. . . . The emanation of proper accidents from their subject is not by way of transmutation, but *by a certain natural resultance*; thus one thing results naturally from another, as colour from light'[34].

The substance, he says, is the *final cause* of the properties: the latter are natural instruments or means which the substance has at its disposal for attaining its ends. They exist only for the sake of the substance.

The substance is the *material cause*, in the sense that it sustains the properties and receives them within itself from the moment they are generated.

But the substance cannot be said to be the efficient cause of its properties, since in no created being is action a substantial reality: created beings act in virtue of their secondary powers or faculties which are the vent for their activity and make it of different kinds. The words '*quodammodo activa*' must then be interpreted in another sense than that of true efficient causality. It is this:—When an extrinsic agent invests matter with an essential form and thereby realizes a new essence, in doing so and by the same action it clothes it with all its necessary accidents. Here the efficient causality of the extrinsic agent has a double effect: namely a principal effect, the new form, and a secondary effect, the natural properties. Now these two effects are indissolubly connected with each other, for the reason that the new substance has an influence upon the activity of the extrinsic agent in so far as it determines the sphere of its action and its power of reaching to the accidental realities that are the necessary resultants of its substantial existence. On this account it does influence their genesis; and the causality which it most closely approaches, though never truly realizes, is efficient causality.

In addition to this immediate physical reason of the connexion between substance and its properties, a remote reason may be drawn from the finality of material beings.

Every being of the inorganic as well as of the organic kingdom has to co-operate by the exercise of its natural energies

[34] 'Dicendum quod subjectum est causa proprii accidentis, et *finalis* et *quodammodo activa*, et etiam *materialis*, in quantum est susceptiva accidentis. . . . Quod emanatio propriorum accidentium a subjecto non est per aliquam transmutationem, sed per *aliquam naturalem resultationem*; sicut ex unc naturaliter aliud resultat, sicut ex luce color'. *Sum. Theol.*, I, q. 77, a. 6, ad 2 and 3.

for the general good (*Gen. Metaphysics*, **182**). Moreover as it is incompatible with the Wisdom of the Creator to make beings without a purpose to fulfil, so it is incompatible that He should leave them for a moment without the means necessary for its attainment. Now properties are these necessary means, they are the immediate principles of action but for which a substance would be without vent for activity. We see then that it would be absurd for a substance to have its powers of action determined simply by the caprice of chance, or, in other words, why the connexion must be more than merely contingent. Thus are we brought back to the necessity of the fact of which the Thomistic theory, as we have just seen, affords the proximate explanation.

II. Closer Study of Properties

§ 1.—*Quantity*

Quantity is the first accident of all to modify a material substance.

54. Definition.—From the concrete point of view, 'quantity' means *a thing divisible into parts which are in it and each of which is capable of existing as an individual*[35]. This definition of Aristotle's is worthy of close attention.

Although he assigns *divisibility* as the chief note, it does not follow that since all quantity is necessarily divisible, therefore wherever there is divisibility there is quantity. Certain conditions must also be verified :—

1. It is necessary, he says, that quantity formally contain the parts to which division gives rise (*insita*). Hence the actual and complete reality of the parts obtained must be antecedent to the division. This is a reservation meant to exclude a mode of division quite foreign to quantity, viz., the dissolution of the chemical body into its component elements. Indeed the inorganic compound, which is essentially one, can under the power of dissolving forces be disintegrated and its elements regain their state of liberty, but this dissolution does not imply the existence of a quantitative whole, since the elements do not exist *as such* in the compound ; they are

[35] Aristotle, *Metaph.*, IV, c. 13. 'Quantum dicitur, quod in insita divisibile, quorum utrumque aut singula unum quid et hoc quid apta sunt esse .

there only in a potential state and are re-instated in their existence only after an essential change [36].

2. As a second necessary condition Aristotle lays down the aptitude of each of the parts to form, after division, a new individual being (' *unum . . . hoc quid* '). If you break up a piece of wood or a bar of iron, you have parts each enjoying its own existence; as the result of division separate complete beings issue from a real quantified whole. This second condition rules out another case of divisibility not indicative of the existence of a quantitative whole, namely the divisibility of a body into its two essential constitutive parts, matter and form. Here, although there is a division inasmuch as the matter can be deprived of its actual form in exchange for another, nevertheless since neither of these principles is capable of existing in isolation, it is not a true sign of a quantitative whole.

On account of this twofold condition limiting divisibility, the Aristotelian definition possesses the great advantage of being applicable to its object and to it alone, whatever may be the various modes of its existence.

55. Kinds of Quantity.—*Discrete* quantity is made up of parts really distinct which have each their own limits. It forms a whole whose unity is purely mental. In reality, since its parts are actually distinct, it is a *multitude* or *number* [37].

Continuous quantity is made up of parts not distinct which adhere to one another in such a way that the limit of one is identical with that of the next. Independently of any act of the mind it has a true unity. It represents *size* or *amount* which has as a property the characteristic of being measurable, either entirely or in part according as it is finite or infinite (*Gen. Metaphysics*, **55**).

Continuous quantity is subdivided into many kinds :—

[36] According to one view, supported by scientific research, we have no sufficient reason for asserting that elements do not actually remain in an inorganic compound and that when they are liberated an essential change takes place (**80**); cp. SCHAAF, *Institutiones Cosmologiae*, p. 339 ff. (Privately printed for the Gregorian University, Rome, 1907). For the Author's proof of the opposite view see reference on p. 105.—TRS.

[37] ' Multitude ' signifies that there are distinct units gathered in a single mental concept; nothing more. It is by its definition neither limited nor unlimited. ' Number,' on the other hand, signifies how many there are of a thing. See *Gen. Metaphysics* **53** f., and MERCIER, *L'unité et le nombre d'après S. Thomas d'Aquin.* (*Revue Néo-Scholastique*, Aug. 1901.)

Successive quantity has its integral parts succeeding one another without interruption according to an order of 'before' and 'after'. Its principal subdivisions are *time* and *movement*.

Permanent quantity has all its parts existing simultaneously and occupying different positions in space. To this kind of quantity belong *extension* and *space*. Extension in its three dimensions represents to us a body as it really is and is called *volume*; considered only under the one aspect of length, it is a *line*; and under the double aspect of length and breadth, a *surface* [38].

56. The Essence of Quantity.—Many attributes may be predicated of a body in virtue of its quantitative state. It appears to us as a complexus of many integral parts, each of which, if separated from the whole, takes with it a fragment, so to speak, of the matter and form; it is moreover subject to ever further divisions; it is by nature impenetrable; it is extended in space, and forms a measurable amount.

Now of these many properties connected with quantity is there one which may be regarded as the foundation of the others, one that cannot be posited without involving also all the others?

Such a primary property of quantity we think to be its *entitative composition*. Being essentially composed of integral parts, quantity by its union with substance communicates to it that composition which it possesses within itself and makes it a whole capable of division. This is not to say that quantity gives to the body the reality of the integral elements of which it is constituted, for an accident cannot produce a substance; but, that quantity is the reason on account of which the substantial mass, of itself indivisible, becomes a whole or, rather, a potential multiple which can be broken up into integral parts [39]. This is the most fundamental of all the attributes of quantity; divisibility, extension in space, measurability and impenetrability all follow naturally from it.

57. There is a Real Distinction between Quantity and Substance.—By the 'essence' of a body we mean that which

[38] For all these notions, compare ARISTOTLE, *Metaphysics*, IV, c. 6, 10–16; c. 13, 1–4. (In Oxford translation, Bk. V.)

[39] ARISTOTLE, *Physic.*, I, c. 2; *Metaph.*, IV, c. 13. — ST. THOMAS, *Sum. Theol.*, I, q. 50, a. 2; cp. III, q. 77, a. 9; *Dist.* 3, q. 1, a. 4.; *Cont. Gent.*, IV, c. 65.

constitutes it, that which is its underlying foundation, the principle and support of all its accidental phenomena. On the other hand the idea of 'quantity' expresses simply a mode of being, that in virtue of which the body has extended mass in space and is capable of division. These two representations of material being are different. The question is: Are these two aspects the result of a mental process or are they really distinct in nature?

With Aristotle and many of the Scholastics we think that substance and quantity are two things really distinct [40].

Argument from Reason.—Substance and quantity appeal to our sense-perception in ways really different: for quantity is directly perceptible by the senses, substance only indirectly. The eye, and even the taste, may indeed mistake for milk chemical substances that are essentially different from it though having certain physical resemblances. But one and the same thing cannot make two mutually exclusive relations with the same term of comparison—our sense-perception. Therefore substance and quantity, which appeal to our cognitive faculty in two different ways are not one and the same thing [41].

Theologico-philosophical Proof.—The proof from reason just given is not without its value. Yet there are many who fail to see in it a convincing proof of the Scholastic theory. However this may be, if reason left to its own natural powers remains in doubt, it can be so no longer when it receives the confirmation afforded by the data of Revelation. The Catholic Faith teaches that by the Consecration at Mass 'the substance of the bread and wine is changed totally into the substance of the Body and Blood of Christ' [42]. Now to sense-perception the natural properties of the substances that have disappeared remain identically the same: the Consecrated Host keeps the same extension in space as the plain bread and is capable of division; in a word, its quantity persists without

[40] ARISTOTLE, *Metaphys.* VII, c. 3. — ST. THOMAS, *In I physic.*, c. 2. — SUAREZ, *Metaphys.* L. 40, sect. 2, n. 8. — P. DE SAN, *Cosmologia*, p. 270 (Louvain, 1881). — MIELLE, *De subst. corp. vi et ratione*, p. 140. — JOHN OF ST. THOMAS, *Logica*, q. 11, a. 1. — SCHIFFINI, *Disp. metaphys. spec.*, p. 182. — PESCH, *Inst. phil. nat.*, Lib. 2, disp. I, sect. 3, p. 401.

[41] Cp. P. DE SAN, *op. cit.*, p. 277.

[42] *Council of Trent*, sess. XIII, ch. 4 and can. 2. Cp. DENZINGER, *Enchiridion Symbolorum*, nn. 877 and 884 (Herder, London, etc., 12th edn., 1913).

any apparent change. But it is impossible that two things really separable—as in this case Christ in the sacramental Real Presence and the quantity of the bread—should not be two realities distinct from one another.

It is true that accidents are intrinsically dependent on their substance, and therefore we may well wonder how realities having such a precarious existence can exist outside their connatural subject. Yet if the reality of quantity is not confounded with that of substance, there appears nothing contradictory in the Almighty supplying the influence of the secondary cause (the substance of the bread) which has temporarily disappeared.

We must now examine the properties of extension.[43]

58. Every Part of an Extended Thing is itself Extended and therefore indefinitely Divisible.—Are the parts resulting from a division, however far it is carried, themselves always extended? To answer in the affirmative is to say that the continuous whole can be broken up indefinitely, for the reason that extension is essentially capable of division. To answer in the negative is to say that the ultimate results of a process of division, themselves impervious to any further division, must be simple points destitute of real extension. Aristotle, St. Thomas and the majority of the older and modern Scholastics agree in holding the first opinion [44].

Proof of the Thesis.—It is impossible for an extended thing to be formed of unextended parts. For either the parts are united according to an order of perfect continuity, or following an order of simple contiguity or contact. But, in either case, the opinion that reduces the extended thing to a collection of simple points leads to conclusions manifestly false.

In the first place, the parts cannot be *continuous*. Indivisible things have no parts. If their boundaries are not separate from each other, the bodies must wholly interpenetrate. To two elements thus interpenetrating add ten, twenty or a hundred others: all of them will interpenetrate alike in a single mathematical point that excludes all real extension.

[43] To avoid an interruption here in the leading ideas of the Scholastic system 'Time' and 'Space' are treated separately at the end of the treatise.

[44] Cp. ARISTOTLE, *Physic.*, III, c. I, 1. — ST. THOMAS, *In VI Physic.* lect. 1 et 6. — MIELLE, *De substantiae corporis vi et ratione*, p. 279. — PESCH, *Inst. phil. nat.*, p. 32. — SCHIFFINI, *Disp. metaphys. spec.*, t. I, thesis 15ª. —LAHOUSSE, *Prael. metaphys. spec.*, *Cosmologia*, pp. 197–207, etc., etc.

In the second place, it is equally impossible for simple parts to be *contiguous*. Objects are contiguous when they touch one another while keeping their respective boundaries. Either, then, a part of one touches a part of the other, or a part of one touches the whole of the other, or they touch one another according to the totality of their being. Now the first two cases are impossible for the reason that an indivisible thing has no parts. And the last case can never result in extension, no matter how many parts be superadded, since it is essential to this quality that its elements occupy different portions of space.

59. The Parts of a Continuous Whole are not Actual but Potential.—Whilst it is evident that the reality of the parts produced by division must be antecedent to it (**56**), it remains a question whether these parts possess their own respective boundaries and are thus really distinct from one another, or whether the elements which constitute extension, instead of being actually distinct parts, form a true unity in which there is no multiplicity until a division, real or ideal, has been made.

Proof of the Thesis.—If each of the elements forming a continuous whole possesses its individual boundaries, we may naturally ask how many parts actually distinct there are in the surface of a square centimetre. We are justified in asking this question, seeing that elements which are distinct are units and therefore capable of being counted. Now there are two alternatives possible: either these elements are *finite* in number or else there is an *infinite* multitude of them. If we say they are finite, we are bound to acknowledge limits to the divisibility of a continuous whole and to reduce it to a collection of unextended points: for the only reason why parts become incapable of further division lies in their simplicity or lack of extension [45]. If we say they are infinite, we are thereby granting an actual infinity in a thing of finite dimensions—which is a contradiction, since 'there is no part, however conceivably small provided it is greater than zero, which repeated an infinite number of times does not make up a quantity greater than any that can be measured'. Hence, as soon as it is admitted that integral parts are really distinct,

[45] ARISTOTLE, *Physic.*, VI, c. 1, 1–4. Cp. ST. THOMAS, *In VI Physic.* lect. 1 et 7.

that they are actual parts, be they finite or infinite in number, the idea of a continuum becomes impossible.

60. Scientific Definition of Mass.—The notion of 'mass' is closely allied to that of quantity. It is generally defined in the natural sciences and particularly in mechanics as: *The constant relation between force and acceleration.*

To determine the acceleration of a body moving under the influence of a moving principle, it is not sufficient to consider only the intensity of the impelling action. Experience establishes the fact that the velocity of the movement imparted during a unit of time depends also on the nature of the moving body to which the force is applied. If two bodies of unequal weights, for instance, are submitted in the same place to the action of the same mechanical force, the velocity communicated to them will be different in each case, and less in proportion to the greater weight of the body. But in the case of a single body moving in a straight line under the influence of a force which does not vary during the experiment, there exists, between the intensity of the force and the amount of velocity produced by it in a unit of time, a relation which is always and everywhere constant; such that if the force is increased, the acceleration increases in proportion. By dividing the force applied to a body by the acceleration which it produces we obtain therefore a quotient which is invariable but proper to the particular body in question. This is called *mass.* Hence the classical definition given above.

61. Criticism of this Definition.—Although there is nothing to be said against this definition from a scientific point of view, it is nevertheless inadequate for philosophy: it does not help us at all in getting to know the intimate nature of this mysterious factor which plays so important a part in cosmic phenomena. For, inasmuch as mass is a kind of intermediary between force and acceleration, we know it as something purely relative; it is a number, a quotient, the value of which is essentially dependent upon two other numbers. In itself it is neither force nor acceleration but a constant relation between these two factors which are themselves alien to it. Yet this relation only expresses the measure of it, it in no way tells us what it is, what is its nature.

That mass is something absolute is clear from the fact that a body possesses it equally in a state of rest as in a state of motion. And were there but one body in existence, it would still have its own mass.

The cosmologist, then, though he be possessed of this well-known formula, is justified in asking, What is the real entity of mass? Is it an accident or a substance? How does it fulfil the function which the scientist assigns to it?

62. Philosophical Definition of Mass.—Since the natural sciences stop on the very threshold of these further questions, it remains for us to appeal to metaphysics.

In metaphysics the only definition which seems capable of bearing the test of facts is this: *The mass of a body is its dimensive quantity*; or, to use a more concrete form: *It is by its quantity that a body fulfils the function of mass and possesses the properties belonging to this mechanical factor.*

1. The chief characteristic of mass is *its power of reducing the velocity of motion.* This is proved by experience: the velocity communicated to a body always undergoes a diminution proportionate to the greatness of the mass, and this reduction of motion is the effect of a passive resistance. This physicists express by saying that if all active resistance on the part of matter ceased, the mass of all bodies would remain exactly the same [46].

Now dimensive quantity, and that alone, is endowed with this power of reducing the velocity of motion.

Quantity, be it observed, is the receptive subject, the common substratum, of all corporeal properties: it communicates to substance the multiplicity of integral parts of which it is itself made up and sets up an internal arrangement which determines the manner according to which all other qualities are received in it; thus all other properties of necessity partake of its manner of being, they all spread over, so to speak, this common foundation [47]. Now if this is so, we can understand how a mechanical impulse communicated to a body has to be dispersed throughout the whole mass, and this dispersion

[46] BALFOUR STEWART, *The Conservation of Energy* (London, 1890). Examples of *active* resistance, or forces of resistance, are friction and the resistance which a body at rest makes against one in motion. If all resistance of this kind ceased, the push given by a fly's wing would be sufficient to set the heaviest wagon in motion. This kind of resistance is no measure of mass.—TRS.

[47] ST. THOMAS, *Sum. Theol.*, III, q. 77, a. 2. Colour, e.g., clearly spreads over the extent of surface. Cp. *General Metaphysics*, 23.—TRS.

of it will be so much the greater as the number of material parts in it is greater; in a word, the dispersion will be proportionate to the quantity. Next consider the truth, which is verified by daily experience, that *the more a force is dispersed, the less is its intensity.* By the hypothesis, the intensity of the acceleration of the motion resulting from the mechanical impulse will in every case suffer a decrease proportionate to the dispersion of the motion imparted; that is, the velocity will bear an inverse ratio to the greatness of the mass. Lastly, the resistance on the part of the moving body is here purely *passive,* as the data of mechanics require. It consists in a simple dispersion which destroys none of the quantity of the motion transmitted. The velocity alone of the moving body is affected by it.

2. By the identification of mass with quantity we are enabled to learn the origin and the cause of its *constancy.* It would seem that everything in the universe changes except mass and the sum-total of energy. How is it that this privilege belongs to mass? Because quantity with which it is identical has its root in that common foundation of all corporeal substances which passes without alteration or change throughout the various stages of the cosmic evolution. Since this material principle—first matter—is ever identical with itself in every substantial state, however diverse, quantity which is its immediate and faithful expression persists with it without being affected by any of the changes to which bodies may be subjected. It is a manifestation not of a body's nature but of its materiality: hence its constancy.

63. Inertia.—Inertia may be taken in different senses. Newton has defined it as *the property in virtue of which a body cannot of itself modify its state, whether of rest or of motion.* Thus understood, it is rather a negative property of matter. It signifies the absolute indifference of a body in respect of two opposite states, rest and motion. The reason of this indifference lies in the fact that a material part, even in the case of living beings, never acts upon itself, but only upon the parts placed in proximity to it. Since the action of inorganic bodies and that of each of the particles of organic beings is always transitive, it is naturally impossible that matter should modify, on its own initiative, the state in which it has been placed.

From a second point of view, inertia signifies a passive resistance, a power that reduces communicated motion. It is this power of reduction that is proper to each body and absolutely constant which physicists call the 'quantity of inertia', 'quantity of mass', 'force of inertia'. Now the concrete reality which has this function is, we have said, none other than dimensive quantity in the strict sense of the word.

The term 'force', so often applied by scientists to signify this passive property of matter, is not a felicitous one. For, whilst the ordinary meaning attached to this word is that of an active principle, an efficient cause, all are agreed that the ideas of inertia, of mass, and of quantity would be falsified, if there were introduced into them any notion of a causality which is not entirely passive.

64. Impenetrability. Scientific Interpretation.—Though subjected to the most violent shocks or the most intense pressure, neither different masses of matter nor the parts of the same body can ever be made to occupy simultaneously one and the same spatial position. Scientists generally make the cause of this impenetrability to consist in the *force of resistance.* According to them, what keeps two bodies from interpenetrating is simply that energy in virtue of which each resists the entrance of the other into its own spatial position.

65. Consequences of this Interpretation.—1. The first and most serious objection to this scientific explanation is that *it introduces life into all the beings of the inorganic world.*

Let us consider the atom of a simple body, that is, the smallest possible chemical individual being.

Like every other extended being, the atom possesses a multiplicity of parts occupying space in such a way that to each there corresponds its own proper spatial position. In a word, all the component elements of the atom are naturally impenetrable among themselves.

Suppose now that the impenetrability arises from the continuous exercise of internal forces of resistance. In this case, the parts of the atomic mass cannot preserve the law of externality to each other that governs them, without acting upon one another, and the atom thus becomes the scene of a multiplicity of actions of which it is at once both the cause and the receptive subject. Yet such activity as has its principle and objective in the same substantial being is none other than immanent or vital activity (*Psychology*, **10**).

2. Moreover this theory leads to another error, namely *the real distinction of parts in a continuous whole.* If all the particles of matter contained in an atom exercise contrary activities upon one another, they must necessarily be realities actually and really distinct.

66. Thomistic Interpretation.—To have recourse to the force of resistance or to any *active* force is to be faced with the above difficulties. Since then impenetrability demands a cause, it remains to look for the reason of it in some *passive* aptitude of matter. In what does this aptitude, or rather this exigency consist?

That a thing cannot be something actually except it first be so potentially, that a subject cannot receive a determination except it be fitted by its nature to be so determined, is a truth of Metaphysics: accordingly extension, which is a certain actuality or determination, presupposes a natural adaptation on the part of the subject which is extended. Now whilst the quantified parts of a body have a natural aptitude to be affected by spatial extension, they have yet no such aptitude to occupy positions in space which are already occupied by other parts. Hence the impossibility of two bodies or of two parts of the same body interpenetrating can be accounted for by the complete absence of this requisite receptive power [48].

However do not let us lose sight of the fact that all matter is seen universally to possess forces of resistance. Such forces we believe even to be indispensable for the maintenance of the cosmic order, for it would be hard to say what would become of the universe if but the least effort sufficed to displace a mountain or to overturn a house. But while we recognize how important their concurrence is for safeguarding the relative stability of bodies and for preventing their too easy displacement, we fail to see here the reason of their natural impenetrability.

§ 2. *Forces or Active and Passive Powers of Bodies.*

All the multifarious elements of the universe, the smallest not excepted, conspire by their joint action to bring about

[48] ST. THOMAS. *Opusc. in Boetium, De Trinit.*, q. 4, a. 3.—*Quodlibetum*, I, c. 21.

the welfare of the whole. All are depositories of certain powers of action corresponding to their respective natures. Now of these natural energies the basic or ultimate principle is always the *substance*. But, since action in any created being is not a substantial perfection, the substance's energy has to be distributed through as many different *accidental powers* or faculties as it has different modes of action. These secondary powers that are intimately connected with substance and are derived from it are the immediate causes of a body's activities. Our present concern is to say what kinds of powers a body has.

67. First Classification.—From the point of view of their origin material powers may be divided into *intrinsic* and *extrinsic*.

Some powers have their root in the very substance of the body and cannot be separated from it. Such are chemical affinity, electricity, magnetism, the energies of heat and light, forces of resistance, elasticity, repulsion and attraction. These are very properly called *intrinsic* forces.

Extrinsic forces are those of which a body is not itself the cause, but which are communicated to it in the course of its existence and subsequently lost without any prejudice to it. An example of this kind of power is the force of impulse communicated to a body at rest by one in motion: the motor energy that is communicated is clearly a borrowed energy.

68. Second Classification.—This comprises *active* and *passive powers*.

Active powers are so named because they have of themselves an immediate and complete adaptation to their effect. It may of course happen that certain *extrinsic* conditions necessary for the development of their energy are lacking; in which case they must necessarily remain inoperative until such time as the realization of these favourable circumstances render their exercise possible. In this sense they are active powers without being always and necessarily in action. Thus when chlorine and antimony are in contact, they exercise a violent action on one another, independently of any outside agency, and discharge an enormous quantity of heat and electricity. It is obvious that these forces existed previously to the contact; they were abiding in the two bodies as active powers, as forces already quite disposed for action; yet they were incapable of exercising their native power as long as the condition of contact was lacking.

Passive powers are likewise powers of action [49], but such that before they can produce their effect they require to be in some way perfected so as to have their *intrinsic* indetermination removed. For example, bodies which in perfect darkness have no colour, when exposed to light assume each one its own; each receives in its own way the influence of the luminous ether and immediately exercises its own particular action upon our visual organ: each therefore possesses a passive power, a natural aptitude for making an impression on us, which cannot however develop its energy except in the measure in which it is itself determined by light.

69. Third Classification.—There is a generic distinction between *purely mechanical* forces and *physical forces properly so called.* By the former are here to be understood weight, the forces of repulsion and attraction, resistance, and motor qualities communicated at the moment of collision between masses of matter. These energies constitute quite a distinctive class from those of light, sound, heat, electricity and magnetism, which we denominate as 'physical forces properly so called'.

Indeed, the only effect which brings before us the activity of mechanical forces is local motion, i.e. simple spatial displacement: weight attracts towards the centre of the earth all bodies in its vicinity; forces of repulsion drive bodies away from one another or keep them at a distance; forces of attraction tend to make them meet; motor qualities arouse bodies from their state of rest. All other effects are manifestations of physical forces. Local motion, it is true, may also appear in the resultant of their action, but it is not the principal and final result, which is rather the appearance of a new state, of a quality *sui generis*, that is irreducible to terms of simple motion. When our eyes rest on the varied colouring of flowers or we inhale their perfume or taste their fruit, or when we feel the pleasure of warmth stealing over our chilled limbs, it is not the local movement accompanying these phenomena which we first advert to, nor any of the common mechanical principles which cause sensation; but it is some

[49] Not to be confused with *potentiality*, also called 'potentia passiva'; cp. *Glossary* in Volume II of this Manual.—Trs.

real manner of being which though perhaps difficult to define bears a character distinct from all the ordinary causes of local movement.

70. Fourth Classification.—Physical forces are themselves *specifically distinct from one another* [50].

1. By our external senses we perceive the world around us and amongst other things the physical forces of matter. These senses are to-day universally admitted to differ from one another both anatomically and physiologically. Now how comes it that each of our senses has been provided by the Creator with its own special constitution and activity, if these properties of the material world that they are to make known to us are all of exactly the same nature?

If the objection be raised that our sense-organs are different in constitution and functional activity because the representative movements of these physical agents are different, we may reply in the first place that what we are conscious of perceiving in these agents is not movement but qualities properly so called; and in the second, that diversity of movements does not justify a diversity of sense-organs, since one and the same sense can inform us of movements that are different both in direction and in speed.

2. We know to-day what quantities of heat, electricity and motor force are absolutely equivalent to one another from the mechanical point of view. Yet these quantities, though quantitatively identical, remain just as much qualitatively distinct from one another as a colour, an electric current, a sound and a smell. This is clear proof that under the mechanical equality there lies some real basis of differentiation.

71. Secondary Aspect of Physical Forces.—Physical forces always have a double efficiency—one, specific and proper to each, such as colour, a thermic state, etc., and another common to all, namely that of imparting a movement to bodies subjected to their influence. Although they are specifically distinct and their primary function is to give bodies diverse qualitative states, they all fulfil, in a secondary way, the rôle of *motor* forces. On this account local movement always accompanies the exercise of these forces and is even the measure of their intensity.

[50] Duhem, *L'évolution de la mécanique*, p. 35 (Paris, 1903). — Hirn, *Analyse élémentaire de l'univers*, pp. 39, 134 et passim (Paris).

Now why this is so is explained by the very manner of being which is proper to physical energies. For since all the qualities of bodies are by their nature extended, as we have already said (**62**), any modification produced in a quality or physical energy must accordingly have its corresponding effect in spatial extension. But change in spatial position is nothing else than movement. Therefore the alteration of properties or physical forces naturally involves a local movement of equal intensity.

The chief error of mechanism has been in recognizing only one of the aspects of material phenomena, namely movement, and denying the existence of the other, which is force or quality.

ART. V. THE PRODUCTION OF MATERIAL SUBSTANCES

72. What is Substantial Change?—Hitherto we have considered corporeal substance from the static point of view; we have investigated the constitutive elements of a body and the nature of the properties which are its visible manifestation, notably quantity and active and passive powers. There is however the dynamic point of view to consider: for material beings are subject to constant changes, some of which modify their outward appearances, some are deeper and concern their very inner nature. When hydrogen and oxygen, for instance, combine to form water, these two bodies lose their specific nature, they are deprived of their essential form or specific principle and in exchange receive a new form common to both, namely the form of water. What has taken place in this case is a substantial transformation: the primary matter of each of the two elements has become merged into one under the influence of a really new determining principle.

A substantial transformation is, then, a complex fact inasmuch as there are two distinct yet inseparable phases, namely the *generation* of the new substance that is brought about at the expense of one or more substances which disappear as such, and the natural *destruction* of the one or more substances that determines the appearance of the new one. To express this the Schoolmen had the aphorism, 'Corruptio unius est generatio alterius et generatio unius est corruptio alterius.'

These two aspects of substantial change call for separate consideration. We will first consider the natural production of a substance or the realization of a new essential form. There are four points to be noticed concerning it.

73. (a) **Process preparatory to the Reception of a New Form.**—Substantial changes of inorganic bodies belong exclusively to the domain of chemistry; we know them only in the facts of combination and decomposition which form the entire subject-matter of that science. If we wish to study an example, we may do so in the combination of chlorine and antimony. What happens is this :—Immediately these bodies come into the same sphere of action, their mechanical forces first of all come into play. They possess strong affinities and therefore the forces of attraction dominate over those of repulsion and the bodies are brought into contact. As soon as this has happened, then their physical forces commence to exert themselves. Heat, electricity, etc., are displayed, and these act of course not on the bodies which put them forth—for such action would be immanent action—but on the bodies with which they are now in opposition. In this exchange of activities each substance tends to communicate its own particular characteristics to its rival and to make it become like itself, 'Omne agens agit sibi simile', for action is the expansion or self-diffusion of a being. But another factor also enters in, inasmuch as the character of an effect depends also to some extent upon the subject in which it is received. 'Quidquid recipitur, ad modum recipientis recipitur': the receptive subject is like a mould which impresses its form on that which it receives. Thus dependent upon two factors, all corporeal activities tend to produce a progressive levelling down of properties, a general qualitative state which has more or less the nature of a common denominator, and which, in the same proportion, lacks all distinctive characteristics of the elemental bodies. In this levelling down process there comes a time when the fundamental harmony that obtains between an elemental substance and its respective connatural means of action has to be broken up; the common resultant becomes incompatible with the two natures mutually reacting and necessitates their being transformed into a new substantial state. It is at this juncture that in the two bodies, now intimately united and predisposed for the reception of a new

common form, the two essential forms disappear and are replaced by a new one compatible with their new state.

It is to be noticed that the formation of the common resultant has the distinctive characteristic of necessitating alike the appearance of the new form and the disappearance of the individual forms.

74. (b) Actual Reception of a New Form, or the Act of Generation.—Generation may be defined as the transition of primary matter from the state of being without a certain substantial form to that of having it [51], if by being without it be understood the absence of a form which the primary matter is capable of having [52].

Primary matter concurs in a real though passive manner in the action of generation, inasmuch as it so sustains the new form at the very moment of its genesis that the form from the commencement relies on the matter for the essential support it needs in order to exist.

The realization of a form which is intrinsically dependent on its subject—which is nothing else than the becoming actually of what the matter was previously potentially—was expressed in mediaeval phraseology as the form being *educed* or drawn forth from the matter, 'eductio formarum e potentia materiae' [53]. By this phrase the Scholastics wished to bring out the absolute dependence of all lower forms upon the material element and to show the great difference that separates these from subsisting forms. Accordingly this saying does not apply to the human soul, seeing that although it is destined to inform matter it is yet directly made by the Creator without the concurrence of any pre-existing material subject; it is dependent only upon its efficient cause, and for this reason, in spite of its natural state being one of union with the body which it animates, it is able to subsist apart from matter after death.

75. (c) The Result of Generation.—The *formal* 'term' or result of generation is a new determining principle introduced into primary matter. But the whole or *integral* result is a body endowed with its own subsistence: for since existence is the

[51] ARISTOTLE, *De Generatione*, I, c. 5.
[52] ST. THOMAS, *In I Physic*, c. 7, lect. 13. — *Opusc. De Principiis naturae*.
[53] *Id.*, *Sum. Theol.*, I, q. 90, a. 2, ad 2. — *Cont. Gent.* II, c. 86.

complement required by an essence, it must always be the final resultant of the act of generation [54].

76. (d) The Efficient Cause of Generation.—It is an ascertained fact throughout the whole of chemistry that the properties of a compound resemble those of its component elements, albeit with a certain modification proportionate to the intensity of the combination. On account of this resemblance between new beings and those from which they are derived, and especially between living beings and the parent-stock from which they are propagated, the Scholastics did not hesitate to attribute the production of essential forms to secondary causes, that is to say, to the natural forces of the beings themselves.

This does not mean to say, however, that substantial forms pre-exist as such in the matter; they are only and wholly possible in the matter until such time as they become actual. Yet it would be foolish on this account, because forms are new realities, to refer them to a creative action and to refuse a generative activity to material agents, for by the same reasoning we should have to deny to such agents all activity whatever, even accidental, since every new accident also passes from a state of non-being to that of being [55].

Furthermore, it would be as great a mistake to take the act of generation for one of strict creation. An act of creation always has as its result a subsisting being that is entirely brought into being from nothing by the sole influence of the efficient cause, and therefore without the concurrence of any presupposed subject. An act of generation, on the other hand, presupposes a material subject which it transforms and brings to a new substantial state by giving it a new specific principle. Here the formal result is only part of the being, and even this part is due to a twofold causality, namely the efficient causality on the part of the agent and the material causality that belongs to the subject receiving the action

ART. VI. THE DESTRUCTION OF MATERIAL SUBSTANCES

77. How do Substantial Forms Disappear?—The disappearance of an essential form is never the direct and immediate result of efficient causality: for every active power tends

[54] St. Thomas, *Sum. Theol.*, I, q. 45, a. 4, and I, q. 66, a. 1.
[55] *Id.*, *De potentia*, q. 3, a. 8.

to communicate the likeness of itself, to bring into the world some definite mode of being. Rather, the reason why a form disappears is that its further existence is incompatible with one or other of the changes undergone by the body. Now this incompatibility in the course of a substantial change arises from a twofold cause: firstly, the properties suffer a diminution and cease to be adapted to the natures from which they spring; and secondly, the new form, which is the ultimate end of the reaction, is the rival of those that have gone before it.

What becomes of these forms? They simply vanish from the world of reality, just as the many movements we see around us disappear and with them the various accidental manners of being.

The birth of a new form and the disappearance of those it supplants are therefore two phenomena at once instantaneous and simultaneous.

78. What Happens to Accidents when a Substantial Change Occurs?—St. Thomas lays down categorically that, 'All accidents share the fate of the form'[56].

It is quite clear that *necessary* properties that form the natural complement of a substance cannot survive the destruction of the compound. Their substance is not only the basis of their existence, but the source whence they draw their energies and derive their distinctive character and the direction of their activity. Such properties are indissolubly united with their form, and therefore disappear with it when the rival form that supplants them brings with it its array of new properties. A succession of essential determinations is thus accompanied by a corresponding succession of accidental perfections.

The same law holds good for *contingent* or transitory accidents. Existing as these accidents do in a substance as their indispensable subject of inherence, they are individualized in it whilst remaining radically and intrinsically dependent upon it. When the essential form disappears, they lose their natural support which is the first condition of their continuation. And it cannot be that primary matter should act as an immediate support for them, for if the essential form, as we have said,

[56] St. Thomas, *De pluralitate formarum*. Difficultates ex philosophia, ad 5. Cf. Cajetan, Comm. in *De ente et essentia*, c. 7, q. 17.

gives to primary matter its first actuation, it is impossible for an accidental form to precede it.

We arrive, then, at the conclusion that no accident is *numerically* the same in a new being.

ART. VII. THE VIRTUAL EXISTENCE OF ELEMENTS IN THE CHEMICAL COMPOUND

79. In What does this Virtual Existence Consist?—In spite of their essential unity chemical compounds possess a natural aptitude to return to the elements from which they were produced. This leads us to ask why it is that beings which are substantially one should, under the influence of a single extrinsic agency, make other beings of different kinds issue from them, sometimes indeed of very many different kinds. The true reason of this, of why it is possible for elements to return to their state of liberty, is that they *remain virtually* in the heart of the compound [57]. And this virtual persistency of the elements is to be explained as follows.

Although the essential form of a compound is one, it is the natural substitute for the elemental forms that have disappeared, and as such it contains in some measure the chief energies possessed by the elements.

Secondly, the new being possesses the real properties, though in a weakened state, of the components so that each of the simple constituent bodies is represented in it by a number of properties that are analogous to those it possessed at the time of the combination.

Thirdly, each group of properties representative of the elements has a definite place in the mass of the compound.

Thus a molecule of common table salt (NaCl) is a body really one and having only one essential form, but it contains two parts, one representing in particular the chlorine, the other the sodium. These parts correspond to the two quantities of matter furnished to the compound by the elements from which it was generated; in each of these parts a number of weakened qualities recalls the element from which it originally came. And here the different groups of forces manage

[57] St. Thomas, *De malo*, q. 5, a. 5, ad 6. — *Sum. Theol.*, I, q. 76, a. 1, ad 4. — *De anima*, q. 1, a. 9, ad 1. — *De natura materiae*, c. 8. — *De mixtione elementorum*.

to agree under the governance of a single form because they have lost their salient characteristics and that particular degree of energy which necessitates an interchange of activities on the part of the elementary masses. After being reduced by the reaction to a kind of mean state they can maintain this stable and permanent equilibrium and thus persist in the compound. Hence, whereas in the case of living beings instability is the condition for existence and development, in inorganic bodies a disturbance of equilibrium is the forerunner of dissolution.

If heat or any other physical cause is brought to bear upon the latent energies of a compound such as the one mentioned, the two groups of properties will clearly each undergo a different development and eventually demand their own respective forms.

ART. VIII. IS THE ESSENTIAL UNITY OF THE COMPOUND A PRINCIPLE OR A MERE APPLICATION OF THE SCHOLASTIC THEORY?

80. A Modern Opinion.—According to the belief of many modern Scholastics, it would be preferable now to abandon the Thomistic doctrine of the unity of the chemical compound and in conformity with the principles of scientific atomism to regard it as a mere *aggregation of elements.* Such a concession, it is argued, merely restricts the field for the application of the general theory without compromising it; simple bodies and beings endowed with life are still asserted to be essential units. Furthermore it seems the easiest and most effectual way of putting an end to the conflict which has so long existed between philosophy and science.

What are we to say of this opinion?

81. (a) The Sacrifice of the Essential Unity of the Compound does not free us from Scientific Difficulties.—The difficulties introduced by modern science come chiefly from chemistry, especially from the structural formulae chemistry so largely uses. The purpose of these formulae is to show how the properties of a compound are a function of the way in which the atomic masses are arranged in the heart of the molecule: in it the different constitutive atoms receive a determined place and upon this their influence on the rest of the molecular mass and ultimately on the reacting bodies depends. These atoms the majority of chemists consider to be true individual substances, and thus the molecule to be a structure *sui generis*.

But if the actual persistency of atoms in the compound is necessary, as it is said, for the understanding of structural formulae and the chemical properties cannot be explained without it, then why maintain that organic beings, whether vegetable, animal or human, are essential units? There are a large number of compounds analysed in the laboratory which are also to be found in living beings, with their distinctive properties and modes of reaction. As surely as the same phenomena demand the same causes, if actual permanence is the only explanation for the properties of non-living bodies, it must also be so for the living being, and this therefore can be only an aggregation of unchanged atoms. Hence, whilst the difficulty may be overcome for the mineral world, it is thus merely transferred into the organic kingdom where it entails many very serious consequences [58].

82. (b) **The New Theory Militates against many Fundamental Principles of the Aristotelian System.**—1. Because substance is of itself inactive and therefore cannot attain its natural ends except by the means of those accidental powers which flow from it and are the immediate sources of its energies, every body possesses a number of proper qualities which are the faithful expression of its nature. It is thus a condition of immanent finality that every body should have active and passive powers suited to its nature and necessarily inherent in it as a substance. Now the new theory contravenes this fundamental doctrine of Thomism. For elements never generate a definite compound without undergoing serious modifications, without assuming new properties from the three points of view of chemistry, physics and crystallography. Indeed so distinct and permanent are their qualities that in chemistry we even call compounds by the name of species. These changes may be multiplied indefinitely and at every stage the simple body receives a new aspect, that is to say, it bears the characteristic features of the compound of which it is a part. Were it true, as our opponents maintain, that

[58] See the large edition *Cosmologie*, chap. V, for a harmony of St. Thomas' theory of the unity of the compound with the formulae of structure as interpreted in the light of *facts*.

throughout the immense number of chemical compounds elements retain their own individuality, these would enjoy the wonderful aptitude of assuming all the possible properties of beings whilst keeping intact their own distinctive nature. In such a hypothesis, where is that necessary and intrinsic relation of the nature of a being to its properties which is so strictly demanded by finality?

2. Secondly, the new theory makes the only criterion we employ in the inorganic world utterly valueless. The classifications made by scientists and philosophers rest on this one basis—the properties of beings. Elements are reckoned to constitute different species on the ground that they possess a group of irreducible properties. Now why may we not apply this criterion of specification to chemical compounds, seeing that as we have no direct knowledge of the inner nature of these bodies it is the only standard at our disposal for discriminating between them? Compounds indeed, no less than elemental substances, afford us a scientific description of themselves: each of them has its specific crystalline form, its own optic, electric and calorific qualities, its clearly defined chemical affinities; and on the score of stability, these properties are in no way second to those of the elements. Either we must, then, give up using the criterion we have mentioned or apply it equally to all bodies of the mineral world, to the atoms of elements and to the molecules of compounds alike.

CHAPTER III

HARMONY OF THE SCHOLASTIC THEORY WITH FACTS

In the inorganic kingdom complete individuality belongs to the *atom* of the element, and to the *molecule* of the compound. All bodies perceptible by the senses are aggregations of individual atoms or of molecules.

ART. I. FACTS OF CHEMISTRY

I. Atomic Weights

83. Difference of Atomic Weights.—The weight of an atom is a property that is really specific inasmuch as each simple body has its own invariable atomic weight in virtue of which it occupies a definite place in the graduated scale that stretches from hydrogen, the lightest body, to uranium, the heaviest.

According to Thomism, this diversity between atomic masses is a natural consequence of each element having a specific nature. Matter and form are necessarily related to one another as potentiality and actuality; and it is quite natural that there should be a perfect adaptation of the one to the other, that to the progressive series of essential forms belonging to the elements there should be a corresponding series of quantities of mass or atomic weights [59].

84. Constancy of Atomic Weights.—In spite of their inequality all atomic masses equally resist division by ordinary physical forces. What does Scholastic cosmology assign as the cause of this fact?

If we consider merely mathematical quantity or quantity in the abstract, there is no reason why bodies should not be capable of ever further divisions and finally all be reduced to the same. But over and above mere quantity, there is the substance with its special exigencies: indeed every being has

[59] St. Thomas, *In I physic.*, lect. 9. 'In corpore naturali invenitur forma naturalis quae requirit determinatam quantitatem sicut et alia accidentia.'

an inherent tendency to preserve the integrity of its mass and in consequence to offer a resistance of its own to any forces that would dissolve it. Hence it is natural for every simple body to have its own special quantity of matter that defies further division [60].

II. Chemical Affinity

Chemical affinity is one of the most striking manifestations of the specific difference between inorganic bodies. It appears at once as (*a*) an *aptitude* of heterogeneous bodies to combine; (*b*) as an *elective* tendency, and (*c*) as a force or *chemical energy*.

85. (a) Affinity Normally Exists only between Heterogeneous Bodies.—'Elements which enter into combination have to be altered to each other; and this happens only to things which have the same matter and can be active and passive in respect of each other' [61]. According to Scholasticism, every compound is a being essentially one and specifically distinct from its component elements. Now before two bodies can, by the exercise of their mutual affinity, proceed to a new substantial state, they have clearly to undergo profound alterations and give place to a resultant of forces which is incompatible with their respective natures: and this supposes the heterogeneity of the reacting bodies, since if they were of the same nature they could only communicate to each other those properties which each already possessed.

86. (b) Affinity is an Elective Tendency.—It is another principle of the Thomistic theory that every being in the universe has been created for a purpose; there is nothing which does not co-operate in realizing and maintaining the order of the world that shall reflect the plan of the Divine Mind. With this aim in view the Creator has endowed every body with natural tendencies which direct their activities and secure the stability of the laws of the universe. 'Nature', says St. Thomas, 'is the principle of a divine art impressed upon things, in virtue of which they move towards determinate ends' [62].

[60] St. Thomas, *De sensu et sensato*, lect. 15. 'Etsi corpora mathematica possint in infinitum dividi, ad certum terminum dividuntur cum unicuique formae determinatur quantitas secundum naturam.'

[61] 'Quae miscentur oportet ad invicem alterata esse; quod non contingit, nisi in his quorum est materia eadem et possunt esse activa et passiva ad invicem'. St. Thomas, *Cont. Gent.* II, c. 56.

[62] 'Natura nihil aliud est quam ratio ejusdem artis scilicet divinae, indita

Chemical affinity, considered as an elective tendency, appears then as the most remarkable manifestation of what the Scholastics called 'immanent finality'.

87. (c) **Affinity Considered as Force or Chemical Energy.**—When bodies act chemically, that is to say, so as to form new compounds, they exercise their energies under the impulse of this intrinsic tendency, and thus chemical energies find the norm of their spontaneous activity in the body itself. Hence the intensity of the action has to be proportionate to the mutual tendency of the reacting masses.

Moreover, since each body has its own specific nature and own proper energies, it is not unnatural that the discharge of calorific, electric and luminous forces should vary in different substances.

III. Valence

88. Relative Constancy of Valence.—Valence or atomicity is nothing more than atomic weight plus affinity, left to the caprices of chance and the varied circumstances in which the activity of matter finds its exercise. It is relatively constant, that is to say, the few variations to which it is subject occur, as we have said (**15**), only in well-defined cases.

Has Scholasticism any explanation to offer of this fact?

According to our theory valence must have some constancy from the fact that it depends on the very nature of a body. The chemical compound is the primary end towards which simple bodies tend, it is the goal of their natural tendencies, and therefore the compound must be of a definite type, bearing an invariable character of its own; its constitution cannot be dependent on the ever varying circumstances under which the combination takes place, or else the natural end of the elements would vary according to the environment of the reaction. Now the nature of a compound results not merely from the kind of elements composing it but also from the number of the atoms which represent them. This number of atoms is itself determined by the valence, since it is their measure. The

rebus, qua ipsae res moventur ad finem determinatum'. *In II physic.*, lect. 14. 'Et per hunc modum omnia naturalia in ea quae eis conveniunt, sunt inclinata, habentia in seipsis aliquod inclinationis principium, ratione cuius eorum inclinatio naturalis est, ita ut quodammodo vadant et non solum ducantur in finos debitos'. *Quaest. disp.*, q. 22, a. 1.

valence then enjoys the same degree of constancy as the compound and is dependent, like the compound itself, upon the nature of the generating elements.

But this constancy is not absolute, such as to admit of no exception. If the relative valence has the nature of the components for its remote cause, it has for its proximate cause the attractions and repulsions which are exercised by the immediate agents of the combination. The contact between one definite number of atoms rather than another clearly presupposes the intervention of these mechanical forces. Now although these intrinsic forces may be governed by immanent finality and follow the direction it gives, they are, nevertheless, of all corporeal energies the most exterior and the most exposed to influences from without; and this is true of all mechanic energies. Hence it would be remarkable if they remained altogether unaffected by the interferences of physical agencies. We may add that the narrow circle of these variations and the exactly determined circumstances in which they take place point to the necessity of referring the relative constancy of valence to the fundamental principles of chemical agents.

IV. Combination

89. Essential Distinction between Combination and Physical Action.—An inorganic combination is the fusion into one body of all the elements that generate it, so that a new species of being results in which they only virtually persist.

Scholasticism attributes a strict unity to the compound and thereby makes an essential difference between a combination and physical actions, particularly a mixture. A combination reaches to the very substance of being, whilst physical actions do not go beyond the sphere of accidental modifications. Hence it explains the radical difference which distinguishes chemistry from the other sciences: it alone is able to be defined as the study of the essential transformations of matter considered from the point of view of their sensible manifestations. Hence, too, the reason of those other distinctions made by scientists between chemical phenomena and physical changes; the former are specific, radical and permanent, the latter general, superficial and transitory: for the former involve a change of nature and species, whilst the latter affect only the surface of a being and at the same time leave unimpaired its substantial integrity together with its natural exigencies.

90. What is the Original Cause of the Heat which Accompanies Combinations and of its Constancy and Intensity?— Speaking generally, the thermal phenomenon produced by a combination results from two different things—from physical causes such as the change of state, exterior pressure, etc., and from a chemical cause, which is the union of the component elements[63]. The latter is absolutely invariable, the former depends upon the circumstances.

According to the Scholastic theory bodies can be drawn into action by extrinsic causes; but at the moment that they begin to interact in virtue of their natural affinity, all their intrinsic forces, and especially heat, are liberated under the exclusive influence of their substantial nature—or, more correctly, of their immanent finality. Bodies move spontaneously towards one another; 'they are not only drawn', says St. Thomas, 'but in some way advance towards one another'[64].

Now if calorific force has the law of its spontaneous activity in the being itself, how can other causes that assist its action make any difference? Must not the thermal phenomenon arising from a chemical origin be as constant as the cause itself?

Further, it is clear that in this case the being throws its whole self into the action keeping back none of its store of energies. It follows the impulses of its nature; nothing can check its pursuit of its end; in a word, it is prodigal of all it can expend. Herein lies the secret of the intensity of thermochemical phenomena, that extraordinary intensity which has not failed to astonish the keenest supporters of mechanism[65].

V. Chemical Decomposition

91. Nature of Decomposition.—Chemical combination deprives the elements of their essential forms to give them in exchange a form common to all; decomposition, the reverse

[63] Muir and Wilson, *Elements of Thermal Chemistry* (London, 1885).
[64] *Quaest. disp.*, see p. 109, n.
[65] Jouffret, *Introduction à la théorie de l'énergie*, p. 52 (Paris, 1883). — Secchi. *Unité des forces physiques*, p. 562.

process, re-invests them with their respective forms whilst at the same time dissolving the unity of the compound. The essential part of decomposition is, strictly speaking, the reviving of the component elements; their disunion is a natural consequence.

92. Particular Character of Decomposition.—When the bodies which have been virtually remaining in an inorganic compound recover their own existence, they take back the whole quantity of heat which they expended in the act of combination.

The Scholastic theory provides an explanation of this apparent mystery without having recourse to new hypotheses; it has merely to turn to its general principles concerning the genetic process of essential forms. According to these principles we saw that a new form becomes realized only in matter predisposed for its reception. Now just as the heat given off on the occasion of the combination is the measure of the alterations required by the exigencies of the specific form of the compound, so the very same law also demands that the lost forms of the elements should not be recovered until there has been restored to the various parts of the compound that exact quantity of energy which characterized them in their natural state as free elements.

We must remember that whilst the compound is a being that has an essential unity, it bears at the same time within itself the forces, though in a modified form, of the component elements, and that each component is an integral part of the compound, surviving there in virtue of certain properties. The perfect harmony brought about by the modification of all the chief properties makes it possible for the compound body to keep its unity, whilst at the same time it allows the specific powers, active and passive, of the several elements to persist in the particular parts which represent them. When, then, heat is brought to play on these latent energies, each part of the compound receives a special quantity of it and thus gradually approaches the elemental state of which it had been deprived, until at length it breaks up the harmony of the compound and regains its own existence.

93. General Conclusion.—The philosophy of chemistry when viewed in the light of the Scholastic theory reduces itself to a small number of principles; thus one single hypothesis—of the *specific nature of every body*—ultimately furnishes the explanation of the whole wonderful order that governs the intimate transformations of matter. It is the natures of bodies, inasmuch as they are the source of all their properties and activities, which rule the constant diversity of *atomic weights*; which preside over the regulated manifestations of *affinity* and *valence*; and which give a definite and invariable constitution to *chemical compounds*. And in the sphere of chemical activities, it is the natures of bodies which put into action the *calorific* and *electric energies*; which set limits to their *discharge*; and which guarantee a *regular decomposition* in the face of no matter what external circumstances. In short, the Scholastic theory explains the order investigated by chemistry by the substantial composition of species, without having to resort to a number of subsidiary hypotheses such as have continually to be invented to meet the weaknesses of the mechanistic position.

ART. II. PHYSICAL FACTS

94. General Outline.—From the physical standpoint every different species of body has its own proper character; every one has its own distinctive group of invariable qualities—its crystalline form, its natural state, its specific weight—and exhibits special phenomena relating to heat, sound, electricity and magnetism. These properties, which are all intimately connected, afford a secure basis of differentiation (see **24**).

95. Explanation of these Facts.—These groups of differentiating qualities that science informs us of, Scholasticism regards as the natural manifestation of the fundamental distinction which it maintains exists between the different substances of beings. Must not natures which are of different kinds possess different groups of properties, seeing that phenomena are but the only visible indication of the unseen, underlying substance? Hence all the distinctions which the classification of species has already made or will yet make were justified in anticipation by Aristotelian physics when it established a correlation between the inner substance of a being and its accidental qualities.

CHAPTER IV

PROOFS OF THE SCHOLASTIC THEORY

I. First Argument, drawn from Immanent Finality

96. Major Premiss : Order Exists in the Inorganic World. —Many striking scientific facts bespeak the orderliness of the world. There are the many laws governing the play of physical forces, such as weight, electricity, sound, heat and light ; the classification of crystalline forms and their invariable relation to the chemical nature of bodies ; the relations of weight and volume observable in chemical combinations ; the laws of affinity and valence ; the historical development of the changes the world has gone through since its nebulous state until the extremely complex conditions required for the appearance and maintenance of vegetable, animal and human life were brought about ; the relations of the earth and the heavens, relations upon which depend the regular succession of the seasons and the due performance of both organic and inorganic activities of matter. All these are witnesses to the existence of order in the universe.

Moreover if we had nothing more than the invariable recurrence of the same chemical species, the material universe would still be more wonderful than the most marvellously well-regulated of the works of man.

No one can hope to trace the infinite number of transformations undergone in the course of the ages by the myriads of bodies that find their place on the surface of our globe or are scattered throughout the atmosphere. The course of nature is one uninterrupted series of substantial changes in which the elements, after being worn away, broken up and stripped of their native properties, assume those of compound bodies, whilst other molecular structures lose their unity and distinctive traits by the release of their constituents.

Furthermore, the regular recurrence of the same mineral species has never been hindered either by the great number of causes whose interplay would, we should think, make the activities of beings capricious and disorderly, or by the intervention of the free-will of man who has power to vary agents and circumstances to suit his purposes, or by the ever-changing forms of environment that may be found. Simple bodies ever reappear with the same train of characteristics they exhibit in their isolated state; compounds that are time and time again destroyed and as often re-formed always contain exactly the same combination of elements and exactly the same number of atoms.

And what is even more striking, all these activities conduce in the same constant way both to the welfare of the individual and to that of the universe as a whole.

97. Minor Premiss: This Order is Explainable only on the Supposition of Immanent Finality in Material Beings.—*First explanation: Materialistic Mechanism.*—The old-world atomists—Leucippus, Democritus, Epicurus—and for the most part modern materialists such as Holbach (1723–1789), Haeckel (b. 1834), Büchner (1824–1899) recognize no telic principle directing the natural activities of matter. According to them all things in the universe are substantially homogeneous and are actuated by local motion alone; they follow blindly the lead given them by the chance impulses they receive through contact with one another. Yet, although without purpose or preconcerted plan, the processes of the universe are orderly because in virtue of mechanical laws matter under the present conditions can act in no other way.

> 'The multitude of living beings', says De Jouvencel, 'presents itself before us, not as the execution of a natural plan, but as an historical result, continually modified by a multitude of causes, which have acted consecutively, and in which every accident, every irregularity, represents the action of a cause. The plan—in the sense in which the expression is employed—does not exist. The forces act necessarily blindly, and from their concurrence beings take their origin. To believe that nature follows a serial plan would be a grave error. The series is a resultant, and not an idea of nature: it is nature itself. The human mind, however, evidently perceives that, if the forces of the universe are continually acting on the globe in the same way, in order to modify their organisms their work

must constitute a complete and perfectly graduated series '[66].

This materialistic explanation is obviously inadequate. If, as is maintained, there is no impulse towards a determined end either within a being or without it; if all things take place blindly, how is it that amidst the confusion of material activities all actions are adapted to a furtherance of the cosmic order? Whence arises this harmonious convergence to an end, and these combinations so suitably adapted for the production of specific types as well as for the general good? To say that each cause is directed by some blind fate to produce its effect is to offer no explanation of the *constant direction of all* corporeal agents towards the individual and the general welfare[67]. There is only one single path by which the activities of matter can effect the state of order we find, whilst there are a million possible ways by which they can effect disorder.

Second explanation: Spiritualistic Mechanism.—Not less dissatisfactory is it to attribute to bodies, as certain spiritualistic philosophers suggest, a communicated tendency derived from impulses received from without. At the beginning, they assert, the Creator gave to each atom its initial position and a fixed quantity of motion. Under the guidance of this primitive direction, the results of which the Divine intelligence forecasted, atoms proceeded to evolve themselves according to mechanical laws, and thus little by little they realized the purposeful series of events which, often repeated and ever orderly, makes up the record of the long history of our globe[68]. In this theory the important thing to notice is that the tendencies of beings are wholly extrinsic and foreign to their natures.

Although such a theory might be tenable if applied to a very limited number of beings under invariable conditions, as in the case of a machine—yet even so, the interference of God would be necessary every time that the regular working of the machine were interrupted by usage or by the deterioration of its many parts—its inadequacy becomes apparent as soon as it is a question of the actual evolution of events as we find them in

[66] *Apud.* BÜCHNER, *Force and Matter*, trs. COLLINGWOOD (London, 1864), which see for the materialistic conception of the Universe. Cp. also LANGE, *History of Materialism*, trs. THOMAS (London, 1892).

[67] Cp. HERBERT SPENCER, *First Principles* (London, 1890), Pt. II, esp. chaps. vi.–viii. and xii.

[68] Cp. MARTIN, *Philosophie de la Nature*, p. 115.

the inorganic world. To take but one example, if all chemical affinities were the result of purely mechanical impulses, man with his powerful means of action, such as heat, electricity, would very soon have changed the focus to which these primitive energies were directed and have given atoms entirely new directions, with the baneful result that bodies hitherto indifferent or without mutual affinities would by chance have combined, essential modifications have been introduced into the constitution of compounds, and an unlimited variation made in species; for nothing is more variable and ductile than a mechanical impulsion. In a word, the vast field of chemistry would have been reduced to a chaos of the most fantastic combinations to the great prejudice of the orderly working of our globe.

98. **Conclusion.**—Since no tendency which is extrinsic in its cause is capable of bringing about the stability of the cosmic order, the conclusion is inevitable that there must be in the very constitution of corporeal beings some principle controlling these activities and these very orderly combinations which by their incessant recurrence make up the history of the universe. In other words, we must recognize in every inorganic body an inherent purpose in virtue of which it tends, in the first place, to maintain the distinctive properties of its species, and, in the second, to exchange in obedience to the laws of chemical affinity its native energies with those of other kindred bodies.

99. **Explanation of the Minor.**—What is the real nature of this immanent finality or, as it is also called, natural tendency? The root error of the opinions we have hitherto considered has been a failure to recognize any natural connexion between the substances of things and the invariable groups of properties which form the basis of differentiation for all inorganic bodies, simple and compound alike. If such a divorce is admitted, the material substrates are by their nature quite indifferent to the properties they always possess when in their free state, and we may ask in vain why the free atom of hydrogen or of oxygen should always reappear with the same invariable properties. The invariable union which makes up a single group, of all these many independent qualities, physical, crystalline and chemical, remains an unexplained phenomenon so long as its cause is not placed in the substantial unity of a being [69]. If

[69] St. Thomas, *In II Physic.*, lect. 14. — *Sum. Theol.* I–II, q. 1, a. 2.

however we make substance the cause of these differentiating groups of qualities, of these tendencies that affinity shows clearly to be truly elective, we are in so far professing the Scholastic theory of the specific diversity alike of elements and of compounds, for it would be maintaining a contradiction to attribute to a *homogeneity* of the substrates the *diversity* of their accidental manifestations. We are thus compelled to admit the existence of natures that are specifically distinct from one another, and to acknowledge that there are as many such natures as there are indissoluble and constant groups of differentiating qualities.

Now this conclusion is merely a statement of the root-principle of Aristotelian physics. The other ideas follow as simple corollaries.

100. Logical Consequences of this Principle.—1. The first consequence of the specific diversity among simple and compound bodies is the *hylomorphic composition* of all natural bodies, that is to say, their composition from matter and form. If we maintain that the elements generating a compound assume when in it a common form and thus share in the same substantial state, we must believe at the same time that these elements lose the specific *form* they previously possessed and receive instead the new common form which gives rise to the new specific compound. On the other hand, since the transformation is not a creation of a being nor its annihilation, there must needs reside beneath the principle that determines the species some underlying *indeterminate substantial substrate* to receive the new essential determinations. These two constituents are the Scholastics' *primary matter* and *substantial form*.

2. The *function of the form* or determining principle stands in consequence clearly defined. It gives substance its primary actuality and distinctive nature, as well as fixes the character of the accidental properties that necessarily result from it. Moreover it holds them indissolubly bound together, since in conjunction with matter it is their common source and the cause necessitating their appearance. And thirdly, it is that which makes the body with its manifold activities tend to the special purpose for which it exists.

3. Lastly, the *order in the universe* ceases to be a mystery, inasmuch as we see that all things contain in themselves an

essential teleological principle which makes them retain their state and guides the trend of their actions [70].

II. Second Argument, drawn from the Unity of Living Beings

101. Statement and Explanation of this Fact.—No one questions the fact that plants and animals are substantial units. The solidarity of the functions necessary for their maintenance in being, the constant convergence of the many activities they possess towards their well-being and normal development, are proofs of this assertion which cannot be lightly brushed aside. And in the case of man, we have in addition to these data of experience the irrefutable testimony of our own consciousness : to one and the same subject do we attribute the sum-total of all our acts, whether pertaining to our sensitive, intellectual or purely vegetative life—a fact that remains entirely without explanation unless there is in us, beyond the immediate powers of actions, a being really one, the single substance of the human compound (*Psychology*, **149**, f.). All living beings, however, in spite of their exalted nature, are dependent upon inorganic bodies ; they derive from them the matter with which they build up their tissues, they are nourished at their expense, and after death return again into chemical bodies either simple or compound. All living beings thus present two characteristics which have to be reconciled, namely *substantial unity* and the *multiplicity of the materials incorporated*.

Now the fact of substantial unity, about which there is no question, is clearly incompatible with an actual persistence of the numerous individual atoms or molecules that combine in an organism's formation : for if they retained their individuality even man himself would be only an accidental aggregation whose manifold activities would be divided between his soul and the millions of atoms making up his body. The only way, then, of avoiding a contradiction and at the same time of preserving the substantial unity of living beings is to allow that all bodies have a dual constitution which permits them to be

[70] St. Thomas, *Cont. Gent.*, IV, c. 19. 'Res naturalis per formam qua perficitur in sua specie, habet inclinationem in proprias operationes et proprium finem quem per operationes consequitur : quale enim est unumquodque talia operatur et in sibi convenientia tendit '.

subjects of essential transformations, i.e. to be deprived of their specific qualities and so to put off their own individual being in exchange for a higher substantial state. Their unification by a single vital principle and the mutual interdependence and harmonious concurrence of all activities will then present no difficulty. Thus are we brought back to the hylomorphic composition of matter and all the consequences we have noticed that follow from it.

III. Examination of some Other Arguments

After having examined the solid and, as we view them, irrefragable foundations of the Aristotelian-Thomistic theory, we may without lack of interest inquire into the validity of some other arguments in vogue at the present day.

102. (a) Argument Drawn from the Specific Diversity of Properties.—Many authors seem to attach a primary importance to this line of proof. They maintain that the qualitative diversity of properties is an ascertained fact of sufficient importance to warrant the immediate inference of all the leading ideas of the Thomistic theory. Their argument is as follows :—

All simple and compound bodies are characterized by a group of really specific properties. Substance is known to us by its accidental manifestations. Therefore all chemical bodies are natures specifically distinct from one another.

Thus presented the argument seems to us of little weight. (*a*) It is scarcely true to experience. Consider physical forces, and see if you can find one which is *qualitatively* different in the various species in which it appears. Does not the *calorific force* of twenty-four chemical elements always and everywhere produce thermal phenomena of the same kind ? Maybe these phenomena are differentiated by their intensity, and it is in this respect we can say that each species has in reserve a special quantity of heat. Nevertheless it would be puerile to distinguish as many specific notes in heat as there are possible degrees of it. Secondly, consider *electricity*, which is also a common property of all inorganic matter. In the alkaline elements it is highly positive, it grows progressively less so in the other metals, it becomes negative with the metalloids, and after an ascending increase attains its maximum of intensity in the halogens, chlorine and fluorine. Here again there is a quantitative difference in both the positive and negative bodies, but from the point of view of effects there is not the slightest qualitative distinction. The same may be said of *light*, of *refractive power*, and in general of *optic properties*. Furthermore, the *state* of a body, whether gaseous, liquid or solid, affords no more sure ground for specification. Long ago it was proved in physics that the state of a body depends entirely upon the relative intensity of the attracting and repelling forces inherent in the ultimate particles of matter; and according as one or other of these energies predominates the particles either adhere (solid state) or tend to disperse (gaseous state), or assume some intermediate (liquid) state. Lastly, what about *crystalline form* with its apparently decisive evidence? Its modes are certainly manifold, yet in reality they are nothing but so many configurations of a common property—extension—which undoubtedly never changes its nature no matter what be the aspects under which it appears. In vain then may we search among the accidental manifestations of chemical species for that *really specific* note which is laid down as the chief ground of the argument.

(*b*) The questionableness of the major is not, however, the only weak point in the argument; the minor also is far from being evident. From the presupposed heterogeneity of properties an immediate inference is made to the heterogeneity of substances, on the ground that the former are the faithful expression of the nature of a being. Now such a proposition may be true enough in the Scholastic theory where the properties are a kind of efflorescence or natural derivation of the essence of a being; but it is a proposition hotly contested by the mechanists. It must therefore first be proved, and the only way of doing this, it seems to us, is to have recourse to immanent finality, or else to the invariable recurrence of the same inorganic species: in which case the main argument loses its own force and is nothing more or less than a more involved form of the proof we gave from the order of the universe.

103. In What Does the Diversity of Properties Consist? Its Importance in Cosmology.—It must not be inferred from this discussion that the study of the appearances of mineral bodies is without its importance in cosmology. Briefly we may say that notwithstanding the absence of all specific distinction in the strict sense of the term, the groups of properties are nevertheless true signs revealing substantial types, that is, are really specific to those who can discover the ultimate reason of their several characteristics.

1. In the first place, among the different groups there is a quantitative difference clearly defined. All simple bodies, for example, have a special calorific force, and when combining, say for the sake of comparison, with a similar element, they cause thermal phenomena of unequal magnitude: KCl liberates 105 calories; NaCl 97.3; LiCl 93.5, etc. The other forces present similar constant figures.

2. The degree of intensity displayed by the energies of a given body is a natural indication of it which is independent of extrinsic influences and accordingly invariable.

3. Each group of powers is subject to certain conditions of activity that are pecular to it. This truth will be evident if we glance over the field of chemistry and verify the infinite variety of circumstances in which chemical combinations take place. Placed in a given environment some bodies spontaneously discharge a considerable quantity of heat, electricity and light; others can be moved from their state of inactivity only with great difficulty; whilst others remain absolutely inert.

4. Lastly, although the properties of a being are each betrayed by their own manifestations, they are all united into one group by a bond so close that they are in fact inseparable.

Now these four features—none of which alone furnishes a basis of specification—admit of no other explanation than the diversity of bodies, when referred to immanent finality (98). Placed in this setting, the purely quantitative differences of properties become a real proof of the Scholastic doctrine.

104. (b) Argument Drawn from the Opposition observed to exist between Certain Corporeal Properties.—A careful inspection of material beings reveals certain antinomies or apparent contradictions; on the one hand there is the undeniable *unity* of each body; on the other, the *multiplicity*, diffusion and reduplication of its parts. We find an *actual indivision* of the whole in conjunction with an indefinite *divisibility*. Again we are encountered with an *inertia*, *passivity*, complete indifference to states of rest or motion at the same time as an *activity* and a kind of *spontaneity* of action. Finally there are certain generic properties *common* to all material beings, side by side with certain specific ones that are *proper* to each individual. Now it is impossible for one and the same basic principle to be acting at once as the foundation of two contradictory qualities or actions. Therefore every body must have a double element in its constitution, i.e. on the one hand a principle of extension, of passivity, quantity, identity, and on the other a principle of unity, activity, quality and specification—or in two words, *primary matter* and *substantial form*[71].

105. Value of the Above Argument.—In criticism of this argument we may say in the first place (*a*) that it will not do to lay too much emphasis upon the opposition of properties which is the chief point of the new proof. If, as seems to be supposed, certain properties are in such opposition to one another that they seem mutually contradictory, it is difficult to understand how they can attach to the same body at one and the same time, and the natural union between the two basic principles on which they rest would thus seem to be impossible.

(*b*) In the second place, the hylomorphic composition of matter, as put forward in the Scholastic theory, can be perfectly reconciled with a certain co-existence of disparate properties; it even gives an easy and plausible explanation of the fact. But does the mere fact, of itself, suffice as a proof of the composition of matter and form? We do not think it does, and for the following reasons:—

1. Although *activity* and *passivity* are for certain reasons opposed to each other, the inference is illogical that they must proceed from two opposite substantial causes. This admixture is found in every creature; even an angelic being, despite the simplicity of its essence, is in many respects both active and passive. It is the fact of being contingent, we believe, which is the ultimate reason of the passivity found in every creature. Yet this imperfection we find to be increasingly great the lower we come in the scale of beings, and thus we see the reason why the element that is the most potential of all, primary matter, is in perfect harmony with the great passivity of bodies, whilst still not its indispensable cause.

2. Again *inertia* and *activity* appear to be two properties

[71] This argument is especially well developed in FARGES, *Matière et forme en présence des sciences modernes*, p. 13 f. (Paris, 1888). Compare SCHNEID, *Naturphilosophie im Geiste des heiligen Thomas von Aquin*. (Paderborn, 1890).

exclusive of one another. Yet in reality this opposition is not so radical as we are at first led to think. The term ' inertia ' is ambiguous. Either it is synonymous with passivity, as in the phrase ' quantity of inertia or quantity of mass', (**63**) and in this case, as we have just shown, we can bring no argument in favour of hylomorphism. Or it means simply the impotency of a body to modify its state of rest or of motion : by the simple fact that an inorganic body has its activities turned in an outward direction, it is impossible for it, on its own initiative, to modify the state in which exterior causes have placed it. Understood in this sense, inertia far from being opposed to activity becomes a necessary consequence of the way in which material beings exercise their action.

3. What have we to say of extension with its antinomies of *unity* and *multiplicity, actual indivision* and *indefinite divisibility*? Assuredly the double aspect of this property agrees in every respect with the distinctive aptitudes of the essential elements of a body ; but we must not forget that extension is not an admixture of two irreducible parts—unity and potential multiplicity ; on the contrary, unity of extension essentially implies a potential many, so that both are but aspects of one and the same reality. Now it would not seem that the constitution of such a reality absolutely demands two substantial parts, namely form and primary matter ; if extension is by its very concept a quality really one, there would be nothing against saying that matter understood as homogeneous in the mechanical sense was endowed with it.

Furthermore, did all these antinomies furnish a real proof of the dual theory of corporeal essence, there would still be the need of finding a firm basis for the fundamental principle of Aristotelian cosmology. For since all the properties enumerated are common to all bodies, the conclusion cannot affirm more than that all material bodies are constituted of two consubstantial elements, namely an indeterminate principle and a determining one. But the fundamental conception of Aristotle's system is far more comprehensive than this : it asserts that in the inorganic world there are natures *specifically* distinct, that bodies by their substantial constitution tend towards their individual ends which they realize by the exercise of appropriate powers ; their constitution out of matter and form is but a deduction from this. Desirous to complete the proof we are considering, many authors make a further appeal to the specific diversity of certain properties; but such a line of argumentation, we have seen (**102**), meets with scientific criticism which nowhere discovers any but quantitative differences.

106. Conclusion.—To us it seems that there is only one complete and convincing proof of the Scholastic theory considered in its application to the inorganic world, and this is to be found in the study of the order that exists in the universe. Aristotle recognized no other, and with reason. The orderliness of the universe, we repeat, with the manifest design and adaptation of its parts, is unmistakable evidence that every body has by its nature an inherent purpose and carries with it throughout its existence a certain invariable, constant group of qualities that are quantitatively different from those in every other such group. This is the one fact which justifies the whole of St. Thomas' physics.

Yet we are far from denying that the argument drawn from the constitution of living beings has value. We believe, however, that this line of proof is incapable of establishing specification among mineral substances without borrowing largely from the preceding argument; alone it can lead us with certainty only to the bipartite constitution of inorganic bodies, and for this reason we have assigned it a secondary place as corroborating, by a new and more direct way, one of the conclusions of our argument. Specification among natures is a doctrine of first importance in cosmology, inasmuch as this study has as its primary end to ascertain the ultimate causes or explanations of the cosmic order and especially to determine the immediate principles of its constancy; hence its task would be but partly fulfilled if it left unexplained the peculiar character and special rôle of the individual factors, and were content with proving in a general manner their composition from matter and form.

Moreover it would be unfair to say that the other arguments mentioned are without any value. Though lacking the force of cogent proofs, they are valuable as declaring the agreement of the Scholastic theory with several facts ascertained by experience.

PART III

Dynamic Atomism

107. Statement of this Theory.—The root ideas of this system may be stated as follows:—

(1) Matter is essentially *homogeneous*.

(2) All material phenomena can be accounted for by *purely mechanical* forces, that is, by forces capable of producing only movement.

(3) Atoms are *unchangeable* and always retain their own being throughout all the phases of their evolution.

The first and the third propositions are borrowed from mechanism and constitute the common principle for both these theories. The second proposition, in which mechanical energies are substituted for local motion, contains the distinctive feature of dynamic atomism. There is a general agreement among authors about these primary tenets, but dissension appears when it is a question of determining the number and nature of the forces put into play by matter. Some authors divide these mechanical forces into three classes: (1) *forces of attraction* and *repulsion*, which act from a distance and tend unceasingly to produce motion; (2) *forces of impulsion*, the peculiarity of which is to communicate motion by shock or pressure; (3) the *force of inertia*, which maintains beings in their state of rest or of movement in a straight line [72]. Other authors endow matter with *gravity* as its one and only essential fundamental force, thus making all other energies different modes of the force of gravity [73]. Others again assert the *force of resistance*, which is essentially inherent in matter, to be the only truly irreducible energy [74]. Finally many scientists

[72] MARTIN, *Philosophie de la nature*, II, p. 87.

[73] JAHR, *Urkraft der Gravitation*: 'Light, heat, magnetism, electricity, chemical force are secondary manifestations of the elementary force of the world' (Berlin, 1889).

[74] TONGIORGI, *Cosmologia*, lib. I, c. 3, a. 2.

find the dual theory that there are only *forces of attraction* and *repulsion* the most satisfactory.

108. Criticism of Dynamic Atomism. First Principle: Homogeneity of Matter.—The great outstanding fact noticeable in all that happens in the universe is the double teleological tendency in organization and destination of the works of Nature. Every body shows itself to be the subject of an immanent tendency in virtue of which it follows its natural purpose according to certain invariable laws. The mechanist fails to recognize this fundamental principle manifested by the orderliness of the universe and the constant recurrence of the same species, and in consequence is encountered by insurmountable difficulties in chemistry, physics and crystallography. So likewise the dynamic atomist by professing the homogeneity of matter *suppresses all intrinsic finality*, or at least deprives it of its chief features. Indeed there can be no place for elective tendencies so long as all matter is the same, seeing that if bodies of the same nature possess inherent tendencies, they cannot tend but towards exactly the same ends. Whereas it is precisely the diversity of intrinsic tendencies which accounts for the diversity of the properties of beings, for the difference in their activities or, in a word, for the order of the universe (**98, 99**).

A second and no less serious consequence of this mitigated form of mechanism is that, if atoms are indestructible and unchangeable, *essential unity* would seem to belong only to atomic masses, and accordingly inorganic compounds together with vegetable, animal and even human structures must be regarded as mere aggregations of individual atoms held together by mechanical forces: a conclusion which is counter to the results both of biology and of metaphysics.

109. Second Principle: All Material Forces are Simply Mechanical.—Although material forces are always accompanied by local movement and on this account can be called mechanical forces, many of them have in addition a specific mode of action. Such are the physical energies of light, electricity, heat and sound. The chief function of these is to produce different qualities which we call thermal state, colour, etc., states which are each manifestly irreducible to a simple displacement of matter and which are therefore essentially distinguished from ordinary mechanical forces, the proper effect of which is solely local motion (69, 70)[75]. So speak facts. Now dynamic atomism, by denying this specific diversity of forces, contradicts the verdict of our senses without being justified by any data from experience in doing so. Indeed there are physicists of the highest repute who do not hesitate to say that not a fact of science has yet been ascertained which warrants the reduction of all material energies to purely mechanical forces[76].

110. An Objection.—Heat, sound, light, etc. are all subject to the same general laws of reflection, refraction, and interference. Now it is difficult to understand such a fact as this if these energies are distinguished from one another by qualities which are specifically distinct.

We reply that whilst it is beyond dispute that many of the physical laws apply to some of the energies we regard as heterogeneous, there is nothing in this fact which either militates against the Scholastic theory or proves the homogeneity of material forces. For all the laws discovered by experimental physics concern the mechanical aspect of phenomena; and according to the Scholastic teaching all activity, whatsoever its nature, is always accompanied by movement. Hence it is not to be wondered at that owing to this common property all forces are subject to certain general laws of physics.

111. Conclusions.—Dynamic atomism is a half measure. As a reaction against mechanism it acknowledges that if matter is despoiled of every internal principle of activity, philosophy cannot hope to give an ultimate explanation of the facts which present themselves and must leave the universe to the caprice of chance. It keeps in view then the order of the universe and allows that matter has forces properly so called. But it denies a substantial diversity between beings and in so far fails to give an explanation of the constant diversity of the groups of accidental properties. It makes a step in the direction of Scholasticism but does not logically arrive at it because it is content to leave the problem of cosmology only partly solved.

[75] Cp. Boutroux, *De la contingence des lois de la nature* (6th ed. Paris, 1908).
[76] Cp. Duhem, *L'Evolution de la méchanique*.

Dynamism and Energism

ART. I. STATEMENT OF DYNAMISM

112. Principal Ideas of this Theory.—The dynamic conception has been put forward under many forms. It was constructed by Leibniz (1646–1716) into a complete system of cosmology, and since has undergone many profound changes, especially during the last century. The chief ideas of the many forms in vogue at the present day may be summed up in the following propositions :—

(1) There exist in the world only simple elements, or groups of them, *really unextended*.

(2) Their whole essence is *simply force*.

(3) According to the majority of dynamists action always takes place '*in distans*', that is to say, without contact.

(4) All phenomena, no matter how different in kind, result from a conflict of elementary forces, and are nothing but *modes of motion* [77].

ART. II. CRITICISM OF DYNAMISM

I. THERE IS FORMAL EXTENSION IN THE MATERIAL WORLD

113. Proof Drawn from the Testimony of Consciousness.—1. All dynamists allow that at least as regards objects of sense-perception bodies appear to be realities having extension. Such phenomenal or subjective extension is a common fact which imposes itself upon the consciousness of everybody and retains its distinctive character even when submitted to reflective consideration. Now we have the duty as well as the right to believe our senses and to take their representations as faithful replicas of the external world until such time as their

[77] For a brief exposition of the principal different dynamist systems—of Leibniz, Kant, Boscovitch, Carbonelle, Hirn, and Palmieri—see *Cosmologie*, 2nd large edition, nn. 337–342.

inexactitude or falsity is proven by convincing demonstrations of science or philosophy; for our senses are passive faculties the vital reactions of which, under normal conditions of exercise, correspond to the impressions they receive. Therefore corresponding to phenomenal extension, the internal effect, there must exist proportionate external cause.

2. In the hypothesis of dynamism the perception of even purely phenomenal extension is an anomaly lacking all explanation. Indeed what can be its cause? Not the senses, for if dynamism is true, the senses themselves are made up of simple unextended elements that do not possess, either formally or in an embryonic state, the integral elements of real extension. Nor can the cause be the combined influence of external agencies, because here again are only simple principles whose unextended actions if they come into contact meet in a single indivisible point.

114. An Objection.—No material body, it may be objected, enjoys a real continuity. The most compact masses are full of lacunae or pores—interatomic or intermolecular spaces. Our organs of sight misinform us when they represent bodies as continuous wholes. Extension is therefore apparent.

This we willingly admit, that in the mineral world true continuity belongs only to atoms and to molecules in the compound. We admit that every sensible mass is a collection of minute particles between which we can without difficulty conceive apparent or real intervals of space. If our senses are incapable of perceiving the small interstices that break up the extension of material bodies it is because they are imperfect instruments. But, we argue, this imperfection in no way diminishes the real objectivity of our perception of extension, since every external agent, atomic and molecular mass alike, if taken as a whole, does really possess this quality. The general effect produced in our sense-organs thus receives a complete explanation in the Scholastic theory: the subjective representation of a continuous extension has a real cause, namely the influence of the particles each of which has itself a continuous extension, whilst the absence of divisions in external objects is due to the natural limitations our faculties have in their perceptions.

115. Proof Drawn from Unity.—The theory of dynamism strikes a fatal blow at the unity of higher beings. For either the simple forces that constitute a being come into contact or they 'act at a distance'. If they come into contact they all coincide in a mathematical point, inasmuch as two indivisible beings in contact touch each other according to the totality of their being. If they do not come into contact, then a living being is a collection of individual particles which are capable of mutual influence only on the supposition that *actio in distans* is possible—an hypothesis physically impossible (**121**) [78].

116. An Objection.—Force is an absolutely simple reality; extension on the contrary is liable indefinitely to division. Force is essentially active, whilst extension is synonymous with passivity or complete inertia. But two contrary properties cannot possibly belong to the same subject [79].

The fallacy of this objection consists in making extension and force two opposed realities whereas they are simply realities of different natures. The idea of force represents *power of action*, and nothing more. It in no way reveals to us the mode of the material being according to which this power is realized. Whether force be actually in form no more than a mathematical point or whether it occupies a definite portion of space, the idea of it remains the same; in a word, it abstracts from all spatial relations. Hence it may be applied either to energies which are extended, such as physical and mechanical forces, or to forces of a simple nature, such as mind and will. The function of extension, on the other hand, is to expand in space the subject, whatsoever be its nature, to which it belongs.

[78] To escape these criticisms Palmieri and some other dynamists allow a *virtual extension* to force. This means to say that the atom is not an entity devoid of all real volume; it fills so much definite space, and in each part of this space it remains whole and entire, defending by its force of resistance the inviolability of its particular spatial department. Now, it is argued, such atoms even though they are simple can touch one another without complete interpenetration, and can thus excite in our sense-organs a perception of apparent extension.

What are we to think of this conception? Like the other dynamic systems, it rules out the *substantial unity of living beings*, since virtually extended atoms cannot be transformed. In the second place, by granting to all beings the same mode of existence, it does away with the essential *difference between the spiritual and material worlds*. The atom would be just like the human soul in occupying a definite portion of space and being its own complete self in each part of it; whereas such a mode of being is peculiar to spiritual substances and is the ultimate principle of their immaterial activities.

[79] Balmès, *Fundamental Philosophy*, trs. Brownson, Vol. II, Bk. 3, chap. 24 (New York, 1864).

Although it does not possess any dynamic power, it tends to spread out material energies as well as passive quantity. Hence force and extension are two distinct realities, but such as to be perfectly compatible with one another.

II. The Essence of a Body is not Force, nor a Collection of Forces: it implies a Passive Element

This proposition, which is the antithesis of dynamism, is none other than the Scholastic doctrine. It is proved by the argument appealed to above in support of the dual constitution of bodies, namely the composition of matter and form.

117. An Objection.—We know bodies only by the actions they exercise on our sense-organs. Any body which is incapable of making an impression upon us must remain unknown. Bodies, therefore, manifest themselves as principles of activity and nothing more [80].

118. Criticism.—All phenomena represented by our senses are characterized by extension. Therefore the external causes determining them must, before they can have the properties belonging to their effects, be forces really *extended in space.* Such is the conclusion to which we are led by the application of the principle dynamists themselves admit, namely that an effect bears the impress and character of the cause which produces it.

Extension, it is true, is not a dynamic power; but if all the forces of nature are affected by this property, it is impossible for them to produce an effect which is unextended, for a force extended in space cannot by mere action lose its manner of being and become a simple force without extension. If then dynamists from the fact of the activities of bodies are justified in making the induction that active substances must exist, we also are equally justified in making the inference, from the fact of extension—the principle of inertia and passivity—that there is in bodies a second constitutive element, very closely united with the first but one which is essentially passive.

Secondly, the passivity of matter, we maintain, is just as manifest as its activity. For all the bodies in the universe stand to one another in the relations of agent and patient. No one body can act without another receiving its activity;

[80] Ostwald, *Natural Philosophy*, trs. Seltzer (London, 1911).

and since the body acted upon re-acts against its motor agent, this original agent changes its rôle and in turn becomes passive. Thus we see that when it is a question of transitive action, activity and passivity are two correlative and inseparable terms; and therefore activity alone does not constitute the whole essence of a body.

III. 'Action at a Distance' is Physically Impossible

119. Meaning of this Statement.—'Distance' here means an absolute vacuum. The question proposed here is whether when two bodies are separated from one another by an interval void of all reality they can exercise a real influence upon each other.

This problem allows of a twofold interpretation:—

1. Is action at a distance in opposition to certain known laws of the material world, or is it not? In other words, is it *physically* possible?

2. Supposing that immediate contact is, in the ordinary course of nature, an indispensable condition for action, is it in the power of the Creator to dispense with this condition? In other words, is action at a distance *metaphysically* possible?

Our opinion is that there are undeniable facts to prove the physical impossibility of such activity, but that up to the present there has been discovered no convincing proof of its metaphysical impossibility.

120. Insufficiency of the A Priori Arguments broguht forward to prove the Absolute, or Metaphysical, Impossibility of 'Action at a Distance'.—The idea of 'transitive activity' neither implies nor excludes the notion of immediate contact. Transitive activity supposes on the one hand an agent which possesses force and exercises a causal influence, and on the other a patient receiving it; and between the effect and the cause a relation of proportion as expressed by the principle of causality. The *force* put into play we cannot conceive to be anywhere but in the agent; for if it is an accidental property it depends upon its subject of inherence, and if a substance, it is identical with the agent. The *effect* is wholly in the recipient subject which occupies a position outside the agent.

Now does action pass from the agent to the patient? Certainly not; the agent does not cause any accidental reality originally belonging to itself to pass over into the recipient subject, otherwise every efficient activity would be reducible to a simple displacement of pre-existing realities, to a passing over of accidents. Therefore no transference takes place, nothing passes from one to the other; the effect is a new birth, and takes place entirely within the patient under the influence of an external cause (*Gen. Metaphysics*, **144**).

In this analysis neither contact nor distance appears as an indispensable condition of activity. There remains little difficulty, therefore, in showing that all a priori arguments rest on a false conception of activity or else beg the question.

First objection.—In the hypothesis of action at a distance, a being acts in a place where it does not exist.

A distinction will help us to answer this objection. To say that if a body acts at a distance (*a*) the action, i.e. the active force, is in a place where the agent is not, is untrue, for this force is inseparable from its substantial subject of inherence. But (*b*) action, i.e. the effect realized under the causal influence, is indeed outside the agent. And this is true no matter what theory you hold. If you mean that the agent must be in contact with the terminus of its activity, you are dogmatizing about the very point at issue.

Second objection.—Action at a distance is possible on the condition that the effect is transmitted across the vacuum from the agent to the patient. But such a supposition is absurd.

In reply, we deny the major. An effect is never transmitted either through a void or through a medium. It can never be outside the subject that receives it, being intrinsically dependent upon it for its birth.

Third objection.—To change the patient, the agent must exercise some influence upon it. But such a thing is inconceivable unless there is contact.

The major certainly no one will dispute. But the minor is precisely the point under discussion; to assert it is not to prove it.

121. The Hypothesis of 'Action at a Distance' is Physically Impossible.—All material forces are governed by a constant law, which may be enunciated thus: 'The intensity of the action that one body exercises on another diminishes in proportion as the distance increases; and conversely, it increases in proportion as the distance is diminished'. Now there is no explanation of this fact if the hypothesis of action at a distance is accepted.

Without altering the internal dispositions of the agent and patient—which moreover cannot be altered by a vacuum whether great or small, since it is nothing—we may vary the distance which separates them. The action, considered in the agent, has an intensity which is invariable and independent of the distance, for the reason that material bodies, being destitute of freedom, cannot change the degree of their intensity on their own initiative. Considered in the patient, where nothing is changed, it has the same degree of intensity as it had in the agent. If there were a change, the medium alone would be the cause of it; yet the vacuum is nothingness, and the action, not having to traverse it, cannot lose any of its power in space [81]. Hence the variations of intensity of which we are informed by experience remain as effects without a cause unless in place of the supposed vacuum we substitute continuous matter, either ponderable or imponderable; and then the progressive diminution of the action depends upon a proportionate cause, namely upon the various resistances of the medium.

ART. III. STATEMENT OF THE THEORY OF ENERGISM

122. General Sketch.—The changes which happen in the material world are of many different kinds; a stone falls, fire burns, electricity drives machinery, lightning rends the clouds, a river bursts its banks, and mysterious affinities of chemical bodies long perhaps inactive occasion under the requisite conditions a great display of heat, electricity and mechanical effects. So different are these changes which take place that we might at first sight think there is not a single feature in common between them; yet a closer investigation, we are told, reveals always and everywhere under the fleeting and varied aspects the same essential content, one indestructible element, namely energy. If there is diversity, it is only in the form of the phenomena; behind the manifold forms and persistent throughout all the phases of change is ever one and

[81] DE. SAN, *Cosmologia*, p. 353 f. (Louvain, 1881).

the same reality—energy. The whole universe as we know it is a complexus of energies, the constituent elements of which we name as extension, volume, form, space, electricity, magnetism, movement, weight, light, heat, matter, etc. Indeed there is not one of these realities which cannot make an impression on us or at least produce mechanical effects.

According to this theory of energetics, then, the only thing in the world is *energy* and all material reality partakes of it, either as a factor of *quantity* or else of *intensity*, or tension. Thus, for example, the energy of gravity comprises two constituent elements, one a quantitative element represented by so many kilogrammes, the other an intensive element expressed by the height of the fall. The product of these two factors constitutes the energy of gravitation. For certainly the magnitude of this energy depends both upon the magnitude of the suspended body and upon the extent of the space traversed.

The manifold forms under which energy presents itself are considered in this theory to constitute real species, among which we notice chiefly energy of motion, electric energy, energy of heat, of gravity, of light, chemical energy, nervous energy, etc. But all these different kinds of energy can be transformed into one another, insomuch that every phenomenon is nothing but a change or transformation of energy. The two principles governing these transformations are (*a*) the principle of the conservation of energy, which asserts that in spite of the changes of form the quantity of energy remains the same; and (*b*) Carnot's principle, which may be enunciated thus: A phenomenon is possible only where there is a difference of intensity or tension; and energy tends to flow from the higher point to the lower. These notions being settled, we may define the theory as one which conceives all the phenomena of the world as the action of energy upon energy.

The theory of energism is a reactionary system against mechanism. The latter reduces the universe to the two factors of local movement and homogeneous matter; it thereby excludes all *quality* from science and interprets the nature of accidental and substantial realities accordingly. As a reaction against this system, the theory of energism re-instates the principle of quality by its avowal of many species of energies. M. Duhem describes it as the mathematical theory of quality.

Further, it forbids any judgment about the nature of the material realities it studies; it is content to describe energies and such transformations as they represent, to measure them and to be able to state, in general or mathematically, the numerical relations which exist between these various degrees, etc.

123. Leading Ideas of this Theory.—Viewed from a purely philosophical standpoint the theory of energism may be summarized in four propositions:—

(1) Energy is the only reality in the world.

(2) All energy is made up of the two factors, quantity and intensity.

(3) There are different kinds of energy.

(4) They can be transformed into one another.

124. Inductions Peculiar to Certain Savants.—Many writers, notably Ostwald and Mach, think that they can find in the theory of energetics a basis for a phenomenalist and monist conception of the universe. According to Ostwald (*a*) the world is nothing but energy, really one, which is spread through space and time or, more accurately, comprises space and time in its synthetic unity, itself remaining a constant reality under various manifestations. (*b*) Substance does not exist, but only a series of phenomena linked together. (*c*) Matter does not exist; what we term matter is in reality only a complexus of three factors of energy—volume, weight and mass[82].

ART. IV. CRITICISM OF THE THEORY OF ENERGISM

125. Points in its Favour.—There are several points in this theory which go a long way to recommend it and it gives a more exact view of nature than either mechanism or pure dynamism. First of all, it rejects the reduction of all phenomena to local movement as unscientific and contrary to every-

[82] For an exposition of this system see OSTWALD, *L'énergie* (Paris, 1910), *L'évolution d'une science* (Paris, 1909) in French Translations; and *Principles of Inorganic Chemistry*, trs. FINLAY (London, 1908); *Principles of General Chemistry*, trs. TAYLOR (London, 1912) — DUHEM, *L'évolution de la méchanique* — L. POINCARÉ, *The New Physics and its Evolution*, III (trs. London, 1907) — REY, *L'énergétique et le mécanisme* (Paris, 1908) — LE BON, *The Evolution of Forces* (London, 1908) — MACH, *Science of Mechanics*, trs. M'CORMACH (London and Chicago, 1893) — NYS, *L'Energétique et la théorie scholastique* (in *Revue Néo-Scholastique*, Aug. 1911 and Feb. 1912).

day experience. It rightly gives a prominent place in physics to quality, and even goes so far as to assert the existence of many qualitative elements. In the second place, it refuses to pass any judgment upon the substantial nature of bodies; it excludes from the sphere of physics a field of research which is beyond its power to investigate, inasmuch as it belongs to metaphysics to solve the problems that relate to the substance of beings. Yet, though it may escape censure on some points, it is not above criticism.

126. Its Defects.—The chief weakness of this theory, which it shares with pure dynamism, consists in assigning to material nature an exaggerated dynamic power, or rather in extending this power to a large number of properties which are in reality destitute of it. On this score it merits the same criticisms as we meted out to the earlier theory. Thus, all corporeal realities, we are told, are constituent elements of energy; extension, volume, space, distance, time, the form of a body, its mass, etc., all help to make up diverse energies. From this it follows, since energy is nothing if not essentially a power of action, that every material reality bears a purely active character or is a resultant of activities. But none of the elements just mentioned, such as space, extension, time, etc., possesses any dynamic character whatever.

We are quite prepared to admit that all properties without exception have, in view of the dynamics of the universe, a certain function to fulfil: some are true dynamic elements, real principles of activity, especially heat, electricity, weight, force of impulsion, chemical affinity, light, etc. Others, although really distinct from this first class, furnish us with the measure of their quantity or of their intensity, as for instance space, mass, etc., whilst others again are conditions which must be present before cosmic agents can act and even in part measure that activity, as do time and space, etc. The term 'energy' is sufficiently elastic to embrace all these various elements, provided however that we attribute to each its natural rôle. The error of the theory consists in considering them all to be *constituents* of that one single complex reality 'energy'.

127. An Objection.—The advocates of this theory warn us against the too common confusion of force with energy. In general, force, they say, is only a part or an element of energy;

and hence there is a real distinction between the theory of energism and pure dynamism.

That there is such a distinction we beg to deny. All quantity of energy can be reckoned in terms of work, and work, in mechanics, is equivalent to the product of the intensity of a force and the space traversed. Now if force is, in this hypothesis, only a part of the energy, the reason is because under the name force is understood only the intensity of an action, whilst under the name of energy is understood the intensity together with the quantity of action. Energy therefore remains a true dynamic power when considered in its twofold aspect of quantity and quality, notwithstanding the fact that it is not a force in the mechanical sense of the word.

128. The Theory of Energism, even were it Established, would lead neither to the Negation of Matter nor to Phenomenalism nor to Monism.—The word 'matter', we are informed by Prof. Ostwald, is applied to whatever is revealed to our senses as a complexus of three fundamental and inseparable qualities—extension, weight and mass. These three properties are three factors of energy the union of which is required for the realities of this world to make up objects of our experience. If these three properties represent the whole of what is contained in our concept of matter, and are moreover the constituent elements of energy, then matter is quite a superfluous idea [83]. This is the solitary argument on which the German professor bases his denial of the existence of matter.

1. Now first of all it is untrue, as we have already said, that these three realities are dynamic elements. And secondly the concept of matter contains more than these three fundamental properties; it is universally admitted to stand for an extremely complex group, a collection of very many elements. It embodies mechanical properties, such as weight, mass, extension, forces of attraction and repulsion; also physical properties—electricity, magnetism, heat, light, and colour; and finally special properties falling under the general name of chemical affinity. Matter is this permanent stable thing endowed with these many different characteristics which are so indissolubly bound together and so intimately connected one with another that they provide every being with a reliable basis of differentiation. Now such a collection of attributes

[83] Ostwald, *L'énergie*, p. 168 f; *L'évolution d'une science*, p. 441 f.

can find no explanation unless we admit the existence of substance as the source and connecting bond and principle of activity of each several group. Thus do we find ourselves again with all the elements, accidental and substantial, which make up the concept of matter.

2. And even the advocates of this theory cannot refuse to acknowledge this conclusion. For they must allow either that all properties are modes or objective aspects of the same substance, or that each property is a substance having its own separate existence. In the first hypothesis, they admit the existence of material substance; in the second, they offer no explanation of the indissoluble grouping of properties and attribute to accidents substantial being the existence of which they denied. Unless then these phenomenalists are willing to restore matter its traditional claims, they have either to multiply substances gratuitously or to subscribe to the flagrant contradictory proposition that a thing exists without that whereby it is enabled to exist. Because they profess to study only phenomena of nature, this is no sufficient reason for refusing these passing realities the permanent substantial substratum which they demand for their existence (cp. *Gen. Metaphysics*, 82 f.).

3. Lastly, their doctrine of monism is the result of a confusion of the ideal order with the real. Because all realities of the material universe can be grouped under the one term 'energy', they imagine that this unification or reduction to unity made by the concept likewise obtains in the real, external world. Or in other words, all ideal representation they take to be such a representation of the real world of experience that whatever is a property of the one must also be found wholly in the other. Herein is the root-error of their professed monism. In reality the truth is this: the proper and essential character of a concept, even though objective, is to represent the things of reality in an abstract way, that is to say, without those many individual notes which particularize them and distinguish them one from another in number if not also in nature. Furthermore the facts of our internal and external experience condemn the reduction of all beings to a single and universal substance which is the professed tenet of some advocates of this theory.

129. The Relation of Energism to Dynamism.—Briefly

we may say that there is only one idea common to these two theories, namely the dynamic conception of the universe, a conception which makes all material realities constituent elements of energy or of a power of action. Questions concerning the extension and manner of activity of material agents do not come within the particular scope of the theory of energetics, or if they are dealt with they can receive a solution even opposed to that of dynamism. For none of the advocates of the new theory, as far as we are aware, has attempted to settle what manner of being belongs to the quantitative or intensive factors of energy—to say whether they are simple, or spread through space and extended. This question is one not raised, much less solved. On the other hand, the concept of force or energy essentially implies a dynamic power, but it does not reveal what kind of being this power of action is. Whilst retaining, then, the fundamental ideas of the theory, one might if so minded make the dynamic elements either extended or simple. So with regard to the question of *actio in distans*: if extension is attributed to the factors of energy, one is not unreasonable in professing the non-existence of action without some kind of contact; not so however if energies are pronounced to be devoid of extension, for then such action is a logical consequence.

RECAPITULATION AND CONCLUSION

130. At the end of this section it will be well to glance over the ground we have traversed. Four systems, each claiming to be based on experience, aspire to solve the intricate problem of the ultimate constitutive causes of the inorganic world. These we have weighed in turn and three of them we have found not to balance the sum of the facts to be explained.

First of all we examined *mechanism* and found that in the domain of chemistry, physics and crystallography its fundamental tenets come into perpetual conflict with the invariable laws of nature, with its diverse yet constant activities, with the indefinitely great variety of species and their stability. The homogeneity of mass and the capricious variability of motion, the absence of any principle of orientation, of activity and of specification, leave the marvellous order found in nature without any explanation.

To meet these deficiences *dynamism* is a re-actionary system which in place of extended and inert mass substitutes a simple element, essentially active, viz. force. Nature thus recovers one of her most noble prerogatives, her internal dynamic power. But this system is too exclusive. Real extension and passivity that are inseparably united to the activity of matter, and the capacity bodies have of combining to form new essential units, are facts established by science and attested by consciousness which condemn the narrowness of dynamism.

Dynamic atomism is a rather weak attempt to reconcile these two systems. From mechanism it borrows extended mass, from dynamism a force-element. By clinging however to the essential homogeneity of all matter, it creates a divorce between substances and their accidental manifestations, since peculiarity of properties and especially the constant specific direction of activities cannot be derived from substance if all material substances are of identically the same nature.

The examination of these theories opens out the way to a right understanding of the material world. It is clear that the order of this world is to be accounted for by the existence of natures that are specifically distinct from one another, that are endowed with extension and appropriate powers of action and that substantially tend to realize particular purposes. This is the conclusion we are led to from the investigation of facts and by the guidance of common sense. And this is a succinct statement of the *Scholastic Theory*

APPENDIX

Time and Space

131. Thomistic Definition of Time.—Time is closely associated with successive continuous quantity ; we know it, whether in the ideal or the concrete, as a reality whose parts pass in a continuous succession from 'future' to 'past'.

Aristotle and, after him, St. Thomas have defined it : '*Tempus est numerus motus secundum prius et posterius*'[84]. Let us try and elucidate this pregnant definition.

132. Connexion Between Time and Movement.—According to these two philosophers time is closely connected with continuous movement ; it is indeed its measure, or perhaps better, a breaking up of it, a numbering—*numerus motus*. Now does this close connexion as a matter of fact seem to be borne out by experience ? Yes : in the first place, for example, it is by the movement of the earth round its axis that we have our standard of measuring the duration of contingent things and the events and actions of our lives. Again, if it happens that we are intensely absorbed in some occupation and no longer have attention for the various movements or changes taking place around or within us, we lose all sense of time. And should we try to reflect, we find we are incapable of calculating even approximately the time that has elapsed, unless we apply our memory to recall one by one the things which have happened during the interval in question. Lastly, to represent time we often make use of the metaphor of a line, extending indefinitely into the past, running uninterruptedly through the continuous development of an ever elusive present and stretching without limit into the future.

133. Why Movement Suggests the Idea of Time.—Move-

[84] St. Thomas, *Opusc. De tempore*, c. 2.— *In IV physic.*, lect. 17. On the subject of Time see also Balmès, *Fundamental Philosophy* III, trs. Brownson (New York, 1864); Spencer, *Principles of Psychology* II (London, 1881); Bergson, *Matter and Memory*, trs. Paul and Palmer (London, 1911).

ment (*motus*) properly so called presents two features: (*a*) Firstly it is the coming into actuality of something which is capable of being realized tending to be further realized, or something perfectible tending to be perfected; an actuality therefore which has a twofold relationship, viz. to the potentiality whose actualization it initiates and to the yet further perfection in which the potentiality finds its completion or by which it may be even replaced [85]. Now so understood, movement is an uninterrupted progress bearing the characteristic of *unity* proper to all continuous quantity, whether successive or permanent (**55**). Under this aspect movement is not identical with time nor does it appear to suggest the idea of time [86]). In fact, as we have just said, it is impossible to notice the elapse of time whilst the mind is so absorbed that it cannot take heed of the different phases which really break up its apparent unity.

(*b*) Secondly, movement possesses another characteristic which is no less essential. Although it does not consist in a collection of parts actually distinct from one another, it nevertheless contains, because it is continuous quantity, the foundation of discrete quantity or of number; it is *virtually multiple*, in this sense that by a simple extrinsic designation one can separate it out into an indefinite number of parts that when viewed by the mind become really and truly actual parts. Movement, then, subjected to a simple mental division becomes a number or a multitude. The parts of this multitude, however, have this distinctive feature, that they are perceived in the movement whose constituent elements follow one another according to a relation of before and after, of past and future.

What our perception of time consists in is in perceiving in this continuous foundation which is real movement parts that succeed one another without interruption and are linked together according to a fixed and invariable relation of before and after: 'cum enim intelligimus extrema diversa alicujus medii, et anima dicat, illa esse duo nunc, hoc prius, illud posterius, quasi numerando prius et postius in motu, tunc hoc dicimus esse tempus' [87].

The '*numerus* motus' of which St. Thomas speaks consists,

[85] For an analysis of 'Movement' see *Gen. Metaphysics*, **115**; and for the three kinds referred to on p. 147, see *Glossary*.

[86] St. Thomas, *In IV physic.*, lect. 17.

[87] *Ibid.*

then, of the parts of the division made by the mind in movement. The two words '*prius*' and '*posterius*' express the two aspects under which these parts are related to one another and come before the mind. The term '*motus*' points out the continuous movement or the real and undivided thread which is presented to the mind for division.

Thus time is made up of two elements, the one *formal*, namely number (numerus), the other *material*, namely movement (motus).

134. Distinction Between Time and Movement.—Between these two notions there is only a logical distinction[88]. As a matter of fact concrete time and movement are one and the same reality. For although continuous movement does not at once appear before the mind under the formal aspect of temporal duration, as it has first to submit it to a process of mental division which brings out the notion of succession, the progressive development of a before and after; nevertheless this division is not a real one, but belongs to the mental order and makes no change in the objective reality of the movement.

135. Abstractions Necessary for the Mind to arrive at the Universal Idea of Time.—The identification of real time with continuous movement does not at first sight seem to be compatible with our ordinary conception of time. We represent to ourselves the duration of time as a single duration, regularly successive and always the same in its continuous prolongation. Whereas, on the other hand, there is a great variety of movements, such as rapid, slow, uniform, vibratory, undulatory, etc. How reconcile contradictory attributes in one and the same thing?

These opposite features are seen to be consistent with one another when we take into account the many abstractions that the mind makes in order to form its concept of time.

1. First of all our mind in perceiving in movement the idea of time abstracts from the qualitative element that is there, from what kind of movement it is. Movement may be quantitative, purely local, or qualitative, according as its result is an increase or diminution of quantity, a simple change in position in space, or a modification in quality. To all these three kinds of movement the notion of time applies equally.

2. Next, the concept of time has nothing to do with the

[88] St. Thomas, *De instantibus*, c. 5. — *Opusc. De tempore* c. 2.

special modes of a determined movement. If it is a question of local movement, it is evident that the direction and the successive directions of the movement which produce undulatory, vibratory or other movements, in no way enter into the idea of time.

3. Again, in the original conception of time, the mind abstracts also from the manner in which the parts of the movement succeed one another, the mode which differentiates it into slow or rapid movements. This is proved by the fact that the idea of rapidity or slowness presupposes a relationship between time and the space covered. A movement is more rapid just in proportion as it covers a greater space in a fixed time. From this it is clear that the idea of rapidity and the opposite idea of slowness become intelligible to us only if we already possess the two ideas of space and time; and hence they cannot be the object of the first conception of temporal duration.

When all these abstractions have been made, what is there that remains in the movement we perceive to give our idea of time an objective reality? It is the continuous succession, the flow of the parts some of which are anterior and others posterior. This is the object of the abstract and universal concept of the mind, a concept which is applicable to every kind of continuous movement, whatever be its nature, its mode of succession or its quality.

136. The Parts of Temporal Duration.—There are three parts in time, the present, the past and the future. The *present* is essentially fleeting. The moment we consciously examine it, it is already in the past. It is impossible to conceive it without putting it into relation with the past which precedes it and of which it will immediately go to form a part, and with the future which follows it and which will immediately replace it. Situated thus between the past and the future, it comes before us as a link, constantly moving, which unites them and disappears with them without interruption.

The other two parts, the *past* and the *future*, constitute the intrinsic elements of time. They are essentially relative, since to conceive them as such we have to connect them with the fleeting present. Compared with the real present which is actually passing, all previous parts are once and for all past, all succeeding parts are really to come.

Hence it follows that time has but an imperfect reality. Of the three kinds of parts that go to form it, the one no longer exists, for it is the past; the other is not yet in existence, for it is the future; there only remains the fleeting present, which has a momentary existence. Therefore a duration of time, however small it may be, requires the bringing of the memory into play, that is to say, the simultaneous representation of a whole of which only one part enjoys a reality and that a fleeting one.

137. Various Acceptations of the Notion of Time.—1. According to St. Thomas' theory, the objective reality of the concept of time is identical with movement. There are then as many particular times as there are distinct movements. In a word, every being that is subject to change has its real time, which is commonly called *intrinsic time*. For although movement, if we leave out of consideration the action of the mind, does not possess in its complete actuality the formal element of time, nevertheless it has a successive existence which is divisible into parts of time; and in this there is, as it were in a rudimentary state, the 'numerus motus' of which Aristotle speaks[89].

2. Time often comes before the mind under the aspect of a successive duration susceptible of being extended indefinitely into the past and of being prolonged at our pleasure into the future, and independent of the real world and of the mode of succession which characterizes the contingent beings that exist. In this respect it is an abstraction from movement; in elaborating its concept the mind ignores in movement all that individualizes it, in such a way that it attends only to the two essential notes of successive duration. It is a universal concept, really and truly one, however manifold it may be in its applications. This is *ideal time* which has no existence except in the mind that conceives it.

3. Another less abstract form of time is that of a successive continuous duration, having a true unity, that we divide into periods of days, months, years: namely, the concrete duration of the apparent movement of the heavenly bodies. With this

[89] 'Et ideo, signanter dicit Philosophus quod tempus, non existente anima, est utcumque ens, id est imperfecte, sicut et si dicatur motum contingit esse sine anima imperfecte'. St. Thomas, *In IV physic.*, lect. 23. — Cp. Suarez, *Met.* Disp. I, sect. IX, n. 6. — St. Augustine, *Confessions*, Bk. III, c. 23.

movement of the heavenly bodies, whether it be real or apparent, time has really no more definite connexion than with other movements that belong to the earth; but by reason of their great regularity and constancy and the extent of their manifestations, their movement has become the type of all movement, the model of duration from which events on the earth take their common measure or standard. Indeed so familiar has become this particular concrete representation of time, this identification of time and movement as it is thought to exist among the heavenly bodies, that any other way of conceiving time appears to us forced and strained from its original meaning. And from this particular, practical point of view we say with reason that there is no time except *real, concrete time*[90].

4. A fourth form of duration is in *imaginary time*. When in our thought we leave out of view the whole world of material beings, continuous time necessarily appears to us as a kind of indestructible reality. It even assumes the characteristic of a being *sui generis*, occupying a place above all that comes into being or disappears, necessary in spite of the uninterrupted succession of the parts that go to form it, embracing at once the past and the future, anterior to all created things and capable of surviving their destruction. This time is called imaginary, for it is a hybrid product of the intelligence and the imagination, being a fusion of the abstract universal time that as such is independent of any particularized existence, and of a vague and indefinite movement represented by the imagination. The imaginative faculty here gives an appearance of reality to the object which is conceived by the mind and exists there alone.

Imaginary time, both in itself and in its unity, belongs wholly to the subjective order.

ART. II. SPACE

I. INTERNAL PLACE

138. Definition of Internal Place.—Every natural body possesses a certain volume and occupies a determined position, a place properly its own, a change of which constitutes local

[90] ST. THOMAS, *Sum. Theol.* I, q. 10, a. 6; *In IV physic*, lect. 23. — CAJETAN, *Comment. in S. Thomam*, q. 10, a. 7.

movement. This portion of space occupied and measured by the real volume of a body is its internal place.

If a material body undergoes a displacement before our eyes, the image of its movement appears to us under the form of a series of positions successively occupied and abandoned. Each of these positions we call a movable or transient place. If the body passes to a state of rest, in so doing it acquires a place of its own, relatively immovable and always proportionate to its real dimensions.

139. Reality and Nature of Internal Place.—Bodies are indifferent with regard to space; they do not require one particular place rather than another, and yet they cannot exist without occupying some one place determined in all its points. How can we account for the fact that every body, which thus shows a general indifference with regard to all the possible places of the world, does actually occupy an individual place reserved to itself? This taking of possession is due, in our opinion, to a real accident that belongs to the body, which we shall henceforth call its *localizing accident* or the 'intrinsic whereness' (*ubicatio*) of a body.

First proof.—The state of rest is not the same as that of motion: apart from any consideration of the mind, the simple displacement in space of a body that is independent of its causes imposes itself upon us as a *real* phenomenon, perhaps even as the one least liable to sense-illusion. We must then recognize, unless we are willing to avow a radical subjectivism, that not only movement but every part or stage of the movement marks a real change in a body. Now, we ask, what is the precise reality which suffers this change? It cannot be the body's substance nor can it be one of those accidental properties such as weight, colour, physical or chemical energies: for we have no experience of such a modification, seeing that a body in motion remains ever itself as well as keeps all its properties the same throughout, excepting perhaps for some alteration for which we can always discover a cause other than the movement itself. Hence there must be some other reality over and above, whose successive, continuous changes constitute the mobile reality of movement; one that we cannot but suppose to be a special real accident whose proper function is to localize the body and confine it to this or that part of space. Indeed, since movement is continuous change of position or place, it can only exist if *place*, whereof it is the change, exists too; if place is not real, movement is an illusion. Every material being, then, appropriates a fixed part of space in virtue of a localizing accident which determines its natural indetermination or indifference and fixes it in a position proper to itself and exclusively its own. When the body is at rest, this accident is stable and unchanged like the place it determines; when the body is in motion, it undergoes continuous modifications and to these is due the body's successive series of positions or places that we understand by 'movement'. Considered in its whole nature, movement has a twofold formality, the one invisible and alone real, namely the continuous changing or incessant renewal of the localizing accident of the body; the other, the succession of positions which the moving subject occupies and then abandons in its path. The latter is the sense-perceived manifestation of the internal and unseen reality of movement.

Second proof.—Between the various bodies of the universe there exist many relations of distance, and these we must regard as objective and real, seeing that by geometry and astronomy we measure and compare them and, in gauging their respective extents, rely on our judgments having more than a mere subjective validity. Now these relations of distance between bodies so clearly marked and carefully estimated are continually changing; bodies move away from one another and approach nearer to one another; distances increase and diminish. We have the clearest evidence of these real changes, indispensable as they are both for the general development of the universe and the continuation of order on our own globe. The only question to determine is, In what precise reality do they take place?

Every relation necessarily implies two terms and, if it is a mutual one, an objective reason as its foundation (*Gen. Meta.* **108 ff.**). In order that a new relation of distance may exist between two bodies, a real change must have been brought about in the bases of this relation; if not, how can we say that the bodies are really nearer or further apart, seeing that relation as such does not exist but draws its whole reality from the two terms which are its foundation? Now in a real change of distance, the only reality that changes is the actual position of the bodies, i.e. their internal place; the distance diminishes or increases because the bodies leave their respective places to occupy new ones. Therefore, unless we are going to deny the objective character of the change, we must admit that localization proceeds from a mobile accident whose essential rôle is to determine a body in a certain position in space. In this case, to every spatial change there corresponds in the body a parallel modification of the localizing accident ; and new relations of distance have an objective aspect because they rest on new foundations, viz., the intrinsic localizing accidents (ubicationes) they acquire as the result of their movement.

Conclusion.—Internal place, considered under its formal aspect, is the portion of space circumscribed by the mass of a body. Considered in its concrete reality, it is a real accident with the function of circumscribing the volume of a material thing and of giving it its peculiar spatial position.

II. External Place

140. Definition.—Had only one single material substance been created, it would still have had its own internal place. Yet it would have been impossible to determine the position of this body, for the reason that all spatial determination is necessarily relative. The position of a thing is settled by certain guiding-marks, or rather by certain relations established between the body in question and those which surround it. Hence in common language 'place' signifies more than the portion of space occupied by the real volume of a material being ; it means its whereabouts or the surroundings in which it is. So viewed, place is external to the body, and is accordingly known as *external place*. This external place of a body we may define more strictly as *the immediate circumference or the first immovable surface which circumscribes a body*[91].

141. Analysis of this Definition.—If a hollow vessel is filled with water, to the question, 'Where is this water ?' the spontaneous reply is, 'In the vessel'. This latter serves for the liquid it contains as a true *place*, a place exterior to the body within it. Here we have a first and fundamental property of place, namely the aptitude to contain within itself a determined volume.

Next, it is clear that by very reason of its character as a

[91] Aristotle, *Physics*, Bk. IV, ch. 4 (6). — St. Thomas, *De natura loci* : 'Locus non solum est terminus corporis continentis, sed etiam est immobilis'. — Id., *Logicae summa*, Tract. VIII, c. 6.

recipient, the vessel must be an individual thing distinct from the thing contained in it, since to contain and to be contained are two contrary attributes implying different subjects. This distinction is a second property of place [92].

Moreover, if we inquire what precisely in the vessel it is which plays the part of recipient, we find it to be only its internal surface. It is a matter of indifference whether it is made of cut-glass or of common glass, or of iron or wood, or whether its sides are fragile or solid; so long as it can contain, it keeps its essential rôle independently of these and other accessory circumstances. Accordingly we may define external place as the immediate material circumference which surrounds a body, the first surface which a material substance encounters at the limits of its extension. Here we are to notice two elements, the one *material*, the internal surface; the other *formal*, the interval or capacity circumscribed. These two elements are indivisibly united in the concept of real place: for the internal surface can be called place only if it has the aptitude to contain, that is to say, if there are relations of distance between the walls of the vessel; and the capacity of the vessel or the distance between its walls is a definite capacity only if it is circumscribed by real limits, by an enveloping surface.

Aristotle adds as a fourth condition that the containing surface be considered as *immovable*. Relative immobility is indispensable for the constitution of external place as conceived by us. How, indeed, do we represent the movement of a body except as a removal from one place into another; the body moves, but the place it abandons remains unmoved. There is however just this difficulty that, if all the beings in the universe are subject to movement, where are we to find this immobility? There are two ways of considering the surface of a localizing body: either we may consider it as a concrete, individual material thing, and then it constitutes a place that is essentially mobile; or we may leave out of consideration all its individual characteristics and conceive it merely as the surface, of any body whatsoever, capable of circumscribing such and such a volume. Looked at in this latter way, the place always keeps its identity in spite of the

[92] St. Thomas, *In IX phys.*, lect. 4. 'Oportet enim primo et per se alterum esse, quod est in aliquo, et in quo aliquid est'.

many different bodies that follow one another in it and fulfil the same office there.

In order to allow external place a true relative immobility it is sufficient to conceive it as related to certain fixed and invariable points, such as the poles and the centre of the earth. As these terms of comparison remain always the same, we are easily enabled to perceive when bodies change their places as well as the identity of the places which they change. In every point this definition of Aristotle has the support of empirical data.

142. Kinds of External Place.—The place we have just defined is called by Aristotle *proper place*. It signifies the material surface or circumference which immediately fits its content and encloses that alone. It is, we may say, the typical form of external place. By *common place* is meant that which contains several bodies, such as a room full of furniture: a name that justly applies, but with a sense derived from the first acceptation.

III. Space

143. Facts of Experience.—To stand on a railway bridge and watch an express train pass by so quickly that scarcely any part of it is seen distinctly, provokes the remark that it flies through *space*; where by space we mean distance and to fly through it to cover a great distance in a short time. Again, I may say that my study is a very pleasant one, that it is pleasing to gaze upon because of the light and the *space*, the notion of space being used in the sense of roominess, of interval enclosed by the walls of the place. Once more, we speak of the early mist being melted by the first warm rays of the sun into vapour which slowly rises until it is dissipated in *space*, meaning to say that it loses itself in the immense capacity or interval that separates the earth from what we speak of as the vault of heaven.

Vary the examples as you will, analyze the various ways that this term is constantly applied by science or ordinary speech, and you will always find that it contains the idea of distance or interval, of real or apparent void, comprised within certain definite limits.

144. Analysis of the Facts, and Definition of Space.—If we carefully reflect upon this concept of space, we discover in it two elements, one a *formal* element, the relation of distance, the capacity, or the relative void comprised within the bodies that limit it ; another, a *material* element, namely the bodies, or more exactly, the surfaces of the bodies that by their distance from one another make a real or apparent void.

We may, then, define *real* or *concrete space* as a *relation of distance in three dimensions, determined by the respective positions of the bodies that limit it.*

In point of fact, every definite interval is always limited by extended bodies ; and between two extended things, however small they may be, there intervenes some room that is measurable according to three dimensions. If the exact sciences, however, notably geometry, deal sometimes with spaces that are of only one or two dimensions—such as a line or a surface—these extents do not really exist apart from the mind, but are the result of a process of abstraction by which it picks out from among several real objective facts one or other of the three dimensions, while disregarding how inseparably connected they are in the world of reality.

145. Connexion Between Space and External and Internal Place.—1. The analysis of space and external place shows the two notions to come really to the same thing. In each we find the same constituent elements, a *material* element or the bodies that limit the distance, and a *formal* element or the interval itself, the distance or capacity. If they are different ideas it is because they differently emphasize one or other of the two elements which they embody ; in the idea of 'space' prominence is given to the relation of distance, in that of 'external place' to the concrete limits or terminal surfaces. Yet just as every definite interval presupposes real limits, so every set of real limits implies a definite interval.

2. 'Internal place' is also closely allied with 'space' inasmuch as the internal places of material substances are the foundations or the formal limits of the spatial relations. For the determination and the extent of these relations depends entirely on the positions occupied by the bodies limiting them ; thus, every change in one or other of these positions involves a corresponding change in the distance between them, in other words, in the space. If, then, space enjoys a real existence, however imperfect this reality may be, it is due to these internal places. If a change in spatial relations appears to us as an

objective fact, it is only the existence of localizing accidents that give us the reason of it. In brief, the reality of these accidents is the objective foundation of spatial relations.

146. Is There Only One Space ?—1. In the real world we distinguish as many particular spaces from one another as there are intervals or distances marked out by concrete limits.

2. Yet, among this innumerable multitude of real spaces the whole series of which makes up the extension of the material world, there is one which seems to have a special claim to be called ' space '—that unmatched and unmeasured, immense interval which stretches from the earth to the vault of heaven. Because it is so imposing on account of its unique dimensions and of its part in the economy of the universe, it occupies a special place in our imagination and in our language and we call it simply ' space '.

3. Outside the world of real things there is still another acceptation of the idea of space. As our senses bring us in touch with concrete and particular spaces, our intellect works upon these data of experience and, by disregarding both the size of the different intervals perceived and the individual nature of the bodies that bound them, retains of the concrete representation only the essential note of limited distance. This is a purely intellectual concept with an indefinite range of application ; it forms an abstract type not determined to correspond to any particular interval but applicable to any interval whatsoever. It is what we call *ideal* or *possible space.* The unity and the universality it possesses depend on the fact that it is an abstraction and exists only in the mind.

4. The last form of space we meet with is *imaginary space.*—The abstractive power of the mind has always to be assisted by representations of the imaginative faculty. When therefore the concept of ideal space is being formed by the mind, an image, more or less vague, accompanies it and serves as a support. Now as distance abstractly conceived is indefinitely elastic, as it can be stretched as far as we wish and the movable limits our intelligence assigns to it are co-extensive with it, the imagination, in playing its part in this work of extension, furnishes under an abstract form a vague and indeterminate image of the extension, it pushes further and further back the horizons it meets, until of abstract space we have a vague concrete image made by the imagination and the illusion that it

is something real, independent of all bodies that exist. Such is the genesis and the nature of *imaginary space*. Like absolute time it has no existence except in our subjective representations.

147. Does the Notion of Space imply a Vacuum or a Plenum? —Space, as such, is indifferent to either of these attributes; whether matter is one continuous whole stretching from the earth to the heavens or whether this immense interval is void of all material reality, space remains exactly the same. Neither a vacuum nor a plenum makes any change in its nature, since this relation of distance according to three dimensions owes both itself and its extent, not to anything within, but to the respective positions of the boundaries that mark its limits. In other words, if there is no change in the limits that mark a place, the capacity or the physical possibility of a definite thing being within it remains the same.

No doubt the notion of space always awakens the idea of a certain vacuity, but the vacuum indicated by the notion of space is not synonymous with the absence of all matter. It is essentially relative to the two bodies which in every case determine the relation of distance. There cannot, indeed, be any space without interval; but between the extreme limits of any particular interval there are any number of positions where these two limits do not exist. Here we have then a relative void, inseparable from distance, although a void which does not exclude the presence of material bodies, with which it is unconcerned.

Thus are two seemingly contradictory facts explained: every representation of space the mind makes contains the idea of a relative vacuum, and yet neither a vacuum nor a plenum are conditions of the real existence of space.

[For another Appendix to Cosmology *see* p. 574.]

PSYCHOLOGY

INTRODUCTION *

1. Object of Psychology.—Psychology (ψυχή, λόγος) is that department of philosophy which contemplates the human soul. The soul, understood in its most general sense, denotes that which makes a being live; it is the first principle of life in a living being. If regard be paid only to the etymology of the word, the object of psychology should be co-extensive with all living beings, vegetable and animal as well as man. Custom, however, has restricted it at the present day, so that psychology is limited to the study of man.

By the greater number of modern psychologists the object of this science is still further restricted to *whatever falls within our consciousness*, that is to say, to what are strictly 'psychical' facts to the exclusion of all that are physical or physiological. This narrower definition of psychology owes its origin to Descartes, who considered the human soul as a mind (or spirit) really and actually distinct from the body; what is essential to the soul is *thought*, that is the enjoyment of conscious states, on the other hand what is essential to body is *extension*. Accordingly the 'science of the mind' came to be reduced to the introspective observation of states of consciousness or *psychic* phenomena.

* Books for study or consultation—

Card. Mercier. Large edition of *Psychologie*, 2 vols. (9th ed., 1912). *The Origins of Contemporary Psychology* (translated by Mitchell, Washbourne, 1917).

M. Maher, *Psychology* (Longmans, London, 8th ed., 1915).

B. Windle. *What is Life?* (Sands, London).

G. H. Ward, *Philosophy of Theism* (Free-will) (Kegan Paul, London, 1884).

Jos. Rickaby, *Free-will and Four English Philosophers* (Hobbes, Locke, Hume, and Mill) (London, 1906).

J. Guibert, *In the Beginning* (*Les Origines*) (chaps. on Origin of Life and Transform sm) (trs. G. S. Whitmarsh, Kegan Paul, London).

A. Vonier, *The Human Soul* (mainly theological), (Herder, London).

Non-Scholastic :—

G. F. Stout, *Manual of Psychology* (Tutorial Press, London).

W. McDougall, *Physiological Psychology* (Dent, London).

W. James, *Principles of Psychology* and *Text-book of Psychology* (Macmillan, London).

In this opposition he set up between the physical and the psychical Descartes was influenced by a preconceived idea and unscientifically formed his judgment before weighing the evidence. The direct testimony of consciousness enables us, without drawing upon conclusions that we have subsequently to establish, to declare at once that the man who is living, sentient and rational is *one* being. It is the *man* who feels and thinks, not his soul only, just as it is the *man* and not his body only that works when his hands are in motion and is nourished and quickened by the food that is taken. Hence we must consider the complete human nature as the seat of life, sensation and thought, and, following Aristotle, look upon the 'human soul' as the first entelechy or first principle in virtue of which we are alive, sentient, and capable of rational thought. Accordingly this treatise will have three parts, dealing respectively with *organic life, sentient life,* and *rational life.*

2. Method of Psychology.—The method employed in psychology is the same as that employed in all the other natural sciences, the double method of induction and deduction, which is summed up in the words : *observation, hypothesis, verification,* followed by *deduction* or *synthesis.*

The physicist *observes* that warmed bodies expand ; he forms the *hypothesis* that heat causes this expansion, and that therefore bodies have the natural property of expanding under the action of heat ; he multiplies his observations and, if possible, makes use of experiments in order to *verify* his hypotheses ; if the results are satisfactory, his hypothesis becomes thereby raised to the rank of a scientifically established theory. In this way physics, and in general the other experimental sciences, make use of inductive methods to discover the *immediate causes* of observed phenomena and to ascertain what are the *properties* of corporeal substances and the *laws* of their action.

Psychology pursues exactly the same method. First of all the phenomena of mental life are carefully *observed,* then *conjectures* are made concerning causes and properties and finally these results are *verified.* The *facts* under observation are both external and internal, embracing the various external movements peculiar to living beings, and internal phenomena, such as our sensations, emotions, and other psychical events. Of these facts the mind strives to find a *cause* or an *immediate principle*, which in psychology is called a *power* or *faculty*. From these faculties the mind, by a further induction, ascends to the very *nature* of the soul which is their *first principle*.

When by means of this final induction we have arrived at the nature of the soul, we are in a better position *to understand*, i.e. to comprehend or gather together in one grasp, the isolated conclusions reached by our several successive inductions: thus does synthesis ensue upon analysis. At this stage it now becomes legitimate to make use of deduction in order to verify the previous inductions, just as in an arithmetical calculation the result is finally verified by reversing the process [1]. Last of all, for completeness' sake, we deduce from the *nature* of man what our reason can tell us about his *origin* and *destiny*.

From this outline we see that *observation* plays a fundamental part in psychology. At the same time this observation is not only of what is interior, as Descartes teaches, nor only of what is exterior, following the positivists; but it is of both kinds at once.

[1] This question of scientific and philosophic method is dealt with *ex professo* in *Logic*, chap. IV.

PART I

Organic or Vegetative Life

CHAPTER I

IDEA OF LIFE

3. As *acts* proceed from the subject which puts them forth, we may logically infer from them the *nature* of their subject. The Scholastic axiom '*operari sequitur esse*' expresses the intimate connexion that exists between the activity of a substance and its nature. Before taking up the study of the inner nature of the vital principle, we must therefore first investigate vital activities, the functions which manifest and characterize life.

I. Popular Idea of Life

4. According to popular ideas the ordinary sign of life is *movement without any apparent external cause.* A bird on the wing, a creeping insect, a fish darting up stream, all awaken in us the idea of life. The untrained mind of the savage and the child fondly imagines that even any piece of automatic mechanism is gifted with life; the child, for instance, wants to see the little animal that makes the ticking inside the watch. On the other hand, as soon as an object that was once seen to live has ceased to move, we consider its life to have departed and immediately declare it dead.

II. Scientific Conception of Life

5. For the scientist, living being is a synonym for organic substance: by life he means the sum-total of the functions peculiar to organized beings, namely nutrition, growth, reproduction, etc. An *organized being* consists either of a single cell or of a compound of several cells. As a matter of fact every living being, however complicated its organized structure, is derived from a single primitive *cell,* and all its organs and

tissues are made up of cells. The *cell* is therefore the primordial element of living beings, and must accordingly be the first object to engage our attention.

6. Morphology of the Cell.—A section of living tissue, when viewed under the microscope, is seen to resemble a piece of honey-comb. This is the reason why the name *cell* has been given to each of the elements composing the tissue. The cell itself may best be compared to a microscopic egg. It has in its composition two fundamental parts, the *protoplasm* or *cytoplasm* and the *nucleus* or kernel (Plate I, Fig. 1*A*).

The protoplasm has the appearance of a firm meshwork, very irregular and floating in a more or less fluid ground-substance. This protoplasm is the fundamental living substance and fills the whole cell. At the exterior it is generally thickened into a permeable membrane or cell-wall that serves to regulate the endosmosis and exosmosis [2], that is the entrance into the cell of nutritive liquids and the rejection of matter that has become useless. In the middle of the cell lives the *nucleus* sheathed in a thin membrane (nuclear membrane) and containing its own protoplasmic reticulum (*karioplasm*). It contains moreover another peculiar substance rich in phosphorus and readily receptive of colouring matter, and is called *chromatin* or *nuclein*.

Although it is enclosed in a membrane, the nucleus is not a body separate from the cell; it does not form an independent element, a new individual. Between the protoplasm and the nucleus there exists such a close relationship that the cell is one complete undivided whole, a single unit.

7. Physiology of the Cell.—The cell is not only the ultimate anatomical element of the organized substance, but it is also the fundamental seat of the vital activities, which may be reduced to the following: *nutrition, growth* and *development, multiplication,* and *irritability.*

Nutrition or metabolism is the name given to the double process of assimilation and dissimilation, or as they are otherwise called, anabolism and catabolism.[3] From the substances

[2] The word *osmosis* is used to signify the diffusion of liquids through a porous wall. If the liquid enters into the porous recipient, we speak of there being *endosmosis*; the opposite process, liquid issuing from the porous vessel, is called *exosmosis*.

[3] Cp. J. T. Merz, *European Thought in the Nineteenth Century*. Vol. II, p. 421 (Edinburgh, 1904).—Trs

by which it is surrounded the cell draws certain materials which it combines into organic molecules of ever increasing complexity and eventually incorporates them into its own substance, by *assimilating* them either wholly or in part. Anabolism is accompanied by the alternating process of *catabolism*, that is the destruction of certain parts of the living substance, the breaking up of the complex organic molecules into simpler bodies, some of which are ejected (e.g. carbonic acid) whilst others provide matter for new combinations and thus re-enter in the course of assimilation.

Growth and *development*. As the result of the double process of nutrition, the cell is subjected to continual modifications in form and structure, to alternate growth and decay which biologists call the *evolution* of the living organism.

Multiplication : When it has reached a certain stage in its evolution, the cell has the power of dividing itself and of generating another cell (Plate I, Fig. 3).

Lastly, *irritability* is a generic property of living protoplasm by virtue of which the protoplasm reacts with intensity to the slightest excitation. This reaction often consists in a displacement or a contraction: it then takes the special name of *motility* ; at other times it manifests itself by a secretion or by a certain definite vital activity according to the nature of the element irritated.

The chief function of cellular life is *nutrition* ; growth and multiplication are the consequences of it, whilst irritability is its indication or expression.

8. The Human Organism and its Functions.—The human organism, like any other organism, is characterized by the harmonious *co-ordination* of its anatomical elements together with the subordination of their functions to a single end, which is the well-being and preservation of the individual and of the species.

In an organism so complicated as that of man, the structure of the cells deviates considerably from the type described above. Owing to the economic law of nature known as the *division of labour*, the primitive cells during their multiplication become differentiated so as to constitute different organs and systems [4].

[4] Any part of the living body that is composed of cells of the same nature is called a *tissue*, e.g. muscular tissue, cartilaginous tissue, adipose tissue,

The more complicated the organs of a living being, the more complex are its vital functions. Every tissue has to be fed; the food-stuffs to be assimilated by our tissues are not provided by nature already prepared; a number of nutritive substances are solid, and consequently have first to be rendered liquid before they can be absorbed; it is the work of *digestion* to dissolve them by means of ferments secreted for the purpose by the glands of the digestive system (saliva, gastric juice, bile, etc.). Once made soluble these substances may pass by osmosis through the intestine and in this way their *absorption* takes place (Plate IV, Fig. 3). The food material that has been received has next to be distributed to the various parts of the organism; this is effected by the double *circulation* of lymph and blood (Plate IV, Fig. 4). For the blood to be of avail, however, its oxidation is first required, and for this purpose the organism provides *respiration.*

In a word all these functions—digestion, absorption, circulation and respiration—are subsidiary to the *assimilation* of food on the part of the cells forming the tissues. On the other hand *dissimilation* takes place by the various *secretions,* some of which (those of the saliva glands, stomach, pancreas, etc.) aid the work of digestion, and others (from the kidneys, liver, and sweat glands) serve to get rid of the waste-matters that are superfluous or harmful to the economy of the organism (Plate IV, Fig. 2).

In the higher organisms no less than in unicellular beings, functions that appear the most diversified may be reduced to nutrition, which is the primordial function of vegetative life. Accordingly, to this subject of nutrition our attention must first be devoted if we intend to make a philosophic investigation of the distinctive functions of the living being. Previously, however, it would be well to notice what are the conditions under which these functions can be carried out and what are the laws to which they are subject.

9. Conditions of Vital Activity.—A superficial observation would lead us to consider the activity of living beings as entirely

etc. Many tissues combine to form an *organ,* i.e. a part of the body having a particular function, such as the stomach, the tongue, etc. A *system* or *apparatus* is a combination of organs adapted for the performance of some special functions; thus the organs of the mouth, œsophagus, stomach, and intestines together form the *digestive system.*

automatic and independent of external agents; to regard the living being as living by its own inherent power and as creating, so to speak, its own activity. But a closer insight dispels any such illusion: vital activity, just like every natural activity of inorganic beings, is subject to fixed conditions. If some of these are so necessary that in their absence it is *absolutely impossible* to live and life, should it be present, ceases, others are only necessary for the normal functioning of life; if they are absent, life is difficult or becomes sluggish and *latent*—as it is in seeds, microbes, or in the dried-up spores of certain plants. As long as they remain in this state such beings are only potentially alive, they are but machines ready for action. For them to become actually alive certain material conditions are needed, such as damp, certain degrees of heat, etc.

Furthermore, vital activity seems subject, exactly as in the case of inorganic nature, to the great laws of the *conservation of matter* and the *conservation of energy*. 'Nothing is ever lost, nothing is ever created'. Man may make use of matter, but he cannot create or annihilate a single particle of it. He may make use of energy in one form to reproduce it in another, but the new form is always exactly proportionate to the old, so that he no more creates or annihilates it than he creates or annihilates matter. Now, the chemical transformations that occur in living bodies are of the very same nature as those which take place in the laboratory; and the physical and mechanical properties manifested by living bodies are the same as those displayed by inorganic bodies. Hence there is no reason for thinking that living bodies do not come under the above general law of matter. Moreover the application of this double law has been verified at least approximately by experiment.

III. Philosophic Definition of Life

10. Vital Movement is Continuous and Immanent.—By the light of facts disclosed to us by scientific observation we have to find what is the peculiar character of vital activity. How is it differentiated from the activity of lifeless matter? We discover that it has two distinguishing features, viz. that it is, by its nature, *continuous* and *immanent*.

1. Vital activity is *continuous*.—Inanimate nature tends to stability: a body left to itself tends to a state of equilibrium ·

of the many possible combinations when chemical bodies are united, invariably that one results which is the most stable. A living being, on the other hand, *tends to keep in continual motion*: nutrition in particular is an incessant movement of alternate assimilation and dissimilation. The albuminoid molecules that compose protoplasm, being extremely complex and highly unstable, are incessantly becoming dissociated or decomposed and as quickly re-combined. This movement, it is true, may become so slight as to be almost imperceptible in the state of latent life, but it never ceases altogether; once it stops, death ensues, or rather has already taken place. This continuousness of vital movement is not however the chief feature of life: its essential characteristic is immanence.

2. Vital activity is *immanent.*—The activity of material bodies is generally *transitive*, that is, it modifies a patient distinct from the agent, it has an object or term other than the subject acting. Vital activity, on the contrary, is not transitive but *immanent.* The patient here is, sooner or later, the agent itself; the organized subject is the object affected by vital activity, it is nourished and developed and the activity, having its effect remaining in it, is immanent (manere in) [5].

We do not mean to say, however, that all physical and chemical phenomena displayed by a living being are immanent; it is obvious that a great many of these phenomena are not so; for instance, all the changes in food-matter, right up to and including the building up of the organic molecule, are transitive; but all these are only so many preparatory stages leading up to assimilation properly so called, and it is this intussusception of the organic molecule into the substantial unit of the cell that really constitutes immanent movement in the strict sense. As assimilation is the essential end or purpose of the nutritive process it remains true to say generally that nutrition is an *immanent movement.*

Likewise the growth and evolution of the living being are unmistakably seen to possess the character of *immanence.*

11. Definition of Living Being.—These two characteristic

[5] 'Duplex est actio. Una quae transit in exteriorem materiam; ut calefacere et secare. Alia quae manet in agente: ut intelligere, sentire et velle. Quarum haec est differentia: quia prima actio non est perfectio agentis quod movet, sed ipsius moti; secunda autem actio est perfectio agentis.' *Sum. Theol.*, I, q. 18, a. 3, ad 1.

notes of life, *continuous and immanent movement*, furnish the materials for a strict definition of living substance. The first element, continuous movement, will represent the proximate *genus* in the definition; the second, immanence, is the *specific difference*.

St. Thomas describes life as the distinctive property of beings which move themselves: a living being is one which possesses by its nature the power of self-movement [6].

Movement, *motus*, in the language of the Schoolmen does not signify merely local movement or change of place, but any action involving change. Hence when the living being is said to move itself, *movet seipsum*, the meaning is that it so acts as to be both the principle of the action and the subject receptive of the change that is at once the completion and the purpose of the action; in other words, the action of the living being is immanent. This is really the idea the ordinary man endeavours to express when he considers any manifestation of movement without an apparent external cause to be a sign of life. This definition is too the conclusion from our scientific analysis of the functions of organized being.

According to the definition of St. Thomas, self-movement is natural to a living being, '*cui convenit secundum suam naturam* movere seipsam': indeed a living being, as we have seen, possesses a natural tendency to move itself, though for the effective realization of this self-movement the presence of certain conditions is required.

In fine, by the words '*secundum aliquam speciem motus* seipsam movens', Aquinas alludes to the particular evolution of life, to the special character peculiar to each different type of living being.

[6] 'Illa proprie sunt viventia quae seipsa secundum aliquam speciem motus movent'. And again: '*Ens vivens est substantia cui convenit secundum suam naturam movere seipsam*'. *Sum. Theol.*, I, q. 18, a. 2.

CHAPTER II

NATURE OF LIVING BEING

12. Statement of the Question.—For the marvellous structure and the harmoniously co-ordinated functions of the living organism a sufficient reason is clearly demanded: there must be a cause alike for this order and for its maintenance. Three hypotheses have been, and continue to be, put forward to solve this problem.

The first, which we may designate by the name of *Exaggerated Vitalism* or Vitalism of the School of Montpellier, posits in the living being vital forces distinct from the chemico-physical forces of inanimate nature.

The second, *Organicism*, is at bottom only a particular application of the mechanical conception of the universe. According to this theory the whole of nature in general, and beings endowed with life in particular, are only aggregations of atoms plus efficient causes which are always reducible to mechanical forces.

Midway between these two opposite systems, comes the theory of Aristotle adopted by Aquinas, viz., *Moderate Vitalism* or Vitalistic Naturalism. A living being, like every other substantial being, is not a mere accidental aggregation of atoms and forces, but is a *nature* tending towards a definite end, for the realization of which it directs, as so many means, the inherent powers with which it is endowed. This nature which is the foundation and first principle of the being's tendencies and activities finds its explanation in what we call the *substantial form*, which, in the case of a living being, is the *soul* or *vital principle*. The statement of the extreme vitalists, that this principle is immaterial and simple, the source of the forces not to be found in the mineral kingdom, stands as a gratuitous assertion.

13. Proof of Scholastic Vitalism.—1. *The first principle of life is a subject composed of matter.*—The nature of a being is revealed by its acts, '*operari sequitur esse*'. In order to be able to predicate an immaterial vital force of a being belonging to the vegetable kingdom, we must first have observed, during some part of its life-history, at least one phenomenon that positively cannot be reduced to the general laws of matter. Now it does not appear that there is a single phenomenon of this kind: the living being is superior to the non-living not on account of the particular nature of the forces it displays, but simply and solely in virtue of that constant harmonious employment of all its forces towards the realization of the intrinsic end of the living being, its own well-being and the preservation of the species.

2. *The first principle of life is a substance possessing a natural tendency.*—Even the most elementary organization, such as that of the unicellular being, presents an amazingly complex yet withal harmonious combination of elements and forces that continually combine together for the formation and preservation of what is termed the *organism.* The existence and especially the stability of this combination must have its sufficient reason. Now this sufficient reason is not found in the *actual organization*: this is the very fact requiring explanation. This immense number of elements and forces now mutually related are by their nature independent of one another; there is needed therefore something more than their mere union to account for the permanent and harmonious character of their combination. Nor is this sufficient reason to be found in external conditions or *environment*: for the very same types can live in entirely different environments, and types of entirely different species in one and the same exterior environment. Further, the incessant struggle that has to be made by the organism against a host of different external disintegrating forces forbids us to assign the *immediate intervention of God* as the reason of the persistence of this orderly combination. For if God's intervention were sought as an explanation, it would be necessary to admit that such immediate and direct intervention takes place without intermission and this would deny the action of secondary causes. There is left then only one plausible explanation of the harmonious and stable combination of elements and forces in the organism: viz., the theory that there exists *within* the organism itself some *principle* making them necessarily tend towards an end that is *intrinsic* to the organism, namely its well-

being; a principle that makes all the forces of the organism converge towards the realization of this end and makes a ceaseless opposition against everything that may hinder it.

Hence we may conclude that the organism is not a simple collection of atoms and forces, but a *substance* endowed with a *natural tendency* to realize and maintain the conditions of its organization; it is a *single substance, one nature*, composed of matter and of a specific substantial principle which we call the *soul* or principle of life.

14. Unity of the Living Substance.—As every organism is composed of cells and every cell performs vital functions, there is the inclination to look upon every cell as a separate organism and to say, as some have actually said, that the larger organism is a mere collection or 'colony' of independent cells. Such a conception, however, is radically false: the living being has always two distinctive features that clearly evince its *substantial unity*, namely, the *co-ordination of its organs* and the *subordination of their functions*.

Every organism is a *continuous whole*. Whether surveyed with the naked eye or scrutinized through the microscope, the elements of which it is made never appear disconnected nor do they suggest that they have been brought together by chance; on the contrary, they are united according to an orderly and regular arrangement, are mutually dependent on one another, and by their different structures help to constitute a single harmonious *whole* of which severally they form so many *parts*.

The unity of *subordination* is not less remarkable. We have already noticed above (8) the close interdependence of all the various functions in the more complex organisms. It is true the various tissues are to some extent independent; but whilst each performs its special function, its activity is always regulated by and subordinated to the needs of the organism. The welfare of the whole organism is always the rule of action for each organ as well as for each single tissue. This unity, or subordination, in structure and function clearly demonstrates a more profound unity, the *unity of nature, substantial unity*.

15. Divisibility of Living Beings.—An objection is sometimes raised against the substantial unity of the living being on the score that it can be divided up into more than one such being. Plants may be reproduced by slips; a sufficient portion detached from a hydra becomes another complete animal; earth-worms can be cut up into sections each of which will continue to live.

The explanation of these facts is to be found in Aristotle's axiom: 'The vegetative soul is *one actually* but *potentially many*'. Unity is not simplicity; what in point of fact is *undivided* is not necessarily *indivisible*. The existence of simple or immaterial forces is in no way disclosed in the development of organic life. There is nothing therefore to prevent the living substance from being divisible, provided every separate portion has whatever is necessary to continue the life lived in the whole. In the lower organisms this condition is easily realized. But in the case of the higher animals such division is impossible owing to the separate functions devolving upon specialized organs which occupy distinct places in the organism.

CHAPTER III

ORIGIN OF ORGANIC LIFE

16. The Immediate Origin of Living Organisms.—Living organisms have the power of reproducing themselves, i.e. of giving birth to a new organism similar to the parent producing it.

1. The most elementary method of propagation is by *fission* or *simple division*. This method is to be found only in the lowest stages of life, among unicellular beings. The entire cell grows to a certain size and then at a given moment in its development divides into two exactly similar twin-cells.

2. Higher in the scale of life we find reproduction by *budding*. According to this second method reproduction is localized in a certain part of the organism; at a definite place some of the cells are multiplied so as to form a *bud*, which sometimes remains united to the parent and lives with it to form a colony, sometimes breaks off and becomes a separate individual. This manner of reproduction is exemplified in a number of polyps.

3. Besides propagation by division and by budding there is also *reproduction in the strict sense of the term*. The parent organism produces germ-cells, which are either *spores* or *gametes*. In reproduction by spores, or sporo-genesis, a germ-cell is made into a new complete individual by means of a process of division and differentiation. In none of the above kinds of reproduction is there required the concurrence of more than one element.

4. The case is otherwise, however, when reproduction takes place by means of *gametes*. Here the fusion of two distinct elements is required. When these two elements are of the same kind, as in the case of certain plants, such as *spyrogyrae*, the method is known as *isogamy*. Here two cells, in appearance the same, are put forth as buds, which sooner or later come into contact and fuse; that is, one of the cells empties

itself into the other through the channel formed at the place of contact and the resultant is a single cell which becomes a new separate alga.

In the cases so far enumerated, where the living being does not require the union of two elements sexually different, male and female, reproduction is *asexual* and, strictly, *agamic*.

5. But, higher still in the series of living beings, where the division of labour is very much greater, reproduction can be effected only by the joint action of the two sexes; it is then *sexual* or *gamic* in the full sense of the word. The female furnishes the *egg* or *ovule*, the male the *spermatozoid* or fertilizing element; both are simple cells formed in special glands, and from their fusion results *conception* or *fecundation* (Plate I, Fig. 2).

17. Heredity.—Fecundation throws a certain amount of light upon the nature of heredity. As the two different elements, supplied respectively by the ovule and the spermatozoid, combine in the formation of the embryonic cell, we can easily understand that the resultant embryo should share the nature and characteristics of both the parent cells. But how precisely the parental traits are represented in the germ-cells and how these manage to transmit the same traits to the embryo which they form, has not yet been exactly determined. Some very ingenious hypotheses have been invented in the endeavour to solve these questions; yet the ultimate explanation of these complex phenomena must be looked for once more in the basic principle of immanent finality, in virtue of which the living being has a natural tendency to the formation, preservation and *reproduction* of its own definite specific type; so that the personal traits of the offspring result from the combined action of the parent-cells.

18. Primary Origin of Living Beings.—It is a well-recognized fact that life has had a beginning on our globe, for there was a time when it was in an incandescent state incompatible with the existence of any living creature. The question arises, Whence did the first organic beings come? One theory, originated by W. Thompson (Lord Kelvin), suggests that germs were received from some other planet—a theory that in spite of its ingenuity does not solve the difficulty by placing it further back. Another theory is that of *spontaneous generation* or, as it is called to-day, *abiogenesis*, which professes that life has sprung from inorganic matter. But in the light of modern research there is not a single scientist to-day who believes that life can be produced by the exclusive action of inorganic agents. The experiments of Redi, Schwann, P. Van Beneden, Pasteur and Tyndall have exploded this ancient fallacy once for all. Wherever new life is manifested it is invariably found connected with previous life: *omne vivum ex vivo*; *omnis cellula a cellula*. Invincible logic forces us, then, to the conclusion that in the first instance life must have owed its origin to a direct intervention of the Author of nature.

PART II

Sensuous or Animal Life

INTRODUCTION

19. Object and Division.—In the preceding section we have studied life in its widest meaning: what has been said applies to all living beings indiscriminately. Indeed there are some beings that cannot be said to get much further than *living*; their function does not rise higher than organic or vegetative life. But there are other beings that are sentient as well as living; of these we predicate not only life but also *animality*. We may begin by distinguishing in our own selves between the functions of vegetative life and those which can be classed under the generic name of sensitive or *sensuous* life. This distinction is based on the three peculiar functions of the animal which are not found in simple organic life, namely *sensation, appetition* and *spontaneous movement*: the animal perceives its object, this perception begets desire, and this desire issues into movements by which the object is secured. However we must notice that sensation and appetition can be directly known only by the subject experiencing them, and this is why we begin by considering these three functions in ourselves first; in animals we have certain evidence of the existence of such phenomena only in the visible spontaneous movements provided by them. Hence, we may say that spontaneous movement is the best general external sign of sensuous life.

To obtain a complete knowledge of sensuous life we must, then, first of all consider its *nature* (Chapter I) and then its *origin* (Chapter II). Chapter I subdivides itself into the investigation of *sensuous acts* (Art. I) and the nature of the *sentient subject* or first principle of these acts (Art. II). Hence of this second part we have the following scheme :—

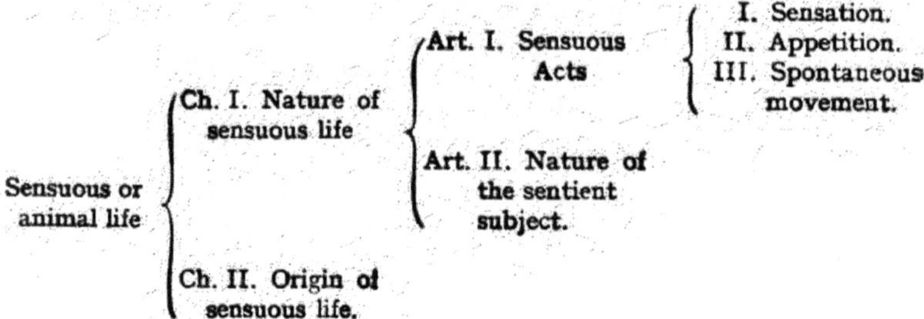

CHAPTER I

NATURE OF SENSUOUS LIFE

ART. I. ACTS OF SENSUOUS LIFE

I. Sensation or Sensuous Cognition

§ 1. *Anatomical and Physiological Aspect of Sensation*

As the functions we have enumerated of animal life depend for their exercise upon special organs—sensation and appetition upon the *nervous system*, and locomotion upon the *muscles* and *bones*—we must commence our investigation of sensation by a glance at the anatomy and physiology of the nervous system.

20. General Sketch.—Of the nervous system there are two different aspects—*ganglia* or *nerve-centres*, which are groups, varying in size, of nervous tissue, and *nerves* or elongated processes that ramify through all parts of the body.

Considered in its entirety, the nervous apparatus of man comprises two systems, that is to say, two groups of centres and of nerves—the *cerebro-spinal* system, to which belong the functions of animal life, and the *sympathetic* system which controls the vegetative life and innervates the viscera, the blood vessels and the glands. However these two systems are not independent of each other : the sympathetic ganglia are bound to the spinal nerves by bundles of nervous fibres known as communicating branches ; so that the whole organism, even in the matter of vegetative life, is under the control of the cerebro-spinal system.

21. Anatomy of the Cerebro-Spinal System.—Of this system are to be noticed three parts : a central, the *cerebro-spinal axis*, a peripheral, the *sense-organs*, and the connective of these two, the *cerebro-spinal nerves*.

The cerebro-spinal axis (Plate II, Fig. 1) is itself popularly divided into two parts, viz., the *brain*, which is a semi-ovular mass filling the cranial box or skull, and the *spinal cord*, which is a cylindrical column running through the vertebral canal from the base of the cranium down as far as the lower border of the first lumbar vertebrae. In the brain are commonly distinguished the *cerebrum* or brain proper, the *cerebellum* and the *medulla oblongata*.

1. The *cerebrum* or large brain (Plate II, Fig. 2) presents the appearance of two symmetrical hemispheres, the surface of which is thrown into folds or *convolutions*. Certain of the clefts or furrows are so pronounced—such as the fissure of Silvius, the fissure of Rolando, the parietal fissure—that each hemisphere is conveniently divided into four lobes: the *frontal* lobe is the portion in front of the fissure of Rolando, the *parietal* on the side on the upper portion, the *temporo-sphenoidal* on the side underneath, and the *occipital* in the rear.

Through the whole of the cerebro-spinal axis are observable two different substances, *grey* matter of the ganglia consisting of nerve-cells, and *white* matter almost entirely composed of nerve-fibres (**23**). In the brain the grey matter is to be found in two places (Plate II, Fig. 3)—a thin envelope covering the whole of the cerebellum, called the *grey cortical envelope*, and clusters of cells lower in the interior called *ganglia of the base*. The centres of the upper cortical surface, on account of the functions attributed to them, are also called *psychico-motor* centres, being regarded as the termini of sensuous impulses received and the region from which spontaneous movements first issue. This grey cortex of the brain is the immediate anatomical substrate of the acts of our sensuous life and, therefore, indirectly of the acts of the intellectual life.

2. The *cerebellum*, or little brain, is situated behind and below the occipital area of the cerebrum. It possesses two large lobes called lateral hemispheres, which are united by a thin vermiform process or median lobe. In front of the cerebellum is the region of the annular protuberance comprising the pons Varolii, the cerebral peduncles and the optic lobes or corpora quadrigemina. In this region are seated the nuclei of the auditory and optic nerves together with the nerves that control the muscles of the eye.

3. Making a continuation with the annular protuberance is the *medulla oblongata*, which is an enlarged prolongation of the spinal cord at its juncture with the brain. It is the centre for the nerves of taste and smell.

22. Anatomy of the Sympathetic System.—The central

portion of the sympathetic system is composed of a chain of ganglia situated at regular intervals on either side of the spinal column along its whole length. They are interconnected by means of nerve-fibres, and at the same time are connected with the cerebro-spinal nervous system by communicating branches. They send out nerve-fibres to the muscular coating of the blood-vessels, of the viscera and of the glands. Other smaller ganglia are to be found in some of the various tissues themselves, as for instance in the muscular walls of the heart; but all these clusters of nerve-cells are in connexion with the spinal-cord and thus so in dependence upon the cerebro-spinal axis that in a real and true sense they form but *one single* nervous system.

23. Histology of the Nervous System.—The essential constituents of nerve matter are *nerve-cells* and *nerve-fibres.* They are not however independent of each other, for the central thread or transmitting part of every nerve-fibre is merely a prolongation of a nerve-cell. Nerve-cells (Plate II, Fig. 4) present in structure a finely reticulated protoplasmic ground-substance and a nucleus with a nuclear membrane, but they do not seem to possess a cell-membrane. They are especially characterized by the numerous processes that pass out from them, some of which deploy into many ramifications, whilst others become what is called the axis-cylinder of nerve-fibres and run to very considerable length. The nerve-cell with all its various processes constitutes an organic unit commonly called a neuron.

Nerve-cells, moreover, are of two kinds, *motor* and *sensory,* or, as they are otherwise called from their different functions, *efferent* and *afferent*; but this distinction, in the present state of science, does not apply to the structure of the cells themselves: it is only a deduction made from the difference of their functions and their anatomical connexions with other organs.

Nerve-fibres, as we have said, are essentially processes from nerve-cells (Plate II, Fig. 4*B*); but they are seldom left simply as a connecting thread along which the nervous impulse travels. Sometimes, as in the nerves of the sympathetic system, the fibre is encased within a tubular membrane called the *membrane of Schwann*; sometimes, as in the fibres of the white matter of the cerebro-spinal axis, it is covered by a sheath of white substance called *myelin*; or, as is generally the case of the peripheral nerves of the cerebro-spinal system, the axis-cylinder has both the sheath of myelin and the membrane of Schwann.

As in the brain (**21**), there is grey matter and white matter also in the spinal cord (Plate II, Fig. 5); the grey matter crosses the centre and also forms four branches or *horns* (cornua), so that a transverse section closely resembles the figure of a capital H. The anterior horns, containing peripheral motor cells, are the centre of the motor nerves, whilst the cells of the peripheral sensory fibres are located in the spinal ganglia close to the posterior horns. White matter surrounds all the grey; it is composed of bundles of nerve-fibres, and is itself surrounded by a covering of myelin. Of these bundles of fibres, some are *motor* or *efferent fibres* for transmitting nervous impulses from the cortex of the brain to the motor centres of the cord, others are *sensory or afferent fibres* conducting impressions received by peripheral nerves to higher psychical centres [7].

24. The Nerves.—From the grey matter of the spinal cord, from the medulla oblongata, the annular protuberance, the cerebral peduncles and the basal ganglia (but not from the grey matter of the cortex) the peripheral nerve-fibres proceed and by their union make up the nerves. If their function is regarded, nerves are either *motor*, which control the contractions of the muscles, or *sensory*—or, to be more accurate, it is the fibres making up the nerves that are *motor* or *sensory*, for most of the nerves are mixed, that is to say, are composed of both kinds of fibres. Motor fibres terminate in the muscles by branching out into a great number of very fine ramifications or dendrites. The sensory fibres have special end-organs peculiar to each of the different senses.

25. The Sense-Organs.—The afferent fibres, together with the central cells to which these lead at the one end and their peripheral terminals at the other, make up the sense-organs

[7] It is worthy of remark that all these fibres, no matter where their path is traced, terminate on the opposite side of the body from where they began; thus any excitations sustained on the left side become affections of the grey cortical matter of the right hemisphere of the brain when they are transmitted into terms of consciousness, and conversely the cortical cells of the left side control the voluntary movements of the muscles of the right side of the body.

properly so called. Each of the senses has its different terminal filaments, adapted to their own normal excitants; they constitute, so to speak, pieces of mechanism especially designed to multiply or magnify external excitations. For the different senses of touch, taste, smell, hearing and sight, they are respectively called the *corpuscles* of touch, the *papillae* of the tongue, the *olfactory cells*, the *organs of Corti*, and the *rods* and *cones* of the retina (Plate III).

Besides these five external senses, there are sensory fibres terminating in each of the muscles and having the contraction of these muscles as their peculiar stimulus. This explains why we are able to feel the contractions of our muscles and consequently the movements of our organs. In addition then to the traditional five external senses *the muscular sense* must be enumerated as a sixth.

By their terminal sensory apparatus the sense-organs receive peripheral excitations which they transmit along the afferent fibres to the central cells and so inform us of what is taking place around us. Owing to the fibres of the sub-centres connecting together all the cells of the central system, owing also to the efferent or motor fibres issuing from the same centres, an impression received at any peripheral locality can be transmitted through the central system to wherever may be its appropriate internal destination and may provoke or suggest any kind of movement. Indeed the senses may well be compared to so many people connected by telephonic wires to an exchange through which they are brought into communication with all the subscribers of the same circuit and are thus enabled to transmit any directions or information they may wish.

26. Physiology of the Nervous System.—The exact functions of the various *nervous centres* have not yet been fully ascertained. We only know that the regular exercise of their activity depends on the composition of the blood by which they are nourished. It is an interesting fact that the action of certain poisons, such as morphia, alcohol, etc., suspends or modifies the functioning of certain cells without interfering with that of others: thus a poison that suspends the action of the cortical centres of the brain does not, for example, affect that of the centres governing respiration. From this it would seem that *all nerve-cells are not of the same nature*—a conclusion that is corroborated by the fact that the centres reacting to light do not react to sound, and vice versa.

Fibres and *nerves* are the organs affording paths for the conduction of impulses. The different fibres that combine to form a nerve do not share direct communication with each other, but each fibre is an insulated conductor. The only essential condition required for being a conductor is that the axis-cylinder be continuous, that is to say, that it is uninterrupted by any constriction of the fibre (Plate II, Fig. 4 *B*).

Normally the conduction of a sensory fibre is centripetal; along an afferent nerve the impression travels inward towards the nerve centre. But it is commonly admitted that an excitation *artificially* provoked at any part of a nerve is transmissible in both directions. Hence nerves are said to be of *indifferent conductivity* (Plate II, Fig. 6).

The speed of the nervous current has been measured, and is gauged to be about 30 metres a second in efferent nerves and 60 metres in afferent nerves. From this it appears the current does not resemble the electric current nor luminous nor sound vibrations. Nevertheless there is in the nerve during transmission an unmistakable display of chemical, thermic and electric phenomena.

27. Physiology of the Senses.—1. *Vision.*—A luminous excitation is received by the rods and cones of the retina (Plate III, Fig. 5), and from thence it is conducted by the fibres of the optic nerves to the sensory centres of the brain. In front of the retina is a crystalline biconvex lens, capable of diminishing or increasing its convexity, through being adjusted by the muscles of the eye, according as the object presented is nearer or further away. The organ of sight has, then, besides its function of *perception* also that of *adapting* itself to luminous stimuli as they are received from varying distances.

2. *Hearing.*—The air vibrations set up by sounding bodies eventually impinge on the nerve-fibres of the organ of Corti (Plate III, Fig. 4) and are transmitted by the acoustic nerve to their appropriate centre. These fibres of Corti are stretched over a membrane, known as the basilar membrane, not unlike the strings of a harp; it is supposed that each of them corresponds to one and only one special vibration, as in the case of the strings of a musical instrument.

3 and 4. *Smell* and *Taste.*—The stimuli of these senses

are chemical. Odorous particles are drawn in with the air breathed and act upon the olfactory cells containing the terminals of the olfactory nerve. Similarly sapid substances dissolved in the saliva act upon the terminals of the gustatory nerve. These two senses, closely alike in their nature, are mutually complementary and so allied in their action that it is often extremely difficult to discriminate between the part played by each in the total sensation. (Plate III, Figs. 2 and 3).

5. *Touch.*—Tactile corpuscles (Plate III, Fig. 1) are distributed over the whole surface of the body, but they are very much more numerous in certain places—such as on the lips, the tip of the tongue, the extremities of the fingers—which on this account are extremely sensitive to touch. The sense of touch really comprises several specifically different senses. To it are attributed *tactile* sensations strictly so called (pressure, contact, shock, etc.) and *thermic* sensations (warmth and cold); also there are connected with it *muscular*, or as they are otherwise called *kinesthetic* sensations (**25**) and those of *pain*. These last it would seem are due to an over-stimulation of any of the sensory nerves.

After this brief study of sensations from the standpoint of anatomy and physiology, it is time to consider the same sensations from the point of view they present to our consciousness, that is to say, under their more strictly psychological aspect.

§ 2. *Cognitional Aspect of Sensation or Sensuous Cognition in General*

28. Meaning of Sensation or Sensuous Cognition.—Sensation denotes a manner of being on the part of a sentient subject; it is a change of state importing to a perceptive subject a cognition concerning something. In sensation the sentient subject is both passive and active: first *passive*, in so far as it receives an impression; then *active*, in so far as it reacts to the impression received. The natural result of this activity is to bring the subject into some sort of contact with something other than itself, something that is brought up against it, an *object* (from *ob-jicere*), something that is objective, as distinct from the merely subjective.

If the *passive* side of the sensation predominates it is often called *feeling*, or simply sensation: we speak for instance of experiencing a sensation of cold, a feeling of discomfort, of well-being, etc. If it is the *active* element that is in prominence, then the sensation goes by the name of *cognition* or *perception*. Sensuous cognitions in general, especially when considered in their subordinate relation to the superior faculty of reason, are referred to as *sense-* or *sensuous experience*.

29. Cognition in General.—In sensation we are confronted with an entirely new phenomenon, something which we did not meet with in the course of our investigation of organic life, namely *knowledge*. If it be asked, What is knowledge? the only answer that can be given is that it is something primordial in its own order which cannot be defined but only described by the enumeration of its peculiarities. It consists in some sort of *resemblance*, achieved in the knower, of the object known—'Omnis cognitio fit secundum similitudinem cogniti in cognoscente'[8]. The thing known is somehow possessed by us *in* ourselves. It is of course impossible that the person knowing should strictly speaking appropriate the thing in its physical reality. He can, then, get possession of it only by the way of imitation, by reproducing it in himself in some manner that is in accordance with his own nature; he begets it afresh, so to speak, under the form of a likeness; and hence the second axiom of the Schoolmen completing the first is:—'Cognitum est in cognoscente, *ad modum cognocentis*'.

But knowledge is more than a mere resemblance; it is an *image*, that is, a resemblance which is an imitation, a reproduction of the thing according to the nature of the knowing subject. The image, however, is not a *material, physical* image, like that of a photograph, but an image of another kind, what is called *psychical, ideal, mental*, or sometimes in Scholastic language *intentional*. But these are only so many words that must speak for themselves; their positive signification cannot be defined; they amount simply to saying that this image is *other* than a physical one, in a word, that it is knowledge.

30. External and Internal Sensibility.—The immediate principles of sensuous cognition are the *external* senses of the subject. A summary account of these external senses by which we are brought into touch with reality around us has already been given (27). Though summary and superficial, that analysis makes it evident that there must also be, in man

[8] St. Thomas, *Cont. Gent.*, II, 77

and in the higher animals, at least one, or perhaps several, *internal senses* [9].

1. *Internal Sense, Common Sense.*—As soon as a sensory impression transmitted along the afferent nerves reaches the higher nerve-centres, it enters into the realm of consciousness: at some particular moment a subject, for example, that is seeing with its external organ becomes aware that it is seeing, or if hearing becomes sensible of the fact that it is hearing. Thus there is reason for postulating the existence of an internal sense of sensations—called also to-day '*sense-consciousness*'.

Again, sensuous cognition is a union and co-ordination of several sensory impressions contained in one total representation which, in the true and fullest sense of the word, is the *perception of an object.* Indeed, to perceive an object is nothing else than to gather together several sensations coming through different senses—the colour of a rose, the smoothness of its petals, its perfume, etc.—and unite them in one common object, this particular rose. Thus there is reason to posit in the higher animal, besides the external senses, also an interior faculty, a *common sense* or *central sense*, a kind of complement to the peripheral organs and needed to *combine* external sensations and to compare them and to *discriminate* between them. According to the mediaeval Scholastics the faculty of perceiving the operations of the external senses which constitutes the *internal sense* is one of the functions of the common sense [10].

2. *Imagination.*—We have the power of representing to ourselves sensible attributes that we have already ceased actually to perceive, and in fact to bring absent objects back into our consciousness. When sense-perception fades away it does not perish altogether, but leaves its traces in the mind, traces that we have the faculty of *preserving*, or *reproducing*, and of *combining*. This faculty the Scholastics have called the *imagination* and

[9] On the use of these terms, see Maher, *op. cit.* p. 93 ff.—TRS.

[10] Cp. ST. THOMAS, *Opusc. de potentiis animae*, c. IV. — 'Ista autem potentia (sensus communis) est animali necessaria propter tria, quae habet facere sensus communis. Primum est quod habet apprehendere omnia sensata communia. . . . Secundus actus sensus communis est apprehendere plura sensibilia propria, quod non potest aliquis sensus proprius: non enim potest animal judicare album esse dulce vel non esse, vel ponere diversitatem inter sensata propria nisi sit aliquis sensus qui cognoscat omnia sensata propria: et hic est sensus communis. Tertius vero actus est sentire actus propriorum sensuum, ut cum sentio me videre. . . .'

they attribute to it the threefold function of *retention, reproduction* and *construction*. The power to retain and reproduce sense-images may also be called ***sensuous memory***, whilst the *imagination* more properly consists in the power of re-forming the residue of past impressions, of building up the elements of previous sensations into novel forms, of associating them in new ways, in a word, the power of construction.

3. *Instinct.*—The lamb flees from the wolf, the fledgeling from the sparrow-hawk, although there is nothing in the colour or external appearance of either the wolf or the hawk to effect an unpleasant sensation in the animals perceiving them. Similarly birds gather bits of straw for building their nests, even though there is in the straw no particular quality to move them to take it. There is reason then to acknowledge in certain animals at least a discriminating power which is not the same as that by which useful and noxious things are perceived as sensible realities; a faculty or sense which *estimates* certain concrete connexions between things, according to St. Thomas, a '*vis aestimativa* percipiens intentiones insensatas'.

4. *Sense-memory.*—This is a faculty which stores not only the images of actual perceptions but also traces of those cognitions which concern utility that have been made by the instinct. It differs from the reproductive imagination in that it comprises besides a certain appreciation of past duration also a *concrete* perception of a succession or interval that has elapsed.

§ 3. *Closer Investigation of the External Senses*

31. Purpose of this Investigation.—Sensations have their own qualities by which they are differentiated from one another. Comparison may reveal a difference in their *quality*, in their *intensity*, or simply in their *localization*, i.e. local relations [11].

We have, then, first of all to consider: (i) the *qualitative* aspect of sensation, or what are the respective objects that

[11] Modern psychologists also observe in the whole complex sensation what they term its *feeling-tone*, that is to say, the additional quality belonging to the sensation of being in some degree pleasing or displeasing, agreeable or disagreeable, or of having no appreciable feeling-tone. This quality will be best treated of when we come to speak of the appetitive faculties (66).

make our sensations qualitatively different; (ii) their *quantitative* aspect, which concerns their intensity and duration; (iii) their *objective exteriority* or *localization*; (iv) next a word must be said about the cerebral centres of sensations or their *cerebral localizations*; and finally (v) by gathering the results of these considerations we shall be in a position to make an induction concerning the *real nature* of sensation.

QUALITY OF SENSATIONS

The *object* of a sensation is what is present to the sense in question. It is not the thing as it is in itself, but as presented to the sense-faculty by means of some change produced within it. The special quality which each sense perceives in the object, to the exclusion of all the others, is the *proper object* of that sense. If we can ascertain the proper object of each sense we shall thereby get to know the nature of the sensitive faculties, seeing that faculties are revealed by their actions and actions are differentiated by their objects.

32. Proper Object of Sight.—The proper object of our visual sensations (27) is *light*. According to the present scientific conception light partakes of the nature of vibrations in a very rarefied fluid called ether. The peripheral endings of the optic nerve, which consist in the rods and cones of the retina, are so delicately arranged as to be readily excited by ether vibrations. What we are pleased to call a ray of light is an imaginary line along which the vibrations are being transmitted. The vibrations themselves are transversal, that is to say, are perpendicular to the direction of the ray of light. According to the duration of the vibrations, or which is the same thing, according to the number of vibrations a second, or again according to the length of the wave, there corresponds a particular sensation and this is *colour*.

The admixture of all the radiations of the sun is white or uncoloured light; which by being made to pass through a prism may be split up into a fixed number of simple vibrations, thus revealing the simple colours of which it is composed and giving us what is called the *solar spectrum*. The number of colours in the spectrum is countless; custom however assigns seven principal ones—red (of rays the least refrangible), orange, yellow, green, blue, indigo, violet (of rays the most refrangible)

Each colour is distinguished by its own hue or tint. Moreover there are discernible in our sensations differences of brightness or luminous *intensity*, as well as differences of *saturation*, according as the particular hue is more or less pronounced or weakened by the admixture of uncoloured light.

The various objects in the world have different colours because they do not equally reflect all the wave-lengths composing the solar light, but absorb one or another, sending back the rest to the eye of the observer.

The physical action of the ether vibrations most probably gives birth to a chemical reaction in the rods and cones of the retina, and this stimulation of the retina in its turn acts as an excitant of the optic nerve and of the cerebral nerve-cells to which the optic nerve conducts.

33. Proper Object of Hearing.—The proper object of auditory sensations is *sound*. Sound is produced by the vibration of elastic corpuscles. The vibrations of sonorous substances penetrate, through the medium of the air, into the auditory canal and set in motion the membrane of the tympanum or drum. The vibrations thus received by the membrane of the tympanum mechanically stimulate the sensory endings of the acoustic nerve and so affect the corresponding centre in the cortex of the brain and give birth to the sensation of sound.

In sounds are to be distinguished the qualities of *intensity*, *pitch* and *timbre*; and of many sounds heard together is the further quality of either *harmony* or *discord*.

What we have spoken of as a vibration, or oscillation, is the movement to and fro of the molecules of a body. The *amplitude* of a vibration is the extent of the movement measured between the vibrating molecule and its position of equilibrium. It is the amplitude of the vibrations that determines the *intensity* or loudness of a sound: the greater it is, or the more the molecules deviate from their position of equilibrium, the more intense is the sound.

The *duration* of a vibration is the time it takes for the molecules to make a complete movement backward and forward. The shorter the duration, the more oscillations will the vibrating molecule be able to accomplish in a definite time: this idea of duration is often conveyed in terms of so many vibrations a second. It is the duration of the vibrations which regulates the *pitch* or altitude of a sound in the musical scale.

The greater number of sound-vibrations actually produced are composite, that is to say, are the fusions of many simple vibrations, and the resulting sensations are the mixture of tones which the ear is able to analyse. As it is seldom that all the simple vibrations composing a composite one are of the same intensity, one generally dominates and gives the *fundamental* sound, whilst the others which produce *partial* sounds are very much weaker. In musical instruments and in the human voice the numbers of vibrations of the partial sounds bear a constant ratio to the number of the vibrations of the fundamental sound. These ratios may be represented by the series of whole numbers 1, 2, 3, 4, etc. . . . ; if, then, a fundamental sound makes one vibration, the first partial sound or overtone makes two, the second three, and so on. These partial sounds are termed *harmonics*. Upon the nature, number, and intensity of the harmonics that supervene upon the fundamental sound depends the *timbre* of a sound, by which for example we distinguish two sounds of the same pitch and intensity but coming from two different instruments.

The peculiar quality of being agreeable or disagreeable, of *harmony* or *discord*, depends on the relation the numbers of the vibrations of notes simultaneously emitted bear to one another. If the relation of the numbers of vibrations is simple, the notes are harmonious ; on the other hand, discord is accentuated the more complex that relation becomes. The physiological explanation of these pleasant or unpleasant sensations lies in the fact that the occurrence of dissonant notes produces interruptions in the sound and in consequence the excitation of the acoustic apparatus is intermittent, whereas in the case of consonant notes the sound, and therefore the excitation, is continuous.

34. Proper Object of Smell.—The normal stimulus of the nerve organs of smell consists in certain extremely fine particles *distributed in the air*, which are termed *odorous substances*. The excitation is of a chemical nature. Our olfactory sensations have so few qualities by which we can describe them that they do not easily admit of classification. We usually think it a sufficient indication if we refer odours to the different substances from which they emanate.

35. Proper Object of Taste.—The proper object of the sense of taste consists in *savours* or *flavours.* Certain *chemical* substances in a state of *solution* are the adequate stimulus, and the excitation itself most likely is also of a chemical nature.

Four qualitative differences are commonly noticed in regard to gustatory sensations, namely, of sweet, bitter, salt and sour. Most of the sensations that go by the name of *taste* are in reality complex, in which smell, touch, and even sight, each play a considerable part.

36. Proper Object of Touch.—It has already been observed (**27**) that the sense of touch embraces several different senses. (1) If the back of the hand is placed flat on a table and a light piece of paper allowed to rest on the upturned fingers, the sole sensation that will result will be that of *contact.* (2) If however for the piece of paper be substituted a book of two or three pounds weight, the sensation of contact will be accompanied by that of *pressure* or even entirely replaced by it. (3) If, again, the hand is raised, a new sensation will be experienced, namely, of resistance to the pressure of the weight, of the necessary effort put forth to support or to move the hand; it will be produced at the same time as the muscles are contracted to lift the hand and the degree of muscular contraction felt by us will help us to measure the sensation of effort or movement: and hence the sense by which the sensation is felt is called the *muscular sense.* (4) When a body in contact with the skin imparts heat to it, we have the sensation of warmth, and when it is moved away, the opposite sensation of cold. Such *sensations of temperature* inform us at first hand of the variations of the temperature of the skin and indirectly of the temperature outside it. (5) Finally sensations of *pain* occur when a sensory nerve is over-stimulated. And here the term sensory nerves comprises not only the nerves of the skin but also all the afferent nerves of the visceral organs.

37. Common Sensibles.—Besides the special sensible qualities which constitute the *proper object* of each of the external senses and which we have just described, there are also '*common sensibles*' or qualities that affect many or all of the senses at once. Of these Aristotle enumerates five, namely, 'movement, repose, measure, form or shape, and size'. We shall have occasion to return to these later (**46**). As yet we have to discover on what it is that the *qualitative character* of our sensations depends; how does it come about that we may predicate *specific* differences between the objects of these sensations.

38. **The Cognitional Determinant.**—The adequate or total cause of sensation is not found simply in the senses themselves. The senses are so many powers or faculties that by themselves are inactive: they have an aptitude to represent objects, but an aptitude that remains in a potential state so long as it lacks an excitant other than itself to stimulate it; for its transition from power to act the sense requires to receive an impression from without to arouse its activity and to determine it in some particular way. Thus, whilst the eye is capable of seeing, it does not actually see until a ray of light has depicted an image upon the retina. A sensory impression is, then, the necessary complement of the sensitive power and the natural determining cause of the act of perception. To this impression the Scholastics gave the name *species intentionalis*, or *species sensibilis* by way of emphasizing the part it plays in determining the activity of the sensitive faculty through bringing it into connexion with the object perceived. Instead of employing the Latin expression for so important a term we propose to use the free translation *cognitional determinant.*

The necessity of this determinant as a factor of perception follows from the very nature of cognition. If knowledge is anything, it is an *immanent union* of the subject knowing with the object known. And for an immanent union to be possible, for this union to be accomplished in and by the one knowing, the object must be somehow united to the subject and, so to speak, incorporated in it. Now it is evident that the material object, the thing in its physical reality, does not enter into the subject or become immanently united to it; it must therefore be somehow replaced by a replica or resemblance or *image*: 'omnis cognitio fit *secundum similitudinem* cogniti in cognoscente'. Hence an act of perception requires a sensory impression coming from the object and conveying a representation of it. This impression produced in the knowing subject by the object is an image (*species*) or sensible form *determining cognition.*

But it may be objected that if what we say is true, then it

is not an extra-mental something that we perceive but only the modification received, the image that replaces it and represents it to us.—The objection, however, has been anticipated by the Scholastics: the intentional species or mental modification, the disposition determining the mind to perception, is not the direct object of perception, but is the *mean* through which the sense-faculty is enabled to perceive the object itself; a mean that does not require to be also an intermediary object that has itself first to be perceived before the mind can pass on to the thing without; but such that is a purely *subjective* mean, a factor intrinsic to the percipient subject, an accidental formal cause of the act of perception. It is a subjective disposition through which extra-mental reality is reached and cognized; it is not *id quod* percipitur, but *id quo* percipitur objectum. To express this St. Thomas makes use of the example of a mirror exactly adjusted and adequately adapted to the dimensions of an object that is portrayed therein: it is not the glass that is seen in the first instance and then the object represented in it; but the object presented by means of the glass is what is directly seen first; the glass simply brings it before you, its function is limited to enabling you to see it.

39. Qualitative Character of Sensation.—From what we have just said it follows that the qualitative character of our sensations must be immediately referred to the subjective modification which we have called the cognitional determinant. To the Scholastics of the Middle Ages this did not present much difficulty, as they regarded the sense-impression as a real image, an actual resemblance of the object perceived. To-day, however, on account of our greater knowledge of the nature of sense-stimuli, it is asked how there can possibly be a resemblance either between the sensation and its immediate excitant or between this excitant and the object from which it proceeds. What for instance is there in common between vibrations in ether and the colours we are aware of and attribute to things? A complete answer to this question is impossible in the present state of physics and physiology. Yet we may see a general explanation of the qualitative difference of our sensations in the double fact of the *specific character of the sense-organs* on the one hand and the *different natures of their stimuli* on the other.

At present, until we have been able to ascertain the exact nature of the *cerebral centres* and of the *organs of conduction*, we cannot affirm with certainty whether these are specifically different or not. The *peripheral terminals* of the sense-organs, however, clearly form *specialized apparatus*. And as it would seem that the special manner of reaction of the sense-organ should vary with the nature of this organ, there is certainly here one basis—an anatomical one—for the qualitative differences of sensations.

The second reason, the varying nature of the stimulus, will be apparent when we remember that the natural excitant of tactual sensations would seem to be exclusively *mechanical*, that of auditory sensations *physical*, of taste and smell *chemical*, the former evoked by soluble substances, the latter by gaseous ones; and the stimulus of vision in all probability is both *physical and chemical*, and by analogy we are led to believe that the same is to be said for sensations of temperature. Such very different objective causes must be expected naturally to evoke equally different effects in the sensory organs. The full explanation must be found in an understanding of the stimulus and the nature of the subject receiving it. Our sense-organs are so formed that each is impressionable only by a certain excitant and its response to it is an *appropriate reaction* that makes the percipient subject experience a definite sensation.

QUANTITY OF SENSATIONS

The quantity of sensations can be looked at from two points of view: *intensity* and *duration*. Sensations, whatever their quality, all possess a certain amount of intensity; by comparing one sensation with another of the same kind it is found to be more or less strong or intense. The point of interest here is whether this intensity can be measured, and if so, how?

Owing to the nature of the case the intensity cannot be measured in itself, for there is no common standard possible by which it can be gauged. The most that can be done is to discover the relation that exists between the intensity of a sensation and its external cause or its stimulus; or else the relation that exists between the intensity of a sensation and its dynamic effects.

40. Intensity of Sensation measured by its Antecedents.

Weber's Law.—It is quite clear that there is a relation between the intensity of a sensation and the quantity of the stimulus evoking it—for two candles give more light than one and a kilogramme weighs heavier in the hand than a pound. Not less certain, however, is it that an increase of the same quantity on the part of the stimulus does not always cause an equal increase in the intensity of the sensation: the brilliancy of a well illuminated room is not perceptibly affected by the addition of a single lighted candle; one gramme added to another single gramme in the hand makes quite an appreciable difference, but there is not the same difference when it is added to a kilogramme. The question is to determine this relation, and it is one that would seem to be without solution seeing that the intensity of sensations, that is one of the terms, does not admit of being measured: we may feel that one sensation is stronger than another, but can we measure how much or how many times stronger it is than the other? To solve the difficulty Weber tried to ascertain in each case what is the minimum increment in the same stimulus that must be added in order to make the subject perceive a difference in his sensations. If I have a weight in my hand, for instance a gramme, he asks, What is the smallest quantity that must be added to it in order to make me conscious that there is a difference of weight? It is found that this quantity is not an absolute but a *relative* one: for example, a third of a gramme will evoke a new distinguishable sensation if it is added to a gramme, but it will have to be a very considerably larger quantity if the initial weight happens to be a kilogramme. Roughly, Weber discovered that the stimulus evoking the initial sensation of pressure must be augmented by a third for a perceptible difference to be noted. In the other sensations—of hearing, sight, etc.—there seems also to be required a *relative increment* in the physical stimulus. Hence the generalization known as Weber's Law, that 'The increase in stimulus that gives rise to an appreciable modification in sensation bears a constant ratio to the quantity of the stimulus to which it is added.'

41. Intensity of Sensation measured by its Effects.—One attempt to measure sensation has been to reckon it by the amount of physical stimulus required to cause it; another method is to start in the opposite direction and calculate it in terms of its own effects.

Experiments made with the *dynamometer* [12] show that sensory excitations are attended by a considerable dynamic action in the organism. To speak only of the sense of sight we may say that colour-sensations, in so far as they have the power to generate nervous activity, arrange themselves in the same order as the spectral colours. In the experiments conducted by M. Féré [13] the dynamometric state of the hand of a subject which normally marks 23, is seen to rise respectively to 42 for red, 35 for orange, 30 for yellow, 28 for green and 24 for blue.

Another class of experiments deals with the change in volume of the members under the influence of peripheral excitations and sensations. According to a general law of physiology the blood is more copious wherever an organ is working; it swells the capillaries and so increases the volume of the whole organ. These changes of volume have been made the subject of study by Mosso [14] by the aid of his *plethysmograph*. This is an instrument consisting of two glass jars of water in which the hands of the patient are placed and then the jars are hermetically sealed with clay so that only the wrists project. By means of a slender tube through the walls of the vessels the level of the water may be seen to rise or fall and every change in volume of the hands observed. Another apparatus made use of by Mosso is the *see-saw bed* arranged on a balance, so that when the blood flows to the head of the subject, the weight is increased there and the balancing bed tips in that direction.

With these experiments should also be taken into consideration those made by Schiff at Florence. This specialist in physiology contrived to embed in the brains of some animals a *thermo-electric* pile [15] sufficiently small to be entirely buried in the cerebral matter. As soon as the wound by which it was inserted healed, he excited the sense-organs of the animal

[12] The dynamometer is an apparatus used for measuring the total force of certain muscles of living organisms, as for instance the contractile power of the hand. The effort of the contraction acts on a spring, the pressure upon which is recorded by an indicator upon a dial. The displacement of the indicator shows the gradual development of the contractile power.

[13] FÉRÉ, *Sensation et mouvement*, ch. VI (Alcan, Paris, 1887).

[14] A. Mosso, *Fear* (tr. Lough and Kiesow), ch. III, IV (Longmans, London, 1896).

[15] A thermo-electric pile is composed of two plates of different metals soldered at one end. A current is produced as soon as the solder is heated

and discovered that to each irritation there corresponded a movement of the galvanometer, thereby indicating that the cerebral matter had become heated.

The records left by these instruments show how it is possible to measure and compare sensations.

42. Duration of Psychical Phenomena.—The nervous phenomena that go to make a psychic act are by no means instantaneous. Attempts have been made to measure the time each part of the process takes. The method pursued has been as follows: A stimulus is applied to a sense-organ and as soon as the person perceives any sensation he has to make known his perception according to a predetermined signal. The exact times both of the stimulation and of the response are duly recorded by special instruments. The interval thus calculated is called the *physiological* or *reaction time.* This reaction-time varies in the case of different sensations: it averages $\frac{1}{7}$ of a second for tactual sensations, $\frac{1}{6}$ for hearing, $\frac{1}{5}$ for visual sensations.

As well as to obtain in this way the duration of the entire phenomena, attempts have also been made to determine the respective times taken in the separate parts of the process. The whole process, as we know, comprises an excitation received on the peripheral nerve-organs, the transmission of this along the sensory nerves to the nerve-centres, and then the elaboration of the psychical act; next a motor current is started, which travels down the efferent nerves to control the muscles and so give the response. Accordingly the reaction-time is made up of the time taken by the afferent current, the time necessary for the elaboration of the action in the nerve-centres, the time taken by the efferent current, together with the time taken for the contraction of the muscles. Now experiment allows us to fix directly the time taken for the contraction of the muscles, as also the time for the transmission of the two currents. By deducting the sum of these partial times from the total reaction-time, we are enabled approximately to arrive at the duration of the action in the nerve-centres, that is to say, the time it takes for a *simple central act.* This simple central act consists at least in the *perception* of the sense-impression (e.g. a contactual irritation, a sound, a flash of light), the *association of a motor image* (e.g. the movement of the right hand) with the previous sense-perception, together with the *motor impulse* controlling the movement imagined.

LOCALIZATION AND EXTERIORIZATION OF SENSATIONS

Sensations, we have seen (28), are *states of feeling* which bring us in touch with various *qualities of objects.* These feelings for the most part have reference to definite parts of the organism ; in other words we can *localize* them. We have now to ask ourselves, How is this localization effected ?

Moreover these qualities and objects we often perceive as distinct from ourselves and we refer them to definite positions outside of us. This is especially the case in sensations of seeing and hearing, and in those of touch, when so strong is the tendency that we even fancy we feel resistance at the end of a stick. We have, then, in addition to ask, What is the process of this *objectivation* or *exteriorization* ?

43. Localization of Sensations.—Localizing a sensation is not unlike finding a place on a geographical map. We are able to map out the body, so to speak, owing to our muscular or kinesthetic sense. We have already noticed that each of the muscles is provided with sensory fibres that acquaint the centres with any of its contractions. Now to the muscular movements of the various organs—of the eyes, hands, vocal organs, etc.—there correspond different sensations, and as memory-images of these are preserved after the muscular sensations have ceased, there becomes inscribed in the imagination a veritable chart of the sensations arising from the different muscles and organs, and by reference to this both new percepts can be classified and localized, and new movements directed.

44. Exteriorization of Sensations.—We seldom have pure muscular sensations ; as a rule they accompany tactual sensations or sensations arising from some other sense. If for instance I hold a sphere of metal in my hand, I experience both the sensation of contact with the round, cold, hard metal and the sensation of muscular effort put forth in supporting the suspended mass. If I raise my head with my eyes shut, I have a pure and simple muscular sensation ; if I open my eyes and they alight on some luminous object such as the sun, I experience in addition to the sensation of the movement of my head, the extra sensation from the light-rays. Thus two classes of sensations become discriminated—the one, muscular, arising from within the organism itself, the other, due to agencies foreign to the ego. This distinction, which begins to impose itself with the dawn of sentient life, is strengthened by *double* sensations. As soon as a child is subject to pressure it has a simple sensation, but when it comes to press its hands together or to rest one hand against another member of its body, its experience is then of a *double* sensation. Similarly when it hears people around talking, it has one, an auditory sensation; but when it tries itself to speak, in addition to the perception of the *sound* which it causes, it has also a second, a sensation of the *effort* required to emit it.

In a word, the upshot of sense-experience is an ever-increasing opposition between muscular sensations and those of another class which are external or objective. The memory-images left by muscular sensations together make up what we have called the muscular chart, or the map by reference to which future *internal* sensations (muscular, organic, painful) can be *localized* or recognized as coming from a certain definite portion of the organism. The memory-images of the objective class of sensations (e.g. visual, auditory and tactual) form another distinct chart in the imagination, by the memory's reference to which we are enabled to *exteriorize*, i.e. to refer to an *objective cause*, all our new *external* sensations.

45. Objective Character of Visual Sensations. Perception of Space.—The spontaneous reference of certain of our perceptions to an external reality is especially characteristic of those of sight. We see objects occupying a definite position, having definite relations of *distance* from other objects and from the perceiving eye; we attribute to them a definite *size* and *shape* or *form*; in a word we locate them in *continuous space of three dimensions*. We have now to explain both the cause and the process of our visual perception of space.

Those who profess a theory of *innate ideas* reckon our sense-perceptions of space as inborn or, more strictly, natural to us. *Empiricists* on the other hand maintain that such perceptions are simply the result of education. Yet to us it would seem that the truth lies in the mean between these two extreme opinions. The sense of sight, it must be acknowledged, by its natural power discriminates in its perception between a *number of elements*, which it is able to distinguish either by their various colours or by the muscular movements of eyes or head required in adjusting the sense-organ to see them. Hence by the use of the eye, besides the perception of light and colours, *extension* also is revealed both by the vision alone as well as in its association with the muscular sensations connected with the visual apparatus.

The simple visual perception of a number of objects is also accompanied by one of *distance*, inasmuch as distance is nothing more than a relation of two points to each other. And from this we have the *size* and *surface-form*.

But how are we to explain the *third dimension*?—It seems clear from the groping and mistakes of young children and of those recently operated upon for blindness, that the faculty of sight is not complete by itself; it needs the sense of touch as its *natural complement*. Hence it would seem that the full idea of the properties of space is due to the association and *co-ordinated education* of these two faculties. We have sensations of the efforts made in reaching objects at various distances from us and of the movements that must be made by us to touch any one object in all the aspects under which it is visible, and these sensations furnish percepts of their distance, size and form. Again we have sensations of sight and can measure with the eye the degrees of luminous intensity of the various objects seen. After repeated experiences of both kinds there gradually springs up an association between the two perceptions, of touch and sight, and at the end of a certain time one recalls the other or may replace it.

Thus, the perception of space appears to be partly natural to vision, as the one school would maintain it to be exclusively, and partly acquired, as indeed the empiricists prefer altogether.

46. Accuracy of Aristotle's Views concerning Common Sensibles.—It has been noticed (37) that besides proper objects of the special senses Aristotle enumerates *size, form, measure, repose* and *movement* as what he calls 'common sensibles', or objects of many or all the senses. Now we have just seen that the perception of *size* and *form* depends on the joint action of sight and touch. It may even be said that the perception of extension is given by all the senses—for smells and tastes would seem to affect several points simultaneously on the nostrils and tongue, and auditory perceptions supply a more or less distinct knowledge of the distance, if not of the form, of the object emitting the sound. Senses, moreover, that perceive the positions and distances of things are equally able to furnish a concrete perception of bodies in *repose* and *movement* and even of the concrete relation existing between one definite quantity and another perceived as a unit; in a word, of the *measure* of so much quantity.

CEREBRAL CENTRES OF SENSATIONS

47. Theory of Cerebral Localization.—It is safe to assert to-day that the brain is not a single organ all the parts of which have to fulfil the same functions. It is a combination of several different organs, each with its own psychological functions and constituting distinct faculties. Accordingly localization of cerebral functions in the brain may be regarded as an ascertained fact.

As a general conception, it may be noted, this is by no means new, for in his *Summa Theologica* and in his smaller work *On the Faculties of the Soul* [16], St. Thomas attributed the different functions of internal sensibility to a special place in the brain. Recent research has been devoted to mapping out the cerebral centres, or at least the nerve-centres, governing the various functions of sensitive or organic life. It would be beyond our scope and trespassing upon physiology to detail the methods employed; it will suffice for our purpose to notice only the following results.

1. The *spinal cord and sympathic system*, as we have already seen, are the nerves chiefly controlling the *viscera*—the anterior horns of the cord being motor-centres, the posterior sensory, and the more important functions of organic life being controlled from the medulla oblongata.

2. The *cerebellum* is commonly thought to be a centre for the co-ordination of movements, a centre of muscular equilibrium.

3. The parts below the cerebral hemispheres seem to play no part in voluntary or conscious life.

4. Concerning cerebral localizations the following has been ascertained: (*a*) The oldest and best-known discovery is that of Broca, who observed in 1861 that the lower frontal convolution is the seat of *articulate speech*: hence the name 'convolution of Broca.' Cases of aphasia have been met with in

[16] *Sum. Theol.*, I, q. 78, a. 4; *De Potentiis Animae*, c. IV.

which the afflicted person though incapable of speaking was able to move the face, to laugh, and even to sing. A post-mortem examination revealed a lesion of the third frontal convolution on the left side (Plate III, Fig. 6). (*b*) It is ascertained that the occipital lobe is the centre for *sight.* (*c*) That of *hearing* is in the temporal lobe, principally in the upper convolution. (*d*) Likewise *taste* and *smell* would seem to have their seat in the temporal lobe. (*e*) The centre for *touch*, which is the most extensive of all, embraces the central convolutions and those of the paracentral lobule and the posterior portion of the three frontal convolutions.

A word must be added on the localization of the *memory*. Most physiologists at one time believed that the same centres served for sensation, imagination and memory. Experiment has shown, however, that the Scholastics were right in their surmise that the memory required a separate organ. Pathological cases have been known in which the sense of hearing has been retained and the persons have been able to repeat words pronounced to them, but they have not understood anything nor been able to remember anything after a few seconds. This is a clear testimony that the memory of auditory images and the perception of the value of words are localized elsewhere than in the area devoted to hearing. This fact, moreover, corroborates the well-founded general distinction made by the Scholastics between the internal and external senses.

With these remarks we must end our analysis of the quality and quantity in sensations ; it remains for us to draw from it a general conclusion concerning *the nature of sensation.*

NATURE OF SENSATION AND OF THE SENSITIVE FACULTY

48. Nature of Sensation in General.—The foregoing study (**38** and **39** in particular) of sensation may be summed up in the following statement : The senses are faculties, or powers, of perceiving material things through a certain determination—*species sensibilis*—being produced in us by the action of the things themselves.

As we have knowledge of material things by our intellect as well as by our senses, the question arises, What is the formal difference between the object of sense and that of intellect ?—The answer is that the object of sense is *concrete* and that of intellect *abstract*: the one is *particular*, determined by being here and not there, existing at this moment, of such and such a colour, distinguished by so many degrees of light or obscurity, or by such a sound, note, etc.; the other is an object considered apart from all these particularizing qualities with which material things are found to exist in the actual order of things, considered in abstraction from any circumstances of place and time. Thus the intellect knows colour—not *this* colour—light, sound, etc.: the first idea that it forms is what this thing is now presented to the mind, *id quod aliquid est.* Hence our definition of the senses will be more complete if we make it: *The senses are faculties by which we perceive material things in their concrete reality, through a cognitional determination*—species sensibilis—*effected in the percipient subject by the action of the things themselves.*

We say that a sense is somehow determined to a perception, or cognition, because something must happen in the sense itself before it begins to experience a sensation. At first a sense is only the capacity to perceive, the power of perceiving: a *power* that is *passive*, incapable of passing into act without receiving some completion. Thus the eye has the power to see but this power is dormant when inactive. To pass, then, from power to act, in order to perceive—and the same may be said of the other senses—the eye needs a psychical awakening to complete its as yet indeterminate capacity of sense-action and thus dispose and determinate it to see an object. Sense-stimulus is the motive cause of this disposition to a definite act of perception. As soon as it is received, the potential faculty becomes an active one. Hence this disposition determines the actual sensation, the perception of a definite object. And hence it is termed the *cognitional determinant, species sensibilis.*

49. Nature of the Sentient Subject.—St. Thomas tells us that sensibility properly belongs neither to the soul nor to the body but to the compound subject made up of both; the senses are therefore faculties of the whole compound animal [17]. This we think an accurate statement, but we should prefer to break it up into the two following propositions which we will endeavour to establish: (i) *Sensuous perception is a hyper-*

[17] 'Sentire non est proprium animae neque corporis sed conjuncti. Potentia ergo sensitiva est in conjuncto sicut in subjecto.' *Sum. Theol.*, I, q. 77, art. 5.

physical operation, i.e. an action of higher nature than that of which brute matter and organic substances of the vegetable kingdom are capable. (ii) *Sensuous perception however requires the intrinsic co-operation of a material organ*, and is therefore essentially in matter as its subject.

50. I. Sensuous Perception is a Hyperphysical Operation.—The proof of this proposition lies wholly in the fact that sense-perception is essentially dependent upon the subject being made psychically disposed or determined to cognition (**29, 38**). This psychical disposition or mode according to which the perceptible object comes to exist in the subject who, so to speak, assimilates it by the act of perception, is of an entirely different nature from any mechanical, physical or chemical process; it is of another *order* altogether, an order that by exclusion we may denominate hyperphysical.

The efforts of materialists to include psychical phenomena in the category of purely material facts have been so remarkably ineffectual that one of the very leaders of experimental science, Du Bois-Reymond, has not hesitated to say: 'What imaginable connexion is there between definite movements of definite atoms of brain and such facts, to me irreducible and undeniable, as my feeling a pain or a pleasure, my perceiving a sweet taste, smelling the perfume of a rose, hearing an organ-note or seeing a red colour? It is impossible to catch even a glimpse of how consciousness can be generated by the combination of atoms'[18].

51. II. Sensuous Perception is essentially in Matter as its Subject.—(*a*) *Argument drawn from the constant relation sensation bears to nervous phenomena*. After the detailed analysis made of sensation from the standpoints of anatomy and physiology there is no need to show that sensuous activity depends upon material conditions; it is evident that it is swayed by affections of the nerves, that it is influenced by organic disorders and, where the nervous functions are disordered, is marked by corresponding defects. But there is no evidence from any source to point to this dependence being indirect and extrinsic. We must therefore conclude that it is *direct* and *intrinsic*, in other words, that it is the organ itself that is the subject of sensation.

[18] Du Bois-Reymond, *Ueber die Grenzen des Naturerkennens; die sieben Welträthsel.* Leipzig, 1884, p. 39.

(*b*) *Argument drawn from the concrete notes of sensation itself.* There is nothing to show that sensation is intrinsically independent of matter. On the contrary, it is intimately connected with the concrete conditions which flow from matter and manifest its presence, notably, for example, its *extension*. Although sensation is one, it is not *simple* but *extended* and divisible. 'If I look before me on my study table, I see books on the left hand, an ink-stand on the right, my manuscript in the middle with a letter, my note-book, and a page I have detached from it: so much I perceive. What happens if I put my hand up and draw it slowly across my face from left to right? The image of the table disappears, and disappears *gradually*. First the perception of the books ceases, next that of the manuscript and last of all that of the ink-stand. Then the whole table vanishes altogether from view. The point to be noticed is that there is no question here of a series of cognitions, one giving place to the other. . . . The perception of the whole table is therefore a phenomenon that can disappear *per partes*; it is therefore divisible and composed of parts, in a word, it is extended'[19]. It would be utterly gratuitous, then, to assert that sensation belongs to a principle entirely disengaged from matter.

Furthermore, our *internal sense* informs us that we do perceive with our *sense-organs*; we know that it is our hand that feels contact, that our eyes see and that it is our ears that are hearing.

The general conclusion, then, is correct, that sensation is the property of a *compound subject*; it is not an act exclusively of the soul, but that of the *animated body*.

§ 4. *Special Study of the Internal Senses*

In our general survey of sensuous cognition we noted (30) the existence of certain internal senses. These now require to be treated in detail. They are respectively (i) the common sense and the internal sense, (ii) imagination, (iii) instinct, (iv) sensuous memory.

COMMON SENSE AND INTERNAL SENSE

52. Existence of a Common Sense and an Internal Sense.— The chief reason inclining us to profess with Aristotle the

[19] De Coster, *Revue Néo-Scolastique*, janvier 1895, p. 58.

existence of a common sense is the fact that the sense-qualities that we perceive with the different senses we *unify* in one object whilst at the same time we *distinguish* them from one another. Consider Aristotle's example of one man having the sensation of the taste of something sweet and another man experiencing the sight of something white; neither of them has any element in their sensations by means of which they can *compare white* and *sweet*: so, if in ourselves the senses of taste and sight were entirely separate without any bond of connexion, we should not be able to *unite* the objects of these sensations in a common substrate, nor to *distinguish* from one another the qualities perceived by the different senses. It is a point of fact, however, that we do so unite these qualities and distinguish them, and therefore there must be in us a *common sense* in addition to and distinct from the external senses.

The existence of an internal sense, of a faculty for perceiving the *acts* of the external senses, is equally necessary. When I have the sensation of sight, I am conscious of seeing; when I hear, I am conscious of hearing. But a sense is incapable of perceiving its own act; for this would be nothing short of an act of real reflection and, as will be seen in Part III, no material faculty is capable of such an act. Logic compels us, then, to posit a special faculty, which may be called an *internal sense*, for this perception of the act of the external senses.

53. Nature of the Common Sense.—Because there has been demonstrated the existence of a distinct function, common sense, it would be false to argue that this sense is a single separate faculty apart from the others, having a special organ, that is to say, definitely localized and possessing like the other senses a function peculiar to itself, viz. of associating and distinguishing sensations. Were such the case, this organ of common sense would itself be composed of parts, each of which would perceive the particular act of an external sense and the object of this act. But then each part would be isolated and must accordingly, as Aristotle observed, be denied the power to associate or distinguish specifically different qualities.

In order to obviate this difficulty, we shall have to regard the common sense not as a special faculty disconnected from the others, but simply as the power of *associating our sensa-*

tions. This power of association we consider not to occupy a special cerebral centre but to depend upon the combined action of the cerebral centres affected by the exercise of the external senses and upon the conduction along the nerve-fibres that connect these various centres. Of course there still remains the need, sooner or later, of some principle of *unity*, to explain this association of sensations, for without some such principle they will be known only as juxtaposed, as somehow successive or contemporaneous, rather than as united. Such a principle, we venture to think, is adequately found in the *oneness of nature* of the first subject to whom all these faculties belong, or in other words the explanation lies in the fact that the person who experiences all the different sensations is one person. This being so, there is no need to call in the aid of a special faculty to combine the various percepts into one object.

54. Nature of the Internal Sense.—The conception of an internal sense situate in a special organ in the brain is fraught with as many difficulties as beset such a conception of the common sense, of which the internal sense is only one function. In what then does this internal sense by which we perceive the acts of the other senses consist? We think it is to be explained as being an association that grows up between the qualitatively different sensations of the various senses and a sensation of a uniform character, namely *muscular sensation*, which accompanies them all. This association is possible, once again, because the subject who experiences the two sets of sensations is one and the same person.

Our meaning will be clear when it is remembered that the active exercise of the external senses is always accompanied by muscular sensations (25). These muscular sensations being contemporaneous with the particular sense-impressions will tend to become associated with them until in time the muscular sensation itself will be an index of the activity of the particular sense with which it is correlated. Hence, in ultimate analysis, the so-called internal sense does not immediately give us a perception of an act of one of the external senses, an act of seeing for instance; but it informs us both that we feel we are acting and that we are at the same time seeing. This association, it may be noticed, is only a function of the common sense. It has also been called sense-consciousness.

THE IMAGINATION

55. Retentive Imagination. Motor Effect of Images.—Consciousness attests that our sensuous states are of two kinds, one of which is accompanied with the assurance that the object with which we are brought into contact through the sensation has an existence in reality independently of our cognition of it, whilst the other kind, in normal circumstances, is devoid of such an assurance; in a word, the difference is between *presentations* and *representations*, or as the contents of them are called, between *percepts* and *images*.

An *image* is the sensuous re-presentation either of qualities or of whole material things that have been previously presented in perception but which are now no longer actually present. The power of storing images is called the *retentive imagination* or the *sensuous memory*.

A notable feature of all images, and of images representative of movement in particular, is their *motor effect*. Every representation of a movement is accompanied by an excitation of the motor centres and thus produces some modification in the state of the muscles that are to perform the movement represented. Further, just as all sense-impressions are accompanied by muscular sensations, so every image has intimately associated with it the images of appropriate movements. Thus, for example, if I direct my attention to some object near my right hand, the image of the movement necessary to grasp it accompanies the first image and innervates my arm to reach out for it.

This motor effect of images has some interesting results. In the first place, the power of *imitation* is only an application of it. The sight of a person yawning or laughing provokes me to do the same. There is a tendency in watching an actor instinctively to imitate his gestures. The same tendency is even displayed when we look at a picture or a statue. Another application is what is commonly known as *thought-reading*. A blindfolded person, for instance, by taking the hand of another person who knows where a certain object is concealed is able to walk straight to it. This is to be explained by the blind person being guided by slight muscular contractions and relaxations on the part of the subject of the experiment.

56. Reproductive Imagination. Laws of Association.—Images do not come isolated into our conscious life, but united to one another like the links of a chain. Thus the revival of one image tends to bring about the revival of a train of others. This phenomenon, of the revival of images and memories through their connexion with an actual image, is called *association*. The question with which we are dealing concerns the conditions requisite for this revival; what are the laws of association and, accordingly, of the *reproduction* of images? Let it be noted that we are not speaking here of those combinations of images and thoughts that are due to volition under the direction of the intellect; for the present Part is devoted exclusively to the study of sensuous life and therefore only contemplates such associations as are independent of any action of the free-will.

According to Alexander Bain (1818–1903), who devoted considerable attention to these phenomena, the laws governing association may be reduced to three :—

1. *Law of Contiguity:* That actions, sensations, thoughts and emotions occurring together or in close succession tend to grow together or cohere, in such a way that when one of them is afterwards presented to the mind, the others are apt to be brought up in the memory. Thus it is a very old dodge to tie a knot in one's handkerchief, that the sight of it may 're-mind' the person of some other business which was in the mind at the time at which it was tied.

2. *Law of Similarity:* That present actions, sensations, thoughts and emotions tend to reproduce their like among previous impressions or states. Thus the sight of the photograph of a friend recalls to memory the image of his person, his gait, his voice, and even the circumstances of a previous meeting.

3. *Law of Composition:* That past actions, sensations, thoughts and emotions are revived more easily when they are associated, either through contiguity or similarity, with more than one present object or impression [20]. Thus the date 1914 brings back to memory the many opening events of the European crisis.

It is to the merit of modern psychologists, especially those of the Associationist school, that the most minute analysis of the facts of association has been made. The reality, however, of many of these facts was not ignored by the leaders of mediaeval

[20] A. Bain. *The Senses and the Intellect*, Ed. 1864, pp. 332, 463, 559.

philosophy. The following passage in Aquinas is significant :—

'A thing may recall another in three ways, by *similarity*, by *contrast*, or by *propinquity*. By similarity, thus Socrates makes me think of Plato, because the one resembles the other in wisdom ; by contrast, the remembrance of Hector recalls that of Achilles ; by some close connexion, for example, the idea of father suggests that of son ; likewise any other connexion—of community, contiguity, concomitance or succession —provokes corresponding associations' [21].

57. Illegitimate Interpretation of Association.—Some psychologists, such as Taine, Ribot, Bain and Herbert Spencer, have maintained the theory that these associations between states of consciousness are purely mechanical events that occur without any influence on the part of the sentient subject. Ribot went so far as to claim to make a ' psychology without a soul '. The error made by the representatives of this view is that of confusing the *fact of the co-existence* of two similar or dissimilar sensations with the *perception* of their similarity or dissimilarity. Even granted that the co-existence of two conscious states is a passive event, it must always remain true that the notion of their resemblance or difference essentially entails an *act of perception*. We must conclude, then, that it is radically impossible for conscious life to exist where there is not the *active* intervention of the subject who is aware of his existence, who on receiving an impression is conscious that he is the subject of it, who compares his impressions and his acts, who associates or dissociates them. In a word, a psychology without a soul, without an apperceptive principle —which most psychologists now agree to call *mind*—is as absurd as it is arbitrary.

58. Constructive Imagination.—The imagination is more than a mere store-house of past images that may revive ; it has also the power of *combining* the images that it preserves, of grouping them into new associations and even into chains of new associations. This remodelling of its own contents it may accomplish by itself, as in dreams and reveries, which are usually wanting in coherence. The fruitful use of the constructive imagination, however, is generally found only when the faculty is employed in conjunction with reflection and under the direction of the higher faculty of reason.

[21] St. Thomas, *De Memoria et Reminiscentia*, lect. 5.

INSTINCT OR THE SENSE OF WHAT MAKES FOR WELL-BEING

59. Sensuous Experience.—Perception and association do not explain the whole of animal psychology. There is a sense in animals which enables them to know what is useful or harmful to the preservation of the individual and the species. We see them pursue what is beneficial and flee from danger and pain. The Schoolmen, as we have said (30), called this the '*vis aestimativa*', or, as St. Thomas termed it, '*animal prudence*'. We might term it the sense of what makes for well-being. As some of the actions which result from its guidance are those promoting the particular species of the animal and transcending its individual experience—such as the weaving of webs by spiders and the building of nests by birds—it is also called *instinct.* There are other actions dictated by it which show an individual initiative and an adaptability that can be trained and perfected by practice. There is a great deal of knowingness displayed by the dog who is hanging about outside the kitchen door, anxious to gain access to where the meat is being dressed; the aroma of the viands is unmistakable even from outside the door and the voices of those who are good to it are audible within; it scratches the door, pushes with its paws, quivers with excitement, runs from one door to another and back again, whining and even barking, until eventually the door is opened and it is allowed to bound in and make up to those who it knows will gratify its hunger. Such behaviour is commonly attributed if not to a power of intellect at least to a 'sort of intelligence'. But the term, in spite of the well-meant distinction, is annoyingly ambiguous, and therefore it is better to call these manifestations of the sense of well-being simply *sensuous experience.*

The origin of this animal-experience is to be found, we think, in the *perception of concrete relations.* The quasi-reasoning process of the animal, if we may be allowed the term, is essentially the union of *concrete actions with a concrete end.* To all appearances the end of the dog's movements is a sensuous, concrete satisfaction, of appeasing its hunger; all the movements are dictated by the desire of this sense-pleasure and directed by the perception of things connected with this pleasure, namely things that procure it. The connexion between the action and the end is always a concrete one; never yet has any action of an animal been observed which, as will be seen in Part III (**125**), presupposes abstract, universal knowledge. The distinction we make will be emphasized by the following illustration :—A gentleman, stepping into his rowing-boat, found it dirty and wet. By means of gesticulations he brought his dog to understand that he wanted a sponge which he habitually used as a mop in these circumstances. The dog ran off and returned with the desired sponge. Had the animal reason ? Certainly not, if the merits of the case are to decide, for nothing more was shown than that it had a perception of certain concrete relations. If, however, the dog had not been able to find the sponge *its master habitually used* and instead of it had fetched a cloth which it *had never seen its master use*, we should indeed have to argue otherwise : its behaviour would then have proved that in the sponge and in the cloth the animal not merely perceived two concrete things but *abstracted* from them the idea of the common property 'capable of absorbing water'.

60. Nature and Origin of Instinct. Mechanistic Hypothesis.—Instinct may be defined as an impulse in an animal, prior to its individual experience, determining it to perform certain uniform external actions that are so co-ordinated as to further its own welfare and that of the species. That it is a *natural* impulse, *prior to individual experience* is immediately patent : the spider straightway weaves its web without ever being taught, the silk-worm makes its cocoon, and the bird its nest. Sometimes, moreover, the actions which they are led to perform are wonderfully ingenious and of extreme complexity.

At first sight there is the temptation to believe that such instinctive actions are purely mechanical, accomplished without prevision either of an end to be attained or of the means to its attainment. This has given rise to the *mechanistic hypothesis*, according to which instincts are derived from acts that in the first instance, as performed by the first individuals, were intelligent ; by frequent repetition they became automatic, were transmitted by heredity and thus in the course of time became *mechanical* : at bottom they are materialized intelligence.

This theory, at least in principle, was adopted by Lamarck, Herbert Spencer, Darwin, and Romanes. It is not however admissible, for : (*a*) There are several facts which go to prove that instinctive actions are not purely mechanical : spiders, for instance, mend their webs when they have been torn, bees repair accidents that happen to the cells they are building—facts which clearly show that circumstances have some determining influence upon the work begun and can cause a work, now accidentally become necessary, to be inserted in the ordinary series of acts. A purely mechanical action cannot be thus suspended and then continue of itself. We must therefore posit in these workings of instinct some *sort of knowledge* and the *guidance from some end in view*. (*b*) Darwin himself honestly confessed the difficulties in the way of attributing the marvellous instincts of 'working' ants and bees to *hereditary transmission* of acquired experience. It is well known that many of the marvellous instincts of ants and bees are shown by the 'workers', that is by those that are sterile insects. Whatever, then, may be the habits these insects acquire or whatever the intelligence that dictated them in the first instance, it is certain that neither can be transmitted if they are without posterity.

61. A Tentative Explanation.—We may take it as certain, on the one hand, that the working of instinct is neither blind nor automatic; and, on the other hand, that an animal is incapable either of conceiving or willing the abstract good. The question to be answered is, then: *What kind of intention* dominates the animal in these instinctive actions?—It seems scarcely probable that animals can imagine the *remote end* for which they work—that the young squirrel should have a prevision of the coming winter with its hardships. What we think happens is that an animal has *an imagination of the acts which have to be performed hic et nunc* and this imagination directs its work each moment during the performance of it. It has been observed that whilst an animal has not the ability to improve something already achieved, it certainly may repair an injury that its work may suffer *during* the process of its achievement: thus it would seem that it *is conscious of its acts whilst it is doing them.* If it be asked what produces these images that control its present action, we should reply that the cause is partly objective and partly subjective: a present external perception or a present internal sensation is an *exciting cause* of the imagination, whilst there is also some subjective *natural disposition*, peculiar to the particular animal type, co-operating towards the effect.

An example of what we mean by the initial *perception* which starts the animal performing the series of co-ordinated actions to which it is determined by its instinct, is the sight of a bit of straw, or of some coloured shape, the hearing of a cry, the scent of a trail, or even some organic internal sensation, such as hunger, the feeling of heat, etc. This is a first excitation. Owing to the animal's particular nature, this perception will immediately conjure up several *other images by association* ; for instance, images of the actions necessary for constructing a nest, for procuring food, for jumping, chasing, fleeing, etc. The association or connexion of these images is entirely independent of individual experience ; their conjunction is a priori synthetic, in Kant's sense. Next the presence of the images of these movements awakens the desire to perform them, and finally the desire acts as determining cause of the movement itself.

SENSUOUS MEMORY

62. Recognition. Reference to the Past.—Whilst to the imagination, as we have seen (**55**, **56**), belongs the power of preserving and reproducing sensuous impressions, the proper act or distinguishing feature of the sense-memory is the recognition of that impression as an impression of the past. This act of memory has in it two elements, either of which may predominate, viz. (1) the recognition of the event, and (2) the reference of it to its place in past time.

1. An act of recognition is the perception that this object now cognized is identical with a previous image that the subject is aware was once his. Besides the element of the resemblance there is entailed the feeling of a previous acquaintance with the object, and this we may explain in the following way. The memory preserves and reproduces not only perceptions made by the external senses but also those of the internal sense. This internal sense takes cognizance of the activities of the other sense-faculties. On the occasion of the remembrance of a past image, the memory will also recall the acts which gave rise to this image and which were perceived previously by the internal sense, and in this way the feeling is generated that the present representation was on a former occasion present to the subject's consciousness. Sometimes it may even happen that the remembrance of the past *activity* is brought back without a distinct revival of the

image received formerly by the external senses: when this occurs a very vague feeling is experienced of having seen something before but without a recognition of the thing in particular.

2. Besides enabling us to recognize objects previously perceived, memory also locates previous perceptions for us in past time. This is probably achieved by the fact that the recollection of a past perception evokes in a more or less clear way the events which have happened since the original perception of the object when it was actually represented; and thus a concrete perception is furnished of the duration of time.

63. Memory in Animals.—There is no reason for denying that animals possess the kind of memory we have just been describing. It is a household truth that a dog *recognizes* its master, just as the horse its stable or the roads along which it has already travelled. Animals moreover seem to have some sort of *an estimation of concrete time*: the animals of the farm-yard, for instance, know very accurately at what time of day to assemble for the food that is given them.

The animals, then, if we are to judge from their external actions, would seem to be endowed with exactly the same sense-memory that we have been describing as possessed by man, with however this one difference that in man this sense-faculty may be subjected in part to the control of his intellect and free-will and its recollections thus be consciously sought after and more accurately defined and referred to the past.

II. Sensuous Appetition and the Sensuous Appetite

§ 1. *Meaning of Sensuous Appetency*

64. Cognition and Appetition.—Conscious life bears two kinds of relation to what is extra-mental, and therefore comprises two classes of acts: one class is of operations which bring the external world before the subject, and these are called *cognitive* acts—apprehension or perception—and the faculties putting them forth *cognitive* faculties; the other class tend to identify the subject with the external reality, to incline it towards something other than itself, and these are *appetitive* acts—of sensuous appetition, of will, or of tendency—and the faculties are called *appetitive* or, in the case of intellectual appetition, *volitional*[22]. Sensuous appetency is, then, an inclination in virtue of which an animal tends to seek, or is drawn towards, some object which is brought before it as a good.

65. Natural Inclination and Spontaneous Inclination.— Every being has from its nature certain inclinations or tendencies; in fact the *nature* of a being is the being itself regarded under the particular aspect of possessing a fundamental inherent tendency towards a definite end which is its good. The *good*, then, is to be defined as the object towards which every being by its nature tends: 'Bonum est id quod omnia appetunt'.

We have already seen (**12, 13**) that it is only in the natural tendency in organic beings that we can find the explanation of the harmonious, persistent order they display throughout their evolution. The uniformity and constancy of physical and chemical laws are clear proofs of the existence of some similar law of tendency in the mineral kingdom. Hence the mediaeval Scholastics spoke of mineral and vegetable substances as endowed with a 'natural *appetite*'; they posited in them some inherent inclination in virtue of which they are drawn towards their particular good. Where the natural tendency is only physical it displays itself blindly and necessarily and its activity is uniform and constant. In the cases of sentient and rational beings the natural inclination is no longer blind and necessary, in the animals and in man it is dependent on a previous cognition made through the senses or the intellect: in other words the object which is the sentient being's good must be known somehow by it, must be presented to its higher faculty of consciousness before that being can tend towards it. These two different manners of tendency, one displayed through

[22] It is over this broad bipartite division of acts and faculties into cognitive and appetitive that Scholasticism chiefly parts company with Modern Philosophy, which admits a tripartite division (See **122**). As Scholasticism makes another fundamental division into sensuous and intellectual acts, the word *perception* may be generally used for sensuous cognition and *apprehension* (to which *judgment* is reducible) for intellectual cognition. Of the appetitive class, *volition* expresses the full deliberate act of the rational will; other tendencies of higher appetency—indeliberate liking, desire, aversion, etc.—and tendencies of the lower faculty can only be designated respectively as rational or as sensuous appetition. The word *conation* might well be used as a synonym for appetition, were it not in vogue to express a member of the modern tripartite division (cognition—feeling—conation) and so made to bear a slightly narrower meaning than Scholasticism desires to assign.—Trs.

consciousness and the other independent of it, may be better understood from the following examples: a needle, when brought into the presence of a magnet invariably moves towards it; an animal in the presence of a vessel of water is attracted to it only if it finds that it is here and now good to drink, and will show itself indifferent to it if it is not thirsty and it does not perceive that it is a good for it here and now. In the latter case, when the inclination is not merely physical but essentially dependent upon a previous cognition the special term 'sensibilis' or 'elicita' was used as an epithet by the Schoolmen; we may use the term *spontaneous appetition*.

Sensuous or spontaneous appetition is, then, an inclination or tendency in an animal in virtue of which it is drawn towards some object apprehended by it as a good.

66. The Emotions or Passions.—Sensuous appetition, which we have just defined as an inclination towards some object, is always, however slight it may be, attended by certain organic modifications—changes, for instance, in the circulation of the blood, in breathing, or in the beating of the heart. From the point of view of this further result, of the agitation set up in the organism, appetency bears the special name of *emotion*, or as the Schoolmen called it, '*passion*'[23]. This latter word, along with *appetition*, has practically fallen into desuetude: modern psychologists prefer the word *emotion*. The word is equally apt as it adds to the idea of inclination the notion of physical agitation which is further cognized as agreeable or disagreeable[24], for we speak in common parlance of being 'moved' by something that affects us physically through the mind. It must be remembered however that whilst *passion* was directly and immediately referred by the Scholastics[25] to the organic display in animals and only indirectly on account of their union in the same subject was applied to the

[23] St. Thomas says, 'Propriissime dicuntur *passiones* animae motus'; and adds: 'In omni passione animae additur aliquid vel diminuitur a naturali motu cordis: in quantum cor intensius vel remissius movetur, secundum systolem aut diastolem, et secundum hoc habet rationem passionis'. *Sum. Theol.*, I-II, q. 22, a. 2.

[24] This phenomenon of pleasure or displeasure which attaches to organic modifications is what we have described (31) as sometimes called the *feeling-tone* of a sensation.

[25] To-day it almost exclusively means a *violent* emotion or emotional tendency.—Trs. This paragraph the translators have adapted, rather than translated, from the original text.

supersensible affections—or sentiments—experienced by man as consequences of his intellectual cognitions, the term *emotion*, which is used by modern writers who neglect the distinction between sense and intellect, is too often employed exclusively in its primary signification, which is in reference only to man's affective states: if adopted, it must formally designate not only the higher feelings but also sensuous, or animal, organic modifications that are agreeable or disagreeable to the subject and are perceived to be such. We may define emotions, then, as certain movements of that appetitive faculty which impels towards what is good and averts from what is evil. Mere sensations of pleasure and pain are respectively the results of the consciousness of this attraction or aversion on the part of the sentient subject. We think modern psychologists are much at fault in postulating in the soul, besides the cognitive and appetitive faculties, a faculty of a third class, to which they apply the vague name of *feeling* or *affective life*, and refer to it the emotions and, sometimes, the experiences of pleasure and pain, which they consider to be elementary processes of affective life; for, as we have just said, the emotions are only movements of the appetitive faculties.

67. Classification and Enumeration of the Emotions.— Of the various classifications which psychologists of different schools have offered of the emotions or passions, that of the Scholastics is perhaps the most reasonable. They distinguish two aspects of sensuous appetency, or perhaps we had better say two appetites in the sensuous soul, one of which they called the *concupiscible* or the tendency towards objects in themselves, and the other the *irascible* or the appetite which seeks objects not directly in themselves but as perceived as subject to some condition of difficulty or danger. The basis for this distinction they found in the fact that the lower emotions have not all the same formal object: some regard a good object precisely as it is cognized as good, an object therefore that is directly sought after as agreeable or avoided as abhorrent—or in other words, that is directly 'loved' or 'hated'. There are others which, though concerned ultimately, it is true, with the good, have as their immediate object the removal of some obstacle that prevents a good from being acquired, or, it may be, an evil from being averted—in other words, the object is not the good simply but the *arduous* good; it is something that is formally presented as difficult to be acquired or avoided and the emotions of 'love' or 'hatred' are now not simple but complicated by a special affective state which the presence of the obstacle gives rise to in the perceptive subject. The objects in the first case are of the concupiscible appetite and in the second of the irascible.

That there is such a distinction of objects may perhaps be clear from the two different meanings in the phrases: 'to have a loving heart' and 'to have a valiant heart',—the one means a going out towards an object and implies the capability of the reverse (concupiscible appetite), the other a form of feeling that exists in respect of difficulties in the way of the possession of some object of desire (irascible appetite).

Of the emotions of the first group we may count six:—*love* and *hatred*, when the agreeable or disagreeable object is regarded absolutely, that is, without any reference to its real presence or absence; *desire* and *aversion*, when the object is known to be absent; *delight* or pleasure and *sadness*, when the object is present.

Those of the second group are five:—*hope* and *despair*, which arise when a desiderated object is difficult of acquisition but whose attainment is judged in the one case to be possible and in the other impossible; *courage* and *fear*, in the presence of a grave danger that has to be averted and when the impulse is either to face it or flee from it; lastly *anger*, which is a vindictive emotion aroused by a present evil either inflicted or threatened.

Of these appetitive states it would seem those of the latter group owe their origin in reality to those of the former; for, the contending against an obstacle is surely simply the making of an effort to obtain or prolong some state of enjoyment. Moreover, as the love of self, of one's own good, is the source of all the movements of the concupiscent faculty, it is right to conclude that this *love of self is the generating principle of all the other passions*.

§ 2. *Nature of Sensuous Appetency*

68. Sensuous Appetite is of a Higher Order of Being than that of the Natural Inclination of Inanimate or of Vegetable Bodies.—The natural tendency inherent in conscious beings depends for its display (**65**) upon the object sought being first represented to the sentient subject through sensation. As the faculty of cognition places a subject which possesses it in a rank of being above those that are by their nature without it, it follows that spontaneous appetition which is formally dependent on it is of a higher order than are the natural inclinations of other things which lack all consciousness [26]. As, moreover, cognition and the chemico-physical phenomena of inanimate bodies are by their nature two totally diverse realities (**50**), the superiority of sensuous appetency over the mere blind tendencies of the lower organic and inorganic bodies is not simply one of degree but of *nature* and marks another, higher order of being.

69. Sensuous Appetite is an Organic Faculty.—There is no more reason for asserting that the sensuous appetite is a spiritual faculty than for saying that the cognitive faculty of sensation on which it depends is spiritual (**51**). Its seat is not in the soul by itself but in the compound of soul and body, in the *animated organism*.

(*a*) *Argument drawn from the close relationship which is seen to exist between the sensuous appetite and the organism.* That some intimate relationship does exist between the two is evident from the physical manifestations which accompany the emotion of delight: the supply of blood becomes more copious in the brain, as a peculiar brightness of eye especially indicates, respiration becomes more active, with the general result that the temperature of the body rises and the nutritive processes are quickened and furthered. Grief and sadness have effects that are almost the opposite: the circulation appears impeded, respiration slackens and is fitful, nutrition in general is retarded, a lack of appetite, indigestion, etc., supervene. These are only two examples but they are sufficient to indicate clearly that the sensuous emotions are indeed modifications of the organism.

(*b*) *Argument drawn from our internal experience.* Our consciousness tells us that besides the aspirations of the rational soul towards supersensible objects and the delight which ensues upon their attainment, we most certainly experience other desires, of an inferior kind, that regard goods of the

[26] 'Sicut igitur formae altiori modo existunt in habentibus cognitionem supra modum formarum naturalium; ita oportet quod in eis sit inclinatio supra modum inclinationis naturalis quae dicitur appetitus naturalis'.

sensuous order, together with pleasures of the same lower type when we secure them. Further, we not infrequently feel that there is a certain antagonism between these two different tendencies, with the result that we can follow the lead of the higher only at the cost of a great struggle against the solicitations and emotions of the lower. These facts establish that there are two faculties of desire or conscious tendency; that besides the rational will there is another distinct appetitive faculty which does not transcend the level of an organic faculty.

70. Sensuous Appetency in Animals.—The states of consciousness we have hitherto been examining and which our own inner experience assures us are ours, may also be attributed to the animals. The great similarity in the structure of organism and the spontaneity discernible in the actions they perform furnish the grounds for such a judgment. We assert, then, that the animals, in varying degrees according to their grades in the scale of living being, share with man all those feelings and passions which depend on and result from the reception of sense-impressions. This does not however amount to saying that they enjoy the power of reasoning, which implies a cognizance of universal ideas (125–126), and the power of will proper, which is dependent upon intellectual knowledge and therefore belongs only to man: we allow that they have all other kinds of conative states than those which are produced by these spiritual faculties. Materialists are very much astray when they think that by citing the facts that their dogs are 'affectionate', 'delighted', 'jealous', 'conceited' and so on, they are thereby disproving an *essential* difference between the intelligence of man and that of the animals.

71. Organ of Sensuous Appetency. Not the Heart.—It is a well attested fact that there is some close connexion between the heart and the emotions. The effect of sorrowful emotions is a slackening of the beatings of the heart, which is betrayed by a blanching of the cheeks and a general depression of the whole organism. Joy and hope have just the opposite effects: the pulsations are quickened, the blood flows more abundantly to all the organs and gives the feeling of contentment and vitality. These common experiences are recorded in all languages by the use of such stock expressions as 'to have a heavy heart', 'to have a broken heart', 'to be light-hearted'.

The question is whether we are right in concluding that the heart is the seat, or organ, of the emotions and affective sensibility. Philosophers of old considered that it was, as indeed the uneducated to-day still consider it to be. But scientifically speaking, it is not so; the heart is nothing more than a muscle and has nothing in common with either sensation or the affective states dependent upon it. The real organ of the sensuous appetite is the nerve-centres, which are indeed the seat of all psychical life; but the present state of physiological-psychology does not allow us to assign any definite area of the brain to this faculty.

The popular error which refers the emotions to the heart is easily explained by the regular corresponding changes in the heart's action which accompany these states of feeling. Roughly the physiological explanation is that the heart comes under the control of the nerve-centres through two groups of nerve-fibres that belong respectively to the pneumogastric nerve and the sympathetic nerve. Any excitation of the former slackens the movements of the heart whilst any excitation of the latter accelerates them. Hence it is clear why the emotions, which act directly upon the nerve-centres, come to have a reacting influence upon the motions of the heart, and why, conversely, modifications in the contractions of the heart, by varying the supply of blood to the brain, have an effect upon the psychic activity of the person.

III. Spontaneous Movement

§ 1. *Anatomical and Physiological Aspect of Movement.*

72. Our Locomotor Apparatus.—Our organs of movement are our *muscles* and *bones*. The latter together form a skeleton or framework of hard calcified tissues, which in themselves are devoid of any power of action but are arranged in relation to one another as so many levers that are mutually connected and capable of being brought into action by another set of organs, the muscles; these have the power of contracting themselves whenever a pull has to be made on the bone-levers. Together the bones and muscles make up the members.

The *muscles* themselves are composed of very slender threads, called muscular fibres, which are derived from separate cells and may be regarded as elongated cells; here and there in them are even to be found cell-nuclei. Two kinds of muscles are distinguished, namely, voluntary or *striated* ones and plain, *unstriated* ones, called involuntary (Plate IV, fig. 1, *A* and *B*).

73. Muscular Contraction.—The muscular fibre has the properties of being *irritable* and *contractile*. Irritability is the characteristic a muscle has of responding to a stimulus by a movement. Under the impulse from a motor nerve a fibre shrinks or contracts itself by diminishing its longitudinal diameter and swelling transversely. This, the great and chief property of muscular tissue, is called its *contractility*. By contracting or relaxing, the muscles alter the position of the bones attached to them and so move the members and set the whole body in motion.

Strictly speaking, the muscles are never entirely relaxed but always partially contracted. Even when the organism is engaged in no apparent movement, the muscles are subject to a continuous nervous excitation which keeps them in a state of tension or *tonicity*.

Muscular contractions are accompanied by certain physical phenomena—a disengagement of heat, electric variations, etc.; as well as by chemical phenomena—the formation of lactic acid and carbonic acid, etc.

§ 2. *Psychological Aspect of Movement: Spontaneous Movement.*

74. Reflex, Automatic and Spontaneous Movements.—In man and animals alike psychologists distinguish three kinds of movements, namely, *reflex*, *automatic*, and *spontaneous*.

A *reflex* movement is one that is made in response to peripheral stimulation, without the intervention of any conscious effort. The classical example of simple reflex action is that of the knee: if a patient is seated on the edge of a table with his legs hanging loosely down, and is gently struck on the forepart of the knee just below the kneecap, the inevitable result will be a jerk forward of the leg.

The stimulation from without is conducted along an afferent nerve to a sensory centre, where it immediately changes or 'turns back' (*reflectere*) along an efferent nerve and so gives rise to the reflex movement. There are reflexes much more complicated than this, such for instance as swallowing, the sucking of the newly-born offspring, and in some animals the action of jumping. Reflex action may be attended by consciousness or not; but it is characteristic that it always takes place without any previous volition or sensuous appetition.

Automatic movement resembles reflex action in that it also is independent of any previous conscious origin; but it differs from it in this, that whereas reflex action is due solely to some peripheral excitation, automatic movement has its origin in some *internal stimulation* of the organ. Thus the heart beats automatically, even though taken out of the organism; so too respiration is automatic.

Spontaneous movement, which is chiefly the concern of the psychologist, differs from the two preceding kinds inasmuch as it *results from an act of sensuous appetency*, and is therefore dependent upon a previous perception. Hence to this class also belong all those actions performed under the direction of the sense which makes for well-being, whether they be dictated by individual experience or class instinct.

75. Existence of Spontaneous Movements in Man and the Animals.—As Descartes recognized in the created world only two kinds of reality—matter whose essence is extension, and mind whose essence is thought—he found himself confronted with a dilemma: either he had to allow that animals are the subjects of sensations, passions and spontaneous movements like man, and to admit in consequence, since psychic phenomena cannot in his theory be attributes of matter, that they have a spiritual soul to which these psychic states may be referred; or, as the only alternative, he had to deny that animals have any sensibility at all. He shrank from conceding to animals a spiritual soul and so chose the second alternative, declaring them to be 'automata' or mere 'moving machines'.

This extraordinary opinion was taken up by Malebranche and to-day is still put forward by the materialistic school. Against such an opinion we have to establish that spontaneous movements do take place both in man and in the animals; movements, that is to say, of which the immediate determining cause is not anything mechanical, physical or chemical, but something psychical. This is best done by a few examples.

A schoolboy plays truant, steals into an orchard, where he gathers fruit and eats it with glee. What is the cause of his actions? The desire of eating the fruit; he remembers the taste of good apples and he easily images to himself a repetition of the same pleasure: the imagination awakens desires, desires determine his movements. Further, what happens when on a sudden the owner of the orchard appears and gives chase to the young intruder? A scampering off with cries of alarm, movements this time provoked by the fear of a cuffing and the hope of escaping it. Here are so many movements having a sensible desire for their determining cause. It is undeniable that a desire has here provoked movements: when it is suppressed they cease, when it becomes more or less intense they become more or less vigorous and rapid. What is true of this particular instance consciousness tells us is equally true of a host of other similar cases. Man at least is, then, the author of really spontaneous actions. Can the same be said of animals? The law of analogy would seem to demand that it can: for, consider the behaviour of a cat which stealthily approaches the meat-safe, pushes the door it sees ajar, seizes a piece of meat and begins to devour it; then steps are heard and an angry voice, it attempts to scurry away, crouching in the distance at the sight of the upraised stick. Are we to say that the movements in the two cases are entirely dissimilar: that the actions of the animal are not, like those of the child, determined by the desire of the dainty morsel and by the fear of the stick? Is there any justification for asserting that the same procedure, the same cries and the same movements are in the one case spontaneous and in the other purely mechanical? Surely we must conclude that animals, just as much as men, are the authors of spontaneous movements, which are set in action by sense-appetitions as their determining cause.

76. Causes of Spontaneous Movement.—In his analysis of spontaneous movement [27] St. Thomas assigns three kinds of causes. The muscles put into action by the nerves are the *immediate efficient* cause executing the movement. The *determining* cause consists in the desires urging the animal, sensuous appetitions that determine the act and regulate the locomotive power appropriate to it. And the third is the *directing* cause, which is some act of sensuous cognition—more often than not of the instinctive faculty that estimates the worth of an object; this cognition awakens and directs conation, which immediately provokes the movement.

[27] *De Potentis Animae*, c. V

Although the external or internal stimulus is not the sole and adequate cause of spontaneous movement, its influence is nevertheless a *real* one in so far as it is necessary to bring the cognitive and appetitive powers into operation. What is not infrequently spoken of as the *environment* of the animal is, then, a remote cause, a stimulus, of the spontaneous movement.

A *corollary* from what has been said is that appetency and the power of external movement are two distinct faculties. That they are, moreover, separable may be seen from facts of everyday experience—from the fact, for instance, that the paralytic desires and tries to command a movement but is unsuccessful in performing it; who, in other words, has will, which is an appetitive faculty, but no power of locomotion.

ART. II. NATURE AND PROPERTIES OF THE FIRST PRINCIPLE OF SENSITIVE LIFE

77. Object of this Article.—In the foregoing article of this chapter we have investigated the functions of sensitive life, first of all from an anatomical and physiological standpoint, then from a psychological one: it has comprised a study of external and internal sensations (I), appetition (II), spontaneous movement (III), and the *faculties* that are the *immediate principles* of these various functions. From sensuous *acts* and their immediate principles we have now to make an induction concerning the *first principle* or the *nature* from which they proceed.

The nature of the first principle of sensibility may be formulated in the following theses:—

I. The first subject of sensibility is a single but compound substance.

II. The first subject of sensibility is of a higher nature than that of a vegetable.

78. I. The First Subject of Sensibility is a Single but Compound Subtance.—To the mechanistic materialist philosopher an animal is nothing more than a collection of material elements and forces; to the spiritualist of the Cartesian type, if he be logical, it is something immaterial and simple; the Scholastic agrees with neither the one nor the other. Against the mechanist the Scholastic doctrine asserts that a being endowed with sensibility is a *single substance actually one,* a *nature*, and that the forces connected with it are only so many accidents and derived principles of activity. Against an exaggerated spiritualism it lays down that the first principle of animal life is not as such a simple substance independent of matter, but one that for its subsistence and activity so depends on primary matter that what is the subsisting subject is a *material compound*. Our first thesis, then, falls into two parts, each of which we must proceed to establish.

79. (i.) The Sentient Subject is a Substantial Unit.—The same reasoning (**13 f.**) that led us to assert the substantial unity of the living being compels us to admit the unity of the sentient subject. But a glance at the animal kingdom affords sufficient evidence that the actions of animals, multifarious as they are, harmoniously and continuously converge towards the realization of the same result, to wit, the maintenance, reproduction, and protection, in a word, the well-being, of the animal. This unity of purpose demands a sufficient reason; and this is to be found not in the *external conditions* or *environment*, for these change with time and place, and the fact to be explained is independent of these variations; nor is it in any incessantly reiterated extrinsic action of Providence, for this would involve a suppression of secondary causes. The sufficient reason is therefore something *internal*, within the sentient subject itself. It is not however in the organs or anatomical elements of the animal, since it is precisely the persistent harmonious combination of these that has to be accounted for. It must therefore be some inherent *first principle* that makes all the elements of the animal's organism and all their respective forces converge towards one and the same end. In other words, the animal is a first subject, a first principle of energy, or, in technical language, one *substance*, a single complete *nature*.

80. (ii.) The first Subject of Sensibility is a Compound Substance.—It has been already proved that sensation (**51**), appetition (**69**) and, consequently, spontaneous movement also, have material organs both as their seat of activity and as their immediate principles. Applying then the axiom: 'operari sequitur esse', that the nature of a being is revealed by its acts, we must assert that the first principle of the various sensitive functions is not a simple soul forming by itself a substance apart, but is a *composite* material substance, of which the sensitive soul is only the formal principle, which is essentially dependent upon matter both for its existence and activity.

The substance of organized beings we saw above (**13**) to be composed of primary matter and a first principle of life that is commonly called the vital principle or soul. The question will present itself whether there are, then, in the animal two first principles, two substantial forms, an organic soul and a sensitive soul.—The answer must be in the negative: that the first principle of sensibility is the same as the first principle of its vegetative life, that *there is only one soul, a single substantial form.* Our reason for this assertion is that the substantial form of a being is nothing else than the nature, or natural tendency of that being towards its intrinsic end; and as the functions of sensibility have obviously the same intrinsic end as the vital functions, namely, the well-being of the animal, these two kinds of functions must proceed from the same intrinsic tendency, from one and the same nature. Hence an animal is a sentient being by the same substantial form as that by which it is a living being; in other words, the animal has only one substantial form.

81. II. The First Subject of Sensibility is of a Higher Nature than that of the Vegetable.—This follows from the impossibility of a faculty to surpass in perfection the nature to which it belongs: for the sensitive faculties of perception (**50**) and appetition (**68**) evidence a perfection that surpasses that of chemico-physical forces. In vain are the attempts of the positivists to reduce psychic phenomena to the category of purely material events; whether it be of a chemical nature that they make them—as for instance a secretion of the brain—or molecular or atomic vibrations, or again, as Taine regards them, the obverse or inner aspect of the physical or chemical phenomena of the nerve-centres. The first two interpretations are, on the confession of sincere positivists, unintelligible. The third suggestion, that sensation is the inner lining, so to speak, of a physical or chemical process, amounts to nothing more than to saying that psychical states are of such a peculiar character that they are entirely different from the ordinary physical and chemical phenomena.

A *corollary* that follows from this superiority of sensation over physical and chemical phenomena is that there is a radical distinction—a distinction of nature or kingdom—between vegetables and animals: the living being possessed of sensation is an animal, the living being without sensation is a vegetable. It is not always easy, however, to recognize this natural demarcation in point of fact: for sensation only betrays itself by spontaneous movement and in the lower degrees of the animal scale the signs which distinguish spontaneous movement from reflex movement or even from the simple irritability of protoplasm are difficult to discern. Hence there are a certain class of doubtful living beings about the nature of which naturalists dare not pronounce.

82. Deduced Properties of Sensitive Nature.—1. The souls of the brute animals begin and cease to exist with the compound. Several modern psychologists, of whom Balmès is representative [28], maintain that the animal soul is *immaterial*. Now there is no reason why we should not call the soul of an animal incorporeal if by this we mean that it surpasses in perfection corporeal substances whose activity produces the forces generally associated with matter; but the use of the word is erroneous if by it we mean that such a soul is in a real and strict sense immaterial, that is, that it is a substance independent of matter.

As the sensitive soul enjoys only the existence of the compound (**80**), it does not exist previously to the existence of the compound nor endure after it. There is consequently no question of its creation or immortality, nor even of its annihilation.

2. The animal soul as such is neither *divisible nor indivisible*, since as such it does not exist; as we have said, it has no subsistence of its own apart from that of the organism which it informs and in which it is, as it were, immersed 'penitus immersa', to use the phrase of St. Thomas.

But one may ask if the sensitive soul may not be divided *indirectly*, 'per accidens', when, that is to say, the animal compound is divided.—To such a query we must make the same reply as in the case of vegetable organisms (**15**). Some animal organisms are divisible in the sense that *certain* parts can regenerate the whole; but with the higher organisms this is not the case, for their parts after separation cannot regenerate the whole nor survive by themselves: hence the higher organisms are entirely indivisible.

[28] *Fund. Phil.*, Bk. 2, chap. 2.

CHAPTER II

ORIGIN OF SENSITIVE LIFE

83. The Origin of Life and the Problem of the Origin of Species.—The *immediate* origin of animated beings has already been stated in the axiom 'Omne vivum ex vivo': every living being comes from one or more living beings endowed with the power of propagation (**16**). After tracing back a definite number of generations we must come ultimately upon some primitive cause. This we have seen (**18**) to have been an intervention of the Creator's power by which He introduced life into His work. The same cause must be assigned for the existence of sensitive life, for sensation cannot be reduced to the functions of vegetative life. Granted then this direct intervention of God, the further question arises, what should be the limits assigned to that intervention? Did *each species* require special creation? or was a single divine action sufficient by which *one or several types* were created so that all other species were derived through the influence of natural causes? This is the much-discussed and interesting problem of the *origin of species.* The solution essentially depends upon the fundamental question, Are natural species permanent and fixed? or are they variable so that one can be transformed into another?

A species in natural history denotes a series of living beings that have come from a common stock and are *inter se* fertile. We can observe in general that the types of the same species visibly remain the same throughout all variations of place and time; in one sense, then, a species is fixed. However this fixity is not absolute, for it is a fact known to and made use of by breeders that specific types can have certain hereditary qualities with the result that in the same species different races or *varieties* may be generated. On this account some would argue that if artificial selection can produce new races, it is not impossible for new *species* to be produced also; and if indeed, owing to changed conditions, it is not possible to-day, it may at least have been possible in bygone periods when influences were more potent and time for the effect unlimited. This is a conception that was unthought of by any of the older naturalists, who were unanimous in professing that there is an impassable barrier between the separate species. It was originated by Darwin (1809–1882) who, following Lamarck, introduced the idea of a *natural selection,* analogous to but more perfect than the artificial selection of breeders; and this he thought would account for all the present species of both kingdoms being derived from certain primitive types.

The doctrine of the fixity of species is sometimes called *fixism* or, on account of the differentiation of species being attributed to the intervention of the Creator, *creationism.* The opposite doctrine is generally known as *evolutionism, the theory of descent,* or *transformism.* The term *Darwinism* expresses only a particular theory of the way in which evolution has taken place, namely, that natural selection is determined by the 'struggle for life': all animals are mutual enemies which live in a perpetual struggle for their food and other necessaries of life; in this struggle those individuals survive which chance to be best fitted by their secondary qualities to the requirements of the situation, while the weaker succumb and become extinct; by 'the survival of the fittest' newly acquired qualities of a useful character are transmitted to posterity, and in this way a new species is progressively formed.

Some materialists (such as Huxley, Spencer, Haeckel) push the theory of evolution to the extreme, making the development of the whole universe, moral and religious as well as cosmic and organic, transformations of an eternal matter that is independent of any supramundane agency either as regards its first origin or as a factor in its evolution. Such a 'materialistic monism' is as false as it is arbitrary: as for matter, cosmology has demonstrated its contingency; the vegetable kingdom we have seen in this treatise cannot be explained by the general forces of inorganic matter; animals moreover are essentially different from vegetables, and soon we shall establish that there is also an essential difference between man and the animals. If there is any question of transformism, it must be restricted to the confines of the same organic kingdom, either vegetable or animal. What is to be said in its favour?

84. Examination of the Theory of Transformism.—Within the range of ascertained facts nothing has yet been known that can be regarded as a decisive proof of the transformation of one species into another. Direct observation and experiment have, on the contrary, positively, universally and constantly borne witness against the transformation of species in the present state of living nature. The *facts* being so, may we *conjecture* that the case was otherwise in the beginning? Does the study of the action of natural forces in the past warrant the *hypothesis* that our present-day species are descended from common ancestral forms?—In favour of it, or at least of its main outlines, stand by far the majority of naturalists. Moreover it can summon an array of facts to support it, the principal of which are—(*a*) the existence of a gradation among the beings that have successively appeared on our globe; (*b*) a unity of plan, discernible by comparative anatomy, in accordance with which the whole series of vertebrates is built; (*c*) a similarity, revealed by embryology, between the successive phases through which the embryo passes and what the transformist makes out to be the series of species which led up to that one of which the developing embryo is a member, in a word, the fact that 'ontogeny, or the development of the individual, is a recapitulation of phylogeny, or the evolution of the species'[29]; (*d*) the persistence of certain rudimentary organs the rôle of which it is difficult, if not impossible, to attribute to the Creator in the creationist theory and which appear to transformists either as traces of previous states or else incipient adaptations towards future more advanced states. Such, for instance, are the rudimentary eyes of the mole.

But (1) not one of the above facts constitutes a demonstrative argument: (*a*) succession cannot be identified with descent; (*b* and *c*) similarity is not identity, nor comparison a basis for inference; (*d*) rudimentary organs furnish only a presumption, and before a proof can be drawn from them

[29] The series of forms through which the embryo of the individual organism passes (ontogeny) appears to the transformist to be a recapitulation of the prolonged succession of transformations undergone by the line of ancestors of this same organism in order to form the present species (phylogeny). Thus in the first periods of their embryonic evolution all mammifers exhibit a conformation very closely resembling the gills that a fish retains throughout life.

evolutionists have first to establish that their proffered explanation is the only plausible one.

(2) Moreover there are several other objections to be raised against the doctrine of evolution. First, were evolution a fact, it would have to be due to an inherent tendency in the living being itself; yet this is also to suppose an intrinsic tendency to self-annihilation, and this involves a contradiction.—If evolution is the general law of living beings, how account for the unvarying continuance in being of many species that are known to have existed from the beginning?—The transformist theory has the weakness of possessing no proofs from observation and experiment. In fine we must conclude that the theory of descent—even if it is confined only to one organic kingdom—is at best only a *working hypothesis.*

This brings us to the close of our study of sensitive or animal life. In Chapter I, we saw in what that life consists—quid est?—or its *nature*; in Chapter II, whence it has sprung—unde est?—or its *origin*; and we have also seen, though not in a separate chapter, its destiny—ad quid?—or its *end*, which is the well-being of the compound in this life inasmuch as the animal soul has no other destiny apart from that of the compound. It remains now to investigate the functions of intellect and will that are peculiar to the soul of man.

PART III

Rational Life

INTRODUCTION

85. Object of Part III.—In this part we have to investigate the *activities* peculiar to man and the *faculties* from which they immediately proceed, with the view of discovering the *nature* from which both are ultimately derived. As in the preceding part, the first chapter will deal with the *nature* of man; the second with his *origin*; while a third will be devoted to the question of his *destiny*.

Chapter I subdivides itself into three articles dealing respectively with the *acts* peculiar to man—of his intellect (I) and will (II), in contrast with the acts of the animal (III); the *mutual influences* of sense and intellect—of imagination and intellect (I) and sensuous appetite and will (II); the *nature* of the human soul, looked at in itself (I), and in its union with matter (II).

Hence of the whole Part we have the following scheme :—

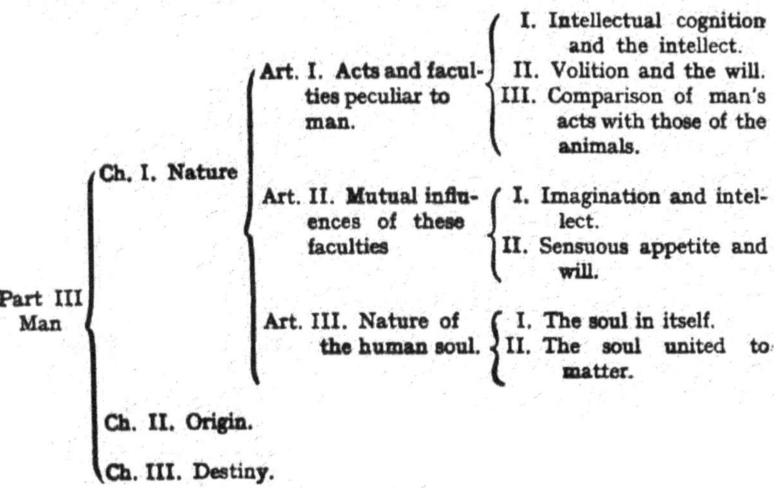

CHAPTER I

NATURE OF THE HUMAN SOUL

ART. I. ACTS AND FACULTIES PECULIAR TO MAN

I. INTELLECTUAL COGNITION AND THE INTELLECT

86. Object of this Section.—Intellectual cognition, like all other cognition, essentially entails the union of an object known with a subject knowing. We have, then, to inquire what in the case of the intellect this *object* may be (§ 1), and how the *union* may be effected between the object of thought and the understanding (§ 2). These two questions concerning the origin of our simple or first thoughts precede a third question, that of the *process of mental development* or of the more complex acts of the mind (§ 3).

§ 1. *Object of Intellectual Knowledge*

87. Material and Formal Objects: Common and Proper Formal Objects.—The question, What is the object of thought? may be understood in two different ways. It may mean: What can we think about? and then it concerns the *material object* and the answer is: Anything whatsoever that the mind can obtain knowledge of. Such intelligible objects are, however, very different in their nature: they may be substances or accidents, material or spiritual, contingent beings or the Necessary Being. The question, then, is patient of another meaning: What is strictly intelligible in all these objects? What is the formality common to them all that makes them fall within the grasp of the understanding? Whatever that formality is may be called the *common formal object* of the intellect. It is *being* or the *true*, for the true is nothing else than being in its relation to mind.

Owing to the great diversity of objects that can be thought of by the mind the common formal object is of two kinds. That is called the *proper* formal object which falls directly within the range of the faculty, namely that for the knowledge of which the faculty is by its nature adapted, which it can therefore know independently of a knowledge of other things and which it uses as a medium for the attaining of any further knowledge. If the proposed question be read, then, as referring to the *proper* formal object—otherwise called *primary, immediate, direct, proportionate* or *connatural* object—the answer, as we shall see shortly, is *material being.*

The *improper* formal object—or *secondary, mediate, indirect* object—is whatever the cognitive faculty cannot know except by the aid of the knowledge it has of its proper object: the chief improper object is all *immaterial being.* The meaning will be clearer when we say that the knowledge of the proper object is *immediate* or furnished directly by the object itself; that of the improper object is *mediate* or gained by way of negation or of analogy from a knowledge of things distinct from it. An example of knowledge obtained by way of *negation* is the notion of the simplicity of the soul; it is a negative idea gained by taking away the imperfection of composition perceived in material beings. By *analogy* is meant the attribution of some proper idea we already have to another object of which it is not the direct expression and to which therefore it can be applied only with the reservation, expressed or implied, that now it is not being used in its plain original sense but only as a sort of comparison[30]; thus we have a proper idea of the co-existence of two superimposed bodies, but only an analogical idea of the presence of the soul in the body.

To repeat: the *common formal object* of the human understanding is, broadly speaking, *being* and the *true.* All *material beings* constitute its *proper object*; *immaterial beings*—the human soul, spiritual realities, God—constitute its *indirect* or *improper* object. These assertions require to be proved.

88. I. The Common Formal Object of the Intellect is Being. —*Positive proof: The intellect knows being.*—Being in general designates everything that exists or may exist. Now whenever the mind thinks, it does so about something that exists or may exist. The *common object* of the thinking faculty, the intellect, is therefore being.

Exclusive proof: The intellect knows nothing but being.— The objects which the mind knows are of diverse natures— substances and accidents, material and immaterial beings,

[30] The word *analogy* is explained in *Logic* 22, 26.

contingent beings and the Necessary Being. Now all these different objects have but one characteristic in common, namely, that they are all beings. Therefore the only formal reason of anything being apprehended by the mind is its being: being is, then, the *common* and *adequate object* of the intellect. The same may be said of the *true.*[31]

89. II. The Proper Object of the Human Intellect is derived from Sense-data; but it is Abstract and Universal. Explanation.—The things of which we have knowledge are of two kinds, sensible and supersensible. Whatever is *positive* in the content of the concepts we have of these, that is, whatever knowledge we gain directly and not by way of negation or analogy, is found realized in sensible things themselves and it is from our sense-experience that in the first place we derive it. This is the meaning of the Scholastic principle 'Nihil est in intellectu quod non prius fuerit in sensu'. It does not mean that of supersensible beings we have no positive knowledge; it only asserts that in the concepts we may form to ourselves of them, there can be no positive element that we have not previously apprehended as realized in some sensible object; in a word, that the concepts we have of supersensible beings can represent to us only such elements in them as they have in common with material ones: our concepts of their being, unity, activity, and knowledge are of this kind. The peculiar or *proper* elements in immaterial beings we cannot know positively but only by means of negatives and analogies,—e.g. the ideas of simplicity, immensity, the localization of spirits. So much for the first part of the thesis.

The second part of the thesis informs us that, although obtained through sense-data, the object of intellectual knowledge is *abstract* and *universal.* This trait is what distinguishes a concept of thought from a perception of sense and from an imagination, both of which are essentially *concrete* and *individual.* What is perceived by the senses is *this object, hoc aliquid,* a material thing determined by certain particularizing notes, this much quantity, such and such qualities,

[31] 'Illud quod primo intellectus concipit quasi notissimum, et in quod omnes conceptiones resolvit, est ens. Verum et ens differunt ratione per hoc quod aliquid est in ratione veri quod non est in ratione entis; non autem ita quod aliquid sit in ratione entis quod non sit in ratione veri'. ST. THOMAS, Quaest. disp. *De veritate,* art. 1. Cp. *Gen. Metaphysics,* 63 f.

situated in such a place, existing at such a particular moment; in short, it is *hoc aliquid, hic et nunc*; and thus determined, it is called *concrete* (cum-crescere). Such a concrete thing stands distinct from all others; it is made singular by these very notes that particularize it. Considered as singular and a whole, a unit, such a being is called an *individual*. The object of sense is then a *particular, concrete, singular individual*. In contrast to this is the object of the intellect: it is the same object as the senses perceive or imagine, but it is represented without reference to any particularizing notes; in thought it is considered *apart* from this quantity, these qualities, this place, this particular time; all its material, spatial, and temporal determinations are prescinded from, and it is regarded in the *abstract—abstracta ab hoc, hic, nunc*. Such an abstract object, as we shall see, can be, and naturally is, *universal*, that is to say, it is applicable to an indefinite number of individual subjects.

It is frequently said that the proper object of the intellect is the 'essence' or 'nature' of material things. Such expressions are not felicitous, as they might lead one to think that we have an immediate knowledge of the *specific essences* of things. Yet who, pray, has been able to know the essence of horse, of oak-tree, of gold, of lead? To a full idea of a *species* the mind must proceed from some less determined, and therefore simpler, notions of *genera* and even of accidents. In order to avoid such a misunderstanding and to imply that the mind's notions of things are at first only the most simple and general, it is better to adopt two Scholastic words and call the object of the intellect the *quiddity* or *inner reason* of a thing. The word *quiddity* signifies in a very general way *what-a-thing-is*; it expresses more or less definitely the *quid* or whatness of a thing; it answers the question: 'What *sort of a being* is this? quid est?' The word *reason* is seldom used in English in this particular sense; in Latin *ratio*—literally *an account*—may stand indefinitely for all those distinctive characteristics which together constitute the formality of a being; if we avail ourselves of an English translation it should then mean the *reason why* any given being is such a being; and as this reason which makes a being specifically different from others is not in any superficial perceptible peculiarities but is in some internal radical principle, we add the epithet inner, intimate, or intrinsic, to remind us that the object the intellect contemplates is something quite different from the external phenomena which constitute the objects of sense-perception.

After these explanations the thesis resolves itself as follows :—

Part I : *The intellect draws its immediate object from the things of sense* and not from essences that exist apart from matter, nor from the spiritual substance of the soul, nor from an intuition of the Divine Being, as the Platonic, the Cartesian, the ontologistic or pantheistic schools have respectively taught.

Part II : *The object of the intellect is abstract*, and is precisely on this account superior to the object of sense-perception and, consequently, can in no way be identified with it, as the sensationalist and positivist schools in general maintain.

90 (i.) The intellect draws its Proper Object from Sensible Things.—Proofs. 1. *Argument drawn from external observation.* —The exercise of our intellect is closely connected with the anatomical and physiological conditions of our nervous system. Thus a lesion of the brain suspends or hinders thought ; a slight increase in the temperature of the blood causes delirium, intense cold renders any mental work impossible ; the action of certain poisons, such as alcohol, morphia and opium, either stimulates or paralyzes the working of the mind.

Now this dependence admits of only two possible explanations : either thought is itself a function of the nervous system, or else it requires the concurrence of another activity which is a function of the nervous system. The first explanation is ruled out by a set of facts that will have to be mentioned in connexion with the second part of the thesis. Hence the second explanation alone remains as the true one : thought is dependent upon the proper functioning of the nervous system, for the reason that it is dependent upon the exercise of the external and internal senses and these have the nervous system as their organs. Pursuing the argument we find that this dependence consists in nothing more than in this, that the object of thought must have been previously perceived by one or other of the external or internal senses. Hence the object of intellectual knowledge is derived from sense-data.

2. *Argument drawn from internal experience or consciousness.* —In support of our thesis consciousness declares the two following incontestable facts :—(*i.*) *Thinking requires the presence of images,* not sometimes merely, but normally, and indeed

always. Aristotle states this by saying that we never have a mental conception that is not accompanied by a 'phantasm', or picture in the imagination. Whenever a thought springs up in the mind, an image simultaneously appears in the imagination, and as long as the thought lasts, so long does the image. Sometimes this image is a sensuous representation of the object of nature; sometimes a geometrical figure or an arithmetical or algebraical symbol; sometimes simply a conventional sign, such as the words of speech. Whatever this image may be, it is so closely bound up with the accompanying concept that it is only by a conscious effort we can distinguish the one from the other; and those who do not make this attempt, such as the materialists, are constantly confusing intellectual thought and the accompanying sensuous image. (*ii.*) *Communication of thought requires the presence of images.*—First of all no simple idea can be transmitted without the use of some sensible medium. Secondly, it is a well-known device in leading any one through a chain of reasoning to insinuate the arguments in a dress that will appeal to the imagination; and, similarly, visual representation is invaluable as a method of instruction.—These two facts attested by consciousness together make up the major of our argument. The minor is as follows: were the object of thought spiritual or in some way supersensible, not only would the mind not require images either for its own operations or for awakening ideas in other minds, but the presence of sense-images on such a supposition would be rather of the nature of a hindrance than a help. We conclude that the proper object of the intelligence has, then, to be something that is perceived or imagined, in a word a sense-object.

An analysis of the content of thought confirms and completes the above declarations of consciousness. Some of our thoughts are of immaterial beings, e.g. of the soul, of God. Now as we have said just above, whatever is positive in the content of these and similar ideas is derived by negation or analogy from the material things we know directly through the senses; we cannot draw directly from such realities an immediate concept that will positively represent to us the qualities by which they are superior to material beings. We have, then, a class of ideas —of the immaterial, the spiritual, the infinite and so on—of which the connotation does not exceed either a negation of the imperfections belonging to material things or a comparison with these material things. This fact confirms the above declaration that the human intellect cannot contemplate immaterial beings directly; that its connatural object is not immaterial but material, sensible realities.

3. *Explanatory argument drawn from the natural character of the union of soul with body.*—The peculiar way in which the soul is united to the body gives us the intrinsic and fundamental reason why the object of the intellect *should be* some object in the first instance perceived through the senses. For, the union of the soul with the body, being natural—witness the instinctive horror of death—it must also be expected that the soul should find in the body a helpmate for the exercise of its faculties, since were it self-sufficient, the body would be a useless burden to it; but, for reasons which will be clear later, the body cannot play an *intrinsic* part either in the act of the intellect or in that of the rational will; the aid therefore which it supplies to the soul must be some *extrinsic co-operation.* And the only way in which it can supply this co-operation according to its nature is by the organic sense-faculties furnishing the materials on which the spiritual faculties may act; in other words, the mind has its proper object in the data with which the senses and the imagination furnish it.

91. (ii.) The Object of the Intellect is Abstract.—Every object perceived by the senses or reproduced by the imagination is invested with certain particularizing notes characteristic of concrete things which exist here or there, at this or that moment, *hoc, hic, nunc,* etc. Now our consciousness declares that besides these cognitions we have another equally large class in which the object is without any of these particularizing notes and which on this account are rightly called *abstract.* This proves that we have a faculty whereby we apprehend the quiddity, or abstract reason, of things; a faculty that we call the *intellect,* having a proper object that is distinguished by being abstract.

In demonstrating the minor of this argument, that we really possess such abstract cognitions, we shall discover that there are three successive degrees of abstraction.

(i.) If I take a walk into a forest I find thousands of trees, say of oak-trees, and on each of them thousands of leaves of which no two are exactly similar: they are different in colour, in shape, in the number and arrangement of their veins, as well as different in the places in which they are, on different oaks, in different parts of the forest, and moreover they differ in point of time from others exactly similar that will come after them. Nevertheless if I wish to compare the leaf of the oak with that of the willow I take no notice of any of these details which I perceive make the separate oak leaves different from one another ; I think only of what they have in common, of what it is that makes the oak leaf an oak leaf. The result of this act of thought is my concept *of what the leaf of the oak tree is*, and the object of that concept is *abstract*, *quod quid est*, the *ratio rei*, namely, the 'whatness' of the oak leaf or that which forms my definition of it. Such a concept as this of oak leaf stripped of its particularizing determinations is the result of a *physical abstraction.*

(ii.) I can see before me, or I can imagine, this triangle, formed of three white strips of wood, lying on the palm of my hand at this particular moment. At the same time I am aware of what 'triangle' means, triangle apart from all the determinations of sensible matter, of place and time ; I am aware of the abstract notion contained in the definition of geometry, that a triangle is a figure with three sides and three angles. This concept of triangle, besides taking no account of individualizing traits, neglects even the sensible qualities of my sense-picture and retains only what is sufficient to represent triangle to the intellect. This is the work of a *mathematical abstraction.*

(iii.) By a third effort of mind we can penetrate further still and arrive at what are called *metaphysical* notions. By mentally stripping a thing of its individual characteristics and by ignoring also its figure and quantity, that is to say, by taking from a thing every quality that will place it in any particular category of being, we get down to *this something hoc aliquid*, to its substance. The substance of things is the object which the intellect apprehends in a confused way when it first comes in contact with any reality, and it is the final resultant with which it is left when it has finished a full analysis of the content of its thought.

It is clear, then, that we have a class of cognitions the object of which possesses characteristics quite opposite to those of sensitive knowledge. And hence the axiom which sums up the first part of the thesis, 'Nihil est in intellectu quod non prius fuerit in sensu,' receives its completion by the addition: ' sed alio modo est in sensu, alio autem modo est in intellectu '.

92. Universality and other Properties of the Abstract Idea.—The concept of the mind is, as we have seen, always naturally accompanied with the presence of some image; hence it is that when the mind takes thought of an idea of abstract type, it naturally and immediately refers it to a concrete subject—the idea ' oak leaf ' is identified with a particular oak leaf, ' triangle ' with this plane or spherical, equilateral, isosceles or scalene triangle, the idea ' thing ' with this or that actual or possible particular thing. There may be found many pictures in the imagination to correspond to the same abstract type; in fact our reason tells us that the same type may be applied to an *indefinite* number of particular subjects—' oak leaf ' is identifiable with any oak leaf whatever, when or where it may be; just as ' triangle ' is with every triangle, and ' substance ' alike with everything. This applicability of an abstract object to any concrete subject constitutes its *universality*; but it is clearly a universality that is *potential* rather than actual.

The abstract ideal type is therefore universal in this sense, that it is applicable to an unlimited number of individual subjects independently of when or where they exist or are imagined to exist. Being thus *independent of time and space*, ideas are in one sense, then, ' immense ' and ' eternal '. But it must be carefully noticed that this twofold independence is in no way the same as that universality in space called ubiquity—which is immensity in the strict sense—nor with that eternity which is co-existent with all time. If these epithets are used of abstract ideas it is not because they exist everywhere and always, but because when they are thought of it is without any relation to place and time.

Lastly, the abstract type is also often said to be ' *necessary* '. Once again this quality of necessity is not an absolute one; it does not imply that the abstract object must exist either in reality or even in thought. But it means that, supposing an abstract type to exist in the mind, it becomes the original exemplar by which we identify all objects which belong to the type, which objects cannot be otherwise than they are: the type is *necessarily* what it is and could not possibly be other than it is. Hence this necessity is only a *hypothetical necessity of relations*, a necessity which is inherent in the hypothesis of type-fellowship.

Inattention to the above qualifications of the properties of abstract ideas misled the ontologists into attempting to identify the universality, necessity, and eternity of 'ideas' or 'intelligible essences' with the attributes of God.

93. Answers to Certain Objections.—*First objection :* The power of abstraction we have been claiming for the intellect is objected to by Berkeley as unreal. 'I can consider the hand, the eye, the nose, each by itself abstracted or separately from the rest of the body. But then whatever hand or eye I imagine, it must have some particular shape and colour. Likewise the idea of man that I frame to myself must be either a white, or a black, or a tawny, or a straight, or a crooked, a tall, or a low, or a middle-sized man'[32].

It may first of all be remarked that there can be no question of imagining an abstract object, for such a feat is obviously impossible. Consequently where Berkeley makes a mistake is in his failure to distinguish the difference between considering things *separately* (separatim considerare) and considering them as being *separate* (considerare separata). Without judging them to be really separated, the mind considers separately certain aspects of a thing which are necessarily united both in reality and in our sense-representations[33]. In thinking of 'man' it conceives an idea that is truly of a type which as it is realized is white or black or tawny, tall or short or of middle-height, but the idea of man represents neither colour nor stature but only human nature. Thus I can conceive a man who is capable of being *indifferently* black or white or yellow or red. Now this is surely because, precisely as I conceive him, he is not white, or he could not also be black; nor is he black, or he could not also be white, etc. In my concept therefore he is considered apart from whiteness or blackness or any other colour.

Second objection : According to the Sensist School there is no such distinction as that of the image and the concept, for the image can be equally universal with the concept.

[32] BERKELEY, *Principles of Human Knowledge*, Introduction, p. 142.

[33] 'Ea quae sunt in sensibilibus abstrahit intellectus, non quidem intelligens ea esse separata, sed separatim vel seorsum ea intelligens'. ST. THOMAS, *De anima*, III, lect. 12.

It is true that at first sight certain images do appear to be universal; but in reality such images are only *confused* or an *uninterrupted succession of fleeting images*;—just as light-stimuli rapidly repeated at short intervals produce the sensation of a continuous luminous line, so a rapid succession of images produces the resultant of apparently one conscious state, a single persistent image. Secondly, if attention be paid to but one feature of these images at a time it will clearly be seen to be definite and concrete and not capable of being applied to many subjects. Lastly, a comparison between the image and the concept shows up the distinction: the *image* is more confused in proportion as it is applicable to a larger number of particular things, whereas the reverse is the case with the idea, which becomes increasingly more clear and distinct [34].

Third objection: Some empirical psychologists attach great importance to generic images or 'composite portraits' obtained by photography. Francis Galton (1822–1911) for instance, by a process of superpositions, ascertains the features of a number of people belonging to the same family or afflicted with the same disease (e.g. tuberculosis), until at length he reaches the 'type' of the family or of victims to tuberculosis. This is compared, as a *material* realization, to the mental process of abstraction. In the essential point this comparison breaks down: this supposed 'portrait-type' is the portrait of a particular person who may perhaps resemble several others but whose own features are certainly determinate and fixed. In most cases such an image is extremely vague and confused.

After investigating the object of thought and discovering the characteristics of the concept we have now to ask ourselves

[34] The difference between an image and an idea is well expressed by Taine: 'We find a wide gulf between the vague and shifting image which the name suggests, and the precise and fixed extract which the name denotes.—The reader may convince himself of this by considering the word myriagon and its meaning. A myriagon is a polygon with ten thousand sides. It is impossible to imagine such a thing even when definite and special, much less when general and abstract. However lucid and comprehensive may be the mind's view; after five or six, twenty or thirty lines drawn out with great difficulty, the image becomes confused and indistinct; and yet my conception of a myriagon has nothing confused or indistinct about it. What I conceive, is not a myriagon like this, incomplete and tumbling to pieces, but a complete myriagon all whose parts co-exist simultaneously; I can hardly imagine the first, but can readily conceive the second. What I conceive, then, differs from what I imagine; and my conception is not the same thing as the shifting figure that accompanies it'. TAINE, *On Intelligence*, trs. Haye, London, 1871, I, p. 9.

concerning the immediate cause of the conceptual object. What is the *origin of concepts*? How do we come to think them? 'Quomodo fit ipsum intelligere?'

§ 2. *Genesis of Intellectual Ideas*

94. General Sketch of Aristotelian and Thomistic Ideogeny. —At the root of the problem of the origin of ideas lies the fact that the formal object of intellectual knowledge is different from that of sense-knowledge. The question is to account for this supersensuous object. Has it an existence outside of and independent of the intellect? and if so, Has the intellect been confronted with these ready-made notions from the beginning? Plato answered both these questions in the affirmative. Not so his disciple, Aristotle, who professed the theory that in the beginning the state of the mind may be compared to an uninscribed tablet—'tabula rasa in qua nihil scriptum'. By his intellect man is *capable* of knowing, but the faculty itself does not provide him with knowledge; potentiality precedes actuality; in itself it is *intellectus possibilis*, signifying that there must be the power of knowledge before there is actual knowledge. Secondly, this power is 'passive' or 'receptive' and is not sufficient by itself to determine itself to act. To be brought into exercise it requires some sort of completion, which has been called by Aristotle and the Scholastics 'species intelligibilis' or, as we had better translate it again, a *cognitional—intellectual, conceptual—determinant* because it has to produce in the faculty a modification or determination which makes an intellectual act immediately possible. These two considerations of Aristotle give us our first proposition: that the intellect *acquires* its ideas.

The determinant that evokes conception must necessarily come from without, since no faculty or power can of itself come into act. We know moreover that our sensuous experience plays at least some part in the production of ideas (**90**): yet it cannot be the sole cause, for sensible objects can only act upon material organs and the intellect has no such organ or else its cognitions would be material and in no way superior to concrete perceptions. There must be, then, some *immaterial* efficient cause acting in concert with the senses. This *principal* efficient cause of the intellectual determinant required to account for the actuation of the intellect is called in Scholastic language the active intellect, *intellectus agens*. As operative under the superior control of this active faculty the imagination is an *instrumental* efficient cause [85]. This combined action of the active intellect and the senses is adequate to move the understanding to an act of intellection; consequently as soon as it is determined by their conjoint action, it cannot but respond by an act of intellection, it begins to know, and to know the quiddity of a thing, what-it-is in the abstract apart from its particular concrete qualifications. Lastly, it must be noticed that any object falling within the range of sensuous experience is capable, under the action of the *intellectus agens*, of moving the understanding to an act of intellectual knowledge, and hence the cognitive intellect is capable of receiving every possible form of knowledge—'intellectus possibilis potens omnia fieri'.

This theory adopted by Aquinas of the origin of intellectual ideas, now but briefly outlined, may be formulated for the convenience of demonstration in the four following propositions:—

First proposition: The understanding, or cognitive intellect, is a passive faculty—potential intelligence—which requires for its actuation, or act of intellection, to be determined by some thing extrinsic to itself.

Second proposition: The power of understanding is determined to intellection by a double efficient cause, namely, the imagination and an immaterial, abstractive force called the active intellect.

Third proposition: As soon as the intellective power is presented with a conceptual determinant effected by the double cause, it is immediately actuated to know and expresses to itself what-a-thing-is.

Fourth proposition: The intellect knows first and directly the quiddities of sensible things, and itself only through reflection.

95. The Chief Historical Theories of Knowledge.—The Scholastic theory of the origin of ideas holds a position exactly

[85] 'In receptione qua intellectus possibilis species rerum accipit a phantasmatibus, phantasmata se habent ut agens instrumentale et secundarium, intellectus vero agens, principale et primum. Et ideo actionis effectus relinquitur in intellectu possibili secundum conditionem utriusque: intellectus possibilis recipit formas ut intellegibiles ex virtute intellectus agentis, sed ut similitudines determinatarum rerum ex cognitione phantasmatum.' St. Thomas, *De verit.*, q. 10, art. 6, ad 7.

midway between the two erroneous extremes of *sensism* on the one hand and an *exaggerated spiritualism* on the other.

Sensism, sensualism or *sensationalism*, is the very general theory that thought has not an object different from that of sentience and that accordingly sense-experience is quite adequate alone to account for all our so-called intellectual knowledge. It is also called *empiricism*, and counts the three following phases of its development in modern philosophy :—

1. *Sensationalism* has had its most prominent advocates in Locke and Condillac. It denies the existence of a radical distinction between the concept and the sense-image; if they differ at all it is not by a difference of nature but of degree, and thus the image is not simply a subordinate cause of the intellectual idea but the principal cause of its production: that is to say, the concept is only another form—a more or less complex transformation—of a sensation. To this system is allied the Psychology of Association—or *associationism* which puts forward the factor of association to account for this transformation of sensations[36].

2. Sensationalism pushed to its ultimate conclusions has become *materialism*, which is a denial on principle of the existence of anything that is not purely and simply material.

3. *Positivism* is less direct than materialism in its denials, but it professes a complete ignorance of whatever is supersensuous, and on this account has justly earned for itself the additional name of *agnosticism*. Its fundamental tenet is that observation and experiment can never penetrate beyond phenomena—hence termed phenomenalism—or facts that are either simultaneous or successive, and that those realities which metaphysics demands beyond these facts—such as substance, cause, spirit, necessary Being—the mind not only does not know but is quite incapable of knowing.

A destructive criticism of these systems is to be found in the fundamental thesis dealing with the proper object of intellectual knowledge (Part II of the thesis, **91**) and in the second part of the above Proposition II yet to be proved (**101**), which declares the necessity of an immaterial efficient cause to

[36] Its chief representative is J. Stuart Mill. A slightly different aspect of the same theory is that of recent *nominalism*, which makes all knowledge to be concrete and allows universality not to any content of the mind but to the names of things alone.—Trs.

explain the actuation of our spiritual faculty, the intellect.

The doctrines of the other extreme, *exaggerated spiritualism*, maintain that the object of thought is something that is directly and of itself knowable by the intellect and that our knowledge of it is not dependent upon experience. It is also called *idealism* and sometimes, though in a special sense of the word, *rationalism*. Its chief forms are represented by *Platonic idealism*, *ontologism*, Descartes' theory of innate ideas or *innatism*, and *traditionalism*. All these theories, which unduly emphasize or take into account only the spiritual element in thought, are opposed by Part I of our fundamental thesis concerning the proper object of intellectual cognition. We shall deal with them separately after establishing Proposition I which is directed against them collectively.

96. First Proposition : Intelligence is a Passive Faculty.— The child who has not yet learnt the elements of arithmetic has the *power* or faculty of understanding some day the relation of equality contained in the proposition '$7+5=12$'. The master who teaches the child, at the moment of teaching him, has an *actual cognition* of this intellectual truth. When the lesson is finished both master and pupil may occupy themselves with other thoughts, but they remain *informed* of this arithmetical truth, with the result that they can think of it again at will.

This example of a class of facts proves our proposition inasmuch as it shows that there are three stages in our understanding—the *radical capacity* or simple power, the *actual intellection* or the act of understanding, and lastly the permanent possession or *habit* of the knowledge. In order to pass from the state of mere capacity to that of actual intellection, the faculty clearly has need of some further determination, which in the case of an already-informed man is to be found in his habitual knowledge. Hence, whilst the intellect is a principle of action, it is one that stands in need of an intrinsic complement for it to be able to exercise its action, that is, it is a *passive power*.

This modification or complementary determination which the intellect requires before it can know, was called in the language of the Schoolmen the *form* (i.e. the determining element: cp. our word 'to *inform* some one') or *species intelligibilis*. In present-day philosophical language it is sometimes called the habitual idea. A more expressive phrase we have ventured to suggest is *intellectual,* or *conceptual, determinant.*

An indirect proof of this first proposition is furnished by the rejection of the opposite theories—Platonic idealism, ontologism, innatism—which are founded on the principle that the thinking mind, or rather the mind capable of thought, either by virtue of its nature or by reason of certain innate forms, is always actuated, always actually thinking.

97. Criticism of Platonic Idealism.—According to Plato what the human mind contemplates as 'ideas' are in reality the pure essences of things, what in things is one, eternal and absolute. Further, he conceives these ideas as having a real existence apart from things, so that the object of the intellect consists in real universals. The way in which our present knowledge of them is accounted for is by the supposition of a pre-natal existence during which the soul was in contact with them, and that in the present existence the person from his birth has retained remembrances of them: thus are they rightly termed innate ideas.

Plato lays undue emphasis upon the features of universality, eternity and immutability presented by our abstract concepts; and since he finds them in evident contradiction to sensuous perception where everything is variable and fleeting, asserts that the only explanation lies in the supposition of a real world of ideas where they exist as universals independent of and prior to our experience of them. He never realized that these universal concepts that are independent of time and space are first *abstracted* from the data of experience and subsequently attributed by acts of reflection to the particular subjects in which they are verified.

98. Criticism of Ontologism.—The ontologists (Malebranche, Gioberti, Ubaghs, etc.) taught that the first act of the intellect is an intuition of God and the first object of that act is God and His divine ideas. This theory owes its origin and its success to an erroneous interpretation of the two following facts:—(*a*) The essences of material things, owing to our abstract manner of apprehending them, may be referred to an indefinite number of individuals, and on this account may become *universals*; and, universal essences form the basis of propositions that, in a sense that is legitimate but needing explanation, are *necessary* and *eternal.* (*b*) Our knowledge penetrates beyond finite things at least some little distance into the regions of the Infinite. The only way the ontologists could account for these two facts—(*a*) the marks of universality, necessity and eternity of the essences of things and of their relations, and (*b*) the presence in us of the idea of the Infinite—was in the supposition that God Himself, the Necessary, the Eternal and the Infinite, is the immediate term and proper object of the human understanding.

1. The fundamental tenet of this theory is clearly belied by many psychological facts : for instance, (*a*) were the knowledge we have of God immediately derived from Him it would be a positive and proper knowledge, whereas our present ideas of Him are all either negative or analogical. (*b*) All our intellectual cognition is dependent, as we have seen, upon the senses ; yet if our intellect has what is supersensible and absolute for its direct and immediate object, how has such a dependence any explanation ?

2. The theory stands also condemned by some of the consequences that may be deduced from it. For, if we enjoyed an intuition of the Divine Essence, (*a*) we should necessarily be in possession of our highest good and complete happiness ; (*b*) there would be no error possible about God, and (*c*) there would be no doubts about His existence and His attributes.

3. It remains then to give the correct interpretation of the two facts which led the ontologists to make their paradoxical statement that we have an intuition of the Deity. (*a*) In regard to the *first fact* they argue that what is contingent, individual, variable and transitory, cannot give rise to what is characteristically necessary, universal, immutable and eternal. But there is an alternate interpretation we have already expounded (**92**) : when the exact signification of these peculiar attributes of our concepts is gauged, it becomes apparent that they cannot be identified with the Divine attributes, and that they are quite adequately explained by the *abstract* character of the manner of our concept-formation. (*b*) In regard to the *second fact,* they argue that the idea of the finite, inasmuch as it is a negative idea formed by way of limitation of the infinite, is necessarily posterior to the idea of the infinite. Yet psychologically the reverse is the truth : our idea of the finite is a positive idea and it is that of the infinite that is negative. The idea of *finite* or limited is that of so much ex-

tension or of such perfection with, in addition, the negation of further extension or perfection; its conception does not necessarily entail a comparison with an *infinite* quantity or perfection, but only with a *greater* quantity or perfection. It is only after abstracting from limited realities the notion of limitation in general that the mind comes to conceive of a being without quantity and of limitless perfection, the infinite.

99. Criticism of Descartes' Ideology.—Descartes lays down that the essence of the soul is *thought*, which is to know the *self* in us, and to find therein the type of all other intelligible reality. Hence for him the first and natural object of the human understanding is the ego.

Instead of regarding the intellect as a faculty of the soul capable of being impressed by external things, Descartes takes it to be an essentially active substance that can excogitate from itself the notion of ego, of the spiritual, of God and of external sensible things. He failed to perceive that the power of thinking is also a *passive* faculty. It is true that during the moments of its conscious activity the mind has an apperception of the fact of its own existence. But between this awareness of its own existence and the intellectual ideas of what the mind is, of what bodies are, of what God is, there is a very great difference indeed: for this wealth of ideas the intellect is indebted to efficient causes, to whose action it is essentially passive.

Whilst the mind, then, is not *by its nature* in a state of activity, may it not nevertheless become so through the medium of certain accidental forms with which it has been endowed from its first beginning by the Creator?

100. Criticism of Innate Ideas.—Urged like the ontologists (98) by the consideration of the peculiar necessity, universality and eternity of ideas and the opposition these notes present to the contingent, concrete, definite character of the object of sensuous cognition, the supporters of the theory of Innate Ideas sought to explain the origin of our ideas by certain 'innate' forms in the mind that have been placed there from the beginning by the Creator. This theory is at variance with the data of consciousness and with itself.

1. It is quite beyond doubt that no one has had his mind stocked from the dawn of his existence with ready-made ideas. On the contrary, it is a well-attested fact of internal experience

that the first state of the human mind is one of pure potentiality, different even from that of habitual knowledge (96), and this fact is irreconcilable with the existence of inborn ideas.

2. The theory is illogical. If we have innate ideas they are presumably for us to make use of in knowing external things. Yet the application of such an idea to an external thing, the discovery that it is realized in it, can only be an act of recognition and if we can re-cognize the idea in the object why can we not cognize it there straightway? As we have seen we can and do cognize our ideas by the process of abstraction.

We have so far proved that the act of thought presupposes some modification of the intellect, some determination of it to the act of intellection by a *species intelligibilis*. Our second proposition is concerned with how this determinant is itself formed.

101. Second Proposition: The Imagination and the Active Intellect produce, as a Prerequisite of Intellection, a Conceptual Determinant of the Understanding.—The imagination is incapable by itself of producing an object in the strict sense intelligible, for the object of the intellect is of a higher type than that of the senses. Moreover the intellect itself is not self-sufficient here, for at first it is nothing more than the possibility of knowledge, it is the mere power of knowing; it cannot therefore determine itself nor produce its own object of knowledge. It is necessary, then, to postulate besides the understanding, or cognitive intellect, a supersensible cause to account for the object of apprehension: a cause that must be intrinsically capable of acting of itself. Further, regarding this active cause we can say this: that as the superiority of the object of thought over that of the senses consists precisely in its being universal, abstract and immaterial instead of individual, concrete and material, the cause which is required to supervene upon the action of the sense-imagination must be a force of abstraction which disengages the object from all individualizing conditions [37]. Such is our definition of the *active intellect*. It remains only to determine the manner of

[37] Fr. Maher (*Psychology*, p. 308), though differing slightly in his account of the part played by the imagination, gives the following definitions of the active intellect: A certain instinctive spiritual force or energy of the mind, which, acting spontaneously on the presentation of objects in the imagination, generates 'species intelligibiles' of them; *or*, 'an active faculty whereby the intellect modifies itself so as to represent in a spiritual or abstract manner what is concretely depicted in the phantasm'.—Trs.

the joint-action of the two causes, to ascertain the respective rôles of the imagination and of this spiritual faculty in the formation of the concept.

There is only one hypothesis which accounts for the combined action of these two factors and remains at the same time true to all the facts observed. It is that the external object as represented in the imagination (phantasma) is a real cause, though an *instrumental* one, whilst the active intellect is the *principal efficient* cause. To this hypothesis we are led from the consideration that whilst the object depicted in the imagination is concrete, it nevertheless contains beneath its individual determinations what later we shall find to be present in the abstract form in thought. St. Thomas with great profundity says: 'Callias is this man': that the person of Callias perceived by the senses is human nature individualized. When the senses perceive this individual Callias, they perceive in a material way all that is contained in human nature. The action of the immaterial faculty, then, supervenes and assimilates for itself the concrete reality whilst wholly ignoring the particularizing determinations attaching to it. The union of the action of this immaterial faculty with that of the imagination accounts for the formation of that *abstract* 'species intelligibilis' which determines the understanding to its act of intellection. Thus we see how this abstract immaterial determinant which is effected, in no way surpasses its cause, since the active intellect is immaterial; yet as an effect it is the faithful reproduction of the object, since the image which is thus at the service of the active intellect really co-operates in the production of the idea. In brief, the active intellect and the imagination together form a complex cause of the conceptual determinant we are seeking to explain, the one playing the part of principal efficient cause, the other that of a subordinate, instrumental cause.

102. An Objection and its Answer.—If the image furnished by the senses is material, as is indeed beyond question, how can it have any influence upon the understanding which is a spiritual faculty? And, moreover, whatsoever be the nature of the influence which you suppose the active intellect to exercise upon it, it must still remain material; so that an efficiency is surely being attributed to it which even in conjunction with the active intellect it does not possess.

The basis of the objection that no matter what modification the material image undergoes it yet will ever remain material, is of course quite true. Yet an *instrumental* cause, precisely as it is instrumental, possesses a power to act in a way which would be impossible to it if it acted independently of the principal cause: the chisel of Phidias carves a master-piece in the marble and therefore really co-operates in the production of that master-piece, although by itself it could not produce it nor any part of it. The action of an instrumental cause is real, although the instrument does not suffer any change in its nature at the hand of the one who employs it. So, whilst the active intellect does not change the nature of the image, it makes use of just that in it which is capable of being conceived in an abstract manner and by means of this produces in the understanding a conceptual representation of the type which in the image is particular and concrete.

103. Third Proposition: When determined to action the Intellect Apprehends What a thing is.—This proposition follows from the two preceding ones. The faculty of the understanding is at first passive, without the power of moving itself to action; once however it is determined in the manner described above, it has everything required for it to come into action: it *knows*, or expresses to itself in its peculiar, intellectual, mental way, an idea or what-an-object-is.

The first notion the mind expresses to itself thus under the combined influence of the imagination and active intellect is, however, only a representation of an abstract object: when and how does it become *universal*? St. Thomas with his usual penetration says that at this first, abstract stage the object of thought is neither individual nor universal[38], but is susceptible of becoming both the one and the other. It will become universal when the mind shall have *reflected* upon the abstract thought-product and when, seeing it stripped of all individualizing characters, it *finds it can represent* an indefinite number

[38] 'Ideo si quaeratur utrum ista natura (natura humana considerata modo absoluto ut abstracta) possit dici una vel plures, neutrum concedendum est, quia utrumque est extra intellectum humanitatis et utrumque potest sibi accidere. Si enim pluralitas esset de ratione ejus, nunquam posset esse una, quum tamen una sit secundum quod est in Socrate. Similiter si unitas esset de intellectu et ratione ejus, tunc esset una et eadem natura Socratis et Platonis, nec posset in pluribus plurificari'.—*De ente et essentia*, IV.

of individual subjects, that it is applicable to each of them inasmuch as it verifies what is common to them all.

104. Fourth Proposition : The Intellect knows its Determinant indirectly and, through it, its own Nature.—The first object the intellect apprehends is what something is. It is clear from consciousness that the mind apperceives its own act of knowing only subsequently to the object presented to it in that act. 'Alius est actus quo intelligo lapidem, alius est actus quo intelligo me intelligere lapidem', says St. Thomas.

The reason for this fact is apparent :—An act alone is knowable ; a power can only be known through its activity. Now the faculty of intellection is essentially a potentiality. It needs therefore to be set in action before it can itself become an object of knowledge.

An importance attaches to this proposition inasmuch as it is in direct opposition to contemporary idealism and more especially to the idealism of Descartes which would make the ego to be the primary object of intelligence. Careful introspection reveals that what is first present to the mind in thought is some *object of experience,* only afterwards the apperception of self as the thinking subject.[39]

A corollary : The active intellect and the understanding are really distinct faculties. They are different for the reason that their acts are specifically different. The active intellect is an efficient cause which produces the intellectual determinant (the 'species intelligibilis') required for the act of cognition ; the understanding is a faculty which when duly determined accomplishes the act of knowledge. To produce an intelligible form and to receive it, differing as they do as 'action and passion', are two irreducible processes, and therefore the faculties which respectively act as principle in the production of this form and as subject of its reception must be two really distinct faculties [40].

[39] The word *ego* is a word open to abuse. It is employed sometimes with a restricted meaning, as here by Descartes, to signify what is opposed to *extra-mental.* If so used the organism, which can be handled and form the content of an idea, is then contrasted with the *ego*—though in reality part of the person—and is an *object of experience.* In **149** ego means body and soul, the one substance, and is opposed to every other substance, non-ego.—Trs.

[40] 'Necesse est igitur in anima intellectiva esse has differentias, ut scilicet unus sit intellectus, in quo possint omnia intelligibilia fieri, et hic est intel-

§ 3. *Process of Intellectual Development*

105. Object of this Section.—As yet we have only ascertained the nature and origin of our *first* intellectual cognitions. The *first* object that the intellect cognizes is the universal, abstract quiddities or *intrinsic reasons* of material things. Through the combined action of the imagination and the active intellect upon the passive intellectual faculty, the latter *acquires an habitual idea*; informed by this habitual idea or *species intelligibilis*, it is capable of expressing what the idea represents, and this mental expression is the formal *act of understanding* or intellection.

This first act, regarded *subjectively*, is an act of *simple apprehension* or mere *conception*, that is, it merely represents what a thing is, without affirming or denying anything about it: the resultant of this simple act is called the *concept* or *idea*. Regarded *objectively*, in the first instance it only conveys to the mind the very indeterminate note of *being*, of something existent or subsistent. In this initial stage of knowledge the mind first of all takes hold of the concrete *accidental qualities*, such as the colour, the resistance, etc., of a body, and it represents them as a *something subsisting*, something luminous, resisting, etc.—the something the child spontaneously denotes by its vague words 'this', 'that'.

Now that we have settled the question of the genesis of the simple concept, there arise the two following questions concerning the advanced stages of intellectual cognition, namely: (i) What is the *subjective* process of mental development? or, What are the different modes which the act of intellection naturally and progressively assumes (judgment, reasoning)? (ii) How does the mind proceed from *material* things, its first and proportionate object, to spiritual substances and to God, which it can know only in some indirect way?

The first question, which deals with all our rational operations from simple apprehension to the most complex train of reasoning and seeks to find how they are all related and developed from one another, forms the subject of formal logic, and reference should therefore be made to that treatise. We need concern ourselves here only with the second question.

lectus possibilis; et alius sit intellectus ad hoc quod possit omnia intelligibilia facere actu, qui vocatur agens'. *De anima*, III, 10.

106. Intellectual Development objectively considered.—1. Knowledge of Substances and Corporeal Essences.—The mind begins with a knowledge of corporeal things and expresses what they are. This it does first of all by apprehending the *qualities* of things in a vague way as a concrete, subsisting something. This first stage of our intellectual knowledge is entirely descriptive—a something coloured, offering resistance, of such a taste, etc. An advance is made when by *comparison* and *induction* we come to distinguish among the qualities of a thing those which are *necessary properties*, or accidents flowing from its substance, from those which are variable and purely contingent. In this way we gradually approach to a knowledge of that primary substantial basis of a thing which remains invariable throughout all the accidental changes to which it is incessantly subject, i.e. to a knowledge of what the thing ultimately is in itself and without which it would not be and could not be what it is, in a word, its *specific essence*. In brief, even material substances are not directly known in their *essence*, but only *mediately* through a knowledge of their qualities—and by way of *induction*.

107. 2. Knowledge of the Soul or of Self.—The essence of the human soul is not thought, as Descartes imagined, but its rôle of informing matter and constituting it one animated body (see **149** ff.). This body which it informs and animates, it also renders *capable* of experiencing sensations, as well as being itself *capable* of thinking and willing dependently on some external or internal sensible experience. At first the soul has only the capability of thinking; it requires to be modified, determined or informed by an intelligible impression or 'species' before it can make use of this power and put forth an *act* of thought.

Now a thing is knowable only as it is actual: 'ens actu et verum convertuntur'. Therefore the soul cannot know itself immediately, since of itself it is not capable of being known.

This conclusion is moreover supported by our conscious experience, which tells us that we have no direct knowledge of ourselves, that we know of our own *existence* only because we act and perceive ourselves acting, and that we know our *nature* only subsequently by an indirect and reflex knowledge.

(a) *The soul knows its own existence in its acts.*—It is a matter of fact that we are conscious of our existence precisely when we are acting; we are aware of ourselves as either engaged in experiencing some sensation, or in thinking or in willing. When we are not conscious of acting, as when in a deep sleep or a faint, we are entirely ignorant of our own existence [41]. Descartes' aphorism, 'Cogito, ergo sum', has, in this sense, a very true meaning.

(*b*) *The soul knows its own nature by reflection on its previous acts.*—(i) Did the soul know itself directly, it would have positive, proper concepts of its own spiritual, simple, incorruptible nature. But in point of fact its ideas of itself are negative and analogical. (ii) An immediate, connatural knowledge is certain and needs no demonstration—witness the knowledge of first principles, such as the principle of contradiction. But concerning the nature of the human soul doubts and errors prevail, not to say ignorance. Hence the human soul is not an object of which our mind has an immediate, connatural knowledge.

108. 3. Knowledge of God.—As we have already seen that God is not the direct object of the human mind (**98**) we have here to ask, By what indirect process do we come to know Him?

First of all we know His *existence* by reasoning to it, by way *of demonstration*: by applying the principle of causality to the existence of contingent things we prove there must be a Necessary Being. Next, to form an idea of God's *nature* or *essence* we have recourse to the triple process of *composition* or *synthesis*, of *negation* or *elimination*, and of *superelevation* or *transcendence*. (i) By the process of *synthesis* we attribute to God all the perfections we see variously realized in His works, on the ground that the Source of these perfections must possess them in Himself. (ii) We know however that in Him these perfections cannot be mixed with the imperfections inherent in created things nor be limited like the perfections of contingent beings; by the process of *negation* we therefore eliminate all imperfection or limit from the Divine perfections. (iii) But even when freed from all imperfections and limitations, created perfections contain nothing that does not attach to finite being and therefore they are not strictly

[41] 'In hoc enim aliquis percipit se animam habere, quod percipit se sentire et intelligere et alia hujusmodi vitae opera exercere'. ST. THOMAS, *De verit.*, q. 10, a. 8, c.

applicable to the Infinite Being. To elaborate a concept which may be exclusively applicable to God we must acknowledge that the created perfections, already stripped of all imperfection and limitation, still infinitely fall short of the Divine reality and therefore have to be predicated to an infinite degree if they are to be true of Him as He is in Himself. This last process of *transcendence* is the complement demanded by the two preceding ones.

II. Volition and the Will

This section falls into three divisions dealing respectively with necessary voluntary acts (§ 1) ; free acts (§ 2) ; emotions and sentiments, the attendants of voluntary acts (§ 3).

§ 1. *Necessary Voluntary Acts*

109. Introductory : The Good ; Will ; Kinds of Good.– The good is defined by Aristotle as ' id quod omnia appetunt , the object which all beings desire, to which they all tend. In common parlance we term *good* what is profitable to a being. As it happens that all beings whatsoever possess an inherent tendency towards what is to their profit, Aristotle's definition appears well grounded and accurate.

Although it is not quite evident at first sight that insensate beings are led towards what is good for them, there is no doubt that conscious beings are drawn towards things they desire and that they experience the desire for them ; for we know this in our own case, through our sensitive faculties, and there is no reason to suppose that animals have not similar desires through the attraction which sense-perceived objects present to them. In the case of animals, however, there is this difference, that the attractive good is the object of a desire arising from a *sense-perception* or *sense-estimation,* and is what is termed a *sensible good.* This sensible good is always a concrete thing : the animal perceives a certain good thing and goes after it. Not so is the usual and proper object of desire in the case of man. Whilst the animal is incapable of distinguishing in the thing perceived *that which precisely constitutes its goodness*, it is the characteristic of man who knows things in an abstract way to consider goodness thus abstractly, and consequently the desire engendered by this knowledge has for its proper object not the concrete good but *the good as such*, the abstract good or that by reason of which concrete things are desirable and worthy to be sought. Further, in the case of the human will, as it is natural to the intellect to generalize the resultant of its process of abstraction, above and beyond all particular goods it conceives an ideal good which shall comprise in itself all that is good in particular objects; and this ideal, the quintessence of finite goods, is commonly called the general good or the *universal good*. Hence the characteristic desire or will of man is an act that has the abstract, universal good as its formal object. *Rational will*, peculiar to man, may then be defined as the faculty which is the immediate principle of those acts by which man moves towards the abstract, universal good.

The good is rightly to be distinguished in various ways:—

1. An object towards which the will moves, because considered in itself it is good, is an *absolute* good. The will may also tend towards an object considered not as good in itself but as leading towards an ulterior good, and this is a relative good or *useful good, bonum utile*. The former, the absolute good, constitutes an *end* for the will, the latter a *means*.

2. Upon gaining possession of its desiderated end the will experiences a certain satisfaction and pleasure. This being so, it may happen that in seeking a good object the will is also seeking this pleasure it will enjoy in its attainment. There is ground here for the distinction of the *objective good*, the object itself, and the *agreeable good*, 'bonum delectabile', the subjective pleasure accruing upon its possession.

3. The objective good towards which the will inclines under the guidance of sound judgment is called by moralists the *upright good*, 'bonum honestum'[42].

110. The Will is a Principle of Necessary Acts.—We must first understand the exact meaning of this assertion before we can attempt to prove it. A being is denominated *necessary* when it is determined by its nature so to exist. Necessary is then in this sense synonymous with *natural*; it is what is demanded by the nature of the subject and so comes about

[42] 'In motu appetitus, id quod est appetibile terminans motum appetitus secundum quid, ut medium, per quod tenditur in aliud, vocatur utile. Id autem quod appetitur ut ultimum terminans totaliter motum appetitus, sicut quaedam res in quam per se appetitus tendit, vocatur honestum; quia honestum dicitur quod per se desideratur. Id autem quod terminat motum appetitus, ut quies in re desiderata, est delectabile'. *Sum. Theol.*, I, q. 5, a. 6, c.

in accordance with the being's fundamental inherent tendency. Thus understood, it is the opposite to what is *forced, constrained*, 'violent', what is wrought through some extrinsic agency and is against the natural tendency of a thing. Thus a stream flows naturally and *necessarily* towards the sea, yet man may force its waters backward towards its source. Both these ideas of necessary and constrained are included in that of *determined*, 'determinatum ad unum', and both alike are opposed to the idea of *liberty*, which signifies the absence of determination on the part of a will to one line of action. With this explanation of terms we may proceed to prove that the will is a principle of necessary acts.

Whenever any object is represented by the intellect as good, upon that representation the will *necessarily* becomes active. Do we not feel ourselves necessarily drawn to side with those who wish us well and to keep aloof from those who are ill-disposed towards us? Sincerity attracts; selfishness, dishonesty, infidelity repel: in a word, we are aware of necessary movements of the will that take place within us *spontaneously* and before there has been any reflection.

Further, there is another class of objects which make such an appeal to the will that *even after reflection* it cannot withstand their attraction. We each form to ourselves in a vague way an ideal that contains within it all desirable good; it is an ideal that we can please ourselves whether we think of or not, but if we do think of it we cannot but desire it. Similarly there are some good things which when considered as the elements or indispensable conditions of the universal good—existence, life, knowledge—never fail to move the will to desire them [43].

§ 2. *Free Acts*

111. Meaning of Free Action. Liberty is rooted in an Indetermination of the Judgment.—Whilst the will, as we have seen, acts of necessity when confronted with a universal

[43] 'Est quoddam bonum quod est propter se appetibile, sicut felicitas, quae habet rationem ultimi finis; et hujusmodi bono ex necessitate inhaeret voluntas: naturali enim quadam necessitate omnes appetunt esse felices . . . Si essent aliqua bona, quibus non existentibus non possit aliquis esse felix, haec etiam essent ex necessitate appetibilia et maxime apud eum qui talem ordinem perciperet: et forte talia sunt *esse, vivere* et *intelligere*, et si qua alia sunt similia'. ST. THOMAS, *In Periherm*. I, 14.

good, it also puts forth acts which are not necessary but free. The voluntary act, in a special sense of the word, is a necessary, determined act: what is judged good has an inevitable attraction for the will. The free act, on the other hand, is one that is not determined, one that even when all the conditions necessary for its production are present depends for its being willed or not willed upon the volitional faculty itself.

As it is a condition for an act of will that something be presented by the intellect as good—'nihil volitum nisi praecognitum'; 'voluntatem non allicit ad faciendum quodlibet', says St. Augustine, 'nisi aliquod visum'[44]—and as the will necessarily seeks what is presented as good, it clearly cannot be free unless the judgment is in some way free also. Hence we assert that the liberty of the free act is rooted in the judgment, is dependent upon a *freedom of judgment*[45]. The point to be determined is what exactly this means: how can our judgment be free when it is determined by evidence which necessarily excludes its contradictory?

In the speculative order it is true enough that evidence, either direct or indirect, compels assent. Thus the general proposition: 'A son must respect his father', necessarily imposes itself upon the reason and its objective value wrings from the will an inevitable consent. Yet any acts the will may be called upon to execute when this and similar dictates of the speculative order come to be interpreted as practical judgments, are all particular, concrete acts. The fact that I am the son, with my tendencies, my particular likes and dislikes, makes a great deal of difference to my judgment; the particular act which under these particular circumstances is demanded of me by way of honouring this my parent may appeal to me or may be very distasteful. In the abstract my reason certainly approves of parents being honoured, but to honour mine in a particular case may be inconvenient and may cost me much. From one point of view, then, it is good for me to do this thing and show my parent the deference

[44] *De libero arbitrio*, P. III, c. XXV, n. 74.

[45] 'Tota ratio libertatis ex modo cognitionis dependet. Appetitus enim cognitionem sequitur, cum appetitus non sit nisi boni, quod sibi per vim cognitivam proponitur. . . . Et ideo si judicium cognitivae virtutis non sit in potestate alicujus, sed sit aliunde determinatum, nec appetitus ejus erit in potestate ejus, et per consequens nec motus vel operatio absolute'. St. Thomas, *De verit.*, q. 22, art. 2.

due; from another it seems better to be more solicitous about my personal interests. Two contradictory practical judgments arise in my mind and I am aware that it rests with me which shall predominate, that I have the liberty of passing a final judgment, that I am free. We are not, however, now proving the freedom of the will but only indicating wherein that freedom lies.

It is the will, then, that ultimately makes the indetermination to cease or, as we may say, 'settles the mind' of the person. In brief, liberty has its root in the intelligence, but resides formally in the will.

112. Proofs of Free-will.—The proofs for the doctrine of free-will may be reduced to the following three:—

1. Introspective analysis of *consciousness* declares the ego to be free.

2. Certain *ethical and social considerations*, interpreted by the common opinion of mankind, corroborate the testimony of the individual consciousness.

3. The *metaphysical reason* of free-will lies in the fact that any particular concrete good is not presented to the will as the absolute, universal good and therefore the deliberating mind can at the same time pronounce it a motive and not a motive for volition.

113. Proof drawn from Consciousness.—It is a commonplace of my conscious life that I am master of myself to choose or to reject a proffered line of action that appears to me good; my deliberative faculty supplies me with motives both for acting and for abstaining from acting. I am aware on these frequent occasions that my will is solicited by these objective motives, yet not determined by them; that it is I who determine myself which way I shall act; in a word, that I am free. One example will suffice as an illustration: It is evident to me that I can bestow of my worldly substance upon the beggar at my door, or I can steel my heart; I can give my money to alleviate distress or to procure my own satisfaction; I can use it to purchase lawful pleasures, or, if I so please, abuse it by pandering to my vicious inclinations.

An objection is made by John Stuart Mill on the ground that 'a direct consciousness of the freedom of the will' is a 'figment' and the feeling of liberty is impossible. 'To be conscious of free-will, must mean, to be conscious, before I have decided, that I am able to decide either way. . . . Consciousness tells me what I do or feel. But what I am *able* to do is not a subject of consciousness' [46]. Indeed we may appear to have said something very similar ourselves when we laid down that only what is actual is knowable and that our powers become disclosed only in the acts they enable us to exercise; for, on this principle, the reputed free act is not knowable until it is actual and as soon as it becomes actual the faculty ceases to be indeterminate and therefore liberty ceases too; in a word, our liberty is unknowable.

Answer: It is true that once an act exists it is settled. It is true also that a power as such is unknowable. But between the power to do and the doing there is something real and knowable, namely the *actuation* of the faculty, the *becoming* of the free act. Let us turn for a moment to introspection: I am aware, on the one hand, of certain acts of will that I feel take place in spite of myself, that are due to and entirely determined by the objective motives which give rise to them. On the other hand, I am equally aware of an entirely different class of acts which I have a motive for willing but to the willing of which I am not at first irresistibly determined by that motive; it is only after a moment's delay that my mind is made up and that I act on the strength of it. In these acts there are two states, of hesitation and of decision, indetermination and determination. By comparing these two states I become conscious that upon the first inefficacious solicitation of the first moment something supervened, something was added, something coming from me, emanating from my will, that converted the desire into a decision, the mere solicitation into a real determination. What is this but the consciousness that the determination of my free-will is in the last resort the real work of my own will?

It must be noticed that the expression: 'When a man acts he is conscious that he is free not to act', does not mean that his power of not acting, as such, is a direct subject of consciousness. But it means: once a decision has been made, he becomes conscious that it is caused by his consent. He knows from other occasions that a motive soliciting his will and to which he refuses his consent, remains a mere solicitation and never becomes a determination. Far from it being

[46] J. Stuart Mill, *Examination of Hamilton's Philosophy*, 6th ed., p. 560.

impossible, it is very true that we have a clear testimony of consciousness that the will has complete control of its acts.

114. Proof corroborating the Argument from Consciousness.—Men in general *praise* those who act well, and they *blame* evil-doers; they offer one another *advice* and issue *commands* to be obeyed; and they live under a system of *laws* the enforcement of which public authority sanctions with *rewards and punishments.* These are so many facts. Their value, however, is not in themselves; for, it is not correct to say that the distinction between good and evil, the giving of advice, the existence of laws, of rewards and punishments, would be meaningless and absurd if the world were determinist [47]: these would still serve as so many objective motives to determine what would then be our spontaneous actions, somewhat in the same way as our coaxing and beating of animals really influences their activity. Their value is rather in the *significance* which men in general attach to them: such facts evidence the universal opinion of mankind that the agent of human acts, good and bad, praiseworthy and blameworthy, is a *responsible* agent and therefore that he is judged to act freely and with control of his own acts. The behaviour of men with their fellowmen shows that they all have the same consciousness of freedom and share the same belief in moral liberty.

115. Intrinsic Proof of Free-will.—To understand this proof there is required a careful knowledge of the antecedents of the act we are claiming as free. First of all, we must take it as a principle we have proved above that the proper object moving the will to action is the attraction the universal good has for it. This being granted, we must next notice the various acts of the cognitive and conative faculties that naturally precede the full voluntary act. The first prerequisite condition is knowledge: sensuous representation gives birth to ideas, among which are one or more objects capable of serving as motives for the will. *Simple representation,* first of all sensuous, afterwards intellectual, is succeeded by *spontaneous judgments* on the part of the sense-instinct or estimating faculty and of the reason proper concerning the goodness and badness of the objects represented. This rough estimation, putting a certain personal value upon the objects, provokes

[47] *Determinism* is the philosophical theory which denies freedom.

spontaneous movements of the lower and higher appetitive faculties so that an incipient yet real liking or disliking is taken for what is in question. These tendencies arouse *attention* and the mind begins to *reflect* upon the advantages and disadvantages of the objects as well as upon the favourable or unfavourable inclinations the different aspects of them produce in the will, and on these matters it forms a series of judgments which together make up the process we call *deliberation* (*librare*, to weigh), *consilium*. This deliberation does not go on for ever; an end is put to it as soon as the reflecting mind cuts short its self-imposed discussion by making a *decision* (*decidere*, to cut); and decision is immediately followed by a deliberate volition of the act decided upon.

A certain freedom is displayed by us first in the deliberation and the making of the decision, for it is irresistibly brought home to us by introspective consciousness that the course of the deliberation leading right up to the final decision is throughout directed and ultimately terminated by ourselves. Further than this, we have the conviction that the *will itself is free, formally*: for whilst the will's determination towards a particular object springs, like a plant from its root, from the freely-made decision, the act of the will, the supervening volition, we are aware, is neither forced upon us by any extrinsic cause nor necessitated in us by any intrinsic law of our being, but alike for its existence and persistence is due to the will itself. Now when we come to give the intrinsic reason of this apparent freedom of self-determination we are bound to conclude that the freedom is not apparent but real: the argument is as follows.

The proper formal object of the will, the presence of which moves it or necessitates it to volition, is the universal good or perfect happiness. But all the objects of experience, all the concrete objects the intellect can represent as attainable by us in this world are particular goods—*this* good and not *the* good. This being so, as the result of its process of reflection and comparison, the intellect can never assert that *this* good with its limitations and imperfections is identical with the ideal, the perfect good, *the* good; the most it can decide is that *this* particular good may be deliberately willed since it is *a* good and that it need not be willed inasmuch as it is not *the* good which alone, as true formal object of the will, necessitates volition [48]. This double judgment—disclosed by analysis as the real content of the act of intellectual decision—leaves the will determined to neither course, i.e. not bound either to tend towards this concrete good represented or not to tend towards it. In the event of an act of volition, the determining cause is not the object alone; the will alone can produce it; it is mistress of its action; it is a self-determining force; it is, in a word, really free.

116. Two Corollaries.—1. It follows from the above explanation that *every spontaneous desire can form the subject-matter for an act of free-will,* not excepting even the fullest happiness we can possess in the present life. For, whereas perfect happiness (which is *the* good necessitating volition and taking away its freedom) implies the possession of what satisfies all the aspirations of our nature and cannot be lost, all goods in the present life are not adequate to satisfy us completely and by their nature are contingent and liable to be lost, and therefore, even all taken together, they are not such as to compel the action of the will but only such as, on account of their desirableness, may serve as objects of its free exercise.

2. A second conclusion from the analysis we have just made is that free choice is always a *choice between means,* not between ends. A person must have some *end* fixed before he is free to choose the means to it. His end, as such, cannot be an object of his free choice; it may, however—and so may every other end but the last end—become matter for deliberation and ultimately be an object for volition, but then it will not be as an end but as a means to some other end. I may, for instance, have decided to go from London to Paris, and in this case, when the end is settled, I am free to choose the means, whether I will travel by Dover or Folkestone or any other route. But was I not free to choose to go to Paris?

[48] 'Si proponatur aliquod objectum voluntati quod sit universaliter bonum et secundum omnem considerationem, ex necessitate voluntas in illud tendet, si aliquid velit: non enim poterit velle oppositum. Si autem proponatur sibi aliquod objectum quod non secundum quamlibet considerationem sit bonum, non ex necessitate voluntas feretur in illud. Et quia defectus cujuscumque boni habet rationem non boni, ideo illud solum bonum quod est perfectum et cui nihil deficit, est tale bonum quod voluntas non potest non velle: quod est beatitudo. Alia autem quaelibet particularia bona, in quantum deficiunt ab aliquo bono, possunt accipi ut non bona; et secundum hanc considerationem, possunt repudiari vel approbari a voluntate, quae potest in idem ferri secundum diversas considerationes'. *Sum. Theol.*, I-II, q. 10, a. 2, c.

Certainly; but only in so far as it appeared a means to something else, because I had previously determined to go to the Riviera: and this end, my journey to the Riviera, was only chosen as a means of benefiting my health, and so on with every choice I make, each is an object of volition precisely inasmuch as it serves as a means to a predetermined end. Now it is clear that such a series cannot be indefinite or choice could never begin. Hence it has been necessary to lay down that all free-will is based on a spontaneous, necessary inclination of the faculty towards the good in general; this indefinite object supplies an ultimate end for the series of particular ends and thus explains how a free choice of means is possible. In accordance with this explanation is St. Thomas' definition of liberty; he calls it 'The faculty of choosing what leads to an end'[49]. Similar to this is the definition of Pope Leo in his encyclical *Libertas*: 'Liberty is the faculty of choosing means suited to the end proposed'[50].

117. Determinist Theories.—Determinism is the theory that the will is not free and that all our acts, even including those apparently free, are adequately and inevitably determined by their antecedents. According to the nature of the antecedents which are held to account for our actions is determinism to be variously denominated. *Mechanical* determinism is not distinguishable from fatalism; it makes the will a material force subject like everything else to inexorable mechanical laws. *Physiological* determinism likens even our noblest volitions to reflex action. Lastly *psychological* determinism is the theory that the will necessarily follows the strongest motive, or what is presented to it as the greatest good.

The first two determinist theories are sufficiently disproved by all that has already been said in support of the freedom of the will and they do not require to be specially reviewed here. Psychological determinism owing to the plausibility given to it by Leibniz calls for more particular attention. According to him the will is bound to seek the greatest good

[49] 'Facultas electiva eorum quae sunt ad finem'. *Sum. Theol.*, I, q. 62, a. 8.

[50] 'Libertas est facultas eligendi res, ad id quod propositum est, idoneas'. For a translation of this encyclical on 'Human Liberty' see *Pope and People*, Cath. Truth Society, London.

offered to it, since to conceive it as making a positive choice whilst indifferent, without being moved by the strongest motive, is to attempt to deny the principle of sufficient reason[61].

118. Refutation of Psychological Determinism.—To assert that the will is always dominated, consciously or unconsciously, by the prevailing motive is, if not tautological, an entirely gratuitous statement. It may happen, as indeed it does happen, that a choice has to be made between two good things that in themselves are absolutely equivalent. Who will doubt that between two glasses of water, between two sovereigns, between two roads of exactly the same length and leading to the same place, the will is objectively swayed in neither direction? In such circumstances, inability to choose would remind us of the ass in the proverb which died of starvation between its two pecks of oats. As the theory of Leibniz stands contradicted by facts, it remains only to consider his criticism that our theory is a contradiction of the principle of sufficient reason.

The value of Leibniz's criticism will best be gauged by an example. The two glasses of water we supposed as exactly similar and equally desirable in every respect are objectively equal motives. If I reach out my hand to the one on the left instead of the one on the right, the sole reason for my action, since it cannot be in any objective quality attaching to one and not to the other, must be my desire to act; I am actuated by my desire to act (to take a glass) which can be realized only on the condition of my making a choice and taking one. My choice, then, which is without an objective motive, has its sufficient reason in something subjective, in my own desire to exercise my will.

All difficulty will vanish as soon as it is remembered that the freedom of the will resides formally not in the selection between different goods (freedom of specification) but in the volition, or rather, the self-determination to move towards a good or not to move towards it (freedom of exercise). Determinists who bring forward the above objection make the mistake of asserting that when the will is presented with two

[61] The *principle of sufficient reason*, on which psychological determinism is grounded, is thus formulated by Leibniz: 'Nothing can be true or real for which there is not a sufficient reason of it being so'.

unequal motives it is compelled to choose the better; an assertion which is only partly true, as can be seen from the example of an artist who is offered the choice of two pictures of unequal value. The act of *preference*, as such, is undoubtedly not free, for it is physically impossible for the will not to prefer that good which the practical reason judges *hic et nunc* to be on the whole the better. Thus, if the deliberative faculty be concentrated upon the *relative* artistic value of the two pictures, the will cannot but prefer the one which is judged the better. Yet if attention is not paid to the superiority of one over the other, so that each is presented *separately* to the will as a particular good which may be chosen because a good and rejected because not the universal good, then a basis for choice exists: the better picture may freely be chosen or rejected as also may the inferior one, seeing that in itself it too is a particular good, yet only a particular good. Of course the man would be foolish to choose the less good, but it is consistent with our explanation to assert that he is free to be foolish; he may refuse to allow attention to be paid to the objective considerations that would change the course of his conduct were he acting reasonably, and instead, if he so will, he may say, 'Stat pro ratione voluntas'. In our explanation, to sum up, choice is founded upon the freedom of exercise, the freedom of willing an act or of abstaining from willing it.

119. Moral Liberty and the Power of Doing Evil.—*Moral liberty* is freedom exercised in respect of *moral* acts, i.e. acts considered in relation to the end of our rational nature. Sometimes moral liberty is defined as 'the power of choosing between good and evil'. In point of fact human liberty does verify this definition, inasmuch as man can choose evil; but, strictly, moral liberty does not imply the power of choosing evil. This power is an imperfection, just as the power of self-deception is an imperfection in our reason.

A man chooses evil under the guise of apparent good. Such an unfortunate action is possible on account of his possession of many faculties each of which has a different proper object; what is the real good of one is not necessarily that of another—as is manifest in the case of the higher and lower appetites, where what is truly the pleasure of the lower is sometimes not at all the good of man as he is a rational being.

When the will seeks an inferior good in place of what is

upright, it violates the law of its nature, thereby acting inconsistently with right order and abusing its liberty. Hence a moral evil is called a defect, unrighteousness, a fall.

Since the liberty to commit evil is an imperfection of the will, to claim it as a right either for one's self or for others is manifestly absurd. When, therefore, a legitimately constituted authority, acting within the limits and observing the precautions demanded by prudence, takes measures to prevent in the family or in society vice or error leading to vice, it is protecting moral liberty and in no way curtailing it. Unbridled liberty is no true liberty but only *licence*, a counterfeit of it.

120. Answer to Certain Objections.—Two sets of facts are adduced by the determinists against the freedom of the will:

1. An irresistible propensity to crime to be met with in criminals.

2. The uniformity and constancy of certain moral facts.

3. A further objection is drawn from the impossibility of reconciling free-will with the law of the conservation of energy. These three objections require to be briefly noticed.

1. We admit that under certain influences—heredity, alcohol, vicious habits, etc.—responsibility is in a large number of cases *lessened*, and indeed so much lessened that it is probable it is not sufficient, or is no longer sufficient, to justify their being called criminals. This granted, it is surely very arbitrary to make the exception a rule and to deny responsibility for all because there are some who are not responsible: as arbitrary as to deny that man is rational because some men are deficient in reason.

2. The second objection runs thus: if the individuals composing the social body were free, their moral acts would vary; yet statistics of such moral events as marriages, illegitimate births, crimes, suicides, etc., show a remarkable constancy [52], which therefore proves that the moral acts considered to be free are as subject to laws as physical events.

To this we reply in the first place that all acts performed by man are not free. Only those acts are free which are the fruit of reflection. A very large percentage of acts, then, even in the most serious life are not free because done without

[52] The number of suicides recorded in France between 1849 and 1860 is as follows: 3583, 3596, 3598, 3676, 3415, 3700, 3810, 4189, 3967, 3903, 3899, 4050.

thought; a large percentage are suggested simply by the imagination, controlled by passion or self-interest or are due to routine. In the second place, it is a mistake to imagine that free acts are purely arbitrary, proceeding from a will that acts without purpose. Truly man may be unreasonable if he like. But in point of fact, in by far the majority of cases, men are not unreasonable, but allow themselves to be actuated by a purpose. Thus, not to speak of the last intention—the seeking after supreme happiness—the instinct of self-preservation, the instinct of propagation, the natural love of parents for children, of children for parents, the striving for well-being or for personal interest, are all so many motors to the will to which it generally responds without making a deliberate choice. It follows that in apparently similar circumstances men will for the most part be led by the same intentions, so that it is in reality the similar spontaneous desire which accounts for men acting in many instances in a uniform and constant fashion.

It must be observed that this relative constancy and approximate uniformity in no way excludes liberty, for every act induced by a spontaneous intention may be the subject for a deliberation either concerning the motives for which it shall be done or concerning the manner or time. Thus we are no doubt each of us free to travel somewhere to-morrow or to stay at home; yet it is absolutely certain that, when to-morrow comes, of the number who have a reason to travel many will freely decide to do so and the number of people travelling by train will be approximately the same to-morrow as on any other day of the year.

Finally, the constant and uniform manner of action of men certainly allows us to deduce laws akin to physical laws, but as their actions are free they are called by the special name of *moral laws*.

3. The materialistic determinist makes it his objection against free-will, that it would militate against the constancy of the energy of the universe [53]. If the will, they argue, were to cause other bodily movements besides those which would

[53] Lavoisier's well-known axiom is that 'nothing is ever lost or created in nature'. This principle, which was enunciated originally by its author in reference to the conservation of mass, applies also to the conservation of the energy of the universe. So applied it means that, of the quantity of energy

occur if the organism were subjected exclusively to the action of material forces, it would thereby introduce so much more energy into the universe and necessarily destroy the constancy of the total energy.

The answer to this is very simple: the will is not an efficient cause producing mechanical effects. All that the will does is to direct the power of local movement possessed by the organism to some action. This effect does not require the expenditure of any active force, for the action of the will is not transitive, having an external effect, but is immanent. All the energy that is put forth externally comes from the sensitive appetite and the locomotive faculty, which are material faculties subject to the law of the conservation of energy.

§ 3. *Attendants of the Voluntary Act: Emotions, Sentiments*

121. Pleasure and Pain.—Acts of will are usually attended by feelings of pleasure or of pain. *Pleasure*—and the same is to be said of *pain*, its contrary—is something that does not admit of explicit definition; the most we can do is to describe it according to the conditions of its existence and the causes which produce it. We may lay down that it is caused by all conscious activity which is *subjectively* and *objectively perfect*. Let us explain these two conditions.

1. An action is *subjectively* perfect when the faculty producing it acts in the fullness of its power. To produce the maximum amount of pleasure of which it is capable, the energy of the faculty must be exerted to its utmost, yet not to the degree of excess that brings fatigue and exhaustion.

2. An action is *objectively* perfect when its object corresponds to the natural end of the subject putting it forth. The intensity of a pleasure, therefore, does not always increase simply in proportion to the energy expended: it is also a requisite condition that the activity exercised serve in some way to forward the subject towards its natural end, since powers of action are possessed by all beings for this purpose. Hence it follows that the activity of a lower faculty must, if it is to be productive of pleasure, be subordinated to the higher faculties. Displeasure or pain is caused when the action of

displayed under the various forms of mechanical movement, sound, heat, light and electricity, whilst one form may give place to another form, *the sum-total in the universe remains constant.*

the lower faculties is antagonistic to respective ends of the higher ones.

This theory of Aristotle and St. Thomas is fully justified by observation. (*a*) We have as many *sources of pleasure* as we have springs of activity—there are the pleasures of health and organic well-being, of sensuous and intellectual cognition and volitional action, the pleasures of the emotions, the pleasure of movement. (*b*) *There is never pleasure without activity*, as Aristotle remarks. The pleasure of idleness summed up in the expressive Italian 'dolce far niente' is not derived from inaction, but from the performance of free and easy actions following upon prolonged effort. (*c*) *Increased activity increases pleasure*. Thus, whereas a dim light at the most does not displease, the full light of day gives considerable pleasure; whereas a trite argument affords little satisfaction, a problem requiring subtle investigation gives an intense delight.

In brief, whenever activity is perfectly exercised, pleasure is an invariable concomitant and the pleasure is proportionately augmented as the activity becomes more perfect. With St. Thomas we may therefore say that pleasure results from the perfection of activity [54].

122. Feeling is not a Distinct Faculty. Psychological Analysis of Emotion.—With modern psychologists the popular classification of psychic phenomena is a threefold one, namely into cognitive, conative or motor, and emotional or states of feeling. Scholastic philosophy knows no such tripartite division of faculties; it recognizes only two broad classes, of cognitive and of appetitive or conative. If we wish to be competent to decide for ourselves which classification is the more reasonable, it will first be necessary to have a clear idea of what these affective states, formerly called passions and to-day emotions, really are.

Emotion may be defined as *an agreeable or disagreeable passive state of consciousness produced by a representation of something good or evil*. The passive impression must be (*a*) in some way agreeable or disagreeable to the subject, that is, must bring about some change that is perceptible to conscious-

[54] 'Si ergo operatio perfecta est delectabilis, perfectissima autem delectabilissima, consequens est quod operatio, in quantum est perfecta, est delectabilis. Delectatio ergo est operationis perfectio'. St. Thomas, *In X Ethic.* lect. 6.

ness as pleasurable or painful. We do not speak of being affected or 'moved'—of feeling in this sense—unless the effect is more or less intense; 'indifferent' feeling is not worthy of the name 'emotion'. Yet the mere element of pleasure or pain is not sufficient to constitute an emotion: a good dinner well digested is as real a source of contentment as a badly digested one is of annoyance or of positive pain, but no one would dream of classing these agreeable or disagreeable sensations as emotions. An essential element of emotion is (*b*) that the strong feeling arise from a mental representation, either directly formed or through the imagination, of something appealing to the subject as good or harmful—such, for instance, is the delight of a child on meeting its mother after a period of separation, or the grief of a mother at the sight of her dying child. (*c*) The last element in the definition is the passivity of the emotional state. It is precisely because it is a passive modification of a person that modern psychologists have been led to contrast it with cognitive and conative states, which are essentially active: on the strength of that contrast depends their threefold classification of faculties.

The mistake upon which their reasoning is based is a confusion concerning the nature of a passive faculty: it is not one that is absolutely inactive; but, on the contrary, one that is active though requiring as a condition for its activity to be determined by the reception of some determination. Granted an emotion is then a 'passion', it is nevertheless a *passion determining to action*, and therefore there is nothing to prevent it from being considered as a phase of the activity of the appetitive faculties. The analysis is then we think as follows.

The operation of the will [55] presents more than one aspect.

[55] In his larger *Psychologie* (8th ed., Vol. II, p. 166), of which this is a summary, the author calls attention to the fact that our emotions are complex states, i.e. made up of sensuous and supersensuous elements—just like human cognition; it may be the lower element or the higher (e.g. patriotic, aesthetic sentiments) which is predominant. As there is reason to distinguish what in fact is found together, consistently with this distinction the physical element in emotions has been treated of under the heading of sensible 'passions' (in Part I, 66 f.). The analysis given in this paragraph of the higher element, appertaining to the spiritual will, applies equally, *mutatis mutandis*, we think, to the sensuous appetite, seeing that the latter is a similar passive faculty and does not cease to act on the attainment of its object. Only if this is borne in mind is the *complex emotional state*, usually not recog-

when seeking an end or choosing means leading to an end, it appears as active—*intentions, desires, resolutions*; when the end is attained, there succeeds another phase, for the movement ceases and the will, in this sense, is at rest, according to the maxim 'quies in bono adepto'—*possession, satisfaction, complacency.* The union of the object sought with the faculty seeking it produces a modification in the will, and to this the will is passive. Yet this passivity does not here mean inaction; it is to the will a determination to fresh activity, to renewed appetition—not this time to the seeking of a new object, but to a closer attachment to the object attained, to an ever increasing complacency in what procures for it the pleasure it has already attained. We see, then, how, on the one hand, emotion is passive, although with that passive impression is closely joined a renewed movement of the appetitive faculties; and how, on the other hand, the will, with the lower appetite, being a passive faculty, requires some such attraction of its object to determine it to action. If this explanation of man's conative faculties is true, we see that there is no reason to assign to emotions a special place apart in a classification of the soul's operations and faculties, for from their nature they are rightly to be considered as manifestations of the appetitive faculties.

123. Nature of Emotion.—When we come to ask what our emotional states really are, we may find, as in the rest of psychology, two extreme theories put forward that are equally erroneous. On the one hand is the *physiological theory* (Lange, William James, Ribot) put forward by materialists, which states that emotions consist simply in physical modifications of the organism, in physical gestures and cries, etc., which are not a vent for internal feeling but on the contrary so condition it that if they are suppressed, it also must cease. As far opposed as possible to this is an ultra *psychical theory* (Leibniz, Herbart) which regards the emotions as something purely psychical; for instance, the disagreement or the harmony of several ideas that occupy the mind simultaneously (Herbart).

Midway between these two theories, verifying once more the truth that 'in medio stat virtus', stands the Scholastic interpretation. According to this the lower, sensuous emo-

nized to contain animal and rational elements, wholly accounted for by us.—Trs.

tions, 'passions', are on the testimony of the internal sense and consciousness at once *both physical and psychical*; the higher intellectual emotions or sentiments are never wholly unaccompanied with sensuous feeling and therefore indirectly come within the range of physical facts. Hence we may say of the emotions what we have said with St. Thomas of sensuous perceptions, that the immediate subject is neither the soul nor the body but the animated organism: 'Sentire non est proprium neque animae neque corporis, sed compositi.'

III. Comparative Psychology of Animal and Man

124. Object of this Section.—We have hitherto considered intellectual cognition and rational volition as *acts peculiar to man*. It remains to prove that they are really so. As, however, volition depends upon intellectual knowledge, attention must chiefly be directed to demonstrating that thought belongs to man and to him only.

Thought, it will be remembered, consists in abstract ideas and the perception of universal necessary relations obtaining between objects thus abstractly conceived. Our task resolves itself then into establishing that man and man alone has abstract universal ideas. This gives us the two propositions to prove: (i) *Man knows the universal*; (ii) *Man alone knows the universal*, i.e. animals show no signs of any such knowledge. If these two propositions can be shown to be true, it will be legitimate to conclude that *man's knowledge of the universal proves that he is of a different nature from that of the animal.*

125. I. Proofs that Man knows the Universal.—1. It is obvious to direct observation that even the most ignorant and degraded of men evince a continual acquaintance with universal ideas. To cite but one example: what man has failed to realize, at least in an implicit way, the necessity and universality of the proposition 'Two and two make four'?

2. Common to all men are *language*, *personal development* due to thought and conscious action, and *moral and religious sentiments*; and these several elements each involve abstract and universal knowledge.—Of the facts forming the major of this argument there can be no doubt for the impartial student of anthropology: nowhere has there yet been found even a single tribe that does not possess a language, that does not either in its present activity or in the traces apparent of

an antecedent civilization show evidence of mental progress, that is devoid of all sense of right and wrong and without any religious principles.

The parts forming the minor are best proved separately: (*a*) For more than one reason *language* involves the power of abstract thinking and generalization. In the first place, the mutual understanding of two minds through the medium of a word supposes that they both conceive the same idea of an object. Now sensible experience pure and simple is unavailing to produce this understanding: a word corresponds to some abstract aspect of a thing and when it is pronounced attention is drawn only to this one aspect, about which the two minds, upon grasping it, are in unison. Secondly, language is not made up of isolated words but of propositions, and in any proposition the predicate is abstract: as Aristotle says, 'What is particular, such as Cleon, Callias, etc., cannot serve as a predicate, but what is universal is predicated of a particular or of a subject less universal, as, for example, man is predicated of Callias, or living being of man'[56]. (*b*) *Personal progress*—'ex propria inquisitione' is the phrase of St. Thomas—likewise presupposes abstract universal ideas. Indeed progress in this sense, as the fruit of the personal initiative of the one achieving it, presupposes a perception of an end to be realized by *different* means, a perception of a *common relation* connecting them all with this end to be attained, and a *reflex knowledge* of personal activity that can be directed to the end and adapted to it. Such ideas and acts of reflection clearly imply the power of abstraction and generalization. (*c*) *Morality* and *religious sentiment*, also characteristic features of the human race, equally imply a perception of what is universal. *Moral laws* and *relations* on the one hand are *universal, necessary principles* bearing upon the direction of free-will towards its supreme end; religion, on the other hand, demands alike a proof, at least by the principle of causality, of God's existence and a knowledge of the natural law by which man is subordinate to God. Hence both moral and religious sentiment rely upon ideas of what is necessary and universal.

126. II. Proofs that Man alone knows the Universal.—1. Animals *show no signs of having* universal ideas: for, (*a*)

[56] *Analyt. pr. I*, 27.

we saw above (59 f.) that even the most wonderful actions of animals can be explained by a concrete perception of images and by associations of images that have concrete relations as their object. Further (*b*) we have just seen that an acquaintance with universal ideas naturally displays itself by external signs that are always and everywhere manifest, to wit, by language, personal progress and some kind of moral and religious conduct. But everybody is ready to grant that animals show none of these exterior signs. They show no indications, then, of forming universal ideas.

2. Animals *show positive signs of not having* universal ideas. The uniformity and invariable sameness in their actions, which show no evidence of personal development, are incompatible with the power of thought proper: beings capable of abstracting and generalizing would necessarily conceive one end or purpose under different aspects and then see that it is realizable by various means. Bossuet aptly observes: 'Is it not a very strange thing that those animals we would accredit with so much ingenuity have never yet invented anything, not even a weapon for their defence nor a signal for uniting and acting in concert against man who is ever ensnaring them? If they think, if they reason, if they are reflecting creatures, how is it that they have not yet agreed about the slightest sign? The deaf and dumb contrive to speak on their fingers. So too manage the most stupid of men; and if we see the animals are incapable of this, it is thereby clear how far they fall short of even the lowest degree of stupidity, and that it is a misconception of reason to allow them the slightest spark of it' [57].

127. Conclusion.—*All* men know universal ideas (Prop. I); men *alone* know universal ideas (Prop. II); therefore, by reason of this acquaintance with the universal, man and animal stand proved to be *essentially* different by nature.

Language, progress, morality and religious sentiment are indeed so many characteristic features of mankind, but they all presuppose abstraction (Prop. II); wherefore abstract universal knowledge alone constitutes a *fundamental characteristic* and realizes all the conditions of a proper and real *note* of man.

[57] *De la connaissance de Dieu et de soi-même*, ch. V, § 7.

ART. II. MUTUAL INFLUENCES OF SENSITIVE AND SUPERSENSITIVE LIFE

128. Object of this Article.—We have noticed more than once, incidentally, that the *sensuous* or *lower* perceptions and appetitions and the *intellectual* or *higher* exercise a mutual influence upon one another. It is now time to gather these isolated observations together and to endeavour to find in this mutual play of sensuous and rational life the explanation of certain psychological states that are particularly difficult to diagnose. In the First Section of this Article we shall consider the mutual influences of sense and reason, and in the Second those of the will and the other manifold activities of the soul. Yet the two sections must inevitably trespass upon each other.

I. The Senses and Reason

129. Solidarity of the Senses and Reason. Its Laws.—We have not in view here the relations existing between what, to use the terminology in vogue, are called 'body and mind'; our purpose is not to recall attention to the dependence of the sensuous psychical life, and consequently of intellectual activity also, upon organic life and in particular upon the functioning of the nerves. We are to investigate the *immediate interdependence* of sense-functions and intellectual acts.

From this point of view sensibility has obviously an influence upon our intellectual acts, inasmuch as the senses, as we have seen, furnish the intellect with the object about which its activity has to be exercised. Contrariwise the higher activities have a bearing upon the sensitive functions, as is apparent from the fact that when a man is absorbed in some intellectual occupation he no longer sees what is happening around him, he no longer hears what is said; we say he is abstracted, absent-minded, his mind gives attention to nothing else but his dominant thought.

This absent-mindedness is at once the result and sign of a concentration of the mind's activity upon some single object. The explanation of this fact, as also of many other similar ones, is to be found in the two following psychological laws: (*a*) Every act of the soul impedes in some degree other acts—'Una operatio', says St. Thomas, 'cum fuerit intensa, impellit aliam'. (*b*) The free-will can command the other activities of the soul and in consequence can draw off, to the advantage of the intellect, energy that would otherwise be expended in sense-activity. These two psychological laws together with the laws governing the association of images (**56**) afford us a partial insight into the nature of certain abnormal or exceptional states, such as dreams and hallucination, madness and delirium, natural somnambulism, magnetism or hypnotism, etc. Before considering these states, however, it would be useful to analyze the normal habitual state of the soul, namely, the state of full consciousness or of being awake, and the opposite state, that of sleep.

130. The State of Wakefulness.—The senses come into play of themselves and effect acts of perception; the imagination and memory awake and associate images or memories of past images; the lower appetitive faculty is drawn of itself to sensible goods; the intellect forms ideas and thinks and reasons, and the will directs itself towards the good. Such various activities of the soul are always clearly distinct from one another, so that in the normal state we are seldom liable to mistake one for another. This is particularly true in the case of a perception of an object and of an imagination or remembrance of it; we are sure that we never confuse these. Further, to speak still of the normal state, all these manifestations are dependent, at least negatively, upon the free-will. That is to say the will can, to a greater or less extent, if the person so choose, apply the activity of the senses or of the reason in a chosen direction or prevent such activity from following the course it would spontaneously take. This *natural opposition* that our consciousness perceives between sensory presentations and imaginative representations, as also the *power the free-will exercises* over all psychical activities, are the two distinctive features of the state of one who is awake. The absence in a more or less complete degree of this double cause constitutes the various psychological states —of sleep, dreaming, hallucination, etc.—which are opposed to the waking state.

131. Sleep, Dreams, Hallucinations.—A man is not always wide awake; the psychical activity that characterizes his fully conscious life is at intervals slackened and periodically even entirely suspended. This state of relaxed or dormant mental life, in which the perception of exterior things fades and we are only half-conscious or not conscious at all of our own acts, is *sleep*.

The state of *reverie* is one in which consciousness is not so fully effaced; it is when we cease to pay attention to external objects and allow the imagination to drift along its own course and guide our thoughts as it pleases.

According as perception is dimmed and more rein given to the imagination, musing gives place to day-dreaming and we fit our actions and words instinctively to the objects holding our fancy. Under the spell of a very vivid imagination, or as the after-effect of some affection of the nerve-centres, a man will allow himself to be led by his subjective states *without comparing them with his perceptions* of his external surroundings and will thus mistake his own imaginations for objective realities. Such a man who objectifies his subjective image in the absence of corresponding reality is the victim of an *hallucination*.

During the time of sleep the will no longer directs a person's attention; images and ideas become associated by causes that are independent of the will; moreover both the imagination and the intellect lack the usual corrective they find in perception. Hence sleep is the time when thought is without direction and without control, the time of *dreams* in the strict sense. The *incoherence* usually characteristic of our dreams is due to a want of voluntary attention; the *unity* on the other hand that we sometimes experience may be explained by mental association. The *illusory* character or the hallucination-element is to be ascribed to the cessation of perception.

132. Madness and Delirium.—In virtue of his free-will man is normally master of his rational and voluntary acts. A lunatic or madman is one who is 'out of his mind' (alienus a se), who has lost this self-possession, this self-consciousness and freedom. Ordinary *madness* is the state in which, owing to the dethronement of the reason, the associations of images and motor-effects are capricious and the imagination, no longer checked by perception, has full licence to follow its own extravagances. *Delirium*, on the other hand—often the attendant of serious illness, such as meningitis, typhoid, epilepsy, etc.—is a passing aberration, the chief feature of which is the frequency of hallucination. Delirium may then be regarded as a derangement of the attention whereas madness is the derangement of the reason. Finally, *raving madness* or *frenzy* is the derangement of the will, the overthrow of its empire over the passions and the confusion of the external acts of the person.

133. Natural Somnambulism.—Natural somnambulism is a very different state from that of dreaming. The somnambulist is not deprived of the use of his senses; he perceives very clearly, especially with his senses of sight and touch; he is even more dexterous in his movements than when awake, which proves that the will has the direction of his motor faculty: but the field of his exterior observation and of his voluntary movements is very limited. This is apparent from the instance quoted of the sleep-walker Castelli who lighted a candle to write by and, when some one lighted other candles and extinguished the one he had lighted, believed himself to be in the dark and felt about to re-light the first one. Somnambulism seems then to be a state of intense pre-occupation; the sleep-walker is an Archimedes wholly taken up with his problem. A further characteristic of this state is that the subject on re-awakening has not the slightest remembrance of what has happened during his sleep; yet strangely when the fit is on him again the recollection of what took place during the last and previous ones revives.

134. Suggestion and Auto-suggestion.—*Suggestion* is an excitation which by directly awakening some image in the imagination indirectly provokes other closely associated images to appear and thus determines the subject to perform the action represented by the first image. The same definition may be expressed in a passive form by saying that suggestion is an impression communicated to a subject and accepted by him without the previous consent of his free-will. *Suggestibility* is the susceptibility to be influenced by a suggestion without offering any resistance. Everybody is amenable to suggestions, though some people are more so than others. Tell a man that he has a fly on his forehead and he immediately makes a movement to knock it off: he believes without weighing what you say and acts accordingly; he is a specimen patient of suggestion. Quacks, mountebanks and, in varying degrees, barristers, teachers, business bargainers, etc., make a practice of inducing suggestion.

Suggestion has not necessarily to come from without: it may be produced, consciously or unconsciously, by the subject himself, and then it goes by the name of *Auto-suggestion*. In this way imaginary illnesses are produced. So too preconceived ideas, fanaticism and routine are to be attributed to self-suggestion.

In brief, suggestion is the awakening of an image that determines to action. Its explanation is to be found in a psychological law already mentioned (55), namely, that *every idea suggested and accepted tends to become actual*; or, in physiological terms, that every cerebral cell excited by a sensation or idea excites the motor nerve-fibres and through them the organs of movement which have to come into play to realize the object of the idea. It must be observed that suggestion has no direct action on the will, but influences it only through the imagination and the sensuous appetite, and this it does by bringing before it an object soliciting it to action [58].

The state in which a person is intensely amenable to suggestion is hypnotism.

135. Hypnotism.—*Hypnotism*, or as it was previously called artificial somnambulism or animal magnetism, is a state midway between waking and sleep, that is capable of being brought on artificially and seems to consist chiefly in a *state of abnormal suggestibility* which renders the hypnotized subject dependent wholly or partially upon the hypnotizer. The processes of hypnotization are almost countless; but they have one common, essential element in suggestion: the patient goes to sleep, or is hypnotized, because it is brought home to him that he ought to sleep, because the sleep, or hypnosis, is suggested to him. Passes, gestures, fixation of the eyes, etc., are of use only as a means of enforcing the suggestion by materializing it in an action suited to concentrate the attention of the patient [59].

[58] St. Thomas tells us that no creature can directly influence the human will; the most one can do is to get at it indirectly by proposing some object to it which will be more or less successful in drawing it on to action; in a word, one can only persuade it. 'Non potest ulla creatura *directe* agere in voluntatem ut eam immutet necessario, vel *qualitercumque* inclinet, quod Deus potest . . . ; potest extrinsecus, aliquid proponendo voluntati, eam aliqualiter inducere, non tamen immutare'. St. Thomas, *De verit.*, q. 22, art. 9.

[59] Such at least is the theory of the Nancy School, expounded by Liébault, Bernheim, Beaunis and Liégeois, which daily gains popularity over the Paris

Whatever be the real nature of hypnotism it is certainly characterized by an increased susceptibility to suggestion. This abnormal suggestibility exhibits itself in a vast variety of ways and can be pushed very far. Accordingly it gives rise to two serious problems :—(1) Can suggestion be induced *against the will* of another? (2) When it has been accepted, is it insistent and *absolute*, to the point of leaving no room for free-will and personal responsibility? Neither question has yet been fully answered.

1. It may be said in general that the operator requires for success the passive assent of the patient to what he is about, and experience has furnished divers cases where in the event of the patient offering a stubborn opposition hypnotization has not ensued. Yet on the other hand a number of instances can be quoted when most obstinate resistance has been overcome. This much we do know, that once a person has given his consent, there becomes less difficulty in hypnotizing him again.

2. With regard to the second question we are told by those who conduct experiments at the Nancy School that there are many instances of somnambulists doing things under the influence of suggestion either during the hypnotic trance or after awaking from it which in their normal state would be acts of theft or forgery or murder. However, Charcot, Delbœuf and the others of the opposite School, whilst admitting the facts, put on them another interpretation: the crimes the patient has been made to commit are 'crimes of the laboratory'; the hypnotized person knows himself as what he is represented to be in his imagination and he plays in good faith the part you assign him in the comedy; you give him what he thinks is a paper-knife to kill the man he is appointed to meet, he takes it as the inoffensive weapon he is led to imagine it and fearlessly strikes it against the breast of his pretended enemy.

Yet cases there may well be in which the patient is utterly devoid of sensibility and his suggestibility is absolute, cases which we may liken to the states in normal life of complete inebriation or of delirium. Even so there is no warrant for making a law of them, so long as there are many other well-

School, represented by Charcot, which sees in hypnotism only a particular phase of a nervous disorder.

attested facts not in accord with them: we see the best subjects victoriously combating powerfully given and often repeated suggestions when these are averse to their past education and habitual sentiments.

The nature of hypnotism we must then confess remains a mystery to us; although it is established that the hypnotic state closely resembles that of sleep but with the difference that it has as its salient characteristic an increased and abnormal suggestibility. The hypnotized person, like the man who is absorbed in an intellectual work and sees and hears nothing of what goes on around him, has his senses closed to the whole exterior world saving the voice and movements of his hypnotizer. The art of hypnotizing consists simply in making a skilful use of the patient's freedom of imagination and of the more or less complete abeyance of his personal will.

136. Mental Suggestion. Telepathy.—A person may imagine an action he wants somebody to perform—for instance lifting up his left arm—and the second person, without coming in any contact with the first, conceives an image of that action and does it. For such *mental suggestion* to be of effect the patient must of course be of an extremely fine if not abnormal nervous sensibility and as detached as possible from ordinary excitations. Granting the facts are true, as indeed they would seem to be, we must make their explanation contain the three following conditions:—That the imagination of the operator produce a cerebral action capable of some sort of transmission; that this action diffuse itself outside the brain of the operator until it reach that of the patient; that in the patient's brain it become the efficient excitant of an image corresponding to that in the mind of the first person.

A similar explanation may possibly account for *telepathy*, which etymologically means sensation at a distance. Of this phenomenon examples are by no means rare. A typical instance is the case of a young man who went bathing and was drowned; his sister, who was several miles away, was at the same moment overcome with emotion and saw the whole tragedy enacted in a small pool close by where she was sitting. It would be difficult to ascribe all cases of telepathy to deceit or to hallucination, and yet its explanation is baffling. It has this much in common with mental suggestion, that the communication between agent and patient takes place without the aid of the sense-organs, and that the agent puts forth a great deal of energy whilst the patient is in a state of excessive nervous excitability. The distance, however, which is sometimes very considerable between the two people, as well as the very diverse forms the phenomena may assume, do not allow us to identify telepathy with simple mental suggestion. It may be that certain natural factors in the events have not yet been disclosed. It may even be that all or part of the effect is due to some preternatural agencies. The solution of the problem remains for the future.

II. The Will and the Other Activities of the Soul

137. Influence of the different Operations of the Soul upon the Will.—Our actions are so bound up with one another that a mutual influence is inevitable. As yet we have only considered the influences of the senses and the reason upon each other; now we come to examine the will in its relations with the other operations of the soul.

1. The *intellect* has the largest influence over the will, and this it exercises *directly* by proposing to it its proper object, which is the abstract good, the goodness of things.

2. The *external* and *internal senses* play only *indirectly* upon the will, namely through the medium of the intellect, to which they present material goods in a more or less attractive way.

3. The *sensitive appetite* affects the will both directly and indirectly. *Directly*, inasmuch as if the object of the will coincides with the object of the lower appetite, the latter strengthens the higher faculty; or, if the two objects are contrary to each other, it subtracts from the will a proportionate amount of energy, in accordance with the Scholastic axiom: 'una actio cum fuerit intensa impedit aliam'. *Indirectly*, inasmuch as the passions of the lower appetite disturb the judgment of the mind.

4. Even the *vegetative life* or state of the organism has a distant influence upon the sensitive and intellectual life in general and upon the will in particular. Facts abound which show how health and organic disorders affect the moral dispositions of the soul, and how, conversely, the latter have an influence, either advantageous or disadvantageous, on the functions of the organism.

138. Influence of the Will on the other Operations of the

Soul.—The will can control all the other activities of the soul, not indeed absolutely but none the less really and efficiently, with a power that the older moralists described as 'politic' rather than 'despotic'.

1. It acts upon the *intellect* by directing its attention to a given object or by diverting it. Moreover the feelings of attraction and repulsion entertained by the will have respectively a strengthening or weakening effect upon the mind's assents in its speculative judgments.

2. The will exercises the same influence over the *sensuous cognitive faculties* and through them, although less efficaciously owing to the organic nature of these faculties, over the lower passions.

3. It has a direct power over the *passions* or emotional states which it can to some extent encourage or restrain, in a way somewhat similar to the influence already mentioned of the passions upon the will.

4. Lastly, it affects the *motions of the body* and may even further or hamper its *vegetative life*.

139. Action of the Will upon Itself.—Its Normal Exercise.—The Virtues.—As the will is a spiritual faculty it has also the power of acting upon itself. Its characteristic is to determine itself to perform any design the intellect may conceive.

The perfection of the will consists in its acting with *uprightness, energy, prudence*, and *perseverance*. It acts uprightly when it sets itself as its purpose the true, real end of human nature and directs towards this end all the energies of the soul as so many subordinate means. Both this end and the means to it the perfect will must embrace with energy, prudence, and constancy.

The frequent repetition of perfect volitions little by little engenders in the will-faculty *habits* or habitual dispositions that increase its energy and facilitate its normal activity, and these are called *virtues*.

Of the *moral* virtues there are four principal ones—*prudence, justice, fortitude* and *temperance* [60]. Temperance moderates the lower passions and through them the senses and the imagination. Fortitude, constancy or courage, is a stimulus against

[60] We speak here only of the natural virtues. In the supernatural order there are distinguished in addition three theological virtues, faith, hope and charity, which regard the supernatural end, God Himself.

sloth or weakness in the face of difficulties. Justice leads us to respect the claims made on us by our relations with our neighbour. And prudence teaches us to make a judicious use of the means at our disposal for the attainment of our end.

140. Abnormal or Pathological States of the Will.—The will may either freely or through some natural defect swerve from its normal exercise which we have just described. The freely chosen deviations from that path are matters for moral philosophy; psychology takes cognizance only of the natural anomalies [61].

The first defect of the will is a *want of constancy* in the pursuit of a purpose deliberately chosen. It is a defect common among persons of whims and fancies, and may be put down to the changeableness and want of co-ordination of their desires and actions.

Another departure from the normal state is that of *irresolution* or a form of defect in energy: the motor organs are intact, the intellect clear and the judgment sound, the person has a consciousness that he ought to act, and yet it is impossible for him to decide to act.

Yet sometimes the will is dominated by an excess of energy and finds itself governed by its own strong impulses, which at times seem quite irresistible. This is an *impulsive* state and in its worst stage reaches what we may call *moral insanity*[62].

Between these pathological states and the healthy, ideal state to which we have opposed it there are possible an almost infinite variety of intermediary states.

All these phenomena are additional proofs of the intimate solidarity, the close binding together and mutual dependence, of the various operations of which man is at once the principle and subject.

[61] The disorder of the will which consists in a deflection from the true end of human nature is *wrong*, in Christian language 'mortal sin'. Just as moral virtues dispose the will to choose the moral end of life and the means leading to it, so the will is subject to bad habits or *vices* which incline it to act in the opposite direction. It is the part of moral education to overcome disorderly tendencies and implant habits of virtue.

[62] Cases are known in which the victims of this disorder have announced the crimes they are going to commit and begged beforehand to be prevented. Maudsley relates the confession of a peasant aged twenty-seven who declared that when the fit was on him he must kill any one, even a child, unless he were stopped.

ART. III. NATURE OF THE FIRST PRINCIPLE OF LIFE IN MAN

I. Spiritual Character of the Rational Soul

141. Substantiality of the Ego.—Taine and the phenomenalists sought to elaborate a 'psychology without a soul'. What we call mind they say is only a collective name for a number of perceptions united by means of certain relations; conscious life is only a succession of phenomena and the ego has no reality beyond that of these phenomena.

Yet it is surely absurd not to suppose that related to these phenomena there is, as Herbert Spencer phrases it, a 'something which serves as a substratum for them'; nutrition must pass into *something* or into *some one* that is nourished by it; seeing, wishing, moving, etc., must necessarily be of *some one* who sees, wishes and moves. Besides, why do we speak of '*we*', of '*our* doings', of '*self*', if there are only happenings, and if the *we* does not exist? There is a necessary substratum, the principle and subject of every vital act—the *ego, myself*.

Inasmuch as the ego puts forth vital acts it is called *nature*, for nature by definition means the inherent *first* principle of the acts peculiar to a being. Inasmuch as it is a *thing existing in itself*, something undivided and distinct from everything else, it is a *substance*.

There are two proofs for demonstrating that what we call a person is really and truly a substance:—

1. In every vital action performed *consciousness* is aware simultaneously of a subject who acts and also, on the occasion of every 'passion', of a subject who suffers the action of another. Granted this testimony of our consciousness, we proceed: a thing must exist either in itself or in another; but we should never arrive at the idea of person if the acts expressed by the verbs 'walk', 'see', 'feel well', were realities subsisting in themselves—for each presupposes someone *who* walks, *who* sees, *who* feels well; such acts are therefore accidents, and in consequence the 'I' who walk, etc., in which they exist, must subsist in itself, must be a substance.

2. If the human soul does not differ from its acts, *memory*, the feeling of *one's own continuity*, and that of *responsibility*, become impossible. 'If all things are but phenomena, we can

only be events unknown to one another; for these events to appear to us as united, for us to be able to declare their succession in us, it is necessary, then, for there to be something other than themselves; and accordingly this other, this bond which connects them, this principle which is aware of their succession, can be nothing but a *non-event*, a *non-phenomonon*, that is to say a substance, the ego substantally distinct from its sensations '[63]. This self, the first principle of the vital acts of a man, is therefore a substance.

What is the nature of this substance?

142. The First Principle of Life in Man is a Material Substance.—In the two preceding parts of this treatise we have shown that the phenomena of nutrition, sensations, images, appetitions and spontaneous movements are functions of material organs. The principle, then, which produces them and in which they are realized must also be material.

143. The First Principle of Rational Life in Man is Spiritual: Explanation.—We call an *action spiritual* which is done neither in nor by an organ. A *spiritual being* is accordingly one capable of existing and acting without depending intrinsically upon an organ, or, in more general terms, upon matter. We say 'without depending intrinsically upon matter' because it is possible for a spiritual being to depend *extrinsically*, or *indirectly*, upon matter. And this is the case with the rational soul which depends on the sense-organs inasmuch as these have to furnish it with a material object for its operations.

The mediaeval Scholastics used to speak of the human soul as a *subsisting* being—'anima humana est *subsistens*', says St. Thomas. According to Scholastic philosophy all corporeal substances are essentially composed of *two* constituents—primary matter and substantial form—neither of which is capable of existing by itself. The human soul, on the contrary, is a form that may subsist without needing a further complement, its material subject, and so is a *subsisting form*.

144. Proofs of the Spirituality of the Rational Soul.—We know a substance by its acts, so the soul by the vital manifestations which it exhibits. In order to prove that the human soul is spiritual, we have accordingly to establish that some acts whereof it is at once the principle and subject are spiritual acts. Now we observe that the acts of the intelligence are

[63] T. FONTAINE, *La sensation et la pensée*, p. 23.

spiritual, and likewise those of the rational will, and in proof we can summon six arguments.

1. *Argument drawn from the abstract nature of intellectual knowledge.*—In order to appreciate the drift of this argument it is necessary to recall to mind the principle that *knowledge is a manner of being of the subject who receives it*; and that consequently the nature of knowledge reveals to us the properties and nature of the subject who knows.

Now knowledge is some modification of the subject knowing; it is received in the person who possesses it—'cognitum est in cognoscente' (**29**). But further, we have said: 'cognitum est in cognoscente ad modum cognoscentis', according to the general principle 'receptum est in recipiente ad modum recipientis'—whatever receives a thing receives it after its own manner of being; water assumes the shape of the vessel into which it is poured; food is converted here into muscular tissue, there into nerve- or bone-tissue, according to the nature of the tissue assimilating it. And knowledge is no exception to this rule: intellectual perception will bear the mark of the subject receiving it; and conversely this mark will indicate to us the nature of the intellectual subject. Hence our argument turns into a twofold one, according as we consider (*a*) *the thought itself*, the subjective modification, or (*b*) the *thought-object* that reveals the nature of its efficient cause, the intellect as agent.

(*a*) *Thought* looked at subjectively is an *abstractive act*, an act which consists in the perception of an abstract object, disengaged from the particular characteristics inherent in material things. But this abstractive act is an immanent one, it is a manner of being, a form, of the subject knowing itself. Therefore the subject modified by this form, receiving this manner of being—and necessarily receiving it in conformity with its nature—is itself free from the qualities inherent in matter, in a word, it is spiritual.

If this were not the case, if a material organ were the subject of intellectual apprehension, it would of necessity make it particular; this apprehension would be spread over so much space, enclosed by the limits of fixed dimensions, capable of definite location in the organism, at an exact moment; it would consequently have a definite concrete object.

(*b*) The idea or object of thought proper is an *abstract object* stripped of all the particular, determining characteristics inherent in matter (91); it is, as such, immaterial. But a material cause can produce only a material effect, to which will attach all the determinations proper to matter. Therefore there must be in us an active faculty capable of *abstracting*, a faculty which itself has not the attributes of material agents, but which is *immaterial*—a faculty that, as we have seen, is called the *active intellect*.

2. *Argument drawn from the power of reflection*.—The human mind can bend back upon itself and *reflect*; it can make its own very act its object, and think of its own thought. But such reflection is beyond the power of a material being. The human soul is therefore immaterial.

The *minor* will present no difficulty if it is remembered that every material action presupposes two bodies or two parts of the same body, such action going from one body to the other or from one part to another, and an agent always producing it and a subject, distinct from the agent, receiving it; whereas, in reflection, he who reflects does not act on another but on himself, the subject 'thinking on' his thought-object, his own thought. Hence reflection is not a material act.

An animal, it is true, would seem to reflect: it sees and is aware that it sees. Yet we have no warrant for saying that the sense of sight perceives the act of vision; the explanation of that perception lies with the 'inner sense'. But in the case of man no such explanation will hold, for not only does man think of his thought, but he can reflect upon his act of reflection and is capable of pursuing this act of reflection indefinitely. Hence unless we are to admit an infinite series of faculties, we must allow that the reflecting faculty is not distinct from that which provides the object of reflection; it does therefore reflect on its own act.

3. *Argument drawn from observation*.—Simple observation can establish that the acts of the understanding are *of a different nature* from those of the senses.

When our senses have been very strongly stimulated, they remain at least for some time insensitive to excitations of lesser intensity; thus, for example, a tremendous bang leaves us temporarily deafened, strong daylight or a glance at the sun dazzles the eyes, violent pain has a benumbing effect. The intellect, on the other hand, gets an insight into the highest and most extensive truths of wisdom and immediately afterwards is none the less able to think of what is simple and familiar.

This profound difference between the behaviour of the senses and the understanding did not pass unobserved by the acute mind of Aristotle, who assigned as its one and only possible reason that the exercise of the senses is a function of organs that are material and so subject to wear and tear, whilst the intelligence is a faculty intrinsically independent of a material organ.

4. *Argument drawn from the will.*—The proper object of the will is not such and such particular good, but the good, the abstract universal good. But if volition were elicited by an organ, it could only be drawn forth by a particular good; for an organ, being material, is incapable of grasping an object without that object being particular. Volition, then, is not elicited by an organ; the will's act is immaterial.

5. *Argument drawn from freedom.*—(*a*) The free act involves an act of reflection, and this we have seen indicates immateriality.

(*b*) Every material action is governed by definite, fixed laws, so that whenever certain conditions are present a certain effect is bound to follow. But the free act of will is different: when all the conditions required for it are present, it may or may not be realized. Therefore it must be of a different nature from that of the acts of a material subject.

6. *Indirect argument.*—The sanction of the moral law (*Ethics*, **51** f.) requires the survival of the soul in another life. Yet the soul cannot survive the body unless it is intrinsically independent of it, unless it is, in other words, *spiritual*.

Conclusion.—Our intellectual knowledge and the free acts of our rational will are immaterial acts. But the immaterial character of acts proves immateriality on the part of the *subject* receiving them and of the *active principle* producing them, according to the axiom of St. Thomas: '*eo modo aliquid operatur quo est*'[44]. Therefore the *human soul*, inasmuch as it is rational, *is immaterial*.

And let us add that it is also *simple*.

[44] 'Ipsum intellectuale principium quod dicitur *mens* vel *intellectus*, habet operationem per se, cui non communicat corpus. . . . Nihil autem potest per se operari, nisi quod per se subsistit. Non enim est operari nisi entis in actu. Unde eo modo aliquid operatur quo est: propter quod non dicimus

145. Meaning of Simplicity.—Simplicity means nothing more or less than the *absence of composition.* If we speak of the soul as simple, we mean that it is not composite, that it cannot be decomposed into parts, that it is *indivisible.*

Yet what does composition mean? A thing may be composed of two kinds of parts—of *constitutive parts* and of *integrant* or *quantitative parts.* We call a thing *matter* or *body* if it can make an impression on our sense-organs. Everything capable of impressing our senses occupies a definite portion of space and in it can be distinguished different parts each occupying a different portion of space, parts situated outside of each other; such parts are *integrant* or quantitative parts. The reason of this superficial composition of quantitative or extensive parts lies in another, much more profound composition, namely a composition in the very substantial reality of a thing: a corporeal substance is essentially made up by the union of component or *constitutive* parts—known as *primary matter and substantial form.* With these ideas we became acquainted in Cosmology (**38**) and to them we shall have to make a further allusion when considering the union of the soul and body (**154**).

The meaning, then, of the proposition that *the human soul is simple* contains two parts: (i) that there are no *quantitative* parts in it, and (ii) that there are no *constitutive* or substantial parts.

146. (i.) The Human Soul is not Composed of Quantitative Parts.—1. The human soul is the subject of acts of knowledge and will which are independent of space. Triangle, as the understanding apprehends it, is not affixed to a definite spot in space; it has not such and such determinate dimensions. Still less have metaphysical notions—of being, reality, substance, causality, potentiality, actuality, etc.—anything in common with the limited conditions of extension and space. So too, the abstract, universal good that is the will's object is not subject to any law of space nor restricted by any definite limitation. But the nature of a subject is known by the nature of the acts it puts forth and receives. Therefore the human soul is not extended or composed of quantitative parts.

2. Furthermore, the human soul is *self-conscious*, it knows its

quod calor calefacit, sed calidum. Relinquitur igitur animam humanam, quae dicitur intellectus vel mens, esse aliquid incorporeum et subsistens'. *Sum. Theol.*, I, q. 75, a. 2.

own acts and can know its own nature by way of true reflection —'reditione completa' of the Scholastics. But an extended body cannot thus bend back on or act on itself; it may indeed apply one of its parts to another, but it is impossible for it to superimpose its whole self upon itself; we may well conceive one part of a body acting upon another part, but not the whole of it acting on the whole of itself (**144**). Hence once more the conclusion that the soul is not extended, that it is not composed of quantitative parts[65].

147. (ii.) The Human Soul is not Composed of Constitutive Parts.—1. It has been proved that the human soul is spiritual. But spirituality consists in being able to subsist independently of any intrinsic or constitutive co-principle. Therefore the soul's spirituality involves its simplicity.

2. Substantial composition of matter and form entails the possession of extension by the compound as a necessary quality. But we have just shown that the soul is not extended. Therefore it is not substantially composed of matter and form.

148. The Manner in which the Soul's Operations Depend upon Matter.—It is unquestionable on the one hand that acts of thought and will are immaterial; on the other, that acts of thought and therefore, too, acts of will, are dependent upon the anatomical and physiological conditions of the nervous system, and even still more immediately upon our sense-faculties which are material. How are these facts to be reconciled? How is this dependence to be explained?

Materialism takes notice only of the organic side of our acts and arbitrarily denies they have a spiritual character at all. *Cartesian spiritualism* is not less arbitrary in its neglect of the material aspect, inasmuch as it attributes the conscious act wholly and entirely to a soul that is simple and spiritual. The only hypothesis which seems to succeed in harmonizing the two classes of facts is the *Scholastic theory*. It agrees with the materialists in recognizing the direct, or subjective, participation of the organism and material agents in acts of *sensuous* cognition and *sensuous* appetition. It even recognizes that the higher manifestations of the soul—intellectual cognition and rational volition—never occur without corresponding phenomena of the sensible order accompanying them. But

[65] The proof that many authors take from sensation we do not think convincing: sensation, as we have said (**51**), is *one* but not simple

on the other hand it is emphatic in its assertion that the *immaterial character* of our acts of thought and volition is a fact attested by consciousness and reflection, and accordingly concludes that the only adequate explanation of our psychical life is to be found in its subject being immaterial. For the dependence of a spiritual activity upon material organs it lays down as the reason that this dependence is not an intrinsic, *subjective* one but an extrinsic, *objective* dependence ; that is to say, considered in the *subject* immediately receiving them, considered subjectively, our intellectual acts are immaterial, inasmuch as the immediate principle causing and receiving them is spiritual ; but their content or the intelligible *object* has to be elaborated through the medium of sense-data, to be abstracted from these, and such data are provided by the material sense-organs. Hence our intellectual ideas and rational volitions are *subjectively independent* but *objectively dependent* upon the organism or, more generally, upon material conditions [66].

Corollaries.—1. Can it be said that the organism is the condition *sine quâ non* of intellectual action ? Yes certainly, but the expression does not convey a complete statement. A condition has not a positive influence upon the effect it conditions. But the organic activity of the sense has a real influence upon the production of the concept ; it is the instrumental efficient cause of the intelligible ' species ', the determinant of apprehension (**101**). Hence the organism is more than a mere condition of thought.

2. Is it true that the brain is the *organ of thought* ?—The answer to this question requires a distinction ; *thought* is a word that may mean two different things. The term is used for *the combined work of the sense* and *intellect* whereof the concept is the product ; and in this sense the brain is the organ of thought, since the work of the senses is partly carried on in the cortical substance of the brain. But thought may also mean the actual result of this work, the *intellectual concept* that is opposed to a percept or image. In this second sense

[66] ' Corpus requiritur ad actionem intellectus,' says St. Thomas, ' non sicut organum quo talis actio exerceatur, sed *ratione objecti*. Phantasma enim comparatur ad intellectum sicut color ad visum. Sic autem indigere corpore non removet intellectum esse subsistentem. Alioquin, animal non esset aliquid subsistens, cum indigeat exterioribus sensibilibus ad sentiendum '. *Sum. Theol.*, I, q. 75, a. 2, ad 3.

thought clearly has no organ, and in fact excludes any co-operation on the part of the organism. If, then, the brain is spoken of as the organ of thought, it must depend on the context whether this ambiguous expression is being rightly or wrongly employed.

Here we may close our study of the human soul as it is in itself and turn to consider its union with matter or how it is that our composite humanity is a single nature.

II. The Ego a Substantial Unit composed of Rational Soul and Body

149. Explanation.—Two main conclusions stand out as the result of our past investigations :—(*a*) One part of us, which is alive, grows, experiences sensations and forms desires, feels pain and pleasure, is a *corporeal substance* ; (*b*) another part of us, which is a principle of spiritual acts—of intellectual abstraction, of self-reflection, of voluntary movement towards the good, of free, rational volitions—is a *spiritual substance*. How are these two conclusions to be reconciled with each other? How is it that the same self, the same ego, is at once both a material and a spiritual substance? Indeed two questions arise to be answered : (i) Is man *really* a single whole, strictly one being, a unit? (ii) And if so, how can his body and rational soul unite to form one whole? The first question concerns the *fact* of the union, and to it we reply that *the corporeal, sentient subject and the rational soul do by their union form one single substance, one nature, one person*. The second concerns the *manner* of this union, which is realized *by the rational soul being the substantial form of this single substance*.

150. I. Meaning of the First Thesis.—The corporeal sentient subject and the rational soul do not form two complete beings each subsisting on its own account, two substances thrown together by an *accidental* union. They are two substantial realities which together constitute by their union a single complete substance, so that their union is in truth a *substantial* union.

Considered as a first, intrinsic principle of action and 'passion', a substance is called a nature. Considered in its individual existence or subsistence, a rational nature is called a person, according to the classical definition of Boetius : 'persona est substantia individua rationalis naturae'. Hence it follows that if the human compound is *one substance*, it is also *one nature, one person*, as St. Thomas tersely says: 'Ex anima et corpore, constituitur in unoquoque nostrum duplex unitas naturae et personae'. This is the thesis we propound and purpose to defend.

151. Views of the Cartesian School Concerning the Union of the Soul and Body.—In the view of Descartes soul and body are two complete substances: the soul is essentially thought, the body essentially extension, each has its respective existence without either sharing in any way the existence of the other. However it is an undeniable fact that certain relations obtain between mind and body, and these give rise to a question as with what the nature of that interaction may be. What is the bridge connecting them? The disciples of Descartes have supplied many different answers.

1. Theory of *Occasionalism*.—The interaction between soul and body, according to the theory of Malebranche, is more apparent than real; things that we take for natural causes are causes simply in the sense that their presence is the 'occasion' for the Author of nature, the one and only real cause, to act with such and such an effect. 'I cannot allow', he says, 'that my will is the cause of the movement of my arm, for I can see no relation between things so different. . . . If you say that the union of my mind with my body consists in this that, when I will my arm to move, God wills that the animal spirits exercise themselves in the muscles composing it so as to move it in the manner I wish, I clearly understand such an explanation, and accept it'[67]. The theory of 'Occasionalism', far from explaining, denies the reality of interaction between soul and body. Further, if not actually involving pantheism, it has a decidedly pantheistic tendency; for if the things of the world have no action that strictly and really comes from themselves, we cannot know that they have a proper existence of their own and we are naturally led to conclude that they and God must be one and the same reality.

2. Theory of '*Pre-established Harmony*'. To avoid what seemed the incessant series of miracles demanded by Malebranche for each of our acts, Leibniz suggested, as an alternative to God's constant intervention to make soul and body act

[67] MALEBRANCHE, *De la recherche de la vérité*. Éclaircissement sur le Ch. III de la IIe Partie du 6e livre, 6e preuve.

in concert, that the two were set once and for all in the first instance to work together and a *harmony* thus *pre-established* between them as between two clocks exactly regulated to keep time with each other. 'The soul was so created by God that it has to reproduce and represent within itself everything in order which goes on in the body; and the body in the same manner, so that it has to do of itself whatever the soul commands '[68].—This theory is as destructive as the one it replaced of any real nexus between the soul and the body. Liberatore pertinently remarks that if man's soul were to dwell ever so far away, even in the stars, while his body remained on earth, the union of soul and body, if Leibniz' conception is true, would be in no way changed.

3. The theory of '*Physical Influx*'.—Realizing that one cannot dispute the existence of a real influence of the soul on the body and vice versa and yet at the same time favouring the view that each is a distinct subject, Locke and his followers maintained that there is a real yet *accidental* union between soul and body, inasmuch as each can influence the actions of the other. This 'Physical Influx' Theory is but a rehabilitation of the Platonic theory which likens the body to a ship under the guidance of the soul as its pilot or to a chariot driven by a charioteer.—This theory is indeed an approach to the truth but it does not allow full weight to the testimony of consciousness, which gives clear evidence that there is more than an *accidental* interchange of actions between soul and body, that—as we shall prove later—man is in his substantial being a single complete whole, a proper unit. There is, then, really no room for the inquiry how the gulf between soul and body is bridged over, for there is no distance to overcome. All the various phenomena that we immediately ascribe now to the body and now to the soul belong to one single nature, *one* person. Hence if there is to be any question raised, it can only be concerning the way the different operations of the same subject can be related to one another[69].

[68] *Théodicée*, 1e Partie, n. 62.

[69] The fundamental doctrine of the substantial unity of man, on which the whole of psychology rests, was declared by the Council of Vienne held under Clement V, was confirmed by the general Council of the Lateran held under Leo X, and has been expressly twice repeated more recently by Pius IX in condemnation of the errors of Günther and Baltzer; see DENZINGER, *Enchiridion Sym. et Def.*, 12th ed., nn. 480 sq., 738, 1655.

152. Modern Solution : Psycho-Physical Parallelism and Monism.—We have already remarked upon the phenomenalistic tendency of contemporary psychology ; it professes that there are only *psychical events* knowable by consciousness and *material phenomena* observable by positive science ; there is no such thing as a soul-substance any more than there is corporeal substance. Now it refuses to identify, as formerly did materialistic empiricism, states of consciousness with their physiological functions ; and it will not allow that the two interact upon each other ; it therefore solves the problem by declaring that psychical and physical events occur side by side and run parallel without ever breaking into each other. This theory, known as that of '*Psycho-physical Parallelism*' comprises three main tenets : (*a*) that our psychical life is only a series of states, without there being any soul-substance ; (*b*) that psychical acts and physiological actions are not the same realities ; (*c*) that there is not and cannot be any efficient influence of the first on the second or vice versa.

The best-known exponent of this theory is Prof. Wundt (b. 1837) of Leipzig, who stoutly denies the reality of substance. There are, however, other supporters of it (e.g. James Sully), who recognize that there must be some subject in which phenomena are lodged and which can account for the harmony they exhibit ; a subject that may be *identified* with the *one substance* of Spinoza [70].

Psycho-physical parallelism, either under the empirical form adopted by Wundt or as part of a monistic metaphysic, stands to-day as the only psychological theory opposed to the Aristotelian and Thomistic theory of substantial unity. The French classical spiritualism that arose from Descartes has had its day ; and the strict materialism of the eighteenth century, although still serving a certain number of naturalists and physicians provisionally, is daily more discountenanced by those who seriously profess philosophy.

153. Proof of the Substantial Unity of Body and Rational Soul.—I. *Argument drawn from the testimony of consciousness.*—This fundamental proof is summed up in St. Thomas' sentence :

[70] According to Spinoza all the objects of the universe are different manifestations of a single substance that enjoys the two irreducible attributes of thought and extension See *History*, **117**.

'Idem ipse homo est qui percipit se intelligere et sentire'[71]. It is an undeniable fact that we predicate all our actions of *one and the same subject*, which we call *ego* or *self*: it is I who think, who reflect, who will and love; it is I who see, hear and touch; I who walk; I who live and grow; in fine, I who am here, in this particular place in space. Now, on the supposition that my rational soul is another substance than the material principle of my sensuous activities, these declarations are unexplainable: sensation and intellection being immanent acts take place wholly within the subject producing them—one *ego* will perceive its sensations, another *ego* will perceive its thoughts; but it will be impossible for a same *ego* to perceive as its own two sets of immanent acts if they belong to two substantially different subjects. Our consciousness, therefore, forces us to confess that man's body and rational soul together form one single substantial subject.

2. *Argument drawn from the constant harmony displayed in all man's actions.*—Man is observed to be an aggregation of material elements and forces and spiritual factors which in a regular and constant way all conspire to one definite end, namely the normal functioning and continuance of *rational* life. By their harmonious co-operation the various mechanical, physical and chemical forces at play in the organism prepare and permit the regular functioning of sensuous life, and this in its turn is wholly at the service of the intellectual faculties. Now this persistent, harmonious concurrence of so many different elements must have a constant cause. To account for this we can either deny all activity to secondary causes and, with Malebranche and Leibniz, put the effect down to the intervention of the Creator, or, as the only possible alternative allow that there is in man a *permanent, inherent principle* that makes all the operations converge to the proper end of the rational being, in a word, that man is *one nature, one substance.*

The substantial unity of man admirably accounts for the manner in which we find soul and body united, as well as for the harmonious working together of their mutual activities; deny it and at once you leave unexplained alike the rôle of the body in human life, the instinctive fear of death, and the possibility of any real commerce between soul and body.

154. II. The Rational Soul is the Substantial Form of the

[71] *Sum. Theol.*, I, q. 76, a. 1.

Human Body. Meaning.—We have noticed above that material bodies, by reason of their extension, are composed of quantitative parts (**145**). Yet what are we to say of this extended thing itself, the substance of a material body: has it also parts or is it simple? Aristotle and after him all the great thinkers of antiquity and of the Middle Ages believed material *substance* to be a compound of two substantial principles, *primary matter* and *substantial form*—a theory now often called *hylomorphism* (ὕλη matter and μορφή form). The way in which these concepts were arrived at is best understood by means of an example.

When food, for instance some bread, is eaten and assimilated it becomes part of one's living substance. Nobody dreams of saying that the bread is annihilated and a fresh piece of living substance is created out of nothing in its place, but rather every one says the food *is transformed* into the person. In virtue of this transformation something that existed in the bread now continues to exist in the living substance. This which persists throughout substantial changes, this *first subject*, gave Aristotle his conception of *primary matter*.

Primary matter is not a complete substance (non est quid), neither is it extended (nec quantum), nor endowed with any qualities (nec quale), since it successively exists as a constitutive part of substances which by their nature and properties are very different. For primary matter to become real and extended and possessed of qualities, it has to be united to a principle of being and activity which makes it form by its conjunction with it a complete substance possessing extension and definite qualities. This consubstantial, specifying principle is given the name *substantial form* or *first actuality* (actus primus, ἐνεργεία), or again *first perfection* (perfectio prima, ἐντελεχεία). It is, then, the substantial form that determines primary matter to be bread; and subsequently, when the bread becomes living substance, the substantial form of bread is replaced by the substantial form of the living substance.

Primary matter is said to be *pure potentiality*, that is to say, by itself it has no determination to be anything in particular but is capable of receiving whatsoever determination a substantial form will give it. Hence that which is real and acts, the material thing or *body*, is the compound of two co-principles, one of which is essentially indeterminate though determinable—

atter—and the other essentially a determinant—the substantial form. From its substantial form a substance derives its nature and its properties, whilst primary matter serves as the first subject receiving them.

Between man and the lower substantial compounds there is, however, this essential difference, that the lower substantial forms, as too their primary matter, are incomplete substances and cannot exist except in an intrinsic union with the matter they inform; whereas in the case of man, the substantial form is a *spiritual soul,* a form which can exist by itself apart from matter.

It may be asked, What is the advantage of this union of soul and body? What has the soul to gain by being united to a body? It must be remembered that the soul is not a pure spirit, as thought has not what is spiritual but what is *abstract* as its direct object; hence it has need of the senses of the body, to bring it in contact with the world of knowable reality. In brief, the natural exercise of the highest activities of the soul require a body; it is *natural* for the soul to be united to a body.

155. Proof of the Thesis.—The thesis we have to establish is that the human body has not an existence of its own, but that man is rational, sensible, living, corporeal and existent by reason of his rational soul. Our proof falls conveniently into two parts:—

(*a*) *This is the only theory that accounts for the fact of the substantial unity of soul and body.* If the body had its own existence and the soul likewise its own, body and soul would necessarily be *two subsisting things.* Now, two subsisting things, no matter how closely they approach to each other or how intimate be their actions, yet ever remain *two* beings and never become *one* substantial unit. Every spiritualistic theory, then, which does not regard the body as a first or primary matter to which the soul communicates its own existence, must fail to account for the substantial unity of man and the *intrinsic union* of matter and mind that is to be found within him.

(*b*) *This theory involves no contradiction.* The assertion that the spiritual soul can at one and the same time act as a constitutive part of a corporeal compound and still remain spiritual or independent of matter, may appear to involve a contradiction, but in reality it does not.

If we assert that the rational soul has the power of informing matter, it is because we recognize that superior forms whilst they surpass also contain the perfection and power of lower forms—just as, says Aristotle, higher numbers comprise all beneath them plus one or more units in addition. Thus the human soul, which is superior to animal and vegetable forms, possesses in an eminent way the power possessed by these lower forms of informing matter. Nevertheless, unlike the inferior forms, when the soul exercises its function of informing matter it does not thereby render itself material, and for the precise reason that it is a superior form. When the lower compounds are formed—mineral, vegetable and animal—the form expends, in communicating itself to the matter, the whole of its perfection, and so becomes, as St. Thomas expresses it, wholly lost or immersed in the matter, and is incapable of exercising any action independently of it. But in the case of the soul, its whole perfection is not exhausted when it informs matter, for it is of a superior nature: it communicates to matter just the vegetative and animal perfections, which it contains eminently, whilst its spiritual powers or faculties are left over and emerge, so to speak, from the material compound it informs, remaining untrammelled by matter and capable of exercise without the direct intervention of any organ.

In a word, whilst the rational soul is a form, it is more than a form—it is essentially *subsistent*[72]. And precisely because the soul is subsistent, it is *incorruptible*. It may have need, as indeed it has, to inform matter for the natural performance of the acts peculiar to it, but its existence is intrinsically independent of the body and, consequently, the destruction of the body does not entail its destruction.

156. Conclusion—Difficulties.—Although the Scholastic theory seems not to involve any contradiction in itself and offers a metaphysical explanation of the substantial unity of the human person such as no other theory can offer, nevertheless it is not a little obscure and labours under the disadvantage of more than one serious difficulty. To examine these difficulties *ex professo* belongs to Cosmology, but it would be useful

[72] 'Anima humana propter suam nobilitatem supergreditur facultatem materiae corporalis, et non potest totaliter includi ab ea. Unde remanet et aliqua actio, in qua materia corporalis non communicat'. St. Thomas, *De anima*, III, lect. 7.

to remark that most of them come from the fact that we cannot *imagine* primary matter nor even form a *positive concept* of it. Our imagination can grasp only what has at some time been perceived by the senses, and the senses never perceive the substantial basis of things. Our intellect has as its object to express in positive ideas what a thing is, and primary matter, as we have seen, is not anything real, with extension and qualities—'est nec quid, nec quale, nec quantum'; so that it is impossible for us to know it in any other way than by negation and analogy. Moreover, if the difficulties in the theory of matter and form amounted to a contradiction, we may surely presume that it would not have escaped the metaphysical acumen of Aristotle, Augustine and Thomas Aquinas.

157. Man has but One Soul, and One Form.—If man is one substance, he must of necessity have only one soul and, which is the same thing, one substantial form.

It was the belief of Plato that man has three souls, and a number of modern psychologists distinguish two, a *spiritual soul* that presides over intellectual life and sensation, and a *vital principle* that is responsible for organic life (Exaggerated Vitalism of the School of Montpellier). Yet both theories are openly at variance with the testimony of our consciousness, as well as with the results of observation which finds all the manifestations of organic, sensitive and rational life to be intimately bound up with one another. Furthermore, a plurality of souls in the same individual would serve no purpose; for, as St. Thomas notices, one and the same principle can inform the body and serve the functions of life in all its degrees, since it is natural for a higher form, like the soul, at once to contain and surpass the perfection and vital energy of the inferior forms.

Not only does it follow from man's substantial unity that he has only one soul, but also, we believe, that he has only one substantial form. Objection has been made to this view by Duns Scotus who, whilst granting the rational soul to be the form of the body, thought that before the latter was so informed the matter already possessed a *forma corporeitatis*; a form which he judged to be incomplete and naturally demanding the rational form, but which he deemed necessary for explaining how after the death of the human compound the body remains the same human body as before. Such an additional form of 'corporeity' seems to us to be useless as well as destructive of the substantial unity of the person. For (*a*) in the first place it is a mistake to suppose with Scotus that a corpse and a living body are the same. A corpse, it is true, preserves for a time an external appearance of a human body, but in reality it does not exhibit any of those characteristics which prove that it is *one* being, the resultant of *one* definite form, that is to say, it no longer exhibits a true unity nor a solidarity of functions towards one common end. A dead body is an accidental aggregation of more or less complex substances that are in the course of decomposition: it is not a real unit but exists as one only in our thought, inasmuch as we group a multitude of distinct substances together and call them by the collective name of corpse [73]. (*b*) In the second place, this form of Scotus is incompatible with the doctrine of man's substantial unity; for, every form that gives matter a definite being necessarily precludes the possibility of its being informed by a further substantial form. Now the *forma corporeitatis* would constitute a substance, as also would the form of the rational soul; and these two beings thus constituted, although they might accidentally unite by the interplay of their activities, could never share the same substantial existence.

158. Consequences.—1. In the substantial unity of man's nature lies the ultimate reason why the intellect has for its *proper object* not directly what is spiritual but the spiritual through the material, the intelligible in the sensible. The reason is that man is a unit made up of matter and spirit, and that every action results from and is proportioned to the agent's being, 'operari sequitur esse'; that action reveals the nature of the substance, 'modus operandi sequitur modum essendi'.

2. Secondly, this theory furnishes us with a *strict definition* of human nature; in affirming its substantial unity, it supplies the genus and specific difference required for definition. Man is, first and foremost, soul and body at once. He is a corporeal, living, sentient being, *informed* and *vivified* by a sensitive soul; so that *animality* is the genus to which he belongs, and this

[73] 'Totum corpus et omnes ejus partes habent esse substantiale et specificum per animam; qua recedente, sicut non manet homo aut animal, aut vivum, ita non manet manus, aut oculus, aut caro, nisi aequivoce, sicut depicta aut lapidea'. St. Thomas, Qq. disp. *De spirit. creat.* art. 4.

genus must be the first term in the definition. But the human soul that is capable of apprehension and reasoning is different from the vegetable and the sensitive soul; it distinguishes man from plant and animal and makes of him a *species* apart; so that *rationality* comes as the second term in the definition. The true definition of man then will be: Man is a *rational animal.*

3. This definition enables us to see also the *place in the universe* that man occupies; inasmuch as he is partly material and partly spiritual, he stands midway where the two great orders of created beings meet.

4. This doctrine of substantial unity sets before us the true notion of *human personality,* inasmuch as it shows that it is not the soul only nor the body only, but the compound subject of soul and body which constitutes the human person. By *person* we generally understand a rational individual considered as the subject of certain distinctive and incommunicable attributes, or as Boëthius concisely defines it: a *complete individual subject gifted with reason,* 'substantia individua rationalis naturae'. In this definition '*individual*' is the genus and '*reason*' the specific difference distinguishing person from individual. A mere individual is a complete subsisting being (ens indivisum in se): a substance, with existence in self and not in another, a being therefore distinct from every other (ens a quolibet alio ente divisum), and one that is neither an integral part nor a constitutive part of some whole. An individual endowed with reason is a distinct species bearing a special name, *person.* Endowed with reason and freedom, a human individual verifies in a very special way the full self-possession that is the essence of individuality: he is unlike other individuals without reason and freedom inasmuch as he is master of his own acts and is free and independent in his direction of them towards his last end [74]. Further, since he is responsible for his destiny he has the *right,* in the society in which he finds himself, to do and to demand whatever the achievement of his end requires; he is the subject of inviolable rights, a *moral* and *juridical* person or individual; in conse-

[74] 'Adhuc quodam specialiori et perfectiori modo invenitur particulare et individuum in substantiis rationabilibus quae habent dominium sui actus, et non solum aguntur sicut alia, sed per se agunt. . . . Et ideo speciale nomen habent . . . et hoc nomen est *persona*'. *Sum. Theol.* I, q. 29, a. 1.

quence, if reason and natural right are regarded, he may not be used as a mere tool, a thing (*res*), or treated, in other words, as a slave.

159. Erroneous Theories of Personality.—Personality was confused by Descartes with *self-consciousness*; and modern empiricists reduce it to a mere *co-ordination of conscious or subconscious states.*

But (*a*) it would be a mistake to allow that personality is adequately defined either as actual or as habitual self-consciousness. Were it identical with *actual* self-consciousness we should have to confess that an infant is not a person, as also that we cease to be persons every time we fall asleep, and surely no one is willing to make such avowals. Nor can *habitual* self-consciousness constitute personality since the ego or individual subject is something prior to such consciousness, which perceives the self as something distinct from psychical state and pre-existing before it. It is true, however, that self-consciousness is a *mark of personality*, for it is a manifestation of reason, and reason it is which differentiates a person from a mere individual, making it a species in the genus individual.

(*b*) The manifold acts which modern empiricists speak of as making up personality by their co-ordination are also posterior to the existence of the person; for, every act must be the act of some principle acting, as also immediate principles or faculties must be the faculties of some first principle; consequently every act of ours presupposes a first principle or person, and therefore the acts in question cannot, even by their co-ordination, constitute personality.

These observations it is important to bear in mind when there is a question of 'variations in personality', 'double or multiple personality', etc. In such cases what happens is not that the first individual subject, or person in the strict sense, varies or is changed or ceases or becomes double; but the forms of activity through which the person comes to know himself vary. For a person knows himself not directly but through his conscious acts. Consequently as these acts vary or become changed, so does the mode under which his personality appears to him vary or become entirely changed. In brief, our *personality* must not be confounded with the *idea* which the consciousness of our own activity affords us of it.

Our conscious states vary with our activity, but these variations do not as a rule make any striking difference in the *habitual idea* of one's self, with which every one is familiar; but in exceptional cases they may so upset this habitual idea as to create the illusion that the ego has become some one else and so produce dual personality.

160. Manner of the Soul's Presence in the Body.—The doctrine of man's substantial unity again supplies us with the answer to the question where and how the soul is present in the body it animates.

Plato and Descartes, who both considered the soul as a substance completely distinct from the body, make it reside in some central part whence, like a pilot at the helm, it can control the movements of the whole organism. By Plato the rational soul is placed in the brain; whilst Descartes relegates it to the minute portion of it called the pineal gland. St. Thomas' opinion, to which we adhere, is entirely different: he lays down that the soul is wholly present in the whole body and in all its parts—'*anima rationalis est tota in toto corpore et tota in qualibet parte corporis*'.

The soul is not simply the motor or controlling agent of the body, but it is its *substantial form*, which communicates to the whole body its very subsistence. Now in order that it may make the body exist, it must be present in accordance with the universally admitted principle: 'actus est in eo cujus est actus'. Therefore it is in the whole body which it actualizes and animates; 'anima est in *toto* corpore'.

Further, as the rational soul on account of its simplicity has no quantitative parts, it cannot be in the body after the manner of an extended thing, with parts corresponding to each part of the organism. Wherever it is it must be there whole and entire; hence it is '*tota* in toto corpore et *tota* in singulis partibus corporis'[78].

But when we assert that the soul is present in every part of the body, we do not wish to imply that it is present in each part *with all the faculties* of which it is the source. Indeed the *vegetative* and *sensitive* faculties attach to the several organs—

[78] 'Totum corpus et omnes ejus partes habent esse substantiale et specificum per animam: . . Sic igitur cum omnis actus sit in eo cujus est actus, oportet animam, quae est actus totius corporis et omnium partium, esse in toto corpore et in qualibet ejus parte'. Qq. disp. *De spirit. creat.*, art. 4.

the power of seeing to the eye, of hearing to the ear, and so on—and can be accordingly localized in the parts of the organism to which they pertain. With the *spiritual* faculties it is different: they have not any organ and consequently cannot be fixed down to any definite part of the body and so are not, in the strict sense, anywhere. When, then, we say that the soul is present in all the body and in all its parts, we speak simply of the *essence* of the soul, which plays the part of substantial form to the body: 'Anima est tota in qualibet parte corporis secundum totalitatem essentiae, sed *non secundum totalitatem virtutis*'.

Now that we have discovered the *nature* of the soul and found it to be in itself spiritual yet substantially united to the body which it informs (Chap. I.), let us turn to the question of its *origin* (Chap. II).

CHAPTER II

ORIGIN OF THE HUMAN SOUL

161. Statement of the Question.—The human soul is evidently a contingent being that does not carry within itself the reason of its own existence; it must therefore have been called into existence by the action of something else. Of the nature of this action two theories are forthcoming: (*a*) *Traducianism* and *generationism* profess that the soul is born by *generation*, that is to say, by the substantial transformation of something pre-existing; the whole man, the soul equally with the body, comes from the parents, either as the one school maintains by the transformation of a material germ, or as the generationists say by the direct action of the parent-soul alone. How one immaterial soul can produce another immaterial soul the generationists confess they cannot explain, but they compare souls to torches which spread their light from one to another. (*b*) The other theory is *creationism*, which on account of the immaterial character of the soul ascribes its origin to a direct *creation* from nothing and thus makes God its immediate author.

The question reduces itself, then, to whether the parents *beget* the soul of their child or God *creates* it. If God creates it, a further question arises concerning the precise time at which He does so.

162. Proof of the Creation-Theory: The Soul is not Begotten by the Parents but Created by God.—I. *Argument drawn from the impossibility of traducianism and generationism.*—If parents beget the soul of their child, then something belonging to them—either (*a*) from their bodies, or (*b*) from their souls—must pass from them into the soul of the child; for if not, the soul must be produced from nothing, which is creation. But neither hypothesis is compatible with the immaterial nature of the soul: (*a*) If the material semen could produce the soul of the child, that soul would need to be *composed* of two constitutive parts, namely of a material part coming from the semen and of a formal part that in conjunction with the matter would confer on the resultant soul its own peculiar nature. But the soul of a child is not made of constitutive parts (**145**), for, as we have seen, it is spiritual and *simple*. Furthermore, it is inconceivable that a corporeal agent should produce a spiritual effect. (*b*) The second hypothesis is equally impossible. As it proposes 'generation' instead of creation it implies that a *part of the souls* of the parents is transmitted to the child. But this is absurd since the souls of the parents are simple and therefore *indivisible*. Hence the soul is in no way begotten by the parents, and from this we infer that it must be created by God.

2. *Argument drawn from the spirituality of the soul.*—The existence of a spiritual, subsistent soul can only be due to creation. For between the 'becoming' and the 'being' of anything there must be a natural proportion, since 'becoming' is really 'being' looked at precisely as issuing from its causes. Now the being of the soul is spiritual, that is, intrinsically independent of any material subject. Hence must its origin likewise be independent of any material subject; and for a thing to come into existence without the use of some pre-existing material subject, it must needs be created. Therefore the human soul is created.

It may perhaps be said that, if the soul is created by God, the parents are not parents in the proper sense of the word; they do not bring into the world a child of the same nature as themselves, but a mere body that lacks a rational soul. This is an apparent rather than a real objection. If man were an accidental combination of two complete substances, body and soul, the parents who would only produce the body would certainly be in no wise the real authors of a human being. But man is *one* single substance, formed by the union of a rational soul with matter furnished by the parents; and, although this union is indeed the work of God inasmuch as He is the author of the creation of the soul, yet it is also the work of the parents inasmuch as by their generative act they are the *determining cause* of the creative one. Hence the parents are in a true sense the cause of the birth of *a human being*.

163. Time of the Soul's Creation.—It was the opinion of both Plato and Origen that the human soul, if not actually eternal, certainly existed a long time before its union with the body. But such an opinion is without any foundation. We have no remembrance of any such previous existence; rather since the union of the soul with the body is natural, it cannot be admitted that God first of all placed souls in a state of isolation contrary to their natural perfection. It is, then, much more reasonable to hold that *God creates souls at the very moment He unites them to the matter* they have to inform.

Does this mean to say that the soul is created at the *moment of conception*? Such may possibly be the case and then from the very beginning the embryo draws its life from the rational soul. But it is equally possible and much more probable that the soul is created *during the course of embryonic life*. In this case the natural evolution of the embryo calls forth a corresponding succession of forms [76]. The organic development of the body is a gradual process; in proportion to its organization life first of all unfolds itself as the result of an organic principle similar to that in plants; next sensibility appears in virtue of an animal form to which the first one has given place; until finally the embryo has attained all the dispositions requisite for its being vivified by a rational soul. The action of the generator continues to be performed until such time as this last condition fitting it for the introduction of the intellectual soul has been reached, and it ceases as soon as this stage supervenes. The course of nature now awaits the intervention of the One who alone can create, and at this point God creates the rational soul infusing it into the body as its substantial form.

Embryology wonderfully corroborates these speculations of the old Scholastics [77]. To-day we know that the formation of a new individual in the human species just as in most of the animal species is due to the fusion of two sexual elements that are simple cells. The first phenomena following fertilization are of the nature of a comparatively simple process of segmentation. At the first development of the fertilized egg the microscope reveals only layers of cells arranged in a regular manner and constituting what are called the germinal laminae (See Plate I). Later, the lineaments of the organs appear

[76] Concerning the origin of the substantial forms of material beings see *Cosmology* 45–50.

[77] St. Thomas in particular has said all that can probably be said. *Sum. Theol.* I, q. 118, a. 2.

and their differentiation becomes apparent. Again, from the standpoint of physiology, vegetative functions—such as the contractions of the heart and circulation of the blood—are first of all exhibited; then follows motility; and lastly, and only lastly, the signs of sensitive life.

As to *what precise moment* the embryo reaches the degree of organization required for its being informed by the rational soul, it is of course quite impossible to determine.

164. Origin of the Body.—Psychology takes account of the whole man and therefore we have to say at least a word about the origin of his *body*.

Its *immediate* origin every one knows to be common with that of animal life in general. Its *first* or remote origin is not so evident; by many transformists it is maintained, in conformity with their system, that man must be a product from lower animal forms. However it is not the place here to examine deeply into this question; we must content ourselves with observing that many scientists who are noted for their sincerity are extremely cautious in their assertions. Virchow, for instance, in a speech not yet forgotten, publicly declared at the Congress of Munich that science does not allow us to doubt of the identity of present man with fossil man nor to assert that the latter was evolved from inferior animal forms [78]. De Quatrefages and Hamy both sanely remark that 'our present knowledge does not yet permit us to pronounce upon the origins of plants, animals and man' [79].

165. Unity of the Human Species.—The question concerning the unity of mankind, which was once the subject of hot discussion among naturalists, is to-day finally decided. Science has definitely ascertained that the variously different groups of men that *at the present moment* are distributed over our globe do not represent many *species*, but are different *races* or *varieties* of one and the same species [80].

May we go further and say, on the authority of natural science and archaeology, that not only is mankind one species, but also that it has had *one origin*? We may certainly say that it is both *possible* and *probable* that the human race sprang from one primitive couple; but if reason is to rely on purely

[78] *Rev. Scient.*, déc. 1887, p. 543.
[79] *Histoire générale des races humaines*, p. 62.
[80] Cp. De Quatrefages, *L'espèce humaine*, 6e éd., p. 64.

scientific arguments alone, it cannot, we think, establish this with certainty.

The plan we originally traced out leads us now to consider last of all the *final cause* of human life.

CHAPTER III

DESTINY OF MAN

166. Object of this Chapter.—In this chapter we have to propose two questions: one concerning the *existence* of an immortal life (Art. I), and the other, the *nature* of this immortal life (Art. II).—To answer the first question we have to show successively (i) that the human soul is *fitted by its nature* to outlive the body; (ii) that *as a matter of fact* it will outlive it; (iii) that its survival will be *without end*, that the soul is *immortal*. To answer the second question we shall show (i) what the destiny of man *would have been* if his state had been purely and simply *natural*; (ii) what in point of fact is his *supernatural* destiny.

ART. I. THE EXISTENCE OF AN IMMORTAL LIFE, OR THE IMMORTALITY OF THE SOUL

167. I. The Human Soul is by its Nature Immortal.—There is no doubt that man is a *contingent* being, that he can be conceived as non-existent; and therefore it is not *essential* for him always to exist. On the other hand, he has it in his *nature* that he should always exist. And this does not merely mean to say that the soul does not tend to self-annihilation; for no being tends to annihilation. But much more is meant, namely, that whilst bodies cease to exist because it is their nature to be transformable, because their substantial decomposition is a natural requisite for the birth of a new substantial compound, the human soul is by its nature not exposed to any kind of decomposition and substantial transformation. It is incapable, as the Scholastics say, of either 'corruption or of generation'; for substantial transformation consists in the cessation or *corruption* of one form and the production or *generation* of a new one. Hence our assertion is that the human soul is by nature *incorruptible*.

The proof is an *argument drawn from the simplicity and*

spirituality of the soul.—There are only two conceivable causes that would make the soul corruptible: it might be itself intrinsically liable to decomposition, 'corruptibilis *per se*'; or it might be essentially dependent upon some other subject the decomposition of which would involve its own disappearance, in which case it would be 'corruptibilis *per accidens*'. But the first supposition is not admissible, since the soul is simple and has no parts into which it could be decomposed. Neither is the second, since the soul is spiritual; consequently the dissolution of the human compound or the destruction of the body affords no reason why the soul should be affected in its own existence. Therefore by its nature the soul is neither directly nor indirectly perishable.

Since the soul is such by its nature, if it should cease to live at the death of the man this would be by annihilation on the part of God or, which comes to the same, by His ceasing to preserve it in being. That it will not be annihilated after the death of the man but will outlive the body, can be proved by the following arguments; arguments which it is obvious implicitly strengthen the proof of this first proposition.

168. II. The Soul will in Point of Fact Outlive the Body.—1. *Argument drawn from the testimony of mankind in favour of the survival of the soul.*—Respect for the dead, funeral rites, the belief in a place of reward and punishment beyond the grave, are all evidence of the belief of mankind in the survival of the soul. Now a belief so universal cannot be explained except by a Divine revelation or unless it is rooted in the general and necessary convictions, and consequently infallible convictions, of our rational nature.

2. *Argument drawn from the wisdom of the Creator.*—The soul is so designed, as we have seen in the preceding proposition, that by its nature it is fitted to survive the dissolution of the human compound. Now this capability would have been given the soul in vain if the soul did not as a matter of fact survive the body. But it is inconsistent, we may argue, with God's wisdom to create anything to no purpose. Therefore the soul will survive the body.

3. *Argument drawn from the holiness and justice of God.*—Because God is holy, He loves moral good and hates evil, and He must have established an adequate sanction to safeguard the observance of the moral law; because He is just, He must

decree that sooner or later the just be rewarded and the wicked punished according to their deserts. Now, whilst there is truly some sort of a sanction of the moral law to be found in this world, this sanction is manifestly inadequate (*General Ethics*, **51–52**) ; and the just man as often lives in affliction of spirit as the wicked in the enjoyment of prosperity. There must therefore be a future life where a sufficient sanction will be assured and where all good and all evil will find their just recompense.

4. *Argument drawn from the goodness of God.*—Every man carries in his heart an abiding and insatiable yearning for happiness, and such a desire must be rooted in the very nature of man and therefore owe its origin to the Author of nature. Now this craving is not satisfied in the present life, which all know as a ' vale of tears '. Unless, then, God is to be blasphemed by the accusation of cruelty towards His creatures and by the denial of His goodness, it must be conceded that there is a better life to supply the joys withheld in the present.

169. III. The Soul is in Point of Fact Immortal.—The same arguments which proved the last proposition also prove this if they are pushed to their ultimate conclusions.

1. *Argument drawn from the wisdom of God.*—The wisdom of God implies that what the soul is fitted for by its very nature should in reality come to pass. Now the soul is not only capable of subsisting alone after the dissolution of the body, but also, by virtue of the same nature which provides for this survival, it is *always* capable of continuing to subsist by itself. Therefore the survival can have no limit ; in other words, the soul is immortal.

2. *Argument drawn from the holiness and justice of God.*—In General Ethics (**53**) it is shown that if the sanction of the moral law is to be sufficient it must be eternal. The future life must therefore be eternal, and the soul immortal.

3. *Argument drawn from the goodness of God.*—God cannot refuse, we have said, to satisfy the innate and insatiable desire for happiness that lies rooted in every human soul. But true happiness is conditioned by its eternal continuance. Therefore the future life of happiness must be eternal. In this argument perhaps the *minor* premiss requires a little amplification : Happiness requires the full and complete satisfaction of all the natural tendencies of the soul. Now if we suppose that the soul's happiness had one day to come to an end, we are met

with three impossible suppositions: either (*a*) the soul would know that its happiness was destined to terminate and then its happiness would obviously not be true happiness, since from the very first it would be marred by the fear of its being lost. Or, (*b*) the soul would be the subject of an illusion, and by an invincible error conceive of its happiness as unfailing; then, in the first place an element is introduced which is inconsistent with the happiness of the rational soul, and, in the second, this illusion would be possible only on the blasphemous hypothesis that God should be responsible for keeping the soul in invincible error. Or again, (*c*) if the error were not an invincible one, if the soul were in a state of doubt concerning its future lot, the very doubt would constitute a source of perpetual unrest and abiding uncertainty about the future. Hence the soul's happiness must be eternal if it is to be true happiness at all. But, as the argument states, the exigences of the soul demand its happiness. Therefore the happiness will be in point of fact eternal, and consequently the human soul will live for ever in the enjoyment of an eternal life [81].

ART. II. NATURE OF IMMORTAL LIFE, OR THE FUTURE DESTINY OF THE SOUL

170. The Natural End of Human Nature, considered without reference to the Supernatural.—In General Ethics it is shown that the end of man, considered objectively, is *God* and, considered subjectively, the *knowledge of God*. Here in Psychology we need only attempt to argue by an *induction* from what we have discovered about man's *nature* to his destiny, supposing it were a purely natural destiny.

First of all it must be remembered that all the faculties of the soul spring from one single nature. Although each faculty considered separately has a proper object that is an

[81] 'Cum enim ipsa beatitudo sit perfectum bonum et sufficiens, oportet quod desiderium hominis quietet, et omne malum excludat. Naturaliter autem homo desiderat retinere bonum quod habet, et quod ejus retinendi securitatem obtineat; alioquin necesse est quod timore amittendi, vel dolore de certitudine amissionis affligatur. Requiritur igitur ad veram beatitudinem, quod homo certam habeat opinionem, bonum quod habet, nunquam se amissurum. Quae quidem opinio si vera sit, consequens est, quod beatitudinem nunquam amittet; si autem falsa sit, hoc ipsum est quoddam malum, falsam opinionem habere; nam falsum est malum intellectus, sicut verum est bonum ipsius; non igitur homo erit beatus, si aliquod malum ei inest'. *Sum. Theol.*, I-II, q. 5, a. 4.

end for it, and accordingly man has as many particular ends as he has different faculties, nevertheless looked at in the fullness of his being and nature he has only *one end*; the object of each faculty is for him rather a *means* than an end, and a means only in proportion as it answers to the one end of his nature, of his whole person. From this it follows that his organic and sensible faculties would play a part in his final destiny just in so far as they are useful, as subordinate faculties, for the exercise of thought and rational volition. The problem of man's natural destiny in a future life, then, becomes restricted to the inquiry into the nature of the higher activity of his soul, *his thought and rational volition* in that future existence.

The soul would exercise its *thought to the highest degree of perfection*; it would have the most perfect knowledge of the formal object of the intellect, namely, a knowledge of all material things through their innermost causes and chiefly through their Supreme Cause, together with a negative, analogical knowledge of spiritual beings and of the Divine Being. In a word, man's natural end would be a *comprehensive knowledge of all things through their Supreme Cause*—which is *Wisdom or 'Philosophy'*. Furthermore, this knowledge would naturally evoke the *perfect activity of the will*, that is, a *love* of God considered as the First Beginning and Last End of the physical and of the moral world. From this twofold perfect activity—perfect contemplation and perfect love—human nature would derive its *perfect felicity*.

There would be, however, one condition to be fulfilled for the possession of this happiness, namely that it would have to be merited. Man is master of his own destiny: he is a free and responsible agent and accordingly *has to merit* by the performance of his duty the happiness God has created for him. Being finite and so subject to limitations and deficiencies, he can, if he choose, prefer the apparent goods that this life offers to the real good of the life to come. Were this his choice and were he to end the days of his trial in a state of wilful opposition to the Supreme Good, he would remain irrevocably out of the right order, deprived for ever of his natural happiness.

171. Length of the Time of Trial: Reincarnations and Metempsychosis.—Man's probation or the time of the trial of his free-will must some time have an end, for if it lasted for ever his natural aspiration for happiness would be vain and the sanction attached to the performance of duty an illusion. Yet it seems difficult to demonstrate by unaided reason that the end of his probation will necessarily coincide with the last moment of this life, and this explains why some people imagine that the soul passes through a more or less lengthy series of existences, or successive reincarnations in which it is able to become more perfect. This theory of *metempsychosis*, provided it allows that the soul retains through its successive reincarnations the consciousness of its own personality, and that the series at some time will have an end, cannot be shown by reason alone, we think, either to be impossible or even to be false. All that can be said is that there is not a single positive argument in its favour, and that our present ignorance of any previous existences is a strong presumption against a plurality of existences in the future.

172. Natural Need of a Resurrection.—A resurrection of the human compound is necessary, we think, for the *complete* happiness of the soul in its future life; and therefore we say that resurrection is something *natural*, not in the sense that the soul will by its nature have the power of re-fashioning a new body for itself after death, but in the sense that the formation of a renewed body by the almighty power of God is required for the perfect happiness of the rational soul. It must be understood, then, that there is no question here of the resurrection that Faith assures us takes place in conditions of glory, but simply of a resurrection of some sort, of a reunion of soul and body.

The proof that a resurrection in the sense explained is a natural necessity rests on the fact that the imagination, and therefore the organized body, is a natural help for the soul in its spiritual activity. For from this it follows that the normal exercise of the soul's activity requires the co-operation of the organism and that the soul when separated from the body is in a state of relative inferiority that is incompatible with the requirements of its perfect happiness. It is true that the body is not *essential* for the soul to act; for, being spiritual, the rational soul can exist without a body, it can share the conditions of existence enjoyed by pure spirits and receive from them or from God its ideas—or rather, its conceptual determinants, *species intelligibiles*—which in the present life are obtained by the co-operation of the senses. Yet, although it is intrinsically possible, the state that this separation entails is nevertheless an *inferior* one to the state of union. For the spirit-world, the world of the pure-intelligible is beyond the natural faculties of the human soul, and consequently, unless God gives a supernatural support to which it has no natural claim, the soul cannot rise to an apprehension of such objects. To use a metaphor of Aristotle's, in the presence of purely immaterial things the soul is like some bird of the night in face of the sun; far from being illumined by the pure light it is dazzled, for its eye is adapted to distinguish truth that is tempered by the shadows of matter. The object that is best suited to the imperfect conditions of our feeble intelligence is what is knowable through the medium of the senses, the intelligible presented in the sensible. Hence the soul's natural activity can be most perfectly exercised only when the soul is united to the body; and therefore a resurrection or reunion with the body is natural to man.

173. Declarations of Faith concerning the Supernatural Destinies of Man.—In every state the objective end of the creature cannot be anything else than God. But God Who is the Truth we may know in two different ways—one *mediate* and natural, the other *immediate* and supernatural, of which we learn from Divine Revelation.

The first way teaches us *that God exists* and also *what He is not*, that He is different from all sensible and contingent beings. Such knowledge is possible to man by means of the triple process of causality, negation and transcendence (**108**); and because it is possible to him by his natural powers it is called *natural* knowledge. The second way teaches us to apprehend *positively what God is*—for example, that He is Father, Son and Holy Ghost, that He is three Persons in one Nature. Man could not attain this knowledge naturally, but it has pleased God to communicate it to him: in the present life He communicates it to him in substance through the medium of faith; in the life of glory it will be without any medium, by direct intuition. This intuition, bringing with it perfect happiness for the will, is called the *Beatific Vision*. Both faith and the beatific vision are called *supernatural* knowledge because they are possible to man, as indeed to any creature, only through a gratuitous assistance accorded by the pleasure of Divine Goodness to our intellect and will and exceeding the powers and requirements of every nature created or capable of being created.

There is no reason why a *purely natural destiny* should not have been possible, but in point of fact it has never been realized; from the first moment that God created the first man He appointed a *supernatural destiny* both for him and his descendants. God also supplies the *supernatural means* necessary for its attainment. As the end of man and the means thereto together make up an order, the order of pure nature cannot be said to have ever been anything more than an hypothesis; his nature elevated to the supernatural order is the only *real, historical* order.

Finally let us say a word about the bodies of the blessed; at their resurrection these will be clothed with glorious qualities and prerogatives; they will be, according to the phrase of St. Paul, in some way 'spiritualized'. The complete happiness of heaven is, as the Apostle again tells us, utterly beyond our powers of imagination: 'Eye hath not seen, nor ear heard, neither hath it entered into the heart of man, what things God hath prepared for them that love Him' (1 Cor. ii. 9). The finest intellects of Christendom have owned their impotence to conceive or to express the nature of the direct contemplation of the Infinite.

RECAPITULATION AND CONCLUSION

Psychology we defined as the philosophical investigation of life as it is manifested in man. Accordingly we have studied life in all its degrees, commencing in Part I with *organic* or vegetative life; then, in Part II, *animal* or *sensitive* life; and last of all, in Part III, *intellectual* or *rational* life, which is the most important subject of the treatise. In Part III itself we considered the two elements of intellectual life, *thought* and *volition*: first we considered them in themselves as *acts* and in their relations with the acts of organic and sensitive life; then from the acts we passed to the *faculties* emitting them, and thence to the *nature* in which the faculties have their source (Chapter I); and we came to the conclusion that the human soul is *spiritual* and *simple*, as also that it is *substantially united by its nature to matter*.

When once an insight has been gained into the nature of the rational soul and into its relationship with the matter of which it is the form, it is an interesting and profitable task, which each one must accomplish for himself, to go back over the various psychological acts and their respective faculties and to explain these effects *by their causes*, these acts *by their principles*, and so acquire that knowledge which alone merits to be called *science*, in the highest sense of the word.

In the two subsequent chapters (II and III), we were able to explain from our knowledge of his nature the *origin* and *destiny* of man.

This *résumé* is sufficiently comprehensive to make it clear that the programme we set ourselves has been fulfilled, since philosophy has accomplished its purpose when it has discovered the *material*, *formal*, *efficient* and *final* causes of the things it contemplates.

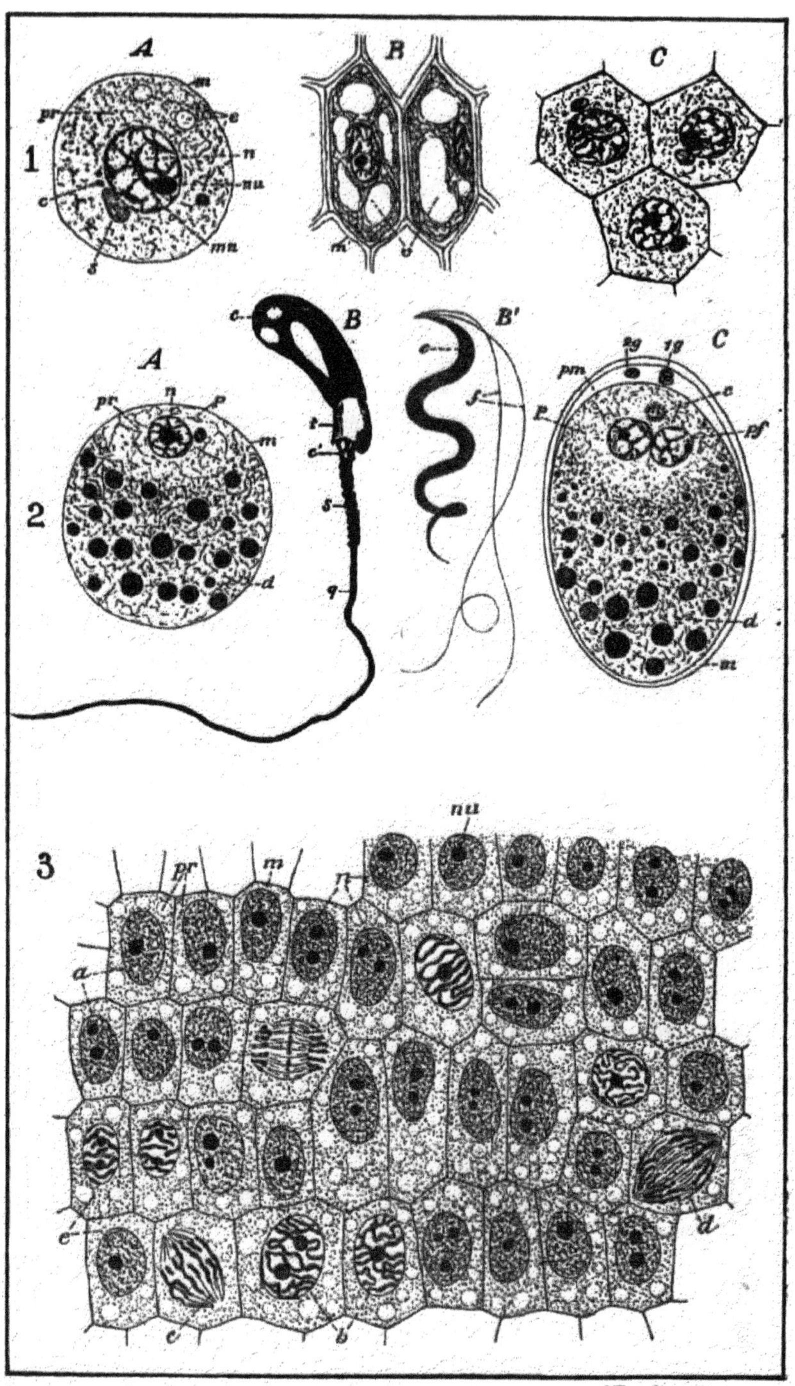
A
B
C
1
m
pr
e
n
nu
c
mn
s
m
v
c
B
B′
A
C
2
pr
n
p
m
d
t
c′
s
q
e
f
2g
1g
pm
p
pf
d
m
3
nu
pr
m
n
a
e
d
c
b

[To face p. 331.

PLATE I

Fig. 1

- *A*. Typical cell
  - *m*. membrane.
  - *n*. nucleus.
  - *pr*. protoplasm.
  - *mn*. nuclear membrane
  - *nu*. nucleolus.
  - *c*. centrosomes.
  - *s*. centrosphere.
  - *e*. reserve matter.
- *B*. Vegetable cells
  - *m* membrane
  - *v*. vacuoles.
- *C*. Animal cells

Fig. 2

- *A*. Ovule
  - *m*. membrane.
  - *n*. nucleolus.
  - *pr*. protoplasm.
  - *p*. pronucleus.
  - *d*. deutoplasm.
- *B*. Spermatozoid (male cell of animals)
  - *c*. hood.
  - *t*. head.
  - *c'*. neck.
  - *s*. spiral.
  - *q*. tail.
- *B'*. Antherozoid (male cell of plants)
  - *c*. body.
  - *f*. filaments.
- *C*. Ovule shortly after union
  - *pm*. male pronucleus.
  - *fp*. female pronucleus.
  - *p*. protoplasm.
  - *m*. membrane.
  - *d*. deutoplasm.
  - *c*. centrosome.
  - *1g*. first polar globule.
  - *2g*. second polar globule.

Fig. 3[1] General view of cells in the growing root-tip of the onion, from a longitudinal section, enlarged about 800 diameters. Here are to be seen the principal stages of indirect cell-division (Plate I *cont.*). *a*, cells at the resting stage, the nucleus has a chromatin-network and deeply-stained nucleoli. *b*, nucleus at the first stage of the prophase. *c*, phase of the equatorial crown of chromosomes. *d*, phase of the polar crowns. *e*, sister-cells, after division. *m*, membrane. *pr*, protoplasm. *n*, nucleus. *nu*, nucleolus.

[1] After Edmund Wilson, *The Cell*, p. 4. London, Macmillan, 1906.

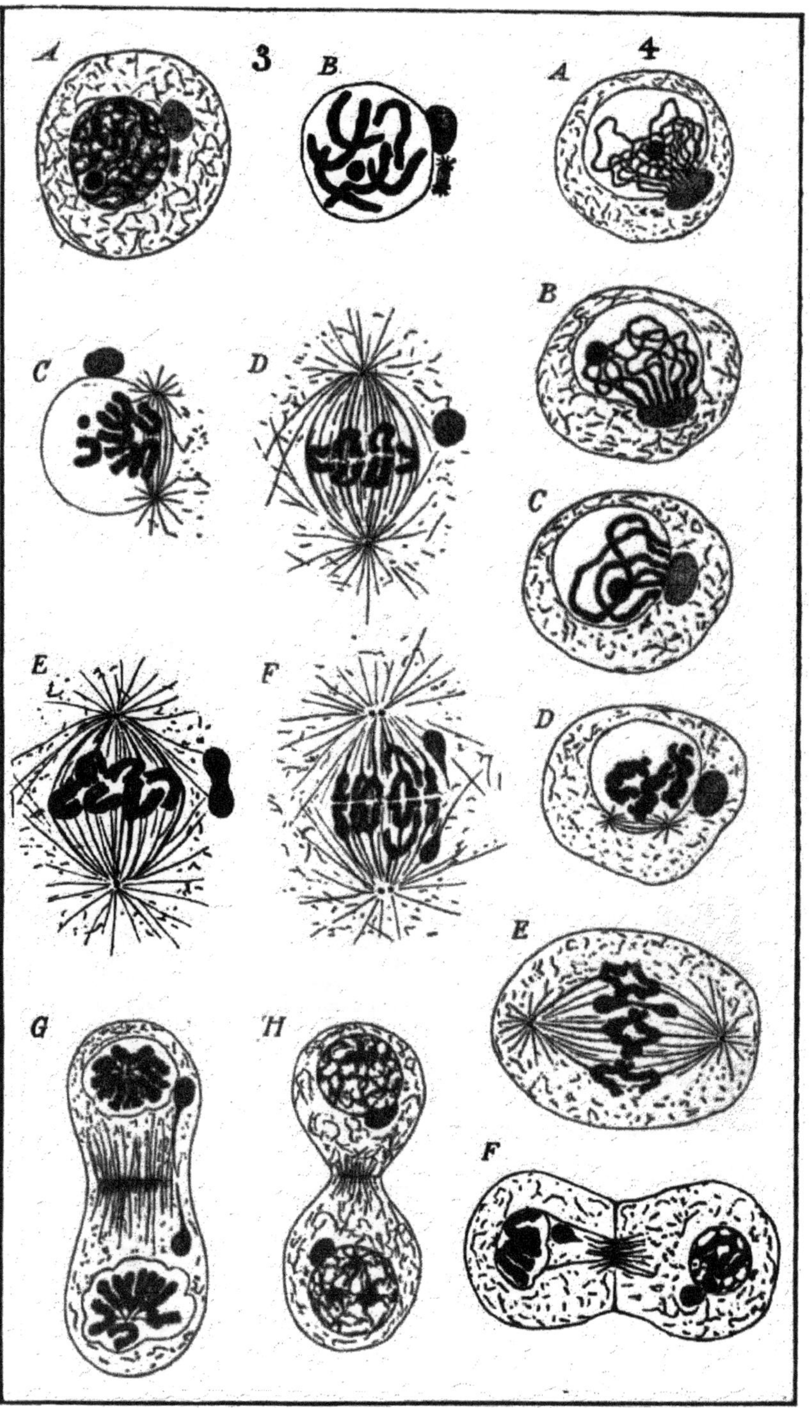

[To face p. 333.

Stages of indirect cell-division or Kariokinesis.

Fig. 3[1]

A. Resting stage.

B. Prophase.—The nuclear chromatin, characterized by its great staining-power, is transformed once more into chromosomes. The centrosomes withdraw from one another gradually to take up their position at opposite poles of the nucleus. Each becomes the centre of an aster. The filaments between the two centrosomes form a spindle-shaped body.

C. Formation of the spindle.—The nuclear membrane disappears. The chromosomes shorten, become thicker and more curved.

D. The chromosomes arrange themselves to form the equatorial plate.—The spindle body is complete; the chromosomes arrange themselves back to back in the form of a ring or plate at the equator of the spindle.

E. Metaphase.—At this stage division begins: the chromosomes split longitudinally into two equal parts.

F. Anaphase.—Some of the spindle filaments, attached to the chromosomes, contract and draw the chromosomes towards their respective poles, forming thus a somewhat compact mass. The centrosomes have already divided for the next cell-division.

G. Telophase.—A nucleus forms at each pole from the chromosomes.

H. When the division of the nucleus is complete, the protoplasm becomes constricted to complete the division of the cell.

Fig. 4[1]

Diagram of the first maturation-division in preparing sexual cells (reduction). In this maturation-division the phenomena are the same as those which are found in ordinary division except in the division of the nucleus.

A. Prophase.—The chromosomes assume the form of long thin loops. In this figure (division of a reproductive animal cell) the ends of the chromosomes are all turned towards the centrosphere. The chromatin accumulates at the same side and forms a *synapsis* stage.

B. The chromosomes attach themselves to one another in pairs beginning at their free ends.

C. The junction of the chromosomes throughout their whole length. The number of loops has been reduced to one half, and they are each twice as thick.

D. Strepsinema and the formation of the spindle.—The double chromosomes become twisted and shorten their length; the two chromosomes separate from each other to a certain extent and thus prepare what corresponds to the metaphase.

E. Beginning of the anaphase.—The chromosomes that were before joined to one another become completely separated in order to withdraw respectively to the poles of the spindle.

F. Telophase and cell division.—Each nucleus contains now only half the number of chromosomes that the original nucleus contained before the division which brought about the reduction.

[1] Original figures from nature, partly diagrammatic. Linear enlargement about 2,400.

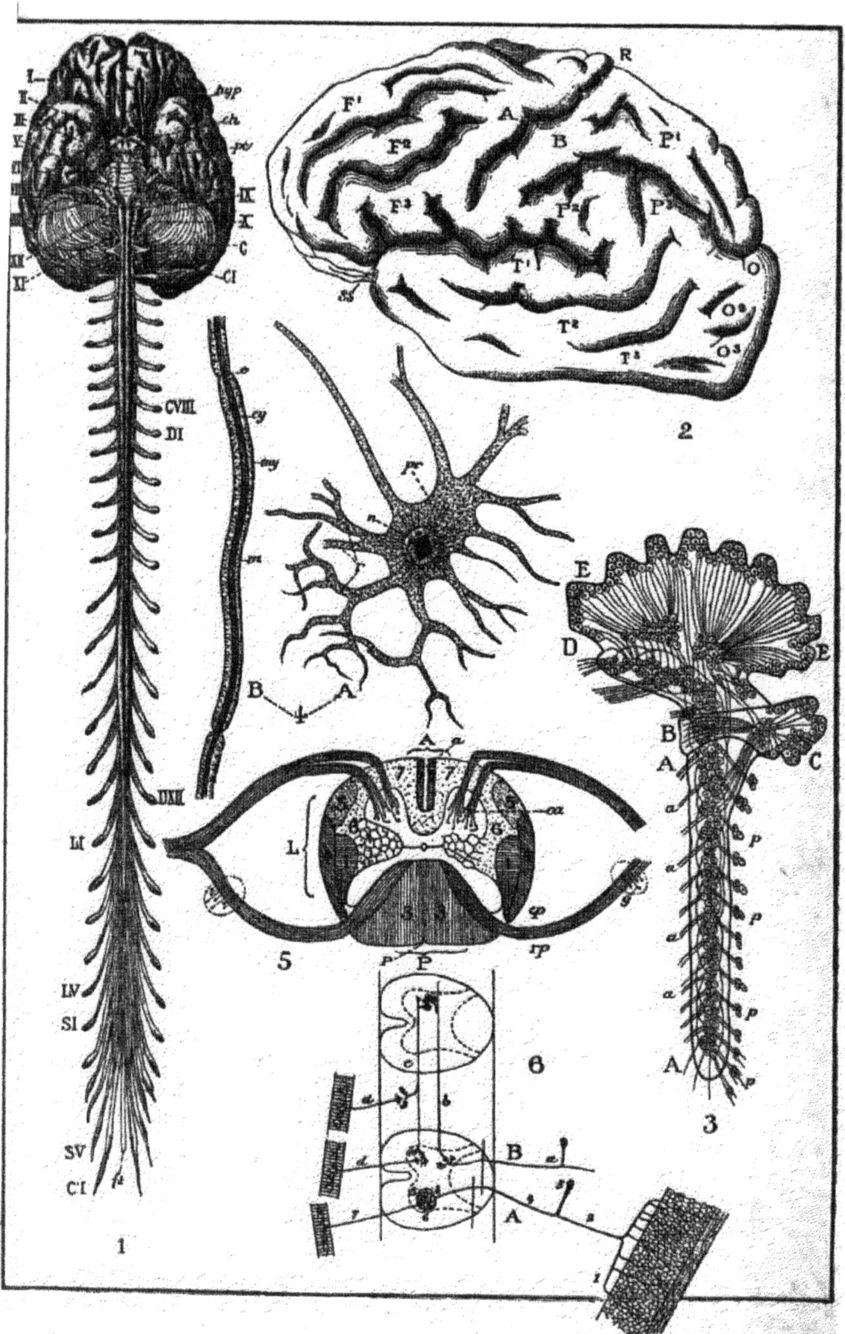
1
2
3
5
6
R
A
B
F¹
F²
F³
P¹
P²
P³
T¹
T²
T³
O
O²
O³
ss
CVIII
DI
DXII
LI
LV
SI
SV
CI
E
D
C
L

[To face p. 335.

PLATE II

Fig. 1[1] The brain and spinal cord (anterior view). ½ natural size.

- I to XII — cerebral nerves
- CI to CVIII — 8 cervical nerves
- DI to DXII — 12 dorsal nerves
- LI to LV — 5 lumbar nerves
- SI to SV — 5 nerves of the sacrum
- C'I — coccyx nerve
- *ft.* — terminal fibre
- *hyp.* — pituitary body.
- *op.* — optic chiasma.
- *pc.* — cerebral peduncles
- *o.* — olivary body.
- *c.* — cerebellum.

Fig. 2[2] Exterior view of the left hemisphere.

- *ss.* — fissure of Sylvius.
- *R.* — fissure of Rolando.
- *ip.* — interparietal fissure.
- F_1 F_2 F_3 — frontal convolutions.
- *A.* — anterior central or ascending frontal convolutions.
- *B.* — posterior central or ascending parietal convolutions.
- P_1 P_2 P_3 — parietal convolutions.
- T_1 T_2 T_3 — temporal or sphenoidal convolutions.
- O_1 O_2 O_3 — occipital convolutions.

Fig. 3[3] Diagram of the distribution of the nerve elements in the central portion of the cerebro-spinal system.

- *AA.* — spinal cord with commissures.
- *B.* — region of the protuberance.
- *C.* — cerebellum.
- *D.* — basal ganglia, optic layer, corpus striatum.
- *EE.* — grey cortical matter, cerebral convolutions.
- *aa.* — anterior roots.
- *pp.* — posterior roots.

Fig. 4

A. Nerve-cell
- *n.* — nucleus.
- *pr.* — protoplasm.
- *r.* — dendrites.

B. Nerve-fibre
- *cy.* — axis-cylinder of the nerve-cell.
- *my.* — myelin.
- *m.* — membrane or sheath of Schwann.
- *e.* — node.

Fig. 5 Diagram of spinal cord.

- *ca.* — anterior cornua with motor (efferent) cells.
- *cp.* — posterior cornua.
- *A. L. P.* — anterior, lateral and posterior cords.
- *1.* — pyramidal tract of the lateral cord.
- *2.* — pyramidal tract of the anterior cord or track of Türck.
- *3.* — posterior cord.
- *4.* — cerebellar tract of the lateral cord.
- *5.* — Gower's tract.
- *6 & 7.* — fundamental tracts of the lateral and anterior cords.
- *a. & p.* — anterior and posterior fissures.
- *ra. & rp.* — anterior and posterior nerve-roots.
- *g.* — spinal ganglion.

Fig. 6

A. Simple reflex arc
- *1.* peripheral endings of sensory nerve-fibre.
- *2.* sensory afferent fibre.
- *3.* sensory cell of the spinal ganglia.
- *4.* efferent dendrites of the grey matter of the cord.
- *5.* protoplasmic branched processes of a motor cell of the anterior cornua.
- *6.* motor cell of the anterior cornua.
- *7.* motor efferent fibre.

B. Compound reflex arc
- *a.* peripheral sensory neuron.
- *b.* central sensory neuron.
- *c.* central motor neuron.
- *d.* peripheral motor neuron.

[1] After M. A. Van Gehuchten, *Anatomie du system nerveux de l'homme*, 3rd ed. (Louvain, Uystpruyst, 1900).
[2] Féré, *Traité élémentaire d'anatomie médicale*, p. 75. [3] Mathias Duval, *Cours de Physiologie*, p. 42.

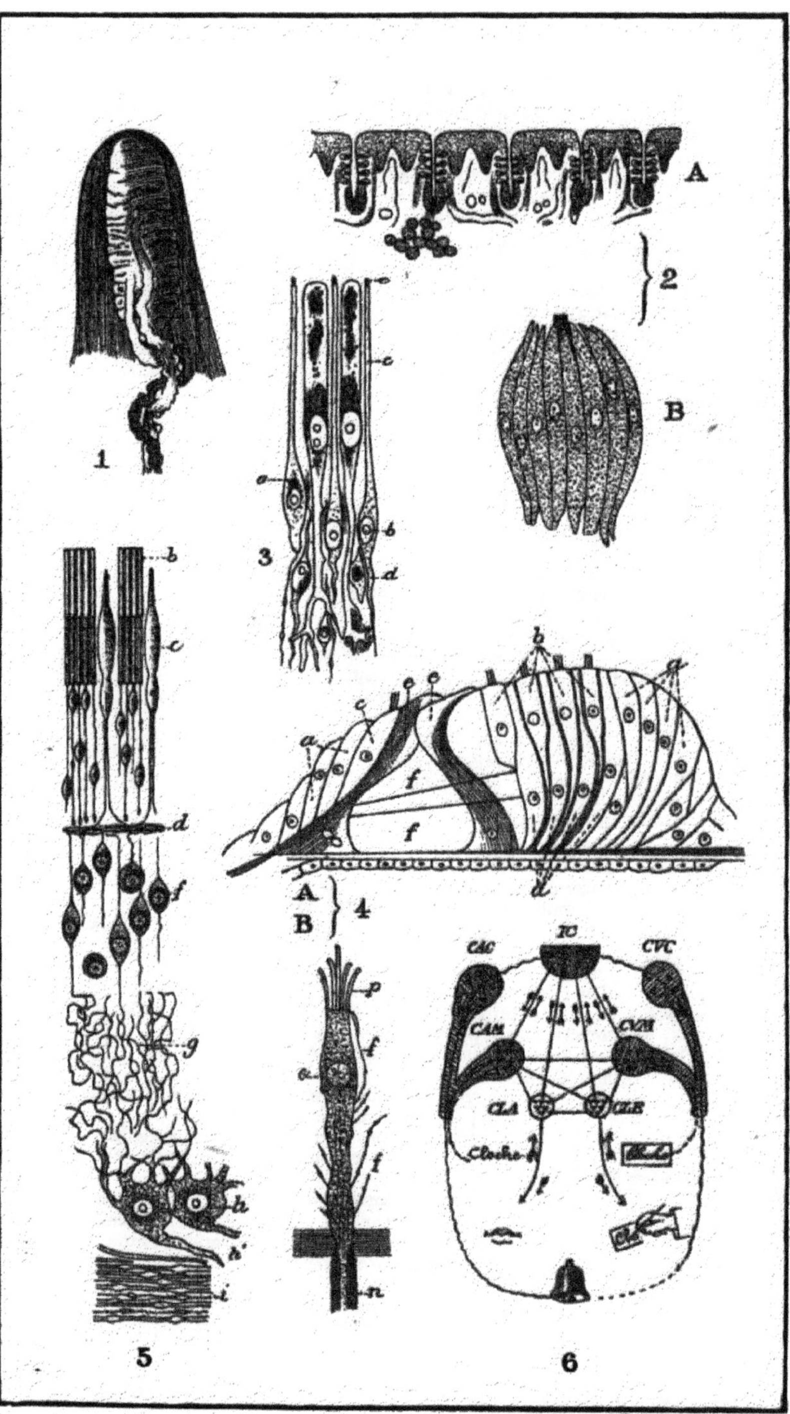

[To face p. 337.

PLATE III

Fig. 1 A nerve-papilla from the front of a man's index finger. In the papilla is the tactile corpuscle, into which the nerve-fibres penetrate (FREY, *Précis d'histologie*).

Fig. 2 *A*. Gustatory organ of a rabbit. Vertical section.
B. Taste corpuscle.

Fig. 3 Cells in the olfactory region in man. FREY, *op. cit.*
- *a*. epithelial cell terminating below in a branch-fibre.
- *b*. olfactory cells with their thin descending filaments.
- *c*. peripheral rod-cell.
- *e*. small vibrating ciliated prolongations.

Fig. 4a Organ of Corti after Retzius; diagrammatic.
- *a*. supporting cells.
- *b*. external acoustic cells.
- *c*. internal acoustic cells.
- *d*. cells of Deiters.
- *e*. pillar of organ of Corti.
- *f*. canal of Corti.

Fig. 4b Auditory cell showing hairs. FREY, *op. cit.*
- *c*. auditory cell.
- *p*. auditory hairs.
- *n*. nerve.
- *f*. nerve fibrils.

Fig. 5 Diagrammatic section of the retina, showing nerves. FREY, *op. cit.*
- *b*. rods.
- *c*. cones.
- *d*. interwoven delicate nervous fibres, from which fine nervous filaments bearing the inner granules or nuclei proceed to the inner surface.
- *f*. inner granular or nuclear layer.
- *g*. interwoven nerve fibrils in the molecular layer.
- *h*. ganglion-cells.
- *h'*. prolongations of the axis-cylinder.
- *i*. layer of nerve fibres.

Fig. 6. Charcot's diagram
- *CAC*. common auditory centre.
- *CAM*. centre for the auditory memory of words, from the lesion of which results word-deafness.
- *CVC*. common visual centre.
- *CVM*. centre for visual memory of words, from the lesion of which results word-blindness.
- *IC*. so-called intellectual centres or centre for the association of images.
- *CLA*. centre for the motor memory of articulation, from the lesion of which results motor aphasia.
- *CLE*. centre for the motor graphic memory, the lesion of which results in agraphia.

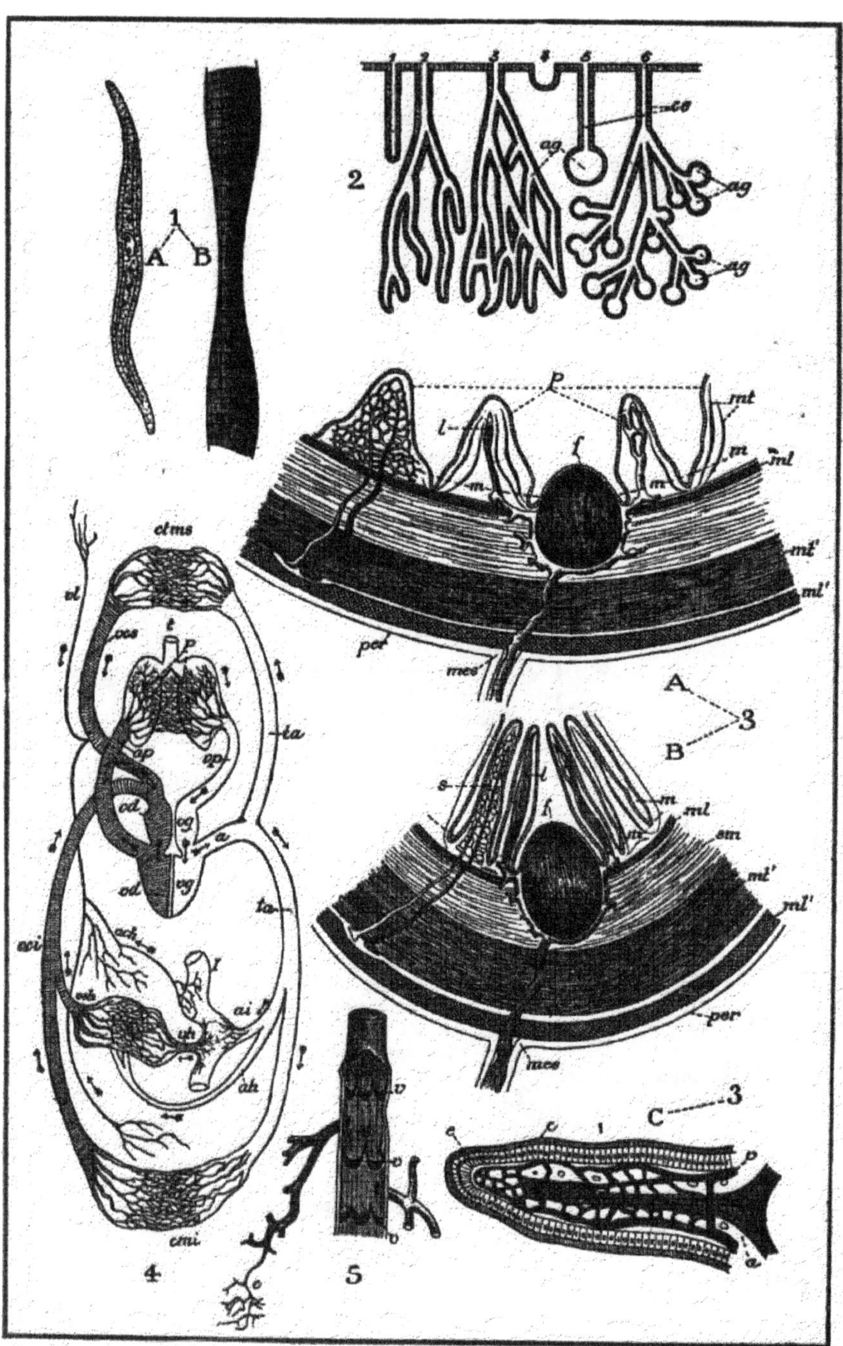
1
A
B
2
ce
ag
ag
ag
P
mt
l
m
ml
f
ml'
ml'
per
mes
A
B
3
s
l
m
ml
f
sm
ml'
ml'
per
mes
C
3
e
c
p
a
ctms
vl
t
p
ta
ap
ap
od
og
a
od
vg
ta
ach
ai
ah
cmi
4
v
v
5

[To face p. 339.

PLATE IV

Fig. 1 — Muscular fibres — *A*. Unstriated muscular fibre. *B*. Striated muscular fibre.

Fig. 2 — Diagram showing the formation of glands.
Glands are formed by an *invagination*, in the underlying tissues, of the epithelial membrane of the embryo. If the glandular tube preserves perceptibly the same diameter throughout its whole passage, it is called a *tubular gland* (1, 2, 3); if it terminates in a swelling, it is called *acinous* (4, 5, 6). When the tube does not branch, the glands are simple (1, 4, 5); otherwise they are composite (2, 3, 6)—*ce*, excretory duct; *ag*, acini.

Fig. 3 — *A*.[1] Portion of a transverse section of the small intestine, muscles relaxed (diagrammatic). Enlarged about 25 diameters.

- *p*. villosities of the intestine.
- *s*. network of blood vessels, formed by the branching of the capillaries from a small artery and a vein.
- *l*. lymphatic caniculus.
- *f*. solitary follicle.
- *m*. mucous membrane.
- *mt*. circular muscles of the mucous membrane.
- *ml*. longitudinal muscles of the same.
- *mt'*. circular muscles of the sub-mucous membrane.
- *m'*. longitudinal muscles of the same.
- *per*. peritoneum.
- *mes*. mesentery.

B.[2] Same section, with muscles contracted.

Fig. 3 — *C*.[3] Villosity of the intestine (enlarged about 70 times).

- *a*. small artery.
- *v*. small vein.
- *l*. lymphatic canal.
- *e*. epithelium.
- *c*. cuticle traversed by very fine caniculi.

Fig. 4 — Diagram showing the circulation of the blood and the lymph; the shaded part shows the passage of the venous blood, the other the passage of arterial blood; the arrows indicate the direction of the flow; *od*. right auricle; *og*. left auricle; *vd*. right ventricle; *vg*. left ventricle; *a*. aorta,; *ta*. arterial trunks; *ai*. artery passing into intestines, I; *ah*. hepatic artery passing into the liver, F; *cmi*. capillaries of the lower members; *cims*. capillaries of the head and upper members; *ap*. pulmonary artery; *vp*. pulmonary vein; *p*. the lungs; *t*. the trachea; *vcs*. superior vena cava; *vci*. inferior vena cava; *vh*. portal vein; *vsh*. hepatic veins; *vch*. chyle ducts; *vl*. lymph vessel.

Fig. 5 — Vein opened.

- *v*. valves.
- *c*. capillaries.

[1] Heitzmann, *Anatomie des Menschen*, IV, p. 267.
[2] Henri Blanc, *L'homme*, p. 124. Lausanne, 1902.
[3] *Ibid*., p. 158.

CRITERIOLOGY

INTRODUCTION*

1. Object of this Treatise. Its place in Philosophy. Criteriology is the *reflex study of our certain knowledge and of the grounds upon which its certitude rests.* The *criterion* (κρίνω, I judge or distinguish) of truth is the test by which we distinguish between truth and error; the word *criteriology* expresses the leading thought, but not the only thought of this branch of study.

It is also called *epistemology* (ἐπιστήμη, *scientia*, knowledge), the scientific study of knowledge. Knowledge is knowing with certitude; epistemology is therefore a *theory of certitude.*

Criteriology is not part of the science of logic. It is therefore erroneous to call it, as is not infrequently done, 'real logic'. This expression comes from Kant. According to him, the mind receives from without passive impressions (matter) which before becoming knowledge must be moulded, as it were, by certain mental *forms.* In such a system a distinction between formal logic and real logic has to be made: the first treating of the presupposed form, the second of the matter moulded by this form. But this Kantian distinction is as false as the system of which it forms a part. The name itself 'real logic' implies a contradiction; for logic studies being as it exists in the mind, that is to say, the attributes with which things become invested in and by the action of the mind, e.g. esse subjicibile, esse praedicabile. It is thus distinguished from metaphysics which has real being for its object. It is therefore a contradiction in terms to speak of 'real logic',

* Books for study or consultation:—

Card. Mercier, *Critériologie générale* (6th ed., 1911, Institut supérieure de Philosophie, Louvain).

St. George Mivart, *On Truth* (Kegan Paul, London 1889).

Rother, *Truth*, and *Certitude* (Herder, London).

Walker, *Theories of Knowledge* (Longmans, London).

Card. Newman, *Grammar of Assent* (Longmans, London).

meaning thereby that logic considers ontological or real things as such.

Criteriology studies certitude, which is a property of the act of knowledge ; hence it is directly connected with ideology and thus with psychology. In view of the importance of this study since the time of Descartes and Kant it is rightly made into a separate treatise.

2. Division of the Treatise.—Criteriology, or the science of certitude, comprises two parts : the first, *general criteriology*, analyses certitude itself, in so far as it is common to all certain knowledge ; the second, *special criteriology*, makes a particular examination of the certitude of the *different kinds* of knowledge possessed by the human mind.

PART I

General Criteriology

3. Outline of Part I.—In the first chapter, after having explained the terms of the problems to be solved, we shall determine the formulation of these problems. Here we shall be brought to recognize that there is a preliminary problem, as well as a fundamental one of a double nature. The second chapter will treat of the solution of the preliminary problem. The third and the fourth with the solution of the two fundamental problems. Hence we may tabulate a scheme of general criteriology as follows:

CHAP. I.	Problems to be solved	1. Terms. 2. Statement.
CHAP. II.	Solution of the preliminary problem.	
CHAP. III.	Solution of the first fundamental problem.	
CHAP. IV.	Solution of the second fundamental problem.	

CHAPTER I

PROBLEMS TO BE SOLVED

I. Terms

Certitude, which is the object of criteriology, signifies, as we shall show, the state of the human mind when it recognizes that it knows the truth. We must begin, then, by inquiring what is truth, what is it to know the truth, what is it to be conscious of knowing the truth or to have certitude.

4. Common Meaning of 'True' and 'Truth'.—In popular language we speak of the objects we know and of things as true just as much as we predicate truth of our knowledge of things. Thus of a certain liquid we say: this is true wine, or, truly this is wine; and we say that: it is a truth that two and two make four. Now what do we mean?

We say this *object* of our knowledge is true, viz., that the parts added together, $2+2$, are the same as their sum 4. Again, as 'wine' is the name given to an alcoholic liquor produced by the fermentation of the juice of the grape, the fermented juice of the grape is *true* wine; any other artificial concoction resembling it is not *true* wine, or is not *truly* wine. Hence a liquid is *true* wine, when it corresponds with the definition we use to express the nature of wine. In general, we apply the predicate 'true' to a thing when it corresponds with that type in our mind by means of which we represent to ourselves its nature; the thing thought of by the mind, we say, *verifies* the idea we have formed of its nature. The *truth* of a thing is therefore its conformity with the nature, already known, of that thing.

Truth, considered as an attribute of objects or of things known by us, is called *objective or ontological* truth, whilst it is *logical or subjective* truth when considered as an attribute of our knowledge.

5. Ontological Truth implies a Relation between Two Terms.—No one uses the word 'true' of a thing considered absolutely, merely in itself. You cannot say 'This wine is true, this poplar is true'; but 'This is true wine, this tree is a true poplar'. Similarly no one says 'Two is true, three is untrue'; but we say 'It is true that 2+2 make 4'. We compare two numerical expressions, and the relation of identity or non-identity which we observe to exist between them is for us a true object, an objective truth. We compare a definite thing, this or that, this tree, etc., with another term, namely, with the type which our mind conceives as realizing the definition of wine or of poplar.

The first term of our comparison—this object, this tree—is given here and now by experience; the second term is an abstract concept already previously present to the mind. When the first term coincides with the definition of the second, we say that it is truly the second, or simply that it is the second: this liquid is true wine, this tree is a poplar.

Objective or ontological truth is therefore the conformity of, or relation of identity between, two thought-objects, one actually perceived and the other a preconceived ideal type. This conformity is objective, inasmuch as it is based on the very content, or the nature of the objects represented.

Such is the exact meaning of the classical definition *Veritas est adaequatio rei et intellectus.* By *res* must be understood a thing actually perceived or an object imagined at the moment. By *intellectus*, the abstract ideal type already conceived of the thing. The exact conformity, *adequatio vel conformitas,* of the thing perceived or imagined with its mental type, is its truth.

The thing, considered in itself, may be termed *fundamentally* true, since it is the real foundation of the relation; but *formal* truth is only in the relation.

To *assert* this relation is to formulate a judgment.

6. Logical Truth or the Truth of the Judgment.—Logical truth is a quality of the judgment when the mind pronounces the identity or non-identity of the contents of two concepts between which there exists, *a parte rei*, an objective conformity or want of conformity. To know the truth, therefore, means to recognize and affirm this relation of identity or non-identity.

When the verdict of the mind is such that it is in accordance with the relation of the two terms as they objectively exist, or when it affirms that a subject has a nature which in point of fact does belong to it, the judgment is true; it enjoys *logical truth*, because it conforms to objective truth. On the other hand, when the mind asserts a relation which does not objectively exist, when it affirms that a subject has a nature which does not belong to it, the judgment is false and tainted with logical error, inasmuch as it does not conform to objective truth.

The knowledge of the truth is, then, not an act of simple apprehension, but what the Scholastics called 'compositio et divisio', a judgment.

7. God is the Foundation of all Truth.—Let us for the moment *suppose* as already demonstrated both the capability of the human mind to know things as they are in themselves, and the validity of the principles which it employs; we shall then be in a position of advantage to view the whole system of truth as it is developed by St. Thomas.

God, the Necessary Being, who exists from all eternity and possesses an infinite mind, knows Himself in an infinite degree, that is to say, as far as He is knowable. His knowledge extends not only to what He is in Himself, but also in so far as He is imitable—though imperfectly—by the finite beings which He has power to create. Everything that He freely creates must be fashioned on the model of these divine ideas, as a work of art is fashioned after the ideal the artist forms of his work before he makes it. It follows that all created things correspond with the eternal idea God formed of their nature; this adequate correspondence is their truth; it is *essential* to them and is immutable. The truth resulting from human knowledge is only a reflection of the truth manifested by God in His works.

Taking this higher view of the order of the universe, we may say that truth resides, in the first place, in the Divine Intelligence which eternally conceives the idea of His works. It belongs, in the second place, to things in so far as they are realized in conformity with their eternal archetypal ideas. And finally, it passes from things into human knowledge as soon as the mind represents to itself things as they are.

This synthetic view, of course, finds its legitimate place at the end of the study of criteriology, as it would be unscientific to postulate it at the outset, during the analytical process, seeing that the existence of an infinitely perfect God needs to be proved by premisses which must themselves first be established.

8. 'Evidence' and 'Certitude'.—Etymologically *evidence* means a bringing to light, a manifestation (*e-videri*); it is the manifestation of objective truth. When objects of representation are compared by the mind, it becomes apparent that they bear to each other certain relations and the manifestation of these makes judgment possible.

Evidence is a quality of objects known; *certitude* is a state of the subject knowing. We say that we are *certain* when we are fully conscious that we know the truth. Certitude therefore implies that some true knowledge, or a judgment, is the object of an intellectual perception. In other words, certitude is the result of reflection.

Sometimes the phrase 'spontaneous certitude' is used to designate the state of the mind pronouncing a judgment under the sole influence of the object, without any reflection having been made. But this state should rather be called 'spontaneous assent', for *true certitude is always the result of reflection*, since in order to be certain we must be conscious of knowing the truth.

In answer to the question 'What is it that gives us certitude?' it will be seen later that it is the perception of the relation of identity or conformity between the two terms of the judgment.

Every judgment brings before me a relation to be established between two terms. If on reflection I see this relation clearly (e.g. if on examining the two terms '2+2' and '4', I see their identity), I declare that I am certain. When, on the contrary, the mind does not clearly perceive the relation between the two terms, it remains in a state of suspense, a state that is termed *doubt*.

We may, then, define certitude as the firm adherence of the mind to a truth after due reflection and because a relation of identity or conformity between two terms has been perceived.

The meaning of these terms being settled, we are in a position to inquire into the exact scope of the problem proposed in criteriology—Have we knowledge of which we are justified in saying that we are certain?

II. Statement of the Problems

9. General Statement.—It is a fact, which even the sceptic will not gainsay, that we are in possession of a number of propositions of which we think, rightly or wrongly, that we are certain, propositions to which we give a spontaneous and even irresistible assent; spontaneous certitude does exist as a subjective fact. The question to be determined is whether this spontaneous assent is justifiable; whether by deliberate reflection upon a proposition to which we spontaneously assent we can show this spontaneous assent to be legitimate, thus obtaining reflex assent and true certitude. If we can find an affirmative answer, then our knowledge stands justified. If we cannot, but have to reply in the negative, then we shall have to confess our nature to possess a radical flaw, inasmuch as our spontaneous assents and those consequent upon reflection are contradictory of each other; we shall have to trust blindly to our spontaneous knowledge without any hope of testing its validity and thus allow the very triumph of scepticism.

Before dealing with the problem, let us first notice a wrong way of setting it forth.

10. False Statement of the Question in the Philosophy of Descartes.—Since the time of Descartes it has been customary to formulate the problem of certitude in this way: Is human reason able to know things as they really are? Or, in other words: Can we attain to a consciousness that our ideas are conformable to things as they are in themselves? How can the mind arrive at an assurance of this conformity?

This manner of formulating the problem must be rejected:—

1. Because it is *incomplete*. It mutilates the problem of certitude in an arbitrary way; for the greatest and certainly most important part of our cognitions is concerned not with external realities but with relations between certain objects, independently of any heed to their contingent existence: of such a nature is the proposition '2+2 make 4' and other mathematical propositions. To formulate the problem in this way thus suppresses the question of certitude in all the abstract truths which make up the rational sciences.

2. Because it *changes the nature of the problem of truth*. In fact it leads to a twofold absurdity. (*a*) On the one hand,

to endeavour to know things as they really are is to aim at establishing an adequate and absolute conformity between our knowledge and a real object such as it is in itself independently of our knowledge of it. Now a thing as it exists considered without reference to our knowledge is, as far as we are concerned, as if it did not exist, a pure non-entity. It is then an absurdity to try, under these conditions, to form a comparison between a mental representation and the-thing-in-itself. (*b*) On the other hand, a cognition is an immanent act which necessarily partakes of the nature of the subject knowing, 'cognitio est in cognoscente ad modum cognoscentis'. To pretend to an adequate conformity between the representation of an object and this object-in-itself is to endeavour to have a cognition in which the subject takes no part at all, in which the nature of the subject is not reflected. This is really wishing to know without knowing.

This error proceeds from the fact that it is forgotten that truth belongs only to an act of judgment, not to a simple concept (6). Consequently, to know the truth does not consist in seeing the identity between a concept and the real thing-in-itself represented by that concept, but it consists in seeing the identity between the subject and the predicate of a judgment, between a subject now apprehended and an abstract note already previously known.

11. The Problems of Criteriology.—The object of the general problem of criteriology is to ascertain the validity of our mental assents, to check our spontaneous judgments. It resolves itself into two fundamental problems, one concerning the *form* of the judgment or the precise meaning of the relationship the two terms subject and predicate bear to each other, the other concerning the *matter* or the terms, subject and predicate, in themselves (Logic, 31).

1. The first question to propose itself concerns the *nature of the mental synthesis* by which we affirm the identity or agreement (*componere* in the language of the Scholastics) of the terms of a judgment. According to Kant this synthesis is determined solely by the nature of the thinking subject. In our opinion it is caused, or motived, by something else than the thinking subject, it is due to an objective manifestation of a relation. In a word the question resolves itself into: Is the mental synthesis subjective or objective?

This first problem to be solved, it must be noticed, leaves out of count the question of the real or fictitious nature of the terms of the relation and considers merely the relation itself. It may rightly be termed, as we shall see later, the question concerning the *objectivity of the ideal order* (Chap. III).

2. When we have proved that the judgment has an objective character, the question then arises about the value of the terms involved in it. Are the two terms pure creations of the mind, with no counterpart in real fact, or are they trustworthy representations of objects which really exist? This second problem is then that of the *objective reality of our concepts* (Chap. IV).

Before however we can embark on either of these two questions, there is a preliminary matter to settle. The object of epistemology is to analyse and to verify our knowledge of truth, and so of every truth. Consequently it is both legitimate and necessary to ask whether at the outset we may presuppose anything at all and what we may presuppose. This is the question concerning *the initial state of mind* of one inquiring into the main problem of certain knowledge (Chap. II). It is the claim of *sceptics* that we must begin the inquiry, if not by denying, at least by calling in question the mind's capability of knowing the truth. Certain *dogmatists*, on the other hand, assert that it is first of all necessary to postulate its capability. Clearly then we must open our inquiry by asking what is the true attitude of mind if we are to start without any unwarrantable assumption.

CHAPTER II

SOLUTION OF THE PRELIMINARY PROBLEM: CONCERNING THE INITIAL STATE OF THE MIND

12. Statement of the Question.—To answer the preliminary question just proposed we must first examine and refute the *theory of universal doubt* (I), according to which we are bound a priori to regard our reason with suspicion, as capable of labouring under invincible error; and next, the *ultra-dogmatic theory* according to which the serious consequences of scepticism can be avoided only by the a priori assumption that the mind is capable of knowing the truth (II). We shall then be in a position to prove our own thesis, of *rational dogmatism* (III), that the true initial state of the mind with regard to the validity of our reason is one of indifference; that is, a priori the mind must necessarily remain in suspense until by an analysis of its act of knowledge it comes to learn the cause of its knowledge.

I. Universal Doubt

13. Real Doubt and Fictitious Doubt.—The partisans of universal doubt may be grouped into two schools. The one, advocating *real* scepticism, actually doubts on the subject of the truth of our knowledge and makes no attempt to dissolve this doubt; its representatives have been many in every age. The other school, whilst assured of ultimately arriving at certitude, maintains the need of a process of a *methodical doubt* about everything. This doubt is of course fictitious; it is a doubt about everything for the express purpose of being better able to justify one's acts of knowledge. The principal representative of methodic doubt is Descartes.

14. Real Scepticism. Its Arguments.—The claim of the real sceptic is that we must regard as doubtful not only each of the acts of the human reason but also its very capability of arriving at a knowledge of the truth; and further that it is impossible to find a way out of this doubt. The two chief arguments that scepticism advances are as follows:—

1. *Argument drawn from fact:* Our consciousness bears witness that we frequently deceive ourselves. In any given case, then, it is the mark of a prudent man to suppose that he may be subject to self-deception. Whence it follows we should necessarily doubt of all our acts of cognition.

2. *Argument drawn from the 'vicious circle':* Before we can affirm a proposition as certain we must, unless we are willing to admit it on mere a priori grounds, verify it by means of some other judgment which shall serve as a criterion of truth. Yet this criterion itself must be in its own turn verified, and this can only be done by means of some other criterion, and so on *ad infinitum*[1]. Thus do we argue in a circle, and are forced to conclude that there is no certain truth and that universal doubt is the law of our mind.

15. The Methodic Doubt of Descartes.—In his *Discours sur la méthode,* Descartes attempted to build up on a solid foundation the whole edifice of human knowledge. For this purpose he commenced by putting in doubt as far as he could all that he had previously admitted.

1. He begins by doubting the *acts* of the senses, of consciousness and of reason. Our senses often deceive us and therefore they cannot be relied upon. Again, when we are sleeping and dreaming, our inner consciousness is not sufficient to enable us to distinguish whether we are asleep or awake. We can call into doubt even the very simplest propositions, such as '2+3 make 5'.

2. He doubts also the very *capability* of our faculties to arrive at the truth, since maybe there is a radical flaw in our nature, or some evil genius maliciously deceives us with his illusions.

Whilst Descartes calls everything in question, he yet believes he can escape from this universal doubt by remarking that he who is doubting must necessarily be something: 'Cogito, ergo sum'. Here then, he says, we have a certain

[1] 'To form a judgment on the appearances we receive of things we must have what will serve as a standard of judgment; to verify this standard we must have a proof; to verify this proof we must have a standard: and so we have a real spinning wheel. Then again our senses alone will not put an end to the difficulty, reason must be brought in; but any argument from reason will not stand without another argument to establish it: and so we go on for ever'. Montaigne's Essays, Bk. II, ch. XII.

and most firm foundation on which all knowledge may be built up.

Whilst the real sceptic remains steadfast in his doubt, Descartes henceforth parts company with him. Yet for all that, as we view the matter, the difference between them is of no great moment, for at any given time Descartes is still himself a sceptic; he not only makes an attempt at doubting but he really doubts, even justifying his doubt by the above general reasons which extend in their application to every kind of knowledge whatsoever (17).

16. Criticism of Real Scepticism.—It is not sufficient for a refutation of scepticism to say, as is commonly done, that the attitude of the sceptic is in contradiction to common sense, since man is by nature dogmatic. For he may reply that he does not deny the existence as a matter of fact of man's spontaneous assents; merely that it is impossible to justify them.

Again the argument has been brought against the sceptic that he is necessarily contradicting himself in his very assertion that he is certain that everything is doubtful. He may answer that he asserts nothing at all, that indeed he doubts about everything, even about his doubt.

The true way of meeting the sceptic is to say that it is quite arbitrary to suppose a priori the inability of the mind to attain to truth. It is just this ability of the mind which is the subject of debate between the sceptic and the dogmatist. And here the two arguments of the sceptic will not stand.

1. The sceptic argues: We deceive ourselves sometimes, therefore we deceive ourselves always. But, he who proves too much proves nothing. It is true that we deceive ourselves sometimes, and therefore we must be cautious in our assertions. But whatever the sceptic may say, if we have a criterion, that is to say, a means of checking and of avoiding errors, we shall be able to determine whether in a given case we have arrived at the truth or must remain in a state of doubt.

2. The argument he draws from the vicious circle wrongly supposes that we must always justify a proposition by means of a criterion distinct from this proposition itself. We shall see later that the act of the mind which unites the predicate of a judgment to its subject can in the majority of cases find its justification by means of itself, and consequently it does not need the assistance of a criterion other than itself.

The sceptic then has no right *to lay down as a principle* that it is doubtful whether the mind is capable of knowing.

17. Criticism of Descartes' Methodic Doubt.—1. The transition from doubt to certitude that Descartes makes is illogical. His doubt is at the beginning purely speculative; but the reasons which he brings forward to justify it have an import so general that his doubt must necessarily become *universal* and *real*. For (*a*) after all the *acts* of consciousness have been brought into doubt, for the same reasons it should be possible to reject its testimony when it assures me of my existence, just as in the case of my doubt. To be logical, Descartes ought to have said: I am aware that I doubt; it is possible that I exist, but I may be deceived. (*b*) When he has called into doubt our very *nature* which is the foundation of all our faculties and the source of all our activities, it is illogical to withdraw any particular acts from the dominion of this doubt. If some evil genius has deceived us in certain cases, it is illogical to assert that we are beyond the power of his dupery when we say 'cogito, ergo sum'. Fictitious or real, *universal* doubt leads nowhere and without a violation of reasoning it can never be a means of leading us to certitude.

2. There are two fundamental errors in Descartes' theory. (*a*) He has misinterpreted his consciousness, for as a matter of fact the doubt which is possible and necessary in the case of certain truths does not exist in the case of others. To arrive at truth it is certainly necessary to push back the doubt as far as possible. But how far back can this doubt go? It is first of all necessary to regard as doubtful all mediate propositions which are capable of as well as need proof. But it is impossible to demonstrate every proposition. For there is no demonstration that does not presuppose two certain premisses; we must then eventually arrive at some indemonstrable principles, some immediate propositions. Now among these immediate propositions there are some whose terms are present to the mind without the bond which unites them being immediately seen. Of these we may still doubt until an attentive examination of the terms reveals their identity or their non-identity. But there are other propositions whose terms are so simple that the very moment they come before the mind the necessary bond uniting them is immediately visible: such for example is the principle of identity. Surely this

latter kind of immediate proposition must from its very nature be excluded from the category of those which are doubtful. Descartes was then wrong in wishing to exclude from this class merely the affirmation that he existed, since we see that quite a number of other truths, notably first principles, ought equally to be excluded for the same reason.—(*b*) The hypothesis of an evil genius does not justify a doubt that is universal. Since the mind is capable of reflecting on its acts, no evil spirit could prevent its seeing the relation of identity or non-identity between two terms. An evil spirit could not, then, deceive us concerning every truth; and especially would the first truths of the ideal order escape his power of deception. To accept the hypothesis of an evil genius or of some deity, good or bad, *before* having studied the acts of the mind and their validity is to be guilty of using a method that must certainly be condemned. Descartes ought, at least for the time being, to have avoided taking his fantastic supposition for granted, and to have abstained from any judgment regarding the ability or inability of the mind to attain to the truth.

Let us add that the claim to justify all our cognitions by referring them to a single principle of which it is impossible to doubt is merely an idle dream.

II. Exaggerated Dogmatism

18. Theory of Three Primary Truths.—Universal doubt, whether real or fictitious, cannot be defended. Does it then follow that we are warranted in commencing our study of epistemology with the postulate that the mind is capable of knowing the truth? A number of philosophers have thought so. Thus Tongiorgi asserts that before any examination can take place, it is necessary, if we are not to fall into scepticism, to affirm *three primary truths*, and three only, to wit: (*a*) a primary fact, *the existence* of him who examines the problem of certitude; (*b*) a primary principle, *the principle of contradiction*; (*c*) a primary condition, *the capability of the mind* to have ideas that are conformable to reality, or, more briefly, *to know the truth*. These truths are primary in the sense that they are incapable of demonstration, since they must be presupposed in every philosophical demonstration. We can neither deny them nor argue against them without implicitly affirming them.[2]

[2] Cp. Tongiorgi, *Institutiones philosophicae*, I, 465.

19. Criticism.—1. Even if this theory were well established, it is useless as a refutation of scepticism, since it takes a wrong view of the real problem of certitude. The theory put briefly is that there are certain indemonstrable truths which the sceptic necessarily affirms in his effort to deny them. Now it is not the necessity of affirming certain propositions that is the problem we are discussing. We are all agreed that these necessary spontaneous assents do exist as a psychological fact. The question at issue is what is the nature of this necessity; we have to find out whether this necessary affirmation is a blind one or one determined by an objective motive.

2. Secondly the theory is not well established, for these supposed primary truths are not fundamental in the sense that they must be presupposed for every demonstration, or in fact for every certain affirmation. By asserting that these three primary truths are at the basis of every demonstration, the advocates of this theory are guilty of confounding the *ontological* order with the *logical*. Of course in the *ontological* order no demonstration can take place unless there exist a person to know the truth; but it is quite a different thing to find out if, before a demonstration takes place, it is necessary, in the *logical* order, to *affirm* positively the existence of the thinker, the principle of contradiction and the capability of the mind to know the truth. Indeed, (*a*) the affirmation of the *existence of the thinking subject* is not at the base of every certain affirmation: truths of the ideal order are independent of it. It is certain that 2+2=4, no matter whether I affirm my existence or not, although of course from the ontological point of view I must necessarily exist before I can know or enunciate this truth. (*b*) The *principle of contradiction* is certainly a primary truth, a primary principle without which we can affirm nothing. Yet this principle is not itself one that can serve as a premiss to a demonstration, for no other truth can be drawn from it; it is rather a light which guides us in the making of all our judgments. (*c*) If the *capability of the mind to know the truth* were not granted as a fact in the ontological order, the mind could never attain to any true knowledge; for an effect can never be produced unless there exists a cause capable of producing it. But, we may ask once again, is it on this account necessary, in the logical order, that the knowledge of the cause should always precede the knowledge of the effect? Evidently not;

on the contrary, it is by the effect that, logically, we know the cause. We conclude then that the affirmation that the mind is capable of knowing the truth does not logically precede the affirmation of other truths, although these are, ontologically, the effects of the capability of the mind being exercised.

These supposed primary truths, if we except the principle of contradiction, are not so self-evident as to call for no proof. If they do not demand demonstration in the strict sense of the word, yet certainly an attentive examination is necessary to bring out their evidence. Especially does the capability of the mind to know the truth need consideration, if not actual demonstration, for is it not the very subject of this treatise? To affirm it a priori is to ignore the problem of certitude instead of solving it.

III. Mitigated or Rational Dogmatism

20. The True Initial State of Mind.—We can, then, assert a priori neither the essential *incapability* of the human reason (universal doubt) nor its general *capability* to know the truth (exaggerated dogmatism.) Between these two extreme theories there is room for an intermediate one which we adopt as our own, one which we shall call mitigated or rational dogmatism. It may be stated thus:—

1. As regards the capability of our *faculties* or powers of acquiring knowledge, mitigated dogmatism *deliberately abstains* from making a judgment, holding that at the beginning of the study of the problem of certitude it is impossible either to affirm or to deny our mental capability of knowing truth. Before a judgment can be pronounced we must first study the value of the mind's acts. The first and immediate subject for our reflection is not the power as such but the acts, from which alone we come to a knowledge of the nature of the faculty that elicits them. If by dint of reflection we can discover that our mental acts, our assents are objective, that is, conformable to things as they are in reality, then and then only shall we be able legitimately to infer that our mind is capable of attaining true knowledge. After all, this manner of procedure is a truly scientific method based upon observation: to use a homely comparison, a good digestion is the only proof of the stomach's ability to digest properly.

2. As regards our judgments or *the acts* of the mind by

which truth is attained, the initial state of the intelligence at the outset of the study of epistemology differs according as these judgments are *mediately* or *immediately* evident. In the case of the former *doubt* cannot be avoided, whilst in that of the latter, which stand firm against any doubt, a state of certitude is always present.

Indeed, when the mind examines the propositions by which it expresses its knowledge, it finds a great number of them in which it does not see the identity or the non-identity between the predicate and the subject. All these propositions are necessarily doubtful, and this doubt is not a methodical one, but one psychologically necessary; it would be against all common sense to affirm an identity which one does not see. They remain doubtful until they have been demonstrated, that is to say, until they have been traced back to more general propositions that are certain. This doubt about *mediate* propositions—for this is what they are called—is not an invention of modern philosophy. Aristotle and St. Thomas have always recognized it in practice, and have been far from overlooking the many advantages it brings.

But it is impossible, as we have said, to demonstrate everything. As St. Thomas says, a proposition cannot be demonstrated by itself but only by means of another proposition. If not, one of two suppositions would follow, both of which are equally absurd. (*a*) Either all propositions are linked to another as it were in the form of a circle, that each one may be proved by another. Yet a proposition by means of which another is proved ought to be better known than this other. Whence in this circle each proposition would be at the same time better known and less known than the others. (*b*) Or else the propositions are united, not in the circle, but in an unlimited straight line. In this supposition, nothing at all could be demonstrated; the conclusion of one demonstration would become certain only when it had been traced back to propositions that were absolutely certain and had themselves no need of demonstration. Therefore, if such were the case, there could be no satisfaction without going back *ad infinitum*, which is of course absurd [3]. Sooner or later, then, the demon-

[3] 'Si enim omnia demonstrarentur, cum idem per seipsum non demonstretur, sed per aliud, oportet esse circulum in demonstrationibus. Quod esse non potest: quia sic idem esset notius et minus notum. Vel oporteret

stration of mediate propositions leads us back to indemonstrable premisses which we call *immediate propositions*: such are all propositions in which the identity or the non-identity of the predicate with the subject is seen by the simple comparison of the terms. These immediate propositions, although indemonstrable, are by no means doubtful: their very evidence makes them indemonstrable, that is to say, incapable of being referred to propositions which are more evident. And when they are reflected upon by the mind, they necessarily draw its assent, *they force their truth upon the mind.*

21. The Data of the Problem of Epistemology.—In setting out to solve the problem of certitude we therefore suppose only *two facts*, which sceptics themselves are willing to admit, namely, the existence of necessary spontaneous assents and the power to examine these by reflection. To disallow these data would make the problem of certitude impossible, inasmuch as to suppress '*id de quo* quaeritur' necessarily involves the suppression of '*id quod* quaeritur'. There is however all the difference in the world between taking these data for granted and the a priori assertion that we are sure to find scepticism wrong, that the result of our investigation must be the dogmatic thesis that the mind is capable of knowing truth.

procedere in infinitum, sed si in infinitum procederetur, non esset demonstratio; quia quaelibet demonstrationis conclusio redditur certa per reductionem ejus in primum demonstrationis principium: quod non esset si in infinitum demonstratio sursum procederet. Patet igitur quod non omnia sunt demonstrabilia'. St. Thomas, *In XII Met.*, IV, lect. 6.

CHAPTER III

OBJECTIVITY OF PROPOSITIONS OF THE IDEAL ORDER

22. Meaning.—To check the judgments of the mind to which we spontaneously assent, the first question to settle is that of the *nature of the synthesis* which is made between the predicate and the subject.

This question arises both in the case of judgments of the *ideal* order in which the relation can be stated independently of experience, and also in the case of judgments of the *real* order in which the statement implies the affirmation that a thing really exists. Now in this chapter, for reasons of method which will become apparent later, we shall deal only with propositions of the ideal order. And further, we shall restrict the problem to *immediate* propositions of the ideal order, since mediate propositions draw their value from these.

The question then to engage our attention for the present is how to establish the value of our simple fundamental propositions, those which furnish an immediate certitude inasmuch as they enunciate the very simplest relations between things, such as for instance, 'The whole is greater than its part'; 'Two things that are equal to the same thing are equal to each other'.

We must bear in mind that the value of these propositions is independent of the real or existential order. Though I were to suppose the material world as non-existent, yet I could still consider as true the *relation* stated in such a proposition as, 'The whole is greater than its part'. Considered in this way, this relation belongs to the ideal order. I may then go on to inquire if there exist in reality quantities capable of division into parts; and if there are, the relationship I have stated then applies also to the real order.

Dealing, then, only with the ideal order, we have to ask: Are our immediate judgments of this order truly valid?—They will be so on condition that we can establish that they have a legitimate motive of certitude, a *certain sign by which the truth is knowable*, a *criterion* of truth.

23. Division.—In the first section (I) we shall prove that the criterion of certitude cannot be *extrinsic* to the truth which it claims to justify; that it cannot be *subjective*, that is to say that it cannot reside solely in the psychological fact of the assent of the mind; that it must be immediate, that is to say, perceptible without a process of reasoning. In the second section (II) we shall see that this criterion—intrinsic, objective and immediate—is none other than an objective manifestation of the identity, total or partial, of the two terms of the judgment. This will be a refutation of the *subjectivism* of Kant. In the third section (III) we shall defend against *positivists* the validity of our judgments of the ideal order.

I. Essential Conditions of the Criterion

The criterion of truth must be *intrinsic*, *objective*, and *immediate*. By establishing this thesis we shall refute the false systems of epistemology which have misconceived one or other of these conditions.

§ 1.—*The Criterion must be Intrinsic*

24. Traditionalism.—The most well-known representatives of this system, de Bonald and La Mennais, in order the better to refute the arguments of rationalism against religion, laid down the principle that the human reason is incapable by itself of attaining to a certain knowledge in matters metaphysical, religious or moral. They maintained that these truths must have been originally revealed by God to humanity, and that this primitive revelation has been handed down by tradition either through *social teaching* (so de Bonald) or by the *general reason* that is the basis of the beliefs admitted by all mankind (so La Mennais).

The last motive of certitude in these matters is thus an *act of faith* in divine revelation. Indeed if we follow the general implication of the arguments brought forward by the traditionalists we find that in its last analysis *all certitude rests on an act of faith.*

To prove the impotence of human reason the traditionalists,

like the sceptics, take their stand upon the weaknesses and errors of the intelligence.

The necessity of an initial revelation, according to de Bonald, is based on the fact of language. He argues thus:—Man possesses language. But man could not have invented it; for to do so the power of thought is necessary, and man is incapable of thinking without inwardly formulating words, according to the celebrated dictum of Rousseau: 'Man must think his word before he can speak his thought'. Therefore to invent language man must first have been in possession of words—which is self-contradictory. He concludes, then, that man received language from without, and this he could have done only from God. Hence did human reason commence to think only by an act of faith in the divine word which revealed at once both language and its meaning. And consequently every certain assent of the mind must rest ultimately on an act of faith in a primitive revelation.

25. Criticism of Traditionalism.—To make *all* certain knowledge rest on an act of faith is to make certitude impossible, unless we are to be guilty of self-contradiction. For, either this act of faith is a blind one, or it is justified. If it is a blind act of faith, it evidently cannot serve as the grounds for any certain knowledge; and thus do we become involved in universal scepticism. If it is justified, if the reason sees the necessity of believing in the infallible testimony of God, then there are truths anterior to the primitive act of faith, namely, the existence of God, His infallibility, the fact of the revelation; and in this case the act of faith is not the basis and the motive of *all* certitude.

With regard to the arguments of the traditionalists:—

1. By agreeing to the impotence of the human reason, the traditionalists necessarily condemn themselves to scepticism. We have answered this argument elsewhere (**16**).

2. The argument of de Bonald drawn from language is radically wrong. It is incorrect to say that the word necessarily precedes the thought: a sound is only a word for us when it is associated with a thought that is anterior to it. Yet even if we suppose that man could not have invented language, it would not follow that the act by which man received language was an act of faith, that is to say, an assent motived by the authority of the testimony of God. It is

much more reasonable to suppose that the divine communication took the form of an act of teaching, to which on the part of man there corresponded an act of intelligence, an assent motived by the intrinsic evidence of the truths taught.

The *social teaching* proposed by de Bonald as the rule of our certain cognitions is a criterion absolutely insufficient, seeing that this teaching transmits errors just as much as it does truths.

The *general reason* of mankind proposed by La Mennais as the expression of the primitive revelation is quite as inefficacious. For how could a man find out practically what is the general belief of mankind, unless he first trusted his own senses and his own individual reason? If the reason of the individual is open to mistrust, surely the general reason, the collection of all individual reasons, is no more trustworthy.

26. Conclusion.—The traditionalists attempted to find the guarantee of certitude outside our intelligence, in other words an *extrinsic criterion*. But if my intellect can attain to the truth, it is within myself that I must find its guarantee. The criterion must be *intrinsic*.

§ 2.—*The Criterion must be Objective*

27. Subjective Criterion of the Scottish Philosophers, of Jacobi and neo-Kantians.—The sensist empiricism advocated by Berkeley (1685–1753) and Hume (1711–1776), by making our knowledge deal only with pure phenomena, declares the mind incapable of knowing immaterial substances, or even any substance whatever. To safeguard our metaphysical cognitions and our religious beliefs several philosophers have attempted to justify them by the introduction of the idea of a subjective impulse which forces us to admit them.

The Scottish School (Reid at Glasgow, 1710–1796) assert that our supersensible cognitions are the object, not of an objective knowledge, but of a kind of natural instinct to which they give the name of *common sense*. Jacobi (1743–1819) makes them depend on a *sentiment* or affective disposition of the mind (Geistes Gefühl).

In France there has recently been developed a line of thought bearing an affinity to these tendencies. This newly formed *neo-Kantian* or *neo-criticist* School, for which Renouvier is chiefly responsible, claims to solve the problem of knowledge by affirming 'the primacy of the practical reason over the speculative reason'. We admit metaphysical truths because our will forces us to admit them; we '*believe*' them. According to the pragmatists we *live* them, we *create* them by our action.

This system finds its inspiration in Kant, who after demolishing in his 'Critique of Pure Reason' the possibility of knowing anything but phenomena, forthw th asserts in his 'Critique of Practical Reason' the necessity of admitting certain fundamental moral and religious truths. These truths force themselves upon us as a logical consequence of the necessity with which moral duty,—'the categorical imperative'—asserts itself within us.

This neo-criticism finds several adherents even among Catholic advocates of a spiritualistic system. We find it in particular as the basis of 'the new Apologetic' that places conviction in the heart rather than in reason, following the thought of Pascal: 'the heart has reasons of which mind itself knows nothing'.

All these different subjective systems make the common mistake of leaving the problem of certitude without solution. Sceptics themselves admit this more or less necessary impulse of our nature to assent to certain truths. But the whole point at issue is to ascertain whether this impulse is blind or justified. If any claim is made to justify it, recourse must be had in the last resort to some other motive than the nature of the subject, to a motive whose foundation the *intellect* can itself perceive, in a word, to a criterion which is objective.

28. Criterion of Herbert Spencer: The Inconceivability of the Contradictory.—Spencer, with the positivist school, makes experience the sole source of knowledge. Experience gives us states of consciousness, modifications of the nervous substance. Further, we have acquired by heredity certain nervous dispositions as the result of the experiences of our ancestors. These states of consciousness are not isolated but associated. Among these associations there are some which, in accordance with the joint experiences of ourselves and our ancestors, are so firmly connected that it is impossible for us to separate them; to separate them by denying them has become 'inconceivable'. Consequently this inconceivability of the negation of a proposition is the supreme guarantee that the association is conformable to the constant experience of humanity; it is the supreme criterion of certitude [4].

Positivism as a psychological system is refuted in the treatise on Psychology (**95, 91**). Here we shall speak of it only from the point of view of criteriology.

Under the name of inconceivability Spencer confounds two notions that are entirely distinct, namely: *subjective* inconceivability and *objective* inconceivability. The inconceivability of an association of concepts can hold good either in the sense that an *object* known excludes its contradictory, or in the sense that the *subject* knowing is incapable of connecting the two together. (*a*) In the first case the inconceivability is *objective*, as for instance a round square is inconceivable. This objective inconceivability of the contradictory is without doubt *a* criterion of truth but it is not the *first* criterion, the ultimate motive for the mind's assent; it presupposes in the object itself a motive of inconceivability. (*b*) In the second case, the inconceivability is *subjective*: for instance we are incapable of conceiving the nature of a spiritual being such as it really is in itself. It is evident that this subjective inconceivability, this incapacity to see how a thing could be otherwise, is no criterion of truth. That we are incapable of conceiving it gives no reason why some higher mind should not conceive it.

29. Conclusion.—No subjective motive—neither an affective disposition of the mind, nor the dominion of the will, nor even the inconceivability of the contradictory—can be a sufficient criterion of the truth. The object of our knowledge itself must of necessity carry with it its own justification: the criterion must be *objective*.

§ 3.—*The Criterion must be Immediate*

30. The Mediate Criterion of Descartes and the Ontologists.—To escape from his universal doubt, Descartes laid down as certain the fact of his own existence: 'Cogito, ergo sum'. He then asked himself why he was certain of this: and found the answer to be because he saw quite clearly, as he said, that thought presupposes existence. 'I judge, then,' he concluded, 'that I may take it as a general rule that whatever things I conceive quite clearly and quite distinctly are true'. Now

[4] Herbert Spencer, *Principles of Psychology*, § 426.

this general rule, we see, is a subjective criterion and as such cannot be first and fundamental. In attempting to justify it, Descartes ultimately has recourse *to the Wisdom and Goodness of God* Who being all Truth cannot give us false knowledge.

The Ontologists also, in accordance with their ideological system which we have examined in Psychology (98), have recourse in the same way to a mediate criterion, namely to the divine ideas, which being the archetypes of ours, are the guarantee of the truth of our cognitions. In making our certitude rest on the divine ideas, they necessarily argue in a vicious circle. Our knowledge of God is not a direct, intuitive knowledge. We can attain a knowledge of His existence and His nature only by a posteriori proofs. But all demonstration presupposes premisses that are certain. If then *all* certitude rests on the divine nature and perfections, the proof by which we seek to establish the existence of God, as also of His goodness and wisdom, must itself also rest on the existence of God and His goodness and wisdom. Thus the conclusion of the proof must first be established before the premisses can be laid down—a flagrant *petitio principii.*

31. General Conclusion.—We have seen that if human reason is capable of reflex certitude, it can only be so on the condition that it has a criterion of truth which is *immediate, intrinsic,* and *objective.* We shall now see in the following section that the real motive of our certitude is *objective evidence,* that is, the objective manifestation of the relation or bond which unites two terms of a proposition. This is a criterion which fulfils all the three requisite conditions we give above: it belongs to the object of the true knowledge itself and is therefore immediate, intrinsic, and objective.

II. Our Immediate Judgments of the Ideal Order are Objective

32. Meaning.—It must be remembered that here we are dealing only with simple propositions, of immediate certitude, expressing relations of the ideal order (22). The enunciation of such propositions—e.g. that 'A whole is equal to the sum of its parts'—entails a mental synthesis or union of two terms by a relation of identity being seen to exist between them. This synthesis is spontaneously made by the mind which is irresistibly impelled to give its assent. In this everybody is in agreement. But the fundamental question arises : What is the *nature* of this synthesis ?

Kant maintained that this synthesis of the two terms subject and predicate results mechanically from the constitution of the mind which is determined by certain invariable laws of understanding. Consequently our judgments are what we ourselves make them, they only make us know our own nature. He is thus led to *subjectivism*, a refined form of scepticism which goes by the name of *criticism*.

We shall prove, against Kant, that these judgments are n the result of a subjective a priori synthesis. We shall show that on the contrary our mind forms the synthesis under the manifest influence of the object itself ; that *the terms of the judgment force our minds to admit the connexion which unites them*. And therefore a judgment formed under the influence of the objective manifestation of this relation of the two terms to each other is not the exclusive product of our mind but is a real effect produced in our mind by the object.

33. Fundamental Thesis.—*When we form immediate judgments of the truth of which we are certain, we as a matter of fact attribute the predicate to the subject precisely on account of the objective identity manifested between the predicate and the subject, and not because this union is demanded exclusively by the natural constitution of our mind.*—The only possible proof of this thesis is the testimony of the fact itself as witnessed *by our consciousness*.

We must, then, proceed to examine, as our consciousness represents it, what takes place within us when we form a certain immediate judgment. What is it that forces me to say, for instance, that a whole is greater than any of its parts ? It is surely the ideas of ' whole ' and ' part ' which come before my mind as bearing a certain relation to each other. The manifestation of what the whole is in relation to its part forces me to judge that the former is greater than the latter.

34. Corroborative Proof drawn from the Successive States through which the Mind passes.—In many cases the mind passes through, in regard to one and the same object, first a state of doubt, then of credible probability, and finally reaches complete certainty. In presence of the two terms of a judgment the mind, left to itself, can remain in a state of suspense as long as it does not see a motive for assent: this is a state of doubt. But as soon as reflection enables it to catch a vague glimpse of this motive, it forms an opinion of greater or less probability. Finally, when the motive becomes evidently manifest, there follows that complete adherence of the mind which is certitude.

Suppose that I doubt if the three angles of a triangle are equal to two right angles; what is the source of this doubt? When shall I cease to doubt? The doubt comes from the fact that I do not perceive in the object of my judgment the identity between its two terms, i.e. the connexion or identity between the attribute 'two right angles' and the subject 'three angles of a triangle' is not clear to my mind; I remain in suspense and am in doubt. But immediately the identity between the two terms of the judgment becomes visible to me, e.g. by my use of some means to discover it, the doubt ceases; I assert that I know the truth of the proposition that the three angles are equal to two right angles; I am certain of it. Thus the necessary and sufficient condition for the exclusion of my doubt and for the possession of certitude is the perception I have of the objective identity of the subject and the predicate of my judgment.

This succession of states of doubt and certainty with regard to the same proposition is inexplicable in the hypothesis of the subjective synthesis of Kant. If, as Kant claims, the mind irresistibly formed a priori syntheses when presented with certain data, we could easily understand that in the presence of the terms of *one* proposition it should remain in suspense, and that it should irresistibly give assent when confronted with the terms of *another* different proposition. But we could not understand that in the presence of the *same* predicate and of the *same* subject, the mind should at one time be in doubt and at another time be certain.

In our theory, on the contrary, this succession of states is explained and justified. If the assent is determined not *subjectively* by the natural constitution of the thinker but *objectively* by the objective identity of the subject and the predicate, then we understand that this assent is proportionate to the manifestation of this identity, as an effect is proportionate to its cause. As long as the identity is not perceived, no mental assent is given. But according to the degree in which the identity becomes apparent, conviction increases until such time as the identity is completely evident, and the certitude of the mind becomes firmly established.

Hence *objective evidence* is the necessary and sufficient cause of certitude: *it gives us the criterion of truth* which we have been endeavouring to find.

35. Conclusion: The Mind is capable of knowing Truth.—We have just shown that in an act of reflex knowledge our mind is determined in the formation of its judgments by the influence of the objective manifestation of the truth. From this well established *fact* we can legitimately *make the induction* that our intellect has by its nature the *power* to assent only on objective motives, which consist, in their last analysis, in the objective clearness that the predicate does belong to the subject of a proposition. Thus the capability of the mind to know the truth becomes for us not indeed a postulate which it is necessary to make a priori, as certain dogmatists would have us think, but the result of an induction based upon observation.

III. Value of our Judgments of the Ideal Order

36. Qualities belonging to Truths of the Ideal Order.—When I assert a truth of the ideal order—e.g. that 'Two quantities equal to a third are equal to one another'—this judgment is independent of experience. To enable me to formulate this relation between the predicate and the subject, I have no need to see it realized as a contingent fact; it is sufficient for me to consider and to *analyse* the mere terms of the proposition to see that my mind is impelled to assent to the relation: and since these terms are abstract, it forces itself upon me *necessarily*, independently of any condition and of any circumstance of time and space.

This kind of judgment is known in Scholastic terminology as a judgment '*in necessary matter*' (Logic, **31**), though to-day it is usually known as an *analytical* judgment.

Distinguished from the analytical judgment in necessary matter is the *synthetic* or *empirical* judgment, or in Scholastic phraseology, a judgment '*in contingent matter*'; e.g. the judgment 'The cause of tuberculosis is a microbe'. The empirical judgment rests essentially on experience, that is to say, an analysis of the terms of the proposition is insufficient to reveal the relation it asserts; to see that relation of predicate to subject we must verify its actual existence as a concrete reality. Such a judgment depends therefore upon a contingent fact, subject to conditions of time, space and matter; it is accordingly *hypothetical* and 'in contingent matter'.

Furthermore as the relation enunciated by an empirical judgment adds to the content of the terms an extrinsic element that is drawn from experience, it is for this reason called *synthetic*.

37. Importance of Truths of the Ideal Order.—Certainty with regard to the truth of our judgments of the ideal order is of extreme importance in science. Not only do the rational sciences belong entirely to this category of cognitions, but even the certitude of truths of experience rests ultimately on truths of the ideal order; at least it is conditioned by the evidence of the principle of contradiction. Further, experimental knowledge becomes scientific only when from contingent facts we can deduce principles, laws of the ideal order.

The value of analytical judgments of the ideal order is denied by *positivists*, who lay it down as a principle that all certitude is one of fact, of observation.

Kant admits, it is true, that we have analytical judgments, but he denies entirely their scientific value by reducing them to mere tautological propositions.

Against Kant we must therefore establish the scientific value of our analytical judgments, at the same time defending their very existence against the positivists.

38. Criticism of Positivism.—By limiting our knowledge to the things of sensible experience positivists deny that we have abstract concepts. What we call an abstract concept is according to them only a collective image. Hence they are not troubled about any question of judgments of the ideal order: all our judgments are concrete, certitude is a question of fact, of sensible experience, either external or internal.

We have proved in Psychology (91) the existence of abstract concepts. When it is a question of establishing relations of the ideal order between these concepts, we cannot deny that the imagination and experience help considerably in enabling us to see them. This assistance is, however, purely extrinsic and accidental, the image exciting and maintaining the action of the intellect, but *without* being *its efficient cause*. Thus geometric demonstrations can be made, without our having recourse to objective figures, whether real or abstract, by a pure act of reasoning upon abstract ideas, although of course the task is very considerably facilitated by an image however badly constructed.

39. Kant's Theory of Analytic and A priori Synthetic Propositions.—Kant admits that we have judgments of the ideal order, that we formulate necessary and universal propositions which do not rest on sensible experience. He calls them a priori. If we consider words merely, Kant recognizes that these propositions are 'objective', for the simple reason that, *in his phraseology*, a necessary and universal proposition is, by definition, *objective*. But he denies that they have the objectivity which, according to the generally accepted use of terms, we allow them, that is to say, the possibility of their enunciation being seen to be founded on reality.

Among necessary propositions, there are some, Kant says, in which the analysis of the subject makes us see the predicate; the predicate is therefore contained in the essential comprehension of the subject. These are his *analytic* judgments, e.g. man is an animal endowed with reason. But these judgments, he continues, are purely *explicative* and they tell us nothing new. They are therefore tautological, without any scientific interest.

There are however other propositions of the ideal order in which the analysis of the subject is not sufficient to make us see the predicate, propositions in which the predicate adds something to the essential comprehension of the subject. Such judgments are formed by a mental synthesis which combines the subject with an idea taken from outside itself. They are *extensive* judgments which give us some new information and thereby increase our knowledge.

Kant calls these latter judgments, conformably with their nature, *synthetic a priori*—synthetic on account of the synthesis they involve, a priori because they are formed independently of experience.

These synthetic a priori judgments, which are the only propositions he allows to be truly scientific, are evidently not motived by reality. Independent of experience on the one hand and not justified by an analysis of the terms on the other, this synthesis is purely subjective; it is an inevitable result of the laws of our understanding.

Kant forthwith applies this theory to all the sciences and endeavours to show that the fundamental principles of arithmetic, geometry, physics and especially of metaphysics, are synthetic a priori judgments and consequently devoid of all objective value.

40. Criticism.—The Kantian theory of knowledge may be summed up in two propositions:—(1) Our analytic judgments are purely explicative; (2) The fundamental principles of the sciences are synthetic a priori judgments.

1. There are, it is true, some judgments that teach us nothing new, but it is false to say that they are all purely explicative. Let us take, for example, the proposition, 'Man is a rational animal'. If we consider that the subject 'man' signifies the specific essence of the individuals called men, it is evident that this proposition is purely tautological, and teaches us nothing. But this is not the obvious and natural meaning of the subject 'man'. Terms of language are spontaneous creations which have for their object not the specific essences of beings but certain sensible properties belonging to them. Thus the word 'man' brings up primarily the idea 'a subject standing erect', 'a subject capable of speech'. Our proposition then means: 'This subject standing erect, capable of speech, is an animal endowed with reason'. It is obvious that in this case there is no tautology, although the language implies a necessary relation with rational animal.

2. Let us next endeavour to show that the principles of the sciences are neither purely a priori nor synthetic.

Although experience cannot enable us to attain necessary universal relations, nevertheless it furnishes us, at least in a material way, with a nature endowed with existence; and it is in this nature the intellect discovers by its work of abstraction the material of necessary universal relations. Experience provides the terms of the relation, reason discovers it. Thus, for example, experience brings before us straight lines and curved or irregular lines; the intellect considers the nature of each of these lines, and as a result perceives and enunciates the judgment that a straight line is the shortest distance between two points. Hence we do not say that the matter from which our principles are drawn is prior to experience; we do not posit their validity a priori.

Secondly, the principles themselves, the necessary universal principles which form the bases of the sciences are analytic and not synthetic. To show this we may begin by remarking that Kant's definition of the analytical judgment is too limited. A judgment is not the apprehension of the two terms but the apprehension of a relation between these two terms. Consequently the analysis of the terms of an analytic proposition has not always the purpose of showing one term to be contained in the other, but it is enough if it reveals how the simultaneous consideration of the two terms implies the necessity of the relation enunciated. In other words, an analytic proposition is a proposition 'in necessary matter' (**36**). From the fact, therefore, that in some primary propositions the subject does not include the predicate, we have no right to conclude that these principles are not analytic.

By way of example, to confine ourselves to the most important, let us examine the principle of causality.

The popular enunciation of this principle—that 'There is no effect without a cause'—is indeed a mere tautology, since 'effect' signifies 'produced by a cause'.

Kant enunciated it: 'Everything *which comes into existence* demands its cause'. This enunciation is true but it is not sufficiently universal: as far as we are concerned commencement in time is without doubt an indication of contingency, but it is not evident a priori that every contingent being has commenced to exist in time.

Let us then exclude all notion of time and attend only to the idea of contingency. We shall then formulate the principle thus: 'A being whose essence is not its existence necessarily demands for the explanation of its existence a cause which brought it into existence'; or more briefly: 'The existence of a contingent being demands a cause'. So enunciated the principle is truly analytical; not because the predicate is formally contained in the subject, but because the mere simultaneous apprehension of the predicate and the subject is sufficient to disclose the necessary connexion which unites them. It could not be denied without a self-contradiction. For let us suppose E to be a contingent being actually existing. This being E may be considered as an essence which of itself is non-existent, whilst in point of fact it is existing. Now either this essence E from these two points of view is formally the same, and then we have a contradiction; or the essence

E in the two cases is formally not the same, which means in other words that from the first point of view E is the essence simply by itself (*essentia nuda*), and from the second point of view E is the essence as submitted to some extrinsic influence (*essentia quatenus substat influxui extrinseco*), that is to say, the essence as having come under the influence of a cause, as caused. The predicate of this analytical judgment is thus seen to belong to the subject upon its analysis. (For further illustration see *Logic*, **32**).

General Conclusion.—Our knowledge is based on universal necessary principles of which we have legitimate certitude, inasmuch as they are analytical and objectively motived.

CHAPTER IV

OBJECTIVE REALITY OF OUR CONCEPTS

41. Meaning.—We have shown in the preceding chapter that when we enunciate a judgment of the ideal order, this is done in virtue of the objective evidence of a relation between the two terms. But this enunciation is quite independent of the fact whether the objects about which the relation is stated exist or not. The question now arises: What is the value of the *terms* which I join together when I make a judgment? Are they concepts having purely fictitious objects, mental beings forged merely by my brain, whose whole nature consists in their being represented? Or have these ideas a *reality independent of my representation of them*? Do they represent things which *really exist* or at least *are possible* in themselves?

That we may have a clear idea of the problem before us, let us observe that it is not a question of proving whether or not our cognitions have an object: a cognition without an object (id quod ob-jicitur), that is, about nothing at all, is surely nonsense. But it is a question of ascertaining whether the object of our cognitions is a *real* being or a *fictitious* one. Once again, it is not a question of the improper and mediate knowledge that we have of supersensible realities, nor of the knowledge of sensible realities as known in their specific essences, seeing that a knowledge of this kind is the fruit of a long intellectual process. What we are considering here is merely the generic ideas of 'being', 'substance', 'subject', 'cause', etc., namely the objects of our primary and most simple cognitions.

42. The Phenomenalism of Kant.—The word *subjectivism* sums up Kant's reply to the first problem of certitude; his reply to this second question we are now considering may be summed up in the word *phenomenalism.*

Subjectivism consists in saying that when we unite a predicate to a subject, we establish this bond in virtue of a subjective law of our nature in conformity with a function or category of the understanding. Phenomenalism consists in saying that the predicate, under the extension of which the subject of our judgments comes, is a pure fiction, and that we do not know whether there exists anything above and beyond this phenomenon.

According to Kant, the characteristic and essential act of the human mind is a spontaneous a priori synthesis of a subjective form with certain unconnected impressions, or matter, supplied through the senses. The senses are purely receptive faculties, the mind on the other hand is an active and spontaneous faculty. We are, he says, in possession of many kinds of impressions and sensations (Empfindung), visual, auditory, etc. To this passive state, which is not a cognition in the strict sense, there corresponds a reaction of the mind which places these impressions in *space* and *time*. The two natural dispositions which bring about this synthesis are called *intuitions* (Anschauung) of sensibility, and by this first reaction of the mind the impression becomes a phenomenon (Erscheinung) in time and space.

As soon as these intuitions have placed things in space and time, the understanding applies certain 'categories'—by which is meant types of connexion between two representative contents—namely those of totality, cause, effect, substance, accident, etc.

By the help of these categories we come to consider phenomena, which are already placed in space and time, as objects of the intellectual faculty.

It follows, from the point of view of criteriology, that so long as our judgments deal only with *phenomena* they are valid. Indeed they are nothing more than the application of categories of the mind to the passive impressions received by our sensitive faculties, such application being made according to the laws of the understanding. When, however, our judgments deal with things-in-themselves—the *noumena* in distinction from phenomena—they lose all objective value, for the noumenon or object is only an a priori synthesis of forms or categories of the understanding applied to the phenomena.

In brief the Kantian theory is that we know only phenomena; noumena, objects of our judgments of the ideal order, are figments of the mind, devoid of all reality.

43. Thomistic Theory.—In opposition to the theory of Kant we lay down the following thesis: *The intelligible forms which furnish our predicates and which we attribute to the subjects of our judgments are endowed with objective reality.* In other words, the object which they present to us is not merely an object known by the mind but a thing-in-itself actually existing, or capable of so existing, in nature.

44. Negative Proof.—There is no reason for thinking that these forms are not endowed with objective reality.

The great difficulty that has given rise to Kant's system is the apparent contradiction which exists between the universal character of our concepts and the individual character of things-in-themselves. This is really the famous *problem of universals,* so much discussed by the different Scholastic schools. The chief solutions of this problem are:—

(1) *Nominalism,* which denies the abstract and universal character of our ideas and, by allowing only their concrete character, finds an easy method of making them exactly correspond with the concrete realities they represent.

(2) *Exaggerated Realism,* which goes to the other extreme and attributes to things-in-themselves the abstract and universal attributes of the ideas which represent them.—We shall have occasion to point out how both nominalism and exaggerated realism shirk the problem instead of solving it.

(3) *Conceptualism,* which admits the fundamental difference between the character of the idea and that of the thing, but maintains that an idea does not apply to a thing.

(4) *Moderate Realism,* known also as Aristotelian or Thomistic Realism, according to which our ideas faithfully represent concrete things without being entirely commensurate with them, the ideas and the things corresponding exactly in nature but not in manner of being.

Moderate realism justifies its position thus: to escape the apparent antinomy between the character of the idea and that of the thing, it is sufficient to consider that universality is not a primary property of our concepts. The essential character of a concept is that it is abstract, that is to say, not limited by any determinating, individualizing notes. A concept by itself is not universal, it becomes so only in consequence of an act of reflection which declares that the abstract note is applicable to an unlimited number of objects.

Again, though it is true that the thing-in-itself is concrete and does not admit of multiplication, yet this is not so in the case of the object-in-itself in so far as it is known to the mind. The object known is itself abstract, taken apart from those particular characteristics inseparable from the concrete thing as presented to the senses; thus it corresponds to the concept and can serve as a basis for its universalization.

45. Positive Proof.—The object of our intelligible forms is contained in the sensible forms from which originally it is derived and to which it is here and now applied by the act of judgment. But the object of sensible forms is endowed with reality. Therefore our intelligible forms are objective realities.

We must prove both the major and the minor of this syllogism.

1. The object of our sensible forms contains the object of our intelligible forms. For, in the object of sensible forms there are certain determinating notes: thus, I see this man, of such a height, with this countenance, etc.; and it is impossible for there to be determinating notes unless there *be* also something that is determined by them, unless there exist a being, a subject, a determined substance. Therefore the object of a sensible form necessarily represents at the same time intelligible forms. It follows, then, that the senses *perceive* in a material fashion all that the intelligence *conceives*; and that consequently, if the object of sensible forms is real, the object of intelligible forms is so also.

2. Now the minor states that the object of our sensible forms is real, that corresponding to them is a thing-in-itself. To prove this we have first to remember that we have already proved the objectivity of our judgments of the ideal order and in particular that of the principle of causality (40); and secondly that the testimony of consciousness has to be granted by sceptics as a fact, as indeed the most advanced do grant it: they may doubt the value of its testimony, but they cannot deny its existence. We then argue:—

It is clear to me from my own consciousness that when I experience a sensation I am the subject of an impression, that there take place within me some passive impressions. Now my sensations, as indeed all contingent beings, require a sufficient cause and, since these phenomena are passive, the cause of their existence is not to be found in any adequate manner within myself. It follows, therefore, that there must be, outside me the subject who feels, one or more real beings capable of producing sensible impressions within me.

This general argument finds a confirmation in the great difference that our consciousness forces us to recognize between the state of sleep and that of wakefulness. We experience a state of dreaminess in which the enfeebled faculties are left to conjure up all kinds of purely subjective images, and the contrast to this state, that of wakefulness, allows us to realize that in addition to internal images we have a perfect assurance that we have also real objective sensations.

46. Reply to Two Objections.—Against this theory the objection is raised, firstly, that the senses are incapable of perceiving the abstract notions of being, substance and the like ; secondly, that we have a direct intuition of the existence of the exterior world without the necessity of having recourse to the principle of causality.

To the first objection, we reply that though of course the senses are incapable of knowing abstract notions formally as such, yet this is no reason why they should not perceive these notions in a concrete state ; they cannot perceive *being* as such, but they do perceive *this* material being. Furthermore, if they are incapable of perceiving being, then either the intelligence has created this notion or else it perceives it from some other source than from sensible things. Yet we have proved in Psychology (**90**) the truth of the Scholastic thesis, 'nihil est in intellectu quod non prius fuerit in sensu'.

To the second objection, we reply that although we can acquire the notion of a real being without having recourse to the principle of causality, and although we can even pass from this to affirm the existence of an internal reality, nevertheless it is impossible to affirm *with certainty* the existence of the external world without having recourse to the principle of causality (**60**). If this is not easily seen, it is because we are so accustomed to have recourse to this line of reasoning that we employ it almost unconsciously and a serious effort of reflection is required to detect it.

47. Refutation of the Phenomenalism of Kant.—The question arises how Kant came to affirm that the object of knowledge is obtained by the synthesis of an a priori form with matter furnished by a sensible impression.

His argument was as follows :—All that comes from experience is particular and contingent. But in all knowledge, even in sensible knowledge, there are elements that are neither particular nor contingent but universal and necessary, namely *time* and *space*. To this premiss he arrived by arguing that we cannot represent to ourselves any sensible object without localizing it somewhere in space and without placing it at some moment of time. And whatever the space is that we represent to ourselves, there is necessarily more beyond; we cannot conceive space as limited: it is therefore *universal*. Moreover, as we can imagine the destruction of all that is contained in space but we cannot conceive the disappearance of space itself, it is therefore *necessary*. Similarly time is shown to be universal and necessary: no matter what the actual time that we consider, there is still a before and after; we may conceive the destruction of all that happens in time, but time itself always goes on.

To continue with the argument: since time and space are necessary and universal, they cannot be furnished by experience, which is particular and contingent; they are *a priori* elements, anterior to all experience, and these unite with experience so as to form *sensible intuition*.

This ideology of Kant is best refuted by our showing that the notions of space and time are not a priori forms but are notions abstracted from the data of experience.

48. Analysis of the Notions of Space and Time.—1. Kant confuses three forms of space which it is necessary carefully to distinguish, viz., *real* space, *ideal* space, and *imaginary* space [5].

When we consider a body before us, we gain by a process of abstraction a notion of position. If there are two bodies, we conceive two positions between which there immediately arises the relation of distance. This notion of distance between two positions or two points is the primary spatial relation. If for one spatial relation I substitute three, one of length, one of breadth, and one of depth, I have the complete notion of space, the concept of space.

If the bodies between which I consider the relations men-

[5] Cp. Appendix to *Cosmology*, which treats of Time and Space.

tioned above are real, the distances are real, and the *space considered is real.* Let us admit that the bodies that really exist are limited in number, then the real space resulting from the relations of distance between these bodies is evidently *limited.*

But the mind conceives that besides really existing bodies there are possible bodies, even an infinite number of possible bodies, which thus give us the notion of a *possible* space; this is *unlimited* or *ideal* space.

Further, parallel with this ideal space conceived by the intelligence, the imagination can picture a space situated between imaginary bodies which has no fixed limits but is capable of being indefinitely increased by the imagination; this is *imaginary space.*

2. The same confusion is found with regard to the notion of time. The notion of time is abstracted from movement. 'Tempus est numerus motus secundum prius et posterius', as the Latin concisely translates Aristotle. When I consider any movement whatsoever, there is before me a succession of parts; the successive duration of this movement (numerus motus) constitutes *intrinsic* time. In order to measure it, I compare it with some other movement which is known as regular, e.g. the course of the sun, and by so doing I obtain *extrinsic* time. From this we see that real time is the duration of a real movement. Next I am able to conceive the successive duration of an unlimited possible time: this is *ideal time* or possible time, to which there corresponds the indefinite course of an *imaginary* time.

This being so, we observe that the whole of Kant's objection applies only to ideal or imaginary space and to ideal or imaginary time. Real time and space are limited and contingent. If, in thought, we banish all existing bodies, real space forthwith disappears, and possible space remains for the mind as if it were a vast reservoir in which possible bodies might be contained. In the same way, if we banish all successive movement, real time disappears; and ideal time alone remains.

We conclude, then, that it is not at all necessary that the notions of time and space should be prior to experience; the analysis of them, on the contrary, shows that they are actually furnished by experience.

49. A Question of Method.—We first checked the objectivity of our judgments (Chap. III) before examining the value of their terms (Chap. IV). We moreover limited the study of the objectivity of judgments to propositions of the ideal order. This method is not only legitimate but necessary. For, the objective evidence of ideal relations does not imply the affirmation that anything exists. The truth that $2+2=4$ is logically anterior to the existence of the subject who makes this judgment or even of any existing thing whatsoever. On the contrary, the affirmation that there exist in nature outside any thinking subject realities of experience that are objects of the terms of our judgments, rests on a judgment of the ideal order, the principle of causality. Hence it is necessary to establish the objective, universal validity of ideal principles before it is possible to arrive at the existence of the external world. As soon as that has been established, there comes the question of the objectivity of judgments of the real order, which is solved like that of the objectivity of judgments of the ideal order.

50. Conclusion of General Criteriology.—The subject of our judgments puts before us a real object. The object presented to the mind by the predicate of our judgment is seen to be realized in the subject itself. Therefore all our predicates have the same real objectivity as our subjects.

We have seen previously that when we unite a predicate to a subject, this union is objective, the affirmation is motived by the manifestation of the fact that the predicate does belong to the subject. In the order of real things no less than in the ideal order, the union of the predicate and the subject is motived. Consequently all human knowledge is justified: we have established the *capability of the mind to know the truth.*

We have been directly considering the case of our reflex knowledge, but we have only to remember that there is no essential difference between this and direct spontaneous knowledge in order to see that by having justified our reflex cognitions we have at the same also justified our direct, spontaneous knowledge (8).

PART II

Special Criteriology: An Analysis of the Kinds of Certitude

51. Survey and Division of Part II.—Most philosophers distinguish three kinds of certitude, namely, *metaphysical, physical* and *moral*, the last comprising also the certitude of faith. Another common division is into *absolute* certitude and *hypothetical* certitude. St. Thomas has another classification: our cognitions must belong to one or other of two groups according as their object is evident or not evident. Adopting this last classification we may call the certitude of those judgments in which it is quite clear to the mind that the predicate belongs to the subject *certitude of evidence*, and that of judgments in which the predicate does not evidently belong to the subject *certitude of authority*.

The certitude of evidence may be of *mediate evidence* or of *immediate* [*] *evidence* according as there is need or not of some stepping-stone to enable us to arrive at the knowledge that the predicate belongs or does not belong to the subject. And further, each kind may be subdivided. The certitude of immediate evidence may be a certainty with regard to ideal truths or to real facts: if it is the former we call it *certitude of principles*; if the latter, *certitude of intuition* or, which is the same thing, certitude of the states of our own consciousness. The certitude arising from mediate evidence or reasoning may be likewise in respect of either the ideal or the real order.

Accordingly Part II of Criteriology will fall into four chapters: one dealing with the certitude of immediate evidence (Chap. I) and treating first of our certainty of principles (I), then of that of our states of consciousness (II); a second dealing with the certitude of mediate evidence (Chap. II) as obtained in the rational sciences (I) and in the experimental sciences (II); a third investigating historical certitude and the certitude of faith (Chap. III); and a last one containing a comparison of these different kinds of certitude (Chap. IV).

[*] Corresponding to the very expressive English word *self-evident*.—Trs.

CHAPTER I

CERTITUDE OF IMMEDIATE EVIDENCE

I. PRINCIPLES

52. Definition and Division of Principles.—Aristotle defines a principle as 'that by which a thing is, becomes or is known'. That by which a thing is or comes into being is a real or *ontological* principle; that by which a thing is known, a *logical* principle.

Logical first principles, with which alone we are concerned here, are then those primary judgments which are indispensable for all further knowledge. Of such there are two kinds:—

1. *Formative principles of each science*, the premisses of a reasoning process which no longer admit of nor need proof; they are first in relation to the definite series of truths comprised by the science in question, and are drawn from its formal object.

2. *General principles of demonstration.* These are primary laws of thought, themselves immediately evident, which direct and govern all reasoning and are accordingly first in relation to all our acts of knowledge.

53. Formative Principles of the Sciences.—1. In any particular science all reasoning and thought-progress rests upon some premisses which *do not admit of proof.* Indeed, the premisses of any particular step are either self-evident, and then they are primary truths; or else to become evident they need to be proved. But *all* the propositions in the chain of reasoning cannot be of the latter class, they cannot all be conclusions and needing to be proved, or we should have to admit one of two alternatives: (*a*) either that all the propositions are provable by other propositions logically prior to them, and then there would not be a single proposition the proof of which would be complete and thus certain knowledge would be out of the question; or (*b*) that the propositions requiring to be proved are limited in number and can be used to demonstrate one another—which involves a contradiction. If, for example, the proposition B is capable of being proved by the proposition A, this latter proposition must be better known than B; yet if, conversely, the proof of A rests on B, the proposition B must be better known than A: an evident contradiction that each of the two propositions depending for its proof upon the other is at the same time less known and better known than the other.

2. All reasoning rests upon premisses that *do not need* to be proved. For, those propositions which *cannot* be proved are self-evident; that is to say, as soon as the mind becomes acquainted with the terms, it directly perceives the relation by which they are united. If it could be that they were not self-evident, then any certain knowledge would be impossible inasmuch as all the conclusions depending on them as premisses for their proof would be still less, or at least never more, evident.

Some propositions neither permitting nor requiring proof must, then, form the foundation of each of the particular sciences. They are known as the *principles of the sciences.* Of such the axioms of Euclid which form the basis of geometry are an instance, and the axiom: 'The whole is equal to the sum of its parts', which is the foundation of Arithmetic.

54. First Principles or Regulative Principles of all Thought.—There are a certain number of judgments which deal with the most elementary relations of *being* and *non-being*. They are of universal application and of evident necessity and therefore serve as directing and controlling principles for *every* assertion and *every* reasoning process, although they are not premisses or sources from which further knowledge may be deduced.

There are three such principles: the *principle of identity*, the *principle of contradiction* and the *principle of excluded middle*. From a *logical*[7] point of view these principles may be respectively formulated as follows:—Truth must be absolutely in conformity with itself—The same attribute cannot be at the same time affirmed and denied of the same subject—Between affirmation and denial there is no middle course.

These first principles cannot be proved, and do not need proof. Once the understanding has apprehended the extremely

[7] For their ontological import see *General Metaphysics* 78–80.

simple concepts contained in them, it directly perceives the connexion between subject and predicate and cannot be deceived in the judgment it formulates. Secondary or derived principles, which entail more complex terms, owe their validity to their being reducible to simple principles, to the very evident ones, the principles of identity, of contradiction or of excluded middle; as was the case with the principle of causality, which we reduced above (**40**).

II. Truths of Consciousness or of Internal Experience

55. Truths of Consciousness admit of no Proof.—Any possible demonstration of a truth of internal experience would necessarily have to be made from premisses that are either of the ideal order or of the real order. But premisses of the ideal order cannot furnish anything more than a logical conclusion and cannot give us certitude of a real fact; and premisses of the real order, if the argument is not to involve a vicious circle, would have to be drawn from facts of external experience, and then the difficulty far from being solved would only be further complicated seeing that our certitude about the external world rests on our certitude about matters of internal experience, on our certainty of our own conscious states. We are able, then, only to point out the immediate evidence of the facts of consciousness, or rather to point out how unreasonable it would be to admit that consciousness is untrustworthy when that very avowal is testimony against its supposed inveracity.

And if the objection be raised that the veracity of consciousness must be called in question on the very ground that its verdicts are contradictory, then we may retort: How can you trust your consciousness when it declares that there is a contradiction and mistrust it when it declares one or other of the contradictory propositions? This is to assert that one is certain about what is complex whilst uncertain about what is simple.

56. Objects of Internal Perception.—Our conscious life or internal experience deals with three classes of objects: our acts of knowledge, our acts of will and our memory-reproductions of both.

1. *Thoughts.*—The intellect knows its own acts directly. Indeed knowledge results from the union of an object known

with the subject knowing through the medium of an intelligible form: when, then, the object to be known is a cognitive act —which is an immanent act—the union can take place immediately, without any medium, and the knowledge is direct.

2. *Acts of the Will.*—Whilst it is an easy matter to see how an act of thought falls directly within the field of internal observation, the same cannot be said about acts of the will. It would even seem that these must escape the observation of the intellect since they proceed from a faculty which is really distinct from it. It is true indeed that every volition is in its foundation present to the intellect in so far as every act of will demands an act of knowledge as a necessary antecedent: 'Nihil volitum nisi praecognitum'. But the real reason which brings acts of the will under the cognizance of the knowing faculty consists in this, that the two faculties, though really distinct, have their common foundation in one and the same subject, the same ego, and are thus intrinsically inseparable.

3. *Memory-reproductions.*—Memory certainly requires as its necessary basis for recalling into consciousness past cognitions the persistent self-identity or continuity of the ego-subject. Nevertheless, whilst this is the ontological reason of memory, it cannot be said that in the logical order a *knowledge* of this identity is required as the basis of certitude concerning these recollections. It is quite possible for me to remember something without having a full consciousness that it is the same 'I' who now re-cognize it and cognized it in the first instance.

An analysis of the complete act of memory shows it to be made up of several elements. In the first place there is a vague awareness that what is now actually known has already been known before; secondly, a more or less definite localization of this act in past time; and thirdly, a true remembrance of it or recognition, either partial or complete. It would seem that the imagination and the intellect, besides storing up the image and the intelligible form of the thing I now actually know, preserve also the cognitional form of my very act whereby I perceived it. Consequently any re-appearance in the mind of the thing known immediately revives a knowledge of the act whereby it was previously known, and so accounts for *reminiscence* or memory in its vaguest form. By reflection upon a phenomenon so reproduced by memory one comes to recollect the successive acts which have followed between this phenomenon and the present moment, and so to localize or set in time the position of this past act with varying degrees of accuracy according as the intermediary landmarks stand out clearly defined or not. Last of all is the act of remembrance proper or *recognition*, whereby is applied to some thing or image or idea a corresponding type which abides habitually in the memory: thus to recognize some man as a man is to advert that this object corresponds to the abstract type of man, and to recognize such and such a particular man is to see that this one corresponds to the image I have stored up of him as an individual.

From this brief analysis it will be gathered that the various acts which go to form the complex act of remembrance are true acts of perception. A fuller analysis of memory finds its proper place in Psychology (62).

CHAPTER II

CERTITUDE OF MEDIATE EVIDENCE

I. Scientific Conclusions of the Ideal Order, or Certitude of the Rational Sciences

57. Science.—Rational and Experimental Sciences.—When a proposition is not self-evident, there is need to make its evidence manifest by the use of some medium or middle term. Such a proposition, which is the conclusion of a reasoning process, was formerly called *science* (scientia conclusionum). At the present day, however, the word 'science' denotes rather a systematic body of propositions deduced from one another and all referring to the same object.

As the basis of a science there stands a certain number of principles from which the conclusions are drawn by way of demonstration. In some of the sciences these principles are simple general propositions which are self-evident: such is the case in the *rational sciences* which are thus wholly deductive. In other sciences these principles are complex truths which have had to be built up by induction from observation or experiment: such is the case in the *experimental sciences* which employ a combined inductive and deductive method (*Logic*, 84 ff.).

Certitude in the case of the rational sciences will be established only if we can show that deductive demonstration under the traditional form of the syllogism as we know it in Logic (49) is a really valid form of argument.

58. Value of the Syllogism.—The chief objections brought against the formal validity of the syllogism have been formulated by John Stuart Mill. All deductive reasoning, he says, may be put in the classical syllogism: All men are mortal; Socrates is a man; therefore Socrates is mortal. But this is no true argumentation, for it teaches us nothing new; moreover it always contains a *petitio principii*. For if we are in a position to assert that all men are mortal, we must have previously ascertained that Socrates is a mortal man; that is to say, for the major to be enunciated the conclusion must be known. Where, then, is there any inferential process? Further it cannot even be said that the conclusion is implicitly contained in the premisses, since an implicit affirmation is one made without proper knowledge, and unless we have real knowledge we have no right to make an explicit statement.

The example given by Mill as a type of syllogistic reasoning is a misleading one; in the form in which he presents it the objections may certainly appear plausible. His major may be taken as a collective proposition, a compendious statement of all particular cases. The fact is, however, that the major of a true syllogism is not an *actually universal* proposition containing the conclusion as a particular instance; but a proposition in which, under the form of an *abstract concept*, a *general* attribute is asserted (Logic, **49**). Then, through the medium of the minor, this general attribute is applied in the conclusion to a *particular subject* which verifies the nature of the abstract concept of the subject of the major.

Mill's example, then, should be formulated thus:—

Human nature is liable to death;
This individual, Socrates, possesses human nature;
Therefore Socrates is mortal.

Here it is clear that the major does not contain the conclusion either explicitly or implicitly, yet that it is the efficient cause of the formation of our judgment—'non est id ex quo elicitur conclusio, sed id quod generat conclusionem'.

In short, Mill's error consists in supposing that the major of every deductive argument is a *collective* proposition containing a number of particular ones; whereas the essential characteristic of reasoning is that it enables us to see that a predicate which naturally belongs to a subject taken in the abstract belongs, as a legitimate consequence, to any concrete instance of that subject.

A better example can be found to illustrate our meaning and to show the weakness of all these objections. Suppose we want to prove that every number ending with 0 or 5 is divisible by 5. This proposition is not evident a priori. Therefore if we demonstrate it satisfactorily, without begging the question, it will at the same time be proved that the syllogism does furnish a new truth in its conclusion and that it really adds something new to our knowledge.

In order to make it evident that every number ending with 0 or 5—e.g., 230 and 235—is divisible by 5, I must find some middle term to which belongs the general attribute of being divisible by 5 and the abstract notion of which is verified by all the particular numbers ending with 0 or 5. Upon reflection I find that the sum of two numbers each of which is divisible by 5 is itself divisible by 5: this is my major. But every number ending with 0 or 5 is the sum of two numbers each of which is divisible by 5: for every such number can be broken up into two parts, into a group of tens and a group of simple units, and the tens-group is evidently divisible by 5 whilst the units-group must be 5 or nothing. Therefore all numbers ending in 0 or 5 are divisible by 5. The conclusion is a legitimate inference and the argument furnishes a real proof which adds a new certain truth to our knowledge.

II. Scientific Conclusions of the Real order, or Certitude of the Experimental Sciences

The subject-matter or, as we prefer to call it, the object with which observation and experiment deal is twofold: the real *existence* of the external world and the *nature* of it.

§ 1. *Certitude concerning the Existence of the External World*

59. The Question Stated.—We give a spontaneous assent to the fact that things exist outside of ourselves and in the same way we are convinced that we know their nature inasmuch as we attribute to what we regard as the non-ego properties which we think belong to it in very reality—extension, resistance, colour and the like. The question is once again the same one we had to answer with regard to certitude in general: Are these spontaneous assents justifiable?

Two answers are given, one by the idealists in the negative, another by ourselves in the affirmative.

It has already been seen (42) how Kant builds up the whole edifice of human knowledge upon passive impressions received in our sense-faculties, with the logical result that we can at most know only modifications of the ego: all that exists, as far as we are concerned, is some state of consciousness together with the permanent possibility of other similar states.

This absolute idealism or subjectivism is best refuted by the establishment of its contradictory, the doctrine of realism.

60. Doctrine of Realism.—The contention of the realists is that *we can be certain of the existence of the external world.*

(*a*) *Argument drawn from the passive character of sensations.*—We are conscious that we are the subject of certain internal experiences in the presence of which we are purely passive. These facts of experience require a sufficient reason for their occurrence. Now since our consciousness bears us testimony that we are passive, this sufficient reason must be, at least in part, exterior to ourselves. Therefore some reality outside the ego must exist, there must be an external world (Cp. 45).

(*b*) *Argument drawn from the contrast between perception and imagination.*—It is universally admitted that of the facts of internal experience there are two distinct classes: perceptions and imaginations. But a slight effort at introspection reveals that I can construct and arrange the images of my imagination at will, that I can travel on the wings of my fancy whithersoever I please; whilst with perceptions the case is *toto caelo* different, for their co-ordination and succession, far from depending upon my will and action, are often forced upon me even against my will. I must conclude, then, that there is a world distinct from myself and my states of consciousness [8].

(*c*) *Argument drawn from the spontaneous belief in the existence of the external world.*—We all of us experience a conviction, arising spontaneously and forced upon us irresistibly, that a world external to ourselves really exists. Now a fact so remarkable requires a sufficient reason for its explanation. But no other sufficient reason can be assigned for that conviction but the real existence of the external world.

The idealist school, it is true, suggests another reason to be found in a habit of thought. But this is really no explanation, as the genesis of the habit has to be accounted for, seeing that a habit is but the result of a number of successive acts. Bain's law of association and Kant's theory of a priori forms are quite inadequate as explanations: neither bridges over the

[8] For the contrast between percepts and images admirably set forth by Balmès see the extract quoted at length in the large edition of *Critériologie Générale.*

[9] For some other proofs of Realism see MAHER, *Psychology*, (Longmans, London), ed. 1900, p. 100.

transition from the simple state of consciousness to the explicit affirmation of the non-ego, from the world as a mere subjective experience to its objective reality.

§ 2. *Certitude concerning the Nature of the External World*

61. Definition of Induction.—Induction is a process of reasoning which sets out with the observation of the many diverse accidents exhibited by a substance, in order to discover which among them are true properties connected necessarily with it.

The property found to have this necessary connexion with its substance then serves as the basis for formulating a universal law which applies to all the phenomena observed: wherever this substance is found, there also will be found this natural property.

Proper induction comprises three separate stages, which will be investigated at greater length in the treatise on Logic (87), namely: (*a*) *observation* of particular facts; (*b*) formation and verification of a *hypothesis*; (*c*) *generalization*, which expresses a universal conclusion that serves as a principle for deduction.

A question arises concerning the rational foundation on which this final generalization is based. What right have we to pass from the particular to the universal? What right have we, for example, after observing a certain number of particular instances in which water freezes at 32° Fahrenheit to declare that this takes place *always*?

62. Logical Grounds of Induction. Erroneous Theories.—1. It is the theory of the *Positivist School* that induction is based exclusively upon observation. They regard the conclusion of an inductive argument as a *probable* proposition inasmuch as it has been verified by repeated experience, and the more probable the more extended the experience; but never more than probable. This theory is, however, contrary to what all scientists implicitly hold, since they are unanimous in their conviction that their researches result in conclusions that are *certain*: there comes a time when further observation adds nothing to their conviction, for the reason that they are already convinced.

2. According to *Reid* and the *Scottish School* the foundation of inductive certitude lies in an instinctive belief in the uni-

formity of the laws of nature. But this is an inadmissible theory, for no instinctive persuasion can be a motive of certitude, since we should require to know the reason of this persuasion. Moreover to believe in the uniformity of nature's laws is to admit the existence of fixed laws in nature and gives no ground for an inference to any law in particular; we are still left without any warrant for asserting that a given number of particular facts present the characteristics essential to a law.

3. A number of *Scholastic* writers find the basis of induction in the principle of causality, or in Divine Wisdom which they regard as a guarantee of the uniformity of the laws of nature. But neither of these explanations is satisfactory, for the reason that neither explains what right we have to assign to any given factor the rôle of cause or to any series of phenomena the character of law.

63. Thomistic Theory.—Since the complex and invariable connexion obtaining between a substance and certain phenomena is not to be explained by chance, the sufficient reason of that connexion must be found in a tendency of the nature of the substance; in other words, in the fact that these accidents are *natural properties* of the substance. Herein, we assert, lies the foundation of the certainty of induction.

In justification of this view of induction may be brought forward, besides an indirect proof in the destructive criticism already given of other opposite theories, a direct proof from an analysis of the inductive process itself.

An analysis of the process of inductive reasoning is best made by the aid of an example. A die thrown down on a table offers equal chances that any one of its six sides may turn up: in this we have an example of an *indifferent cause*, 'ad utrumlibet contingens,' as St. Thomas puts it. If however two dice are thrown down ten times and ten times in succession show double six, all will admit that this is clearly no instance of an indifferent cause, but one of loaded dice, that the repetition is due to some underhand play. Applying this reasoning generally, we may say that if a certain subject invariably displays the same phenomenon, such a subject cannot be indifferent but must be predetermined to exhibit this phenomenon; it must be its *natural cause*. An effect that is consistent and constant is due, then, to no indifferent cause, it is the manifestation of no contingent accident, but of some property arising from a natural tendency on the part of the being exhibiting it. Consequently wheresoever this kind of being, endowed with this natural tendency, is to be found, there too will the corresponding property be displayed; its appearance is a fixed *law* of nature.

The conclusion of an inductive argument is certain, not indeed with absolute or metaphysical certainty, but with *physical certainty*. It may happen that a conflict of natural causes or the intervention of some higher cause may stand in the way of the manifestation of some property; yet such cases will be exceptional and in no wise derogatory to the fixity of the law.

64. Certitude of Sense-experience.—Now that we have justified the inductive method used in the experimental sciences to pass from the observation of particular instances to the statement of general laws, it remains for us to examine the certitude which the senses give us in their observation of phenomena.

It must first be noticed that the senses themselves are incapable of attaining certitude. They can possess what is sometimes distinguished as subjective certitude, a firmness of adherence to their object; but they can offer no explanation of the motive of this firm adherence. The intellect alone is capable of attaining objective certitude, even in matters of sense-experience. Moreover, a simple perception is neither true nor false, inasmuch as these attributes, truth and falsity, belong to the judgment which the intellect pronounces when confronted with a particular perception.

Sensation is a complex phenomenon depending upon three essential factors—an object, a subject, and the use of a medium. To discern the proper part played by each of these three factors in any given sensation is not the part of the senses whose function is merely to present the person with a concrete phenomenon, but the part of the intellect which judges whether this or that quality does really belong to the object before it.

65. The Doctrine of Realism.—*Induction affords a certain knowledge of the permanent properties of sense-objects.* Sensuous perception is *relative*, that is, it varies according to the different conditions that may affect the object perceived, the subject perceiving, or the medium. This is beyond question. An object, according as it is viewed from afar or near, is seen as small or great, confused or distinct; a subject, according as he comes from a dark or a brilliantly lighted room, finds the daylight to be dazzling or dull; whilst blue glasses as a medium make everything blue.

In spite of all this, man's common sense is not deceived; he is perfectly able to distinguish between the habitual or normal perception of an object and what is abnormal or accidental. The question which concerns us is, What is the process he employs in making this distinction?

It is by means of an induction, either spontaneous or upon reflection. He varies his own observations and he compares them with the observations made by others. At length he is enabled to distinguish, among the manifold accidents perceived as belonging to a sense-object, between two distinct kinds of accidents; one kind variable, because the conditions of his observations have varied, and another kind stable, because they belong really and indeed to the object itself. He knows he is right in attributing the latter to the object; he has the absolute physical certitude which we have shown to belong to the process of induction [10].

66. Errors of the Senses do not invalidate the Certitude of Sense-experience.—Induction, as we have shown, is necessary that we may acquire certitude in matters of sense-experience. If this induction is not made or is faulty, the mind is then left at the mercy of mere appearances and may of course make an error of judgment. But it is almost needless to point out that such an error is by way of accident and does not render suspect the essential capability of the intellect to arrive at a knowledge of the truth.

[10] The further question of the exact nature of these properties disclosed by induction as belonging to external things is beyond the sphere of spontaneous experience; it is to be answered by the patient investigations of scientific inquiry.

CHAPTER III

HISTORICAL CERTITUDE AND THE CERTITUDE OF FAITH

67. Nature and Grounds of Historical Certitude.—In the certitude of immediate or mediate evidence, of which we have been treating up to this, the motive determining my assent appeals directly to my own mind; the evidence is *intrinsic*. It may happen however that I assent to a proposition when the motive determining me to do so is not apparent to me at all but only to somebody else; and then the motive or rational grounds for assent reach me only in an indirect way, through the medium of another's testimony. The motive for the assent in this latter case is *extrinsic*.

Historical knowledge and faith both rest on extrinsic evidence. Although this is so, there is this marked difference between them, that whilst the certitude of faith is based on the *authority alone* of a witness, historical certitude, which is also concerned with objects known only by the testimony of others, *relies on evidence* in so far as it is this which moves the person to give assent.

That historical certainty is not founded on authority one's own consciousness clearly testifies: in order to be certain of the existence of South America I have no need to make inquiries about the authority of those who tell me about it. Moreover certitude based on human authority is never more than a strong probability, at best a practical certainty, whereas historical certitude is nothing short of absolute certainty.

The foundation of historical certitude would seem to be a train of real reasoning by way of a *reductio ad absurdum*, something after the following style:—A large number of facts and circumstances all converging to one conclusion are brought to my notice—the regular arrival and departure of vessels with their passengers and cargoes; letters, books, etc. Now such a coincidence of facts and circumstances cannot be explained unless the country called, e.g., South America really exists. Therefore that country must exist, and those who declare they have seen it are speaking the truth. Such certitude is a certitude of mediate evidence.

68. Nature of the Certitude of Faith.—Faith is the giving of assent through the motive of another's authority to a proposition which is formally not evident. Here the motive of certitude is no longer my own reasoning but something extrinsic, namely *authority*, which is the formal object of faith.

The authority of a witness is never evident in itself; it requires establishing, and this is done by means of extrinsic signs. We have no means but external signs by which to determine whether what a man says is in accordance with what he thinks and whether his thoughts are in accordance with reality.

Hence, in the matter of human faith in the strict sense, no matter how numerous and authoritative be the witnesses, absolute certitude can never be attained. Divine faith alone can furnish absolute certainty.

69. Certitude of Divine Faith: its Reconciliation with Freedom.—The Divine Authority (based on the Knowledge and Veracity of God) in itself is evidently absolute. If therefore we can only assure ourselves on the strength of some evidence of the fact that God has spoken on any matter, our faith is certain.

As we know by the teaching of the Catholic Church that faith on the Divine word is both certain and free, the question arises, How are these two qualities of our assent to be reconciled with each other?

According to de Lugo the fact of divine revelation is never evident to us; and for this reason therefore we are free to assent or not. Divine faith however remains certain because it is supernatural, grace preventing us from assenting to error.—But this theory offers no rational explanation of the certitude of faith. Ontologically it is true that grace guarantees us certitude and immunity from error in the matters of faith, but logically the existence of grace is known to us only by faith; and hence by justifying the latter by the former de Lugo is guilty of begging the question.

According to Suarez the act of faith is free because the authority of Revelation is not evident to the believer and is admitted not in virtue of its own evidence but by an act of faith.—Yet to accept the authority of another in virtue of an act of faith is surely only to defer the difficulty, not to solve it: this act of faith, if it is to be rational, must itself rely on the proof of the authority of him to whom appeal is made and we therefore find ourselves just where we started.

In our opinion, in order to show that we can know the fact of Divine Revelation with certainty, we must make use either of the argument *ad absurdum* leading to historical certitude or of the consideration that Divine Providence could never allow a prudent man to fall into error in so momentous a matter. Hence the fact of Revelation once being ascertained, our faith is certain for the reason mentioned above.

Yet at the same time *the act of faith remains free on account of the absence of intrinsic evidence in its object.* The human mind is so made that only intrinsic evidence *necessarily* compels assent. As long as such evidence is absent no assent is necessitated; to procure it the intervention of the will is required. Careful introspection of our own consciousness reveals this as an indisputable fact: no matter how great be the authority of the witness, so long as the object to which he is testifying is not evident to us, we may believe or not as we choose, we are capable of giving or of withholding our assent.

If it be asked how is it that the will acts upon the intellect so as to constrain it to assent to what, if left to itself, it would not assent to, we should say that the part played by the will is both that of withdrawing the reason from a too close scrutiny of difficulties which naturally arise from the obscurity of the material object and also that of concentrating attention on the consideration of motives which make the proposition certain: that a revealed truth can be believed by a prudent man and ought to be believed. When the firmness of our assents surpasses the cogency of the rational motives, this bespeaks within us some action above ourselves, of an action called by theologians the effect of *supernatural grace.*

CHAPTER IV

COMPARISON OF THE DIFFERENT KINDS OF CERTITUDE

70. Various Kinds of Certitude.—Is certitude always specifically the same, or may we distinguish various kinds of certitude?

It has already been said that certitude means the firmness of adherence on the part of an individual to a given object, *determinatio ad unum.* According as there are formally different causes of this determination of the mind there will be formally distinct forms of certitude. As there are two causes of the mind's firm adherence that are formally distinct—one *intrinsic,* namely evidence; the other *extrinsic,* the intervention of the will—so there must be two distinct species of certitude, the certitude of *evidence* and the certitude of *authority* or *faith,* a certitude that is due partly to the intervention of the will.

Certainty arising from evidence is subdivided into *metaphysical* certainty and *physical* certainty, according as the bond of connexion which unites predicate and subject is educed from a mere analysis of the terms of the proposition or is the result of an inductive argument.

71. Order of Subordination among Different Kinds of Certitude.—The certitude of *faith,* it is not difficult to see, comes after that arising from other sources, since faith presupposes the intrinsic proof of the authority on which it rests. The certitude produced by a *process of reasoning,* it is also easy to see, is not a primary certitude, seeing that all conclusions rest upon other truths, ultimately upon immediate truths. The certitude of *experience,* embracing all certain knowledge of the external world, again is seen to presuppose the certainty of internal facts. The certitude of *consciousness,* although indeed able to assure us of our internal states, requires the necessary condition that these states should become the object of a judgment of the mind. Hence it belongs to our *understanding of principles* to furnish us with strict certainty regarding all reality, by our applying immediate judgments to concrete facts experimentally perceived. We may conclude, then, that the criterion of understanding, that is to say, of *immediate evidence*, is the first of all, every other presupposing it whilst it presupposes no other: it is both *fundamental* and *first*.

RECAPITULATION AND CONCLUSION

We began our investigation by taking as the data for the problems of Criteriology acts spontaneously considered by all to be certain, and these acts we submitted to rational reflection with the result that we have been able to show that the human mind has in its nature the capability of knowing truth with certainty in the various spheres to which its knowledge extends.

We may now complete this analytic study by taking a *synthetic* view and determining the relation that exists between the human mind, capable of arriving at truth and certitude, and its supreme Cause. This supreme Cause is God, considered under the threefold aspect of the *final* cause, *exemplary* cause and *efficient* cause of the human intelligence.

1. God, the Uncreated Truth, is the *last end* of man. From this it follows that if the human mind pursues the tendency of its nature, it must eventually arrive at a certain knowledge of the truth—at knowledge that is adequate when the end shall be fully attained, inadequate but nevertheless real during such time as the end is being sought.

2. God created man to His own image and likeness. But the Infinite Intelligence is proportioned to the infinite knowability of the Divine Essence. Therefore the human mind, inasmuch as it is the image of the Divine Intelligence which is thus its *exemplary cause,* must be capable of knowing the truth.

3. God, who is infinite Wisdom, is the *efficient cause* of human nature. But wisdom consists in exactly proportioning means to end. Therefore God's Wisdom is the warrant that our cognitive faculty is capable of attaining its end, which is none other than to know the truth.

By its nature, then, the human mind is capable of always knowing the truth: if error exist, it must be due only to *accidental* causes and does not in any way destroy the *natural* complete reliability of human reason.

GENERAL METAPHYSICS
or
ONTOLOGY

INTRODUCTION*

1. Position of Metaphysics in Philosophy.—The science now claiming our attention has been variously styled during the course of the history of philosophy. To-day it is often called *Ontology*—a word introduced by Wolff, signifying the science of Being (ὄν, ὄντος, being; λόγος, concept, doctrine)—or *General Metaphysics.* Aristotle's name for it was *First Philosophy*, ἡ πρώτη φιλοσοφία, and he defined it as the science of being and of its essential attributes. If we inquire into the significance of this appellation of Aristotle we shall see from the answer what place metaphysics holds among the departmental sciences of philosophy, and also how these various branches are to be classified according to their relative importance.

The first thoughts of the mind are *spontaneous*; the mind is exercised in the first instance under the guiding influence of external objects and events. This initial stage of cognition is succeeded by one of *reflection*, when from the consciousness of the value of this spontaneous knowledge attention is *deliberately* directed to definite objects of special interest—to the phenomena, for instance, of the activity displayed by inorganic substances, or of vegetative, animal or intellectual life; or again, to the history of the earth or humanity. Such systematized thought, where knowledge is grouped round respective formal objects, gives rise to the *particular sciences.* In the construction of these special sciences the method pursued by the mind is *analytic*; it confines itself to the investigation of a particular group of facts, first describing, then comparing and finally making inductions; in other words, the progress is from the accidental manifestations to the nature of their

* Books for study or consultation—

Card. Mercier, *Métaphysique générale ou Ontologie* (5th ed., 1910, Institut supérieur de Philosophie, Louvain).

P. Coffey, *Ontology* (Longmans, London, 1914).

Harper, *Metaphysics of the School* (out of print).

Rother, *Being* (Herder, London).

John Rickaby, *General Metaphysics* (Longmans, London, 1890).

subjects, from effects to their causes. When this much has been achieved the trend of further reflection is of an entirely new kind, towards the discovery of what is *common* among the various *formal objects* of these particular sciences: an effort is made to unify the whole of human knowledge by connecting the separate sciences through this common object, and this effort at complete unification is the work of *philosophy*. Philosophy endeavours to attain an abstract knowledge of what is common to the diverse beings of the universe in order that it may then explain them in terms of this common object; its method is therefore *synthetic*; it descends from principles to consequences, from causes to their effects. Now, in point of fact, the result of the mind's gradual process of abstraction is the discovery that the object common to all beings falling within the scope of its observation is threefold, namely, *movement, quantity* and *substance*; philosophy accordingly falls into the three subdivisions of physics, mathematics and first philosophy.

(1) Under the name of *movement* (*κίνησις*) must be understood change in general, alike of accidental modifications and of substantial transformations of natural bodies. Once the nature of movement is clearly apprehended, the science of physics uses this knowledge to account for the many different phenomena of movement in the universe. (2) The second stage of abstraction is reached when, by prescinding from all changes, accidental and substantial, the mind finds itself faced by another property common to all bodies, viz., *quantity*, which in the Aristotelian division of philosophy is the object of mathematics. This second common property is different from the former inasmuch as it is permanent, and belongs exclusively to material things. (3) Lastly, by ceasing to pay regard either to the movement or quantity in corporeal beings, the human intelligence finds only one common trait left, viz. that in virtue of which each is a self-subsistent being and distinct from every other being. Here, in this third degree of abstraction, we contemplate *substance* in general, or as it may be called 'beingness' or 'being in general' since substance is *par excellence* being, as we shall later have occasion to establish. It is because this object, substance in general—this reality apprehended in all corporeal beings—is conceived without movement or quantity, and indeed is conceived without

matter (since quantity is the peculiarity of material beings), that the philosophic science which contemplates it is the deepest of all and merits from Aristotle the title of *First Philosophy*.

Aristotle also called this fundamental part of philosophy the '*theological science*', on the ground that 'if there really exists a substance absolutely immaterial and immutable, it must be some Divine Being, the first and supreme principle of all things'[1]. We shall see shortly (**11** and **12**) why the science which treats specifically of the Divine Being does not differ formally from that which considers substance in general.

The term *metaphysics* now usually applied to First Philosophy does not come to us from Aristotle, but in all probability owes its origin to Andronicus of Rhodes who edited the works of the Master. It signifies simply the place this treatise occupies in the Aristotelian *corpus*, coming as it does *after* the Physics (μετὰ τὰ φυσικά). Ingenious minds however were not long in discovering a singular appropriateness in the word, for what is studied after physics must surely be something hyperphysical, and so metaphysics comes to denote the science of what is beyond nature, of an object *above* the mere material[2].

2. Modern Meanings of 'Metaphysics'.—Of the four names which this particular branch of philosophy has borne, two alone have survived to it. 'First Philosophy' is now a title carrying only an historical interest, and 'theology' has become a term relegated to the distinct department of rational, or natural, theology. Of the two remaining expressions, *ontology* and *general metaphysics*, the latter, 'metaphysic', is one that has suffered very much abuse at the hands of contemporary philosophers. The new erroneous conception of metaphysics is to be ascribed to the influence of Auguste Comte and Emmanuel Kant.

It is a fundamental axiom of the positivist school, among the founders of which Comte ranks foremost, that the human mind can know only facts of experience, their conditions of concomitance and succession, and that it is impossible for it

[1] *Met.*, X, c. VII, 5 and 6.

[2] This double idea, of being subsequent and superior to physics, is tersely expressed by Aquinas in the following lines: 'Dicitur metaphysica, id est transphysica, quia post physicam discenda occurrit nobis, quibus ex sensibilibus competit in insensibilia devenire'. *In lib. Boetii de Trinitate*, q. 5, a. 1.

to know anything beyond; the nature of beings, their causes and their ends are not knowable but are placed in opposition to 'positive science' and are contemptuously dubbed 'metaphysical entities or conceptions'. Those who adhere to the tenets of positivism, as also often unconsciously many of those who reason with them, accordingly term 'metaphysical' whatever transcends the experimental sciences.

According to Kant all the furniture of the mind must be stamped with the sense-forms of time and space; any object, then, denuded of spatial and temporal conditions cannot be an object of that strict knowledge which alone is properly scientific. In the Kantian philosophy there is therefore no room for a metaphysic in the strict sense. If indeed any such science can be entertained among philosophic speculation it can only be one enjoying a negative rôle, assigning to the human intellect those boundaries beyond which its knowledge will not and cannot be scientific.

3. General and Special Metaphysics.—Being is looked at by the metaphysician altogether apart from matter; he does not deny that it may be subject to the conditions of material existence, but the consideration of any of its material attributes simply does not concern him: the abstraction he employs *prescinds from*, rather than *excludes*, any material element. From this study of these realities which he conceives of in this immaterial way, he next infers that beings positively immaterial are not inconceivable or impossible. It is however elsewhere, in that section of philosophy called theodicy or rational theology, that the conditions for the existence and for the activity of these immaterial beings is specifically considered, and there proofs are adduced for the necessary existence of one immaterial Being who is immutable and the First Cause of all changing, contingent things. Metaphysics is, then, the science as well of material things disengaged by thought from the conditions of matter, as of things which are by their nature untrammelled by such conditions: or more briefly, it is the *science of things either negatively or positively immaterial.* The science of what is negatively immaterial constitutes *general* metaphysics and that of what is positively immaterial *special* metaphysics. Yet this is a division that does not prevent metaphysics from being, like every other science, a *single* science, contemplating an object that is *formally* one : the reason is that whatever *positive* knowledge we have of immaterial things is in no way dissimilar from our ideas concerning the material world. There will be occasion later (**11** and **12**) for insisting upon this unity of metaphysics as one science.

4. Place of Metaphysics in the Modern Division of Philosophy.—The division introduced by Wolff of the departments of philosophy retains the distinction just mentioned, but whilst general metaphysics or ontology is the same, special metaphysics no longer treats exclusively of beings that are positively immaterial. For him and for those who prefer his new division, special metaphysics is made to embrace, under the respective names of transcendental cosmology and rational psychology, the particular study of the first principles of corporeal beings and that of living ones. Accordingly *general* metaphysics may also now mean the wider science of being in general and of its attributes, and *special* metaphysics the science of how these principles gathered in general metaphysics *apply* to corporeal substances, to souls and to God.

5. Subdivision of General Metaphysics.—When an object of sensation has been divested by thought of its changes and quantity, it stands in the mind as something conceived in an indefinite way, something subsisting by itself, distinct from all others and forming a single individual : it is a substance, simple being, being in general. It is, moreover, the subject of certain adventitious determinations or accidents ; it is patient of certain changes and displays certain activities that serve to indicate to us the nature, origin and end of their subject. Hence general metaphysics has to consider being in general ; its necessary attributes—which go by the name of transcendentals because they are of far wider extension than all other properties, which are either specific or generic ; the principal determinations of being ; and lastly, the causes of being and of its active and passive manifestations. Dealing respectively with these topics, the treatise will have four parts :—

PART I : **Being.**
PART II : **The metaphysical attributes of being.**
PART III : **The principal determinations of being.**
PART IV : **The causes of being.**

PART I

Being

I. METAPHYSICAL OBJECTS OF THOUGHT AND THE ASSUMPTIONS OF AGNOSTICISM

6. Present-day Prejudice against Metaphysics.—As a result of the phenomenalism of Hume, of the positivism of Comte, J. S. Mill, Littré and Taine, and of the criticism of Kant, there exists in the intellectual atmosphere of the present day a prejudice against a science of metaphysics on the score of there being no special object for such a science to contemplate. Nothing is knowable, it is said, but what the senses can inform us about, and therefore what is supersensible, should any such reality exist, has no interest for the mind; what is unknowable had best be left in its obscurity. This fundamental assumption goes by the name of *agnosticism*. The philosophic theories which give birth to this agnostic attitude have been reviewed and discussed in Criteriology.

That substance as it is known and studied by metaphysics is not identical with the adventitious manifestations which fall immediately under our senses, in a word, that its formal object is not phenomena, will be duly established by direct and positive proof in the course of this treatise. Just at present it will be sufficient for us to dispel the false notions which the agnostics make use of to show that the metaphysician has no right even to assert or prove the existence of his science. Let us first show that the object of metaphysics is nothing foreign to the things of nature, and secondly indicate the methods which it professes to use in studying this object; it must then be apparent to any but a biased mind that it does in reality verify the definition of a true science.

7. The Object of Metaphysics is Individual Substance.—According to Aristotelian views the principal object of metaphysics is the *substance of individual things* which exist in nature and afford us experience. These things which form the subject-matter of our experience do not possess in themselves, as actual beings, those general characteristics they assume when the mind reflects upon them as abstract objects of thought; on the contrary they are individual and concrete, such that they can be pointed out by the hand, that they can arrest our gaze and be felt by our organs of touch. These concrete things existing in nature form in the *ontological* order the staple of all reality, and in the *logical* order the ultimate subjects of all predication; consequently they are termed *primary substance* (οὐσία πρώτη, substantia prima).

What the ontological sense of primary substance is will be clear if we examine any concrete individual being. Of the full reality disclosed by such an examination we perceive that not all belongs to that being in identically the same way, but rather that there is an invariant, a persisting substrate upon which there successively supervene other accessory and transitory realities or modalities—let us suppose, for example, a being passing from a state of rest to a state of activity: this man whom we see sleeping begins to walk about, eats and thinks, yet no one doubts that it is the same individual being despite the reality of the changes that come and go within him. This primordial foundation, this persisting substrate to which further realities attach, is primary substance in its ontological meaning.

Its logical significance will be equally clear when we consider that all our judgments are intelligible only because the subjects of them can be sooner or later referred to individual substances as *first subjects*. For, as will be seen clearly in Logic (29 f.), every predicate of our judgments, and also sometimes their subject, is an abstract, universal concept; when the subject is universal, to be intelligible it has to refer to a subject less universal than itself, which in turn must refer to another until ultimately the abstract universal concept is recognized as an immediate attribute of an individual subject. Thus all our concepts ultimately refer to primary substances, which are concrete individualizations, perceived by the senses, of abstract natures.

Individual or primary substance that forms the subject-matter of metaphysics—the persistent reality of a thing amid accidental realities modifying it and inhering in it, and the ultimate or ' first ' subject of an assertion—is what the mind is aware of indistinctly when it first awakens to consciousness, and it is the residue with which the mind is left when, by reflection, it has completely analysed its concept. What the mind first perceives, when it first comes in contact with any actual thing of experience, is to it merely an indistinct something, coloured and extended, situated in a definite place; the distinctions of genus and species, of substance and accidents, are not yet made; the mind is aware of something simply in a confused way, though aware of it as an independent thing, something subsisting, *per se stans*. The first elementary concept of anything, no matter what be its real nature, is always thus indeterminate, as indeed is testified by the utterances of the child mind which are always the same: ' this, that ', ' ceci, cela, ça ', ' dies, das ', ' dit, dat ', etc. This indistinct, confused knowledge is subsequently decomposed by successive processes of abstraction and all that is contained in the thought-object is gradually disentangled. The mind, by its characteristic action of abstraction, considers separately the various realities it apprehends: it eliminates successively from the object its particular traits, its specific and generic features, change and quantity, until finally it is left with nothing but *primary substance*—the special object which the science of metaphysics sets itself to contemplate.

From this explanation of the object of metaphysics and of the process of reaching it, it is evident, firstly, that though this object is abstract it is none the less supplied us by experience; and, secondly, that metaphysics, thus understood, is indeed ' First Philosophy ' (1) and not comparable to any of the departmental sciences: for (1) it carefully inspects our *first notions* and (2) it furnishes all the special sciences with their *first principles*. Let us further explain these two reasons.

1. Metaphysics treats of the very general notions of being, of real thing, of unity, etc., which it seizes at the first awakening of thought. These are ideas that cannot be construed by other previously-formed and simpler ideas, they are themselves intelligible whilst everything else that comes into the realms of intellectual knowledge can do so only by passing through them. Moreover whatever is known is never known but as a being, as some-thing, which is one. These notions are described by St. Thomas as the beginning and end of intellectual

knowledge, 'illud quod primo intellectus concipit quasi notissimum et in quod omnes conceptiones resolvit est ens'.

2. The mind is not content to acquire concepts; it compares them, unites and separates them, thereby forming judgments (*Logic*, **28** ff.). Thus it confronts its first notions with one another and from their agreement or disagreement derives universal principles, which are the most general of all principles and serve as the foundation of all its demonstrations—such for instance are, 'That which is, is', 'A whole is equal to the sum of its parts', 'The whole is greater than any of its parts'. These principles, like the first notions from which they are derived, are spontaneously formed and understood by all men; they are indeed essential to all further intellectual acts, alike of judgment and reasoning, and the mind is left with these same general principles after the construction of all science and philosophy has been completed and when it turns back upon itself to question the validity of its own demonstrations.

8. Two Difficulties.—Here some one may not unreasonably break in with a twofold difficulty that naturally arises from the preceding thesis: How can an individual thing be the object of a science that is by definition the most abstract of all the sciences? How is this same object to be met with at the very beginning of intellectual activity and in its last achievement?

9. Solution of the First Difficulty.—Concrete individual substances form the object of metaphysics in the sense that they provide its *material* object. In these substances the mind, by its highest act of abstraction, apprehends *substance entirely in general*, with its properties and determinations. Among these latter is the *general* notion of individuality. Metaphysics does not take any account of the multifarious concrete substances as concrete realities, it is not concerned with the features which distinguish one substance from another. Its work is to apprehend its formal object—substance in general, which is the fruit of the highest mental abstraction.

10. Solution of the Second Difficulty. Proof of the Strictly Scientific Character of Metaphysics.—Our objector asserts that it is surely a contradiction to say that the last effort of metaphysical study is engaged on the same object as that of our first, spontaneous thoughts. To this the reply is that the identity of the two objects is only apparent. Our *initial* conception of a subsisting being is the most imperfect of all the ideas we possess, whilst the *metaphysical* notion of subsisting being is the most perfect possible for us to acquire; the former is superficial, obscure and of little cognitional value, the latter most profound, quite distinct and pregnant.

The first object the intellect grasps on awaking to activity is, we have seen, an extended and coloured something, occupying a definite position in space and having separate existence. No more than this indistinct information is reached at the first step of knowledge. Subsequently many abstractions are made and in increasing degrees the mind comes to sift the full reality of beings and by the aid of several synthetic processes is eventually enabled to form a more perfect conception of it. The first spontaneous cognitions thus give place to reflection, and reflection creates the special sciences and then it crowns these with philosophy.

At the highest stage of our inquiry we find ourselves contemplating substance in general. This conception, in the first place, is an eminently *distinct* one; it stands out as a clearly defined idea against the numerous different notions the mind has formed during the course of observation and reflection. Secondly, it is the most *penetrating* of all our ideas, reaching as it does to the ultimate substrate of things to substance in general. And thirdly, it is a conception most *fruitful* in its consequences. This is so because philosophy, as we have already seen (1), is synthetic in its method: it regards the various objects of the special sciences from the point of view of some feature which they have in common and proceeds to explain these various objects as so many particular instances of that common feature. Thus in that branch of philosophy called physics, it deals with movement in all its phases; in mathematics, quantity is considered in all its forms; and finally in metaphysics, the most general and the most abstract feature becomes the object of consideration, namely substance, a notion which prescinds from concrete features, from material change and from quantity. Thus the notion with which metaphysics deals, the object of this department of philosophy, is that which gives us the *last word of explanation* concerning all beings and all the reality which exists in each of them.

11. Does Substance constitute the Adequate Object of General Metaphysics ?—With the deeper views of Aristotle in accordance with which we have assigned substance in general as the formal object of metaphysics, modern philosophers do not entirely agree. Preferring to adhere too closely to the etymological meaning of ontology they assert it to be the science of 'being in general' understanding thereby being which is neither substance nor accident, neither real nor logical, but that minimum of identity which is just not nothing. This is however a misconception. Such an idea of being in general is purely analogical: it extends to nature-objects very diverse, to substance, to accident, even to notional being. Now *notional*, or *logical, being* is of no concern to metaphysics; it belongs to the special philosophical department of logic. *Accidental being,* it is true, does to some extent pertain to metaphysics, for metaphysics is opposed to logic and takes cognizance of the real and therefore of everything that is real; but, as the reality of an accident is not its own but borrowed from the substance of which it is an adjunct, as it is rather the 'being of a being' than a being—'accidens non tam ens quam ens entis'—it does not fall within the scope of metaphysics on its own account but solely by reason of its connexion with substance. There remains, then, *substance* as the true object of metaphysics; albeit, for completeness' sake, after it has been studied *in itself* as the principal object, it may also, as a secondary object, be considered in its *accidental determinations.* To repeat, metaphysics does not concern itself with notional being, inasmuch as it does not belong to the order of reality; nor with being in general in as far as it extends beyond the limits of the real; nor with accident-being for its own sake, since it is only superficial reality relying for its existence upon substance, which enjoys its own reality.

We might go further and say that the substance or substantial being we abstract from the world of sensible nature forms the object of *all* metaphysics both special and general. If there exist substances of a higher nature than sensible things, we have no proper and direct knowledge of them to enable us to make another science of them, a separate science of the immaterial.

12. There is no Special Science of Immaterial Beings.—That there is no special science of immaterial beings is evident from the consideration of what is the requisite for a special science. Science, according to the definition given by Aristotle and universally accepted, is the knowledge of a thing through its causes. We have all that is required for a science when we know, either immediately or mediately, what a thing is so as to be able to define it and when from the definition of the nature of this thing we can arrive at the intimate reason of its properties. Now in determining whether we can have a special science of immaterial beings, the questions which are all-important are, Are we in a position to give a definition of what immaterial being is? And have we any special principles that apply to this kind of being and to it alone, whereby to construct a science? Both these questions must be answered in the negative, and for this reason we have no hesitation in declaring that we can possess no special science, in the strict sense, of the immaterial.

In the first place, we are unable to define immaterial beings. The proper object of our understanding is what we abstract from sensible things (*Psychology*, **89**, **90**), so that all our concepts apply positively and properly to material things and cannot apply to immaterial things, since by hypothesis these two orders of being have nothing in common. In the second place, we are without special principles based upon the nature or upon the distinctive properties of immaterial beings. Indeed the principles which are the necessary foundation for the growth of knowledge are acquired by comparing our primary notions and seeing their agreement or disagreement, and in point of fact our first notions are abstracted from sensible things. Not having any first notions of immaterial things, we are necessarily without the principles indispensable for the construction of a science of the immaterial.

We see, then, that special metaphysics does not constitute a science distinct from first philosophy, but that it is only a subdivision of it, an applied metaphysic.

II. General Analysis of the Idea of First Substance

13. General Analysis.—When the mind comes in contact with a subsisting thing, or, to use the word of Aristotle, with a *first substance*, it endeavours to find out all that it is. It asks itself, What is this thing? and in answer discovers the various notes which constitute its essence or what-the-thing-is.

These notes however are not a full answer to the question, they do not exhaust all the reality contained in the substance: substance has *existence* and the idea of existence is not contained in the essential definition of a thing. Thus it is disclosed that substantial being involves a complementary element, the ground of its being existent, the principle making the essence exist [3].

We have, then, to distinguish two elements in substance, 'duae rationes objectivae', first the *thing* itself that is capable of being classified in this or that category of things, and second, *that in virtue of which this thing exists*; first *id quod res est*, then *id quo est*; the *essence* and the *existence*.

Furthermore, of quiddity itself (quod quid est), apart from existence, there is place for another subdivision, namely, into *essential* being properly so called and *possible* being. Of these various notions we will speak in turn.

III. Existence

14. Meaning of 'Being' and 'Actual'.—If we carefully consider the idea of being or existence we shall see that it connotes the notion of *actualness*. When we say of a being that it *is*, *exists*, we contrast it with itself as a mere possible entity and affirm that it is now an *actual* thing. Yet, this is not tantamount to saying that we can *define* the idea of being by that of actuality. When for the sake of throwing light upon each other we compare the two notions of being and actual, we are not doing more than putting forward two corresponding terms of two groups of ideas: *existent* being is correlative to *possible* being in the same way as *actual* being is correlative to *potential* being.

An essence or essential being is in respect of existence indeterminate; it is incomplete without it, it is a subject capable of having it, that could be perfected by it; existence, on the other hand, takes away this indetermination of mere essence, adding to it just that which will make it cease to be merely possible. It is this rôle of existence that we express by the term *actuality* (ἐνέργεια). By calling existence the actuality

[3] As the word being (*ens*) expresses alike essence and existence, we may use for the sake of distinction the expressions *essential being* and *existential being* that correspond respectively to the terms *οὐσία*, *essentia* and *εἶναι*, *esse*.

of a thing we wish to convey that it is the formal principle determining the essence, completing and perfecting it (ἐντελέχεια).

IV. Essence

15. Meanings of Essence.—The essence of a thing is that whereby it is constituted this kind of thing and not that. We may define it as what-a-thing-is. Looked at in its relation to existence, essence is a subject that is indeterminate, incomplete, requiring to be perfected (*id quod*), bearing a relation to its actuality, which determines, completes and perfects it (*id quo*). In other words, as apart from its existence, a thing may be called *real being, essence, quiddity*; whereas, in as far as it is an existing thing, it is called *existential, actual* being.

Of essence we can gain three aspects corresponding to the threefold rôle we attribute to it when we come closely to inspect any reality.

1. Our first and constant desire is to know what things are; concerning everything we come across in our experience we ask ourselves, What is this? Quid est? and we find a satisfactory answer only in the *definition* of the thing in question. We cannot however give all at once the definition of what a thing is; we do not grasp it all by one act of apprehension, but by degrees, by a succession of objective concepts. What strikes us as the foremost element in it, as fundamentally constituting the being, is the *essence* in the strictest sense; it is what above all else makes the thing to be what it is, it is the *first constituent of a thing.*

2. But when we notice a thing as some kind of thing, by the same glance we also, *indirectly*, observe what it is not and how it is *differentiated* from other things. Thus we see that, in the second place, the essence is that which distinguishes a being from all others and gives it its place in the scale of beings; it is the distinctive feature, *the first characteristic of a thing.*

3. Lastly, since the essence is the first foundation of the reality of a being, the further perfections which the thing is susceptible of receiving and capable of acquiring must be the complement or manifestation of its essential perfection. Thus essence, in the third place, also discloses itself as the *primary source of all the perfections of a thing.*

16 Abstract Essence and Concrete Essence.—Human thought is essentially an abstractive process; it lays hold one by one of the notes that make up the essences of things. When first an object is placed before it, it deals with those features in it which it shares with other things of a more or less wide class, of a genus or a species; only subsequently does it narrow down its concepts and distinguish different individuals in the same species. The essence as the object of apprehension when the mind has in view only the notes characteristic of the genus or the species, goes by the name of the *abstract* essence—either *specific* or *generic*. That which our knowledge of the individual represents is the *concrete* essence; it is the essence of the *individual* or *person*.

17. Synonymous Terms for Abstract Essence.—Synonyms to be found in Scholastic Latin for essence, *essentia*, are *quod quid est, quod quid erat esse, species, natura, ratio rei, substantia*; in English, *quiddity, specific essence, nature, substance*. The first, the phrase *quod quid est, quod quid erat esse* and its derivative *quiddity*, what-a-thing-is, stands for the answer to the question *quid est hoc?* and accordingly is used for essence in so far as it is the object of our investigations. Similarly the question *quid est hoc?* may be answered by its definition or the *ratio rei*. The words *species, specific essence*, expressly signify that the object of the definition is abstract. *Substance* is essence in its principal signification; whilst *nature* is essence regarded precisely as the principle of a thing's activity.

Now that we understand what is meant by existing or actual being and by real being or essence, it remains to notice possible being and to see how it is different from both.

V. Possible Being

18. Possible Being.—Possible being and real being or essence are not the same; both are the opposite of actual or existing being, but in different ways. We are free either not to consider the existence of a thing or to consider it as not existing; in other words, the mind may simply not *include* the formality of existence in its concept or it may positively *exclude* it. In the first case the abstractive act of the mind is an act of mental *precision* (*abstractio praecisiva*, praecidere); in the second, it is an act of *exclusion* (*abstractio exclusiva*).

The term of the first abstraction is a *real essence*; that of the second is *possible essence, possible being*—essence considered as not existing.

Possible being is opposed on the one hand to actual being, and on the other to logical being. It is to be distinguished from the one, actual being, inasmuch as it does not exist in nature; and from mere logical being inasmuch as it conceivably may exist.

Further, the possibility of a possible being may be considered from two points of view, namely as intrinsic or extrinsic, internal or external, negative or positive. *Intrinsic* possibility is that capacity of a being for existence which is simply due to the absence of contradiction in the essential notes by which it would be constituted if an actual being, powerful enough to produce it, were to make it exist. *Negative* well describes this sort of possibility; it is a non-impossibility. On the other hand, for a thing to be *extrinsically* and *positively* possible more is required than mere absence of inconsistency: extrinsic possibility is the capacity of a being for existence owing to the presence of a cause which is a sufficient reason for its production. This may be called 'possibility of being' meaning thereby 'possibility of actual existence'.

But what does possibility depend on? What is the ultimate foundation of the possibility of things?

19. Ground of Extrinsic Possibility.—The immediate reason of extrinsic possibility of a thing lies in the *existence* of an efficient cause capable of producing it. As, however, all the efficient causes of which we have experience are contingent, they demand that there be above them a Being which by its very essence is actual and capable of serving as efficient cause. God, Pure Actuality, the Prime Mover of the universe, is therefore the ultimate reason of the extrinsic possibility of things.

20. Ground of Intrinsic Possibility.—Must we also have recourse to God as the immediate foundation of the intrinsic possibility of beings? Many modern Scholastic philosophers are of the opinion that we must, that possibles and the features they display cannot be satisfactorily accounted for unless they be referred to God as the prototype of all beings. In the first place, they observe, possibles appear quite independent of actual finite beings: were the material universe annihilated and all finite minds with it, things would still be intrinsically possible. They are then necessary, universal and immutable, whilst existing things are contingent, particular and changeable. Their number is indefinitely great. Moreover, they serve us as types by which we judge actual things and pronounce whether they are as they should be; thus, for instance, we say that an action is not good, reckoning by a rule of justice which is prior to and independent of human actions. It would seem then from these characteristics that possibles are distinct from, and independent of, things of experience; whereas if they are referred to God as their source—which is the only alternative—a satisfactory explanation is forthcoming. If, indeed, all things were swept out of existence, God, who would remain, would be still essentially susceptible of imitation by the creation of beings other than Himself. The immutability, too, of possibles is explained by their being imitations of the Divine essence which is necessary and immutable; so likewise their infinity. And finally, since God is the exemplary cause of the universe, it is easy to understand why we naturally make use of possibles, the imitations of the Divine Being, as standards by which to judge created things.

This argument, however, is a congeries of equivocal statements. Moreover an immediate basis for the intrinsic possibility of beings is, in our opinion, afforded us in the contingent beings to which our experience extends. When by observation we have grasped some being and by abstraction drawn out its constitutive notes for separate consideration, immediately there begin to appear certain relations between these notes, namely, relations of mutual compatibility or of discrepancy. In the first place it is evident that the notes involved in a thing already existing are compatible, and hence we can say that the essences which these existing things realize are possible—for, *ab esse ad posse valet illatio*. Next we perceive that some essences, made up of notes we have drawn from *diverse* existing things, have in them nothing mutually antagonistic. Of such the classical example is the concept of a golden mountain: 'I have never seen a golden mountain, but I have seen at one time a mountain and at another gold'; by comparing the data of my two experiences I am enabled to say that 'a golden mountain is possible'. In brief, contingent beings that surround us in nature and that we have or may have experience of, are adequate to offer us an immediate explanation of the intrinsic possibility of beings.

Yet there are many modern Scholastics loth to allow that this foundation affords an adequate explanation of possible essences: for them they are a world of realities quite independent of beings falling under our experience, and consequently must be rooted in God as the exemplary Cause of all that is, the supreme Archetype of beings, existing and possible alike. But there is no such need to refer them to God: the existence of the sensible world coupled with the mind's inherent power of abstraction can perfectly account for the existence of possible essences and their characteristics: a sufficient reason is furnished for the compatibility we recognize in the concepts we draw from things of experience, as well also for the other properties belonging to possible essences [4].

It need hardly be mentioned that the above explanation of possible being is analytical. There is, also, of course, the synthetic or, as the Scholastics called it, the regressive explanation, which shows how the outcome of our analysis stands in relation to the Divine Essence and its imitability. When we have proved by analytical reasoning that God is the Author of all things, that He is intelligent, infinite and the rest, it is natural to assume that He is the Exemplar and Archetype of all His works, whether actual or possible. Nevertheless the importance of this corroborative view in itself can very easily be exaggerated. For such knowledge as we may attain of God, being negative and analogical (*Psychology*, **108**), will not be of much help in enabling us to understand, by way of contrast, the characteristics of finite possibles; between God and the world of possibles the most able metaphysician will only find those necessarily obscure relations which obtain between a principal analogue and its derivatives.

21. Corollaries.—1. Things are not intrinsically possible because they are conceivable, but they are conceivable because they are intrinsically possible. An object, indeed, must be thinkable before it is thought; a thought without a thought-object is impossible. Now any object which is thought of may be analysed and this analysis reveals the compatibility

[4] A full proof of these last statements will be found in the larger edition, 5th ed. pp. 36–51. Cp. also the treatise on *Natural Theology*, **19** and references there given.

of its notes, which allows us to say that it is intrinsically possible and in consequence intelligible; on the contrary, notes that are mutually incompatible cannot be united in one thought-object, together they are inconceivable. Try, for instance, to conceive 'round-square'; 'round' is conceivable and so is 'square', but it is physically impossible to form a concept embodying them both: the human mind cannot conceive one object made up of contradictory elements. Hence the *intrinsic possibility of a being is logically prior to its conceivability*; and similarly *the intrinsic impossibility is logically prior to its inconceivability.*

2. Turning to extrinsic possibility, which is a being's possibility of actual existence, its producibleness, we may say that, since existence is the actualization of an essence—'esse est id quo aliquid est, esse est ultimus actus'—and existence accordingly presupposes an essence to receive the 'act' of existence, this kind of possibility logically presupposes the intrinsic possibility of the essential type susceptible of existing. Likewise the extrinsic impossibility of a being is logically posterior to its intrinsic impossibility. In brief, *the conceivability and the extrinsic possibility of beings are both subsequent to their intrinsic possibility.*

VI. Closer Analysis of First Substance

22. Sequence of the Questions to be Treated.—A first analysis of particular subsisting being that falls under experience and is the object of metaphysical speculation gave us grounds for distinguishing the *actual existence* by which essence is made to subsist and *essence* which is rendered actual by existence. This essence, moreover, we have considered under two aspects, firstly in abstraction from existence, as *quiddity*, real essence, and secondly as exclusive of existence, as mere *possible* essence. We may now push our analysis of first substance still further.

Whenever we want to know or understand some subsistent object of experience, we ask ourselves, 'What is it'? and the answer gives us the essence of the thing. But this essence is abstract, in the sense that it gives only those characteristics which the subsistent thing has in common with a number of other individual things of the same genus or species. Since however each one of the things we see around us—and they are the object of all metaphysics—is a concrete individual independent of the rest, we are led naturally to inquire into the principle of individuation of the 'specific type'. For instance, every man is alike to the mind under the abstract concept of a material, living, subsistent, rational substance; yet each man is *this* sentient body with this particular rational soul and he can share them with nobody. What is there in the individual that is not in the type?

A second problem before us relates to the constitutive parts of being disclosed by our first analysis of individual substance, namely *essence* which stands for what-it-is and *actual existence* which accounts for why-it-is. What is the relation these two parts bear to each other? Are they two parts distinct? And if so, by what do they differ?

23. Some Prerequisite Ideas from Scholastic Cosmology.—For an understanding of the problem of the individuation of specific types an acquaintance is required with certain ideas of Scholastic cosmology. We need merely recall these now, as we have already established their truth in Cosmology (**37** ff.).

Bodies, according to the Scholastic theory, are composed of two constitutive parts, one that endures, *matter*, and one that takes the place of another which succeeds it, *form*. The former, primary matter, is a substantial element that is absolutely indeterminate but essentially determinable; the latter, substantial form, is the substantial element conferring determination on the matter: from the union of matter with an appropriate form results the constitution of a body. Both matter and substantial form are essentially dependent upon each other, in such wise that their compound alone is what may exist. So, too, it is the complete substance alone which has the properties. First and foremost among these ranks quantity: it consists essentially in the distribution and internal arrangement of the parts of the body. From *intrinsic* quantity flows, in the natural order of things, extension—which is the *extrinsic* manifestation of quantity—divisibility and localization in space. The qualitative properties of a body presuppose quantity and depend on it; and on this account it is named by Scholastics as the *first accident* of corporeal substance.

It is also worthy of notice that the *quantity proper* to a body is not absolute but may vary, though only within certain limits. Each species of body has a minimum of quantity assigned to it without which it is physically impossible for a body of that species to exist, and also as an opposite extreme a maximum in excess of which the type would be lost. As a consequence of this the qualities of the compound likewise admit of degrees within certain limits well defined for each species.

24. The Individual Philosophically Considered presents Three Distinct Points of View.—The question we are now setting ourselves to consider is, How is it that the being we know in an abstract way is an individual subject? A complete solution of this problem requires that we should break it up into three separate questions according to three different points of view from which the individual may be looked at:—

(1) What are the *signs* by which an individual is recognized as such? This concerns the logical viewpoint.

(2) What *constitutes* individuality? This deals with the formal or ontological viewpoint.

(3) What is the *source* of the individualizing characteristics, the root of individuation? The genetic viewpoint.

25. The Individual is known chiefly by its Dimensions in Space.—If we ask ourselves what is the usual sign we go by in distinguishing one singular thing we meet with from another of a similar kind, we shall find that it is mostly by its extension, and the properties depending upon its extension, that is, by its dimensions and its shape or form, its position in a definite place, and its age or position in a definite moment of time. Take any example that you can call to mind. Two oak trees that stand side by side in this avenue of a forest are distinguished for us indeed to some extent by the colour of their leaves but above all by the position in which they stand, by their height and the girth of their trunks, the different shapes of their branches, etc.—in a word, by their extension and the qualities flowing from it.

Sense and intellect both act alike in the means of distinction they employ. The intellect, not having a direct intuition of the essences of things, distinguishes them according to their properties, and of these the fundamental property of matter, the 'primum accidens', is quantity inasmuch as it is the ground in which all other accidents are rooted.

But notice that we do not say that extension constitutes individuality, for the individual is a substance whereas extension is an accident; and it is impossible that an accident should be a constituent of substance. All that we state is that extension and its derivative accidents are the chief and usual signs by which we know an individual. What it is that constitutes individuality we have yet to inquire.

26. The Formal Reason of the Individuality of a Being is its own Entity.—If, on conceiving the essence of some subsisting being in nature, we refer it to that particular being whence we drew the notion, we shall discover that the concept does not include the individual traits of the thing, but is made up only of notes that are common to all the individuals of the same species. The question presents itself, then, What is it that makes this universal essence individual?

In the first place, we must note that whilst the concept by which we express the essence of substantial being is abstract, the abstract character of its notes must not lead us astray. As abstract, essence is only a product of thought, a mental reality. As realized in nature essence is affected by particular determinations which the intellect waives when forming its representative concept; as a realized type it is both concrete and individual. These determinations that the understanding ignores in summing up a reality are singular determinations relating to quantity and quality, together with the act of existence. In point of fact essence is thus determinate: in Socrates, for example, the matter is *this* definite matter, *these* organized tissues, *these* bones, *this* flesh; the soul, *this* soul; in a word, *one and the same reality* makes Socrates to be Socrates, a man, an animal, a substance, and a being. Thus a being is one single, concrete, individual whole.

To return, then, to the question, What individualizes an essence? we have only one answer to offer: That an essence is individual because it is *so*. We can say no more. If it is a senseless question, as Aristotle says, to ask why a man is a man, it is surely equally so to ask why this man is this man. All that can be replied to the question, To what is a thing's individuality due? is that its individuality is constituted by its very entity itself.

Nevertheless, closely allied to this question there are two others that suggest themselves. What, we may first ask are the constituent elements of individuality; what conditions must be verified for an individual to be called such? Ask secondly, How is it that there can be many individuals in the same species? Both of these points are worthy of special attention.

27. Elements essential to the Constitution of an Individual.—An individual we may best define by the classical definition: 'Individuum est ens in se indivisum et ab omni alio ente divisum'. An individual is a complete substance, this thing here, that thing there. By the fact that it is complete, one thing, it is also distinct from every other thing; it is this substance, and thereby not others. But is there no intrinsic reason for this unity of the individual whereby it is a whole and ranks distinct from all other particular substances? The ultimate reason lies in the fact that the individual substance is complete in itself, self-sufficient in respect of its existence and action. Because self-sufficient, it constitutes a complete thing possessed of unity and incommunicable to others.

These features of the individual distinguish it from accident, from generic and specific types, and from constitutive or integral parts of a being. None of these various realities can exist by themselves; they can exist only on condition of participating in the reality of some individual subject. An accident is the being of a being, of a substance; it has to share something in common before it can exist. Likewise generic types do not exist alone, but in conjunction with the species subordinate to them; and species do not exist except in the individuals in which they are realized. Neither genus nor species has the note of being incommunicable. As for integral or constitutive parts, these belong to an individual, and therefore do not by their nature constitute distinct and independent realities. Thus it is seen that the individual *alone* of all the beings of nature possesses the double perfection which is comprised in being self-sufficient without requiring to belong to another being. This completeness of the individual is primarily in respect of its substantiality, but also, secondarily and by way of consequence, in respect of its action, since—as will be shown in due time—every substance is made for action and its reality is proportioned to the rôle which has been assigned to it in the order of nature, 'omne ens propter suam operationem'.

Synonyms for the individual in Scholastic language are *suppositum*, and *hypostasis*. An individual endowed with a artional mind is called a *person*. Accordingly personality is that perfection in virtue of which an intelligent being is capable of existing and acting alone, independently of being attached to any other being. Indeed is not 'to assert one's personality' nothing more or less than to show proof of one's originality and independence? And in the moral sphere, is not personality the capability of directing one's self towards one's own destiny? In the juridical order it consists in being 'sui juris'—a phrase which owes its origin to the distinction by which a slave was considered to be not a person but a 'res', 'juris alieni'. In fine, a *person* is a *rational concrete substance*, according to the classical definition of Boetius: 'Rationalis naturae individua substantia'.

28. The Principle of Individuation. Statement of the Question.—Among the elements that go to form this self-sufficient, incommunicable whole which we call the individual, is there not one with the special part assigned to it of individualizing the concrete essence? Moreover, since we notice that in the same species there are *numerically* several individuals —Peter and Paul, for instance, possessing the same nature but none the less two numerically distinct representatives of it—a second question presents itself: To what is this *numerical* multiplicity of individuals in one species due[5]? These two questions, as we shall see, together make up one fundamental problem which has been known in the history of philosophy as that of the *principle of individuation.*

29. Solution.—The Thomistic thesis, to which we adhere, concerning the principle of individuation is the following:— The individualizing principle of a being is its primary matter; the intrinsic reason of a multiplicity of individuals in the same species is primary matter as the foundation of quantity—or in brief, *principium individuationis est materia quantitate signata.*

Proof of the first part of the thesis: The individuating principle of a being is its primary matter.—Our first object, then, is to ascertain what is the principle by reason of which an essence when realized constitutes a singular thing complete in itself, incommunicable and, in consequence, differentiated

[5] 'Duo quaeruntur concurrentia ad individuationem, scilicet quo primo natura specifica reddatur incommunicabilis et quo primo realiter distinguatur ab aliis ejusdem speciei'. CAJETAN, *Comment. De ente et essentia*, c. IV

from every other. 'Individuum est ens in se indivisum et ab omni alio ente divisum'.

In an individual thing of nature there is ground for distinguishing its substantial form, its primary matter, its accidents and its existence. Now existence does not constitute individuality, for it presupposes a subject that it actualizes. Accidents are realities consequent upon the constitution of the individual, since by their nature they inhere in it. Nor can the form be invoked as the principle of individuation; for by definition the form is the intrinsic principle of the *specific* difference in bodies; hence a difference of form entails a difference in essence, i.e. a specific difference [6]. Individual differences, however, as we have seen, are not formal: bodies individually distinct may belong to the same species of body. Individualization then which has nothing to do with essential differences cannot come from the form. It is to the matter, then, that we must look for the source of individualization in virtue of which things that are the same essentially are distinct from one another. Now primary matter is admirably adapted to be this principle. In the first place it is wholly indeterminate in itself and so could not possibly confer any specific perfection on a subject in which one might imagine it to be received. Secondly, it is not received in any subject, but is, by definition, the subject in which the form is received; by being received in *this* matter the specific form is precluded from being received in or communicated to other subject-matter [7]—in other words, it is through the union of form with matter that we get the individual—the 'hoc aliquid'.

Matter, then, explains how a material being has no essential perfection beyond what is common to the species and yet is something complete in itself and incapable of being an attribute of any other subject.

Proof of the second part: The principle of the multiplicity of individuals in one and the same species is primary matter serving as the foundation of quantity.—We must now endeavour

[6] 'Gradus perfectionis in recipiendo eamdem formam non diversificat speciem, sed diversis gradibus perfectionis in ipsis formis seu naturis participatis diversificat speciem'. *De ente et ess.* c. VI.

[7] 'Dicitur materia principium individuationis quatenus est ultimum subjectum ultra quod non fit communicatio . . . et sic principium incommunicandi est principium individuandi'. JOHN OF ST. THOMAS, *Phil. Nat.*, P. II, q. IX, a. 3.

to find out more precisely what distinguishes an individual from others of the same species as itself, what is the reason for the multiplicity of individuals in one and the same species.

This reason is to be found in the matter; yet not this time in the matter considered as the ultimate receptive subject of the specific form, but in the matter considered as the source of quantity and the root of the divisibility of the corporeal compound.

On account of its being composed of matter, the compound necessarily possesses parts of which some are outside of others; and this composition of parts is due to the accident quantity. These parts, in the natural order of things, give rise to continuous extension; an extended body is divisible, either really or theoretically, into parts mutually distinct from one another; and finally, division is the basis of number—'numerus sequitur divisionem'. Now division of an extended body into extended parts does not furnish any specific determination; it does not bring about a diversity of nature; the beings that result from a quantitative division are of the same species. Hence primary matter, inasmuch as it is the source of quantity, is the reason of there being numerically many individuals in the same species [8].

Primary matter is, then, the principle of individuation. It fulfils the double rôle of that principle: as the ultimate receptive subject of the specific form, it explains why the concrete thing is complete in itself and possesses an independent reality that it shares with no other; as the foundation of intrinsic quantity and, as a natural consequence, of the extension of the body in space and of its divisibility, it explains how it happens that there are many individuals in the same species. This general conclusion is in accord with the teaching of St. Thomas which we may sum up with him in the following words: 'Cum *duo* sint de ratione individui, scilicet *incommunicabilitas*, et *distinctio* materialis ab aliis, unius horum principium est materia, alterius vero quantitas, et sic *totale individuationis principium* est materia signata, id est *materia sub*

[8] 'Materia est ratio habendi individuationem (i.e. multiplicitatem diversorum in eadem specie) quatenus est principium non communicandi aliis subjectis seu partibus materiæ quatenus ultimum subjectum est. Tamen non exercet hanc incommunicabilitatem inter partes materiæ nisi supposita separatione et divisione quæ fit per signationem materiæ tanquam conditionem requisitam'. JOHN OF ST. THOMAS, *l.c.*

quantitate, quae signum ejus dicitur, eo quod per ipsum sensibilis fiat et determinata ad hic et nunc '[9].

Now that we have discovered the reason of the individualization of a being and solved the first problem presented by the individual, it remains to compare the individual with its existence. In the following pages then we shall consider whether there is a distinction between individual substance and existence.

30. Preliminary Ideas concerning Different Kinds of Distinction.—When treating presently of the subject of *unity* among the attributes of metaphysical being, we shall make a special examination of the different distinctions which correspond to real compositions of nature or which are conceivable by the mind. The following ideas will suffice for the meantime.

There are some compositions entirely independent of our thought: such, for example, as the composition of the thinking faculty with the thought itself; and these are called *real* and the distinction corresponding to them is also called *real*. Distinctions that do not exist independently of the mind are called *logical* distinctions: an example is the distinction between the concepts of man and rational animal, and between the notion of the spirituality of the human soul and of its immortality. Logical distinction, or the distinction of reason, may be either the result of an entirely subjective conception, and in this case it is known as *purely logical* or a distinction of *pure reason*: an example is the distinction between the ideas of man and rational animal. Or it may be founded on reality, in this sense that one reality may serve as a common material object for two formally different conceptions; it is then called a *virtual* logical distinction: of this an example is the latter of the two just given, for the same human soul according to the point of view from which it is regarded furnishes two different ideas, namely one representing its independent subsistence or its spirituality and the other the capacity it has, in virtue of its spirituality, of outliving the body it animates. This latter kind of logical distinction is also known as that based upon reality, *distinctio cum fundamento in re*.

31. Distinction between Essence and Existence. Statement

[9] *In* IV *Sent.*, dist. 12, q. 1, a. 1. Cp. *Tractatus de principio individuationis.*

of the Question.—Between the *concept* of essence and the *concept* of existence there is clearly *some* distinction; they do not mean the same thing, they have different objective meanings. This no one disputes. Neither is there any question about there being a distinction between an abstract essence, essence mentally conceived, and the same essence considered as actualized in nature. The present question is concerned with the individual essence of a concrete thing in reference to its existence: are we to say, when the essence of an existing thing is contrasted with the actuality whereby it is existent, that the existence actualizing the essence is really identical with the essence so made actual, or are we to declare the two really distinct?

The answer to this question we hold with St. Thomas to be that the composition of essence and existence is a real one.

But notice, in the first place, that we do not assert their separability: distinction and separability are not the same. Separability is one of the indications of real distinction, but it is not the same thing nor a necessary consequent of it. Two things that are separable are really distinct from each other; but it may happen that two distinct realities composing the same something are inseparable from each other, that is to say, they could not be subjects of existence apart from each other. Thus we profess that the faculties of thought and of will really differ from each other whilst both of them are also really distinct from substance of the human soul; yet both are incapable of being separated from the substance in which they inhere.

And in the second place, we must not be so foolish as to expect to have a *direct perception in any actual thing* of essence apart from existence and existence apart from essence. We have no clear ideas, no immediate proper notions, of these metaphysical objects, but only mediate notions, indirectly acquired by reason arguing that the essence of an existing thing is not identical with its existence; it is by a *discursive* process that we attain to a knowledge of the manner of their composition.

32. Direct Proof of the Real Composition of Essence and Existence.—*First argument:* Essence—what a thing is—is the sum of the notes expressed in the definition of a thing. Existence is existence, we cannot translate it by any other equivalent idea. Now, on the one hand, never does a definition of any object, however perfect, comprise in it the existence of the object defined. Represent anything you like in nature, not only with the notes characteristic of its species but also with its individual features; attribute to it all the reality that is requisite to give an adequate answer to the question, 'What is it?' and the thing will still be destitute of existence, it will still be something capable of existing, not something actually so. On the other hand, the existence of any actual thing, though it also extends over the whole object, is one and indivisible, it is existence and only existence; and indeed this is so true that we cannot employ any synonym whereby to express it, and when we want to represent it more distinctly we have to be satisfied with opposing it to its contradictory, non-existence or nothing. Hence essence does not include existence, nor existence essence; between the two there is an adequate diversity, corresponding as they do, according to the remark of St. Thomas, to two different questions—existence to the question, '*An est?*' and essence to the question, '*Quid est?*' In fine, therefore, the being which is at once the object of two adequately distinct concepts cannot be simple but must be a compound being; or, in other words, essence and existence are two component elements of an existing being [10].

Second argument: Beings that fall under our experience are obviously finite; moreover they are many. But a being whose essence is identical with its existence is necessarily infinite and unique. Therefore the essences of things to which our experience extends are really distinct from their existence.

Proof of the minor:—(i) A being whose essence is identical with its existence is necessarily infinite. The reason for this is tersely assigned by St. Thomas: 'Esse subsistens oportet esse infinitum; quia non terminatur aliquo recipiente' [11].

That being whose essence is identical with its existence is by definition being; it necessarily possesses, then, whatever is included in the concept of being, that is to say all possible being: it is therefore being without limit, infinite being.

[10] 'Nulla essentia sine his quae sunt partes essentiae intelligi potest. Omnis autem essentia intelligi potest sine hoc, quod aliquid intelligatur de esse suo acto. Ergo patet, quod esse est aliud ab essentia'. *De ente et essentia*, c.V.

[11] *Cont. Gent.*, II, 52.

Again, limitation as such implies non-being. But it would be a contradiction in terms to suppose that the being whose essence is existence is affected by non-being, for this would be to place in being *quâ* being the intrinsic reason of non-being. We conclude, then, that the being whose essence is existence is not subject to limitation.

The reason why the perfection of a being does not transcend a certain degree lies not in that perfection itself, but in this further circumstance that a finite being has a limited receptive capacity and this limitation of capacity involves a corresponding limitation in the actual existence it may receive. The reason of the limitation of finite beings thus makes a counter-proof to the argument just given. The intrinsic limitation of finite beings has its sufficient reason in that they are not the being in virtue of which they subsist. Indeed, precisely because they are subjects to which existence is given, they can only receive existence in proportion to their capacity as subjects for receiving it: 'Esse participatum finitur ad capacitatem participantis [12]'. The conception of a content surpassing the capacity of the container is an impossible one. The intrinsic limitation of finite beings follows then as a necessary consequence from the contingency of their existence.

Hence we have the double conclusion, on the one hand, that the being which is its own subsistence cannot be otherwise than infinite; and on the other, that the sufficient reason of the finiteness of finite beings is in their real composition of essence and existence [13].

Proof of the minor: (ii) The being whose essence is its existence is necessarily unique. Beings are not diverse from one another by the fact that they are existent, but by being *what they are*. Plurality of beings results from the fact that there are many essential subjects—stone, plant, man—endowed with existence. But on the supposition of no distinction between *what* exists and the existence itself, there would no longer be any ground for diversification: since the 'act' of existence in virtue of

[12] *Sum. Theol.*, I, q. 75, a. 5, ad 4.

[13] 'Manifestum est quod primum ens, Deus, est actus infinitus, utpote habens in se totum essendi plenitudinem, non contractam ad aliquam naturam generis vel speciei. . . . Omne quod est post primum ens, cum non sit suum esse, habet esse in aliquo receptum; per quod ipsum esse contrahitur, et sic in quolibet creato aliud est natura rei quae participat esse, et aliud ipsum esse participatum'. *De spirit. creat.*, a. 1.

which each thing would exist and thereby be opposed to nothing would be in all cases one and the same, there would be but one being.

33. Indirect Proof of the Real Composition of Existing Things.—This proof lies in the logical connexion that obtains between the doctrine of the real composition of essence and existence and certain other propositions that are fundamental in Scholastic and other spiritualistic philosophy.

All Scholastics are agreed in recognizing that in nature there are some *really composite beings* which are also real *units*. Now it is impossible for elements that are *actually distinct* to contribute *really* to the formation of a true unit unless they are unified by some principle that is *one*; and such a principle of unity can only be existence, inasmuch as it is the sole determining 'act' that is received by all the elements of the compound. Hence the doctrine of the real composition of essence and existence is at the bottom of several generally admitted fundamental truths.

This general reasoning finds its application in the substantial unity of bodies and, in particular, of the human compound; as also in the doctrine that the soul has faculties.

1. Bodies are made up of two intrinsic elements, primary matter and substantial form, which *together* constitute what is *one* body. Now if every reality had its existence, and accordingly the matter and form constitutive of any body each had its own, how could they ever together make up a body substantially *one*? There would be no ground for calling their union an *intrinsic* one. It is therefore necessary, if we are to account for the unity of the corporeal compound, to acknowledge that one act of existence determines both of the component parts. And from this it is apparent that the two constituent principles of the essence are really distinct from their common existence. Thus our contention stands proved from a consideration of the composition of physical bodies [14].

2. Likewise can the unity of the human person be reconciled with its real composition of the two real parts, matter and

[14] 'In natura rerum corporearum materia est ut potentia respectu formae et forma est actus ejus; et iterum natura constituta ex materia et forma est ut potentia respectu ipsius esse, inquantum est susceptiva ejus'. *De spirit. creat.*, a. 1.

spiritual soul, only by having recourse to a single act of existence whereby the composite whole is unified.

3. In Psychology we proved that the soul possesses faculties that are all, even the spiritual ones, really distinct from one another. Intellect we saw to be different from will, and the active intellect to be really distinct from the potential intellect. Nevertheless although these several faculties are different, they all confessedly belong to *one and the same soul*. The human person is one despite his manifold capabilities. How explain these apparently irreconcilable facts except on the hypothesis that the faculties are distinct from one another by reason of their several *realities* and are reduced to unity by virtue of the *single existence* that envelops at once both the substance and its accidents.

Gathering together the various separate conclusions of this argument, we may say that the substantial composition of bodies and especially the intrinsic union of soul and body in the human compound, together with the real distinction of the several faculties of the same soul, bear witness to the reality of the composition of essence and existence.

34. Recapitulation of the Metaphysical Analysis of First Substance.—This concrete *something* which comes within our experience, which is found in every existing reality and forms therefore the main object of metaphysical study, is what we mean by an individual substance, that is complete in itself alike for subsistence and the exercise of its proper activities and is endowed with existence. Substance as thus understood is what answers in the first place to the idea of '*being*'.

VII. Various Meanings of Being

35. Principal and Derived Meanings of the Word Being.—The word being, as Aristotle observes, has many meanings.

1. In its first sense 'being' means this particular concrete thing that comes within the experience of our senses and makes the first object of the understanding when intellectual knowledge commences. To speak in the terms of the grammarian, being in this sense is a *noun* or substantive. In this sense being admits of three subdistinctions: (*a*) Being is the whole compound, comprising at once the substance that exists and the actuality whereby it exists—expressed by the word 'being' (used substantively), *ens*, *τό ὄν*.

(*b*) Being is the thing which is said to exist, *id quod* ens est—*essence*, or nature, *essentia*, οὐσία—which is divided into ten categories. (*c*) Being is the *existence*, *id quo* ens est, the final *actuality* of a thing, εἶναι. Ipsum enim esse *quo* aliquid est.

In the second of these senses, being sometimes designates the *specific* essence, sometimes the *individual* or *personal* essence. If the *individual* essence be compared with the *specific*, or *abstract*, essence, the former is called *first substance*, πρώτη οὐσία—substance, that is, in the primary and principal meaning of the word—whilst abstract essences are substances in a secondary sense and are called *second substances*.

With regard to individual essence itself, we may consider the individual substance strictly so called together with the accidents that inhere in it or modify it. The substance alone merits the name of being, since the accidents cannot claim to be beings at all except on the condition that there be a subject in which they may inhere; they are rather beings of a being, *ens entis*.

2. In the foregoing senses we understand being as *real*. Whether we consider it as existent, or whether we prescind from its existence, or even regard it as possible, it is what it is, independently of the mind considering it. Opposed to real being is unreal being, *notional* being, the objectivity of which is solely the fruit of the mind's thought. It is never realized nor realizable in nature, but is an object only of the mind's creation. Examples of these *beings of reason*, as they are also called, are *negation*, *privation* (e.g. blindness), *genera* and *species* inasmuch as they are the relations a universal idea bears to an inferior to which it is applicable, and also the quality of being *subject* or *predicate* in a judgment. These beings of reason, entia rationis vel entia secundae intentionis, form the whole subject-matter of logic.

3. Being, alike real and notional, may either signify something actual, or something potential; hence there is another division into *actual* being and *potential* being.

4. (*a*) The word 'is' may signify merely truth: thus we say that 'the whole *is* equal to the sum of its parts', and that 'the whole *is not* identical with any of its parts'. A predicate sometimes is identical with its subject or belongs to it, sometimes it is not identical with it, does not belong to it; accordingly it has to be united with its subject or to be separated

from it. The words 'to be', 'not to be', are expressive of these relations of the identity or of non-identity, of the belonging or not belonging, of the terms of a proposition and so of the union or separation of the subject and predicate; thus their sense is only that of the copula. 'Being' in this sense is purely notional. It is however consequent to real being, forasmuch as it is in beings of nature that we are given our basis for the order we put into our thoughts, for our union or separation of terms in the judgment. (*b*) Besides being used in this copulative sense, the *verb* 'to be' may have the additional meaning of possession on the part of the subject of *actual existence*. Thus, 'I am', 'Peter is', are equivalent to: 'I am an existing being', 'Peter is an existing being'.

The following table sums up the different meanings:—The word 'being' may be a *noun* or a *verb*. As a *noun* it stands either for *real* being or for *notional* being [15]. As a *verb* it may bear either of two meanings: as the *copula* it is the nexus between subject and predicate in the judgment; or it has the substantial import of attributing *actual existence* to a subject [16].

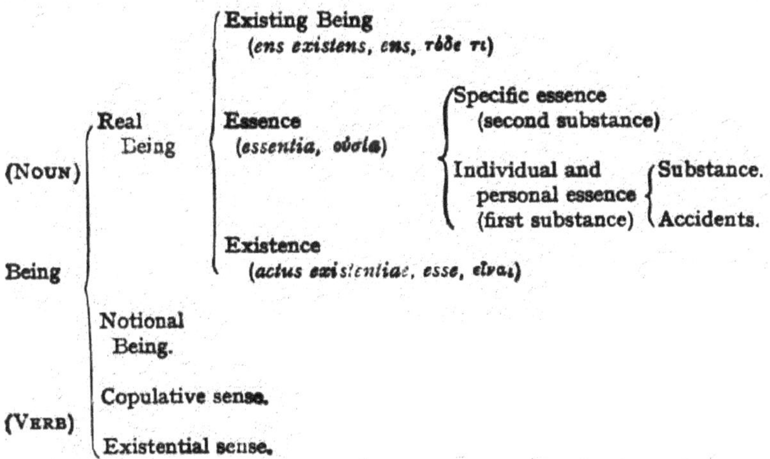

[15] 'Simpliciter dicitur res hoc modo, accepto nomine *res* secundum quod habet quidditatem vel *essentiam* quamdam; *ens* vero secundum quod habet *esse*. Sed quia res per essentiam cognoscibilis est, transsumptum est nomen rei ad omne id quod in cognitione vel intellectu cadere potest. Et per hunc modum dicuntur *res rationis* quae in natura ratum esse non habent'. *In II Sent.*, dist. 37, q. 1, a. 1.

[16] 'Esse dupliciter dicitur. Uno modo secundum quod est *copula verbalis* significans compositionem cujuslibet enuntiationis, quam anima facit, unde hoc

36. Reconsideration of the Object of General Metaphysics.—Metaphysics has nothing to do with the *verb* 'to be' nor with *notional being*, which it leaves to be treated of in grammar and logic; it deals solely with *real* being. Further, it does not make a specific consideration of *accidental* being but notices it only indirectly, for its proper object is *first substance* in the fullness of its being. Of this object we have in this Part taken a general view; in Parts II, III and IV, we shall consider it under its different aspects, in its relations, in its divisions and in its causes.

esse non est aliquid in rerum natura, sed tantum in actu animae componentis et dividentis. Alio modo *esse* dicitur *actus entis*, in quantum est ens, i.e. quo denominatur aliquid ens actu in rerum natura'. *Quodlib.* 9, a. 3.

PART II

The Transcendental Properties of Being

I. General Sketch

37. Introductory.—In the preceding pages we have considered being in its primary acceptation; we have subjected it to analysis and contrasted the several realities comprised in it. But, besides these, the essence of being has attached to it diverse *properties* or *attributes* which on account of their belonging to being *as such*, to *every* real being, whether corporeal or immaterial, rightly bear the name of metaphysical properties; they are indeed common to all beings and, inasmuch as they belong exclusively to no one category of being, surpass in extension every genus, ' transcendunt omne genus ', and in this sense are *transcendental*. These transcendental properties are to occupy our attention in this second Part.

The study of these transcendental properties is truly a *scientific* one; for scientific demonstration, as will be seen in Logic (64 f.), proceeds from the definition of the essence of a thing, as middle term, to show how this essence is the reason of the properties that flow from it.

38. Enumeration of the Transcendental Attributes of Being.—In an illuminating passage at the beginning of his treatise *De Veritate* [17], St. Thomas makes the observation

[17] ' Illud quod primo intellectus concipit quasi notissimum et in quod omnes conceptiones resolvit, est ens. Unde oportet quod omnes aliae conceptiones intellectus accipiantur ex additione ad ens. Sed enti non potest addi aliquid quasi extranea natura; quia quaelibet natura essentialiter ess ens. Sed aliqua dicuntur addere supra ens, inquantum exprimunt ipsiu: modum, qui nomine ipsius entis non exprimitur. Quod dupliciter contingit, uno modo, ut modus expressus sit aliquis specialis modus entis . . . (sicut) nomine substantiae exprimitur quidam specialis modus essendi. Alio modot ita quod modus expressus sit modus generaliter consequens omne ens; et hic modus *dupliciter* accipi potest: uno modo secundum quod consequitur omne ens *in se*, alio modo secundum quod consequitur unumquodque ens *in ordine ad aliud*. Si primo modo, hoc dicitur, quia exprimit in ente aliquid *affirmative* vel *negative*. Non autem invenitur aliquid *affirmative* dictum

that according as it is regarded from different viewpoints being may be distributed into genera, ' diversa rerum genera ', or may be assigned various *transcendental* properties. In Part III we shall consider these genera or categories of being; we shall devote our present attention to the study of the *transcendentals.*

From this point of view all being may be considered either *in itself, absolutely*, or *in relation to something else, relatively.*

Considered in itself, absolutely, being is—(*a*) positively—an *essence, a thing, essentia, res*; (*b*) negatively—it is something *non-divided*, a *unit*: for unity is what it is by reason of indivision.

Considered in relation to something else, relatively, being is—(*a*) negatively—*something distinct from another, some thing, ' divisum ab alio ', ' aliud quid '*, St. Thomas calls it; (*b*) positively—it is *true* and *good*: true inasmuch as to some intellect knowing it, it is intelligible or knowable as what it is; it is good inasmuch as when related as object to the natural tendency of some being, it is appropriate to that tendency.

39. Division of Part II.—St. Thomas we thus see counts six transcendental notions: *ens, res, unum, aliquid, verum, bonum.* As the notions importing *ens, essentia, subsisting thing of nature, essence*, have already been studied in Part I, and as moreover they are not so much the properties of being as being itself, we need examine in Part II only the remaining ideas that are expressed by the terms *aliquid, distinct thing, something that is not another*; *unum, one*; *verum, true*; *bonum, good.* These several ideas will furnish us with so many separate sections. When we have considered each of them separately, it will be time to inquire whether there have been properties of being overlooked by St. Thomas and to ascertain in what sense these transcendental notions may be predicated

absolute quod possit accipi in omni ente nisi *essentia* ejus. *Negatio* autem, quae est consequens omne ens *absolute* est *indivisio* et hanc exprimit hoc nomen *unum*: nihil enim est aliud unum quam ens indivisum. Si autem modus entis accipiatur *secundum ordinem unius ad alterum*, hoc potest esse dupliciter. Uno modo, *secundum divisionem unius ab altero* et hoc exprimit hoc nomen *aliquid.* Alio modo, secundum convenientiam unius entis ad aliud et hoc quidem non potest esse nisi accipiatur aliquid quod natum sit convenire cum omni ente. Hoc autem est anima quae quodammodo est omnia. In anima autem est vis cognitiva et appetitiva: *Convenientiam ergo entis ad appetitum* exprimit hoc nomen *bonum. Convenientiam entis ad intellectum* exprimit hoc nomen *verum* '. ST. THOMAS, *De veritate*, q. 1, a. 1.

of being in general, of all things. Finally we shall have to review the *first principles* which spontaneously arise in the mind from its conception of being. Accordingly Part II will fall into seven sections: the first is this sketch and enumeration of the transcendentals, and the subsequent ones will treat respectively of distinction (II), unity (III), truth (IV), goodness (V), of the sense in which these fundamental attributes belong to being (VI), and of first principles (VII).

II. Distinction

40. Genesis of the Ideas of Non-being, Distinction, Plurality.—The object of the mind's first act is the very indefinite idea *thing, something existing*. With the variation of its sensible impressions a second act of thought occurs and once again it apprehends thing, something existing. The diverse sensible impressions produced in us by the two objects enable us to perceive that they are not identical, to make distinction between them, and thus give birth to the ideas of non-being, distinction and plurality.

To illustrate this mental process let us imagine a young child coming in contact with something rough and cold; he immediately begets the intellectual idea of being, thing. A moment later he feels the warm, caressing hand of his mother and a new idea springs up; this time also of being, of thing, but derived from new sensible impressions. Here we see the young mind twice grasping the notion of being or thing, yet each time associating it with different sensible impressions. The concrete thing that the first sensations present is not the concrete thing presented by the second: the one and the other are not perceived as the same; neither, therefore, does the intellect confuse its corresponding ideas, but on the contrary it *distinguishes* them (from a forcible Greco-Latin word, *dis* and *stinguere*, meaning to prick or mark, στίζω, separately).

Here we have the explanation of the origin of our ideas of non-being, nonentity, negation, as also those of distinction and plurality. *Nonentity* is by definition the negation of thing. Negation may refer to certain things or to some aspect of a thing, in either of which cases it is *partial*; or it may be of all things, when it is *complete* nothingness; or it may be even further the negation of possibility as well as of existence—*absolute* nonentity, the most perfect contrast with being. The discernment between one thing and another thing which it is not gives us the idea of that thing as *some one thing* in opposition to *some other thing*, as something *distinct*. Finally the repetition of this act by which the mind represents to itself distinct thing engenders the new idea *many things*, the notion of *indefinite plurality*.

III. Unity

First of all we must see what is meant by unity and now it is a common property of all beings (§ 1). It will then be important to notice that the unity of a being is not contradicted by its intrinsic composition (§ 2). And lastly we shall contrast transcendental unity with predicamental unity (§ 3).

§ 1. *Transcendental Unity and Kindred Notions*

41. Unity is the Indivision of a Being.—We now understand that when we perceive any object of nature, we perceive it as *something, being distinct from other beings*. We know this oak, or this man, as something; but we also know this forest, or this crowd, as something. We have now to inquire whether this idea 'something' applies to all these objects in the same sense.

The process of distinction to which we spontaneously have recourse in order better to grasp what a thing is, primarily makes an object stand out as something apart from all others. But, further, our attention may be directed to examining this object itself as apart from other objects and we may submit it to a similar process of distinction, and we shall find that it may be capable of being divided. For example, this forest, this crowd, is each something wherein the mind can distinguish many things. Yet, whilst this is true, the oaks, taken singly, we find are not capable of further division. The mind has separated each oak from other oaks but finds each now undivided. So, speaking in general, after we have by a first process separated a being from what it is not, it would seem that eventually there will always come a time when, in our process of distinction, we are faced with a being capable of no further division; this undivided being we call *one*: 'Unum nihil aliud significat quam ens indivisum' [18].

[18] *Sum. Theol.*, I, q. 11, a. 1, c.

Yet is unity nothing more than a negation, the negation of division ?—There is room indeed here for misunderstanding. The being which is one is something positive, the very substance of the being: the formal concept of unity (*ratio unius*) alone is indivision, undividedness. The notion of unity is negative, but the reality of which it represents to us one aspect is positive.

Now that we have seen what unity means, it remains to show that it is a transcendental property of being and that, consequently, the ideas of 'being' and of 'one' are convertible, *unum et ens convertuntur*. If they are convertible, then it will follow that unity is not the addition of any positive perfection.

42. Every Being is a Unit.—Take any being you like and it is either simple, that is to say, it cannot be further broken up, or it is not. If it cannot be further decomposed this must be because it is itself not divided but *one*. If it can be decomposed, then, by the supposition, decomposition must be either a possibility or actually effected. Now in the first case the being is one, for it is not yet divided; it enjoys the unity of a compound: its parts are considered *formally as parts*, i.e. as belonging to one and the same whole, of which they are the components. In the second case we are no longer dealing with the same being about which we are asking whether it is one or many, for now we are confronted with many other beings which result from the division of the being first considered; and thus the question regarding the unity of being has now to be asked with reference to each of these resultant beings: can they be split up or not? If they cannot be, they constitute so many units. If they can, their parts, for the reason that they are parts, united together form a composite being; and then the subject is still one and can be only one [19].

Hence unity is a true transcendental property of being; it is a property of all and every being. And from this it follows that unity does not confer any positive perfection on a be ng,

[19] 'Unum nihil aliud significat quam ens indivisum. Et ex hoc ipso apparet quod unum convertitur cum ente. Nam omne ens aut est simplex aut compositum. Quod autem est simplex, est indivisum et actu et potentia. Quod autem est compositum, non habet esse, quamdiu partes ejus sunt divisae, sed postquam constituunt et componunt ipsum compositum. Unde manifestum est quod esse cujuslibet rei consistit in indivisione'. *Sum. Theol.*, I, q. 11, a. 1, c.

but it is nothing more or less than its own undividedness. Indeed if unity were the addition of any positive perfection, this perfection inasmuch as it would be positive would be something real, itself a being. Now, we have just seen that every being is a unit; wherefore this being too would be a unit. Yet the supposition is that unity adds positive perfection, so that this new unit implies still another and so on indefinitely, perfection requiring to be piled on perfection in order to explain the unity of the first subject.

In brief, unity is a property common to every being and adds no positive perfection to it; it is merely one of the many aspects of being which the mind apprehends by its power of abstraction.

43. Being and Nonentity, Distinction, Indefinite Plurality and Unity, Multitude.—Our first conception is of *being* as such; this we further conceive by means of negation as something other than what it is not, we *distinguish* it from *nonentity*; next, by considering it in itself, we see that the division that separates being from non-being has no application in the thing itself, but that in itself the thing is undivided, a *unit.*

The distinction between being and non-being gives us our first notion of plurality (**40**); but we must notice that it is of *indefinite plurality*, since the idea non-entity, as such, does not furnish the mind with any positive content, still less any distinct positive content. By our mental contrast of being with non-being the only notion we get of plurality is of being, on the one hand, and all that is not being, on the other.

Nevertheless from the concept of unity the mind can derive a clearly defined notion of plurality. By considering a being as one, a unit, it can by repeated acts represent other beings similarly undivided in themselves, other units; it can compare these units and see them as so many things distinct from one another. And this gives us the notion of *multitude*, which is simply that of several distinct units. Thus intrinsic unity can give rise to the notion of *definite* plurality or multitude. It is to be noted that this idea of multitude implies a mental connecting together of the beings conceived as distinct units; this nexus constitutes the notion of plurality which is a single notion and allows us to speak of the unity of plurality. From this we see that indefinite plurality, as a vague notion, has quite a distinct content from the notion of plurality meaning 'a multitude of distinct units'. The former arises in the mind from its entertaining *merely* the positive notion of being together with the spontaneous act by which it vaguely marks it off from all non-being; the latter brings in the further notions, besides the above two, of several unities, distinct in themselves, but now considered by the mind as forming one multitude, or a unity of plurality. Indeed for being to stand opposed in the mind to non-being, it is not necessary to know whether non-being excludes one or more positive realities; but, to conceive the diversity of the distinct units making up multitude, it is necessary to have a positive conception of these units, to have them simultaneously before the mind and to compare them [20].

44. Unicity.—From this positive notion of plurality or multitude the mind reaches to its negation, namely unicity or uniqueness, which signifies that a being is alone in its own order; thus unicity is an attribute of God.

45. Identity.—The mind can look at a thing from different points of view; it may consider chiefly the substance, either as individual or as specific or generic, or it may regard the quantity of a substance or its quality. If we regard their quantity, things are *equal* or *unequal*; if their qualities, they are *similar* or *dissimilar*; if their substance, they are the *same* or *diverse*. Now the negation of diversity is identity; the negation of specific diversity, identity of nature; the negation of individual diversity, *identity* in the strict sense.

46. Unity of Composition: A Problem to be Solved.—Unity is not the same as simplicity. A simple being is one that is not divisible, whereas a being that is still an actual unit may be a compound and, in consequence, be divisible; for unity only connotes actual indivision. There is room then to distinguish unity of indivision—the peculiarity of the being that is undivided but divisible, *ens indivisum actu*—and unity of *simplicity*, which is characteristic of what is at once undivided and indivisible, *ens indivisum actu et potentia*.

Now, it is easy to understand that a simple being, in which

[20] 'Primo in intellectum nostrum cadit *ens* et deinde *divisio* et post hoc *unum* quod divisione privat et ultimo *multitudo* quae ex unitatibus constituitur. Nam licet ea quae sunt divisa, multa sint, non habent tamen rationem multorum nisi postquam huic vel illi attribuitur quod sit unum. Quamvis etiam nihil prohiberet dici rationem multitudinis dependere ex uno, secundum quod est mensurata per unum, quod jam ad rationem *numeri* pertinet'. ST. THOMAS, *In X Metaph.* lect. 4.

there neither are nor can be parts, is one being or a *unit* of existence; but how are we to conceive as also a real and true *unit* the *compound* being, in which there are more than one component realities? We ask, How can the composition of beings be reconciled with their unity? And this resolves itself into two particular questions:—

First question: Since essence is the compound of what are called *metaphysical* parts, how can we reconcile the unity of an essence with the composition of such parts?

Second question: Actually existing beings are made up of *physical* parts, some substantial, some accidental; how can the unity of a being be reconciled with its physical composition?

Before, however, these intricate questions can be fully discussed, the ideas involved in them require to be made quite clear.

47 Meaning of Composition.—Being allows of two kinds of real composition—physical and metaphysical. When the parts that constitute a compound are *physically* distinct from one another, that is, are distinct in the actual order and are parts independently of thought, they are called *physical parts* and their composition is physical and the whole which results from it is a *physical whole.*

An example of physical composition is the union, proved and examined in Cosmology, of the two elements, *primary matter* and *substantial form,* that together constitute corporeal substance. Another instance of the same is the composition of *essence* and *existence* that is realized by all things in the natural order.

On the other hand, when the parts of a being correspond only to distinct *concepts* of the same thing, their composition is logical, and may be either purely logical or metaphysical. It is *purely logical* if it is exclusively the product of the mind's working and does not presuppose any composition prior to the act of thought. It is *metaphysical* composition if it presupposes some sort of foundation in the object itself; such composition is the outcome of the mind's relative incapacity when confronted with the wealth of attributes that are included in the connotation of any object. Do we not, when we strive to gain a complete idea of the complex perfection of some contingent being, avail ourselves of many concepts which, under the form of *genera* or *differentiae*, make an advance on each other in explicitness? Metaphysical composition is the composition of these manifold concepts, and the resultant idea is a *metaphysical whole*.

Of metaphysical composition we have an example in the various objective reasons or formalities—the *proximate genus* and *ultimate specific difference*—which constitute the essence of man. The mind's definition of human nature is corporeal substance endowed with life, sensation and thought. The elements of this definition—different formalities—together exemplify metaphysical composition.

It need hardly be added that the being whose composition we are to investigate is substance, which alone rigorously speaking realizes the concept of unity (*unum simpliciter*); incidentally we shall have to speak of the composition of beings that are possessed only of a *relative* or *accidental* unity (*unum secundum quid, unum per accidens*). Before however we do so, it will be well to define our idea of something closely connected with composition, namely *distinction* [21].

48. Kinds of Distinction.—1. In a being that is substantially one but physically compound there exists a *real* distinction between the physical parts composing it. Such a distinction is real since independently of any mental consideration it involves elements that are not one another; which proves that in nature itself there is distinction *inter rem et rem*, or real distinction.

2. *Logical* distinction (*distinctio rationis*), on the other hand, depends for its existence upon an act of cognition, and is found when two different concepts serve to represent one and the same object.

(*a*) It is a *purely logical* distinction, or a distinction of *pure reason*, when the two concepts have not only the same material object but exactly the same formal object, although they present it, may be, with different degrees of clearness: e.g. the distinction between the concepts of man and rational animal.

(*b*) It is a *virtual* distinction or one *founded on reality*, or 'metaphysical', when the two concepts answer to something

[21] Metaphysics, the science of real being, does not concern itself with *logical* composition (*Logic* 17) which is the exclusive fruit of the mind. An example of it is to be found in the *logical whole* made up of all the individuals to which the mind applies a universal concept.

that is one but with points of resemblance to several and they represent it to the mind under *different formal aspects*. In this case the two concepts have the same material object, but the notes of it they each express are different. Further, this virtual distinction may be complete or incomplete; (α) It is *complete* when the formal object of each of the distinct concepts can be found realized separately in nature. (β) It is *incomplete* when the formal term of each of the concepts differs *expressly* from the others but is nevertheless so indissolubly bound up with them that it is impossible for it to be realized in nature apart from them. Of the complete virtual distinction an example is the distinction between the concepts of the vegetative soul and the intellectual soul, which both help to give us our idea of human nature. An incomplete virtual distinction exists between the transcendental properties of being: they are truly distinct aspects, but always realized together, in every being.

49. Unity taken in its Secondary or Accidental Sense.—Hitherto we have been considering unity in its strict and proper sense; that is, as the notion is essentially verified in substance. Unity however may be also predicated, though improperly, of other beings. Thus we speak of *a* forest, *a* crowd, *a* nation. Unity applies then to individuals which though in one respect distinct are united into a single group or collective body by a perception or some indistinct thought. This is rather an apparent unity.

On the other hand a real though accidental unity exists between two or more substances or between two or more accidents which concur by their activities in producing one total effect: as for instance, the pulling of a pair of horses harnessed in the same shafts. This may be called *dynamic* unity. Further, when this concert of activities is of physical agents and due to the constraint of their nature, the unity is a *physical* one. Whilst it is *moral* when the actions are of free moral agents—such as the family, civil society, the Church, each of which is not uncommonly spoken of as a 'moral being', a 'moral body', a 'juridical person'.

After these preliminary remarks on accidental unity we may now return to the transcendental unity of substance and try to solve the difficulty we set out to answer, namely, How is the composition of a being to be reconciled with its unity?

Seeing that there are two kinds of composition, it will be better to break up the problem into two questions: (i) How is the metaphysical composition of an abstract essence to be reconciled with the unity of that essence? (ii) How is the physical composition of things in nature to be reconciled with their individual unity?

§ 2. *Unity Compatible with Composition*

50. I. Metaphysical Composition is not incompatible with Unity.—The real unity of a being is not destroyed by its metaphysical composition for the reason that the distinction between its metaphysical parts is nothing more than a *virtual* one. Let us show that these metaphysical parts are only virtually distinct.

We are certain that a being which subsists in itself is a unit: it is only *one* human individual who is a substance, corporeal, living, sentient and rational. In such a being we cannot admit any *real* distinction, for on such a supposition it would not be one substance but *several*.

Yet the things of nature have for the most part various kinds of activity: the same thing impresses us in various different ways. Now, we do not take in at one glance, we have no direct insight into, what is the essence of any object of experience; we come to know it by induction, by progressing from the activities it displays to a knowledge of the essential principle of which they are the manifestations. Accordingly we proceed to build up our notion of a being's essence by the use of as many concepts as it has diverse activities. Between these various notes representing the different aspects of any particular substance the mind perforce makes a distinction, but a distinction that is evidently only a *virtual* one: for the substance in question from which the various notes are drawn is in itself a real unit; and its active manifestations alone are diverse.

51. II. Physical Composition is not incompatible with Substantial Unity.—Were there many realities in a being each of which was a complete reality, without doubt we should have not unity but multiplicity. But the physical parts of a compound, if considered in themselves, are incomplete, as is proved by the fact that only the compound as a whole has existence. This we may explain by saying that a *part* as such, by its very definition, is what is capable of forming, with other parts, one compound reality. This *potential* character in respect of the whole which it helps to make up is imperfection which is distinctive of what we term the 'part' of a compound. Thus imperfect, incomplete in themselves, physical parts cannot enjoy a separate existence of their own, and therefore they cannot be detrimental to the substantial unity of the being which they compose.

If we look for the intrinsic reason of the incompleteness of the physical parts that enter into the composition of beings, it is to be found in the relations of *potentiality* and *actuality* uniting them and serving as the ground of their mutual dependence. Primary matter is a subject in a state of *potentiality*; that is to say, it has of its essence to be determined by a specific form, which on its part determines or *actualizes* the matter on which it essentially depends as its subject. Again, when an essence has been constituted by the union of matter and form, it is yet in a state of potentiality in respect of the accidental determinations that are necessary for its perfection of being and which on this account may be called so many further actualities of being. And lastly the essence, thus fully determined by its accidents, is only a *potential* being in respect of the final and crowning determination—*actual* existence.

That the unity of a being is not violated by its having physical parts is also guaranteed by the fact that all the different formalities of a thing, both substantial and accidental, are determined by and share one and the same *single* actuality of existence. The full examination, however, of this question and the proof that each individual being has only one *actus existentiae* we must defer until Part III.

52. Simplicity.—Simplicity is the *exclusion of intrinsic composition*. In reality it is a positive perfection, but we know it only as a negation.

A being is *physically* simple when physical parts are excluded from its nature; and *metaphysically* simple when it has no metaphysical parts. God alone is absolutely simple, excluding both kinds of composition, as will be demonstrated in Natural Theology (**41**).

§ 3. *Transcendental Unity and Predicamental Unity*

53. Unity, Multitude, Number.—Every being is *one*, a unit, something in itself undivided and distinct from everything else.

The idea of *multitude* involves more than one being; it comprises *some* beings which, though when considered separately each is in itself undivided and distinct from all others, when considered together form one object of thought. The idea 'multiple' or 'manifold' is therefore as clearly distinct from that of unity as many beings stand apart in reality from one being. Yet as the mind cannot represent to itself a multitude of things precisely as they are multiple, to get them together into one concept of multitude it needs to consider them all *under some one aspect*, in such a way that, although materially many, they are presented as *formally one*.

Whilst the content of multitude is indefinite, *number* means multitude composed of a definite sum of units. The mind, after thinking successively of several distinct units and still aware that it has so conceived them, can combine them in thought, and the resultant addition is a number, which stands then for a *sum of units*; the mind can conceive of these successive units as so many parts of the same whole, can totalize them, and their number is then a *total of units*. To the elements involved in multitude—various units, distinction between them, their formal unity due to the action of the mind—number requires as a fourth element that there be a limitation to the units, that they be terminated by a last one. Hence number is finite, whereas the concept of multitude has no definite bounds.

The formal aspect by reason of which distinct objects become units of one and the same number is to be found in the transcendental unity of beings: a unity which belongs to every being whatsoever—individual or class, species or genus, substance or accident, real being or logical. As soon as a transcendental unit is united by the mind with another or others, it becomes a numerical unit. Thus Peter, James and John, three individual beings of the same species, together make up a number. Two apple-trees and two pear-trees make four trees. Two apple-trees and two caterpillars are four living beings. Two caterpillars and two pebbles are four material beings. In short, in proportion as we can distinguish more formalities in a being, as Cajetan observes, so often can we regard it as a unit and so often count it as a unit of number.

54. Infinite and Indefinite.—Whereas number, as we have just seen, is essentially finite, multitude does not seem necessarily to be so: that the concept of infinite multitude cannot be proved to involve a contradiction we think we have elsewhere been able to show [22]. These two ideas of *infinite* and of *indefinite*, the latter of which we say is essential to multitude and the former not repugnant to it, it is important not to confuse.

Infinite means the negation of limit. Number is by its definition a collection that is limited by a last unit, whereas the utter negation of a last term constitutes what is essential to the concept of infinite. The idea *indefinite*, on the other hand, implies a limit, but one that is *variable*. For instance compare the recurring decimal $\cdot\dot{6}$ with the vulgar fraction $\frac{2}{3}$: the one is as approximately the other as can be wished, yet is never quite the same; it goes on increasing indefinitely, yet is ever finite.

55. Predicamental Unity, the Unity of Measure; Number, the Expression of Measured Units.—Hitherto our attention has been engaged with transcendental unity that is to be found in every being, corporeal and spiritual, substantial and accidental. Yet there is another conception of unity, namely that which we arrive at by the division of an extended thing. Thus understood, unity can be predicated only of one special category of objects, namely, quantified objects, and for this reason it is called 'predicamental' unity.

An extended thing, inasmuch as it is continuous, is divisible, really or mentally, into distinct parts of exactly similar nature. And these parts can be considered as units forming one and the same whole and, taken together, form a number. So formed, a number has its basis in the division of an extended thing: "numerus sequitur divisionem'.

A part admits of *amount* more or less. The amounts or greatness of parts we compare in order to see whether they are equal or unequal. For any such comparison of sizes, no

[22] See large edition *Métaphysique générale*, 5th ed. pp. 193–198.

matter what be the objects compared, a size-type or standard is required, which is some arbitrarily selected size suitable as a basis for the counting or measurement of things of the same class: this is called the *unit of measure* [23]. Number is now the expression of how many times the size of the thing measured contains the unit of measure.

Of size or, as we had better call it, amount there are three fundamental kinds—*length*, *mass* and *time*; and corresponding to them there are, by more general acceptance, also three arbitrary fundamental units—the *centimetre*, the *gramme* and the *second*.

As these three units have this much in common between them that they always measure greatness or quantity, we are enabled by this to form an idea of unity in the *abstract* with nevertheless a *predicamental* signification; i.e. an idea of unity which is applicable indifferently to extended surface, mass and time, each of which are measurable into amounts.

The distinction between *predicamental* unity and *transcendental* unity is of importance and deserving of further consideration.

56. Two Meanings of Number.—Number stands in general for a total of units. In the last paragraph we have just seen that besides unity of being there is measured unity—units of size or amount. Hence number is susceptible of two different meanings: according to the first it signifies a total of transcendental units, counting all objects of whatever kind or category—substances, qualities, relations, actions, etc.; all realities, material and immaterial. According to the second it counts measured units. This latter use, where number means a total of quantified units, is a narrower sense of the word.

There are still two further points to consider: Are transcendental and predicamental alike both synonymous with numerical unity? Or, to put the question more in the concrete: Does what is a transcendental unit or what is a predicamental unit form a unit of a number? And secondly, is

[23] 'Mensura nihil aliud est quam id quo quantitas rei cognoscitur: quantitas vero rei cognoscitur per unum et numerum. Per unum quidem sicut cum dicimus unum stadium vel unum pedem; per numerum autem sicut cum dicimus tria stadia vel tres pedes; ulterius autem omnis numerus cognoscitur per unum, eo quod unitas aliquoties sumpta quemlibet numerum reddit'. St. Thomas, *In X Metaph.* lect. 2.

predicamental unity exactly the same as the unity of a continuum?

57. Numerical Unity.—A numerical unit is any unit that forms part of a number. Now, a transcendental unit as such is not essentially a part of any number, but is only capable of being such a part. It may be called a numerical unit, that is, when it is regarded as forming part of, or capable of forming part of, a set of objects sharing a common formality.

The case is otherwise with the predicamental, or measured, unit. Measurement essentially implies a relation to other sizes or amounts with which a comparison is made. Such a unit is therefore formally a numerical unit.

58. The Unity of a Continuum.—Care must be taken not to confuse the unity of a measured thing with the unity of a continuous thing. *Continuity* is the undividedness of an *extended* thing and consequently its unity. As such it is a particular application of transcendental unity; for unity, or the indivision of a being, is applicable to every being, substance and accident alike, and therefore to quantity, and continuity is the indivision proper to a quantified, or extended, thing.

Unity of measure is posterior to the unity of a continuous undivided thing. It is itself a continuous quantity, namely the last unit, indivisible or at least regarded as indivisible, and regarded as a standard of counting or measurement of other continuous quantities. Therefore the concept of unity of measure includes within it the unity of a continuum, but it further adds the relation of measurement. The unity of a continuum or an undivided extended body then is *absolute* in its character, whereas as a unit of measurement it is *relative* and follows the former. The first is predicable of any and every quantity, the second only of a *determined* quantity, namely the least quantity which is divisible or at least regarded as such.

59. Recapitulation.—In this section we have had to consider transcendental unity. We have seen it to be an *absolute* attribute of being as such: it surpasses every genus and therefore justly merits to be called transcendental (§ 1). Neither metaphysical composition nor physical composition are incompatible with the unity of being (§ 2). The unity that consists in the internal indivision or undividedness of a being is not the same as the unity which serves as a measure for divisible quantity and which, consequently, is the foundation of number in a special and strict sense of the word. The former is transcendental, the latter predicamental unity (§ 3).

IV. Truth

In this section we have first to see what is meant by truth, and by metaphysical truth in particular (§ 1); then to show that truth is a transcendental property of being (§ 2).

§ 1. *Analysis of the Idea of Truth*

60. Popular Meaning of True and Truth.—What is generally meant when something is said to be true? Let us take some examples. We call 'wine' an alcoholic liquor produced from the fermentation of the juice of the grape: the fermented juice of the grape is *true* wine; every substance which is not fermented juice of the grape is not *true* wine; and from this we may conclude that every artificial production is not *truly* wine. The moral character of a man usually betrays itself in his features: mien, gait and general bearing distinguish the honest man from the knave. If, then, some person is represented to us as a blackguard, to know whether he is truly like one we apply our usual test: of our two type-ideas, of our type of the honest face and our type of the criminal face, we see which the countenance of this man resembles, and if it is to the latter, we pronounce that he *truly* looks like a villain. A liquid, then, is *true* wine when it is conformable to the definition by which we express the nature of wine; a production that does not answer exactly to this ideal type or definition is not *truly* wine. Similarly the physiognomy resembling the ideal type we have in our mind of the honest man or of the rogue is the *true* physiognomy of the honest man or of the rogue. Hence we may conclude that a thing is *true* which is conformable to the ideal type by which we represent its nature. This is the sense in which we predicate truth of things. The truth of a being is therefore *the conformity of this being actually considered with its nature as already presupposed to be known* [24]. The truth of a thing is called *ontological* or *objective* truth, by way of emphasizing that this

[24] 'Denominantur res verae a veritate quae est in ipsa re (quae nihil est aliud quam intellectui adaequata, vel intellectum sibi adaequans) sicut a forma inhaerente, sicut cibus denominatur sanus a qualitate sua, a qua sanus dicitur'. St. Thomas, *De veritate*, q. 1, a. 4.

truth is an attribute not of the thought but of the thing, the object of thought. It is also called *metaphysical* or *transcendental* to show that it is an attribute that belongs to being as such, that is common to each and every being.

61. Ontological Truth is a Relation of Conformity with an Ideal Type abstracted from Sensible Reality.—It follows from the analysis we have just made that the attribute '*true*' is not applied to a thing considered in its absolute state, but is applicable to it only when it is referred to its ideal type that is supposed to be known by some one, and is judged to correspond with it. *Ontological truth* we may accordingly define as a relation of identity of nature between a thing presented to the mind and an ideal type previously known there. This is the meaning of the universally accepted definition of truth: *veritas est adaequatio rei et intellectus.* For by 'res' is to be understood something perceived or imagined at the present moment; by 'intellectus' the previously existing idea in the mind of the thing perceived or imagined; whilst the exact conformity, 'adequatio vel conformitas' of the subject perceived or imagined with its mental type is its truth.

It may be asked, What is this mental type spoken of? Where does it exist or come from? If this is a difficulty, the reader may refer to Psychology (**90**) where he will see that these ideal types are drawn from things of experience. Before approving of this glass of wine, before considering the appearance of this blackguard, we have already intellectually grasped the specific qualities of wine and the characteristic features of a villain.

Ontological truth exists when this glass of wine and the particular physiognomy of this man, now objects of perception, are conformed to ideal types previously apprehended by some really existing mind.

62. Ontological Truth and Logical Truth contrasted.—The truth of a thing we have just seen to reside in a relation of conformity. Now from this it follows that since a relation implies two terms, the intellectual act whereby the mind expresses truth is not an act of simple apprehension but a complex act of 'composition and division', a judgment. For, when it attains truth the mind has to ascertain a relation between a thing and the presupposed idea of its nature: the presupposed idea is the predicate of a judgment, the thing judged conformable to it the subject, and the attribution of the predicate to the subject is a formal act of the judgment.

Besides attributing truth to things, i.e. *ontological* truth, which lies in the relation of conformity of reality to mental type, we also attribute truth to knowledge: this is *logical* truth. When in interpreting reality the mind attributes a nature to a subject which truly, in the ontological sense, belongs to it, its judgment possesses logical truth; and when on the contrary it attributes to it a nature which does not really belong to it, its judgment is logically false. Logical truth and error will be dealt with in Logic.

§ 2. *Truth is a Transcendental Property of Being*

63. Truth is a Transcendental Property of Being: Inductive Proof.—If we go through the categories of being, we shall find that there is not one of them of which truth may not be predicated. We predicate it of *substances*: we commonly speak of true gold, a true diamond, true crystal. Also of *quantity*: the number ten is in truth twice five. Of *quality*: affinity is a true chemical property; to risk one's life for one's country is true patriotism. Of *relation*: talent creates a true superiority. Of *time* and of *place*: a pure spirit's sphere of action is not a true place, nor does the continuance of its duration constitute true time. Of *action* and '*passion*': gravitation is in truth the mutual attraction of bodies, or rather it is a true extrinsic propulsion of one body towards another. And finally we predicate it of an *active attitude* and of *passive intransitive states*: a soldier may have a true martial spirit; a man may be truly overburdened [25]. 'True' we predicate alike of things of nature and of things produced by industry and art: a watch we speak of as being true, a mansion may be a veritable palace, a play is true to life. We predicate it even of *logical* beings: we may raise the question, for instance, whether analogy is a true abstraction and if it can be truly universal. From all these examples it is easy to see that the definition of ontological truth we gave at the beginning is found to hold good in the case of every being whatsoever, no matter to what category of being it belongs; in other words, we have found, arguing a posteriori, that truth is a transcendental property. We have yet another proof.

[25] Regarding these two categories, cp. *Logic*, 15.

64. Truth is a Transcendental Property of Being: A Priori Proof.—In the order of nature there are two terms correlated with each other: namely, on the one hand there is being, actual or possible, to which non-being is the only limit; and, on the other, is the human mind, the capacity of which is as wide as being itself, according to the axiom of Aristotle, 'intellectus potens omnia fieri'. There is no being that, given the requisite conditions, cannot be known by our mind; nothing, nonentity, is alone unintelligible; of everything else, that is to say of everything, mind is physically capable of knowing the nature. Now all that is required for ontological truth is that a thing engender the idea of its nature in some mind and that this ideal type tally, when compared, with some subject which falls within the extension of the idea. Ontological truth is therefore the property of every being.

It must be observed however that this relation of conformity between the human mind and all being is not *actual*, but merely *possible*. Hence when we say that all being is true, we do not really mean anything more than that truth *may* be attributed to every being. Such a reservation is implicitly admitted in all language. When we say of any particular wine that it is true wine, we are aware that ontological truth belongs to something only when it is verifying the actual relation of conformity with the ideal type of its nature. We mean, then, that when a being is not actually related to an intellect apprehending its essential definition, ontological truth belongs only *potentially* to it.

65. Can anything in Nature be False?—We have just seen that everything is true, and yet we speak of a false diamond, a bad coin, a sham scientist, etc.: is this not a paradox requiring explanation?

Whilst every being has specific properties whereby its *true* nature can be discerned, it sometimes happens that the properties of two beings specifically different present superficial resemblances that give occasion for mistakes to be made: unless care is taken we are liable to judge the nature of a thing by certain misleading appearances [26]; and then we say

[26] 'Res notitiam sui facit in anima per ea quae exterius apparent, quia cognitio nostra initium a sensu sumit cujus per se objectum sunt sensibiles qualitates. Et ideo, quando in aliqua re apparent sensibiles qualitates demonstrantes naturam quae eis non subest, dicitur res illa esse falsa. Unde illa

the thing has deceived us and call it false; whereas the only correct thing to say is that we have deceived ourselves. The answer, then, to the paradox is that there are no false things in nature, that everything is true; and that when we predicate falsity of things, we are speaking really of the falsity of our judgment of which these things have been the cause: a falsity that we attribute to the cause, whereas it is really only a property of the effect.

V. Goodness

In this section we propose to follow the same order as in the preceding one, namely, first to consider the idea of goodness (§ 1), and then to show that it is a transcendental property of being (§ 2).

§ 1. *Analysis of the Idea of Goodness.*

66. Popular Meaning of Good.—The child who says of some sweetmeat: 'Good; it is good', is voicing a sensible satisfaction it is experiencing. '*Good*' is its expression for *whatever gratifies its senses.* It is greedy for whatever will gratify them; it *desires* to *enjoy* such things, it *likes* and *loves* them. As age increases, 'good' comes to signify not only what is pleasing to the senses, but in general whatever, things or persons, answers to a need or is in any way useful. Food is good because it answers to a physical craving; learning is good because the mind thirsts for knowledge; friendship is good because it satisfies the wider need of the heart. We apply the epithet 'good' to a host of things that in any way supply a want. The goodness, then, of a thing is that which makes it pleasing or useful to us.

67. First Philosophical Conception: A Good is what serves as the Object of some Natural Tendency.—The following considerations led Aristotle to define the good, from the point of view of its effects, as *the object of a being's natural tendency.* According to his system, every being naturally tends, either consciously or unconsciously, towards some end, 'its natural end'; this it pursues and, if it is a being endowed with sensibility, upon possession enjoys. And that

dicuntur falsa quae nata sunt videri aut qualia non sunt, aut quae non sunt. Nec tamen res est hoc modo causa falsitatis in anima quod necessario falsitatem causet; quia veritas et falsitas praecipue in judicio animae existunt'. St. Thomas, *De veritate*, q. 1, a. 10.

object he termed good towards which the natural tendency of a being leads it and the attainment of which, if it be conscious, produces pleasure. The *good*, then, is alike the object of the blind tendency of insensate beings and of the conscious appetency of conscious ones: the good is that which is '*appetibile*' or 'desirable', which things tend to or seek, *bonum est quod omnia appetunt.*

In proportion as the will is confronted with its end or good, it *desires* it; when it attains possession of it, it *enjoys* it; concomitantly with both states, it *loves* it in the broadest sense of the term. We may then define the good more explicitly as that which a will desires or takes its satisfaction in and which forms the object of its love. For there is no reason why we should not liken the unconscious tendencies of beings to the appetent faculty of will which puts forth conscious desires and affections and so predicate of inferior beings, in analogical language, that they, too, aspire to their ends and on the attainment of them repose therein.

68. Second Philosophical Conception: Goodness is the Adaptation of a Being to its End.—Even in popular language good has also a more objective signification. We are accustomed to call a watch that keeps exact time, a *good* watch; and a soldier who displays all the essential virtues of a military man, a *good* soldier. Such examples lead us to ask what *good* and *goodness* mean?

Both men and things we estimate according to their *purpose.* A watch is not a useless piece of mechanism, but is *for* telling the time. So too a soldier is a person *for* defending the country. Accordingly when a watch so works as to realize the effect in view of which it was constructed and answers the purpose for which it was made, then it is a *good* watch. And the soldier who possesses the physical and moral qualities required for the fulfilment of his function in a society and who can defend his country when needed, is a *good* soldier. In general then we may say of all beings, whether persons or things, that goodness consists in the adaptation of a being to the end or purpose for which it was made.

Now in the philosophy of Aristotle *nature,* as we have seen, means the substance of a being considered precisely as the first principle of all its activities. It stands at once for what a being is and what it is capable of doing; it embraces both its constitution and its powers of action. A more concise definition then is: the goodness of a being is the adaptation of its *nature* to its end, and this is true either of a thing or a person.

However, as what is adapted to an end is called a *means*, the good of a thing is its adaptation as a means to its end, and accordingly we may substitute for the above definition the yet more general one: *goodness is the fitness of means to end*.

The idea of goodness, we see, is correlative to that of purpose or end: if there is no end, there is no good; deny teleology and the word *goodness* means nothing [27].

69. Combination of the two Preceding Ideas.—Are the two definitions of goodness—'A good is what serves as the object of a natural tendency of a being', and 'goodness is the adaptation of a being to its end'—in reality the same? And if so, how is the one to be reduced to the other?

The answer to the first question is simple: what is good is an object of desire; what is desirable is something appropriate to the nature of the subject desiring it; therefore the definitions independently discovered do coincide. Yet what is the logical connexion, what the common ground on which the one passes over into the other?

If a thing is good, this is not because it is desirable; nay rather, it is desirable because it is good, and it is good because it suits the needs and is adapted to the nature of the subject for whom it is good. Hence, ontologically, the 'suitable' has a priority in nature to the 'desirable'. What comes first in the actual order is the tendency of the being towards the end for which it is adapted. In the case of conscious beings the display of this tendency is usually attended by a sensation or some feeling of pleasure: 'delectatio sequitur operationem debitam'. This pleasure reveals to the subject experiencing it the influence that the good has for it, it is the sign by which it is known to it. Logically, then, the notion 'pleasurable' is prior to that of 'suitable'; the one leads us to the other.

Since the good is that which is suitable or appropriate to the nature of a thing, we may ask *what* this suitability or fitness

[27] 'Bonum autem, cum habeat rationem appetibilis, importat habitudinem causae finalis'. St. Thomas, *Sum Theol.*, I, q. 5, art. 2, ad. 1.

of good things to the nature of the subject desiring them consists in? And further, since a good thing is what is adapted to its end, *how* the end of a thing can make the nature adapted to it good?

70. The End belonging to each Being perfects its Nature.— We speak of a good watch and a good soldier when the watch is one in which the mechanism is nicely adjusted for showing the hour and the soldier one who has the qualities necessary for the defence of his country. Yet in both cases the goodness is only a derived goodness, arising from the end assigned to them and being communicated from the goodness of that end. To have the hour marked exactly for us is a good thing and therefore the instrument so marking it is a good instrument; just as it is a good thing for the country to be defended in case of danger and, for this reason, the organization of an army of soldiers for its defence is a good thing. The watch is good because its purpose is good and the soldier because his mission is good.

The goodness of a watch and of a soldier is then a derived, *relative* goodness, the goodness of a means *in relation to its end.* What have we to say of the goodness of the end: why is it good that instruments should keep the time correctly? Why is it good that the fatherland should be protected in the hour of danger? The question is the same one put further back. The final answer to the series of questions that one might thus pose, is that good things have some end which must be wished for its own sake alone and which does not derive its goodness from any other end ulterior to itself. Indeed were there no absolute good there would be no relative good, for a relative good cannot be conceived that has no reference to anything. Neither can we conceive a *means* that is not so in respect of *some end.* It would be beside the point to determine here what is the absolute good and if there are many such. It is enough for our purpose to know that at the top of every series of mutually subordinated means there is some absolute end, something that is good in itself. Now a thing is good because its nature is more or less immediately adapted to this absolute good, because its activities conduce to this absolute good.

But how is it that the absolute good confers goodness on the being which is adapted to it? How is it that the acquisition of diverse particular goods makes the being acquiring them good? The answer is that the good, which is an end, *perfects* the nature tending towards it; in this *perfecting* lies the formal reason of the goodness of beings. What, we must ask then, do the *perfection* of a thing and this *being perfected* (perfectionnement) mean?

71. How the Good perfects the Nature of a Thing.—The word *perfection* comes from the Latin word *perficere, perfectum* (*per-factum*), perfect, and signifies that which is completely made. A thing to be perfected is something yet incomplete, that is to say, it is something having if we may be allowed the expression, so much reality yet requiring so much more before its capacity for being is filled up, before all its potentialities are exhausted and it has all the actuality of which it is capable.

Strictly speaking, only finite beings allow of being pert fected, for they alone have the capacity to be further com pleted. Yet we do not say that they can ever possess all reality; contingent things are essentially, and must always remain, finite; but perfection adds to their being just that which the finite nature of each is capable of receiving and stands in need of for its completion.

Every substance of the material universe enjoys at its first existence just that much reality which constitutes its present, actual perfection; but in addition it has certain powers of action the gradual exercise of which progressively effects its further perfection. Now of these powers of action the first principle is the *end* or purpose for which the being exists: for, the end is the goal of its natural tendency, its natural tendency determines the action of its active powers, and the action of these effects, directly or indirectly, the actualization of its 'passive powers' or potentialities, wherein its complete perfection consists. Hence the end makes the nature adapted to it good because, inasmuch as the end is the first principle of the actualization of the nature's potentialities, it is the source of its natural increase in reality; it is the source and explanation of the process whereby the nature is brought to its perfection. Thus do we see how the end of a being or its good, the object appropriate to and befitting its nature and towards which it tends, is the first principle of its perfection, of its fuller realization, is that whereby it is rendered perfect and good. *Bonum est perfectivum: the good is the perfecting principle of reality.* The end is the 'good bringing perfection', *bonum quod*; the 'perfecting' is the formal reason of the goodness of the being that is perfected, *bonum quo*; the 'being itself which is perfected', and therefore ameliorated or increased in goodness, is the *bonum cui*.

In brief, the good is that which beings naturally seek. And as beings naturally seek and tend towards objects because these objects are adapted to their nature and are suitable as means whereby they can realize their natural ends, for this new and deeper reason objects are also called good. But if the suitability of an object to the end of something makes the object good, it is a borrowed goodness: it is good by reason of the end it subserves. The end, then, makes the means adapted to it good, because the end is the principle of a nature's being perfected and, in consequence, of its goodness.

72. Different Kinds of Goods.—The good, we have seen, is the object of the natural tendency of a being. Now the acquisition of a good is a source of enjoyment for the subject acquiring it. This enjoyment may itself become an object of a further desire; and if so, the natural tendency of the thing will then have for its object alike that which is suited to it and the enjoyment resulting from the possession of it. The thing or object adapted and suited to its nature is called the *objective* good or the 'convenient', *suitable* good; the enjoyment resulting is the *subjective* or the delectable, delight-giving, '*agreeable*' good.

Whether we speak of the objective or of the 'agreeable' good, the good is either the ultimate terminus, the real *end*, in the possession of which the natural appetite of a being finds its repose, 'bonum quiescens appetitum', something *absolutely good, good in itself*, 'bonum per se'; or else it is some intermediary step towards an end, a means to the attainment of something further, and is only a *relative* or *useful* good, 'bonum utile'.

Lastly, the natural, objective good proper to a being endowed with reason and freedom is called the *upright*, or *moral*, good, 'bonum honestum'.

§ 2. *Goodness is a Transcendental Property of Being*

73. Every Being is Good: Meaning.—This statement

does not mean that beings are good in all respects. Rather something very different: that every being of the universe has its own good. So far are we from denying the existence of evil in the world that we only say that every being possesses some goodness.

Further, when we state that goodness is a transcendental attribute of being, we mean that every being is good in itself and for itself. We speak of *formal* goodness, or that quality by reason of which a person or thing is good in itself. This is to be distinguished from *active* goodness which is directly serviceable for the perfecting of some other thing and only indirectly contributes to the perfection of the agent. Thus a virtuous man is good in himself, and a benevolent man is good to others. When we say that every being is good, we are speaking only of formal goodness.

Lastly, that 'every being is good' is a proposition referring to actual and concrete real beings and one which has no application to abstract, possible beings. Indeed who has ever heard of a good or of a bad mathematical axiom. Moreover the notion of goodness, as we have said, is correlative with that of finality, and only beings actually in existence tend towards an end.

74. Every Being is Good: Proof.—I. *Argument from induction.*—Every being has either a conscious or unconscious natural tendency towards some end. Now this adaptation of a subject to its end constitutes its goodness. Therefore every substantial being is good.

Consider by way of example some living organism. Normally the organs are adjusted to the constitution of the subject, and their functioning is adapted to the needs of its maintenance and development. Its organs are therefore good, as also their functioning; the whole organism, thus adapted to its natural end, is good.

But what have we to say of a cancer in the stomach: the epithelial cells are multiplied in that region out of all regular proportion, to the detriment of the tissues of the digestive system and with the result that the nutrition of the entire organism is deranged; may we say that the nature of the organized subject has now become bad? By no means; the organism fights against the new, obnoxious formations invading it, it still tends towards the realization of its natural end and its own preservation in being, and even if eventually it has to succumb and allow the evil to gain the mastery, the tendency of its nature is yet real to the finish and inclines it to self-preservation: inasmuch as it continues to exist, it is good.

Every being having a natural tendency to its end is good. Its tendencies are regularly directed to its good. If abnormally they fail to be so, this want of adaptation is but partial and accidental, and consequently the nature of the being ever remains good. Every substance, then, is good.

2. *Intrinsic argument.*—Every action is, directly or indirectly, a natural principle of perfection for the agent that exercises it. Now there is no being that does not put forth some activities. Therefore there is no being that is not good.

Every action has a positive result: that is, it produces a reality and, according to the natural course of things, thus contributes towards the making perfect of the agent. If the act is an immanent one, it directly augments the perfection of the agent. If it is transitive, it obviously in the first place effects perfection in something else, and secondly, in virtue of the general law of action and reaction, reacts upon the agent, thereby perfecting it. So that every action does effect the perfection of the subject performing it.—Now all substances of the universe are principles of activity. They have also potentialities, which permit or favour the exercise of their activities.—The conclusion, that every substantial being is good, is therefore warranted.

3. *Another intrinsic argument.*—To find out whether beings are good, it is not necessary to proceed inductively from accidents to substance nor to consider accidents in themselves as perfecting the substantial subject supporting them; it is quite enough to consider substance in itself. For, existence is an actuality perfecting essence; and every perfective actuality is a principle of goodness: what need then is there of further proof that a being is good so long as it have existence?

But whilst we demonstrate that every being is good, what are we going to say about evil? What is evil?

75. Evil is Something Relative: it is the Privation of a Good.—The existence of evil in the world is an undeniable fact that meets us at every turn. How are we to reconcile this with our statement that every nature is good?

In a loose sense we sometimes speak of evil as the mere

negation of a greater good. In strict language this 'metaphysical' evil is called *imperfection*.

The proper meaning of evil is that which is opposed to the nature of a subject. It does not constitute any absolute entity, but is essentially *relative*; it is the absence of some good required for the normal development of the nature of a being. This Scholastics termed *privation*. Privation, 'privatio', 'defectus', we may then say, implies some subject and is the lack of some perfection that should naturally belong to it: 'privatio est negatio debiti inesse alicui subjecto'. St. Thomas describes evil as the absence of a good natural to some being: 'malum est defectus boni quod natum est et debet habere. Malum est privatio ordinis ad finem debitum'[28].

In its concrete acceptation, evil supposes positive reality on the part of the subject to which it attaches; whilst in its formal acceptation or *qua* evil, *malitia*, it consists in the privation of a good natural to the given subject. Blindness, for instance, is an evil, inasmuch as it is the deprivation of sight in a subject that naturally should see. So too is cancer an evil: it is an abnormal multiplication of the epithelial cells, which invade the adjacent tissues where their presence and action cause havoc; it is thus the introduction of disorder into an organic substance, the privation of that indispensable orderliness demanded by its nature for the good functioning of its organs and for its life. It is not right to say that the epithelial cells which by their excessive multiplication have produced the cancer are in themselves so many absolute evils. Indeed in themselves they are good, for neither in their nature nor in the manner of their formation do they differ from the normal epitheliums of the organism. They are evil only *relatively*, that is, relatively to the organized being they have deprived of the requisite conditions for life.

Evil, we see then, is relative and consists in the deprivation of some natural good, and its existence in no way militates against the general proposition that every nature is good in itself.

VI. Being and its Transcendental Properties

76. Distinction between Being and its Transcendental Properties.—We first of all considered the six transcendental

[28] *Sum. Theol.*, I, q. 49, a. 1, c.

notions in general, then made a further special inquiry into the last three, namely the properties of unity, truth and goodness. The question now arises whether the transcendental properties are really distinct from being. We must say that they are not; for they are something, they are beings, and therefore are one and the same thing as being. May we say, then, that they are formally identical with it? Again we must say that they are not; for whilst, as we have seen, they belong to every being and therefore are co-extensive with it, and also have the same connotation, yet of the notes comprised in that connotation each of them brings out one part cular aspect. Between being, then, and its transcendental properties there is a *logical* distinction, albeit not a purely logical, but an *incomplete, virtual* distinction, in the sense defined above (**48**).

77. There are Three and only Three Transcendental Properties.—The transcendental properties of being have the same connotation as being; accordingly they do not add any positive determination to it: in what way, then, can they affect it? In two ways—firstly, in its *absolute* entity, they may attach to it by a *negation*; secondly, without interfering with its absolute entity, they may signify some *relation* attaching to it. Any third way of modifying being without adding reality to it cannot be conceived. Now, as affected by a *negation*, being is considered as *one*: unity is negation of division. As affected by a *relation*, being is *true* and *good*. To understand this, we have to remember that, whilst a relation demands two correlative terms, and one of them here—being—is co-extensive with all things and therefore requires that the other correlative be equally co-extensive, there is, even apart from God, something in the world which can extend to all things, namely, the human mind that is capable of knowing everything and the human will that is capable of desiring everything. Being, then, as affected by the relation of conformity with the idea that a human mind forms when representing it as it is, is true; as affected by the relation of suitability to an appetition of will, it is good. There are, therefore, three transcendental properties of being, and only three

VII. First Principles

78. Meaning of First Principles.—When the mind has gained possession of the transcendental notions, it does not rest content with merely simply apprehending them but juxtaposes them and compares them, and from their comparison there spring into evidence certain relations between them. *First principles* are these elementary, primordial relations that arise from the comparison of the transcendental notions.

For a first principle to be such two conditions are essential: first, each of its terms must be a transcendental idea; and second, the relation between them must be immediate [29]. They are thus to be carefully distinguished from the *principles of the particular sciences* (*Logic*, **51**; *Criteriology*, **52**), which are first principles only in a restricted field of knowledge and which are derived from an analysis of some object that is more or less known and is made the subject-matter of a special investigation; principles too which have not the quality of being immediately evident and above all discussion.

79. Three First Principles.—As a first principle is defined to be an immediate relation between two transcendental notions, there must be as many first principles as there are possible ways of juxtaposing the transcendental ideas. The subject of each of these principles may assume an abstract form or a universal form. The notions are six in number—being, something (essence), distinct, one, true, good. The following propositions therefore will show us the number of first principles there are:—

Being is what it is: every being is what it is.
Being is something: every being is something.
Being is one: every being is one.
Being is true: every being is true.
Being is good: every being is good.

Each of these transcendental notions is convertible with any other; thus for example:—

Whatever is something, is a being: every something is a being.

[29] We are considering 'first principles' here only from the metaphysical standpoint and not a means whereby to discover the truth or falsity of propositions. For a fuller development of our theory, see larger edition pp. 261–267.

Whatever is something, is one: every something is one.

Whatever is true, is a being: every true thing is a being.

These notions are only logically distinct from one another, inasmuch as they have all the same connotation.

1. Now when we reduce to their simplest expressions the manifold identical propositions which enunciate the immediate relations between the transcendentals, we are left with the proposition or first principle: *Being is what it is.* This is the *principle of identity.*

2. Among the transcendental ideas there is one we purposely omitted to mention just now, namely *non-being*, which it will be remembered is bound up with the idea of *distinct, other* thing. Now a being is not what it is not, or in other words, being excludes non-being. Hence that every being is distinct from what it is not, is the *principle of contradiction.* Enunciated by Aristotle it runs: 'The same attribute cannot belong and not belong to a being formally regarded as the same'.

Each of the transcendental ideas—thing, one, true, good—can be opposed to its negation and so furnish matter for a contradictory proposition.

The principle of contradiction entails another mental operation besides the first apprehension of being, namely the *division* of it from every other being or *negation.* It is therefore posterior to the principle of identity and must not be confounded with it.

3. Negation—the exclusion of non-being, distinction—follows immediately after the apprehension of being. Between the two operations of the mind there is no other idea generated. Hence between being and non-being, between a thing and the negation of it, there is no middle thing; this is a truth known as the *principle of excluded middle.*

This principle of excluded middle is posterior to that of contradiction, since an application of the principle of contradiction forms one of the terms in the judgment giving rise to it.

Of the three principles then, that of identity is the first; i.e. the first in the order of the mind's analysis or genetically first. But in the regressive order, when it is question of the firm foundation of the certitude of our knowledge, the principle of contradiction is the last, the touchstone of all certitude, according to the theory we developed in Criteriology

80. The Principle of Contradiction prescinds from Time.—Very frequently we meet with the principle of contradiction enunciated thus: A thing cannot be and not be *at the same time*. Strictly, however, the circumstance of time has nothing to do with the principle. The correct enunciation merely lays down that one and the same subject cannot have two contradictory attributes. It is obvious that neither at a given moment nor at different moments can a subject which is the *same* receive contradictory attributes. The foundation of the principle lies therefore in the identity of the subject, and accordingly it is to this idea that we must look and not to the circumstance of time, which does not enter into the principle. Besides, how could the principle have a *transcendental* character, how could it surpass all the categories in extension if it were subordinate to the category of time?

The temptation to restrict the principle of contradiction by the condition that the subject must be considered in any single moment springs from the fact that things of nature are 'in a perpetual flux' and one is never sure that at two successive moments they are still the same. If however the thing is formally *regarded as the same*, it cannot now or at any other time admit of contradictory attributes.

PART III

Substance and its Determinations, or the Principal Divisions of Being

81. Introductory.—In this Part it will be our endeavour to make a comparison of the various acceptations of being that we enumerated above. Of these our attention will be chiefly devoted to substance and its accidents (*Chap. I*); actual and potential being or actuality and potentiality (*Chap. II*); created substance, the object of our first intellectual cognitions, and its contrast, the Necessary, Infinite Being the existence of which contingent, finite beings demonstrate (*Chap. III*). Certain further remarks that will be called for, principally concerning the pre-eminence of substance and the relation of the other kinds of being to it, and concerning the unity of the object of metaphysics, will be dealt with in a last chapter (*Chap. IV*).

Chapter I subdivides itself into four sections, which will treat respectively of substance (I), accident (II), the nature of the distinction between substance and accident (III), the various kinds of accidents (IV).

CHAPTER I

SUBSTANCE AND ITS ACCIDENTS

I. SUBSTANCE

82. General Meaning of Substance and Accident.—Our acquaintance with the things of nature reveals that there are different sorts of reality. Some things exist only on the condition that something else exists; such realities, for instance, as the actions of walking, sitting, feeling, thinking, willing, etc., cannot exist or even be conceived of except in dependence upon some presupposed being: such actions we are bound to attribute to something or somebody who walks, who sits, feels, thinks or wills. Still more is it true that such manners or modes of being as length, breadth, the rectangular or circular shape of an extended body, cannot be realized and conceived except as belonging to something that is long and broad and of rectangular or circular shape. Now such beings as depend alike for their real and conceptual existence upon some presupposed being go by the name of *accidents*; and the being which the accidents presuppose is their *subject* or *substance*.

83. Existence of Substances.—Absolute phenomenalism recognizes the existence only of internal states and external phenomena; we are told that any dogmatic statement of the existence of subjects supporting these phenomenal realities must ever be unfounded. Against these phenomenalists, then, we have to show that the doctrine of substance is well founded, by proving that substances do exist.

1. *Argument drawn from consciousness.*—Every time that the intellect, under the influence of the external senses or of the internal sense, knows something in nature, it knows it first of all as something standing by itself, *aliquid per se stans*—which is exactly what a substance is defined to be. The man yonder, the chair, this table, all appear as things existing

in themselves. Even things that by their nature are not capable of existing on their own account—the blue of the sky, the sound of a voice, the scent of flowers—we think of at first as subsisting objects. Wherefore, either what we take to be a substance is really one, and then our assertion is proved; or what we take for one is not really such but is a reality inhering in something else anterior to it—just as extension necessarily entails the existence of an extended body and the actions of sitting and walking a person who sits and walks—and in this case the immediate object of intellectual perception is not a substance, but the subject in which it inheres is a substance—unless we are to conceive accidents as inhering in other accidents, in a series having no first subject at the end of it. But such a supposition is inadmissible since each reality discovered in nature would entail an actually infinite multitude of interdependent entities. The testimony of consciousness is therefore not fallacious when it declares that the object of every intellectual perception is either a substance or presupposes one. And therefore in nature there do exist substances.

2. *Argument drawn from the existence of accidents.*—There are such things as accidental realities, that is to say, beings which by their very nature do not exist in themselves. Since such beings exist, there must be subjects in which they exist. Try, for example, to conceive motion without a body that moves; or nutrition without an organism which is nourished Sensations and desires, thoughts and volitions, are nothing if not the acts of something or somebody who feels, desires, thinks or wills. It is obvious, then, that the existence of accidents necessarily implies the existence of a substantial subject in which they exist. The ultra-phenomenalists themselves even cannot steer free of a contradiction, inasmuch as on the one hand they allow the existence of accidents and on the other deny the reality of substance and thereby logically also deny accidents which depend for their existence upon some presupposed subject.

Having satisfied ourselves as to the *existence* of substance, we must ascertain more concerning its *nature*, concerning what it is. We will then consider the relations it bears to its accidents.

84. Nature of Substance.—Substance presents itself with

a double characteristic: it serves as a subject for accidents and it is something existing in itself. In the *logical* order its character of subject reveals itself first, but in the *ontological* order the trait of existence-in-self is its principal perfection.

In the logical order the existence of realities incapable of existing without a subject leads us to posit a subject necessary for the existence of accidents. The names *substance, subject* (sub-stans, sub-jectum) are taken from this apparent characteristic of substance—namely that of rendering the existence of accidents possible. Such is indeed the general law of language that the primitive word does not express the essential perfection of the being but one of its apparent properties. But in the ontological order the perfection by reason of which a being exists in itself comes first. For, to exist independently of another being, to be sufficient of one's self to have existence, is an absolute perfection, whereas to serve as a subject for others is a relative property; and the absolute is prior to the relative.

85. Substance in its Relation to its Accidents.—1. Substance is often crudely imagined as a sort of core or kernel of which the accidents form the rind, so that if these can be stripped off the substance will be exposed to view. Such an erroneous conception of the relation of substance to accidents may be ascribed partly to certain consecrated expressions of speech which inform us that substance is the 'support' or what 'underlies' accidents, whilst accidents in their turn 'rest upon', 'reside in' or 'inhere in' substance. Such metaphors have led the unthinking to conceive of accidents as realities superimposed upon substance. In reality there is no superposition or joining together of a concrete substance with concrete accidents: there is the one substance, a subject determinable by its various accidents, which are so many actualizations of its potentialities; its relation to them is a particular case of the potential to the actual, of a material, determinable element to formal, determining principles (**114**). The accidental variations, however, never occur in the same concrete being: when they take place, a concrete reality is succeeded by *another* concrete reality, in such a manner that they do not compromise the physical unity of the being which actually exists. Let an illustration make our meaning clearer: Take a bar of iron and heat it in a crucible until it is white hot.

What has happened? It appears with new accidents: different temperature, colour, volume, etc. But no one would say these are new realities superimposed upon the iron without affecting the iron itself: it is the iron which is luminous and heated and thus expanded. The new accidents have manifested themselves in it, they are intrinsic, intimate determinations of it.

2. Descartes incorrectly defined substance as an inert substratum lying beneath or behind active phenomena. It is true that when the metaphysician speaks of substance, he abstracts from the actions it produces, the changes it undergoes; for him *in his thought* it is something static. But it does not follow that *in reality* substance is devoid of activity and change. The real order presents a dynamic character that it would be arbitrary to deny.

3. This dynamic aspect of reality was emphasized by Leibniz by way of reaction against Cartesian mechanism. He rightly pointed out that substance, whether spiritual or corporeal, is not the inert subject that the geometrically-minded Descartes had conceived it to be. Indeed it is endowed with a natural tendency towards an end and directs all its inherent forces or faculties to the realization of that end. But Leibniz erred by the opposite excess: substance *qua* substance is not active: the tendency of a substance ought not to enter into the definition of substance, for by the name substance we mean a thing precisely *as it is in itself*; considered as capable of acting or of being acted upon, it bears strictly another name, namely, that of *nature* (87).

4. Substance is often defined as the 'stable', 'permanent', 'persisting' subject of 'fleeting', transient realities that, by way of distinction, are termed accidents. Such a definition has come into vogue through the influence of Kant's *Critique of Pure Reason*, and it is now the idea of many present-day philosophers, of whom Herbert Spencer may be cited as an example [30].—Yet 'permanence of duration' is not essential to substance. Existence-in-self, should it be but momentary, none the less for that moment verifies substance; and, on the other hand, beings that are inherent in a subject, though they be so preserved in being for an indefinitely long period of time are still merely accidents.

[30] Principles of Psychology, Pt. II, ch. I, § 59.

5. Spinoza, following here the footsteps of Descartes, gave as his definition that 'substance is that which is in itself and that which is conceived by itself, that is to say, that which can be conceived of without our having to conceive something else '[31].—Yet this, too, is an erroneous notion. Substance is being in so far as it stands by itself, implying existence-in-self, *ens in se, ens per se stans*, not necessarily self-existent being, *ens a se*. The peculiarity, or proper perfection, of substance consists in being *intrinsically* independent of a subject in which to inhere, independent of a material cause —*id ex quo aliquid fit, id quo aliquid recipitur*; it does not consist in being independent of an *extrinsic*, efficient cause— *id a quo aliquid est.* All substances, except the Divine Being, are dependent equally with accidents upon some other being alike for their first existence and for their continuance in existence, *sunt entia ab alio.* They differ from accidents in their not being dependent intrinsically upon a material cause, *substantiae debetur esse non in alio.*

Now that we have analysed the notion of substance and contrasted it with that of accident, it remains to compare it with the ideas of essence, nature, and individual or person.

86. First Substance and Second Substance.—Specific and generic essences of substantial things do not inhere, after the manner of accidents, in a subject, and therefore they may rightly be called *substances*. But inasmuch as we cannot conceive them without logically presupposing an individual subject to which to attribute them, they do not possess the same right to be called substances as do individual singular substances, and accordingly as distinguished from the latter, which alone verify substance in its fullest sense, they are called *second substances*. The reason is patent: substance, as Cajetan observes, means, according to its etymology, *negatively* that which has no subject and serves as a subject to something else; the individual realizes this twofold characteristic better than species or genus; therefore the individual lays foremost claim to the title of substance. Indeed the individual in the ontological order has no subject of *inherence* (subjectum *inhaesionis*) after the manner of accidents; and in the logical order it is not an attribute of a subject (subjectum

[31] SPINOZA, *Ethics*, Pt. I, Definitions.

praedicationis) after the manner of genus and species. For genus and species, though they have no subject of inherence, nevertheless have a subject of *predication* to which the mind has necessarily to refer them. For this reason, then, the individual alone has the first title to be called substance—*first* substance—whilst generic and specific essences merit the name only secondarily—*second* substances [32].

87. Substance, Nature, Essence.—1. The *substance* of a being is the collection of those notes which are so necessary to the individual that were all or any one of them absent the individual would not be able to exist.

The *essence* of a being sometimes means exactly the same as substance, and it is then called also the *quiddity* or whatness of the thing, inasmuch as it is that which corresponds to the question, *Quid est?* What is the thing present to my thought? the answer to which is the definition of the thing, *definitio rei, ratio rei.* But in its strict sense essence has a distinctly different meaning from substance: it does not signify the individual but it expresses those notes that are logically primordial and fundamental. Moreover substance is a correlative idea with accident, whereas essence bears no reference whatever to accidents.

2. *Nature* designates substantial being considered as a principle of action. Everything that exists exists for action—'omne agens est propter suam operationem'. When things come into existence they are in some measure incomplete and naturally render themselves more complete by the exercise of their activities. Yet in such a way do they act that the result is not chaos but a cosmos, not confusion but an orderly world. The reason of this is because the activity of each substance is directed towards an end that is intrinsic to it: so that the harmonious order of the universe is the co-ordination of all these specific activities of beings in so far as each is directed by an end proper to each being. Considered thus from a *dynamic* point of view, as a principle of activity working towards an inherent end, a being is a *nature*: considered from

[32] 'Quantum ad haec tria differt substantia particularis ab universali. Primo quidem quia substantia particularis non praedicatur de aliquo inferiori, sicut universalis. Secundo quia substantia universalis non subsistit nisi ratione singularis quae per se subsistit. Tertio quia substantia universalis est in multis, non autem singularis quae est ab omnibus separabilis et distincta'. St. Thomas, *In V Metaph.* lect. 10.

a *static* point of view, *in so far as it exists* it is an essence, quiddity, substance. Between nature and substance, as also between nature and essence, there is only a difference of aspect: the real entity designated by these terms is one and the same.

Now how does this real entity—call it substance or nature—differ from the complete individual, variously styled by philosophers as *suppositum, subsisting being, hypostasis* (ὑπόστασις) or *person?* [33]

88. First Substance and Subsisting Being or Person.—First substance, this particular subject, *hoc aliquid*, which directly falls within my experience, presents itself to my thought as something that exists in itself and is distinct from all else. So considered, namely under this formal aspect of a complete reality and not belonging to another reality, first substance is known in Scholastic language as a *suppositum* or *hypostasis*, a *subsisting* thing, and further, when it is endowed with reason, as a *person*. Now this notion of subsisting or personal being gives rise to two questions: (i) What is the formal reason of subsistence or personality; what do they mean? (ii) What is the distinction between subsistence or personality and existence?

89. I. The Formal Reason of Subsistence or of Personality.—When we come to consider what constitutes first substance as something existing in itself, we recognize that there are two elements—the being distinct from everything else and the self-sufficiency in possessing existence. Of these two perfections the former, incommunicability, is a *negative* characteristic and implies a *positive* reason: an individual

[33] 'Substantia dicitur dupliciter: Uno modo dicitur substantia *quidditas* rei quam significat *definitio* secundum quod dicimus quod definitio significat substantiam rei. Quam quidem substantiam Graeci οὐσίαν vocant: quod nos *essentiam* dicere possumus. Alio modo dicitur substantia subjectum vel *suppositum* quod subsistit in genere substantiae. Et hoc quidem communiter accipiendo, nominari potest nomine significante intentionem et sic dicitur suppositum. Nominatur etiam tribus nominibus significantibus rem: quae quidem sunt: res naturae, subsistentia et hypostasis, secundum triplicem considerationem substantiae sic dictae. Secundum enim quod per se existit et non in alio, vocatur *subsistentia*. Illa enim subsistere dicimus, quae non in alio sed in se existunt. Secundum quod supponitur alicui naturae communi, sic dicitur *res naturae*; sicut hic homo est res naturae humanae. Secundum vero quod supponitur accidentibus, dicitur *hypostasis* vel *substantia*. Quod autem haec tria nomina significant communiter in toto genere substantiarum, hoc nomen *persona* significat in genere rationalium substantiarum'. ST. THOMAS, *Sum. Theol.*, I. q. 29, a. 2.

has the trait of incommunicability because it is complete in itself, because it is sufficient in itself for existence. To be complete in self, to be self-sufficient, is then the formal reason of subsistence.

Yet in this analysis of the subsistence of first substance we have paid regard only to its existence; there remains the other point of view—that of its action. Now power of action is proportionate to existence: a thing acts according as it is, 'res agit in quantum est actu'. Hence a subject that is complete in its subsistence is likewise the first principle or source of action. Because it is self-sufficient in its existence, its activity must also be attributed to it and accordingly belong to it. Whence the axiom of the Schools: *Actiones sunt suppositorum*, action belongs to subsisting being. Indeed, we never predicate activity of an accident or of a part of a substance: we always assign the efficient cause of a thing to a subject that exists in itself. Hence the characteristic perfection of hypostasis, the formal reason of subsistence, consists in this, that it is complete in self, alike for existence and action, and does not need to be communicated to some other entity.

Personality entails a further idea, namely that the being complete in itself is an intelligent being. For a *person*, according to the classical definition of Boëthius, is nothing else than an individual substance of a rational nature, 'persona est *rationalis* naturae individua substantia'. Nor is it to be wondered at that the subsistence of a being endowed with reason should enjoy the privilege of a special name: it is a free agent, and master of its own actions and responsible author of its own destiny; it is the sole kind of being that is conscious of its own individuality; and accordingly it realizes in a way beyond all other things that fullness and independence of being and action which constitute the characteristic of subsistence.

90. Corollary. The Human Soul is not a Person.—The individual nature of man—this man, Peter, Paul—is not a soul, nor even a soul *plus* a body, but a being composed of matter and soul: the compound is the first principle of action, the first subject to which all the activities must be attributed, in a word, the rational *suppositum* or person. From this it follows that the soul, whether considered in its state of union with the body or as separated from it after the dissolution of the compound by death, has never the quality of being a subject complete from the double point of view of subsistence and action, and consequently may never be called a person (*Psychology*, **158** f.).

91. II. Individual Substance and Existence.—So far as experience and metaphysical analysis show, we never know an existing substance which is not subsisting and incommunicable: from this it follows that subsistence is naturally inseparable from individualized substance; but it does not follow that the former is identical with the latter, and therefore there is room for the question whether the distinction between an existing substance and its subsistence is a *logical* or a *real* distinction. This is an inquiry into what may be the real foundation of subsistence. If it is only a special aspect under which we may regard individual essence or nature, the distinction is logical; if the real foundation lies elsewhere, the distinction is real.

It is to be observed that this question is not a matter of purely philosophical speculation, but one with a bearing upon theology. According to revealed truth, there are in Jesus Christ two natures, the nature of man and the nature of God. The human nature is complete with all its own faculties and its perfections. And yet the human nature does not subsist in itself but in the Divine Person of the Incarnate Word. Presented with these data, what solution is the Christian philosopher to offer to the problem of the distinction between the individual nature and the person or subsistence?

The distinction in question would seem to be not merely one of different aspects. For bodies are composed of matter and form, of substance and accidents; and immaterial substances, though essentially simple, have various accidents. Now how are these diverse realities—matter and form, substance and accidents—so unified as to constitute one being possessed of unity and distinct from every other? Can it be the possessing of one actual existence that unifies all the elements of which it is composed? Surely not, for existence actualizes what is real, yet leaves that reality intact: how could it unify what is multiple? We must perforce admit, then, in every substance some unifying principle by reason of which the subject is rendered immediately capable of receiving existence; an intrinsic principle, attaching to the individual essence, which, to use a Latin word, we might call *suppositality*, or *personality* or *subsistence*. Unified by this inherent principle a substance is complete and requires only its one actuality of existence to have its crowning determination: 'esse est ultimus actus'.

Many Scholastics (e.g. Cardinal Billot [34]) however do not see the need to have recourse to such a principle of unification, to this *modus substantialis* as Cajetan terms it. This rôle is fulfilled, they say, by the substantial existence, whilst accidents possess their own accidental existence and do not militate against the unity of the compound.

Both the one and the other view seem to be in perfect accord with Catholic doctrine. In the hypostatic union of the Word with the human nature of Christ, the human nature has not its proper connatural subsistence, but the rôle of this is fulfilled, in a supernatural and higher way, by the subsistence of the Divine Person.

II. Accident

92. Meaning of Accident.—An accident is a being that does not subsist in itself but presupposes a subject in which it exists [35]. This presupposition of a subject of inherence would seem to be necessary and philosophy, if left to deal only with natural phenomena, would never suspect the possibility of exceptions to this law. But Theology teaches otherwise when it lays down that in the Holy Eucharist God preserves by a miracle the accidents of the bread and wine without their substance. A departure from this general law whereby accidents inhere in a subject is therefore possible.

St. Thomas, in his double character of philosopher and theologian, was careful to notice in his definition of accident this possibility of a supernatural exception to the law, and accordingly worded his definition thus: '*In the natural course*

[34] Cp. Commentary on St. Thomas, *De Verbo Incarnato*, Rome, 1904, 4th ed., p. 129 ff.

[35] 'Accidentia non dicuntur entia quasi ipsa sint sed quia eis aliquid est. Unde accidens magis proprie dicitur entis quam ens. Igitur accidentia et alia hujusmodi quae non subsistunt, magis sunt coexistentia quam entia, ita magis debent dici concreata quam creata'. St. Thomas, *Sum. Theol.*, I, q 45, a. 4.

of things, an accident exists in another being which serves as a subject'; or again: 'An accident is a being that exists in another, *in so far as it obeys the natural law*—accidens est res cui *debetur* esse in alio' [86].

The accident we are now speaking of is, of course, *ontological, real, categorical* or *predicamental* accident, which must not be confused with *logical, categorematic* or *predicable* accident. In Logic (**16**) it will be seen that our concepts admit of a fivefold classification on the basis of the necessary or contingent nexus binding them to the subject of a judgment: namely into genus, specific difference, species, property and accident. The first three predicables express the notes which constitute the specific essence of a thing; those notes which do not are *ontological accidents*, either necessary or common. *Necessary accidents*, although not contained in the essential or specific definition of a subject, are nevertheless necessarily bound up with it; whereas *common accidents* have only a contingent connexion, and for the sake of emphasizing this contingency are often called simply *accidents* in distinction from the former class which are called *properties*. Accordingly in its logical meaning 'accident' is not in immediate contrast to substance, but to another class of ontological accident, viz., property. In its ontological meaning it is opposed to 'being of the first category', i.e. substance, and comprises nine genera of non-substantial realities, the remaining nine of the Aristotelian categories. Between accident thus understood and substance there is no other intermediary kind of being. An example of an *ontological accident* is the faculty of speech in man; which from a logical point of view is a *property*, not an *accident*.

93. The Existence of Accident.—Has each of the accidents which modify a substance *its own* existence distinct from that of the substance? Or is there only *one* existence shared by the substance and its accidents? Two reasons lead us to adopt the second opinion:—

1. This theory alone is in accord with the unity of being.—Every individual or person—that oak yonder with its spreading branches, and the woodman preparing to fell it with his axe—is *one*. Now a thing that is truly one cannot have two existences. It is impossible, says Aquinas, for one thing to have more than one existence—'impossibile est quod unius rei

[86] ST. THOMAS, *In IV Sent.*, Dist. 12, q. 1, a. 2, solut. 1, ad 2.

non sit unum esse ' [37]. Hence every subsisting thing in nature has only one existence; and therefore the accidents of every substantial being have one and the same existence with the substance.—Indeed how could the case be otherwise? Suppose the substance of the oak to have one existence and its quantity another; the compound making up this man, this woodcutter, to have his existence and each of his accidents, his mind and his will, his size and build, etc., to have theirs: there would no longer be an oak and a woodcutter, but instead a plurality of realities as great in number as that of existences.

2. Another reason, drawn from the definition of accident.—Strictly speaking, an accident is not a being so much as 'a being of a being; a reality or, as it were, a facet of a being: non ens, sed aliquid entis'. When, then, we speak of the size of a tree, we say: 'This oak *is* large', and not: 'This oak *has* largeness'. Similarly if we wish to remark that the man is working hard, we say that 'he *is* vigorous' and not that 'he has vigour'. In short, accidents modify the substantial being in which they are inherent.—Suppose on the other hand that accident has its own existence, then why should we refuse to say that it is a 'being', that is to say being without qualification, purely and simply? And where then would be the fundamental distinction between substance which is intrinsically self-sufficient for existence and accident which is necessarily dependent upon a subject for its existence?

Unless we are to banish the idea of the true unity of being and, instead, make it a collection of beings, some profound and others superficial, we must allow to a whole being, its substance and its accidents together, but one single existence, Indeed, is not existence the *last* actuality, 'esse ultimus actus'? Substance, as such, has not actual existence, it is yet determinable by the accidents which complete it; only substance completely determined by its accidents and modes is the subject of existence, of that last actuality that requires nothing further.

III. Nature of the Distinction between Substance and Accident

94. The Question.—Several authors assert that the Catholic doctrine of the transubstantiation of the bread and wine into

[37] *Sum. Theol.* III, q. 17, a. 2, c.

the Body and Blood of Jesus Christ in the Holy Eucharist and the continuance of the accidents of the bread and wine in the absence of their connatural substances is the only warrant we have for declaring that substance and accidents are really distinct. This opinion, however, we think erroneous: it is the *separability* of accidents from their substance that is made clear to us from the doctrine of the Eucharist; the question of the nature of the *distinction* between accidents and their substance presents itself to natural reason apart from any theological consideration and is capable of receiving a purely rational answer.

The question chiefly concerns quantity and quality which are not relative but absolute accidents, not extrinsic but intrinsic accidents.

According to Cartesian speculation accidents do not differ really from substance; they are relative modes of being, adding no intrinsic determination to substance; consequently they do not constitute a real compound with substance and there can be accordingly no question of a real distinction between them and their substance. In opposition to this we maintain that accidents add a *real perfection* to substance, and we predicate, in consequence, a *real* composition of these accidents and the substance they determine.

95. Proof of the Real Composition of Substance with certain of its Accidents.—1. *Argument drawn from change in ourselves.*—Taken in its generality the Cartesian theory cannot for a moment be maintained. Consciousness invincibly refuses to identify the ego with its acts. To contend that 'thought' or any other state of consciousness, which can be but transitory, is the substance of the ego is to own one's self the victim of a priori suppositions.

But there is no reason why we should limit ourselves to internal facts and not apply the same line of argument directly to all corporeal substances.

2. *Argument drawn from change in other things.*—It will surely be denied by no one that there occur in nature changes which modify things *intrinsically.* An intrinsic change means nothing if not the loss or the acquisition of reality. But a thing can be identical neither with a reality it ceases to possess nor with one it has yet to acquire. The existence, then, of intrinsic changes in nature points to the fact that substance

and the accidents which modify it form a real composition.

The alternative to professing that accidents truly add some reality to the substance they modify entails an acceptance of one of these three propositions: that the changes which take place in things are all substantial changes; that no changes take place in nature; that contradictories are identical.

3. *Argument directed against the Cartesian contention.*—It is inconceivable that all accidents are reducible, as Cartesian philosophers would have us believe, to simple relations with no foundation in the subject in which they are found. For, real relations are ever appearing and disappearing amongst things of nature. And every real relation necessarily has a foundation. This foundation cannot be a previous relation itself resting upon some other and so on *ad infinitum*, since this series of relations without any first basis would ultimately have nothing on which to rest; and such an hypothesis would therefore be a virtual denial of the real objectivity of these same relations. This foundation required for every relation must then be absolute. We may suppose it either a substance or an accident. If a substance, then every change of relations between things will mean a substantial change—which is what no Cartesian is willing to admit. We are forced therefore to conclude that the foundation of the real relations observable in nature is in certain absolute accidents which intrinsically modify their substances and are really different from them.

96. Separability of Accidents from their Connatural Substance.—The Council of Trent, summing up the teaching of the Fathers and Theologians, declares that in the mystery of the Holy Eucharist there takes place the 'conversio totius substantiae panis in corpus et totius substantiae vini in sanguine Domini nostri Jesu Christ, *manentibus dumtaxat speciebus panis et vini*'[38].

This official decision of the Council asserts the separability of accidents from their natural substance. The possibility of this separation philosophy, left to itself and guided by experience, would most likely never have suspected. But enlightened by the doctrinal authority of the Church, the *Christian* philosopher professes not only the possibility but the fact.

[38] Sess. XIII, cap. 2.

IV. Kinds of Accidents

97. Introductory.—Beings can be divided into ten classes: substance and nine classes of accidents. Of these nine kinds of accidents some are studied in rational physics or cosmology —viz. the categories of *quantity, place* and *time* which modify only corporeal substances.

Differing from these are the categories of *quality, relation, action* and *passion* which are true not only of bodies but also of spiritual substances; and which in consequence of this universal application fall within the domain of metaphysics.

Of these four kinds of accidents the latter two, *action* and *passion*, will be dealt with under the general division of being into 'act' and 'power' and also later in Part IV in connexion causes; here we need speak only of *quality* (§ 1) and *relation* (§ 2).

§ 1. *Quality*

98. Meaning of Quality.—In its widest meaning quality is opposed to subject and means all that which can be attributed to it: any kind of determination, whether substantial or accidental, is in this sense a quality. But in a stricter sense *quality* designates in the philosophy of Aristotle a distinct category of being, standing in especial opposition to substance, quantity and relation: it denotes an accidental determination that formally modifies substance and allows us to say of *what kind* (*qualis*) it is. 'Haec est ratio formalis qualitatis per quam respondemus interroganti *qualis* res sit', is St. Thomas' definition. But rigorously speaking this is not a definition, as the notion is too elementary to be strictly definable. A true definition requires that a thing be reduced to a simpler genus than itself and a specific difference that serves as a complement to that genus, and very elementary ideas, like the one in question, will not allow of being thus reduced. But to attempt to throw light on the abstract idea of quality by means of the concrete terms *such, sort, kind* is useful inasmuch as the concrete, owing to its being closely connected with our senses, helps us better to understand what is abstract.

99. Classification of Qualities.—By Aristotle and the Scholastics the different qualities that can be predicated of a subject were classified under four heads. (1) Under the first they put '*habits*' and '*dispositions*' which concern the subject's nature and dispose it well or ill in respect of its last end. Such are health, science, sincerity. (2) *Capability*, or an intrinsic principle of action, and *incapability* form the second group. Thus when we say a man is skilful or the reverse at making something, we are attributing him a quality. (3) The third group comprises the sensuous '*passions*,' or emotional states, which are accompanied by an organic change, and also their corresponding *passive faculties*: e.g. pleasure, pain, anger. (4) The last class consists of the quality of *shape* or, as it is usually called, *figure and form*. These four groups of qualities were summed up by the words: *habitus; potentia naturalis activa et impotentia; passibiles qualitates, potentiae passivae et passiones; figura et forma.*

100. Characteristics of Qualities.—1. *Qualities admit of contraries.*—Thus health has its contrary sickness, virtue vice. But not every quality has a contrary; shapes, for instance, enumerated by Aristotle as the fourth class, have none.

2. *Qualities are the basis of similarity or dissimilarity.* Two things we say resemble each other when they possess the same quality or qualities; they are dissimilar when they have different ones.

3. *Qualities admit of degrees.* They are more or they are less, they can be increased or decreased. Thus there are degrees in light, in heat, in knowledge, in virtue. Individual substances, as such, do not allow of degrees.

101. Qualities of the First Class: Habits and Dispositions.—A habit is a permanent disposition which furthers or hinders the movement of a being towards its natural end. In the words of Aristotle 'habitus dicitur dispositio difficile mobilis, secundum quam bene vel male disponitur dispositum aut secundum se aut in ordine ad aliud'.

Strictly speaking only a spiritual nature and its immaterial faculties of understanding and will are the subjects of *habits*. Adaptations of the material faculties go rather by the name of *dispositions* than that of habits. Indeed a habit, according to the idea of the Scholastics, means a permanent modification of the faculty itself, and of this material things do not allow. To be the subject of a habit, the powers of a thing must be capable of being directed in different ways—'potentia determinabilis ad diversa'. Now if we examine bodies we find that they do not admit of any subjective modification, for each is drawn blindly towards its special end. Chemically simple bodies thus have neither habits nor dispositions. As for complex bodies resulting from the combination of simple bodies we find them capable of acquiring 'dispositions' for action: the sensitive faculties become more or less serviceable instruments of the higher faculties; animals can be *habituated* to certain actions, we can *train* them to behave in certain ways; organs *adapt* themselves to their functions; exotic plants become *acclimatized*; metals become *pliant* and easy to work in respect of some shape impressed upon them, an organism has its dispositions of health or sickness, of weakness or strength. Nevertheless all these dispositions do not merit the name of 'habits', for they lack that characteristic stability which is essential to the notion. This is wanting to them precisely on account of the nature of the material subject which acquires them. Every material thing is the resultant of a happy combination of diverse elements with a view to some end; but so numerous are the elements and so great the complexity upon which this concurrence depends, that of necessity its stability is extremely slight. They must not, then, be denominated habits but rather dispositions; and so, too, must be termed health and sickness and the acquired adaptation of organs or of tissues. Habit, in virtue of its characteristic of permanence, implies a subject that is substantially unchangeable and incorruptible.

But every disposition of an immaterial being is not a habit: the name is reserved for those that are difficult of attainment—'difficile mobilis'. Hence mere opinion as distinct from science in the intellectual order, and inclination as distinct from virtue or vice in the moral order, resulting as they do from but a few isolated acts, are not habits but dispositions (διάθεσις). A habit (habitus, ἕξις) is a permanent quality belonging to the nature or spiritual faculties of a subject and determining it favourably or unfavourably in respect of its end [39].

[39] 'Dispositio et habitus possunt distingui sicut diversae species unius generis subalterni, ut dicantur *dispositiones* illae qualitates primae speciei quibus convenit secundum propriam rationem ut de facili amittantur, quia haben causas mutabiles, ut aegritudo et sanitas; *habitus* vero dicantur illae qualitates quae secundum suam rationem habent quod non de facili transmutentur quia habent causas immobiles, sicut scientiae et virtutes; et secun-

102. Psychological Aspect of Habit. Classification of the Habits of the Human Soul.—1. *Origin of habit:* A habit derives its origin from the very act which commences it. It resides in a passive faculty, and this it modifies. If, indeed, the first act did not introduce some modification into the subject, the second would be no easier than the first and the third no easier than the second and so on, and no habit would ever be formed.

2. *Effect of habit:* A habit perfects a faculty and increases its energy, and on this account the repetition of the act to which it disposes is easier and quicker.

Further, it gives rise to and develops a *need* for action. Acts contrary to the habit present more difficulty than those which are in accordance with it so that the faculty leaves them to follow the line of least resistance.

Finally, in proportion as the exercise of an act requires less effort, it is less noticed; habit therefore gradually makes the subject less conscious of action.

3. *Classification of the habits of the human soul:* We may consider the human soul in its essence or in its faculties, and again in its natural condition or in the supernatural state whereunto Faith declares it is elevated.

Supernatural habits, which are said to be 'infused', pertain either to the nature of the human soul or to its powers of action. *Natural* habits, on the other hand, are acquired and do not affect the essence of the soul but the faculties of intellect and will whereby it acts.

Of *intellectual* habits—called by the ancients 'intellectual virtues'—we can count five: knowledge of first principles, science, wisdom, prudence and art. The stability of these habits is due to necessary truths.

The habits of the *will* or moral habits, which nowadays are alone called *virtues*, are prudence, justice, fortitude and temperance, together with the other virtues embraced by these [40].

103. Qualities of the Second Class.—In the second group

dum hoc dispositio non fit habitus'. St. Thomas, *Sum. Theol.*, I–II, q. 49, a. 2, ad 3.

[40] St. Thomas observes that the moral virtue of prudence relies on a prudent judgment of reason. 'Est enim prudentia recta ratio agibilium', to which he later adds, 'prudentia, secundum essentiam suam, est virtus intellectualis, sed, secundum materiam, convenit cum virtutibus moralibus'. *Sum. Theol.*, I–II, q. 58, a. 3, ad 1.

of qualities come *powers of action*. A *power*, capacity or faculty, renders the substance possessing it capable either of putting forth action or of receiving the effect of an action and so of reacting; it is the immediate principle of action or of 'passion'. *Incapacity, impotence, impotentia*, in this connexion does not mean the negation of the power of acting, but that a power is paralyzed or more or less hindered in its exercise; it is weak or weakened power of action. For instance a child's being unable to walk, an old man's inability to see, does not signify the negation of the active power so much as some defect in the conditions required for the exercise of their respective powers.

Powers of operation belong to their subject in virtue of its nature; they are *properties* of a nature. On this account they differ amongst other things from habits, which only accrue to a being through the exercise of its activity.

A faculty or power we have just described as the *proximate* or *immediate* principle of action. This was to distinguish it from the *remote* or *first* principle, which according to the various points of view from which it is regarded is styled *hypostasis, person* or *nature*. Person or hypostasis is the first principle that acts, *principium quod agit*; and it acts in virtue of another principle—its nature, *principium quo agit*. Yet never does a created nature act by itself, but through its powers or faculties. *Nature* is *first, remote* principle, *primum* principium *quo*; *faculties* or *powers* are principles flowing from it, *derived, proximate*, or *immediate* principles of action.

Has this distinction between a first principle and its derived principles of action any foundation in fact? Are powers of action distinct from nature?

104. Proof of a Real Distinction between a Substance and its Powers.—1. Where there are actualities that are specifically different the corresponding potentialities must be really distinct. Now in the case of every created being, existence and action are different actualities—the one of an essence, the other of an operative power or faculty. Therefore, we may conclude, what is actuated by existence (substance) is really distinct from what is actuated by action (faculty).

Of this syllogism perhaps the major requires a little explanation. Actuality is such that it is communicated to the subject it actualizes; it is an intrinsic determination of the subject.

Now this requires on the part of the subject actualized and receiving the determination, that it be capable of receiving it, that it be in potentiality in regard to it; so that different actualities require different conditions for reception on the part of the subject. Clearly then actualities so obviously diverse as existence and action necessarily presuppose a corresponding diversity in the subjects receiving them, and that is to say between substance on the one hand and a capacity or power on the other. A real distinction, therefore, exists between a substance and its powers of action [41].

2. The real distinction is particularly evident in the case of the human soul. It is impossible for a thing to be identical with several things distinct from one another. The several faculties of the human soul are distinct from one another. Therefore it is impossible for the human soul to be identical with any of its faculties.

Here it is the minor that requires proof, and this is to be found in Psychology (**13, 51, 144**), There we saw that some of man's acts, such as nutrition, sensation, etc., proceed from a compound of matter and vital principle, whilst others, such as acts of understanding and of will, spring from immaterial spiritual principles. Now these spiritual principles or faculties are necessarily distinct from those whence material acts proceed. Furthermore, the examination of spiritual acts shows that they are not all to be referred to one faculty, but to different faculties, namely intellect and will.

3. If it be supposed that substance is not really distinct from its powers and that in man there is only *one* active faculty, then the actuality of substance would have to be such that in it must be found realized all the forms of activity whereof that faculty, as supposed, would be capable; and in that case we should be conscious of the existence of one actuality com-

[41] 'Impossibile est quod alicujus substantiae creatae sua essentia sit sua potentia operativa. Manifestum est enim, quod diversi actus diversorum sunt: semper enim actus proportionatur ei cujus est actus. Sicut autem ipsum esse est actualitas quaedam essentiae, ita operari est actualitas operativae potentiae seu virtutis. Secundum enim hoc, utrumque eorum est in actu, essentia quidem secundum esse, potentia vero secundum operari. Unde cum in nulla creatura suum operari sit suum esse, sed hoc sit proprium solius Dei, sequitur quod nullius creaturae operativa potentia sit ejus essentia sed solius Dei proprium est ut sua essentia sit sua potentia'. St. Thomas, *Qq. disp. de spir. creat.*, a. 11.

bining all our vegetative, sensitive and intellective operations. But as a matter of fact the soul puts forth its power only part by part, we are conscious of various forms of vital activity. It therefore follows that human nature is not a *single* power, but is that which has different powers or capacities for the exercise of its activities.

We may now ask, What are these powers of which we are speaking? And what is the basis of their distinction?

105. Classification of Faculties. *There is a valid basis for the classification of faculties.*—1. *Meaning.* The principle governing the classification of operative faculties is that *to acts adequately distinct there correspond really distinct faculties.* Now what distinguishes acts from one another is their different *formal objects.* Let us consider some examples.

If I look at this tree planted in the ground, or again if at the ground in which its roots are buried, I have a perception of light. In these two cases, although the *material* object of my perception is different (tree, ground), the *formal* object (light) is exactly the same; in both cases the sensation I experience, my act (seeing), is the same; only one organ (eye) is employed as the instrument, and the faculty (sight) is the same for both operations.

But, if I press my hand against the tree, my muscular sense comes into play and by it I perceive resistance just as by my eyes I perceived light. Of these two sensations the *material* object is the same (the tree) but the *formal* objects (light, resistance) are different; the acts therefore are of a different kind; and from this diversity of acts it is lawful to infer a diversity on the part of the faculties putting them forth.

The material object of any act is the thing to which it is directed, about which it is concerned, the thing itself apart from any special aspect of it. The aspect of it or that in it which a faculty directly and specially affects or is affected by, *ratio attingendi,* is the *formal* object. Now it is by its formal object, not by the material, that the *specific* character of an action is determined; by the difference of their formal objects are our operations distinguished from one another; on the presence and absence of its formal object depends whether or not a faculty can be put into exercise. Hence we argue from the specific diversity of the objects of our acts to the diversity of the acts, and inductively from the diversity of our acts to that of the principles or faculties whence they proceed.

For the line of argument to be legitimate it is essential that the *formal* distinction of the acts be an *adequate* one. There are some acts formally distinct—such as the necessary willing of the good in general and free volitions of particular goods—which belong to one faculty; in which case the formal distinction is an inadequate one, inasmuch as all acts of the will have the same generic formal object—the good. Only an act considered under a formality *adequately* distinct from every other constitutes the direct *terminus* of a faculty and the reason for its being classified as distinct from other faculties.

2. *Proof.* Every act proceeds from some faculty of operation as its efficient cause. But the nature of a cause is reflected in its effect. It is legitimate then to go from effect to cause to know the latter: effect and cause, an action and the power producing it, are two correlative terms. From this it follows that to classify acts is at the same time to make a classification of faculties which are their principles, for there is one and the same ground for both classifications. But the basis for the real distinction of acts is the adequate formal distinction of their objects. Therefore this same adequate formal distinction of objects reveals a real distinction of faculties.

Besides this proof from efficient causality another may be drawn from a teleological consideration of faculties. A faculty or power of action is a means having action as its end; it is a capability or *tendency* to realize an end. Accordingly it is so constituted as to realize that end. It is impossible therefore for any *one* tendency to move towards two ends that have nothing in common or, as we have just called them above, towards two objects adequately distinct. To objects adequately distinct, then, there correspond diverse natural tendencies, really distinct faculties [42].

106. Qualities of the Third and Fourth Classes.—We need not say much here about these qualities, since on account

[42] 'Cum essentia animae sit unum principium, non potest esse immediatum principium omnium suarum actionum sed oportet quod anima habeat plures et diversas potentias correspondentes diversitati suarum actionum: potentia enim ad actum dicitur correlative: unde secundum diversitatem actionum oportet esse diversitatem potentiarum'. ST. THOMAS, *Qq. disp. de anima*, a. 12.

of their material character they do not strictly fall within the domain of metaphysics.

'Passion', the third class, denotes every quality which modifies a subject by some material change. The actions of the sensitive appetite and whatever, either in the agent and immediate cause or in the patient itself, furthers them are qualities of this class.

Shape or *external form and figure* of extended bodies makes up the fourth class. These are the result of the different arrangements with respect to one another which the parts of the same body may assume; e.g. the figure of a triangle, the form of a building. In the natural sciences this quality is of great importance, as a difference of species is recognized by a difference of form (*Cosmology*, **23**).

II. Relation

107. Importance of the Idea of Relation.—The study of relation is one of real importance. The universe is not a multitude of atoms or isolated individuals, but an harmonious whole whereof the parts are inter-related and by their mutual co-ordinations and sub-ordinations effect the good of the whole. It constitutes accordingly a system of relations. Hence relation will fall within the scope of metaphysics inasmuch as this contemplates everything real.

108. Meaning of Relation.—Consider two lines A B and C D each measuring a yard in length: they are *equal*, and between them there exists a *relation of equality*. The number 4 is *double* of 2; 2 is *half* of 4: double is double of that which is its half, and the two terms are not only opposed but are each necessary for the explanation of the other; they are said to be *correlatives*, and between them is a *relation of quantity*. If two twin-brothers, Peter and Paul, are alike in every respect, there is between them a *relation of resemblance, of quality*. The steam driving an engine gives rise to a *relation of causality*, namely of efficient causality to an effect. The adaptation of the eye to the function of seeing is a *relation of finality*.

Aristotle distinguishes *absolute* things—substance and the absolute accidents, quantity and quality—from *relative* things, which are characterized by their reference to something else other than themselves. The entity of beings of the first class belongs to substance considered apart by itself; whereas a *relative* being cannot exist nor even be conceived except in connexion with a *correlative* being, to which in some way it is also opposed.

Absolute accidents were deemed by the Scholastics to be 'something', *aliquid*, and relation to be *ad aliquid*, 'something in order to' something else, towards another. Absolute accidents are inherent in a subject, 'habent *esse in* subjecto'; relative being, precisely as such, has an *esse ad*, its formal reason or definition, says St. Thomas, is 'respectus ad alterum', or we might say in a word its *otherness*.

If we consider the examples of relations quoted above, we shall find that in each case the co-existence of two absolute terms is indispensable. Thus whilst the length of a yard is an absolute accident of quantity inherent in the line A B considered in itself, as also is the line C D so considered, *equality* belongs to the two lines only in so far as they are regarded as connected with, or are 'in order to', each other.

Care must be taken not to confuse predicamental relation with transcendental relation, e.g. such relation as that of truth and goodness. In the concept of *transcendental* relation there is formally contained the thing that we call true or good, and moreover the relation applies to all beings. *Predicamental* relation, on the other hand, applies only to a restricted group of beings, and in its formal concept does not include the nature of the subject on which it is founded but is really distinct from it.

Are there real relations existing in nature? or is relation only a product of thought, a logical entity?

109. There are Real Relations.—There are certainly some relations that are entirely the outcome of thought: by reflecting upon the content of my consciousness and upon the manner in which I conceive of objects, I create relations between the entities of my mind, relations that are *logical* relations. But as direct perception precedes reflex thought, as I must know individual things before I can consider my acts of knowing, the question may be asked whether between individual things there are only logical relations or whether there are *real* ones, independent of my thought. We assert that there is such a thing as a real relation existing previously to any act on the part of the mind: one that the intellect finds in nature, and does not put there [43]; or, as St. Thomas defines it, a connexion between two things in virtue of something found in both—'habitudo inter aliqua duo secundum aliquid realiter conveniens utrique' [44].

The proof that real relations exist lies in the fact that, whether we think or not, two real things which each measure a yard in length are equal, that a relation of equality *exists* between them; that two twin-brothers are *really* alike, apart from what anybody thinks; this too is the case with all the other various relations enumerated above. Hence in nature itself there do exist real relations. The universe is made up of individual beings that are not entirely absolute but which are interconnected with one another, long before we have any knowledge of them, by a number of relations that constitute the order of the universe [45].

Opposed to this theory of relation stands Kant's idealistic conception of relation as a *subjective category of the mind* which appertains to phenomena only as the mind introduces it into them. The argument he uses to support this view is that without a subjective operation of the understanding we can never perceive a relation, there can be no relation for us; or, in other words, because we are never aware of a relation except by a mental action, therefore it must be that the mind introduces into phenomena the relations and laws which govern them. This argument, however, sins through being ambiguous and is besides erroneous. In the first place, whilst it may be true that a relation does not 'exist for us', that we do not know it as long as we fail to apprehend its two terms and to perceive its foundation, nevertheless there are relations the

[43] 'Respectus ad aliud aliquando est in ipsa natura rerum utpote quando aliquae res secundum suam naturam ad invicem ordinatae sunt et ad invicem inclinationem habent; et hujusmodi relationes oportet esse *reales*. . . . Aliquando vero respectus significatus per ea quae dicuntur ad aliquid est tantum in ipsa apprehensione rationis conferentis unum alteri et tunc est relatio rationis tantum, sicut cum comparat ratio hominem animali ut speciem ad genus'. ST. THOMAS, *Sum. Theol.*, I, q. 28, a. 1.

[44] ST. THOMAS, *Sum. Theol.*, I, q. 13, a. 7.

[45] 'Perfectio et bonum quae sunt in rebus extra animam, non solum attenduntur secundum aliquid absolute inhaerens rebus, sed etiam secundum ordinem unius rei ad aliam, sicut etiam in ordine partium exercitus, bonum exercitus consistit; huic etiam ordini comparat philosophus ordinem universi. Igitur oportet in ipsis rebus ordinem quemdam esse. Hic autem ordo relatio quaedam est. Unde oportet in rebus ipsis relationes quasdam esse, secundum quas unum ordinatur ad aliud'. ST. THOMAS, *De potentia Dei*, q. 7, a. 9.

terms and foundation of which are anterior to any thought and in consequence are not due to the mind. In the second place, besides all the arguments that militate against idealism in general, we may urge against this idealistic theory of relation a special difficulty. Every relation considered a priori, without application to anything real, is capable of being either affirmative or negative. How then does it happen that in certain particular cases we adhere to one of such alternatives instead of to the other? What, for instance, makes us judge that two particular phenomena are alike rather than not alike? Even if the faculty of judging likeness and difference is an internal law of the mind, the particular applications of such a generic faculty can only come from external things themselves. And if this is so, it must be allowed that some relations have a real, objective foundation that is independent our minds and of its modes of knowing.

110. Classifications of Relations.—From an *accidental* standpoint, relations may be divided into *mutual* relations and *non-mutual* or *unilateral* relations. (*a*) A relation is *mutual* when the two terms bear to each other a relation which is of the same order, that is to say, when on both sides it is real or on both sides logical: e.g. paternity and sonship, the relations of genus and species, are mutual relations, the one couple being real, the other logical. (*b*) The relation is *unilateral* or *non-mutual* when there is a real relation properly so called only on one side: e.g., the relation of the creature to the Creator, of sensation to its object. The creature is essentially dependent upon the Creator, as sensation is upon its object; but the converse is not true: God does not depend upon creatures, nor does a sensible thing upon a sensation.

From an *essential* standpoint, from the point of view of their foundations, relations may be distinguished into three groups according as we take as bases for division a measure and what is measured, action and passion, unity and number. (*a*) *Measure* can be the foundation of a relation: for example, it is the basis of the relation between our faculties and their objects, for all operative powers are measured by, are essentially ordinated to or are commensurate with, their objects and so specified by them. (*b*) Again the couple *action* and *passion* can serve as an adequate basis of relation, inasmuch as the patient is formally dependent upon the action affecting it whilst the agent is in its turn in some way the better for the action: thus between father and son there exists a relation that is real and twofold, on the one side that of the son to the father inasmuch as the son owes his life to the father, and on the other in a sense that of the father to the son since the father continues in the son inasmuch as generation perpetuates the specific type and in this sense perfects the generator. Further, it should be observed, that whilst the relation grounded on efficient causality may be a real one, it is not necessarily so: thus an act of sensation or of apprehension is ground for a real relation on the part of the subject of the sensation or the thought, but the thing perceived or thought about bears only a logical relation to the subject of the acts. (*c*) The categories of quantity, and of action and passion, we have said, can be the foundation of real relations, but not so those of substance and quality: before relations can exist between substances or qualities—relations of identity or difference, of similarity or dissimilarity—they must be possessed of the attribute of quantity, of unity or number. Thus the relation of identity rests upon the oneness of substance, just as diversity does upon a plurality of substances; and resemblance upon the unity of a quality, just as dissimilarity upon plurality of qualities.

111. Meaning of Absolute and Relative.—The terms *absolute* and *relative* fill a prominent place in the philosophical vocabulary of the day, coming as they do so frequently from the pen of contemporary writers; it is important then to understand exactly what they mean.

Absolute (*absolutum*, from *ab* and *solvo*, and *solvo* from λύω with se—*e* changed to *o*—prefixed) etymologically means *unbound, free from ties*, and so means what is not bound to another thing, what is self-sufficient. *Relative*, its opposite, therefore designates something that is in some way bound, something that is in some way dependent on another. Now both words may be taken in two senses. In the *ontological* sense, absolute means what is self-sufficient in the matter of existence, and relative what depends on another being for existence. In the *logical* sense or from the standpoint of knowledge, absolute is that which can be known by itself; relative that which depends for its being known upon something else being known. This distinction between metaphysical 'absolute' and 'relative' and logical is a fundamental one. It is the former aspect only which will interest us here in a treatise on Metaphysics. Examples of relative things, or beings that depend upon others in the matter of their existence, are the germination of a seed inasmuch as it depends upon rain; rain which depends upon water-vapour produced by condensation; water-vapour which comes from the evaporation of the ocean, which in turn relies on the heat of the sun and the heat of the sun upon chemical combustion. As absolute is a negative idea, a thing may be absolute from one point of view and not from another: an example is substance, which is absolute in the sense that it does not require to inhere in another being for existence, but which is not absolute in the possession of existence—it is an *ens in se* but not an *ens a se*. God alone is absolute in the sense of depending upon nothing for His existence: He alone is the Absolute.

CHAPTER II

ACTUAL BEING AND POTENTIAL BEING

112. Introductory.—Metaphysics contemplates real being; and the ground covered by real being divides itself into ten categories. Now no matter in what category it be found, real being allows of a further division, namely into *actual being* and *potential being*, into *actus* and *potentia*. For example, to say that a being sees, Aristotle observes, may mean that it has the power of seeing or that it does see; to know may mean equally well to be able to make use of knowledge and to be actually making use of it. The same distinction applies to substantial beings: we can say that the statue of Mercury is in the marble from which it will be sculptured, that the centre of a line is in it before it has been marked, that there is so much wheat where as yet none has matured [46]. After considering in the preceding chapter the partition of real being into ten categories and making a special study of those whose object is not essentially bound to matter and which therefore fall particularly within the scope of metaphysics, we come to examine in this chapter *actual* being and *potential* being. And as this new division of real being is best learnt from the study of '*movement*' or *evolution*, we will begin first of all with that.

113. 'Movement' or Evolution. Matter and Form.—If we consider all the things that go to make up the universe, we notice that they are subject to the general law of change. We observe that they acquire new perfections which previously they had not, or lose perfections which a moment before they possessed. These incessant changes that all beings around us undergo, and we too amongst them, were called by the Scholastics by the generic name of *motus, movement*, corresponding to the Aristotelian word *κίνησις*; and the same

[46] *Aristotle Metaph.*, IV, 7.

idea, still prominent in contemporary philosophy and science, is to-day spoken of as *evolution*.

An analysis of 'movement' or the evolution of material substances compels us to distinguish two kinds of changes, namely *accidental* changes and *substantial*. In change of temperature or of light-reflection we see an example of an accidental change, which does not get down to the inner structure of a body and so allows it to maintain its specific constitution. An example of a substantial change is the combination of two chemical bodies into a new body specifically distinct from either of its components.

What is the explanation of these accidental and substantial changes?

In all changes some new reality appears and some old reality remains. What happens when a thing formerly cold under the action of heat becomes warm is that birth is given to a new accidental determination whilst the thing itself still remains this particular substance, the object of our experience. When oxygen and hydrogen combine in definite proportions and become water, new specific determinations appear before us, a new chemical body springs into existence, yet in such a way that the component elements are not annihilated but that something passes from them into the compound they engender.

What remains in every change is called *matter*, ὕλη, *materia*; what appears, *form*, μορφή or εἶδος, *forma*. *Matter* is that reality which receives one or another form; *form* is that which by its communication to matter determines it to be a body of such or such a kind. From these two correlative realities revealed to us through analysis of material change spring the two ideas of *actual* and *potential*. For, the concepts of *matter* and *form* that we derive from the material world have been extended by analogy to the immaterial world and even into the logical order. As change necessarily implies two realities, one that persists and one that supervenes, matter and form, it is inferred that changes in spiritual beings likewise entail these two correlative realities. St. Bonaventure did not hesitate to call the subject of the changes in immaterial beings *matter*, and the intrinsic principles alike of accidental and substantial determinations *forms*, thus extending the pair of ideas originally taken from corporeal change analogically to spiritual beings. The same two notions have also been transported to Logic. Concepts that are the simplest and of the most universal application can be progressively determined by the mind adding note after note to them: from substance, the topmost genus on Porphyry's tree, to the individual at the bottom, there is a constant, progressive determination of thought-object (*Logic*, **18**), and between any two degrees of this gradation there is a relation of *matter* and *form*. These two correlative notions, then, which in the first instance stood for the principles of *material* change or movement have now an extended application to the whole of the real order and to the logical order. Hence they have acquired a metaphysical signification. With this widened extension and this simplified comprehension, *matter* and *form* mean respectively an *indeterminate, perfectible subject* and *determining, perfective principle*. And so defined they exactly coincide with the two ideas, *potential* and *actual*.

114. Analysis of the Metaphysical Ideas of Potential Being and Actual Being.—Metaphysics ignores the material, quantitative conditions to which the things of nature are subject, and therefore, when studying change, it studies it precisely as change, independently of the determinations which accompany it in the material world; it regards the principles of 'movement', whilst prescinding from every notion that has reference only to material objects.

Now, in Aristotelian metaphysics, that which changes, otherwise called the determinable or the perfectible, goes by the name of *potential being*, and the determining, perfective principle by the name *actual being*.

Potential being must not be confused with mere *possible* being. A thing is possible which does not involve in it notes that are contradictory; possible being is something belonging to the ideal order, not to the physical; it is said to be potential 'objectively'[47], whereas *potential being* belongs to the physical order; it presupposes the existence of a subject not yet perfected; its potency yet to be perfected is 'subjective'.

Potential being and its correlative, actual being, are both alike incapable of being defined, for like other objects of our

[47] In modern philosophy *subjective* denotes what is to be referred to the thinking subject; *objective*, to the non-ego. Formerly *subject* meant a substance of the physical world; and *object*, what in the mind answers to the act of knowledge.

primary concepts they defy analysis. The most that can be done is to contrast them, in order the better thereby to set off each correlative by the light of the other. *Potential being*, then, is being in so far as it can receive a perfection; answering to this—the perfection filling the capacity of the *potentia*—is *actus*. *Potentiality* is the receptive, perfectible quality, perfectibility; *actuality*, its fulfilment, the perfective quality, perfection [48]. St. Thomas with admirable precision says, 'Actus est complementum et perfectio et finis potentiae.'

In fine, the acquisition of actuality by a potential being—of a perfection by a perfectible subject—is change or evolution or 'movement' in the metaphysical acceptation of the word.

115. Metaphysical Concept of Movement.—'Movement' was defined by Aristotle as the '*actuality of a subject that is formally potential*', and again as the '*actuality of an imperfect subject*' [49]. Movement is, then, some *actuality*: far from being the negation of some perfection, it is a *positive perfection*; the thing passes from one manner of being to another manner of being; it acquires a new perfection that previously it had not. Nevertheless movement is not actuality under all respects: the being that undergoes a change, precisely in the very change is still in potentiality with respect to further actuality or perfection which it has yet to receive. It is, then, the actualization of a potentiality not fully completed, 'actus imperfecti', the *actus* of a potential being in so far as it is still *in potentia*. In other words, between the simple aptitude to movement, or *pure potentiality*, on the one hand, and complete actualization which supposes the aptitude fully satisfied, or *potentiality actuated*, on the other, there is an intermediary reality composed of *both 'act' and 'power'*, and this is movement: it is *actuality* inasmuch as it implies a potency in part realized, and it is *potentiality* inasmuch as the subject, partly

[48] The English word 'act' now bears only the same meaning as 'action', which signifies the *process* or operation by which a change is wrought, and will no longer translate the Latin word 'actus' (ἐντελέχεια) which means rather the *resultant* of 'actio' the complement or actuality of passive potentiality 'potentia passiva'.—*Actio* (and 'actus' in this sense also) is of course the correlative of 'potentia activa seu operativa' 'potestas agendi' (ἐνέργεια) power of action, faculty. Further, some faculties, owing to the need of some determination to action, as explained below, are termed 'passive faculties'—TRS.

[49] *Phys.*, III, 1; *De Anima*, III, 7.

actualized, is susceptible of further actuality; it is the actuality of a potential subject, 'actus imperfecti'.

To form an accurate conception of movement we must therefore keep in view a double relation on the part of the subject, namely, with a previous potentiality now become actual, and with an actuality yet acquirable; movement is at once the actualization of a certain potentiality and the capacity for further, more complete actualization; in a word, the *actus* of a *potentia* that is still *in potentia* [50].

116. The Principle of Movement: Nothing can move Itself; the Potential cannot Actualize Itself.—The material universe is made up of things which change, which from being potential become actual. Now the law governing this change or movement is that none of these imperfect beings can move itself; or, as the Scholastics expressed the principle: '*Quidquid movetur ab alio movetur*—every movement requires a mover distinct from the moved thing'; '*Nihil transit de potentia ad actum nisi per aliquod ens actu*—every change which occurs in a subject requires the action of some actual being'.

This principle was regarded by Suarez as the fruit of an inductive argument; and therefore he considered it to apply only to the physical world and to be devoid of metaphysical value. In reality it is a principle 'in necessary matter' [51], an analytical proposition, one which is self-evidently true and the denial of which would be a violation of the principle of causality. For: as a subject which is capable of receiving a perfection does not actually possess it—or it would no longer

[50] 'Considerandum est, quod aliquid est in actu tantum, aliquid vero in potentia tantum, aliquid vero medio modo se habens inter potentiam puram et actum perfectum. Quod igitur est in potentia tantum, nondum movetur: quod autem jam est in actu perfecto, non movetur, sed jam motum est. Illud igitur movetur, quod medio modo se habet inter puram potentiam et actum; quod quidem partim est in potentia, et partim in actu, ut patet in alteratione. Cum enim aqua est solum in potentia calida, nondum movetur: cum vero est jam calefacta, terminatus est motus calefactionis; cum vero jam participat aliquid de calore sed imperfecte, tunc movetur ad calorem: nam quod calefit paulatim, participat calorem, magis ac magis. Ipse igitur actus imperfectus caloris in calefactibili existens, est motus; non quidem secundum id quod actu tantum est, sed secundum quod jam in actu existens, habet ordinem in ulteriorem actum: quia si tolleretur ordo ad ulteriorem actum, ipse actus quantumcumque imperfectus, esset terminus, et non motus: sicut accidit cum aliquid semiplene calefit'. ST. THOMAS, *In III Phys.*, lect. 2.

[51] For the meaning of this phrase see *Logic*, 31–33.

be capable—one of two things must have happened for it to become possessed of it: either it must have been subjected to the action of an extrinsic cause which made it acquire it, and this verifies the principle that no subject is sufficient to perfect itself; or it need not have been subjected to any extrinsic agency, and this involves a contradiction inasmuch as, on the one hand, the subject did not possess the perfection since it had to acquire it and, on the other hand, what is *formally the same* subject does possess it.

Unless this flagrant contradiction is to be entertained, it must be allowed that the actualization of a perfection in a subject capable of receiving it requires an extrinsic influence: 'Nihil reducitur de potentia ad actum nisi per aliquod ens actu'.

117. Various Kinds of Potentiality and, accordingly, of Actuality.—The potential subject receptive of actuality may be either substantial or accidental.

In the case of *substantial* changes that give place to one another in the general evolution of nature there is presupposed some *potential first subject—'materia prima'*; of which the '*first actualities*' are the *substantial forms* specifying the various material substances. Here, then, we see at the bottom of a substantial *essence* a fundamental relation of 'act and power'.

However, substantial essence does not include the whole of physical being: it is also the subject of *accidental* realities, as well as the subject of *existence*. Now in respect of its own accidental determinations, substance is a potential subject, a '*potentia*' actualized by its accidents as so many correlative '*actus*' (85). Whilst substantial form is the 'first actuality, *actus primus*' of 'primary matter', these accessory determinations of substance are further, 'second actualities, *actus secundi*'.

But from another point of view accident itself may be an 'actus *primus*'. Thus, for example, extension is a *first* actuality in respect of the exterior form that circumscribes it, whilst the latter is a second actuality of the former. Again, a power of action, 'potentia operativa', is an actuality, a perfection, of substance, yet it is also a *first* actuality in as far as the action it puts forth is a *second* actuality in relation to itself. Once more; of these operative powers which we call 'passive' faculties, there exists an intermediary actuality between the power to act and the action, between the 'potentia' and the 'actus': e.g. before the cognitive faculties come into exercise, are actuated, they must first be intrinsically determined, they must first receive an intrinsic complement (*Psychology*, **38, 100** f.), and therefore they are 'in power' not only in respect of their final operation—the act of knowledge—but also in respect of this complementary determination which has to put them in the proximate possibility of acting. As a complete illustration consider the human soul, which is a substance endowed with passive faculties. The soul is a *first* actuality in relation to the primary matter which it informs; and in relation to it, its passive powers of action —such as the power of understanding—are *second* actualities. These passive faculties are in their turn *first* actualities in relation to the determination they require to receive as a requisite for action—the understanding in relation to its determinant to knowledge. And after receiving their prerequisite determination, the faculties are again related as potentiality to actuality in respect of their final operation. Lastly, habits, compared to the faculties or powers of which they are habits, are actual; whilst they are potential compared to the actions the exercise of which they facilitate.

Furthermore, it may well be without involving any contradiction, that the same being may be actual with respect to something previous and at the same time in a state of potentiality with respect to something yet to come: The relations of 'act and potency' we have just been considering all arise with reference to substance as an *essence*; but substance, with its quantitative and qualitative determinations, is a subject of *existence*; hence from this new point of view, substance considered in the fullness of its individual or personal determinations, is *potential* with respect to the *actuality of existence*: 'Esse est ultimus actus'.

It was seen above (**32** f.) that there is a real composition of essence and existence in all finite beings. Their 'actus existentiae' is, then, received in a subject, it is 'actus *receptus*, actus *participatus*. In God existence is *subsisting actuality*, actus *irreceptus*' [52].

[52] From our study of cosmology and psychology we learn that a *substantial* being may be *subsistent* in itself or *essentially united to matter*. Further, a

118. Potentiality and Actuality in their Relation to Efficiency.—Our examination of change, or 'movement', as it is in itself, has led us to distinguish that which persists, on the one hand, and that which passes away together with that which newly appears, on the other. From this standpoint, potentiality (potentia passiva) is receptive, passive; and actuality (actus) is the intrinsic principle of perfection communicated to it. Now besides this aspect, which alone we have so far considered and which is the chief one for metaphysics, there is another.

Movement may be considered precisely as not produced by itself—'Nihil reducitur de potentia ad actum nisi per aliquod ens actu'. The principle from which a movement or change proceeds is likewise called a *potentia*, potency, but a *potentia operativa*, a power of action, corresponding to which

subsistent actuality may be *complete* or *incomplete*: e.g. an angel or pure spirit is a complete subsisting form; a disembodied human soul is an incomplete subsisting form, inasmuch as, though there is nothing essentially impossible for it so to exist in separation from matter, the natural conditions for its complete perfection demand that it should be united with matter. The second kind of actuality, *non-subsistent* actuality, requires conjunction with its corresponding potentiality, and cannot exist but with its matter: e.g. the souls of plants and of animals, the substantial forms of minerals. Besides substantial, or specific, forms, there are of course also *accidental* forms, which are also non-subsistent actualities. We may make out, then, the following table of the different kinds of actuality or perfection or completeness in being (ἐντελέχεια):—

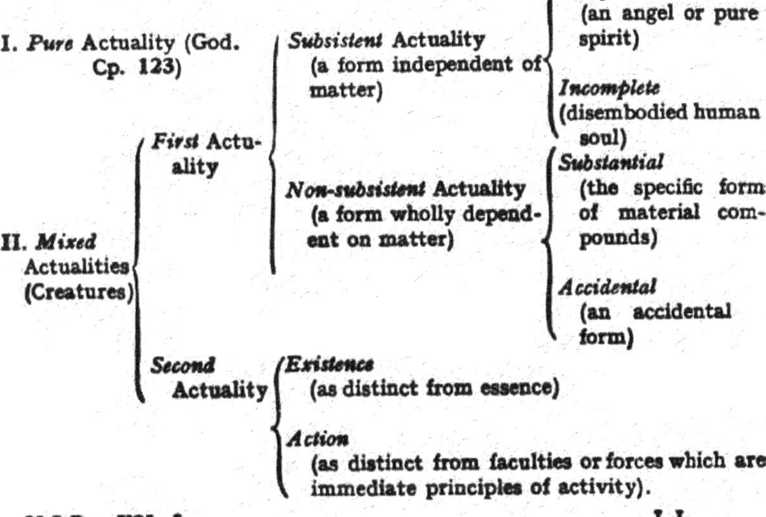

- I. *Pure* Actuality (God. Cp. 123)
- II. *Mixed* Actualities (Creatures)
  - *First* Actuality
    - *Subsistent* Actuality (a form independent of matter)
      - *Complete* (an angel or pure spirit)
      - *Incomplete* (disembodied human soul)
    - *Non-subsistent* Actuality (a form wholly dependent on matter)
      - *Substantial* (the specific form of material compounds)
      - *Accidental* (an accidental form)
  - *Second* Actuality
    - *Existence* (as distinct from essence)
    - *Action* (as distinct from faculties or forces which are immediate principles of activity).

—its exercise or *operation*—is some *action, act* (*actio, actus*). The definition of 'active power' given by Aristotle and adopted by the Scholastics is: *Principium transmutationis in aliud secundum quod est aliud.* Different words for the same thing are '*force*' and '*faculty*', the former being used for the active powers of inanimate nature, the latter when it is a question of those peculiar to animals and man.

The difference between these two meanings of power and 'act' is a fundamental one: on the one hand is '*passive* power', capacity of being perfected (potentiality), and an *intrinsic* principle of perfection (actuality); on the other, an *active* principle of effecting something in a subject that is other than, or *extrinsic to,* the active principle. In point of fact the two kinds of 'power'—passive and active—are always given simultaneously in nature; and the very dependence of the first upon the second provides the reason why the same word, 'potentia' in Latin, is employed for both [58]. The reason why the two always accompany each other is seen if the two ideas are put together: for what use would it be to have the capacity to possess a perfection, 'passive power', if to meet it there did not exist any force able to make it acquire that perfection?

119. The Double Meaning of 'Act and Power' contrasted.—The pair of words 'actus et potentia' are used to express two kinds of relations really distinct: *power,* or as we have usually called it potentiality, considered as synonymous with potential subject is that which is perfectible by some intrinsic determination, and its determination is its *formal* '*act*', or actuality; operative *power*—synonymous with *force* or *faculty*—is an immediate principle of action, and the action effected is its *act.* Now in both cases the couple 'act and power' bears an analogous signification. The question is to determine the

[58] 'Potentia primo imposita est ad significandum principium actionis, sed secundo translatum est ad hoc, ut illud etiam, quod recipit actionem agentis, potentiam habere dicatur. Et haec est potentia passiva; ut sicut potentiae activae respondet operatio vel actio in qua completur potentia activa, ita etiam illud quod respondet potentiae passivae quasi perfectio et complementum, actus dicatur. Et propter hoc omnis forma actus dicitur, etiam ipsae formae separatae et illud quod est principium perfectionis totius, quod est Deus, vocatur actus primus et purus, cui maxime illa potentia convenit'. St. Thomas, *I Sent.*, dist. 42, a. 1, ad 1.

point of contact where the two partially different senses meet. A closer examination of movement will supply the answer.

Consider some reality that is the resultant of movement—for example, a bud that makes its appearance on the branch of a tree. Before it actually existed, this reality was possible, not merely *logically* like an abstract essence inasmuch as its constitutive notes do not involve a contradiction—like winged horse and hydra-headed monster—but possible *really*, as a being that an existing cause in nature is capable of producing. As such, it existed potentially in its causes. Now these causes are of two kinds: one cause is capable of being the subject of the phenomenon, 'subjectum natum pati hoc'; and one cause is capable of producing the phenomenon in the subject capable of receiving it, 'agens natum operari hoc'. These two causes—receptive or material cause and efficient cause—contain potentially the new phenomenon which depends on them for its appearance. They are, then, both *potentiae*, the one being called *potentia subjectiva*, the other *potentia operativa*. Furthermore, the movement is the resultant of the activity of the efficient cause received in the material cause; and hence it is the correlative of both the *potentiae* at once, and, in consequence, has a twofold relation—namely, with the subject in which it is produced, on the one hand, and with the principle producing it on the other: according to this twofold relation it bears the double name of '*passio*' (relation to the material cause) and of '*actio*' (relation to the efficient cause). Movement, then, simply in itself, is the object of two distinct concepts.

120. The Consequence of Ignoring the Metaphysical Distinction of 'Act and Power'.—The philosophy of Descartes professes an absolute mechanism in Cosmology and dualism in Psychology. Matter it makes to be essentially extension, and all corporeal activity to be nothing more than modes of extrinsic, mechanical movement.

Now this mechanical conception is clearly false. Bodies of nature are not material points subjected to the action of extrinsic motors called mechanical forces; they have their own distinctive properties, their own peculiar nature, and they are subject to intrinsic accidental variations as also to substantial transformations. All this implies within them an intrinsic principle capable of receiving determination, passive potentialities, in a word, a potential ground-matter determinable by accidental or substantial actuality. This false conception of the material universe arose from losing sight of the metaphysical distinction of potentiality and actuality: Descartes studied beings only *as they are*, statically; he ignored what they can become, their potentiality.

In the second place, his dualistic psychology with the host of inextricable errors to which it gives rise likewise owes its origin to the same neglect of this fundamental distinction. Neither he nor his followers, Malebranche, Leibniz, Spinoza, were able to offer any reasonable account of the interaction of soul and body: for if, as he maintained, the soul is essentially thought and the body essentially extension, there can obviously be nothing in common between the two realities; two substances so distinct and opposed can in no conceivable way act upon each other. This insuperable difficulty arose from mistaking the action of the soul upon the body for the action of an efficient cause upon an extrinsic subject; whereas it is the *formal cause*, the *actuality* of a potential subject—the soul being nothing else, as we saw in Psychology (**154, 155**), than the substantial perfection of a subject which in itself is only potentially a living body of nature.

121. Conclusion of Part III.—Real being, which is the object contemplated by metaphysics, allows of a twofold fundamental division, namely, into the ten categories and, as a cross-division of each of the ten categories, into potential being and actual being. In Part III we have been engaged on these divisions. We are now in a position to consider, in Part IV, the causes of being. Before doing so, however, it would be suitable, after speaking of movement, which is a mark of the imperfection of created beings, to glance at the characteristics of such beings and contrast them with those of the all-perfect, infinite Being, who is God.

CHAPTER III

CREATED BEINGS AND THE UNCREATED BEING

122. Potential, Contingent, Dependent and Finite Beings.—The things which fall under our experience are *changing* beings, 'entia *mobilia*'; they contain potentiality to be other reality; in short they are made up of potentiality and actuality.

Now, to be potential means to be capable of becoming something, of being in some way further perfected; as such then these beings are not fully complete, they are *imperfect*.

Further, changing beings pass away, they become something new and they cease to be what they were; their existence is not essential to them: hence, in this respect, they are *contingent*. For a contingent being is by definition one whose essence entails neither existence nor non-existence; or again, it is that which has not in its essence the sufficient reason of its existence.

When a contingent being does exist, the existence that it has, since it does not belong to it in virtue of its essence, must have been conferred upon it by some extrinsic efficient cause: hence this kind of being is essentially *dependent*, inasmuch as it is the effect of an efficient cause.

Lastly, the composition of potentiality and actuality that attaches to contingent, changing beings is an intrinsic principle of limitation, for actual existence cannot actualize a subject except in so far as it is capable of actualization: hence every subject that is actualized and produced is *finite*.

123. The Purely Actual, Necessary, Independent and Infinite Being.—In Natural Theology it is shown that the existence of subjects composed of potentiality and actuality implies the existence of a being that has no potentiality, which is *purely Actual, Actus purus*.

Not being capable of becoming any further perfected, inasmuch as It is in no way potential, the purely Actual Being was spoken of by the Scholastics as the Immovable, '*Ens Immobile*'; and as It is the first cause of 'movement' in changing beings, It is further styled the *Immovable Mover, Motor Immobilis.*

Whilst potential beings are, according to their potentiality, imperfect, the Being who is actuality by essence is the *All-perfect.*

Again, composition of essence and existence, the reason of contingency, is excluded from Pure Actuality, since essence and existence are related to each other as potentiality and actuality. Hence the essence of the Perfect Being is identical with Its existence, which is essential to It, and It is therefore *independent* of every other being.

Lastly, since beings in which there is admixture of potentiality and actuality are finite for the reason that the essential perfection of a being is less in proportion to its potentiality and its actual existence is limited by the limitation of the essence receiving it, the Being in which there is no such admixture but which is Pure Actuality must be entirely perfect, perfect without any limitation, with all the perfection enclosed in the concept of being, in a word, must be *infinite* [54].

These ideas will be found more fully developed in their proper place in Natural Theology.

[54] 'Deus est actus infinitus; quod patet ex hoc quod actus non finitur nisi dupliciter. Uno modo ex parte agentis . . . alio modo ex parte recipientis. . . . Ipse autem divinus actus non finitur ex aliquo agente, quia non est ab alio sed a seipso; neque finitur ex aliquo recipiente, quia cum nihil potentiae passivae ei admisceatur, ipse est actus purus, non receptus in aliquo; est enim Deus ipsum esse suum in nullo receptum'. ST. THOMAS, *De potentia*, q. 1, a. 2.

CHAPTER IV

THE UNITY OF THE OBJECT OF META-PHYSICS

124. General Conclusion of the First Three Parts of the Treatise.—The formal object of metaphysics we laid down (7) to be individual substance, or substance as realized in things of experience. This substance we first of all, in Part I, studied in itself; then, in Part II, in its transcendental properties; and lastly, in Part III, in its determinations—its manifold accidental determinations and its metaphysical components, potential subject and its actuality. But this investigation of being under these aspects has not exhausted the subject-matter, or as we have called it the object, of metaphysics: there still remain to be considered substantial and accidental changes (*generatio et corruptio, motus*) as well as privation and negation of being (Part IV).

A difficulty, however, may here suggest itself, namely, How is it that these different points of view from which we study being do not compromise the unity of metaphysics? What is there in common among objects so different as substance and accident, potential being and actual, and substance on the one hand and change, privation and negation on the other?

The answer to this difficulty is contained in the two following propositions:—(*a*) The chief object of metaphysics is substance; (*b*) Beings have in common a certain analogousness.

125. The Principal Object of Metaphysics is Substance.—Metaphysics is chiefly occupied with substance, but non-substantial being also claims attention on account of its subordination to substance—'Ens multipliciter dicitur; sed tamen omne ens dicitur per respectum ad unum primum, scilicet subjectum'[55].

[55] St. Thomas, *In IV Metaph.* lect. 7.

The reason why substance takes the principal place will be clear when we class beings into four groups :—(1) *Negations* and *privations* are at the bottom of the scale; nevertheless they are beings since reason takes account of them and in both affirmative and negative judgments predicates attributes of them. (2) Next comes *change*; it comprises reality plus a privation or negation of reality; it is imperfect actuality, as will be explained *ex professo* in Part IV. (3) *Accidents* do not entail non-being, but such being as they enjoy belongs to them 'in another', '*ens in alio*'. (4) *Substance* alone has its own being, existence in itself: it entails neither negation nor privation and it does not exist in another subject. Since substance then is being *par excellence*, it is obviously legitimate to accord it the first place in the study of Being.

On the other hand, the beings of the first three groups are by their nature necessarily referred to substance: accidents —qualities and quantity—are inherent in it; generation and movement or change respectively give birth to it or produce a new quantitative or qualitative determination in it; and negation and privation are the exclusion of it or of one of its determinations. If we add that the Supreme Being also is connected with substance, in so far as He is its first cause and last end, it becomes evident that everything to which the name *being* belongs, for one reason or another pertains to substance. Hence the fundamental unity of metaphysics is explained.

126. The Various Kinds of Being have in common a Certain Analogousness.—If the various kinds of being we have just enumerated merit the same name of *being*, it is with different significations according as it stands for different things or different aspects: the term is therefore certainly not *univocal*, it does not keep the same meaning throughout for all the objects of which it is used. But is it entirely equivocal, or is it an analogical term?

An *equivocal* term is one which stands for things or concepts which have nothing whatever in common beyond the mere name. An *analogical* term is one that designates objects different by nature but similar in certain common traits or possessing a real relationship to one another for instance, the word 'leaf' is used analogically of paper because in thinness of texture it resembles the leaf of a tree; or again, food is said by analogy to be healthy, as also a climate and a régime and a person's appearance, because food and air and a mode of life are favourable to health and because one's looks betray it.

Now the term 'being' is *not equivocal*, for 'being' in its principal acceptation means this particular concrete thing which we meet in nature; and accordingly the elements which go to make its constitution and which analysis discloses—essence, existence, substance, accident, potentiality and actuality—belong to this being and bear the same name as it. Yet essence, existence, substance, accident, and potential and actual being do not realize the idea of 'being' all in the same way, and therefore the word applies to them all not in a univocal but in an *analogical* sense. God and creatures share the name, but God is Being *per se* and all-being, *esse irreceptum*, whereas creatures have received such being as they possess and possess it dependently and in a certain degree only, *esse participatum*; substance alone merits the name in the strict, proper sense, inasmuch as it is *ens in se*, whereas accident is *ens in alio* and inheres in some other being; potential being requires to be determined by its correlative actuality and cannot be known except through it. Yet various as they are, these beings nevertheless present a certain analogousness in having a certain connexion between them: the being of creatures depends upon the being of God, and the being of accidents upon that substance, and potency is the subject of the 'act' determining it.

These considerations have their importance in showing, on the one hand, how one and the same concept may be predicated of all things and, on the other hand, how it can subsequently be determined by a progressive work of thought and so be applied differently to different things.

The failure to perceive that the concept of being is an analogous one has led the idealistic pantheists into the belief that everything to which the name 'being' applies is one and the same object, and from this they draw their inference that there is only one substance in the universe.

And on the other hand the failure to realize that the analogy is based on real relations between the analogical beings accounts for the agnosticism of the positivists which asserts that things of experience cannot lead us to a knowledge of beings beyond experience.

We may now pass on to the study of the *causes of being*. In this new quest substance alone will engage our attention; yet not substance as it is, but from the point of view of *how it became what it is* and *how it acts* in the manner in which we see it acting. In other words, we leave the static point of view (*substance*) and regard it from the genetic (its *constitution*) and dynamic (its *nature*) standpoints.

PART IV

The Causes of Being

CHAPTER I

GENERAL OUTLINE

127. A Glance at the Material Universe.—The material universe is agitated by a constant *motion*, it is the scene of incessant *changes*. Yet its motion is governed by a *constant law* and its changes are grounded on something permanent. Together the changes and the stable law behind them constitute the *order of nature*. These are fundamental ideas worthy of further attention.

128. ' Movement ' in Nature.—All bodies of nature, inorganic and organic alike, whether considered individually or collectively, are subject to movement. (*a*) *Inorganic matter*, alike in its three stages, liquid, gaseous and solid, is perpetually in movement: in Cosmology (**12** ff.), where the different specific activities of beings were studied, some idea was gained of the unending exchanges of chemical, physical and mechanical activities that we observe to take place in beings of the inorganic kingdom. (*b*) *Organic life* too is continual movement: in Psychology (**10**) it was disclosed that the natural law of living being is constant self-movement. Regarded either in the individual or in the species, life is a cycle of incessant operations that eventuate in the perfection of the said individual or species. (*c*) Thirdly, *our globe*, considered as a whole, is ceaselessly borne along by the double movement of its daily rotation on its own axis and of its yearly revolution round the sun. (*d*) So too *the sun* with its train of *planets* is subject to this law of perpetual motion. (*f*) And it is also probable that the same is the case with all the *stars* that are scattered throughout the immensity of space. All nature, then, is seen to be in movement. So striking indeed is this fact that at the very beginnings of Greek philosophy we find Heraclitus asking himself if his search after reality is not a vain quest. Can anything be found to exist besides what is only becoming? His verdict was in the negative: that 'all things are in perpetual flux', everything changes, nothing is which also is not.

This is a first aspect for consideration. But it is only one aspect. Change is not the whole of reality: there are some things which *are*, which are stable and permanent and persist throughout.

129. Stability in Nature.—In the first place there is permanency in the universe in the sense that the changes which succeed one another do so only after intervals.

Secondly, and in a more strict sense, there is something permanent inasmuch as the countless movements taking place are dominated by stable principles. Thus, to consider the universe *quantitatively*, all the forms of activity put forth therein are subject to the two great laws of the *conservation of matter* and the *conservation of energy*. To consider it *qualitatively*, despite all their changes the *specific types* of the mineral, vegetable and animal kingdoms are maintained. Moreover the spectroscope has even revealed that in the solar matter there permanently exist most of the chemical substances that enter into the constitution of our own planet.

Whilst, then, Heraclitus could find nothing existing but everything becoming, Parmenides was able to proclaim the stability of nature, asserting that things did not become but remained for ever unchangeable. As a third observer more careful than both, Aristotle arrived at a middle conclusion, namely, that the material universe undergoes *perpetual changes*, but through them all is an enduring element which manifests itself in the *laws* and *order of nature*.

The task of explaining this order of the universe devolves upon the philosopher. To whatever explains it, at least in part, he gives the name cause, and herein we see the general object of the metaphysic of causes.

130. Two Opposite Conceptions of the Order of the Universe: Mechanism and Aristotelian Naturalism.—After noticing in outline movement and order in the material world, it remains for us now to find the necessary and sufficient causes of this universal order. Hitherto two theories have been advanced in explanation, namely, that of mechanism and the theory of Aristotle and the Scholastics.

The theory of mechanism may be summed up in the following points :—(*a*) The universe is made up entirely of homogeneous matter. (*b*) The activities of the various masses are simply mechanical forces ; natural agents can produce only local movement, and therefore to it all material energies are reducible. (*c*) Modifications which occur in bodies consist in a quantitative change of mass plus local movement. (*d*) It admits of neither formal nor final causes, but only of efficient causality ; the universal order is the *result* of mechanical movements that have their seat in matter. In short, *local movement* and *efficient* causality that produces it in a fatalistic way, are the sole factors of the order of nature.

Opposed to this theory, which has already been criticized in Cosmology (**30**), is the *naturalistic* theory of Aristotle and the Scholastics ; that is to say, the theory founded on the idea that every being in the world has *a nature.* Its main tenets are :—(*a*) The substances of existing things are specifically distinct, thus forming distinct *species.* (*b*) Each has special *properties* which manifest a distinct specific principle. (*c*) Of the changes that occur in nature some are superficial and *accidental,* whilst others are profound and *substantial,* reaching down to the very substance of the body. (*d*) The reason of these changes lies in *two intrinsic causes*—one *material* and the other *formal*—and an *extrinsic* cause, the *motor* or *efficient* cause. (*e*) Yet natural agents are not mere efficient causes : the perpetual recurrence of the phenomena the laws of which it is the endeavour of the physical and natural sciences to discover, and the permanence of specific types in the mineral and organic kingdoms, cannot be adequately explained unless efficient causes are drawn by *final causes* to act in a definite direction and to make their native forces converge to one and the same purpose. Purpose or end thus constitutes a fourth cause, although in reality the very first, 'causa causarum'.

This doctrine of the *four causes* whereby we profess to explain the evolution of the material universe furnishes ground for a convenient division of the metaphysic of causes into three chapters, dealing respectively with an *analysis* of the causes (Chap. II), the *relations* they bear to one another (Chap. III), and their *general effect,* which is the *order of nature* (Chap. IV).

Chapter II, which is an analytic study of the causes, will comprise five sections, concerning the *material* and *formal* causes (I), the *efficient* cause (II), the *final* cause (III), the place to be assigned to the *exemplary* cause (IV), and cause *in general* (V).

CHAPTER II

ANALYSIS OF THE FOUR CAUSES

I. The Material and Formal Causes

131. Reason for this Inquiry in General Metaphysics.—Since the material and the formal cause are constituent principles of corporeal substances, it may perhaps be thought that they should remain foreign to metaphysics, which is by definition the science of the immaterial. Yet not so: for, whilst cosmology studies material substances, metaphysics has for its principal object that which makes these same objects of experience substances, their substantiality; now substance as such, looked at quite indeterminately, apart from the sensible qualities and specific characteristics it may happen to have, is an object of experience, and therefore to the study which contemplates substance as it comes within our experience (7) must belong the consideration of the intrinsic constitution which is essential to it.

The existence and nature of the material and formal causes of bodies is best revealed by a close inspection of change. Accordingly let us consider the various kinds of changes that take place in material things.

132. The Peripatetic-Scholastic Account of Accidental and Substantial Changes.—All *change*, *mutatio*, Aristotle expressed by the generic name of μεταβολή: it is the transition from being something into being something else. His usual synonym for it is *κίνησις*, *motus*, *movement*.

This 'movement' or change may be *accidental* or it may be *substantial*. Of the former the most apparent kind is *local movement* or *translation*. But there are other kinds too, namely, *alteration*, which is a modification in a subject's *qualities*, and *increase* or *decrease*, which is a change in its *quantity*.

These different kinds of accidental changes are to be explained by two principles: one, inasmuch as they produce themselves in something that remains, *matter* or *material* cause; the other, a *form* or *formal* cause, since they consist in something new appearing in the matter. In these changes the *matter* is a body already substantially complete. This the Scholastics sometimes call 'second matter, *materia secunda*' in distinction from 'first matter, *materia prima*', of which we have also to speak.

For there are some changes that go deeper than into the accidents, that affect the very substance of bodies, and these substantial changes in their turn require for their explanation two intrinsic principles. Here the subject is matter in the sense in which the word is principally used in philosophy; what Aristotle calls ἡ πρώτη ὕλη or simply ὕλη, the *materia prima* or *materia* of the Scholastics. The forms too, in this case, that give place to each other in the matter are forms in the principal sense of the word, *substantial* or *specific forms*, εἶδος. The two phases of the change marked by the birth of one form and the disappearance of a previous one were respectively styled by Aristotle γένεσις and φθορά, which the Scholastics translated as 'generation' and 'corruption'. Substantial transformations, then, reveal to us that all bodies are substantially composed of two principles, namely, first or primary matter (ὕλη) and a substantial form (μορφή).

The nature of these two intrinsic principles of substantial changes which are also the constituent principles of bodies, was more fully examined in Cosmology (37 ff.). Sufficient has been said to allow us to proceed with our study of the material and formal causes. Let us consider the nature of each more in detail with a view to discovering their metaphysical significance.

133. Nature and Causality of the Material Cause.—The material cause exhibits three distinct though inseparable features: (*a*) Firstly, the subject is made to experience from the generator or agent an action which alters the compound: *the matter is altered by an action.* (*b*) Secondly, the alteration in the subject made the introduction of the form of a new compound possible: *the matter receives a new form.* (*c*) Lastly, the reception of this new form realizes a new compound: *the union of matter and form constitutes a new compound substance.*

Now the alteration itself is not material causality but a pre-requisite of it; the latter comes into play in the reception of the new form and the constitution of the new compound. Material causality, then, really consists in two things: it receives the form and, as the result of its intrinsic union with it, constitutes the new being. These two functions of the material cause, however, are not of equal importance: it is *primarily* receptive, and *secondarily* unitive. For, the reception of the form by the matter precedes—by a priority of nature, not of time—the union of the matter and form in the unity of the compound. In a word, the primordial and chief rôle of matter is to be the recipient subject of the form; nevertheless it is more than merely receptive since, though it receives the form, it does not receive the compound. The adequate exposition of this causality is, then, that matter receives the form and unites itself to it to constitute a composite substance: *materia est id in quo recipitur forma et ex quo fit quod generatur.*

134. Applications of Material Causality.—Matter fulfils its function of receptive cause principally in respect of the forms of corporeal compounds. Nevertheless material cause has also a metaphysical application, in so far as every imperfect substance, incorporeal as well as corporeal, plays the part of receptive or 'material' cause in respect of the accidental determinations which perfect it. Even an accident may be a material cause in relation to another accident—as for example extension in relation to light and heat; a power or faculty in relation to the complementary determination it requires for its exercise, in relation to its habits, and in relation to the action that is ultimately effected in it. Moreover the individual is the subject of actual existence, and as such is to be termed *matter* in a metaphysical sense. And likewise in the same sense do the parts of a compound, considered in relation to the compound itself, assume a *material* character. Furthermore the idea of matter is taken over by analogy even into logic (**113**).

135. Nature and Causality of the Formal Cause.—The idea of 'form' we originally derive from corporeal things. Here, in its principal signification, form is the intrinsic first principle of a substance's perfection. Its causality is exercised *primarily* in the perfecting of the essence of the substance, and *secondarily* in respect of its existence. In the fulfilment of its first function, the form bears a relation to the matter and to the compound: *to the matter* inasmuch as, whilst matter may receive indifferently any specific form, the form does away with this indifference and makes it to share the nature of some specific, determinate compound; *to the compound* inasmuch as it is a constitutive part of it and is the source of its perfection and energies. For this primordial rôle of form by which it perfects the *essence* of the compound substance the traditional definition runs: 'Forma est quo ens est id quod est'. In its secondary function, form is the principle of *existence*, in the sense that it provides an immediate subject for actual existence.

The nature of form reveals its causality: it is a cause in that it is communicated intrinsically to matter and, by its union with it, constitutes a substance of a definite kind [56]. Note that in respect of its material subject the formal cause bears the relation of actuality to potentiality, and this explains their intimate interpenetration—for a form may be said to give itself to the matter, it communicates itself to it and determines it intrinsically [57].

136. Applications of Formal Causality. Subsistent Forms.—The distinctive feature of matter, we have just seen, is the capacity of *receiving, of being perfected*, and that of form the capability of *being communicated, of perfecting*. Now these characteristics are to be found in immaterial finite beings as well as in material ones. For in every finite subject is verified the distinction of potential and actual. In material substances it is verified in a double way: firstly, in the substantial composition out of primary matter and substantial form, and secondly in the composition of the substantial subject with its accidents, and again of concrete essence (made up of substance with its accidents) with the actual existence that deter-

[56] 'Materia est causa formae, inquantum forma non est nisi in materia et similiter forma est causa materiae inquantum materia non habet esse in actu, nisi per formam; materia enim et forma dicuntur relative ad invicem; dicuntur etiam relative ad compositum sicut pars ad totum'. St. Thomas, *Cont. Gent.*, II, 59.

[57] 'Forma per seipsam facit rem esse in actu cum per essentiam suam sit actus, nec dat esse per aliquod medium. Unde unitas rei compositae ex materia et forma est per ipsam formam quae secundum seipsam unitur materiae ut actus ejus'. St. Thomas, *Sum. Theol.*, I, q. 76, a. 7.

mines it. In immaterial substances there is no composition of primary matter and substantial form, for the form is what is called a *subsistent* one, a *simple* or *pure form*; nevertheless such subsistent finite forms are capable of being made more perfect by the reception of accidental determinations, and also by the actuality of existence: hence this potential, perfectible subject may be spoken of as *matter* and the perfective actuality as *form* (**113**). One Being alone stands absolutely aloof from all material composition, even understanding the term in this extended, analogical sense; namely, God, who alone is an absolutely pure form.

As this consideration of matter and form brings us back upon the correlative terms 'act' and 'power', it would be as well to determine their exact relations to each other.

137. The Relations between 'Power and Act'.—1. *'Power' is the correlative of 'act'* (**114**).

2. *There is no 'power' without 'act'*; but the converse, there is no 'act' without 'power', is not true.

3. *A 'power' and its correlative 'act' are of the same genus.*

4. *A passive power calls, in the natural order of things, for a corresponding active cause* (**118**).

5. *Ontologically 'act' excels 'power'.* That which becomes tends to an end, and this end is the actuality or action for which the 'power' is. Accordingly, the perfect excels the imperfect, and the whole its parts inasmuch as they exist for it.

6. *Logically and psychologically 'act' is prior to 'power'.* For, firstly, to say that a thing is *in potentia* is the same as to say that it can become *actual*; we know it, then, by relation to its perfective 'act': it is therefore necessary that the definition and concept of the 'act' precede the definition and concept of the 'power'. In the second place, the psychological explanation of this logical priority of 'act' to 'power' lies in the fact that our powers of knowledge are passive (*Psychology*, **38, 96**), that is to say, for them to know they require something actual to determine their potentiality. Hence potential being, as such, is incapable of influencing our faculties of knowledge, and therefore is unknowable. Primary matter, for instance, since it is only potentiality, is for this reason unknowable.

7. *Genetically and in the order of time 'power' is prior to 'act' in the individual, but 'act' is prior to 'power' in the*

series of beings. Before any contingent thing can be actually or in action, it must of course first be such potentially or 'in power'; nevertheless each time that, in the natural order of things, a 'power' passes to 'act', some 'act' must have preceded the transition, for the reason that a potential being can never become actual except through the influence of the action of some being already actual (116). Hence at the head of each series of acquired perfections the perfection which is variously realized in the different terms of the series must actually exist.

138. Form as the Principle of Unity.—Form, we have said, provides the subject for actual existence. Now every existing being is *one.* The form, then, is the principle of unity: 'Ab eodem habet res *esse* et *unitatem.* Manifestum est autem quod res habet esse per formam. Unde et per formam res habet unitatem '[58].

Before the teaching of St. Thomas Scholastics were generally agreed that created substances possessed several substantial forms. But St. Thomas recognized that a plurality of forms would compromise the unity of a substantial compound: for, as soon as a form determines primary matter, it makes by its union with it a substance, a subject capable of receiving actual existence, and the union of another form with this already substantial compound could only result in an accidental determination; the substance and the form so added would thus form an *accidental* whole, not a *substantial* unit. Substantial unity, he concludes then, demands that there be only *one* form: a conclusion that is a characteristic and noteworthy advance of Thomism [59].

[58] St. Thomas, *Quodlib.* I, a. 6.

[59] 'Dicunt . . . quod quaedam forma substantialis est per quam est substantia tantum, et postea est quaedam alia per quam est corpus, deinde est et alia per quam est animatum et alia per quam est animal et alia per quam est homo et sic dicunt de aliis formis substantialibus rerum. Sed haec positio stare non potest: quia, cum forma substantialis sit quae facit hoc aliquid et dat esse substantiale rei, tunc sola prima forma esset substantialis, cum ipsa sola daret esset substantiale rei et faceret hoc aliquid; omnes autem post primam essent accidentaliter advenientes, nec darent esse rei simpliciter sed esse tale, et sic in amissione vel acquisitione ipsarum non esset generatio et corruptio sed tantum alteratio. Unde patet hoc non esse verum'. St. Thomas, *Quodlib.* XI, q. 5, a. 5.

II. The Efficient Cause

139. Nature and Causality of the Efficient Cause.—The efficient cause is the principle which produces the innumerable accidental and substantial transformations that happen in nature. By Aristotle it was called the active principle of 'movement'; and by the Scholastics was defined as '*Id quo aliquid fit*'—*fieri* meaning to *become*, the passing from one kind of being to another or from non-being into being. It is contrasted with 'matter and form', the *intrinsic principles of material being*, inasmuch as it is the *extrinsic principle of its becoming*.

The result of movement or becoming is called *effect* (efficere, effectum); and as the movement itself draws its origin from the efficient cause, the peculiar causality of that cause, its influence upon the becoming of a being, is in the production of movement, in *action*: 'efficiens est causa inquantum agit'[60].

The power of acting is called *activity*. In created beings it is distinct both from their nature and from action (**104**).

Of action there are two kinds, *transitive* and *intransitive*. Action is the former when the change produced by some agent is received in another subject; e.g. the action of heat on the wood it consumes. It is intransitive, or *immanent*, when its subject is none other than the agent itself; e.g. an act of volition (*Psychology*, **120**). In short, transitive action perfects a patient, immanent perfects the agent. Moreover, the verbs 'to act', 'to operate', strictly speaking, apply to immanent action; and the verb 'to make or do (*facio*)' to transitive action. 'To produce' and 'to effect' rather emphasize that the resultant of the action is dependent upon the active principle.

We may hope to obtain more light upon the concept of efficient cause if we contrast it with other kindred though distinct ideas.

140. Condition and Cause.—Whilst the cause has a positive influence upon the appearance of the fact we call its effect, the *condition* is that which is needed for the cause to be allowed to act; it does not itself positively influence the production of the effect, but is rather of the nature of a removal of an obstacle so that the cause, being thus unimpeded, has liberty to act.

[60] St. Thomas, *In I Metaph.* lect. 2.

A condition may be a *simple condition*, one which is not indispensable for action but only makes a possible action more perfect; or it may be a *conditio sine quâ non*, without which a given action cannot take place and which cannot be supplied for by the presence of any other condition. By way of example consider the action of seeing in a room: unless there is a window to allow the entrance of light seeing is impossible; the aperture is the removal of an obstacle to the passing in of light, and is therefore a *condition* (*removens prohibens*) of seeing; the light and the organ of sight are *causes*—the one an objective cause, the other a subjective one.

141. Occasion and Cause.—An occasion can exist only in reference to free causes. It may be defined as *a circumstance or combination of circumstances favourable to the action of a free cause*: e.g. night is an occasion of theft. The occasion has a positive influence upon the effect, if not upon the exterior efficiency at least upon the positive determination of the person's will which precedes it; and for this reason amongst others it differs from the condition. But it is not necessary for the production of the effect, whereas the cause is necessary. Yet in accepted language it is often called a *moral* cause, in contradiction to physical, of which we have been speaking.

142. The Cause in the Proper Sense and the Accidental Cause.—The causes which act in nature, as we shall see presently, are directed towards an end; to this, when acting naturally, they either attain or approach. When however this natural action of a cause comes in collision with that of another cause, there results what is called an 'accidental' effect, an effect different from that which the cause would have produced had its exercise not been thwarted (**157**). The action resulting from the encounter is often attributed to the natural cause, but it is so only through a loose use of language since the natural cause is not the cause of this effect, which is different from what its intrinsic end solicits it to produce and which in reality is due to the chance encounter of two causes, one of which deflects the action of the other. In a word, accidental effects are coincidences. We see an example in nourishment taken by the body which naturally is beneficial but for a weak stomach may be an 'accidental' cause of indigestion.

143. Various Kinds of Efficient Causes.—Besides the division already mentioned, into transitive and immanent causes, there are several other subdivisions of efficient causes, of which the following are the chief:—

1. *Principal cause and instrumental cause.*—When two causes conjoin to produce an effect, that is the *principal* one which makes use of the power of the inferior and directs its exercise; and that one which helps in the production of the effect under the impulse and direction of the other is the *instrumental* one. For example, the surgeon is the principal cause of an operation, the lance he uses is the instrumental cause. From this it will be seen that the principal cause acts by its own native power and the instrumental cause by the power of the principal cause which employs it: the lance does not play its part except in the hand of the surgeon, which is the source of its power; left to itself, it would never perform the operation required. Hence the instrumental cause produces an effect that, if left unassisted, it would be incapable of producing; and in consequence this effect that surpasses its nature and is to be explained by the motion of a higher cause can be but transitory, lasting just so long as the action of the principal cause continues to be exerted.

2. *'Dispositive' and 'perfective' causes.*—A *'dispositive'* cause is one that produces in some subject an ultimate disposition which demands the introduction into it of some definite form, yet does not itself produce that form. The cause which produces the form is, according to the terminology of St. Thomas, a *perfective* cause. An example of the former is a father as cause of his son: he does not procreate the soul of his child, but so disposes the matter as to determine God to intervene and create a rational soul to inform the matter thus predisposed to receive it. God is the 'perfective' cause of the new creature (*Psychology*, **162**).

3. *First and second causes.*—A *first* cause is one whose action is independent of any previous cause and to which one or several other causes are subordinate. A *second*, or as it is often called *secondary*, cause is one subordinate in its action to a higher cause. This subordination of one cause to a higher one may be *essential* or *accidental*: it is essential when the second cause, either for its existence or for the complement necessary for its action, necessarily relies *throughout* upon the

action of the higher cause; it is accidental when it is no longer dependent for its existence or action upon the continued presence of the higher cause although it did receive from it either its existence or its power of acting. Thus, the creature is essentially subordinate to the Creator who even now has to maintain it in being and assist its every action; whilst accidentally subordinate are living organisms to their parental organisms, inasmuch as they derived their existence from them but in their maturity both exist and act independently. It is worthy of note that every instrumental cause is a second cause essentially subordinate to its principal cause. But the converse is not true—principal cause may not be identified with first cause: for whilst every second cause is instrumental inasmuch as it is under the action of the absolutely First Cause, a second cause may yet be considered to be principal cause in respect of the instruments it itself employs. To God alone, who is independent of any anterior cause, does the name 'first cause' properly belong.

4. *Proximate and remote, or immediate and mediate, causes.*—A cause is *proximate* when between it and its effect no other agent interposes its action; otherwise it is a more or less *remote* cause.

5. *Physical and moral causes.*—A *physical* cause produces its effect by its own power, which it exercises immediately or by means of an instrument. A *moral* cause is one which acts upon the will of another by the presentation of something good or evil to it.

We have yet to determine where precisely the efficiency of this cause is formally completed: Is it in the cause or in the effect?

144. The Action of a Created Agent is in the Patient.—This may at first sight seem rather paradoxical, *actio fit in passo,* but the explanation is quite simple. The action of a creature presupposes a material cause, in which it works some change, accidental or substantial, some 'movement'. Now movement, being the actuality of a potential subject, takes place in the thing moved. Therefore action affects, not the agent or mover, but the thing moved, and is received in it as in a subject.

To this it may be objected that if movement does not touch the motor, how is it that a force expends itself by acting? The answer is that if the source of energy becomes exhausted, it is not from suffering anything from the action, but by the *reaction* that follows upon it. Every time a patient suffers an action, it reacts upon the agent, which in its turn then becomes the passive subject and suffers accordingly a diminution of its energy. All material activities are regulated by the law of action and reaction.

Action, then, is in the patient; it is received in it. From this it follows that every movement comprises a double relation, inasmuch as it reaches to the patient and proceeds from the agent. Under the latter aspect it is called *actio*, under the former *passio*. However 'action' and 'passion' (or perhaps it may be translated *endurance*) constitute one and the same reality, and are identical with movement; but they are different *concepts* of the same reality looked at from different points of view. Now, as the categories are not the direct expression of the things of nature, but are logical classifications of the concepts by which we represent them, 'action' and 'passion' are two different categories. As says St. Thomas, 'Actio et passio conveniunt in una substantia motus; differunt tamen secundum habitudines diversas'[61].

145. Has Aristotle's Theory of Movement, of Actio et Passio, a Universal Application?—The Aristotelian theory of movement, of 'action' and 'passion', is derived from an analysis of material movement. Now (*a*), whereas the production of this is a *transitive* action, can it be asserted that vital action, which is *immanent*, is also movement? And (*b*) furthermore, whilst second causes act upon matter, alike in the physical and metaphysical sense of the word, God, the First Cause, does not require matter as a subject necessary for creation, since in creation the creature is previously nothing actual; divine action therefore does not produce a 'movement': how then can creation that does not issue in movement be called action? In what sense is action applicable both to the efficient causality of movement and to creation?

146. The Sense in which Immanent Action is Movement.—The operations of a living body are immanent only in rela-

[61] St. Thomas, Cp. *Sum. Theol.*, I, q. 28, a. 3, ad 1; q. 45, a. 2, ad 2; II-II, q. 90, a. 3, c.

tion to the organism looked at in its entirety; the various material parts act upon one another, and their action is transitive. Hence the theory of movement applies every bit as much to organic beings as to inanimate bodies.

It is likewise applicable, though with a reservation, to psychical activities. Both knowledge and appetition are movements, inasmuch as they are the actuation respectively of the power of knowing and, in its widest sense, of moving towards. In the case of knowledge, the mind is influenced by some excitant and thereby determined to know: now this determination, considered in the knowing mind, is a *passio*, something suffered by it; considered as proceeding from the excitant, it is an *action*; and the actuation of the cognitive power by it is *movement*. Similarly appetition is a movement, the actuation of the will by a final cause: the inclination it feels when influenced by the presentation of the desirable good is, considered in the faculty receiving it, a *passio*, and considered in relation to the final cause to which it tends, some sort of *action*. The concept of movement does then apply also to psychical activities, but with one restriction: namely, that cognition and appetition are *immanent* activities and perfect the subject of the action and accordingly knowledge *does not react* upon the stimulus producing it nor appetition upon the good that motives it.

147. Creative Action.—Creative action, we have seen, cannot have as its resultant a 'movement', for unlike the action of creatures which makes some already existing thing pass from one manner of being to another and presupposes a subject that receives these modes of being, creative action excludes the pre-existence of a recipient subject. Considered, then, in the thing created, creation is not some change endured, a *passio*; nor, considered from the side of the creating cause, is it an *action* producing change. Looked at actively, expressed by 'to create', creation is the production of a substance in its entirety, primary matter and substantial form; looked at passively, expressed by 'to be created', it means a simple dependence of origin [62].

[62] 'Creatio non est mutatio nisi secundum modum intelligendi tantum. Nam de ratione mutationis est quod aliquid idem se habeat aliter nunc et prius. . . . Sed in creatione per quam producitur tota substantia rei non potest accipi aliquid idem aliter se habens nunc et prius nisi secundum intellectum tantum'. ST. THOMAS, *Sum. Theol.*, I, q. 45, a. 2, ad 2.

148. Action in General.—That action, considered in general, is wrongly imagined as some sort of passing of the cause into the effect our metaphysical analysis of movement makes evident: action does not modify the agent and therefore nothing passes out from the cause into the effect. What then is action? If we look to the different activities of inanimate and animate bodies, of spiritual faculties and to creative activity, we find that what is common is that *something is made to be which previously was not,* that *something is made to become*: *becoming* would seem therefore to be the formal resultant of all efficiency. 'If we take away motion, action implies nothing more than order of origin, in so far as action proceeds from some cause or principle to what is from that principle'[63].

149. Occasionalism.—According to the theory of occasionalism, invented by Malebranche (1638–1715), God is the one and only efficient cause; creatures are not true causes, but only 'occasional' causes, that is to say, they afford God occasions for acting but are not themselves possessed of any real native power of acting: 'they act only by the force and efficiency of the Divine Will'[64]. To this occasionalism Malebranche made just one exception, namely he allowed to the human will free action though without external efficacy.

150. Criticism.—*First proof that the creature is an efficient cause.* If I consider myself acting, I become conscious of two things: first, that my act is real and, secondly, that until it is over and done with, it is throughout dependent upon me. This double consciousness affords a valid proof of my own causal power. Moreover I observe that between certain external phenomena and my internal acts there is a constant correlation: which is evident proof that the former are caused by the latter. I will, for instance, to move my arm and it moves, or that it should remain still and it does not move; I determine the force with which it shall move and it moves to a nicety. What more complete inductive proof of the efficiency of our will-action upon the external world?

Second proof that the creature is an efficient cause.—1. If

[63] 'Remoto motu, actio nihil aliud importat quam ordinem originis, secundum quod a causa aliqua vel principio procedit in id quod est a principio.' ST. THOMAS, *Sum. Theol.* I, q. 41, a. 1, ad 2.

[64] *De la recherche de la vérité*, liv. 6me, 2 Partie, ch. III.

we study the things of nature we see a marvellous variety in type, in internal constitution and in function. Now what is all this profuse variety in their natures for, if they are not efficient causes? Such richness would be purposeless and a meaningless prodigality. Malebranche who makes the distinguishing mark of the Creator as opposed to the creature to consist in His being the sole efficient cause, here undoubtedly shows us a most unskilful and unreasonable Architect.

2. *Occasionalism compromises free-will.*—Again by attempting to safeguard the free causality of the human will, Malebranche is inconsistent with his general system. If God alone enjoys the dignity of cause and it is derogatory to Him for finite creatures to be causes of their actions, why still allow that man is master of such acts as take place in his will?

3. *Occasionalism leads to idealism.*—It was seen in Criteriology (**45**, **60**) that we cannot come at the existence of things outside ourselves except by establishing that these beings make impressions upon us by their activity. Now, if we deny that they are efficient causes, what validity is left to our proof that real things exist in the external world? Still more are we unable to say anything about the nature of the realities forming the world. We can never get beyond ourselves and our own mental states.

4. *Occasionalism leads to pantheism.*—If God is the only cause, what utility has the world? Why not straightway deny its real existence and assert phenomena to be but manifestations of one divine substance? The step is a short one to confounding creatures with the personal God.

151. The Principle of Causality.—The Principle of Causality is often regarded by scientists to be nothing more than a general law of physics: that is to say, no material manifestation—mechanical, physical or chemical—ever occurs without having a material antecedent, or efficient, cause. So enunciated, the principle applies only to the physical world and has no *metaphysical* signification. Yet is it not patient of another enunciation with this wider sense? Understood in a metaphysical sense we think that the principle may be stated thus: *The existent being to which existence is not essential exists in virtue of some action external to it.* Other proposed enunciations the reader will find we have discussed in Criteriology (**40**).

III. The Final Cause

152. Introductory.—A general conclusion we have reached from our study in the last few pages is that for 'movement' there is required the intervention of two intrinsic causes—the material and formal causes—and one extrinsic, the efficient cause. Now are these three sufficient for the production of 'movement'? Some, the mechanists, assert that they are. Teleologists, on the other hand, require the additional influence of a final cause, if the order of universe is to be adequately explained. Design, purpose, finality, they find to be an evident fact in the world, and this must be the immediate effect of a final cause. That *there are final causes*, then, they are at one in asserting; but whether there is one in every particular case and what may be its nature and what the precise extent of its finality they do not determine.

As to the *character* of the finality which is realized in the world there is a divergence of opinion among teleologists: Descartes, Leibniz, and the French Eclectics profess that it is *extrinsic*; Aristotle, St. Thomas and Scholastics in general that it is above all *intrinsic* and *immanent*. This does not however imply that Scholastic philosophy denies extrinsic finality: on the contrary, it considers that some things of nature are made for others, that they are 'useful' to one another. For example, the elements that go to make up our atmosphere are so nicely mixed that in every climate organic life is rendered possible; the organic kingdom is subordinate to the animal kingdom; our globe is just so situated in relation to the sun as to conduce to the maintenance and development of organic life. What is meant is that these relations of extrinsic purpose are the result of a much deeper finality that is *inherent* in every substantial being. Whereas, then, according to the Cartesian theory the *extrinsic* order of nature is achieved by God solely by the means of efficient causes and maintained solely by the external action of His Divine Providence, for Aristotle and St. Thomas there is in the very depths of all beings a tendency which draws them to their ends and directs thereto the exercise of their forces and, while they are thus all pursuing their own intrinsic ends, other relations of extrinsic finality exist between them and constitute the harmony of the universe. In the Scholastic theory the extrinsic finality of the universe follows from the internal orientation and disposition of each individual being.

Before justifying this conception of nature, it will be profitable first to analyse some of the ideas involved.

153. A Fuller Concept of Final Cause. Voluntary and Physical Finality.—Let us take an example in which the causality of the final cause is apparent :—A young man decides to become a doctor. He sets himself to attend lectures and to read the branches of study specified for the medical profession. Why does he do this if not to obtain his degree, which will admit him to the profession. Because to be a doctor is a career in life that appeals to him and is a good for him, he pursues the studies which lead to it.

Purpose (finis) is a desired good which, because it is desired, determines the will to choose an action or line of action judged to be necessary or useful for its attainment. Aristotle defines it as *that for the sake of which* something is done or made, *id cujus gratia aliquid fit.*

The end or purpose is a *cause,* since besides the fact that in the absence of the volition of it certain definite actions would not occur (which is also the case with a *conditio sine quâ non*), it exercises a *positive influence* upon the manifestation of certain actions and upon the order of their succession; and to exercise a positive influence is characteristic of a cause.

Furthermore, in the example we have just given the final cause is a *known* good; the finality or tendency towards a willed end is directed by a judgment; it is, as the Scholastics say, 'elicita', a 'psychical' act. Our fellow men as well as ourselves order their actions to some final result, which is their purpose and influences their actions as means leading to it. Similarly do animals seek things they *perceive* and *want,* and adapt their actions with a view to the attainment of them.

But outside and beyond conscious volition and appetitions we can discern in the physical world this same causality. There we see a wonderful interplay of countless, varied and ever-renewed operations issuing into results that are *consistently good and useful.* This constant repetition of the same results alike in the vegetable and mineral kingdoms, as well as in the animal and human, demands for its causal explanation the influence of a final cause.

In both cases, in the subject possessing an inner sense or

consciousness, where finality is conscious and voluntary and the influence of a purpose known and willed, and also in the physical world, where it is neither known nor voluntary, the influence is the effect of one and the same fundamental cause, the finality of a *final cause*.

What is the nature of this causality?

Let us try and determine the nature of this causality.

154. The Causality of the Final Cause.—The final cause exercises an attraction upon the active powers of beings and determines these powers or forces so attracted to will or to tend towards the good offered to them. From this it is clear that the causality of the final cause consists in an *attraction* which it exercises upon the will and a consequent *tendency* in the same power or faculty towards the good offered. Regarded from the side of the final cause, it is an *attraction* exercised by the end upon the appetitive faculty; regarded from the side of the faculty suffering this attraction, it is a *passive modification*. This modification gives rise to a desire in the will towards its good, a *tendency* or, as we call it, an '*intention*' (in-tendere). The intention of a purpose involves, as a natural consequence, the desire of the means which lead to its attainment; and, finally, this desire is the determining cause of such actions as have to be performed for the end first entertained and willed to be realized.

For a right conception of the causality of the final cause we must avoid imagining that the attraction it exercises is a physical *effect* of an *efficient cause*: for precisely when considered as an end, the good does not yet really exist in nature, and therefore it cannot exercise a physical action on the subject who is pursuing his desires. Similarly we must guard against representing it as the physical effect of an act of knowledge: for knowledge of the good to be obtained is the *condition* without which the attraction of the object would not influence the conscious subject, whereas the attraction is something belonging to the good itself. The final cause is, then, the good presented to the will, and its causality consists in the attraction which the good has for the appetitive faculty and in the inclination which it engenders there. 'Sicut influere causae efficientis est agere, ita influere causae finalis est appeti et desiderari', is St. Thomas' summing up[65].

[65] *De veritate*, q. 22.

This theory of finality is not limited to conscious volitions and appetitions, but applies also to the final cause as manifested in the domain of unconscious nature. Here it is still always a passive inclination, an 'intention', but the conditions of its exercise are different. Here, unlike the voluntary inclination which is evoked through the perception or imagination of a good end, the tendency is *natural* and innate to the subject. Again, whilst the voluntary inclination is an accidental formal cause, the natural tendency is *identical with the substantial form* of the specific type[66]. This tendency which unconscious beings possess towards their ends the mediaeval Scholastics did not hesitate to call *intentio naturae* or *appetitus naturalis*.

This analysis of final cause will aid us to a better understanding of the meaning of *nature* and *natural law*.

155. The Meaning of 'Nature'.—Nature is in reality identical with substance. Nevertheless we must not conceive it, as the mechanists do, as any sort of substance endowed with any sort of forces; it is substance considered precisely as an *intrinsic, first principle of operations that are proper to the being which produces or undergoes them.* According to Aristotle 'natura est principium quoddam (est causa) motus et quietis, quatenus ad ipsum pertinet primo per se, et non per accidens'[67].

Most of what is comprised in this definition has already been explained above when we considered the idea of *nature* (87), so that only a few points remain to be considered here.

Nature is called a *first* principle of action to distinguish it from natural forces or faculties which are *derived* and *immediate* principles of action. Further, it is called *intrinsic* to distinguish it from the efficient cause and the exemplary cause, both of which are extrinsic, the one to the effect and the other to the work completed after it as model. Lastly, it is said to be the principle of operations *proper* to the subject, for the reason that not every operation of which a being may be the subject is 'natural': some there are that are contrary to its nature and on this account are termed 'violent' or 'unnatural'.

[66] 'Res naturalis per *formam* qua perficitur in sua specie, habet inclinationem in proprias operationes et proprium finem, quem per operationes consequitur: quale est enim unumquodque, talia operatur et in sibi convenientia tendit'. ST. THOMAS, *Cont. Gent.*, IV, 19.

[67] *Phys.*, II, c. 1.

Only those manifestations of activity are natural to a subject which subserve the purpose for which it exists.

Every being that finds a place in the real world has an end of its own, a purpose it is to fulfil. To enable it to obtain this, it requires some suitable, or 'proper', powers of action; powers which, since the end of the being remains the same throughout, remain the distinctive properties of the being throughout its existence. Now for their stability these powers require, in each being, a persistent substrate in which they have their foundation; a substantial substrate that is their ultimate principle, and to which the tendency towards the being's natural end must in last analysis be attributed. Such a substrate, substance so conceived, Aristotle calls 'nature'.

After these explanations there should be little difficulty in understanding what are *laws of nature.*

156. Teleological Conception of Natural Law.—According to mechanistic philosophy *law* means the regular and constant appearance of certain phenomena as the necessary consequent of certain material antecedents. It is a law, for example, that every living being derives its origin from a living cell; which means to say, placed in certain conditions necessary for its division or reproduction, a cell will divide or reproduce itself and inevitably give birth to a new organic individual. In the regular recurrence of natural phenomena the chief feature that strikes the mechanist is the rigid determinism: from such and such antecedents such and such consequents must inevitably follow.

Now mechanism states a fact but does not explain it, or rather it explains it only up to a point. Whilst the main object of experimental science is indeed to assign to a phenomenon its material antecedents and to notice the invariable character of the bond connecting them, there is yet beyond the scientific question a further problem which the experimental sciences cannot face and which falls properly within the domain of metaphysics. When we have learnt that certain antecedents are inevitably followed by a certain phenomenon, and have further observed that these various antecedents, these forces whose exercise is the reason of the phenomenon, are in far the greater number of cases productive of useful effects, the question arises why it is that in spite of differences of place, time and circumstances the same useful types—types that are beautiful and good—ever recur. For this felicitous behaviour of all the forces of nature, for this regular recurrence of the same effects, a sufficient reason must exist; and it does exist, according to the teleological conception of nature, in *final causes.*

These must not, however, be thought to take the place of efficient causes: the actual presence of the conditions required for a force to act are the *determining reason* of its doing so in any particular case. It is the constant, harmonious direction of the manifold forces of a subject to one end that the final cause, the fundamental inclination of nature towards this end, is required to explain.

In brief, then, a *law of nature* is an internal fundamental determination in virtue of which a substance, as a first principle of action, tends to realize a determinate effect. When the effect for which a thing's nature is made becomes realized, the thing is said to be *obeying*, or *following, its law.*

It may happen, however, that a thing does not follow the law of its nature, that some other effect than that aimed at by its nature is attained, and in this case an *accidental effect* occurs.

157. Accidental Effects.—*Natural* causes and effects must be carefully distinguished from *accidental* causes and effects.

A *natural* effect is one determined by the very nature of the efficient cause. 'Effectus *per se* causae naturalis est id quod consequitur secundum exigentiam suae formae', or again: 'effectus *per se* causae naturalis est quod evenit ex intentione naturae'. When the agent has knowledge and can will the effect, when it is 'ex proposito', prepense, it is said to be *intentional*: 'effectus causae agentis a proposito est illud quod accidit ex intentione agentis'.

An *accidental* effect is opposed alike to natural and intentional effects: 'quidquid provenit in effectu praeter intentionem est *per accidens*'. It is one which happens contrary to the natural tendency of the agent; in fact one we commonly speak of as an *accident,* a chance-event or a coincidence. Just as a cause is said to be *natural* when it produces an effect in accordance with its proper end, so the same cause is said to be *accidental* when there attaches either to it or its effect some event that is incidental, something not included in the scope of its end[68]. An accidental effect, then, is not the product of any one particular cause alone: for, if the teleological conception of the universe is true, every real being is bound to produce its own definite kind of effect, its 'natural effect', and can produce no other. If an accident happens, it can do so only by some second cause concurrently acting—in accordance with its own nature—and counteracting the production of the natural effect of a first cause. Hence it would be wrong to speak of the natural cause of an accident; it may be explained by the coincident action of two or more natural causes, but the coincidence itself, strictly speaking, has no cause: there is nothing in nature predetermining it. Observe how this leaves the principle of causality intact: the accidental effect results from two causes or two series of natural causes which 'fall out' together and react upon each other.

Let it also be noted that when we say that natural causes combine and produce an accidental effect without there being any objective bond uniting them, we are taking up a purely *relative* standpoint; we are viewing the coincidence of natural causes as we know them, from the point of view of *human knowledge*, not from that of the Divine knowledge. Divine Providence must have taken into account the encounter of two or more causes and the resulting event of their conjoined activities.

Lastly, notice that only that event may be called an accidental effect which does not occur regularly and constantly. When an event that hitherto we have put down to the fortuitous meeting of two or more natural causes occurs with constant regularity, we change our opinion of it, since the coincidence-theory no longer satisfies our need of a causal explanation, and we find ourselves compelled to ascribe it to an habitual cause, to a law of nature.

[68] 'Sicut entium quoddam est per se et quoddam per accidens, ita et causarum: sicut per se domus causa est ars aedificatoria, per accidens vero album et musicum. Sed considerandum est quod causa per accidens dicitur dupliciter: Uno modo ex parte causæ, alio modo ex parte effectus. Ex parte quidem causæ, quando illud quod dicitur causa per accidens, conjungitur causæ per se, sicut si album vel musicum dicatur causa domus, quia accidentaliter conjungitur ædificatori. Ex parte autem effectus, quando accipitur aliquid quod accidentaliter conjungitur effectui: ut si dicamus quod ædificator est causa discordiæ, quia ex domo facta accidit discordia'. ST. THOMAS *In. II Phys.* lect. 8.

158. Corollary: Three Meanings of Natural Law.—Since the order, or orderliness, of a whole makes a far more vivid appeal to the imagination than that of the parts of a whole, the human mind has ever spontaneously considered the order of the whole universe as the work of a supreme Master who imposes His will upon the several elements of which it is made; and thus it would seem, as Suarez suggests, that 'law' originally presented itself to the human mind as a commandment—i.e. of the Creator. Only secondly do the various scientific conceptions of law come to be formed and accordingly by way of metaphor. We may then, by proceeding deductively, distinguish three kinds of law:—

1. In its most fundamental sense law designates the *natural inclination* of a being towards the end appropriated to it by the Author of nature, an inclination or inherent tendency which is the internal reason of all its activities converging to this end.

2. As the result of all the forces of a being converging to one and the same end is a constant and uniform manner of action on the part of the being, law denotes in a more superficial acceptation *this uniform and constant manner of action* of the things in the universe.

3. Lastly, as the uniformity and constancy of action depends on certain extrinsic conditions, the relation of an action to the conditions of its exercise must be taken into account in the formulation of a law, and this gives us a third, and the usual, meaning of law as *the expression of the relation between an action and its extrinsic conditions.* An example of such is the law of gravitation that enunciates that bodies attract one another in direct proportion to their masses and in inverse proportion to the square of their distances.

159. Necessity of the Laws of Nature.—We may now inquire what is meant when the laws of nature are said to be necessary.

A thing is said to be *necessary* which cannot but exist or be so, and to be *contingent* which can not-be or be otherwise. Moreover necessity may be *absolute* or *conditional.* An event is *absolutely* necessary when this necessity is due to an *antecedent* cause—material, formal or efficient—of its appearance; it is *conditionally* necessary when its appearance depends upon a free end: for example, although you need not build a house, although there is no absolute necessity for you to build it, yet *if* you will do so, you are bound—by a *consequent* necessity depending on the condition of your willing it—to make use of materials requisite for building.

Now mechanists consider natural phenomena to be effects of a rigid determinism, to be necessarily produced by efficient causes, and in consequence natural laws to be *absolutely* necessary by an *antecedent* necessity. On the other hand, the teleological conception is that phenomena are ruled by the natural ends beings possess, and that since these ends need not have been willed, the laws of nature are only *conditionally* necessary by a *consequent* necessity.

Adopting this latter view, how far are we to say that this conditional necessity extends?

We say that law in its deepest, fundamental sense, as denoting the *natural inclination* of a being towards its end, is necessary. Does it, however, follow from this that the being which by the law of its nature is directed always to one and the same end is bound with the same necessity and constancy to put forth its activity; in other words, that law in the sense signifying the *uniform manner of action* of a being in nature is also necessary? By no means: the activity of beings depends on the presence of certain conditions, in default of which the effect will not occur. In some cases indeed these requisite conditions belong of their nature to the most general qualities of matter, and so are to be found always and everywhere realized in nature. But in other cases the conditions upon which phenomena depend are many and complex and bound up with special qualities of certain bodies, and therefore are to be met with only at some times and in some places; and hence the laws governing phenomena of this kind will admit of exceptions. There are, then, two distinct classes of laws in nature: one universal and without exception, the other special to certain classes of beings and allowing of exceptions [69].

These exceptions to natural laws we must not neglect to consider, but let us do so after briefly comparing the different ways in which a being may act.

160. Comparison of the Different Ways in which Material Beings may act.—'Natural' movements are those whereof the determining cause is an inclination of nature. Opposed to them are movements determined by some cause extrinsic

[69] Cp. large edition, n. 245.

to the moving being; these are not natural but 'communicated', such, e.g., as the movement of an engine under the action of steam. Further, if the external impulse goes against the being's natural tendency, the movement so produced is *forced* or *by constraint*, or as the Scholastics used to call it, *violent*: e.g. the movement of a stone thrown into the air by some force opposed to that of gravity.

161. Chance, or Fortune.—An accidental effect we have seen (157) to result from the coincidence of two natural causes which are independent of each other. Now among these effects are to be found those that happen by '*chance*' or '*luck*' (good or bad). According to Aristotle a *fortuitous* event is one which happens contrary to the intention either of nature or of a person's deliberate will. When in our examination of phenomena we discover regular and constant relations, we attribute them to an 'intentional', or final, cause; when there is no sign of a purposive cause having sought or willed them, we immediately ascribe them to chance. 'Casus accidit in his quae sunt praeter aliquid. . . . Cum aliquid fit extra naturam in operationibus naturae, puta cum nascitur sextus digitus, dicimus quod est a casu'[70].

It might be noticed that there is room for a distinction to be made between *casus* and *fortuna*—perhaps we might say between *chance* and *luck* (good and bad). To the former is ascribed an event which happens beside the purpose of nature, 'accidit praeter intentionem naturae'; whilst that which happens beyond what a conscious voluntary cause foresees and intends is put down to good or bad fortune.

Because a chance-event in general has not an intentional cause, we must not therefore say it is an effect without a cause. Being an accidental effect it is produced by the coincidence of two or more purposive causes, moral or physical: 'casus et fortuna sunt causae per accidens eorum quorum intellectus et natura sunt causae per se'.

Just as accidental effects enter into the plan of Providence (157), so chance-effects are such only in respect of our limited intelligence: they are willed by God and accordingly have in Him their intention or purpose, which however escapes us. As we judge things only as they are in the ordinary course, we fail to discover any purpose they subserve when

[70] ST. THOMAS, *In Phys.* II, lect. 10; cp. ARISTOTLE, *Physic.* III, 5.

they are not in accordance with the habitual 'intentions' of nature.

IV. The Exemplary Cause

162. Meaning of Exemplary Cause.—We have so far distinguished four kinds of causes—material, formal, efficient and final—and yet it would seem, at first sight, that we have not mentioned all the causes. In a work of art, for instance a statue, we may have learnt the efficient cause, the artist, and the material and formal causes, the marble of which it is made and the special form the artist gives it by his chisel, and the final cause, the aesthetic charm of the finished work. Still there remains, other and above, another cause, namely the *idea* which has guided the sculptor throughout his work and which he has striven to make real. And this is a true *cause* inasmuch as it has a positive influence upon the production of the work.

This, then, is what is meant by the *exemplary* or *ideal* cause. It is *the mental type according to which an intelligent efficient cause produces his effect.* Or, as St. Thomas describes it: 'Idea est forma, quam aliquis imitatur ex intentione agentis determinante sibi finem' [71].

After this definition let us inquire into the nature of its causality.

163. Causality of the Idea.—Ought the exemplary cause to be classed as a separate cause, or may we reduce it to one or more of the four causes already studied?

Its nature is complex, for it may be regarded from two different points of view: from a subjective standpoint it is an intellectual act of the efficient cause, and from an objective standpoint it is an ideal which is realized in the object effected by the efficient cause. From the first point of view it is obviously an *efficient* cause: for it is an act of the intellect, and every act of the intellect effects an inclination in the will. And from the objective point of view—which is of chief interest to us here—the exemplary cause is both a *final* cause and an *extrinsic formal* cause.

The exemplary cause is a *final* cause inasmuch as it is towards this ideal that the artist tends when he is sculpturing his statue. Nor does it make any difference that an end, as a

[71] *De veritate*, q. 3, a. 1.

final cause, is always a concrete good, whereas an ideal is a representation of an abstract type. For the artist regards his ideal *in so far as it is capable of concrete realization*; he represents it to himself not only by an abstract idea but also by his imagination and in so far as it can be reproduced in his work: and it is as such that it is an object of attraction for his will. Hence with reason St. Thomas says: 'Forma exemplaris habet quodammodo rationem finis'[72].

Yet whilst the idea is a final cause, it is one of a particular nature. Truly it is *that for which* a thing is done, yet it is also *that after which* the agent strives and which rules his acts. It is a model to which he strives to conform in realizing his work, an end which entails imitation and which, as such, determines the features of the work produced under its influence; and for this reason it deserves to be classed as a *formal* cause. Nevertheless it is not a formal cause that is intrinsically part of the subject, but one that determines it from without; it is therefore an *extrinsic formal* cause, and herein lies the peculiar nature of its causality.

In short, the exemplary cause has a complex causal influence; it is at once an efficient, final and, in a fashion, a formal cause. Hence its causality partakes of more than one kind of cause and cannot be reduced exclusively to any one of the traditional four causes.

V. Comparison of the Four Causes

164. Cause in General.—In the preceding pages we have examined the different kinds of causes and endeavoured to determine the nature of the causality peculiar to each. It is time now to inquire what they have in common; to ask, What is cause in general? What is its generic meaning?

Each of the four causes has clearly its own peculiar causality: *matter* is that which receives a form and by union with it helps to compose a substance (**133**); *form* is that which is intrinsically communicated to matter and by union with it constitutes a substance of a determinate kind (**135**); the *efficient* cause is an extrinsic principle of 'movement' (**139**); the *final* cause or purpose that which exercises an attraction or inclination upon a subject (**153**). Now to these four causes there appears to belong no single common element. It follows

[72] *De veritate*, q. 3, a. 1, c.

therefore that cause is not a genus whereof the four causes are species. The most there is amongst them is an *analogical* resemblance, and this it behoves us further to determine.

165. Principle ; Cause ; Element ; Reason.—The idea of *cause* is contained in the more general idea of *principle* : every cause is a principle, though not every principle is a cause.

Principle may be taken according to its etymological signification or in its strict, philosophical sense. In the former sense, which is more frequent in Latin (principium) and French (principe) than in English, it involves the idea of *priority* of one thing in respect of another ; not necessarily of being first (*primum esse*), but of being anterior to something coming after (*prius esse*) : e.g. the starting point of the different local positions of a thing moving might be called in this sense the ' principle ', or beginning, of movement. In its philosophical signification principle implies in addition a relation of *dependence* borne by the second thing in respect of the first : so that in this sense the first hour of the day is not the principle of the second, since there is only an extrinsic relation between the one and the other. Moreover this dependence must be one of a positive influence of the first thing over the second : and hence ' privation ', for example, which although really connected with the introduction of a new form into matter does not positively influence the generation of that form (*Cosmology*, 74), is not a principle. In this strict sense it has reference either to the intrinsic *constitution* of a thing, to its *production* or to *knowledge* ; as Aristotle says, ' It is common to all beginnings (principles) to be the first point from which a thing either is or comes to be or is known '[73]. Principles of being and becoming are known as *ontological* or *real* principles ; judgments leading to the knowledge of further judgments as *logical* principles. It is with the former we are especially concerned here.

Although priority is essential to a principle, it need not necessarily be a *priority of time*, which implies simply chronological succession, but may be a *priority of nature*, which consists in the existence of the derived thing (principatum) depending upon the existence of the antecedent principle, whilst the existence of the latter in no way depends upon that of the former. For example, the union of the soul with the body naturally pre-

[73] *Metaph.*, IV, c. 1 (Tra. Ross, Bk. V, c. 1).

supposes the creation of the soul and the presence of the requisite dispositions in the matter, whilst the creation is not in point of time subsequent to its union with the body.

Ontological principles are in reality identical with causes, since a *cause* (*causa*, *αἴτια*) is whatever a thing is positively dependent upon either for its reality or becoming: 'Causae dicuntur ex quibus res dependet secundum esse suum vel fieri'.

Element is a kindred notion, inasmuch as it means one of the first internal components of a thing—'Elementum est ex quo componitur res primo, et est in eo'; and material cause is defined to be that of which a thing is made. Elements therefore are the material cause.

Lastly, the principles and causes, including elements, constitute the *reasons* of things. Whatever belonging to a thing's essence or contributing to its existence we require to know in order to understand a thing, is its reason. The reasons of things are then their principles and causes considered in relation to a mind endeavouring to understand them. Thus the reason of a thing is the same as its explanation; and its explanation lies in the internal principles which constitute it and in the causes which determine its existence. Furthermore, the sum of these principles upon which a being depends is the *sufficient reason* of that being; and therefore to know the full reason of anything we must know all the principles that constitute it and make it the actual thing that it is.

CHAPTER III

THE RELATIONS OF THE FOUR CAUSES TO ONE ANOTHER

166. The Final Cause exercises its Causality First.—Any change or 'movement' taking place in nature involves the introduction of a new accidental or substantial form into a subject through the action of an efficient cause. The *material and formal* causes therefore exercise their causality in dependence upon the action of the *efficient* cause. Yet the efficient cause is directed by the *final* cause; therefore this last is the *first* of the causes, the cause of the other causes, 'causa causarum'[74].

167. The Order of Execution is the Opposite to that of Intention.—Consider the case of an engineer who forms the intention of constructing a railway engine: his *purpose* is to have coaches drawn along the railroad; in order to realize this, he makes designs, considers the interworking of the various parts and calculates the weight that must be drawn, etc.; he then makes the engine; and last of all when everything has been done, the engine is set going and the whole train moves. Here we see that the first intention of the engineer was the last thing to be realized, 'primum intentione,

[74] 'Causa efficiens et finis sibi correspondent invicem, quia efficiens est principium motus, finis autem terminus. Et similiter materia et forma: nam forma dat esse, materia autem recipit. Est igitur efficiens causa finis, finis autem causa efficientis. Efficiens est causa finis quantum ad esse, quidem, quia movendo perducit efficiens ad hoc, quod *sit* finis. Finis autem est causa efficientis non quantum ad esse sed quantum ad *rationem causalitatis*. Nam efficiens est causa in quantum agit; non autem agit nisi causa finis (gratia finis). Unde ex fine habet suam causalitatem efficiens'. St. Thomas, *In V Metaph.* lect. 2.—'Sciendum quod licet finis sit ultimus in esse in quibusdam, in causalitate tamen est prior semper, unde dicitur *causa causarum*, quia est causa causalitatis in omnibus causis. Est enim causa causalitatis efficientis, ut jam dictum est. Efficiens autem est causa causalitatis et materiae et formae'. *Ibid.*, lect. 3.

ultimum in executione; ordo intentionis et ordo executionis ad invicem opponuntur'.

After studying causes (Chap. II) and their relations (Chap. III), we may now consider their general effect, namely, *the order of nature* (Chap. IV). Now this order of the universe has its foundation in the intrinsic finality or purpose that is inherent in nature. This *intrinsic, immanent* order realized in everything in nature we shall consider first (Art. I); and next the order that results from the relations of extrinsic finality between the various beings, or the *extrinsic universal order* (Art. II).

CHAPTER IV

THE GENERAL EFFECT OF THE CAUSES: THE ORDER OF NATURE

ART. I. THE IMMEDIATE EFFECT OF THE CAUSES: THE INHERENT ORDER IN THE WORKS OF NATURE

I. The Idea of Order

168. The Meaning of Order.—The regular interplay of causes produces a number of relations which together make up the order of nature. Now order implies: (1) several things distinct from one another; (2) certain relations of succession between them; (3) some single principle which governs these relations. 'Ordo nihil aliud dicit quam rationem prioris et posterioris in distinctis sub aliquo uno principio'[75]. Consider books on a shelf: to be put in order they have to be taken one after another and arranged according to some one principle of unity.

If we inquire what is this principle of unity necessary for order, we see that it is the purpose for which the work is 'ordained' or set about. In the example, the order of the books will vary as one chooses to arrange them according to contents or according to their size. In a word, the first principle of unity of order is the *end* of the work into which order is introduced. Hence St. Thomas has the further definition: *Order is the exact adaptation of things to their ends*—Recta ratio rerum ad finem'[76].

169. Teleological Order and Aesthetical Order, or Order of Subordination and of Co-ordination. General Definition of Order.—As things 'in order' are arranged with a view to some purpose, they may be considered as so many means making for its realization. Now the relation of a means to

[75] St. Thomas, *Sum. Theol.*, I, q. 47, a. 2, c.
[76] *Id.*, *In II Phys.*, lect. 13.

an end is one of subordination; therefore 'order' designates first and chiefly the *order of subordination*. The various parts, however, that are arranged may be regarded not only as means to an end but also as elements of a whole; and so regarded they give rise to an order of composition or constitution, an *order of co-ordination*. These two kinds of order bear different names: the former, that of subordination, being by excellence that of utility or purposive, *teleological order*; the latter, that of co-ordination, the orderliness or harmony of beauty, in a word *aesthetical order*. In reality the two kinds are only different aspects of one and the same order; but the former, inasmuch as the end is the principle reducing many things to the unity of a single whole, dominates the latter; the teleological, the aesthetic.

These two aspects which order presents enable us to define order generically as the exact arrangement of things, in the relations required by their end. The comma is inserted designedly to mark off the first part which refers to the order of co-ordination, from the second part which refers to that of subordination.

170. The Order in the Universe proves the Existence of Final Causes.—In the universe, alike in its parts and as a whole, we see exhibited order that is at once complex and constant. Now such order could neither exist nor persist unless there were final causes. Therefore there do exist such causes.

Proof of the major.—We perceive in the universe (1) manifestations of an *absolute* order; (2) of a *relative* order among its parts and also between all parts and the whole; (3) a *persistent* order, absolute and relative, maintained by the continuous renewal of the factors which go to form it. Of these three kinds of orderliness which it is convenient to distinguish let us take examples:—

1. The order that reigns in organic individuals is an example of what we mean by *absolute* order. In Psychology (**13**) we described the *co-ordination* of the various parts which together form a living cell and the wonderful *subordination* of its functions to the welfare of the organism. And this same double order, this same unity and convergence of functions is displayed in the highest organisms and in man (*Psychology*, **79** and **153**).

2. Besides having this order in their internal constitution, things of nature are related 'in order' to one another also. Thus, for instance, the chlorophyl action of plants and the breathing of animals maintain just that mixture of oxygen and carbon in the atmosphere as to allow both kingdoms to live. This is an example of what we may call *particular relative order*. But there is also a *universal relative* order, striking examples of which are the laws of the universe: the universal law of gravitation, the laws of the balance of natural forces and of the constancy of energy, etc.

3. The universe is the scene of incessant change so that at no two moments is it the same; yet in spite of this incessant change, its order ever remains: the same natural types with their same internal order continue to appear, and between the various beings the same relations of co-ordination and subordination are maintained.

In short there is order in the universe, both in individual beings and amongst them. And its most notable feature is its persistence.

Proof of the minor.—In explanation of the order of the universe two theories have been put forward: namely, that of mechanism and the teleological theory of Aristotle and Aquinas.

According to mechanism there are only efficient causes and no final ones: the elements out of which the universe is made have no inclination or tendency to form any order whatsoever, they are indifferent to order and to disorder. But this explanation is in reality no explanation:—

1. In the first place consider phenomena exhibiting *absolute* order. According to the mechanists, the chemical bodies that make up living organisms are in no way *predisposed* to form part of the organic whole, but are *indifferent* to entering into any combination, organic or inorganic. Yet what explanation is forthcoming of these utterly indifferent bodies entering *regularly* into such definite combinations as those which form the chemical basis of an organism? Every effect demands its adequate cause; and therefore elements which are perfectly indifferent cannot explain why definite compounds are formed.—Furthermore material elements, left to themselves, are actually *opposed* to the absolute order of the being which they unite to form: they display activities that

in many respects are of an opposite character to those of living beings. Thus some chemical combinations when in the inorganic world present a maximum of stability, whereas the same chemical forms in organic beings are highly unstable. From this it is clear that, if left to themselves, the chemical elements of living bodies would render any specific activity on the part of the latter impossible.

2. Similarly purely indifferent forces would not only fail to account for the phenomena we perceive of *relative* order but would militate against it. Take for example that nice composition of the atmosphere which allows vegetable and animal life to be maintained in every latitude. In the first place, to attribute to elements that in themselves are entirely indifferent a phenomenon which is no less than the *regular converging* of diverse forces towards a joint good end, the continuance of vegetable and animal life, is to fail utterly in assigning a sufficient reason. On the contrary, if the principles supposed to produce the phenomenon of relative order be not inherently adapted and ordained to produce it, they would make it impossible. Animals would go on giving off carbonic acid gas indefinitely and plants would go on indefinitely absorbing it by their green matter, but the two kingdoms, acting independently of each other, would be bound together by none of those relations of purpose which make for the present state of the atmosphere that is indispensable for the normal functioning of life. In short, indifferent causes would militate against the order obtaining between the various things of nature and making them dependent upon one another.

3. The *persistency* of the order in the universe above all would remain without any causal explanation if there were simply efficient causes. Nay more, it would be destroyed by them. For if order be supposed by some chance once to exist in the universe it would immediately be followed by disorder, since indifferent causes, as we have just seen, neither make nor allow perpetually changing actions consistently to converge towards good and useful results such as those we see constantly realized in nature.

We may take it then as demonstrated that mechanism is unable to explain the order, alike absolute and relative, in the universe, and still less its persistence. We must therefore have recourse to some principle of finality, of inherent purpose, if things do make for and achieve ends and a sufficient reason is to be found for these phenomena. The order of the universe is inexplicable except by principles which assert a compelling movement of all elements towards the maintenance of their specific type, an active tendency in each particular order of beings towards the well-being of its species or kingdom and, in general, a persistent impulsive movement towards the universal good [77].

171. Purpose is a Sign of Intelligence.—As soon as we become aware that there is order in a work, we instinctively feel the presence of a mind, of an intellectual cause behind it. Indeed if a number of things are arranged in fitting proportion so as to be subordinate to one end, we have clear evidence that a mind has been at work. Furthermore, we appraise the intellectual qualities of our fellows by the order or purpose they exhibit in what they do, by the way in which they make means subserve their ends: the half-witted man is known by the incoherence of his words and actions, and the sane man judged to be of superior or lower intelligence according as his deeds have a greater or less purposive bearing upon one another and together are adapted to his main object. In Natural Theology we speak of this subject again, when we come to prove in the proper place that the order in the universe bespeaks eminent wisdom on the part of the First Cause who established it.

172. Specific Form is the Principle of a Being's Inherent Purpose.—We have already often observed that substances act in accordance with their natures. Now the substantial form is that which makes a being to have specific qualities, to be of such a nature. Therefore it is the substantial form

[77] 'Quidam enim antiquissimi philosophi tantum posuerunt causam materialem. . . . Alii autem posteriores ponebant causam agentem, nihil dicentes de causa finali. Et secundum utrosque omnia procedebant de necessitate causarum procedentium, vel materiae, vel agentis. Sed haec positio hoc modo a philosophis improbatur. Causae enim materialis et agens, inquantum hujusmodi, sunt effectui causa essendi; non autem sufficiunt ad causandum bonitatem in effectu, secundum quam sit conveniens et in se ipso, ut permanere possit; et in aliis, ut opituletur; verbi gratia, calor de sui ratione, quantum de se est, habet dissolvere; dissolutio autem non est conveniens et bona nisi secundum aliquem certum terminum et modum; unde si non poneremus aliam causam praeter calorem . . . non possemus assignare causam quare res convenienter fiant et bene'. St. Thomas, *De veritate*, q. 5, a. 2, c.

which determines the character of a being's activity and makes it tend to what is its end or good.

Furthermore, since the qualities of the respective specific types are the foundation of the numerous relations obtaining between the beings of the universe—relations indeed that we express as the laws of nature—it follows that it is in the substantial forms of beings that the deep intrinsic reason of the order of the universe lies.

II. Perfection, the Fulfilment of Order

173. Meaning of Perfection. The Natural Perfection of Beings.—*Perfect* (=*perfectum, per-facere*) means that which is *completely made* or *finished off*. Accordingly a thing is perfect when it has all that it requires, everything that befits it; and the abstract, *perfection*, designates everything that befits a being. Now if we ask what that everything is, what is suited to a being, the answer is obviously: whatever is required for it to realize its destiny. In short, to be perfect means to be in possession of one's end or at least in a position to realize it.

Every being in the universe has its end to fulfil. That end is the measure of reality the being can hope to attain or does attain, and its attainment in philosophical language is called its *natural perfection*. Conversely beings are *imperfect* in proportion as they are in a state removed from that of their natural perfection. A child born blind is thus 'imperfect' by a 'natural defect'.

Yet the newly born child who has no natural imperfection only possesses its *essential* or *constitutive* perfection, or what St. Thomas calls *first* perfection; it is as yet only *capable* of fulfilling its destiny, and will not possess its *final* or *second* perfection until it enjoys the full exercise of *all* its faculties and powers.

In the present life man, then, is perfect only in a relative sense: as he cannot yet reach his final goal and come into possession of his end, he must continue in a partially imperfect state, lacking the complete perfection of which his nature is capable.

174. Absolute Perfection.—Only that being is perfect which has attained its end, and of it alone can absolute perfection be predicated. Yet even this absolute perfection is in one sense *relative*—when, that is, the being enjoying its end is compared to higher beings or to the Highest of all beings. Indeed we may consider any particular perfection in itself without paying regard to the limitations attaching to it as it is found realized in contingent beings, and as such it is *unlimited* and *absolute* and an abstract ideal in comparison with which the same perfection in a contingent being is *relative*. We may, too, by combining ideas conceive of a single perfection which contains in a supereminent way all absolute perfections, and by doing so we arrive at the idea of the *Absolutely Perfect* being or the *Infinite*. In respect of this Supreme Being all contingent beings are imperfect, or to change the word, they are finite and limited in contrast to infinite.

The imperfection which is opposed to absolute perfection is not the same as that which is the absence or *privation* of a definite being's natural perfection; it is the *negation* of some higher perfection which exists or may exist in another being or is realized in the All-perfect Being.

175. Kinds of Perfection.—In forming our ideas of any thing we make use of successive abstractions, by each of which we partially represent its total perfection. Now some complex perfections we thus build up we find formally to contain imperfection: such for example is the power of reasoning possessed by man. Such perfections are known as *mixed* inasmuch as they are an admixture of perfection and imperfection, and are opposed to *simple* ones, which we find formally neither imply imperfection nor exclude it. An instance of this class is ' life ', in the concept of which are neither implied the essential imperfections of vegetative life nor are they excluded. *Absolutely simple* perfections, ' perfectiones simpliciter simplices ', are those in the concept of which an imperfection is formally excluded. To rise to the idea of the Divine Being we unite into one concept all absolute simple perfections.

In the foregoing pages we have investigated order and perfection, the fulfilment or complement of order. We must now briefly consider the effect of the manifestation of perfection and order to our perceptive faculties, which effect is the sentiment of the beautiful.

III. The Beautiful, the Expression of Order and Perfection

176. Method of Procedure.—We might begin our study of the beautiful with a metaphysical definition of it, but to do so would lay us open to the suspicion of starting from a priori conceptions. Instead, then, let us begin with observation, and ask ourselves, When is it that man, face to face with some object of nature or art, spontaneously says, 'That is *beautiful*'? And when, in the same conditions, '*That is not beautiful*', 'This is *more beautiful* than that', 'This is exquisite, it is *beauty itself*'? By so proceeding we may apply to the facts of the aesthetic order the inductive methods, of concordance, of difference and of concomitant variations [78], with a view to discovering what are for the mind the distinctive characteristics of the beautiful. Should we find one or more such characteristics, we may then subject them to metaphysical analysis. Thus may we hope to reach a definition of the beautiful. When we have found it, it will be of interest to consider briefly a new question, of particular importance to-day, concerning the relations between art and morality.

177. Analysis of our Experience of the Beautiful—When and in what conditions does a thing affect us as beautiful?—A literary masterpiece, Dante's *Divina Commedia*, Shakespeare's *Macbeth*; a fine painting, the *Coronation of the Virgin* of Fra Angelico; an architectural wonder, the Gothic cathedrals of York or Salisbury; a symphony of Beethoven: are all works of art that captivate and enthral; the more we gaze or listen, the more eager we become to see them or hear them again. The landscape too, its vast prospect with sweeping lines, draws admiration and spellbound wonderment at its inherent charm. On the other hand there are sights and productions that we call 'commonplace', 'vulgar' or 'ugly', which leave us indifferent or even give positive displeasure. These facts make it sufficiently evident, as a first conclusion, that *the beautiful pleases us and the plain and the ugly leave us indifferent or displease us.*

But the *good* pleases us and affects us agreeably; it is by definition that which is the object of desire, the possession of which brings delight, 'bonum est quod omnia appetunt'. Is

[78] For the procedure and validity of inductive reasoning, see *Logic*, 88 ff.

the beautiful, then, identical with the good? No; for not all that is good is beautiful; all pleasure is not aesthetic pleasure. The enjoyment the epicure derives from a good dinner has nothing in common with the pleasure aroused by the beautiful. A mother loves her child, and even if deformed loves it still and perhaps the more. Thus whilst the beautiful causes pleasure, not everything that causes pleasure is beautiful. What is beautiful is good, but not all that is good is beautiful. Where then comes the difference between aesthetic pleasure and pleasure in general? In what does the beautiful differ from the good?

Aesthetic pleasure in anything always begins with the *knowledge* of it; it springs up in the soul at the presentation to it of things observed, heard, understood, contemplated, according to the definition of St. Thomas: 'Pulchra dicuntur quae *visa* placent'[79]. It is moreover a disinterested pleasure, springing from the *perception* of an object. The lover of the beautiful is moved by no desire to be physically possessed of the delighting object. It is one thing to contemplate with pleasure the beautiful demesne of another, when the artistic delight consists mainly in an exercise of the cognitive powers, and another thing to experience the pleasure of proprietorship which results from the possession of such demesnes[80].

Must we think, then, if aesthetic pleasure is derived from cognitive activity, that the beautiful is the same as the *true*, the object of knowledge? No, this is again inadmissible inasmuch as not all knowledge is a source of aesthetic enjoyment: little pleasure, for instance, is aroused by the learning of the tenses and moods of irregular verbs. Aesthetic pleasure requires that the perception of the object call for a more or

[79] *Sum. Theol.*, I, q. 5, a. 4, ad 1. In this a posteriori definition *videre* has a wider meaning than of seeing with the eyes; it means a 'perception' of the cognitive faculties in general—what we called a 'comprehension'. Elsewhere (I–II, q. 27, a. 1, ad 3) St. Thomas says: 'Ad rationem pulchri pertinet, quod in ejus aspectu seu *cognitione* quietetur appetitus . . . , ita quod pulchrum dicatur id cujus ipsa *apprehensio* placet'.

[80] 'Pulchrum et bonum in subjecto quidem sunt idem quia super eandem rem fundantur, scilicet super formam et propter hoc, bonum laudatur ut pulchrum. Sed ratione differunt, nam bonum proprie respicit appetitum, est enim bonum quod omnia appetunt; et ideo habet rationem finis, nam appetitus est quidam motus ad rem; pulchrum enim respicit vim cognoscitivam; pulchra enim dicuntur quae visa placent: unde pulchrum in debita proportione consistit, quia sensus delectantur in rebus debite proportionatis sicut in sibi similibus'. ST. THOMAS, *Sum. Theol.*, I, q. 5, a. 4, ad 2.

less intense exercise of activity on the part of the mind; and a person becomes *active* in the contemplation of the beautiful only when the object is by its nature relatively complex. When the representations are of a simple sort, needing for their comprehension no intensity of action, for instance, the elementary truth that 'two and two make four', little or no pleasure is forthcoming, for the intellect is scarcely more than awakened. In proportion, however, as the relations are multiplied and varied, and so long as they do not require an excess of effort to be understood, the pleasure is increased. Thus a well-worked-out, clear and convincing proof of a geometrical theorem is a real source of aesthetic enjoyment. The classical dramas of the great writers, the masterpieces of the great artists, the grand symphonies of the great composers, the plans of campaign of the great generals, the marvellous inventions of modern mechanical art are for the initiated inexhaustible funds of aesthetic pleasure. The same wonders leave the philistine, if not entirely unmoved, at most but little affected. The reason of the difference is that the former understands and grasps their meaning, whilst the latter never comprehends them. Hence we may form a second conclusion: That *aesthetic pleasure springs from the active perception of certain relations that a work realizes.*

If it be asked, What are these relations we speak of? it will be found that they are relations of the concrete work to an ideal type which enables us to grasp the perfection of the work. By the perception of these relations to the 'ideal' of what it should be to be perfect do we come to know its beauty.

To be able to conceive the perfection a work of art can and should reach, there is need of certain natural qualifications and some training. A journalist, let us say, knows what is right and essential in a dramatic work. Writing a review of a particular piece, he expresses his appreciation of its beauty in this fashion: 'There are moments in this play when the action drags and the dialogue is too slow; the author gives too free a rein to his lyrical faculties. On the other hand, the characters are well conceived and brought into fine relief and the pathos of some of the scenes is intense!' By a judgment of this sort, a critic shows that he appreciates the fine points of a drama and can judge from them its relative beauty. He makes comparison between what he sees in it and the established requirements of a dramatic work. Some of these he finds present and others wanting. Conversely, a stranger to the theatre will only find in the play a superficial enjoyment: he has not enough knowledge to appreciate it rightly. A third conclusion, then, is that *the perception which gives rise to aesthetic pleasure consists in an understanding of the value of the elements which make up the perfection of a work; and it therefore entails a comparison between the work and the ideal to which it was meant to give expression.*

From these three conclusions a *corollary* is immediately evident: That although the aesthetic sentiment is not capricious, it nevertheless depends upon subjective conditions. On the one hand it is not wholly capricious, since the perfection of a work is something *objective*; different essential conditions have to be realized in it which are quite independent of our personal tastes. On the other hand the aesthetic sentiment is, at least to some extent, dependent upon *subjective* conditions, inasmuch as the beauty of a thing consists in its correspondence with an ideal and this ideal we each form for ourselves in accordance with our personal dispositions and taste. Indeed, our aesthetic judgments are never stable; they are subjects of discussion and we are always weighing in the balance our ideal of perfection and its realization in a work of art.

178. Objective Factors of the Beautiful.—Our analysis has so far enabled us to discover that the source of aesthetic pleasure lies with the perceptive faculties. They afford us this pleasure when by their exercise we come to appreciate the perfection of a work by the standard of its ideal. From this we see that aesthetic qualities must be those which make up the type- or ideal perfection of a work and enable us the better to comprehend it. We may now seek to learn from the manner in which the beautiful manifests itself to us, that is by again making use of the standpoint of experience, what are these objective factors which render a thing beautiful.

1. In the first place, the perception of the beautiful implies a vigorous action on the part of the cognitive faculties. Now only an object possessing a certain breadth or largeness, a certain power and life, is capable of energetically stimulating those faculties to action. The little, the paltry, the insignificant evoke no feeling of admiration. For a work to be beauti-

ful it must first of all have its own completeness and not be a fragment of itself. And in addition to this negative condition, it must present also a certain fullness of being, or *perfection*. Yet since, as we must remember, the power of energetic appeal which the object has on account of its fullness of being must be always in proportion to the capacity of our perceptive faculties, it must act upon us within the limits of our power of comprehension.

2. In order to bring the perceptive faculties into full play, the manifold different elements which make up the external appearance of an object must be *orderly*, well arranged, in some way *co-ordinated* so as to form an harmonious *whole*. Order is surely the aesthetic quality par excellence. Aesthetic order—which is the order of co-ordination called harmony and proportion—consists in a number of different things or actions forming one whole. These two constituent elements of aesthetic order—*unity* in *variety*—are essential to beauty. On the one hand a multiplicity or *variety* of factors is required to arouse the cognitive faculties to anything like intense action : the same excitation constantly repeated simply begets ennui. Yet on the other hand mere multiplicity distracts the attention and dissipates the powers of the mind: *unity* is therefore needed to keep the mind vigorously concentrated upon its object of contemplation, and in proportion as it effects this the aesthetic pleasure is increased.

The reduction of the many elements of a work into a whole is not effected in an arbitrary way by the one who contemplates it but by the artist, who conceives the perfection he seeks to express and keeps it before him as the exemplary cause. This ideal type in the mind of the artist is the principle of unity which blends and binds together into a single whole the various elements comprised in the work. The order which constitutes the aesthetic quality by excellence is not any order, but an order preconceived and willed by somebody; what St. Thomas calls *debita proportio* [81].

3. The more eminently and brilliantly the order and unity among the various parts of a work *shine forth*, the more fully and easily is its perfection grasped and, in consequence, the more vivid and intense is the aesthetic pleasure of contem-

[81] For a further analysis of what constitutes this order see large edition 5th ed. p. 586 ff.

plating it. The chief cause of a work's perfection standing out clearly and vividly is the unity of co-ordination of all its several parts. On this account the third aesthetic quality, of *clearness*, or brilliancy, or, if we may be allowed to call it so, 'striking force', is a consequent from the two preceding ones.

In brief, every work of art is in some measure complete, with its parts well arranged, and clearly possesses these two qualities. Or, in the words of St. Thomas, the objective conditions of the beautiful are three: *integrity* or *perfection*; *due order*, or *proportion*, *harmony*; and *clarity* or *splendour*. 'Ad pulchritudinem tria requiritur: primo quidem *integritas* sive *perfectio*: quae enim diminuta sunt, hoc ipso turpia sunt; et *debita proportio sive consonantia*; et iterum *claritas*; unde quae habent colorem nitidum pulchra esse dicuntur'[82].

179. Definition of Beauty.—A work is beautiful in so far as it corresponds to an idea which is the exemplary cause after which it is conceived and effected. This idea, the exemplary cause of an external work, has a concrete internal expression in images of the imagination; and therefore it is to the *imaginative faculty* that the construction of a work of art immediately belongs. The means for the external expression of the idea consist of the *materials* out of which the thing is made—form, colour, sound, imagery, etc.; their *orderly arrangement* with regard to one another; their *power of appeal* on account of their good arrangement: means which correspond to the three objective conditions of the beautiful we have just noticed. By uniting all these elements in one definition we may say that *beauty is that quality of a work whereby, on account of a happy co-ordination of its various parts, an ideal type to which it is related is given intense expression and made to excite admiration.*

180. The Connexion between Art and Morality.—On the plea that science is neither moral nor immoral but entirely unconcerned with good and evil, it has sometimes been claimed that there should be a complete divorce also between art and morality. But the parallel between science and art is not a good one, for between them there is a fundamental difference. Science seeks simply what is true, it deals with facts, not with ideals, and so interests reason alone and even precludes

[82] *Sum. Theol.*, I, q. 39, a. 8, c.

emotion. Emotion indeed, far from aiding, may result in obscuring a clear view of reality; too often it leads the judgment rather to pronounce in favour of its desires than to follow the leading of truth. Art, on the contrary, being the expression of an ideal in terms of a concrete work, has a wider appeal and can so impress the one who contemplates it as to make him cling to the ideal which imposes itself upon his admiration. When confronted with a work of art, we do not think of studying it as an objective reality, of forming an abstract concept of it; its artistic qualities lead us to admire in it an ideal substantially realized. Consequently a work of art does not appeal to the intelligence only but to the whole soul of a man. He does not content himself with studying the beautiful; he admires it and loves it. There is a world of difference between a masterpiece of Rubens and a problem of geometry. The artist grows enthusiastic over his conception and works long years to bring it to life on the canvas or in the marble, in the poem or the sonata, and hopes that the expert public will love it as well as he does himself.

In the same way the connoisseur passes from the examination of a work of art to admiration; with him also, as with the artist, imagination and passion play an important part in aesthetic pleasure. But passion is blind and under its guidance our free-will, which should be ruled by the principles of morality, is apt to seek its object without thought of the good or evil, the moral or the immoral. Every image that moves us, moves us to an act and always seeks to realize itself in the concrete. Hence, whenever the object which excites the imagination and stirs the emotions is conformable to the end of one's rational nature, the impulse to the free-will is wholesome; its author is on the side of virtue; his art preaches morality. If, however, the object is not in accord with recognized canons of decency, the effect of emotion on the free-will will be as powerful an inducement to evil as it might have been for good, and the work of art in such a case is immoral. Thus we see that art has a very definite bearing on morality; and that it is untrue to say that art, like science, has no concern with the distinction of right and wrong.

Does it follow from what we have said that the artist is bound positively to use his art as a moralizing force? By no means; provided that his ideal and his production are not immoral, he fulfils his mission, for the artist as such is not a preacher. Indeed the field of art is as wide as the beautiful. The beautiful is the manifestation of order in whatever province it be realized, moral or non-moral, profane or religious; order, no matter in what, is beautiful and its expression is ever worthy of the artist's talent. Moreover, by the mere fact of his directly pursuing the beautiful for its own sake, provided he observe the claims of the moral law, the artist is furthering the cause of the good, inasmuch as he is helping to raise the standards of pleasure by substituting real, aesthetic enjoyment for the gratification of lower, sensual appetites; hence whilst the artist pursues objects which are in themselves morally indifferent, he is indirectly working for the cause of righteousness.

ART. II. THE MEDIATE EFFECT OF THE CAUSES OR THE ORDER OF THE UNIVERSE

I. The Relative End of the Universe

181. We have established that all beings of nature have within them an intrinsic purpose. Every substance has its proper activity and is determined in its exercise of it by an inherent impulse which makes it tend towards what is its good, towards the purpose of its existence. Things in this world however do not stand in isolation but are intimately bound up with one another by various relations of interdependence, thus showing that there exists a *relative* finality. This relative finality, if the whole of nature is regarded as one system, is the cause of the 'relative order' and the beauty of the universe, which was designated by the Greeks as the Cosmos.

In this teleological conception it will be seen that internal finality is the foundation of external finality inasmuch as the specific nature of individual things and the particular tendency directing their activities along a given line are the basis of the relations which unite them together as one whole. The intrinsic order belonging to each particular type is therefore the basis of this relative, extrinsic order which is the characteristic feature of their interplay. This universal order has as its end the good of all beings. But it is also subordinated to a higher end, a transcendent end. Hence the universe looked at as a whole has a double end, one that we may call *immanent* as concerning all beings in general, the other a *transcendent* one.

II. The Immanent Relative End of the Universe

182. The larger classes or kingdoms of beings in the universe are subordinate to one another, whilst each such class is composed of smaller sub-classes or species dependent upon one another in wonderful gradations. We are enabled to lay down general laws of the universe, the laws of gravitation, of conservation of mass and energy, of the equivalence of forms of energy, etc. Accordingly the universe constitutes *one whole*, all the various parts of which conspire by their mutual relations to bring about good order and the good of the whole.

But we may ask further, has this universal order itself an end, a good which is one, by virtue of which all things are set in order? St. Thomas says, 'The universe has the good of order and another distinct good '[83].

III. The Transcendent Relative End of the Universe

183. Everything in nature, we say, has its own particular intrinsic end, and all things by fulfilling their own ends contribute to the good of one another and of the whole. Now whence is this convergence of all beings towards the realization of universal order if not from some higher principle of unity which determines it? This universal tendency of all nature cannot be explained except by a principle directing all things to conspire to the good of the whole. To unite all the elements of the universe into one harmonious and orderly system or cosmos a single supreme Intelligence must have been at work, to conceive it, to arrange the parts, and to calculate their nice subordination as means to this end. We reach this, then, as a final conclusion, that the supreme, transcendent end of the universe is the realization of the plan of the First Cause. 'The whole order of the universe', writes St. Thomas, developing the thought of Aristotle, 'is for the Prime Mover thereof;

[83] 'Universum habet bonum ordinis et bonum separatum'. St. Thomas, *In XII Metaph.* lect. 12.

this order has for its purpose the working out in an orderly universe of the plan conceived and willed by the Prime Mover. And hence the Prime Mover is the principle of this universal order '[84].

[84] Totus ordo universi est propter primum moventem, ut scilicet explicetur in universo ordinato id quod est in intellectu et voluntate primi moventis. Et sic oportet quod a primo movente sit tota ordinatio universi '. *Ibid.*

APPENDIX TO COSMOLOGY

MODERN CONCEPTIONS OF THE ATOM*

A comparison of the findings of experimental science twenty years ago concerning the constitution of matter with those in our possession to-day certainly affords one of the most splendid examples of the fecundity of scientific research. The way in which different theories have rapidly followed upon one another is a more striking proof than ever that far from being "bankrupt" modern science is achieving extraordinarily rapid success. The question of the constitution of matter has been given three progressive answers: the molecular-atomic theory, or that of grains of matter: the electronic theory, or that of grains of electricity; and the theory of quanta, or grains of energy.

I. The Atomic Theory.

The atomic theory, which has been a metaphysical conception from ancient times, was put upon an experimental basis by Dalton's application of it to interpret the fundamental laws of chemistry. The discontinuity and fixity of the proportions by weight according to which elements combine is to be accounted for by the fact that the indivisible particles or atoms which make up simple bodies are permanent. Compound bodies are made up of molecules resulting from the union of a definite number of different atoms.

The molecular hypothesis formulated by Avogadro and Ampère explains the laws of combination of gases by volume by assuming that the number of molecules contained in a fixed volume of any gas under the same physical conditions is constant.

As the whole of chemistry relies on these two hypotheses for its exposition, it furnishes the first guarantee of their truth. But chemistry is not the only field where the molecular hypothesis has been applied. The kinetic theory of gases, to which it serves as foundation, gives it a fresh confirmation. But the cogent argument

* Books for study or consultation :—

Reiche, *The Quantum Theory* (trs. Hatfield & Brose, Methuen, London, 1922).

Perrin, *Atoms* (Constable, London, 1916; later editions in French).

Aston, *Isotopes* (Arnold, London, 1922).

Millikan, *The Electron* (Chicago University Press, 1918).

Stoek, *The Structure of Atoms* (trs. Sugden, Methuen, London, 1923).

Mills, *Within the Atom* (Routledge, London, 1922).

Bohr, *The Theory of Spectra and Atomic Constitution* (University Press, Cambridge, 1922).

demonstrating the molecular hypothesis is the manner in which the several determinations of Avogadro's number all agree. This constant, or the number of molecules contained in a gramme-molecule of any body whatever, has been determined by a score of quite different methods. We can state with an error not exceeding two per cent. that there are 610,000 milliard-milliard molecules in a gramme-molecule. By certain experiments we can ascertain directly the effect of one single molecule: in fact the motion caused by a molecule of water on an oil-droplet can be observed. So also can be detected the scintillation or the deflection of an electrometer produced by a single atom of helium.

II. The Electronic Theory.

The hypothesis of a granular structure of electricity was suggested and definitely confirmed by a series of observations which we may with profit recount.

Electrolysis.—Aqueous solutions of acids, salts or bases (electrolytes) are conductors of electricity. The passing of an electric current through these solutions is always accompanied by a chemical decomposition. This decomposition takes place in accordance with Faraday's Law: whatever the conditions of the experiment (dilution, temperature, intensity of the current, etc.) the passage through the solution of a fixed quantity of electricity (96,540 coulombs) liberates an "equivalent" at each electrode. (The equivalent of an element is equal to its atomic weight in grammes divided by its valency: 1·008 grs. of hydrogen, $16/2 = 8$ grs. of oxygen, $27/3 = 9$ grs. of aluminium.)

According to the theory of Arrhenius the molecules of an electrolyte in solution are dissociated into parts charged with electricity, or ions, that exist in a free state ($H^{+}O^{--}Ba^{++}SO_4^{--}Al^{+++}$).

We must therefore assume that each monovalent ion carries an elementary electric charge that is always equal. Di- or trivalent ions carry two or three of these charges.

Cathode Rays.—When an electric charge is passed through a rarefied gas (Crookes' tube), the cathode, or negative pole, emits radiations which are given off in a straight line and produce a bright fluorescence where they strike the walls of the tube. These rays can be deflected by an electric or magnetic field, and consist of negative charged particles. This latter point is made clear by the fact that they introduce negative electricity into a completely closed metal enclosure. Hence the particles of the cathode rays carry a negative charge which cannot be separated from them even by making them pass through a sheet of metal.

Positive Rays.—If a canal is pierced through the cathode of a Crookes' tube there is detectable in the space behind the cathode another emanation or radiation which manifests its arrival on the walls of the tube by a dull fluorescence. This radiation is charged with positive electricity, as is shown by its deflection when under the influence of an electric or magnetic field. These rays are really charged atoms whose velocity and ratio of charge to mass can be determined by the amount of the deflection produced by an electric or magnetic field.

Radioactivity.—There are some elements, namely uranium, thorium, radium and their products after atomic disintegration, which are characterized by the spontaneous emission of rays that are capable of affecting a photographic plate and of rendering gases conductors of electricity. By applying a magnetic field we have been enabled to divide this emanation into three kinds of rays: γ rays which are not deflected, and which therefore do not carry any electric charge; β rays which have a negative charge, and α rays which have a positive charge.

α rays are a stream of particles. For we can observe the scintillation produced by a single particle on a screen of zinc sulphide or even trace its passage by the deflection of a sensitive electrometer. Photographs have been taken of the track of particles which in an atmosphere of super-saturated vapour leave rows of condensed droplets as their traces. These α particles are atoms of helium charged with positive electricity. Direct and immediate proof of this has been furnished by our being able to re-unite a sufficient number of these particles to recognize the physical properties of helium gas by ordinary methods.

β rays are of the same nature as the cathode rays. They are particles like these, but travel with a much higher velocity. As in the case of the α rays the trajectory described by a β particle can be rendered visible by the condensation of droplets.

Measurement of Elementary Charge of Electricity.—The experiments just mentioned prove the existence of extremely minute particles carrying very small charges of electricity. Now before we can assert the existence of an "atom of electricity," or electron, we must show that what we observe is always the same elementary quantity of electricity or some whole multiple of this quantity.

Our first method of proving this is by *electrolysis*. If we divide the quantity of electricity required for a decomposition by the number of monovalent atoms liberated at one electrode, we obtain a first value for the electron. For, in order to obtain the same number of di- or trivalent atoms we must multiply the strength of our current by either two or three. This would argue that the charge carried by these atoms is two or three electrons respectively.

A second method is to measure the charge of the α particles.

We can determine the number of particles introduced into an electrometer and the charge which they carry into it. By dividing the one by the other we find that the positive charge of each particle is equivalent to double the quantity determined for electrolysis.

The *positive rays* permit of very accurate measurement. They usually travel in a straight line and affect a photographic plate. These rays can be deflected by means of an electric and magnetic field which curve the trajectory in two rectangular directions in the plane normal to the initial velocity. This displacement depends upon the velocity, mass and charge of the particle. The points marked by deflected particles which differ only in velocity are to be found on a parabola. Particles which differ in mass or in charge produce different parabolas on the plate. The results obtained by measurement of the parabolas are just those to be expected if the positive charge on the positive rays is a small multiple of the unit already determined by the previous method.

The *cathode rays* or *β particles* can be observed individually. Between the two plates of a condenser producing an electrical field of the order of several thousand volts per centimetre there is introduced an oil-droplet carrying an electric charge. The motion of this droplet is observed by means of an ultramicroscope and the electric field can be adjusted so that the particle remains stationary between the plates. If by suitable means this oil-droplet receive one extra β particle, it will begin to move. When the electric field is readjusted it again takes up a stationary position. If the acceleration or the value of the electric field is known and also the dimensions of the droplet, the magnitude of the added charge is easily calculated. The results of this experiment prove directly that the charge (1) varies in a discontinuous manner and (2) that each increase is always a small multiple of the unit already mentioned. The error of these determinations does not exceed 1 in a 1000 and from these experiments is derived the accepted value for the unit charge, viz. $4{\cdot}77 \times 10^{-10}$ electrostatic units.

Measurements therefore of electrolytic ions, of α particles, of positive rays, of cathode rays and of β particles give evidence of the existence of a minimum electric charge together with the existence of integral multiples only of this charge. Put briefly these experiments lead us to assert the granular structure of electricity. Just as matter is made up of atoms, so too electricity is built up of particles or discrete quantities, the negative unit being an electron.

It would seem that electrons are not associated with matter. Their mass—about $\frac{1}{2000}$ of that of the hydrogen atom—is of purely magnetic origin. This mass increases with the electron's velocity as predicted by the Principle of Relativity.

Isotopy and Atomic Number.—The experiments described

above show how we have been led to recognize the existence of indivisible particles of matter and electricity. But we are also able to state the very close connexion there is between the properties of atoms and the presence of electrical changes and to raise the question of the constitution of the atoms themselves.

Our knowledge of radioactivity has provided the first proof of the part played by electrons in the properties of matter. We all know that Mendeleef, relying on the periodicity of all the physical and chemical properties of elements, classified them into a table wherein bodies were written down in the order of increasing atomic weights. They so become arranged in vertical columns or groups of like elements. Several places where there were gaps have since been filled in by discoveries since Mendeleef's day, to mention as instances among others, the places of radioactive bodies.

Now by studying the relationship of these elements we have been enabled to enunciate a very important law. Whenever a change occurs which is accompanied by the emission of α particles the element moves two places in the direction of decreasing atomic weight; whenever there is an emission of β particles, it shifts one place in the direction of increasing weight.

The emission of charged particles indicates, as much as electrolytic dissociation, that in every atom there are electrical charges; the law enunciated above proves that there is some intimate relation between the physical and chemical properties of an atom and its internal charge. By this discovery we are admitted to a close knowledge of the atom and led, not without a clue, to a new problem. For, if an atom lose first an α particle and then two β ones, the atomic weight will be diminished by four units but the new body, occupying the same place in Mendeleef's table, will have exactly the same properties as the initial body, which indeed is indistinguishable from it; they are what are termed two isotopes.

From this an immediate conclusion follows: the constant to be used for designating a group of physical and chemical properties characteristic of an atom is its place or number in Mendeleef's table and not its atomic mass. And further, the same number can correspond to two atoms which are chemically indistinguishable but which have different masses.

Radioactive bodies are not the only ones which exhibit this phenomenon of isotopy. We have already mentioned the experiment for measuring the velocity and mass of particles charged with electrons and forming the positive rays of Crookes' tube. By using this process for studying simple bodies we find that nearly all of them are a mixture of atoms of different masses. For example: neon, with an atomic weight of 20·2, is a mixture of atoms of 20 and 22 atomic weight; mercury (200·6) is a mixture of at least four isotopes of 197, 200, 202, 204 weight; krypton (82·9) consists of six isotopes of 78, 80, 82, 83, 84, and 86 weight. All the atomic weights determined by this method, with the exception of that of hydrogen, are whole numbers in relation to oxygen, the atomic weight of which is equal to 16.

Atomic Number and Electric Charge.—Atoms are electrically neutral. Yet they contain both positive and negative electricity (ions of electrolytes, ions of helium in α particles, emission of charges by radioactive elements). Moreover the electric charge has a close connexion with both physical and chemical properties. The question which now arises is how to reconcile these experimental results so as to account for the properties of bodies and to give a physical meaning to the atomic number. The question has been progressively answered in the light of experiments suggested by successive conceptions of the models after which atoms are constituted.

The Atom according to Thomson.—The first model was conceived by Sir J. J. Thomson. According to him the atom consists of a mass of positive electricity spread uniformly over a sphere having atomic dimensions and containing the negative electrons regularly distributed on concentric surfaces. To a certain extent the periodicity of the properties of the elements becomes intelligible by calculating the equilibrium position of such systems as the number of electrons and, therefore, the positive mass vary. E.g. corresponding to two successive periods we have two successive surfaces containing similar electrons. Granted the existence of free electrons in the atom, a practical means is suggested of determining the total number of electrons in an atom. Certain results obtained by studying the "scattering" of X-rays indicate that this number is approximately equal to the atomic number.

Nevertheless this model has to be given up. For it is known that the α particles projected from radioactive bodies can travel through several centimetres in air or through a thin sheet of metal. Yet these particles are generally deflected very slightly even though they must pass through many atoms. This is easily intelligible with J. J. Thomson's atom since the electrical density of the positive sphere is small and the mass of an electron is small compared with that particle. However, accurate observation shows that some of these α particles are deflected through large angles, sometimes exceeding 90°. Such scattering reveals the existence of a field of force of enormous intensity, a condition which is not satisfied by J. J. Thomson's model atom.

Rutherford's Atomic Model.—Sir E. Rutherford thereupon conceived that the positive charge is concentrated in a very small space constituting the atomic nucleus endowed with mass and that the electrons are distributed in concentric rings over a relatively large area corresponding to the volume of the atom. In order not to fall on the nucleus which attracts them the electrons move round the nucleus just as planets move round the sun.

This new conception allows one to determine the positive charge of the nucleus—and thereby also the number of the outer electrons —by measuring the number of the α particles deflected from a given angle in passing through a sheet of metal. Theoretical forecasts have been exactly verified: the nuclear charge is equal in electrons to the atomic number.

From many points of view Rutherford's conception of the atom answers what experiment calls for. The planetary system of the nucleus and of the electrons shows how both the existence and emission by the atom of positive material particles as well as of β particles is possible. The Periodic Law of Mendeleef is to be interpreted by the constitution of successive spheres of electrons the periodic arrangement of which will be the basis for the recurrence of analogous properties. The considerable yet rare deflections of certain α particles can be foreseen by calculation, the important electrical charge and the smallness of the nucleus being given. The atomic number receives a precise physical signification inasmuch as it measures the charge of the nucleus in electrons. The phenomena of isotopy is easily understood seeing that after the expulsion of one α and two β particles by the nucleus the net nuclear charge becomes the same, the number and, in consequence, the stable arrangement of the outer electrons must be the same; and therefore also the chemical properties.

Negative electricity would seem to have an existence which is independent of what is generally meant by matter. On the other hand no one has ever established the isolated existence of positive electricity. On the contrary, as far as we can ascertain, the nucleus of hydrogen would be its smallest material support. This nucleus would be, like the electron, one of the ultimate constituents of all bodies: for some phenomena seem to be explicable only as expelled particles of mass which are positively charged. Under an intense bombardment of swift α particles nuclei of hydrogen have been thought to have been driven out from certain atoms such as boron, nitrogen, fluorine, sodium, aluminium and phosphorus.

This model of Rutherford would also account for certain luminous phenomena. The frequency of rotation of the electrons which make little oscillators would be measured by the frequency of the luminous lines they emit. The doubling of the spectral lines (Zeeman effect) produced by atoms placed in a magnetic field is explained by the positive or negative variation of the radii of the orbit according to the direction of the rotation.

The structure of the atom thought out by Rutherford is, however, not yet perfected. Indeed, if electrons gravitate around a nucleus, they must radiate like every other oscillator and, in consequence, lose energy and so fall on the nucleus. From this it follows that as the electrons draw nearer the nucleus, the frequency in their rotation will increase and the radiation will diminish in wave-length. If, therefore, the laws of electrodynamics are applicable to the intra-atomic motion of an electron, Rutherford's atom is unstable and the rays emitted by the incandescent bodies cannot correspond to wave-lengths that are invariably fixed. To explain the permanence and complexity of the luminous spectra, Niels Bohr and A. Sommerfeld applied Max Planck's quantum theory to Rutherford's atom.

III. The Quantum Theory.

The want of success which attended all attempts to explain "black-body" radiation by applying the laws of classical electrodynamics led Planck to propose the hypothesis that the energy of an electrical oscillator varies only by abrupt leaps or quanta. A quantum of energy is moreover not a fixed quantity: it increases in proportion to the frequency of the oscillator, the co-efficient of the proportionality being a universal constant termed Planck's constant: it measures the quantum of action which is itself absolutely invariable.

Bohr's Conception of the Atom.—According to Rutherford's idea, since an electron gravitates in equilibrium around a nucleus, the centrifugal force must be equal to the attraction of the nucleus. This equality—the masses and the charges being given—furnishes a relation between the velocity of the electron and the radius of its *circular* orbit. Bohr postulates that in these conditions the electron does not emit radiant energy. He further lays down, in accordance with the quantum theory, that the energy required to bring an electron from rest at an infinite distance to its position and velocity near the nucleus around which it gravitates is equal to a whole number of quanta.

From this it follows at once that the radius of the orbit of an electron can vary only in a discontinuous way; the circles which the electrons can describe are therefore only those for which the number of the quanta is a whole 1, 2, 3 . . . etc. The radii of these circles are proportional to the squares of these whole numbers.

It is then possible to write a general formula determining the radius of the orbits. This formula contains a symbol which can take the values 1, 2, 3 . . . etc., and the orbits are to be numbered by the values given to this symbol: these are stationary orbits. When through the influence of some external cause an electron passes from one of these stationary orbits to another of smaller radius, it loses a certain quantity of energy which is liberated in the form of rays. This quantity, i.e. the difference of the electron's energy in the initial orbit and that of the final orbit, is expressed as a function of the order-numbers of these orbits.

By a further application of the theory of the quanta Bohr assumes that this energy is a quantum equal to the product of Planck's constant and the frequency of the rays emitted.

If then we know the value of Planck's constant, the mass and the charge of an electron, and the charge of the nucleus, we can predict by calculation the lengths of all the waves an atom can emit. Experimental verification of this theory is directly possible.

The simplest case is that of the hydrogen atom the nuclear charge of which is equal to one electron and which has only one gravitating negative corpuscle. Now, forty years ago Balmer found that the frequencies of the spectral lines of the luminous spectrum of hydrogen obey a law the form of which is identically that which Bohr's theory arrives at. Balmer's formula contains a constant that is empirically determined and which coincides to $\frac{1}{1000}$ with that deduced by Bohr through employing the exact results of the measurements connected with the electron.

Under normal temperature and pressure atoms of hydrogen are so close to one another that the electron cannot circulate except along the most central of Bohr's orbits. In fact, under these conditions we observe only three lines, the wave-length of which verifies Bohr's law.

At normal temperature but under pressure of only $\frac{1}{1000}$ atmosphere, the distances between atoms are such that the electron can only describe the 15th of Bohr's orbits. Thirteen lines are clearly observable corresponding to the leaps from the orbits 3 to 15 on number 2 orbit; and the wave-lengths verify Bohr's law.

In certain nebulæ hydrogen is so rarefied that the electron can circulate on the 23rd orbit. All the lines have been discovered from the 13th to the 31st in the luminous spectrum of these nebulæ and Bohr's law remains proven.

All these lines are related to electrons arriving on the number 2 orbit. There have also been found in the infra-red and the ultra-violet, lines produced by electrons arriving respectively on numbers 3 and 1 orbits.

In addition to this startling confirmation in the case of hydrogen Bohr's theory is also completely verified by the spectrum of helium. This result, showing that the charges of the hydrogen and the helium nuclei are respectively one and two electrons, excludes the possibility of any unknown elements lighter than helium, the case of isotopy being excepted.

The Bohr-Sommerfeld Atom.—By a very accurate observation with a spectrograph of great dispersive power it has been ascertained that the lines of hydrogen and helium are not simple but are made up of several closely allied components. Sommerfeld assumes that the paths of the electrons are ellipses with the nucleus as focus. By applying the theory of quanta both to the azimuthal and the radial motion of the electron and taking into account the variation of the mass of the electron with its velocity (theory of relativity), he has established a theory of the fine-structure of the spectral lines which has received a remarkable experimental verification.

The same principles are now being applied to the study of radiations of much higher frequency, viz. the X-rays. They are produced by the electrons of the inner layers of heavy atoms. The theoretical problem is clearly much more complex, but Bohr's theories, while leaving room for further precision, are verified by experiment.

The exactness with which the spectrum of hydrogen confirms the Bohr-Sommerfeld theories is so perfect that the problem of determining physical constants has become inverted. Instead of starting with the charge and the mass of the electron and Planck's constant already determined and then predicting what will be the results of optical experiment, we can now start from these results in order to determine the fundamental constants. The charge of the electron is equal to $4{\cdot}77 \times 10^{-10}$ electrostatic units, the ratio $\frac{e}{m}$ of its charge to its mass is $5{\cdot}31 \times 10^{17}$ electromagnetic units, and the quantum of action or Planck's constant has a value of $6{\cdot}55 \times 10^{-27}$ erg-seconds.

We may summarize by stating that the smallest representatives of simple bodies or atoms bear an astonishing resemblance to very minute solar systems, all the planets of which (electrons) are exactly the same. These electrons—the elementary quantities of negative electricity,—gravitate round a positively charged nucleus wherein is concentrated almost the whole of the atomic mass. The number of planetary electrons is determined by the positive charge of the nucleus and is equal to the atomic number (1 to 92). Positive electricity is thus always localized in the nucleus in a proportional quantity, viz. one electron for a mass equal to 1 in the system O = 16 (*mass*). The net positive charge of the nucleus expresses the difference between the positive quantities determining the mass and the nuclear negative electrons (*isotopy*). The outer electrons, the number of which is thus determined, are arranged in successive layers, and Mendeleef's Periodic Law is explicable by supposing that chemical properties depend on the peripheral layer alone (*valency*). Two different atoms unite in a molecule as the result of the tendency atoms have to make a complete exterior crown or shell, i.e. a shell formed by eight electrons (*affinity*). Granting Bohr's postulates, the radiation of atoms may be explained by distinguishing sharply those orbits which are the only ones along which an electron may travel, so that its energy can only vary in finite quantities (*rays*).

The ingenuity of physicists and the delicate processes of measurement have combined to aid us in constructing a complex and stable atomic model which accounts at once for atomic masses, the phenomena of isotopy in the periodic system, the valency and affinity of simple bodies, and for the radiation of atoms. This model is made up of two irreducible elements, the nucleus of heavy mass and carrying a net positive charge and the negative electrons; the relations of these two elements are governed by the laws of mechanics and electrodynamics of Relativity supplemented by the quantum theory.

Now do these new theories weaken the Aristotelian and Thomistic conception of matter? By no means. To-day as much as before the discovery of the electronic theory the atom remains as the real type of the simple body. It is presented to us with the same group of physical and chemical properties which, in conjunction with its constancy, its indissolubility and its specific qualities, allows us to distinguish one species from another. Furthermore, even up to the present, we have never yet managed to find the sufficient explanatory reason for such characteristics except in the very nature of the atom.

We must admit that the atomic structure conceived by scientists is a little difficult to reconcile with the hypothesis of the essential unity or rather of the continuity of the atom. But we must never forget that a physical theory may render great service without adequately reflecting reality. Besides, in spite of its success what a number of obscurities are still left by the electronic theory to be cleared up, even on fundamental points. What account are we to give of the inner nature of positive electricity which is so indissolubly knit with matter, or of the electron which is free of any material subject, or of the structure of the nucleus upon which in ultimate analysis the whole atomic edifice depends? These are all problems of the first importance and which are not yet solved. Whilst then facts force us to maintain the specific unity of the atom, prudence counsels us to wait for further light for their complete explanation.

Printed in Great Britain by Butler & Tanner Ltd., *Frome and London*